Lecture Notes in Computer Science 8756

Commenced Publication in 1973
Founding and Former Series Editors:
Gerhard Goos, Juris Hartmanis, and Jan van Leeuwen

Pascal Felber   Vijay Garg (Eds.)

Stabilization, Safety, and Security of Distributed Systems

16th International Symposium, SSS 2014
Paderborn, Germany, September 28 – October 1, 2014
Proceedings

 Springer

Volume Editors

Pascal Felber
Université de Neuchâtel
Institut d'informatique
Rue Emile-Argand 11
2000 Neuchâtel, Switzerland
E-mail: pascal.felber@unine.ch

Vijay Garg
University of Texas at Austin
Electrical and Computer Engineering Department
1 University Station
Austin, TX 78712-0240, USA
E-mail: garg@ece.utexas.edu

ISSN 0302-9743   e-ISSN 1611-3349
ISBN 978-3-319-11763-8   e-ISBN 978-3-319-11764-5
DOI 10.1007/978-3-319-11764-5
Springer Cham Heidelberg New York Dordrecht London

Library of Congress Control Number: 2014949157

LNCS Sublibrary: SL 1 – Theoretical Computer Science and General Issues

Typesetting: Camera-ready by author, data conversion by Scientific Publishing Services, Chennai, India

Printed on acid-free paper

Springer is part of Springer Science+Business Media (www.springer.com)

Preface

The papers in this volume were presented at the 16th International Symposium on Stabilization, Safety, and Security of Distributed Systems (SSS), held during September 28 to October 1, 2014 in Paderborn, Germany.

SSS is an international forum for researchers and practitioners in the design and development of distributed systems with self-* properties: (classical) self-stabilizing, self-configuring, self-organizing, self-managing, self-repairing, self-healing, self-optimizing, self-adaptive, and self-protecting. Research in distributed systems is now at a crucial point in its evolution, marked by the importance of dynamic systems such as peer-to-peer networks, large-scale wireless sensor networks, mobile ad-hoc networks, cloud computing, robotic networks, etc. Moreover, new applications such as grid and web services, banking and e-commerce, e-health and robotics, aerospace and avionics, automotive, industrial process control, etc. have joined the traditional applications of distributed systems.

The theory of self-stabilization has been enriched in the last 30 years by high quality research contributions in the areas of algorithmic techniques, formal methodologies, model theoretic issues, and composition techniques. All these areas are essential to the understanding and maintenance of self-* properties in fault-tolerant distributed systems.

This year the Program Committee was organized into several tracks reflecting most topics related to self-* systems. The tracks were: (i) Self-Stabilization, (ii) Ad-Hoc, Sensor and Mobile Networks, Cyberphysical Systems (iii) Fault-Tolerant and Dependable Systems, (iv) Formal Methods, Safety and Security, and (v) Cloud Computing, P2P, Self-organizing and Autonomous Systems.

We received 44 submissions from 20 countries. Each submission was reviewed by at least three Program Committee members with the help of external reviewers. Out of the 44 submissions, 21 papers were selected as regular papers, and 8 papers were accepted as brief announcements. Among the 21 regular papers, we considered 2 papers for special awards. The best paper award was given to Giang T. Nguyen, Mathias Fischer and Thorsten Strufe for "On the Resilience of Pull-based P2P Streaming Systems against DoS Attacks", and the best student paper award was given to Fathiyeh Faghih and Borzoo Bonakdarpour for "SMT-based Synthesis of Distributed Self-Stabilizing Systems". This year, we were very fortunate to have three distinguished keynote speakers: Christian Cachin, Pierre Fraigniaud, and Nir Shavit.

On behalf of the Program Committee, we would like to thank all the authors who submitted their work to SSS. We sincerely acknowledge the tremendous time and effort the program track chairs and the Program Committee members invested in the symposium. We are also grateful to the external reviewers for their valuable and insightful comments and to Easychair for tremendously simplifying the review process and the generation of the proceedings. Finally, we also thank the Steering Committee members for their valuable advice and the Organizing Committee members for their time and effort to ensure a successful meeting.

Organizing this event would not have been possible without the financial support of the German Research Foundation (DFG).

October 2014   Pascal Felber
                                                               Vijay K. Garg

Organization

Program Committee

James Aspnes	Yale University, USA
Chen Avin	Ben-Gurion University, Israel
Lelia Blin	LIP6-UPMC and University of Evry-Val d'Essonne, France
Borzoo Bonakdarpour	McMaster University, Canada
Janna Burman	Université Paris-Sud, France
Costas Busch	Louisiana State University, USA
Fei Chen	BloomReach Inc., USA
Sylvie Delaët	Université Paris Sud, France
Murat Demirbas	University at Buffalo, USA
Stéphane Devismes	Université Grenoble-Alpes, France
Danny Dolev	Hebrew University, Israel
Ittay Eyal	Cornell University, USA
Pascal Felber	University of Neuchatel, Switzerland
Felix Freiling	Friedrich-Alexander-Universität Erlangen-Nürnberg (FAU), Germany
Vijay Garg	The University of Texas at Austin, USA
Seth Gilbert	National University of Singapore, Singapore
Jason Hallstrom	Clemson University, USA
Urs Hengartner	University of Waterloo, Canada
Ted Herman	University of Iowa, USA
Matti Hiltunen	AT&T Labs - Research, USA
Taisuke Izumi	Nagoya Institute of Technology, Japan
Arshad Jhumka	University of Warwick, UK
Sayaka Kamei	Hiroshima University, Japan
Erez Kantor	MIT, USA
Adrian Kosowski	Inria, Université Paris Diderot, France
Sandeep Kulkarni	Michigan State University, USA
Petr Kuznetsov	Telecom ParisTech, France
Sven Köhler	Tel Aviv University, Israel
Mikel Larrea	University of the Basque Country UPV/EHU, Spain
Xiaolin Li	University of Florida, USA
Victor Luchangco	Oracle Labs, USA
Raimundo Macêdo	Federal University of Bahia (UFBA), Brazil
Tom Maibaum	McMaster University, Canada
Stephan Merz	Inria Nancy, France
Mikhail Nesterenko	Kent State University, USA

Table of Contents

Separating Data and Control: Asynchronous BFT Storage with $2t + 1$ Data Replicas

Christian Cachin[1], Dan Dobre[2], and Marko Vukolić[3]

[1] IBM Research - Zurich, Switzerland
cca@zurich.ibm.com
[2] Work done at NEC Labs Europe, Germany
dan@dobre.net
[3] Eurécom, France
vukolic@eurecom.fr

Abstract. The overhead of Byzantine fault tolerant (BFT) storage is a primary concern that prevents its adoption in practice. The cost stems from the need to maintain at least $3t + 1$ copies of the data at different storage replicas in the asynchronous model, so that t Byzantine replica faults can be tolerated. This paper presents *MDStore*, the first fully asynchronous BFT storage protocol that reduces the number of replicas that store the payload data to as few as $2t + 1$ and maintains metadata at $3t+1$ replicas on (possibly) different servers. At the heart of *MDStore* lies a metadata service built upon a new abstraction called "timestamped storage." Timestamped storage allows for conditional writes (facilitating the implementation of the metadata service) and has consensus number one (making it implementable with wait-free semantics in an asynchronous system despite faults). In addition to its low replication overhead, *MDStore* offers strong guarantees by emulating a multi-writer multi-reader atomic register, providing wait-free termination, and tolerating any number of Byzantine readers and crash-faulty writers.

1 Introduction

Byzantine fault-tolerant (BFT) protocols are notoriously costly to deploy. Their overhead stems from the extra resources that must be installed compared to systems that tolerate less severe faults, such as crashes. For example, in the asynchronous communication model, BFT storage protocols that emulate a simple register abstraction need at least $N > 3t$ server replicas so that t faults can be tolerated [32]. This stands in contrast to the required number of replicas when only server crashes are tolerated, where $2t + 1$ replicas suffice. Such crash-tolerant systems based on quorums [34] are in production use today, in cloud-storage systems and other contexts. But the additional cost of handling Byzantine faults compared to crashes represents one of the main concerns for the adoption of BFT systems in practice.

In this paper, we show that the gap between crash-tolerance and Byzantine-tolerance in distributed storage can be reduced significantly. By separating the functions that handle metadata from those that store the payload data, the number of expensive servers with large storage capacity can be reduced to $N > 2t$ while tolerating Byzantine faults. We introduce protocol *MDStore*, which emulates a storage register abstraction in an

P. Felber and V. Garg (Eds.): SSS 2014, LNCS 8756, pp. 1–17, 2014.
© Springer International Publishing Switzerland 2014

asynchronous message-passing model; it requires only $N > 2t$ *storage replicas* that store payload data (of which t may be Byzantine) and $M > 3f$ *metadata replicas* that maintain short control information (of which f may be Byzantine). Storage and metadata replicas may be separated physically or co-hosted on the same servers.

Despite achieving lower replication cost, *MDStore* does not sacrifice other desirable features: *MDStore* implements a multi-writer multi-reader (MWMR) *atomic* register [21, 24] with *wait-free* semantics [20], tolerates any number of Byzantine readers and crash-faulty writers, and works *without any synchrony assumption*. Compared to other BFT storage protocols that reduce the number of storage replicas to $3t$ or less [11, 12, 22, 33], *MDStore* is the first one that achieves this without trusted hardware components. Moreover, because *MDStore* is fully asynchronous and does not employ a consensus primitive, it fundamentally differs from other related systems that separate the control plane from the data plane for providing, e.g., consensus [19], state-machine replication [26, 37], and distributed storage [2] — these are all subject to the FLP impossibility result [17] and require partial synchrony [15].

Protocol *MDStore* has a modular architecture. The clients exchange metadata about the stored data through a *metadata service (MDS)*. The metadata related to a stored value v consists of a cryptographic hash of v, a logical timestamp, and pointers to $t + 1$ among the N storage replicas that store v. Our MDS implementation contains an array of simple read/write registers with safe semantics for the hash values and a novel *timestamped storage* function for the other metadata. Timestamped storage offers conditional operations to multiple readers and writers, is linearizable, and has wait-free semantics. The storage replicas, on the other hand, simply store data values associated to timestamps.

The timestamped storage function is very similar to a classical atomic register [24], except that it also exposes a timestamp associated with the stored value. This permits the clients to execute conditional writes, i.e., write operations that take effect depending on the timestamp value. Interestingly, despite its support of conditional writes, timestamped storage has consensus number equal to one [20], and this paves the way for a wait-free BFT distributed implementation of the MDS in the asynchronous model. We show how to realize the MDS for *MDStore* from asynchronous BFT safe [1, 18, 31] and atomic [3, 9, 13, 30] single-writer storage protocols using $M > 3f$ metadata replicas.

In a preliminary version of this work [6], we also show why the number N of storage replicas cannot be reduced to $2t$ or less, even when only crashes are tolerated. Furthermore, we argue that cryptographic techniques, in particular, collision-free hash functions, appear to be necessary for any BFT storage emulation that uses $3t$ or fewer replicas.

The rest of the paper is organized as follows. The next section further discusses the relation of *MDStore* to other work; Section 3 introduces the system model and definitions. In Section 4, protocol *MDStore* is presented with an overview, pseudocode, an example execution, and a formal correctness argument.

2   Related Work

The formal study of *registers* as abstractions for concurrently accessed read/write storage starts with Lamport's classical paper [24]; this work also introduced safe, regular, and atomic consistency properties. Martin et al. [32] establish a tight lower bound of $3t + 1$ replicas for any register implementation that tolerates t Byzantine replicas in an asynchronous system. Their bound applies even to a single-writer single-reader safe register, where the reader and the writer may only fail by crashing. In this paper, we refine our understanding of this bound by logically separating the replicas into storage replicas and metadata replicas. Protocol *MDStore* shows that the lower bound of $3t + 1$ replicas [32] applies only to metadata replicas that exercise a control function. The number of storage replicas, which take care of storing the data, can be lowered to $2t + 1$ in the presence of t Byzantine faults, assuming cryptographic techniques.

Some elements of *MDStore* are similar to mechanisms in Farsite [2], a virtual file service that tolerates some Byzantine nodes, and Hybris [14], a recent hybrid cloud storage system. In particular, Farsite and Hybris separate metadata from data, they store cryptographic hashes and maintain directory information in a metadata service, and they both use only $2t+1$ storage replicas that are subject to Byzantine faults. However, unlike *MDStore*, the metadata services of Farsite and Hybris are based on a generic service implemented by a replicated state machine. Hence, Farsite and Hybris are subject to the FLP impossibility result [17] and require at least partial synchrony [15], whereas *MDStore* is asynchronous. The replication mechanism in Farsite assumes there is a single writer and uses read/write locks for concurrency control. On the other hand, Hybris is not wait-free as it only provides reads that are live in the presence of finitely many concurrent writes (so-called *FW-termination* [1]). Protocol *MDStore*, in contrast, supports multiple concurrent writers, offers atomic semantics, and provides wait-free termination without resorting to locks.

Many practical storage systems separate data and control for reasons related to performance and modularity [36]. In an asynchronous model where nodes are subject to crashes, several replicated storage systems have divided the control path for metadata from the data path for bulk data [10, 16, 35]. Interestingly, on a conceptual level, this separation does not pay off with crash-faulty replicas, as it does not allow to lower the number of storage replicas to below $2t + 1$. These related systems all require $2t + 1$ storage replicas. It can be shown that this is inherent: $2t + 1$ storage replicas are necessary, even with a fault-free metadata service [6].

In the context of state-machine replication and the consensus problem, separating data from control functions is a well-known technique. Lamport's Paxos consensus algorithm [25, 26] introduces three roles for the participant processes and distinguishes between proposers, acceptors, and learners. The lower bound of $3t + 1$ replicas for partially synchronous BFT consensus only applies to the acceptors but not to proposers or learners [27]. For example, there is a partially synchronous BFT consensus protocol in which any number of proposers and learners may be Byzantine [19]. Yin et al. [37] separate the agreement function from an execution component in a BFT system for generic state-machine replication, with $3t + 1$ replicas needed for agreement and $2t + 1$ replicas for storing state and executing commands. However, just like Farsite [2] and Hybris [14], these designs are fundamentally different from the principle underlying *MDStore*. As these are based on consensus, they are subject to the impossibility of consensus in asynchronous systems [17]; therefore, they rely on stronger timing assumptions [15].

3   System Model and Definitions

System model. We consider an asynchronous distributed system of *process abstractions* that communicate with each other. There are at least four kinds of processes: (1) a set $\mathcal{M} = \{m_1, \ldots, m_M\}$ of M *metadata replicas* that act as servers for (small) metadata, (2) a set $\mathcal{S} = \{s_1, \ldots, s_N\}$ of N *storage replicas* that store (large) values, (3) a set $\mathcal{W}$ of *writers* and (4) a set $\mathcal{R}$ of *readers*. The readers and writers together form the set $\mathcal{C}$ of *clients*, which run operations on the storage service. The set $\mathcal{R} = \mathcal{M} \cup \mathcal{S}$ denotes all *replicas*, which provide the storage service. Clients are disjoint from replicas. Processes may be *correct*, *benign*, or *Byzantine*, as defined later.

The processes interact asynchronously by exchanging events. A protocol specifies a collection of algorithms with instructions for all processes; equivalently, a distributed algorithm can be seen as a collection of deterministic automata, where each process is assigned an automaton. An *execution* of an algorithm is an infinite sequence of the *steps* taken by the correct and benign processes according to their algorithms, together with the actions of the Byzantine processes. More formal descriptions appear in the literature [7, 29].

A process may fail by *crashing* or by exhibiting *Byzantine* faults. A *benign* process executes its algorithm until it crashes and takes no further steps. A *Byzantine* process may perform arbitrary actions, such as sending arbitrary messages or changing its state in an arbitrary manner (NR-arbitrary faults). We assume an *adversary* that coordinates the Byzantine processes and controls the scheduling of events.

All writers are benign (they are correct or may crash), readers may be Byzantine, up to f metadata replicas are Byzantine, where $M > 3f$, and up to t storage replicas are Byzantine, where $N > 2t$. Processes that do not fail are called *correct*.

Channels. We assume that every process can communicate with every other process over point-to-point perfect asynchronous communication channels with FIFO order [7]. Perfect channels guarantee reliable communication among correct processes, i.e., that every message sent from a correct process is eventually delivered to a correct receiver exactly once. In an actual implementation, the channels between clients and replicas are *authenticated* in the sense that the adversary cannot modify or insert messages on the channels. Using point-to-point channels and a message-authentication code (MAC) [23], such authenticated channels can be implemented easily.

Notation. Protocols are presented in a modular way using an event-based notation [7]. A process exposes an *interface* to other processes, which defines the events that it exposes. Processes are specified either through abstract *properties* or via an *implementation*. A process may react to a received event by doing computation and triggering further events. Every process is named by an identifier. Events are qualified by the process identifier to which the event belongs and may take parameters. An event *Sample* of a process m with a parameter x is denoted by $\langle m\text{-}Sample \mid x \rangle$.

Objects and histories. An *object* is a special type of process for which every input event (called an *invocation* in this context) triggers exactly one output event (called a *response*). Every such pair of invocation and response define an *operation* of the object. An operation *completes* when its response occurs.

A *history* σ of an execution of an object O consists of the sequence of invocations and responses of O occurring in σ. An operation is called *complete* in a history if it has a matching response. An operation *o precedes* another operation o' in a sequence of events σ, denoted $o <_\sigma o'$, whenever o completes before o' is invoked in σ. If o precedes o' then o' *follows* o. A sequence of events π *preserves the real-time order* of a history σ if for every two operations o and o' in π, if $o <_\sigma o'$ then $o <_\pi o'$. Two operations are *concurrent* if neither one of them precedes the other. A sequence of events is *sequential* if it does not contain concurrent operations.

An execution is *well-formed* if the events at every object are alternating invocations and matching responses, starting with an invocation. An execution is *fair*, informally, if it does not halt prematurely when there are still steps to be taken or triggered events to be consumed (see the standard literature for a formal definition [28]).

Registers. A *read/write register* r is an object that stores a value from a domain $\mathcal{V}$ and supports exactly two operations, for writing and reading the value. More precisely:

- A *Write* operation to r is triggered by an invocation $\langle$ *r-Write* $|$ v $\rangle$ that takes a value $v \in \mathcal{V}$ as parameter and terminates by generating a response $\langle$ *r-WriteAck* $\rangle$ with no parameter.
- A *Read* operation from r is triggered by an invocation $\langle$ *r-Read* $\rangle$ with no parameter; the register signals that the read operation completes by triggering a response $\langle$ *r-ReadVal* $|$ v $\rangle$, which contains a parameter $v \in \mathcal{V}$.

The behavior of a register is given through its sequential specification, which requires that every *r-Read* operation returns the value written by the last preceding *r-Write* operation in the execution, or the special symbol $\bot \notin \mathcal{V}$ if no such operation exists. For simplicity, we will assume that every distinct value is written only once.

In this work, there are multiple readers and writers for the emulated storage, but only readers may invoke *Read* operations and only writers may invoke *Write* operations on the emulated register. Such a register is also called a *multi-writer multi-reader (MWMR) register* (we will also use a *single-writer* variant, abbreviated *SWMR*). Furthermore, we assume that all clients invoke a *well-formed* sequence of operations.

Consistency and availability. Recall that clients interact with an object O through its operations, defined in terms of an invocation and a response event of O. We say that a client c *executes* an operation between the corresponding invocation and response events. When accessed concurrently by multiple processes, executions of objects considered in this work are *linearizable*, that is, the object appears to execute all operations *atomically*.

More formally, a sequence of events π is called a *view* of a history σ at a client c w.r.t. an object O whenever:

1. π is a sequential permutation of some subsequence of complete operations in σ;
2. all complete operations executed by c appear in π; and
3. π satisfies the sequential specification of O.

Definition 1 (Linearizability [21]). *A history σ is linearizable w.r.t. an object O if there exists a sequence of events π such that:*

1. π is a view of σ at all clients w.r.t. O; and
2. π preserves the real-time order of σ.

The goal of this work is to describe a protocol that emulates a linearizable register abstraction among the clients; such a register is also called *atomic*. Some of the clients may crash and some replicas may be Byzantine, but every client operation should terminate in all cases, irrespective of how other clients and replica behave.

Definition 2 (Wait-freedom [20]). *A protocol is called* wait-free *if every operation invoked by a correct client eventually completes.*

Cryptography. We make use of cryptographic hash functions. One can imagine that these are implemented by a distributed oracle accessible to all processes [7]. A hash function H maps an input value x of arbitrary length (e.g., represented as a bit string) to a short, unique representation in a small domain (e.g., a bit string of fixed length). We use a *collision-free* hash function; this property means that no process, not even a Byzantine process, can find two distinct values x and x' such that $H(x) = H(x')$.

4   Protocol *MDStore*

MDStore emulates a MWMR atomic wait-free register. Our implementation of *MDStore* is modular. We begin this section by specifying an abstract metadata service (MDS). Then we given an overview of *MDStore*, which uses the MDS abstraction and $N > 2t$ storage replicas, describe its implementation, and illustrate it through a sample execution. Subsequently we discuss possible implementations of the MDS in a distributed system from $M > 3f$ metadata replicas. Finally, we argue why *MDStore* provides a wait-free atomic register.

4.1   Timestamped Storage and the Metadata Service

The metadata service used by *MDStore* is assumed to be a wait-free abstraction provided by a correct process. The MDS comprises two independent functions: the first is a storage abstraction called *timestamped storage*, which resembles a register object with a versioned interface and a particular sequential specification; the second one models an *array of registers* for storing hash values associated to timestamps.

The specification of the MDS appears in Alg. 1. The timestamped storage function is accessed through the *MDS-WriteTs* and *MDS-ReadMax* operations and maintains a timestamp ts and a value $data$. In order to write a timestamped value, a client supplies a write-timestamp wts and a data value v. The MDS stores (wts, v) in its state $(ts, data)$ if and only if $wts \geq ts$. In a read operation for the timestamped value, the MDS returns the stored ts and $data$.

In the specification of timestamped storage it is critical that the guard for a *MDS-WriteTs* operation to "take effect" requires wts to be *greater than or equal to* the stored ts. With this condition, timestamped storage has consensus number *one* [20] and can be implemented from simple atomic registers, as discussed later in Section 4.4.

In contrast, Cachin et al. [8] define a "replica" object that is the same as the times-tamped storage function, except that the guard for the conditional write requires the write-timestamp to be *strictly greater* than the stored timestamp; this object, however, is much more powerful and more difficult to implement, as it has an infinite consensus number [8].

The second function of the MDS stores an array of independent hash values associated with timestamps. The operations *MDS-WriteHash* and *MDS-ReadHash* implement these in the canonical way.

Algorithm 1. Timestamped-storage metadata service *MDS*.

1: **Types**
2:     $TS = \mathbb{N}_0 \times (\mathcal{C} \cup \{\bot\})$, with fields *num* and *c*   // $ts = (ts.num, ts.c)$ for $ts \in TS$

3: **State**
4:     $ts \in TS$, initially $(0, \bot)$ // Timestamp of stored value
5:     $data \in \Sigma^*$, initially $\bot$ // Stored metadata associated with ts
6:     $hashes[ts] \in \Sigma^*$, initially $\bot$, for $ts \in TS$ // Hash values associated to timestamps

7: **upon** $\langle$ *MDS-WriteTs* $\mid wts, v \rangle$ **do**
8:     **if** $wts > ts$ **then**
9:         $(ts, data) \leftarrow (wts, v)$
10:     **invoke** $\langle$ *MDS-WriteTsAck* $\rangle$

11: **upon** $\langle$ *MDS-ReadMax* $\rangle$ **do**
12:     **invoke** $\langle$ *MDS-ReadMaxVal* $\mid ts, data \rangle$

13: **upon** $\langle$ *MDS-WriteHash* $\mid ts, h \rangle$ **do**
14:     $hashes[ts] \leftarrow h$
15:     **invoke** $\langle$ *MDS-WriteHashAck* $\mid ts \rangle$

16: **upon** $\langle$ *MDS-ReadHash* $\mid ts \rangle$ **do**
17:     **invoke** $\langle$ *MDS-ReadHashVal* $\mid ts, hashes[ts] \rangle$

4.2 Description

Protocol *MDStore* operates similar to related algorithms and associates an increasing timestamp, chosen by the writer, to every written value. It employs the MDS for storing metadata of two kinds according to the previous section. First, the timestamped storage function of the MDS maintains the *authoritative* timestamp ts, i.e., the one of the most recently written value; it also acts as a *directory* by pointing to a set of $t + 1$ storage replicas that store the value associated with ts. This resembles the role of metadata in Farsite [2] and LDR [16]. The second function of the MDS permits to store hash values associated with timestamps, and writers in *MDStore* store the hash of a written value there, indexed by the timestamp. The hash ensures the integrity of the value towards readers, as a majority of the storage replicas may be Byzantine. Every client may write to and read from the MDS, but the hash values for a particular timestamp is written only once by a single client.

A timestamp ts in *MDStore* (see also Alg. 1) is a classical multi-writer timestamp [5, 7], consisting of a pair (num, c), where num is an integer and c is a client identifier (of the writer). The latter serves to break ties. Comparison of timestamps uses lexicographic ordering such that $ts_1 > ts_2$ if and only if $ts_1.num > ts_2.num$ or $ts_1.num = ts_2.num$ and $ts_1.c > ts_2.c$.

The pseudocode for clients is given in Alg. 2 and the pseudocode for storage replicas appears in Alg. 3. At a high level, a *r-Write* operation that writes value v to register r proceeds as follows (Alg. 2): (1) the writer c_w invokes *MDS-ReadMax* and obtains the latest timestamp ts from the MDS (line 22); (2) it produces a write-timestamp wts by incrementing ts and writes the hash of v to the MDS under wts (lines 23–25); (3) c_w now invokes s_i-*Write* on all storage replicas s_i for $i \in [1, N]$ with wts and v, and waits for a set Q of $t + 1$ replicas to acknowledge the write (lines 26–30); (4) c_w writes (wts, Q) to MDS with the timestamped storage function (line 31); (5) c_w now invokes s_i-*Commit* on all storage replicas with parameter wts, such that they may garbage collect the stored values associated to timestamps smaller than ts (lines 32–33); and, finally, (6) the writer resets its internal state (lines 34–35). In response to a s_i-*Write* operation, a storage replica saves the written value indexed by the write-timestamp, as long as the write-timestamp exceeds the most recently committed timestamp at s_i. This means that a storage replica may store multiple values at one time.

On the other hand, when a reader c_r invokes *r-Read*, it first obtains the authoritative metadata $(ts, replicas)$ from the MDS, where $replicas$ denotes the $t + 1$ storage replicas which have stored the value and acknowledged it to the writer (Alg. 2, line 38). The reader then invokes s_i-*Read* with parameter $rts = ts$ on s_i for $i \in replicas$ (lines 42–44). The storage replica s_i responds with the value indexed by the timestamp rts supplied by c_r; however, if s_i has already committed a higher timestamp than rts and thus deleted the corresponding value, then it advances the timestamp to the committed timestamp and responds with that value (lines 61–64, Alg. 3). Hence, the reader c_r obtains a value associated to timestamp rts or to a higher one.

Since clients cannot trust replicas, the reader *validates* the value received through s_i-*ReadVal* from the replica. To this end, c_r consults the MDS and verifies that the hash of the value v with timestamp ts received from the replica matches the hash stored at the MDS as follows (lines 45–51): (1) c_r retrieves the hash value h' corresponding to ts from the MDS; (2) c_r will check that $H(v) = h'$ (line 51); (3) if ts (which was obtained from s_i) is higher than rts (which the reader requested) due to a concurrent write operation, then c_r validates ts by retrieving the authoritative metadata with the currently highest timestamp $\overline{ts}$ from the MDS and by checking that ts lies between rts and $\overline{ts}$ (lines 47–51).

As a side remark to Alg. 2, the values $data$ and $data'$ obtained in lines 22 and 48, respectively, are ignored.

Intuitively, the register emulation preserves safety because the MDS stores an authoritative hash of the value stored by the (Byzantine) storage replicas. Furthermore, client operations are linearizable because of the atomic operations on the MDS primitive. For

Algorithm 2. Protocol *MDStore*, atomic register instance r for client c.

18: **State**
19:     $wts, rts \in TS$, initially $(0, \perp)$ // Timestamp of written and read value, resp.
20:     $Q \in 2^{\mathbb{N}}$, initially $\emptyset$ // Storage replicas that have acknowledged write

21: **upon** $\langle$ *r-Write* $| v \rangle$ **do**
22:     **invoke** $\langle$ *MDS-ReadMax* $\rangle$; **wait for** $\langle$ *MDS-ReadMaxVal* $| ts, data \rangle$
23:     $wts \leftarrow (ts.num + 1, c)$
24:     **invoke** $\langle$ *MDS-WriteHash* $| wts, H(v) \rangle$
25:     **wait for** $\langle$ *MDS-WriteHashAck* $| ts' \rangle$ **such that** $ts' = wts$
26:     **forall** $i \in [1, N]$ **do**
27:         **invoke** $\langle$ s_i-*Write* $| wts, v \rangle$

28: **upon** $\langle$ s_i-*WriteAck* $| ts \rangle$ **such that** $ts = wts$ **do**
29:     $Q \leftarrow Q \cup \{i\}$
30:     **if** $|Q| > t$ **then**
31:         **invoke** $\langle$ *MDS-WriteTs* $| wts, Q \rangle$; **wait for** $\langle$ *MDS-WriteTsAck* $\rangle$
32:         **forall** $i \in [1, N]$ **do**
33:             **invoke** $\langle$ s_i-*Commit* $| wts \rangle$
34:         $wts \leftarrow (0, \perp)$
35:         $Q \leftarrow \emptyset$
36:         **invoke** $\langle$ *r-WriteAck* $\rangle$

37: **upon** $\langle$ *r-Read* $\rangle$ **do**
38:     **invoke** $\langle$ *MDS-ReadMax* $\rangle$; **wait for** $\langle$ *MDS-ReadMaxVal* $| ts, replicas \rangle$
39:     **if** $ts = (0, \perp)$ **then**
40:         **invoke** $\langle$ *r-ReadVal* $| \perp \rangle$
41:     $rts \leftarrow ts$
42:     **forall** $i \in replicas$ **do**
43:         **invoke** $\langle$ s_i-*Read* $| rts \rangle$

44: **upon** $\langle$ s_i-*ReadVal* $| ts, v \rangle$ **do**
45:     **invoke** $\langle$ *MDS-ReadHash* $| ts \rangle$
46:     **wait for** $\langle$ *MDS-ReadHashVal* $| ts', h' \rangle$ **such that** $ts' = ts$
47:     **if** $ts > rts$ **then**
48:         **invoke** $\langle$ *MDS-ReadMax* $\rangle$; **wait for** $\langle$ *MDS-ReadMaxVal* $| \overline{ts}, data' \rangle$
49:     **else**
50:         $\overline{ts} \leftarrow rts$
51:     **if** $rts \leq ts \leq \overline{ts} \wedge H(v) = h'$ **then**
52:         $rts \leftarrow (0, \perp)$
53:         **invoke** $\langle$ *r-ReadVal* $| v \rangle$

showing liveness and that the emulation is wait-free, note that the writer never blocks, assuming a wait-free MDS abstraction. Moreover, the timestamp *ts* obtained by the reader together with v is higher and therefore "more recent" than the timestamp *rts*, which the reader initially requested, due to the protocol logic at the storage replicas.

Algorithm 3. Protocol *MDStore*, implementation of storage replica s_i.

54: **State**
55:     $ts \in TS$, initially $(0, \perp)$ // Committed timestamp
56:     $values[ts] \in \mathcal{V}$, initially $\perp$, for $ts \in TS$ // Map of stored values

57: **upon** $\langle\ s_i\text{-}Write \mid wts, v\ \rangle$ **do**
58:     **if** $wts > ts$ **then**
59:         $values[wts] \leftarrow v$
60:     **invoke** $\langle\ s_i\text{-}WriteAck \mid wts\ \rangle$

61: **upon** $\langle\ s_i\text{-}Read \mid rts\ \rangle$ **do**
62:     **if** $rts < ts$ **then**
63:         $rts \leftarrow ts$
64:     **invoke** $\langle\ s_i\text{-}ReadVal \mid rts, values[rts]\ \rangle$

65: **upon** $\langle\ s_i\text{-}Commit \mid cts\ \rangle$ **do**
66:     **if** $cts > ts \wedge values[cts] \neq \perp$ **then**
67:         $ts \leftarrow cts$
68:         **forall** $freets \in TS$ **such that** $freets < ts$ **do**
69:             $values[freets] \leftarrow \perp$
70:     **invoke** $\langle\ s_i\text{-}CommitAck \mid cts\ \rangle$

The range check $rts \leq ts \leq \overline{ts}$ by the reader ensures that ts is also permitted with respect to the authoritative timestamp $\overline{ts}$. The formal analysis appears in Section 4.5.

4.3   Illustration

We illustrate *MDStore* using an execution σ, depicted in Figure 1. In σ, we assume $t = 1$ and $N = 3$ storage replicas. Replica s_1 does not receive any message due to asynchrony in a timely manner, whereas replica s_3 is Byzantine.

The execution starts with a complete operation $o_{w,1} = r\text{-}Write(v_1)$ that writes (ts_1, v_1) to the storage replicas s_2 and s_3; the timestamp ts_1 is a pair $(1, w_1)$ that the writer w_1 generated in line 23 during $o_{w,1}$. The operation $o_{w,1}$ is not contained in the figure, only the state of the MDS upon completion of $o_{w,1}$ is shown.

The initial write $o_{w,1}$ is followed by two concurrent operations shown in Figure 1: first, $o_{w,2} = r\text{-}Write(v_2)$ by a writer w_2, and, second, $o_r = r\text{-}Read$ by a reader r_1. Upon invoking $o_{w,2}$, writer w_2 in Step ① (referring to the numbers in Fig. 1) first invokes *MDS-ReadMax* on the MDS (line 22). When the MDS responds, the writer w_2 obtains the highest timestamp $ts_1 = (1, w_1)$. Then, w_2 computes the timestamp of its operation as $ts_2 = (2, w_2)$ (line 23) and invokes *MDS-WriteHash* with ts_2 and $H(v_2)$ in Step ② (line 24). Notice that the hash is written to the MDS *before* the write $o_{w,2}$ is exposed to other clients via the timestamp through the MDS; this will prevent a Byzantine storage replica from forging values with a given timestamp. Eventually, the MDS responds and w_2 then invokes $s_i\text{-}Write(ts_2, v_2)$ on the storage replicas for $i = 1, \ldots, 3$ in Step ③

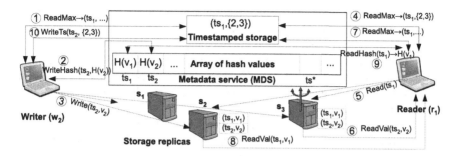

Fig. 1. An execution of *MDStore* with a concurrent r-*Write* and r-*Read* operation

(lines 26–27). The messages carrying these operations are received only by the storage replicas s_2 and s_3 (but recall that s_3 is Byzantine). Since s_2 is correct, it stores v_2 in *values*$[ts_2]$ (line 59). At this point in the execution, the writer w_2 stalls, waiting for two s_i-*WriteAck* replies from the storage replicas.

Concurrently with $o_{w,2}$, a reader r_1 invokes $o_r = r$-*Read*. The reader first queries the MDS through a *MDS-ReadMax* operation in Step ④ to determine the latest time stamp *rts* and the set *replicas*, which store the corresponding value (line 38). The MDS responds such that *rts* = ts_1 and *replicas* = $\{2,3\}$. Next, in Step ⑤, r_1 invokes s_i-*Read*(ts_1) on the storage replicas s_2 and s_3 (lines 42–44). According to the algorithm, a storage replica responds to this with the value that it stores under ts_1 or under its committed timestamp *cts*, and not necessarily with the value from *data* with the highest timestamp at the replica; for instance, at this time in σ, for replica s_2, it holds *cts* = ts_1 since no s_2-*Commit*(ts_2) has been invoked yet. However, the Byzantine replica s_3 could mount a sophisticated attack and include (ts_2, v_2) in its s_3-*ReadVal* response, see Step ⑥. Although value v_2 is in fact being written concurrently, it would be wrong for r_1 to return v_2, since readers do not write back data in *MDStore* and the write of v_2 is not yet complete — this may violate atomicity. For preventing this attack, the reader subsequently invokes *MDS-ReadMax* again to determine whether ts_2 (or a higher timestamp) has become authoritative meanwhile, in Step ⑦ (lines 47–48). Since this is not the case here, client r_1 discards the response from s_3 (after the test in line 51) and waits for an additional reply (this will arrive from s_2).

An alternative attack by the Byzantine replica s_3 could be to make up a value v^* with a large timestamp, say $ts^* = (100, w_2)$. In this case, r_1 would also check with the MDS whether ts^* or a higher timestamp has been written (just like in Step ⑦). Moreover, r_1 would check the integrity of the value reported by s_3 by retrieving the hash at ts^* from the MDS and by checking if it matches the hash of v^* (lines 45–51). As the hash function is collision-free and the MDS is correct, this check will fail.

Returning to σ, in Step ⑧, s_2 eventually responds to r_1 with the pair (ts_1, v_1) (lines 61–64). According to the protocol, r_1 successfully verifies the integrity of v_1 after obtaining the hash value at ts_1 from the MDS in Step ⑨ (lines 45–51), and the r-*Read* of r_1 returns v_1.

Eventually, the writer w_2 in $o_{w,2}$ receives two s_i-*WriteAck* responses from replicas s_2 and s_3. Then, it invokes *MDS-WriteTs* with ts_2 and the set $\{2,3\}$ in Step ⑩ (line 31). Note that the write of v_2 only "takes effect" at this point in time; in other words, the linearization point of $o_{w,2}$ coincides with the linearization point of the *MDS-WriteTs* operation with ts_2, and it is safe subsequently for readers to read v_2 from r.

Finally, the writer invokes s_i-*Commit* on all storage replicas, so as to allow them to garbage collect stale data (lines 32–33). Storage replicas update their local variable ts, which determines the value that they will send to a reader, only upon processing this s_i-*Commit* operation (lines 65–70).

Let us point out that *MDStore* uses timestamped storage at the MDS as a way to avoid storing an entire history of values at the storage replicas. One could not achieve this saving if the MDS would only expose a standard read/write register interface, since this would allow that a stored value is overwritten by a value with a lower timestamp. Given the implementation of storage replicas (notably lines 57–60) and our goal of avoiding to store entire histories, such an overwrite might cause inconsistent states between the MDS and the storage replicas.

4.4   Implementation of the Metadata Service

We show how to implement the MDS abstraction with existing asynchronous BFT storage protocols that rely on $M > 3f$ metadata replicas. In order to qualify for the implementation, such a BFT protocol should also tolerate an arbitrary number of Byzantine readers, permit multiple benign writers (which may crash), and, ideally, make no cryptographic assumptions. Recall that the MDS has two completely independent functions, providing the timestamped storage and the array of hash values. Hence, we will implement them through different components.

First, the wait-free atomic timestamped storage function can be implemented as a straightforward extension of the classical SWMR to MWMR transformation on atomic storage objects (e.g., [7, page 163]). In this transformation, there is one SWMR storage object per writer and every writer maintains a timestamp/value pair in "its" storage object, after first reading and incrementing the highest timestamp found in any other storage object. In our extension, the reader determines the timestamp/value pair with the highest timestamp among the SWMR storage objects as usual, and simply returns also the timestamp together with the value. This implementation may be realized from existing SWMR atomic wait-free storage (using $M > 3f$ replicas); some permit a computationally unbounded adversary [3, 13], whereas others assume cryptography, that is, they tolerate only a computationally bounded adversary [9, 30].

Second, the function related to the hash values consists simply of an array of SWMR safe storage objects. These may be directly implemented from the protocols with atomic semantics mentioned above. Furthermore, as one may relax the consistency guarantee for them to safe semantics, one might also employ protocols with weaker semantics, such as (1) SWMR safe wait-free storage [1] or (2) its regular variant, both without cryptographic assumptions [18], or (3) regular storage with digital signatures [31].

Finally, note that more efficient, direct, implementations of the *MDStore* metadata service can be obtained easily, but these are beyond the scope of this paper.

4.5   Analysis

In this section we prove that protocol *MDStore* in Alg. 2–3 emulates an atomic MWMR register and is wait-free.

We define the *timestamp of an operation o* on the register as follows: If o is *r-Write*, then its timestamp is the value of variable *wts* after the assignment in line 23; otherwise, if o is *r-Read*, its timestamp is the value of variable *ts* obtained through s_i-*ReadVal* (line 44) at the time when o returns by invoking *r-ReadVal*.

Lemma 1 (Monotonicity of timestamped storage). *Consider the timestamped storage function of the MDS and suppose an operation* $o_r = $ *MDS-ReadMax returns* (ts', v'). *If* o_r *follows an operation* $o_w = $ *MDS-WriteTs(ts, v) or an operation* $o'_r = $ *MDS-ReadMax that returns* (ts, v) *then* $ts' \geq ts$.

Proof. This follows directly from the sequential specification of timestamped storage in Alg. 1.   □

Lemma 2 (Sandwich). *Let* o_r *be a complete r-Read operation with timestamp ts, let rts denote the timestamp returned by the MDS in line 38 and let rts' denote the timestamp returned by the MDS in line 48. Then* $rts \leq ts \leq rts'$.

Proof. According to the definition of the operation timestamp, the timestamp of o_r is the value of the variable *ts* at line 53. Consider the test that $rts \leq ts \leq \overline{ts}$ in line 51. According to the algorithm, if $ts > rts$, then the variable $\overline{ts}$ contains rts'.   □

Lemma 3 (Partial Order). *Let* o *and* o' *be two operations with timestamps ts and ts', respectively, such that o precedes* o'. *Then* $ts \leq ts'$ *and if* o' *is a r-Write operation, then* $ts < ts'$.

Proof. Suppose o is a *r-Read* operation. Then its timestamp is either equal to *rts*, which is returned by *MDS-ReadMax* in line 38, or *ts* is not larger than $\overline{ts}$, which is returned by *MDS-ReadMax* in line 48. On the other hand, if o is a *r-Write* operation, its timestamp is written to the MDS through *MDS-WriteTs*. Hence, at the time when o completes, the monotonicity of the timestamped storage (Lemma 1) implies that any subsequent *MDS-ReadMax* operation returns a timestamp that is at least as large as *ts*.

In the following we consider operation o' that follows o and distinguish two cases:

1. Suppose o' is a *r-Read* operation. Then its timestamp ts' is at least as large as the timestamp *rts*, which is returned by *MDS-ReadMax* in line 38, and the lemma follows.

2. Otherwise, o' is a *r-Write* operation. Then its timestamp $ts' = wts$ is computed in line 23 from the timestamp returned by *MDS-ReadMax* by incrementing its first component. Hence *wts* and the timestamp of o' are strictly larger than the timestamp returned by *MDS-ReadMax* and, hence, also strictly larger than *ts*.

Lemma 4 (Unique writes). *If* o *and* o' *are two r-Write operations with timestamps ts and ts', respectively, then* $ts \neq ts'$.

Proof. If o and o' are executed by different clients, then the two timestamps differ in their second component. If o and o' are executed by the same client, then the client executed them sequentially. By Lemma 3, it follows $ts \neq ts'$.

Lemma 5 (Integrity). *Let o_r be a r-Read with timestamp ts_r that returns a value $v \neq \bot$. Then there exists a unique r-Write operation o_w that writes v such that its timestamp ts_w is equal to ts_r. Furthermore o_w does not follow after o_r.*

Proof. Since o_r returns v and has timestamp ts_r, the reader receives a s_i-*ReadVal* response containing ts_r and v from one of the storage replicas. Suppose for the purpose of contradiction that v was never written. Then, then by the collision resistance of H, the check in line 51 fails and o_r does not return v. Therefore, we conclude that some *r-Write* operation o_w has invoked s_i-*Write*(ts_r, v) on a storage replica in line 27. Since this timestamp ts_r is equal to variable *wts* and the timestamp ts_w of o_w, it follows that $ts_w = ts_r$. Finally, by Lemma 4, no other *r-Write* operation has the same timestamp, which completes the proof.

Theorem 1 (Linearizability). *Every execution of protocol MDStore is linearizable.*

Proof. Let σ be the history of any execution of *MDStore*. By Lemma 5 the timestamp of a *r-Read* operation has either been written by some *r-Write* operation or the *r-Read* operation returns $\bot$.

We first construct σ' from σ by completing all operations of the form *r-Write*(v) such that v has been returned by some complete *r-Read*. Then we construct a sequential permutation π of σ' by ordering all operations in σ', excluding the *r-Read* operations that returned $\bot$, according to their timestamps and by placing all *r-Read* operations that did not return $\bot$ immediately after the *r-Write* operation with the same timestamp. The *r-Read* operations that returned $\bot$ are placed at the beginning of π. Note that (concurrent) *r-Read* operations with the same timestamp may appear in any order, whereas all other *r-Read* operations appear in the same order as in σ'.

To prove that π preserves the sequential specification of a MWMR register we must show that every *r-Read* returns the value written by the latest *r-Write* that precedes it in π, or the initial value $\bot$ if there is no preceding *r-Write* in π. Let o_r be a *r-Read* operation returning a value v. If $v = \bot$, then by construction o_r is ordered before any *r-Write* in π.

Otherwise, $v \neq \bot$, and by Lemma 5, there exists a *r-Write*(v) operation with the same timestamp ts_r. In this case, this write is placed in π before o_r by construction. According to Lemma 4, every other *r-Write* in π has a different timestamp and, therefore, appears in π either before *r-Write*(v) or after o_r.

It remains to show that π preserves real-time order of σ. Consider two complete operations o and o' in σ' such that o precedes o' with timestamps ts and ts', respectively. Lemma 3 implies that $ts' \geq ts$. If $ts' \geq ts$, then o' follows o in π by construction. Otherwise $ts' = ts$ and Lemma 3 implies that o' is a *r-Read* operation. If o is a *r-Write* operation, then o' appears after o since we placed every *r-Read* after the *r-Write* with the same timestamp. Otherwise, if o is a *r-Read*, then it appears in π before o', as it does in σ'.

Theorem 2 (Wait-freedom). *Every execution of protocol MDStore is wait-free.*

Proof. Since the MDS abstraction used by Alg. 2 is wait-free, every operation invoked on the MDS eventually completes. It remains to show that no *r-Write* always fails the test in line 30 and that no *r-Read* operation permanently fails the check of line 51 and never returns a value.

For a *r-Write* operation o_w, the condition in line 30 is eventually satisfied because there is a time after which all correct storage replicas have responded with s_i-*WriteAck* and because there are more than t correct replicas, from the assumption $N > 2t$.

On the other hand, let o_r be a *r-Read* operation and suppose for the sake of contradiction that the condition in line 51 is never satisfied — therefore, o_r never returns. Let s_i be a correct storage replica with $i \in replicas$. Since the reader has previously invoked s_i-*Read* on s_i during o_r, it eventually receives a s_i-*ReadVal*(ts, v) in response.

If ts satisfies the clause $rts \leq ts \leq \overline{ts}$ in line 51, then the second clause of the condition, $H(v) = h'$, is also true because s_i is correct, and o_r would return. Therefore, we continue the argument assuming that $ts < rts$ or that $ts > \overline{ts}$. Recall that the reader requested timestamp rts in s_i-*Read*. If $ts < rts$, then s_i has replied with a smaller timestamp than rts, which is not possible according to the algorithm for a replica (lines 62–64). Otherwise, if $ts > \overline{ts}$, then by Lemma 2, it holds $ts > rts$, and therefore s_i has replied from its committed timestamp variable; to avoid confusion, we call this value ts^* and note that $ts^* = ts$. According to the replica code, line 67 is the only place where its committed timestamp variable may change. Furthermore, if the replica sets this variable to ts^*, then there exists a *r-Write* operation o_w^* that committed with timestamp ts^*. According to the *r-Write* code, o_w^* commits only after invoking *MDS-WriteTs* containing timestamp ts^*. Hence, if $ts > \overline{ts}$, then o_r invokes *MDS-ReadMax* in line 48 and does so after the corresponding *r-Write* wrote ts^* to the MDS. According to Lemma 1, the reader obtains from the MDS in line 48 a timestamp $\overline{ts}$ that is a least as large as ts^*. This implies that $\overline{ts} \geq ts^* = ts$, which contradicts the assumption that $ts > \overline{ts}$, and the result follows.

5 Conclusion

This paper has explored how to separate the maintenance of metadata from the storage of bulk-data in distributed storage. It introduces *MDStore*, the first fully asynchronous wait-free BFT storage protocol that reduces the number of replicas that store bulk data to as few as $2t + 1$, with t Byzantine faults. Recent work shows that the same approach also improves erasure-coded protocols for distributed storage that tolerate Byzantine faults [4], reducing the storage overhead even further.

Acknowledgment. We thank Elli Androulaki, Alessandro Sorniotti, and Nikola Knežević for inspiring discussions about this work. This work is supported in part by the EU CLOUDSPACES (FP7-317555) and SECCRIT (FP7-312758) projects.

References

[1] Abraham, I., Chockler, G., Keidar, I., Malkhi, D.: Byzantine disk Paxos: Optimal resilience with Byzantine shared memory. Distributed Computing 18(5), 387–408 (2006)
[2] Adya, A., Bolosky, W.J., Castro, M., et al.: FARSITE: Federated, available, and reliable storage for an incompletely trusted environment. In: Proc. 5th Symp. Operating Systems Design and Implementation, OSDI (2002)

[3] Aiyer, A.S., Alvisi, L., Bazzi, R.A.: Bounded wait-free implementation of optimally resilient Byzantine storage without (unproven) cryptographic assumptions. In: Pelc, A. (ed.) DISC 2007. LNCS, vol. 4731, pp. 7–19. Springer, Heidelberg (2007)

[4] Androulaki, E., Cachin, C., Dobre, D., Vukolić, M.: Erasure-coded Byzantine storage with separate metadata. Report ArXiv:1402.4958, CoRR (2014)

[5] Attiya, H., Welch, J.: Distributed Computing: Fundamentals, Simulations and Advanced Topics. McGraw-Hill, London (1998)

[6] Cachin, C., Dobre, D., Vukolić, M.: BFT storage with 2t + 1 data replicas. Report ArXiv:1305.4868, CoRR (2013)

[7] Cachin, C., Guerraoui, R., Rodrigues, L.: Introduction to Reliable and Secure Distributed Programming, 2nd edn. Springer (2011)

[8] Cachin, C., Junker, B., Sorniotti, A.: On limitations of using cloud storage for data replication. In: Proc. 6th Workshop on Recent Advances in Intrusion Tolerance and reSilience, WRAITS 2012 (2012)

[9] Cachin, C., Tessaro, S.: Optimal resilience for erasure-coded Byzantine distributed storage. In: Proc. International Conference on Dependable Systems and Networks (DSN-DCCS), pp. 115–124 (2006)

[10] Cho, B., Aguilera, M.K.: Surviving congestion in geo-distributed storage systems. In: Proc. USENIX Annual Technical Conference, pp. 439–451 (2012)

[11] Chun, B.-G., Maniatis, P., Shenker, S., Kubiatowicz, J.: Attested append-only memory: Making adversaries stick to their word. In: Proc. 21st ACM Symposium on Operating Systems Principles (SOSP), pp. 189–204 (2007)

[12] Correia, M., Neves, N.F., Veríssimo, P.: How to tolerate half less one Byzantine nodes in practical distributed systems. In: Proc. 23rd Symposium on Reliable Distributed Systems (SRDS), pp. 174–183 (2004)

[13] Dobre, D., Karame, G., Li, W., Majuntke, M., Suri, N., Vukolić, M.: PoWerStore: Proofs of writing for efficient and robust storage. In: Proc. ACM Conference on Computer and Communications Security, CCS (2013)

[14] Dobre, D., Viotti, P., Vukolić, M.: Hybris: Consistency hardening in robust hybrid cloud storage. Research Report RR-13-291, Eurécom (2013)

[15] Dwork, C., Lynch, N., Stockmeyer, L.: Consensus in the presence of partial synchrony. Journal of the ACM 35(2), 288–323 (1988)

[16] Fan, R., Lynch, N.A.: Efficient replication of large data objects. In: Fich, F.E. (ed.) DISC 2003. LNCS, vol. 2848, pp. 75–91. Springer, Heidelberg (2003)

[17] Fischer, M.J., Lynch, N.A., Paterson, M.S.: Impossibility of distributed consensus with one faulty process. Journal of the ACM 32(2), 374–382 (1985)

[18] Guerraoui, R., Vukolić, M.: How fast can a very robust read be. In: Proc. 25th ACM Symposium on Principles of Distributed Computing (PODC), pp. 248–257 (2006)

[19] Guerraoui, R., Vukolić, M.: Refined quorum systems. Distributed Computing 23(1), 1–42 (2010)

[20] Herlihy, M.: Wait-free synchronization. ACM Transactions on Programming Languages and Systems 11(1), 124–149 (1991)

[21] Herlihy, M.P., Wing, J.M.: Linearizability: A correctness condition for concurrent objects. ACM Transactions on Programming Languages and Systems 12(3), 463–492 (1990)

[22] Kapitza, R., Behl, J., Cachin, C., Distler, T., Kuhnle, S., Mohammadi, S.V., Schröder-Preikschat, W., Stengel, K.: CheapBFT: Resource-efficient Byzantine fault tolerance. In: Proc. 7th European Conference on Computer Systems (EuroSys), pp. 295–308 (April 2012)

[23] Katz, J., Lindell, Y.: Introduction to Modern Cryptography: Principles and Protocols. Chapman & Hall/CRC (2007)

[24] Lamport, L.: On interprocess communication. Distributed Computing 1(2), 77–85, 86–101 (1986)

[25] Lamport, L.: The part-time parliament. ACM Transactions on Computer Systems 16(2), 133–169 (1998)

[26] Lamport, L.: Paxos made simple. SIGACT News 32(4), 51–58 (2001)

[27] Lamport, L.: Lower bounds for asynchronous consensus. In: Schiper, A., Shvartsman, M.M.A.A., Weatherspoon, H., Zhao, B.Y. (eds.) Future Directions in Distributed Computing. LNCS, vol. 2584, pp. 22–23. Springer, Heidelberg (2003)

[28] Lynch, N.A.: Distributed Algorithms. Morgan Kaufmann, San Francisco (1996)

[29] Lynch, N.A., Tuttle, M.R.: An introduction to input/output automata. CWI Quaterly 2(3), 219–246 (1989)

[30] Malkhi, D., Reiter, M.: Secure and scalable replication in Phalanx. In: Proc. 17th Symposium on Reliable Distributed Systems, SRDS (1998)

[31] Malkhi, D., Reiter, M.K.: Byzantine quorum systems. Distributed Computing 11(4), 203–213 (1998)

[32] Martin, J.-P., Alvisi, L., Dahlin, M.: Minimal Byzantine storage. In: Malkhi, D. (ed.) DISC 2002. LNCS, vol. 2508, pp. 311–325. Springer, Heidelberg (2002)

[33] Veronese, G.S., Correia, M., Bessani, A., Lung, L.C., Veríssimo, P.: Efficient Byzantine fault tolerance. IEEE Transactions on Computers 62(1), 16–30 (2011)

[34] Vukolić, M.: Quorum Systems: With Applications to Storage and Consensus. Synthesis Lectures on Distributed Computing Theory. Morgan & Claypool Publishers (2012)

[35] Wang, Y., Alvisi, L., Dahlin, M.: Gnothi: Separating data and metadata for efficient and available storage replication. In: Proc. USENIX Annual Technical Conference, pp. 413–424 (2012)

[36] Wilkes, J., Hoover, C., Keer, B., Mehra, P., Veitch, A.: Storage, Data, and Information Systems. HP Laboratories (2008)

[37] Yin, J., Martin, J.-P., Venkataramani, A., Alvisi, L., Dahlin, M.: Separating agreement from execution for Byzantine fault-tolerant services. In: Proc. 19th ACM Symposium on Operating Systems Principles (SOSP), pp. 253–268 (2003)

On Proof-Labeling Schemes versus Silent Self-stabilizing Algorithms

Lélia Blin[1,*], Pierre Fraigniaud[2,**], and Boaz Patt-Shamir[3,***]

[1] LIP6-UPMC, University of Evry-Val d'Essonne, France
[2] CNRS and University Paris Diderot, France
[3] Department of Electrical Engineering, Tel-Aviv University, Israel

Abstract. It follows from the definition of *silent* self-stabilization, and from the definition of *proof-labeling* scheme, that if there exists a silent self-stabilizing algorithm using ℓ-bit registers for solving a task $\mathcal{T}$, then there exists a proof-labeling scheme for $\mathcal{T}$ using registers of at most ℓ bits. The first result in this paper is the converse to this statement. We show that if there exists a proof-labeling scheme for a task $\mathcal{T}$, using ℓ-bit registers, then there exists a silent self-stabilizing algorithm using registers of at most $O(\ell + \log n)$ bits for solving $\mathcal{T}$, where n is the number of processes in the system. Therefore, as far as memory space is concerned, the design of silent self-stabilizing algorithms essentially boils down to the design of compact proof-labeling schemes. The second result in this paper addresses time complexity. We show that, for every task $\mathcal{T}$ with k-bits output size in n-node networks, there exists a silent self-stabilizing algorithm solving $\mathcal{T}$ in $O(n)$ rounds, using registers of $O(n^2 + kn)$ bits. Therefore, as far as running time is concerned, *every* task has a silent self-stabilizing algorithm converging in a linear number of rounds.

1 Introduction

1.1 Context and Objective

A distributed algorithm is *self-stabilizing* [12] if it eventually reaches a legal state starting from any arbitrary state, and remains in a legal state whenever starting from a legal state. A self-stabilizing algorithm is therefore well suited to withstand transient failures in which the content of the variables can be arbitrarily corrupted. In the context of network algorithms, and assuming a computational model in which every node has atomic read/write access to its single-writer multiple-readers public register, and atomic read-only access to the public register of each of its neighbors in the network, three main criteria have been considered for measuring the quality of algorithms:

---

* Additional supports from ANR project IRIS.
** Additional support from ANR project DISPLEXITY, INRIA project GANG, and the French-Israeli Laboratory on Foundations of Computer Science (FILOFOCS).
*** Additional support from the French-Israeli Laboratory on Foundations of Computer Science (FILOFOCS).

P. Felber and V. Garg (Eds.): SSS 2014, LNCS 8756, pp. 18–32, 2014.
© Springer International Publishing Switzerland 2014

1. Time, i.e., either the number of individual steps, or the number of collective rounds, or both, required to reach a legal state;
2. Compactness, i.e., the size of the public registers;
3. Silence, i.e., the fact that nodes keep their registers unmodified once a legal state has been reached.

Minimizing time is crucial for evident efficiency reasons. Nevertheless, compactness and silentness are also crucial in many contexts. In particular, keeping the registers small enables to limit the amount of data exchanged between the processors, and hence it avoids overloading the system with a heavy traffic among nodes [1]. Silentness is also desirable as it guarantees that, whenever the system is in a legal state, nodes stop taking unnecessary steps, and hence it enables self-stabilization not to burden the system with unnecessary computations [13]. Silentness can be viewed as a kind of *termination* mechanism combined with a *trigger* mechanism, the former insuring that the self-stabilization protocol becomes quiet when the system is in legal state, while the latter insures that the self-stabilization protocol wakes up in case the system enters an illegal state.

In this paper we address the issue of designing fast and/or compact silent self-stabilizing network algorithms for *arbitrary* tasks.

There is an abundant literature (see Section 1.3) on the design of compact silent self-stabilizing network algorithms for specific tasks, including the election of a leader, and the construction of various types of spanning trees (BFS, min-degree, MST, etc.). In each of these algorithms, silentness is guaranteed thanks to the — implicit or explicit — use of a mechanism known as *proof-labeling scheme* [19]. This mechanism provides each solution of the considered task with a distributed *certificate* consisting of a collection of individual certificates (also called *labels*) assigned to all nodes. When each node has its own certificate as well as the certificates of its neighbors at hand, the nodes can collectively decide whether the current state is legal or not. More precisely, in a proof-labeling scheme, each node has a local predicate over its label and its neighbors' labels, such that the state is legal if and only if all local predicates are satisfied. That is, if a state is not legal then the scheme must insure that some inconsistencies between the certificates will be detected locally by some node(s). In the context of self-stabilization, a node detecting some local inconsistency between the certificates *rejects*. In the spirit of [2], the rejection of a state by some process(es) leads the processes to continue their attempt to reach a legal state, potentially resetting the entire system, or just carrying on the execution leading to eventual convergence to a legal state.

It follows from the definition of the aforementioned concepts that any mechanism insuring silent self-stabilization is essentially equivalent to a proof-labeling scheme. Slight differences may occur because of small variants in the computational model, including, e.g., (1) link-registers versus node-registers, or (2) the ability to read only the certificates of the neighbors versus the ability to read the certificates as well as the data stored by these neighbors, etc. Nevertheless, conceptually, silentness mechanisms and proof-labeling schemes are essentially equivalent under all reasonable variants.

More specifically, it follows from the definition of silent self-stabilization and of proof-labeling scheme that, if there exists a silent self-stabilizing algorithm using ℓ-bit node-registers for solving some task $\mathcal{T}$, then there exists a proof-labeling scheme for $\mathcal{T}$ using registers of at most ℓ bits. An important consequence of this result is that any lower bound B on the size of certificates in a proof-labeling scheme for a task $\mathcal{T}$ implies a lower bound B on the size of the registers required for any silent stabilizing implementation of $\mathcal{T}$. Establishing such kind of space lower bounds for silent self-stabilizing algorithms was, among others, one motivation for introducing proof-labeling schemes [19].

This paper is concerned with converses of this latter statement. More generally, we study the issue of designing fast and/or compact silent self-stabilizing algorithms for *arbitrary* tasks, taking advantage of various kinds of proof-labeling schemes for these tasks. Table 1 summarizes our results, which are detailed next.

Table 1. *Space and time complexities of silent self-stabilizing algorithms in n-node networks for an arbitrary task $\mathcal{T}$, as a function of the minimum size ℓ of a proof-labeling scheme for $\mathcal{T}$, or of the output size k of $\mathcal{T}$.*

	size of registers	number of rounds
lower bound	$\Omega(\ell)$	–
algorithm CSSS	$O(\ell + \log n)$	$O(n2^{n\ell})$
algorithm FSSS	$O(n^2 + nk)$	$O(n)$

1.2   Our Results

First, we show that if there exists a proof-labeling scheme for a task $\mathcal{T}$, using ℓ-bit node-registers, then there exists a silent self-stabilizing algorithm using node-registers of at most $O(\ell + \log n)$ bits for solving $\mathcal{T}$, where n is the number of processes in the network. Therefore, as far as memory space is concerned, the design of silent self-stabilizing algorithms essentially boils down to the design of compact proof-labeling schemes. Note that the latter is significantly easier than the former. Indeed, proof-labeling schemes just deal with the set up of *static* distributed data structures, while self-stabilization must cope with *dynamic* corruptions of variables, and with the actions of the *scheduler* governing the way processes take steps.

Second, we prove that, for every task $\mathcal{T}$ with k-bits output size at each node in n-node networks, there exists a silent self-stabilizing algorithm solving $\mathcal{T}$ in $O(n)$ rounds with registers of $O(n^2 + kn)$ bits. Therefore, we prove that *every* task enjoys a silent self-stabilizing algorithm converging in a linear number of rounds. This algorithm uses register of polynomial size, which can be larger than the optimal for some tasks. Nevertheless, the bound $O(n^2 + kn)$ bits for the size of the registers is existentially optimal in the sense that for some tasks, $\Omega(n^2 + kn)$ bits are required by any proof-labeling scheme (see [3,14,15]).

All our results are constructive, in the sense that we provide explicit descriptions of algorithms reaching these bounds, respectively called CSSS and FSSS, for *compact* and *fast* silent self-stabilizing algorithm, respectively. The complexity analysis of the algorithms is done with respect to an unfair scheduler.

1.3   Related Work

The reader is referred to the textbook [12] for an introduction to the main techniques used for designing self-stabilizing algorithms. There is a large volume of literature focussing on the design of silent self-stabilizing protocols for various kinds of tasks. In particular, a significant effort has been dedicated to different forms of spanning tree constructions, as the presence of a spanning tree is an effective tool for the design of many self-stabilizing algorithms (this is the case of the algorithms in this paper as well). It is thus worth mentioning the construction of spanning trees in [9,20], as well as the construction of breadth-first search (BFS) trees in [1,10,16]. These constructions have optimal $\Theta(\log n)$-bit space-complexity.

The case of minimum-weight spanning tree (MST) construction is also worth being mentioned here as well, because of the non-trivial lower bound established in [17], which proves that any silent MST construction algorithm requires registers on $\Omega(\log^2 n)$ bits. Proof-labeling schemes matching this bound can be found in [17] and [19]. Papers [5,7,18] have proposed compact self-stabilizing constructions, using just $O(\log n)$ bits of memory per node. These compact algorithms are however not silent. ([18] is uniform and converges in $O(n)$ rounds, while [7] is just semi-uniform, and converges in $O(n^3)$ rounds). Recently [6] designed a space-optimal $\Theta(\log n)$-bit register silent self-stabilizing algorithm for approximating minimum-degree spanning tree within additive 1 from the optimal, converging in a polynomial number of rounds. The techniques in [6] can be generalized to design a silent self-stabilizing MST construction using registers of optimal size $\Theta(\log^2 n)$ bits.

In addition, several papers address the leader election task, which is inherently related to spanning tree construction. In particular, [4,11] have proposed silent self-stabilizing leader election algorithms. See also [8] for an exponential gap between the size of the registers in silent and non-silent leader election algorithms. More generally, the reader is especially referred to [13] where the interplay between space complexity and silentness is thoroughly investigated, for various problems, including tree construction and leader election, under different hypotheses.

Before completing this non exhaustive survey of related work, it is worth pointing out that there are subtle but important differences between the notion of proof-labeling scheme [19] and the notion of non-deterministic local distributed decision [14]. Both are assuming the ability to use distributed certificates. However, the latter does not impose restriction on the number of communication rounds before taking decision, while, in essence, proof-labeling scheme performs in one single rounds. Nevertheless, the theory of proof-labeling scheme can easily be extended to allowing more rounds [15]. In fact, the main difference between the two concepts is that, in a proof-labeling scheme, the certificate may depend on the current identity of the node, while, in non-deterministic local distributed decision, the certificates must not depend on this identity. That is, in particular, proof-labeling scheme allows the certificates to be functions of the node IDs, while non-deterministic local distributed decision does not.

Finally, [3] recently aimed at investigating possible generalizations of proof-labeling scheme, and of local distributed decision, where legality is not necessarily the logical conjunction of the local predicates.

2   Framework

In this section, we specify our computational model. More importantly, we also precisely define the different concepts of *configurations*, *states*, *tasks*, *self-stabilization*, and *proof-labeling schemes*, so that to appropriately formulate our general results in Sections 3 and 4.

2.1   Computational Model

We are dealing with a system in which each computational entity is the node of an asynchronous network modeled as a simple connected n-node graph $G = (V, E)$. The nodes act as autonomous computing entities. More specifically, every node $u \in V$ has a distinct identity, denoted by $id(u) \in \{1, \ldots, n^c\}$ for some constant $c \geq 1$, and is a processor with read/write access to a single-writer multiple-readers *public* register. In one atomic *step*, every node can (1) read its own register as well as the registers of its neighbors in G, (2) perform individual computations, and (3) update its register accordingly.

Describing self-stabilizing distributed algorithms is often done by describing the actions of an *abstract state machine*. Each node executes the same instruction set which consists in one or more *rules* of the form:

$$\text{name-of-rule} : guard \longrightarrow command \tag{1}$$

where *guard* is a boolean predicate over the variables in the registers of the node as well as in the registers of its neighbors, and *command* is a statement assigning new values to the variables of the node. An *enabled*, or *activatable*, node is a node for which at least one guard is true. A non activatable node is *idle*. The network is asynchronous in the sense that nodes take step of computation in arbitrary order, under the control of a *scheduler*. For instance, an *unfair* scheduler is free to make arbitrary choices about which node to activate among the set of activatable nodes. It is only bounded to activate one of the currently activatable nodes. Such scheduler is indeed "unfair" because a node may be perpetually activatable, yet the scheduler may never activate it.

The model described above is sometime called the *node-register state model*. Some results in this paper extend to the *link-register* version of the model. In this latter (stronger) model, instead of one public register per node, every node has one single-writer multiple-reader public register for each of its incident *links*, readable by the node at the other extremity of the link.

A *fault* is the corruption of some variable(s) in the register(s) of one or more node(s) in the network. After a fault has occurred, the system may be in an illegal state (to be formalized in the next section). It is the role of the algorithm to detect the illegality of the current state, and to make sure that the system returns to a legal state.

Remark. The algorithms described in this paper could be expressed in the abstract state machine format of Eq. (1). However, in this paper, we shall not provide such algorithm descriptions because, although conceptually not difficult, this would result in long and tedious codes which would not enlighten the main ideas in our contributions. Nevertheless, the reader aware of the programming methodology in the context of self-stabilization can easily convince himself or herself that our algorithms can be implemented appropriately so that to run under any unfair scheduler.

2.2   Configurations, Tasks, and States

In this subsection, we formalize the concept of *tasks*. For this purpose, we distinguish two closely related notions: *configuration* and *state*. While the former focusses solely on the value of the outputs, the latter also focusses on the local variables used to compute these outputs.

a) Configurations. An *identity assignment*, *id*, to the nodes of a graph G is the assignment to every node $u \in V(G)$ of an identity, $id(u) \in \mathbb{N}$, such that $id(u) \neq id(v)$ for every two distinct nodes u and v. Following the terminology of [14], we call *configuration* any triple

$$C = (G, id, x)$$

where G is an n-node connected graph, *id* is an identity assignment to the nodes of G, and x is a set of n binary strings, $x = \{x(u) \in \{0,1\}^*, u \in V(G)\}$.

b) Tasks. A *task* is defined as a collection $\mathcal{T}$ of configurations satisfying the following two properties:

1. Feasibility: for every connected graph G, and any identity assignment *id* to the nodes of G, there must exist x such that $(G, id, x) \in \mathcal{T}$;
2. Computability: $\mathcal{T}$ is computable, in the classical sense of (sequential) computability theory, that is, there exists an algorithm which, given (G, id, x), decides whether $(G, id, x) \in \mathcal{T}$.

We insist on computable tasks since, otherwise, even a system aware of an entire configuration may not be able to decide whether it is legal or not. Intuitively, the feasibility property guaranties that, for each possible system (G, id) consisting of a network G with node-identities provided by id, there exists a possible "output" x for the nodes such that $(G, id, x) \in \mathcal{T}$.

The configurations in $\mathcal{T}$ are said to be *legal* for $\mathcal{T}$, and configurations not in $\mathcal{T}$ are said to be *illegal* for $\mathcal{T}$.

For instance, the task of constructing a spanning tree can be specified by the set of configurations (G, id, x) where, for every node u, $x(u)$ is either $\perp$ or the identity of some neighbor v of u, and the 1-factor

$$\{(u, x(u)) : u \in V(G) \text{ and } x(u) \neq \perp\} \tag{2}$$

forms a rooted spanning tree of G. (Hence, $x(u)$ is the parent of u, each arc $(u, x(u))$ points upward in the tree, and the root r satisfies $x(r) = \perp$). Note that a task needs not to depend on the identity assignments, in which case, for every n-node connected graph G, and any n-dimensional vector x of binary strings, we have:

$$(G, id, x) \in \mathcal{T} \Rightarrow (G, id', x) \in \mathcal{T}$$

for any two identity assignments id and id'. On typical example is the leader election task specified as the set of configurations (G, id, x) where, for every node u, $x(u) \in \{0, 1\}$, and there is a unique node u in G satisfying $x(u) = 1$. (In this latter setting, one does not insist on having every node know the identity of the leader).

In some contexts, the collection of networks under consideration may not be the class of all connected graphs, but be restricted to some families of graphs, like, e.g., planar graphs, trees, rings, etc. All what follow also holds if networks are a priori restricted to belong to some arbitrary class $\mathcal{G}$ of networks.

c) **States.** In the node-register state model, the *state* of a node u is a pair

$$S(u) = (x(u), y(u))$$

of binary strings, respectively called the *output* string and the *auxiliary* string. The *state* of a network G with identity assignment id is then represented as the triple $(G, id, (x, y))$ where x and y are two sets of n binary strings. The legality of a state depends on the task $\mathcal{T}$ to be solved, but, above all, on the actual algorithm A solving that task. The legality property must satisfy the following two properties:

1. Soundness: if a state $(G, id, (x, y))$ is legal for A, then the configuration (G, id, x) must be legal for $\mathcal{T}$;
2. Completeness: if a configuration (G, id, x) is legal for $\mathcal{T}$, then there must exist y such that $(G, id, (x, y))$ is legal for A.

The soundness property simply states that the algorithm cannot consider as legal a state that does not fit with any legal configuration of the task, and the completeness property simply states that the algorithm must not disqualify any legal configuration of the task.

2.3 Self-stabilization

A *self-stabilizing* algorithm solving a task $\mathcal{T}$ is a distributed algorithm A satisfying the following two properties:

1. Convergence: starting from an arbitrary state, A eventually reaches a legal state;

2. Closure: starting from a legal state, A remains in legal states.

The *register-space complexity* of the algorithm is usually expressed as a function of the number of nodes n. It is the maximum, taken over all initial states $(G, id, (x_0, y_0))$ on networks with at most n nodes, all possible execution starting from $(G, id, (x_0, y_0))$, and all nodes u, of the size of u's register. The latter is the amount of bits $|x(u)| + |y(u)|$ used to store the current output string $x(u)$ and the current auxiliary string $y(u)$ of node u, where $|s|$ denotes the number of bits in a binary string s.

Note that the size of a register cannot be made arbitrarily large by a corruption of the variables once the range of each variable is well specified. For instance, a variable storing a node-identity cannot exceed $\lceil \log_2(id_{max}) \rceil$ bits where id_{max} is the largest node-identity in the network. In our context in which nodes have identities that are polynomially bounded by the size of the network, a variable storing a node-identity cannot exceed $O(\log n)$ bits.

In any execution of a self-stabilizing algorithm A, a *round* is any shortest sequence of steps of the execution in which every activatable node at the beginning of the round was activated by the scheduler by the end of the round. If A constructs and stabilizes on the states in some family F of states, then the round-complexity of A is the maximum, taken over all initial states γ, and over all executions $\mathcal{E}$ of A starting from γ and ending in a state $\gamma' \in F$, of the number of rounds in $\mathcal{E}$. The latter is the integer k such that $\mathcal{E}$ can be decomposed in a sequence $\gamma_0 = \gamma, \gamma_1, \ldots, \gamma_k = \gamma'$ such that, for every $i = 0, \ldots, k - 1$, the round of $\mathcal{E}$ starting from γ_i ends in γ_{i+1}.

A self-stabilizing algorithm is *silent* if, once the algorithm has reached a legal state, the content of the register at each node remains unchanged. Hence, in particular, starting from a legal state, a silent self-stabilizing algorithm A remains the same state.

Since the algorithm must converge starting from any state, being silent requires a mechanism that is performed locally at each node, which enables the nodes to collectively detect whether a global state is legal or not. Indeed, if the state is illegal then some action(s) has to be performed at some node(s) in order to update their states, which requires to modify the content of some register(s). Instead, if the state is legal then no actions have to be performed, and the registers must not be modified. Such a mechanism is well captured by the notion of *proof-labeling schemes*, partially introduced in [17], extensively studied in [19], and recalled below.

2.4 Proof-Labeling Schemes

A proof-labeling scheme for a task $\mathcal{T}$ is a pair (p, v) where p is called the *prover*, and v the *verifier*. The prover has unlimited computational power, and assigns a *certificate* $z(u) \in \{0, 1\}^*$ to every node u of each configuration $(G, id, x) \in \mathcal{T}$. Such a certificate may depend on the whole configuration (G, id, x). The verifier is a distributed algorithm running at every node u, which takes as input the local information available at u, i.e., the triple $(id(u), x(u), z(u))$, as well as the set $\{(x(v), z(v)), v \in N(u)\}$, where $N(u)$ denotes set of neighborhs of node u in G. Based on this input, every node u must decide either to *accept* or to *reject*.

To be correct, the proof-labeling scheme must satisfy the following two conditions:

- if (G, id, x) is legal for $\mathcal{T}$, then the prover p must assign certificates to the nodes such that the verifier v accepts at all nodes;
- if (G, id, x) is illegal for $\mathcal{T}$, then, for every certificates assigned to the nodes, the verifier v must reject in at least one node.

For instance, a proof-labeling scheme for the aforementioned spanning tree construction task, specified in Section 2.2, consists, for the prover, to endow each node u of every legal configuration with the certificate $z(u) = (id(r), d(u))$ where r is the root of the tree, and $d(u)$ is the distance of u from r in the tree. The verifier then checks at each node u that u agrees with all its neighbors regarding the identity of the root, and that $x(u)$ satisfies $d(x(u)) = d(u) - 1$ (a root, i.e., a node with $x(u) = \bot$, checks that $d(u) = 0$). If this is the case, then u accepts, otherwise u rejects. It is easy to check that, if the configuration is illegal, that is, if the 1-factor of Eq. (2) does not form a spanning tree (i.e., it is disconnected, or has a cycle), then no certificates can make the prover accepting such a configuration.

The *size* of a proof-labeling scheme is usually expressed as a function of the number of nodes n. It is the maximum, taken over all legal configurations (G, id, x) on networks with at most n nodes, of $\max_{u \in V(G)}(|x(u)| + |z(u)|)$. When looking for a proof-labeling scheme for a task $\mathcal{T}$, one is therefore interested in using certificates whose sizes do not exceed the size of the output at each node. This is however not always possible, even for natural problems, at witnessed by the minimum-weight spanning tree (MST) construction task. Indeed, while encoding the tree consumes only $O(\log n)$ bits at each node (using the pointer-to-parent encoding), proving the correctness of the tree requires certificates on $\Omega(\log^2 n)$ bits [17].

3 A Compact Universal Silent Self-stabilizing Algorithm

The following result is to the least implicit in most papers on silent self-stabilization. For the sake of completeness, we provide a formal proof of it.

Theorem 1. *If there exists a silent self-stabilizing algorithm solving a task $\mathcal{T}$ with register-space complexity at most k bits, then there exists a proof-labeling scheme for $\mathcal{T}$ with size at most k bits.*

Proof. Let A be a silent self-stabilizing algorithm solving $\mathcal{T}$ with k-bit register. We define a proof-labeling scheme for $\mathcal{T}$ as follows. First, the certificate assignment by the prover acts like this. Let (G, id, x) be a legal configuration for $\mathcal{T}$. By the completeness property, there exists y such that $(G, id, (x, y))$ is a legal state for A. The prover sets $z(u) = y(u)$ for every node u. The verifier is then essentially A. More specifically, given an arbitrary state $(G, id, (x, y))$, if node u is idle in that state, then the verifier at u decides to accept, otherwise, i.e., if node u is activatable in that state, then the verifier at u decides to reject.

By construction, the size of this proof-labeling scheme is at most k bits. It just remains to show that it is correct. Let (G, id, x) be a legal configuration, and let $(G, id, (x, y))$ be any corresponding legal state. Since A is silent, no nodes are activatable in this state. Therefore, all nodes accept. In particular, all nodes accepts in state $(G, id, (x, z))$, as desired. Instead, let (G, id, x) be an illegal configuration. By the soundness property, the state $(G, id, (x, y))$ is illegal, for every y. Therefore, at least one node is activatable in state $(G, id, (x, y))$, and thus at least one node decides to reject, as desired. □

As we already pointed out in the introduction, Theorem 1 is mostly interesting for it enables to derive lower bounds on the size of the registers to be used by a silent self-stabilizing algorithm. For instance, since any proof-labeling scheme for MST requires certificates on $\Omega(\log^2 n)$ bits [17], it follows that any silent self-stabilizing algorithm for MST construction must use registers of $\Omega(\log^2 n)$ bits. Designing self-stabilizing algorithms for MST using logarithmic-size registers is doable [5,7,18] , but such an algorithm cannot be silent.

Our first main result is a reciprocal to Theorem 1.

Theorem 2. *If there exists a proof-labeling scheme for $\mathcal{T}$ with size at most k bits, then there exists a silent self-stabilizing algorithm solving $\mathcal{T}$ with register-space complexity $O(k + \log n)$ bits in n-node networks.*

Proof. Let $\mathcal{T}$ be a task for which there exists a proof-labeling scheme (p, v) of size at most k bits. We describe a silent self-stabilizing algorithm CSSS, for *Compact Silent Self-Stabilization*, solving $\mathcal{T}$ with registers of at most $O(k + \log n)$ bits in n-node networks. Let (G, id, x) be a valid configuration for $\mathcal{T}$. We denote by $\mathsf{p}(G, id, x)$ the certificates assigned by the prover p to the nodes of the n-node graph G with identities assigned by id. We define the new task $\widehat{\mathcal{T}}$ as:

$$\widehat{\mathcal{T}} = \{(G, id, (x, z)) : (G, id, x) \in \mathcal{T} \text{ and } \mathsf{p}(G, id, x) = z\}$$

Note that, for every configuration $(G, id, (x, z))$ in $\widehat{\mathcal{T}}$, and for every node $u \in V(G)$, we have $|x(u)| + |z(u)| \leq k$. Algorithm CSSS solves task $\widehat{\mathcal{T}}$. For this purpose, it handles states of the form $(G, id, ((x, z), y))$, using an additional auxiliary string $y(u)$ of length $O(\log k + \log n)$ bits at each node u.

Given a k-bit string σ, we use $2\lceil \log_2 k \rceil$ bits of the auxiliary string $y(u)$ at node u to position two commas at two indexes i and j in σ so that to get $\sigma = (\sigma', \sigma'', \sigma''')$ where $|\sigma'| + |\sigma''| + |\sigma'''| = k$. In essence, Algorithm CSSS is aiming at testing all pairs $(x(u), z(u))$ with $|x(u)| + |z(u)| \leq k$ at every node

$u \in V(G)$. This is achieved by enumerating all binary strings $s(u) = (\sigma_u, i_u, j_u)$ of length $k + 2\lceil \log_2 k \rceil$ bits at every node $u \in V(G)$, where $x(u)$ is expected to be the sub-string of $s(u)$ from index 1 to i_u, and $z(u)$ is expected to be the sub-string of $s(u)$ from index $i_u + 1$ to j_u. For a given n-dimensional vector $s = (s(u))_{u \in V(G)}$ whose every entry is a $(k + 2\lceil \log_2 k \rceil)$-bit string, Algorithm CSSS tests whether the verifier v accepts s, that is, whether $s(u)$ is accepted at every node u. If one node rejects s, then CSSS proceeds with another vector. Instead, if all nodes accept s, then an appropriate pair $s = (x, z)$ has been found, satisfying $(G, id, (x, z)) \in \widehat{\mathcal{T}}$. Indeed, by the definition of proof-labeling scheme, for an x such that $(G, id, x) \notin \mathcal{T}$, the verifier cannot be fooled by any distributed certificate z.

Hence, our problem boils down to enumerating and testing all n-dimensional vectors of q-bit strings, with $q = k + 2\lceil \log_2 k \rceil$, in a silent self-stabilizing manner. Algorithm CSSS uses the k-bit proof-labeling scheme (p, v) as a black box. It proceeds with enumerating all vectors, and testing them. (Note that q need not be constant, but may be a function of n. Thus, to derive the actual value of q, Algorithm CSSS may also need to compute n). For enumerating and testing all n-dimensional vectors of q-bit strings, CSSS builds up a spanning tree T of the network, and labels the nodes of T from 1 to n according to some DFS traversal of T. Each n-dimensional vector s of q-bit strings is viewed as a non negative integer $s = s_n s_{n-1} \ldots s_2 s_1$ on qn bits where s_i are the q bits handled by the node with DFS number i. To test all vectors, Algorithm CSSS actually successively considers all integers from 0 to $2^{nq} - 1$, and, for each of them, tests whether the verifier accepts or reject, until it eventually accepts.

The skeleton of Algorithm CSSS is displayed in Algorithm 1.

Algorithm 1. Skeleton of Algorithm CSSS

1: construct a spanning tree T of G, and let r be its root
2: label the nodes from 1 to n according to some DFS traversal of T starting from r
3: for every $i = 1, \ldots, n$, set $s_i = 0$ at node labeled i
4: **while** verifier v rejects $s = s_n s_{n-1} \ldots s_1$ **do**
5:      update s to $s + 1$
6: **end while**

Instruction 1 can be implemented by the silent algorithm in [11] using registers on $O(\log n)$ bits. (Alternatively, one can also use the recent simple tree construction algorithm in [6]). The setting of the DFS labeling of the nodes in the resulting tree T in Instruction 2 can be implemented by having every node v computing the size $|T_v|$ of the subtree T_v of T rooted at v. This can be done by a convergecast operation from the leaves to the root. Silentness is here achieved by having every node v verifying that $|T_v| = \sum_{u \in \mathrm{ch}(v)} |T_u|$ where $\mathrm{ch}(v)$ denotes the children of v in T, and verifying that the DFS numbers of its children are correct. The verification in Instruction 4 is performed by applying the verifier v bottom-up, along the tree T. If one descendent of a node v rejects, then v must reject. The root eventually accepts or rejects. If the root rejects, Instruction 5 is performed. That is, the root triggers the update of the current value of the string s. The root has DFS number 1, and holds s_1. If adding 1 to s_1 generates a carry, then this carry is propagated to the node with DFS number 2, which performs $s_2 \leftarrow s_2 + 1$. And so on. In general if the node v_i with DFS number i generates a carry when updating s_i to $s_i + 1$, then this carry is propagated to the node v_{i+1} with DFS number $i + 1$ as follows. If v_{i+1} is a child of v_i, this is immediate. Instead, if v_{i+1} is not a child of v_i, then the carry must be "routed" to v_{i+1}. However, routing in T can be easily implemented thanks to the DFS numbering of T.

Of course, there are several implementation details to fix, in particular for avoiding overlappings between the update phases, and the verification phases. Nevertheless, fixing these details does not offer any conceptual challenges.

Note that the implementation of Algorithm CSSS can me made under an unfair scheduler because the algorithm proceeds by bottom-up waves of updates, or by executing a "sequential" addition, where nodes perform one after the other, respecting the DFS ordering.

Eventually, the verifier will accept at all nodes, and Algorithm CSSS becomes quiet, until some fault eventually occurs. □

Algorithm CSSS described in the proof of Theorem 2 is very compact, but may stabilize in an exponential number of rounds. In the next section, we address the issue of designing fast silent self-stabilizing algorithms.

4   A Fast Universal Silent Self-stabilizing Algorithm

Having in mind that every task with k-bits output size in n-node networks has a proof-labeling scheme using certificates on $O(n^2 + kn)$ bits, an immediate corollary of Theorem 2 is that, for every task $\mathcal{T}$ with k-bits output size in n-node networks, there exists a silent self-stabilizing algorithm solving $\mathcal{T}$ with register of $O(n^2 + kn)$ bits. Interestingly enough, since the certificates of the aforementioned proof-labeling scheme are easily computable, one can even bound the number of rounds of the algorithm. This is our second main result:

Theorem 3. *For every task $\mathcal{T}$ with output on at most k bits at every node of n-node networks, there exists a silent self-stabilizing algorithm solving $\mathcal{T}$ and converging in $O(n)$ rounds, with register-space complexity $O(n^2 + kn)$ bits.*

Proof. Let $\mathcal{T}$ be a task with k-bits output size in n-node networks. We describe a silent self-stabilizing algorithm FSSS, for *Fast Silent Self-Stabilization*, solving $\mathcal{T}$ in $O(n)$ rounds, using registers of at most $O(n^2 + kn)$ bits in n-node networks.

It is known [3,14,15] that any task $\mathcal{T}$ with k-bits output size in n-node networks has a proof-labeling scheme (p, v) using certificates on $O(n^2 + kn)$ bits. Specifically, in an n-node graph G with identity assignment id, the certificate at each node u assigned by p consists in the following:

- an $n \times n$ adjacency matrix M of G, and
- an array X with n entries, $X[i] = (id_i, x_i)$ for $i = 1, \ldots, n$, where id_i is the identity of the node corresponding to the ith row and ith column in M, and x_i is the output of that node.

The verifier v acts as follows. Every node checks that the certificates are locally consistent (i.e., in particular, that the neighbors have identities and outputs such as specified in the certificate). Whenever a node notices some inconsistencies, it rejects. Otherwise, it carries on the verification by checking whether $(G, id, x) \in \mathcal{T}$. Note that every node is aware of the triple (G, id, x), since all the required information are available in its certificate (M, X). Thus checking whether $(G, id, x) \in \mathcal{T}$ can be done since tasks were defined as a *computable* sets.

Hence, our problem boils down to construct the certificate (M, X) in a silent self stabilizing manner. The skeleton of Algorithm CSSS is displayed in Algorithm 2.

Algorithm 2. Skeleton of Algorithm FSSS

1: construct a spanning tree T of G, and let r be its root
2: gather all edges at r along T, and root r assembles (G, id)
3: root r computes x such that $(G, id, x) \in \mathcal{T}$, and sets the pair (M, X) accordingly
4: broadcast (M, X) from r to all nodes along T
5: every node u sets $(x(u), (M, X))$ as its pair (output,certificate)
6: **if** verifier v rejects $(x, (M, X))$ **then**
7:     reset
8: **end if**

Again, Instruction 1 can be implemented by any of the silent algorithms in [6,11], both using registers on $O(\log n)$ bits. All gatherings and broadcasts (cf. Instruction 2 and 4) can be implemented by convergecast and divergecast operations, under an unfair scheduler. The computation of x in Instruction 3 can be done since tasks are computable.   □

Note that, in the statement of Theorem 3, we only refer to the size of the *public* registers, but do not intend to reflect the space complexity (in the usual sense of computational complexity theory) required to perform "internal" individual computations. Obviously, in order for the proof of Theorem 3 to apply, we must allow each process to use arbitrarily large private memory for performing arbitrarily complex computations, e.g., for computing x such that $(G, id, x) \in \mathcal{T}$, as well as for deciding whether $(G, id, x) \in \mathcal{T}$ given any x.

5   Discussion and Open Problem

On the one hand, our "compact" algorithm CSSS is optimizing the size of the registers, and is in fact almost as compact as the most compact proof-labeling scheme for each considered task. It uses registers on $O(\ell + \log n)$ bits in n-node networks, with a lower bound of $\Omega(\ell)$ bits, where ℓ is the minimum size of a proof-labeling scheme for the task. On the down side, CSSS suffers from an exponential number of rounds, even in the case in which it is built upon a proof-labeling scheme of constant size. As it was already mentioned in the introduction of this paper, there exist many tasks (e.g., spanning tree construction, leader election, MST construction, etc.) for which space-efficient *and* time-efficient silent self-stabilizing algorithms do exist. However, each of these algorithms is tuned and optimized for one specific task. Instead, our algorithm is generic, and applies to *all* tasks. It may thus not be surprising that one has to pay for this generality.

On the other hand, our "fast" algorithm FSSS performs in a linear number of rounds, but it uses registers on $O(n^2 + nk)$ bits, where k is the size of the output. Hence, for some tasks, like the aforementioned ones, the size of the registers used by algorithm FSSS is much larger than the size of the registers used by dedicated algorithms. However, it is known [15] that there are tasks requiring certificates on $\Omega(n^2 + nk)$ bits for every proof-labeling scheme, and this holds even if the interpretation of the individual decision by the verifier is relaxed compared to the logical conjunction interpretation of proof-labeling schemes [3]. Therefore, the space-complexity of Algorithm FSSS is actually optimal, from a worst-case analysis perspective.

Open problem. Does there exist a universal compact *and* fast silent self-stabilizing algorithm?

In particular, for tasks with proof-labeling schemes of size at most ℓ bits, we question the existence of a universal silent self-stabilizing algorithm converging in $poly(n)$ number of rounds, with registers of $O(\ell) + o(n^2 + kn)$ bits, where k is the size of the output.

References

1. Afek, Y., Kutten, S., Yung, M.: Memory-efficient self stabilizing protocols for general networks. In: van Leeuwen, J., Santoro, N. (eds.) WDAG 1990. LNCS, vol. 486, pp. 15–28. Springer, Heidelberg (1991)
2. Afek, Y., Kutten, S., Yung, M.: The local detection paradigm and its applications to self-stabilization. Theoretical Computer Science 186(1-2), 199–229 (1997)
3. Arfaoui, H., Fraigniaud, P., Pelc, A.: Local Decision and Verification with Bounded-Size Outputs. In: 15th International Symposium on Stabilization, Safety, and Security of Distributed Systems, SSS, pp. 133–147 (2013)
4. Arora, A., Gouda, M.: Distributed reset. IEEE Trans. Computers 43(9), 1026–1038 (1994)
5. Blin, L., Dolev, S., Potop-Butucaru, M.G., Rovedakis, S.: Fast self-stabilizing minimum spanning tree construction – using compact nearest common ancestor labeling scheme. In: Lynch, N.A., Shvartsman, A.A. (eds.) DISC 2010. LNCS, vol. 6343, pp. 480–494. Springer, Heidelberg (2010)
6. Blin, L., Fraigniaud, P.: Polynomial-Time Space-Optimal Silent Self-Stabilizing Minimum-Degree Spanning Tree Construction. Tech. Report arXiv 1402.2496 (2014)

7. Blin, L., Potop-Butucaru, M., Rovedakis, S., Tixeuil, S.: A new self-stabilizing minimum spanning tree construction with loop-free property. In: Keidar, I. (ed.) DISC 2009. LNCS, vol. 5805, pp. 407–422. Springer, Heidelberg (2009)
8. Blin, L., Tixeuil, S.: Compact Deterministic Self-stabilizing Leader Election – The Exponential Advantage of Being Talkative. In: Afek, Y. (ed.) DISC 2013. LNCS, vol. 8205, pp. 76–90. Springer, Heidelberg (2013)
9. Cournier, A.: A new polynomial silent stabilizing spanning-tree construction algorithm. In: Kutten, S., Žerovnik, J. (eds.) SIROCCO 2009. LNCS, vol. 5869, pp. 141–153. Springer, Heidelberg (2010)
10. Cournier, A., Rovedakis, S., Villain, V.: The first fully polynomial stabilizing algorithm for bfs tree construction. In: Fernàndez Anta, A., Lipari, G., Roy, M. (eds.) OPODIS 2011. LNCS, vol. 7109, pp. 159–174. Springer, Heidelberg (2011)
11. Datta, A., Larmore, L., Vemula, P.: Self-stabilizing leader election in optimal space under an arbitrary scheduler. Theor. Comput. Sci. 412(40), 5541–5561 (2011)
12. Dolev, S.: Self-Stabilization. MIT Press (2000)
13. Dolev, S., Gouda, M.G., Schneider, M.: Memory Requirements for Silent Stabilization. Acta Inf. 36(6), 447–462 (1999)
14. Fraigniaud, P., Korman, A., Peleg, D.: Towards a complexity theory for local distributed computing. J. ACM 60(5), 35 (2013)
15. Göös, M., Suomela, J.: Locally checkable proofs. In: 30th ACM Symposium on Principles of Distributed Computing (PODC), pp. 159–168 (2011)
16. Huang, S.-T., Chen, N.-S.: A self-stabilizing algorithm for constructing breadth-first trees. Inf. Process. Lett. 41(2), 109–117 (1992)
17. Korman, A., Kutten, S.: Distributed verification of minimum spanning tree. Distributed Computing 20, 253–266 (2007)
18. Korman, A., Kutten, S., Masuzawa, T.: Fast and compact self stabilizing verification, computation, and fault detection of an MST. In: 30th ACM Symp. on Principles of Distributed Computing (PODC), pp. 311–320 (2011)
19. Korman, A., Kutten, S., Peleg, D.: Proof labeling schemes. Distributed Computing 22(4), 215–233 (2010)
20. Kosowski, A., Kuszner, Ł.: A self-stabilizing algorithm for finding a spanning tree in a polynomial number of moves. In: Wyrzykowski, R., Dongarra, J., Meyer, N., Waśniewski, J. (eds.) PPAM 2005. LNCS, vol. 3911, pp. 75–82. Springer, Heidelberg (2006)

On the Resilience of Pull-Based P2P Streaming Systems against DoS Attacks

Giang Nguyen[1], Mathias Fischer[1], and Thorsten Strufe[2]

[1] Department of Computer Science, TU Darmstadt
{nguyen,fischer}@cs.tu-darmstadt.de
[2] Department of Computer Science, TU Dresden
thorsten.strufe@tu-dresden.de

Abstract. The robustness of pull-based streaming systems to node failure and churn has been extensively analyzed. Their resistance to sabotage, however, is not well understood, so far. Recent measurement studies on a large deployed pull-based system have discovered stable source-to-peer paths and the convergence of the content dissemination to rather static topologies over time. Thus, an attack on central nodes within these static topologies, which causes serious service disruptions, is feasible. This paper demonstrates attacks that significantly reduce the system's performance. As a countermeasure, we introduce a novel striping scheme, which decreases the dependencies between peers and thus the impact of attacks. A thorough simulation study indicates that our scheme achieves a high resistance against sabotage attacks at negligible overhead and performance penalties.

Keywords: Resilience, pull-based P2P streaming, DoS attacks.

1 Introduction

Peer-to-Peer (P2P) streaming has been becoming a viable solution to distribute live streaming content over the Internet. Systems following this paradigm incorporate peers in the content distribution and make use of their upload bandwidth. Therefore, the provision for server resources is reduced and the service scales with an increasing number of users.

Most popular P2P streaming systems in practical deployment, e.g., PPLive[1] and Sopcast[2], can be classified as pull-based. In such systems [5,8] the stream is divided into equally sized chunks and peers download and forward those chunks between each other. This requires that each peer establishes and maintains partnership with other peers via bidirectional connections. This results in an unstructured and randomized mesh overlay. Peers inform others about the chunks that are downloaded and stored in the video buffers via Buffer Maps (BMs). A BM is a signaling packet containing an array of binary-valued elements that indicates

---

[1] http://www.pplive.com

[2] http://www.sopcast.com

P. Felber and V. Garg (Eds.): SSS 2014, LNCS 8756, pp. 33–47, 2014.

chunk availability. After receiving BMs from its partners, a peer needs to decide from which partners it requests which chunks, e.g., via a Rarest-First scheduling strategy. Hence, a randomized distribution tree is formed implicitly per chunk, but in case of failures the mesh topology provides redundant connectivity via alternative source-to-peer paths. Even when one or several partners fail, each peer can quickly react to failures by downloading the video chunks from other partners. For this reason, pull-based systems are inherently *robust* to node churn and peer failures.

However, measurement studies [6,13] of one of the largest pull-based P2P streaming systems reveal that peers form different *tiers* in terms of play-out lags. The *stable* tiering effect allows for inferring the flow of the video content distribution. As stable source-to-peer paths evolve, the topologies established for subsequent chunks become highly similar. This might not affect the robustness of these systems to node churn and failures, but is of concern during attacks, e.g., DDoS attacks, on the most relevant nodes in the content distribution. As in tree structures the majority of nodes is residing in leaf positions and close to them, random failures of nodes will affect only few other nodes in average. However, attacks on nodes in the tier close to the source of the stream will affect nearly the whole overlay. Trees are robust against random failures, but not very resilient against attacks that target the most relevant nodes, e.g., nodes adjacent to the source (so-called head nodes). For this reason, we suggest to study the *total resilience* which we define as the *robustness* to failures as well as the *resistance* to attacks. For that, we assume an attacker with global knowledge that attacks head nodes only. To the best of our knowledge, this paper is the first that addresses this problem.

Our contributions in this paper are two-fold: (*i*) First, we demonstrate that the performance of pull-based systems is significantly affected by practical and simple attacks. (*ii*) Second, we introduce a striping scheme that *enforces diversification* as a countermeasure. Aiming at *reducing the direct dependency* between peers, our scheme divides the video stream into several stripes and enforces each peer to request the stripes from diversified groups of partners. Simulation results indicate that the striping scheme effectively reduces the maximum and average chunk miss ratios by 50% and 30% respectively, even with a conservative number of two stripes.

The remainder of this paper is structured as follow: Section 2 discusses related work. The striping scheme is described in Section 3. After discussing the results in Section 4, Section 5 concludes the paper.

2   Related Work

Studies on the resilience of P2P streaming systems mostly address either failure recovery or the resistance to attacks.

To prevent overlay partitioning, Probabilistic Resilient Multicast (PRM) [1] allows for redundant connections alongside a single multicast tree. Each peer can establish additional connections, with a low probability, to a few others and forward video chunks to them. It has been shown that the whole system can maintain a high delivery ratio.

In FatNemo [2] nodes with higher bandwidth are placed closer to the source, while nodes with lower bandwidth are placed further away. The resulting tree topology is low and broad. Intuitively, the less number of predecessors a peer has the more likely the peer can receive a stable video stream.

The above approaches are not resistant to targeted attacks since they introduce relevant nodes that are close to the source. Attacks on them can disrupt the whole system.

DagStream [10] introduces directed links on top of a mesh overlay. Each peer separates its mesh partners into parents and children. The peer requests chunks from its parents and sends chunks upon requests from its children. To optimize the topology, each peer has a level that is calculated from the ones of its parents. The farther the peer is from the source, the higher its level is. To avoid loops, a peer has to find a parent whose levels are lower than its level. This way of ordering peers hinders the collaboration between peers when there is a disruption in the overlay. Furthermore, the parent selection policies in DagStream prioritize peers that are close to the source. As a result, many peers might depend on a few parents. Attacks on those nodes can cause a heavy impact on a large fraction of peers.

To tackle both problems of node failure and sabotage, systems such as [3,4] extend the publish-subscribe design and minimize the direct dependency between any two peers. Each peer has multiple parents. Those forward a fraction of the whole video stream, so-called a stripe, to their children. Peers are organized into inner-node disjoint spanning trees, each delivers the chunks in one stripe. The resilience of those systems was proven theoretically, but they have not been adopted in a wide real-world deployment.

To summarize the discussion, building a resilient P2P streaming system is an open question. One promising approach to achieve system's resilience to both random failure and targeted attacks is to: (i) leverage the resilience properties of pull-based systems with the mesh topology and (ii) reduce the direct dependency between peers.

3   Striping Scheme

The tiering effect in pull-based systems allows an outsider to gain information on the structure of the whole network and to infer the flow of video chunks between tiers. Attacks by shutting down peers on a certain tier can disrupt the flow of the video distribution. Furthermore, the damage can be severe when an attacker targets head nodes, which are the peers adjacent to the source in the overlay topology.

There are two potential approaches to mitigate the damage caused by attacking head nodes: (i) To decrease the direct dependency between peers by increasing the connectivity among them, which consequently increases the number of head nodes; and (ii) To remove the tiering effect completely. We reserve the second approach for future work and instead, in this paper, focus on the first approach which allows us to answer a more urgent question: *Assuming that the structure is revealed, what can we do to mitigate the damaging effect when head nodes are attacked?* We also assume that recovery measures, such as rejoining upon isolation or disconnection are always available.

Increasing connectivity among the source and peers is challenging due to resource constraints and inherent behavior of the pull-based protocol. Without increasing the bandwidth of the source and peers, the straightforward method that increases their number of partners does not work. Head nodes might gradually prefer to download chunks directly from the source due to its high availability of chunks. The higher the number of head nodes, the more likely that they have to compete with each other for a fixed source bandwidth. This leads to increasing delay and probably chunk miss since the source cannot response timely to all chunk requests.

In this section, we present our striping scheme for pull-based P2P streaming systems that reduces the direct dependency between peers. This scheme mitigates the negative effects of attacking on head nodes, which we demonstrate in Section 4. We begin with the idea of the scheme first. After that, we describe the design and the specification of the scheme.

3.1   Idea to Enforce Diversification by Out Striping Scheme

Current pull-based protocols do not diversify chunk requests exhaustively, i.e. peers can steadily download chunks from a few among several partners as long as they respond reliably. This leads to an implicit yet direct dependency between peers. To reduce this dependency, each peer needs to download video chunks from diverse partners. This implies that it needs to send chunk requests to more diverse partners. Towards this end, each peer enforces itself to request subsets of the required chunks from different groups of partners.

At this point there are three methods to diversify the requests. (*i*) *In the first method, each peer alternates between different groups of partners to request chunks at different scheduling cycles.* Over the long run, the average number of requested chunks per peer is reduced. However, certain peers might, by chance, receive many chunk requests in a short period. Consequently, local overloading might happen, which affects the overall chunk dissemination. (*ii*) *The second method is to split the needed set of chunks by their play-out deadlines, from most to least urgent.* On-time delivery of the most urgent chunks is more critical since there might not be enough time to request them again in the next scheduling cycles. When the peer requests the most urgent chunks from a subset of partners that is not reliable, the urgent chunks might not be delivered on time. This leads to more missed chunks. (*iii*) *The third method is to divide the video stream in an interleaved manner into stripes.* This way, diversification is achieved while avoiding the drawbacks of the above two methods.

Subsequently to dividing chunks into stripes, each peer needs to *locally* separate its partners into different groups. There are two methods: (*i*) *In the first method, the grouping is based on partners' identities, e.g., the IP addresses.*

This partner grouping is inflexible because it depends highly on the fluctuation of the partner list. A group might not have partners with certain identities among the peer's available partners. *(ii) In the second method, each peer assigns its partners into different logical groups, regardless of partners' identities.* Fluctuation of partners in each group can be quickly compensated by adjusting partners among the groups or even by reassigning.

We summarize our idea to enforce diversification as follows:

1. *The video stream is divided into stripes.*
2. *Each peer logically forms separate groups of partners.*
3. *Each peer enforces itself to request a certain stripe from a certain group of partners*

By doing that, the chunk downloading demand to a peer from its partners can be efficiently reduced. In conventional pull-based systems, a peer with m partners can, in principal, receive chunk requests of m times the streaming rate in the worst case. However, the demand for each peer with striping is reduced by a factor of k, the number of stripes, when the number of partners is fixed.

Consequently, the diversification enforcement allows a peer to have more partners, given the same upload bandwidth. Thus, the peer has more source-to-peer paths and at the same time avoids overloading itself. More importantly, the source can significantly increase its number of partners, or the number of head nodes, with the same upload bandwidth. The critical connectivity between the source and the peers is therefore enhanced, thus, potentially strengthens the resilience of the system against both failures and attacks.

In the coming section, we elaborate the idea of diversification enforcement into the design of the striping scheme.

3.2 Design of the Striping Scheme

Following the high-level sketch discussed in Section 3.1, this section details the design of the striping scheme. This includes the division of the video stream into stripes and the assignment of partners to different groups.

First, a stripe i consists of chunks whose sequence numbers equal to $i \bmod k$. Second, partners of a peer are assigned to k groups, each contains a subset of the partner list. This way, a peer requests chunks of the stripe i from partners of the group i. Figure 1 illustrates the design of our scheme for a generic peer. In this example, the video stream is divided into three stripes. Accordingly, seven partners are assigned to three groups.

The assignment of partners to groups has to satisfy several constraints. (i) First, every group has at least one partner to ensure the existence of chunk providers for the respective stripe. (ii) Second, all partners should be assigned to groups since partners that are not assigned to any group are not considered in requesting chunks. (iii) Third, the difference in the number of partners of any two groups should be minimized. Otherwise, chunks in the stripe whose respective group has very few partners have a lower chance to be requested and

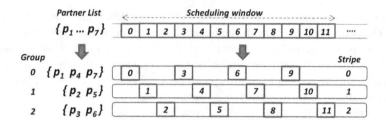

Fig. 1. An example of grouping and striping: partners in each group receives requests for chunks of the respective stripe

delivered successfully. (*iv*) Lastly, the assignment should minimize the difference between the number of groups assigned to each partner. Assigning a partner to several groups increases its chance to be requested more frequently, which might overloads it. We formulate the above assignment problem as follows.

Given the set of partners $P = \{p_1, ..., p_m\}$ and the set of groups $G = \{g_1, .., g_k\}$, and let $a_{ij} \in \{0,1\}$ ($1 \leq i \leq k$ and $1 \leq j \leq m$) denotes the assignment of partner p_j to group g_i, where $a_{ij} = 1$ if group g_i has partner p_j and $a_{ij} = 0$ otherwise. Define $N_i^P = \sum_{j=1}^{m} a_{ij}$ as the total number of partners assigned to group g_i, and $N_j^G = \sum_{i=1}^{k} a_{ij}$ as the total number of groups to which partner p_j is assigned.

Consequently, the problem of assigning partners to groups is to find a_{ij} such that:

$$z = minimize \left\{ \sum_{i=1}^{k} \sum_{j=1}^{m} a_{ij} \right\} \tag{1}$$

$$s.t. \quad \sum_{j=1}^{m} a_{ij} \geq 1, \quad i = 1..k \tag{2}$$

$$\sum_{i=1}^{k} a_{ij} \geq 1, \quad j = 1..m \tag{3}$$

$$\operatorname*{argmax}_{i}\{\sum_{j=1}^{m} a_{ij}\} - \operatorname*{argmin}_{i}\{\sum_{j=1}^{m} a_{ij}\} \leq 1 \tag{4}$$

$$\operatorname*{argmax}_{j}\{\sum_{i=1}^{k} a_{ij}\} - \operatorname*{argmin}_{j}\{\sum_{i=1}^{k} a_{ij}\} \leq 1 \tag{5}$$

In this formulation, the objective function in (1) is to minimize the total number of assignments of partners to groups. The constraints in (2) & (3) ensure that every partner is assigned to groups and every group has partners. The constraints in (4) & (5) are used to prevent groups from having too many partners and assigning a partner to many groups.

With the *Round-Robin assignment* of partners to groups, we achieve the optimal solution [14] with $min\{\sum_{i=1}^{k} \sum_{j=1}^{m} a_{ij}\} = max(k, m)$.

Determining Parameters. Following the above design, in this section, we discuss the constraints for the two system parameters introduced in the design of the striping scheme.

The first parameter is the number of stripes k. Its value is constrained by the number of requested chunks C in each scheduling cycle which is asymptotically proportional to the streaming rate (in chunks per second) and the scheduling interval. When $k > C$, over-striping happens, i.e. one or more stripes contain no chunks. Consequently, there are groups of partners that are redundant for chunk request. The striping in this case is not efficient. At the other extreme, when $k = 1$, all partners are in the same group. The striping scheme operates similarly to a conventional pull-based system. The second parameter is the number of partners m. When m is too small, diversification is eventually limited because there are a few options for each chunks request. When m is too large, the necessary communication overhead can overload the system.

In the coming section, we refine the design of the striping scheme with specifications to integrate it into conventional pull-based systems.

3.3 Specification

Integrating the striping scheme into current pull-based protocols requires a few modification. At the source, the number of partners scales up with the number of stripes k. At each peer, the chunk scheduling operation does not search exhaustively available chunks from all partners. Instead, for a chunk with the sequence number s, the peer only considers partners in the group $s \bmod k$. Additionally, the assignment of partners to groups needs to be adapted when there are updates on the partner list. The adjustment should be fast to react promptly to the dynamics of peers to minimize the computational cost. The simple Round-Robin assignment introduces little computational cost. Even with a naive implementation when partners are re-assigned upon each update of the partner list, the cost would be negligible.

In the next section, we integrate the striping scheme with Round-Robin assignment into DONet – a conventional pull-based protocol and evaluate its performance.

4   Evaluation

In this section, the proposed striping scheme for pull-based systems is evaluated with respect to its provided resilience against attacks on head nodes. In addition, the efficiency of the proposed scheme is evaluated in detail. The evaluation aims at answering the following three questions:

1. *What damage does attacking head nodes cause to the performance of the conventional pull-based systems?*

2. *What resilience against the head node attacks is provided by our striping scheme?*
3. *What trade-offs in terms of signaling overhead does the striping scheme introduce?*

To answer the above questions, we need to identify metrics to quantify the performance of the streaming system and an accurate simulation model with realistic settings. Their in-depth discussions are presented next.

4.1 Metrics

In live streaming, timely delivery of video chunks is critical to ensure that the video stream can be played out smoothly. Therefore, each video chunk has its own play-out deadline for decoding. When a chunk arrives after its deadline it is considered missing. A missed chunk causes the video player to either stall or skip the chunk. In the former case, the smooth video play-out is not achieved. In the later case, the visual display of the video is impaired. Both cases reduce the perceived quality of the decoded video.

There are several methods to estimate the quality of a streaming system. Among them, the amount of missed chunks is one useful indicator because it tells how properly the system is working. It is also convenient since the calculation is straight-forward. The disadvantage of this method is that it hardly reflects the quality of experience (QoE) from users' perspective. To better quantify system's performance as perceived by users, studies in the literature [7] use QoE metrics, such as the Peak Signal-to-Noise Ratio (PSNR) which compares the decoded video at end users with the original one. However, this method has several drawbacks: First, calculating this metric is costly since it requires a considerable CPU power to decode the video. Second, the calculation depends on the video codec types and the benchmark video. It is therefore difficult to make general statements on the performance of a protocol.

From the above discussion, we select chunk miss to quantify system's performance for simplicity and flexibility. Specifically, we define the *chunk miss ratio* as the fraction of chunks that missed their play-out deadline divided by all chunks that should be played out. Note that the ratio is complementary to the Continuity Index that is commonly used in the literature. The chunk miss ratio is favored in this paper because it is more intuitive to quantify the damages caused by the attackers to the system's performance.

Furthermore, to comprehend the effects to the system after being attacked, we introduce three additional micro metrics to look at chunk miss ratio from three different perspectives:

– *Average Miss Ratio* which is the average miss ratio over a significant period of time after the attack.
– *Maximum Miss Ratio* which is the maximum instantaneous chunk miss ratio per second. It estimates the upper limit of damage that the attacks can cause to the system.

– **Per-chunk Miss Ratio** which is the fraction of peers missing a certain chunk. The metric quantifies how significantly missing a specific chunk can affect the system.

One immediate concern over the striping scheme is its signaling overhead. Due to an increased size of the partner list, additional overhead arises as (i) each peer sends more chunk requests to its partners and (ii) peers exchange more BMs with each other. Subsequently, we introduce the **Signaling Overhead Ratio** metric, which is the fraction of the volume coming from signaling packets divided by the total volume of both video and signaling packets.

4.2   Simulation Model

Simulation framework: To evaluate the resilience of pull-based P2P streaming against attacks, we developed OSSim, our generic simulation framework for P2P streaming, which is built on top of OMNeT++[3]. The framework allows packet-level simulations of different classes of P2P streaming systems. Its source code, including the one used in this study, is available online [4].

Representative pull-based P2P streaming system: Using the OSSim framework we developed DONet [16] – a popular deployed pull-based system in the literature. We select DONet as the benchmark system due to several reasons. (i) First, the design and protocol description of DONet is described in detail, which supports a verifiable implementation of the system in simulation. (ii) Second, its Rarest-First chunk scheduling strategy produces comparable performance to the state-of-the-art algorithms [17]. (iii) Third, the simulation model of DONet is also validated in our previous study [11].

Underlying networks: To emulate the characteristics of the underlying Internet, we used the GT-ITM [15] topology generator to generate a transit-stub core network consisting out of 20 core and 400 edge routers that are inter-connected by 1212 links. In particular, we use the following parameters for the topology generator: diameter 14, node degree 2.843, and path length 6.231. The latencies in the links connecting the routers are uniformly distributed in the range [1, 60] ms. Peers are randomly attached to the 400 edge routers at the beginning of each simulation.

Workload: We use a synthetic churn model from a measurement study in [12], in which the authors analyze traces from a popular live program over a period of 90 days. From this model, the distributions of inter-arrival times of users and session durations are Pareto and Lognormal respectively. Specifically, we use $a = 2.52$ and $b = 0.35$ for the Pareto distribution and $\mu = 1.44$ and $\lambda = 5.19$ for the Lognormal one. In addition, we allow leaving peers to rejoin the system after a random period, to maintain a rather stable peer population.

---

[3] http://omnetpp.org
[4] http://www.p2p.tu-darmstadt.de/research/ossim

Attack strategy: We assume that the strength of the attacker is represented by a budget (A). This tells the maximum number of head nodes the attackers can shut down simultaneously or in a relatively short period. We assume that the head nodes can be identified. For example, the attackers can apply a similar technique which was introduced in [6]. The implementation of such technique is, however, beyond the scope of this study. Given a list of head nodes, the attacker randomly selects nodes to shut down simultaneously. The attacker stops attacking when either all head nodes are shut down or the number of selected head nodes reaches its budget.

Parameters: In all experiments, the following parameters are used unless otherwise stated. The streaming rate is 400 kbps. Each video buffer stores up to 30 seconds of video chunks whose sizes are 2500 Bytes. A peer starts playing out video chunks when the downloaded chunks are equivalent to around six seconds. We simulate one source and 1000 peers. The upload bandwidth of the source and peers are 8 Mbps and 800 kbps respectively. Even though it is not realistic to assume that all peers have the same, it is reasonable as we are only interested in the resilience of pull-based systems against attacks. Using an homogeneous peer bandwidth eliminates the impact of the peers' characteristics in the results. The simulation duration is 1200 seconds. In the first 500 seconds, no data is collected to avoid unstable system behavior. We repeat each simulation setting at least 35 times.

4.3   Results

In the following, we summarize our main simulation findings and describe the effects of attacking head nodes first. Afterwards, we present a comparison of the striping scheme to a conventional protocol – DONet. Finally, we investigate the tradeoff of the striping scheme in terms of signaling overhead.

Effects of Attacking Head Nodes: In the following, we answer the question: *What damage does attacking head nodes cause to the performance of the conventional pull-based systems?*

In this experiment, the maximum number of partners of the peers and the source was eight and ten respectively. To perform the attack, all of the ten head nodes which are the partners of the source were shut down simultaneously at the 900th second, after the system has reached its steady-state. The instantaneous chunk miss ratio per second were plotted in dependence on time.

Figure 2 presents chunk miss ratio for DONet under the attack. For clarity, the figure includes only the relevant period after the attacks. It can be seen that, during the first 20 seconds, the chunk miss ratio remains as low as 1% . In the next 20 seconds, the miss ratio increases dramatically to reach its maximum of almost 35%. It then reduces quickly and remain low since the 960th second.

Intuitively, the results have agreed with expectation on the behavior of pull-based protocols and can be explained as follows: Head nodes serve as intermediate sources of video chunks for the rest of the peers. When they are shut down,

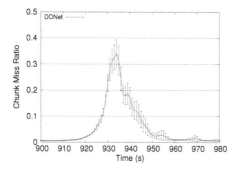 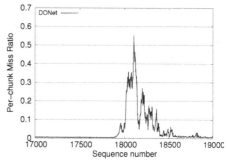

Fig. 2. Instantaneous chunk miss ratio of DONet versus time, after attacking all ten head nodes

Fig. 3. Chunk miss ratio of DONet versus sequence number of chunks, after attacking all ten head nodes

their partners cannot request chunks from them. However, chunk missing does not occur immediately after the attack, because the peers have large buffers. Chunk missing might start from the peers connecting to the head nodes previously. It then spreads to other peers that locate further away from the source. Chunk missing reduces when the connections between the source and the peers are established again.

To estimate more precisely the impact of missed chunks to the system's performance we recorded the sequence number of all missed chunks and calculate the chunk miss ratio per chunk's sequence number. The results are plotted in Figure 3. The figure shows that the chunk miss ratio increases sharply from around 1% to a maximum of 55% in accordance with an increase in sequence number from around 18000 to 18100. It diminishes steadily for subsequent chunks and remains low for sequence numbers greater than 18500.

The spread of missed chunks to a significant fraction of peers as shown in Figure 3 indicates the strong and negative impact to the system's performance. A certain chunk can be more important than others, depending on whether it carries an intra-coded (I), a predictive-coded (P) or a bidirectionally predictive-coded (B) frame. A successfully decoded I-frame is required to decode the P-frames and B-frames in the same Group of Picture (GoP). Losing an I frame, therefore, fails the decoding of the GoP, which leads to a perceptible picture degradation at users. More severely, given the small number of head nodes a malicious party can periodically trigger attacks. Perceived quality by users in this case can be further degraded.

Comparing the Striping Scheme with a Conventional Protocol: The second question we studied was: *What resilience against the head node attacks is provided by our striping scheme?*

In this experiment, we compare the effect of attacking head nodes on the conventional DONet ($k = 1$) versus the adapted one with striping ($k = 2, 3, 4$). The number of partners of the source and peers in the striping scheme scales with the number of stripes. The attacker budget in terms of the number of nodes that is attacked varies between 5 and 60. Maximum chunk miss ratio and average chunk miss ratio over a period of 60 seconds have been recorded and plotted.

We expect that the impact of attacks with the same budget is stronger in the conventional DONet than in the striping scheme. Since the number of head nodes in DONet is less than in the striping scheme, the same number of attacked head nodes reduces a larger portion of the number of connections for distributing video chunks from the source to the peers. Consequently, chunk miss ratio in DONet is larger than in the striping scheme.

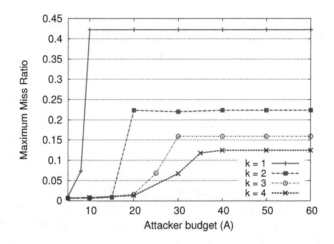

Fig. 4. Comparing the conventional DONet ($k = 1$) to the adapted one with Striping ($k = 2, 3, 4$) in terms of maximum chunk miss ratio after attacks

Figure 4 plots maximum chunk miss ratio of DONet and the striping scheme in dependence on the attacker budget. The results agree with our expectation. First, it can be observed that when more stripes are applied, the attacker needs significantly larger budget to achieve the same damage to the system. The miss ratios reach their maxima when the attacker budget equals to the number of head nodes, at least. Second, it is also shown that even a conservative diversification with two stripes can reduce the maximum chunk miss ratio by around 50%.

To comprehend better the effect of attacks on the system, we plot in Figure 5 the average chunk miss ratio over a period of 60 seconds after attacks in dependence on the attacker budget. The figure compares the conventional DONet ($k = 1$) versus the adapted one with striping ($k = 2, 3, 4$). As seen from the figure, the striping scheme reduces the maximum of the average chunk miss ratio from 30% to 50% when the number of stripes varies from two to four. Additionally, the attacker budget has to increase proportionally to the number of stripes to maximize the damage.

One unanticipated but interesting finding in Figures 4 and 5 was that the striping scheme effectively reduced the maximum damage even when all head

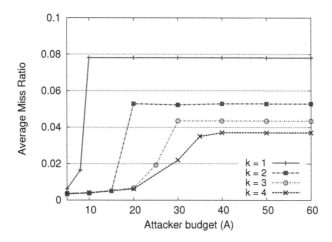

Fig. 5. Comparing the conventional DONet ($k = 1$) to the adapted one with Striping ($k = 2, 3, 4$) in terms of average chunk miss ratio over 60 seconds after attacks

nodes are attacked. Note that in all experiments we applied the same process and parameters for recovering a node from isolation. The finding can be explained by two reasons: (i) The striping scheme disseminates chunks better due to the diversification enforcement. When chunks are requested in small numbers from diverse partners, they can be quickly downloaded. Consequently, chunk availability in the whole network is improved. (ii) The increased number of partners that each peer has also allows it to connect to partners that have its required chunks with a higher probability.

Trade-off of the Striping Scheme. In this section, we studied the tradeoff of the striping scheme in terms of signaling overhead when there is no attacks. We varied the number of stripes from two to nine. We expect that the striping scheme produces more signaling overhead since each peer has more partners. The exchanged BMs are increased subsequently. Furthermore, each peer probably sends more chunk requests per scheduling cycle because the peer should diversify the requests to different partners.

Figure 6 shows the signaling overhead in dependence on the number of stripes. In this figure, the lower horizontal line represents the average signaling overhead of DONet. As expected, the overhead increases steadily with an increasing number of stripes. Specifically, for each additional stripe, the signaling overhead increases by around one percent. The total signaling overhead is less than 10% when the number of stripes equals to four, which significantly reduces damages caused by attacks. Note that a significant portion of the total signaling overhead would stem from exchanging BMs. This overhead, however, can be strongly reduced by techniques such as one described in [9].

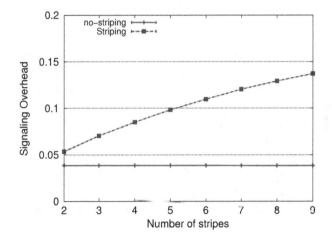

Fig. 6. Comparing the signaling overhead of the conventional DONet (no-striping) and the adapted one with striping when there is no attacks

5   Conclusion

In this paper, we investigated how attacks on head nodes affect pull-based P2P streaming systems. Results demonstrate that conventional pull-based streaming systems exhibit serious vulnerabilities to these rather simple attacks.

Subsequently, we introduced a striping scheme as a countermeasure against such attacks. The scheme enforces peers to request separate sets of chunks from diverse groups of partners. Simulation results reveal that the striping scheme effectively reduces both the maximum and average chunk miss ratios by 50% and 30% respectively. The scheme is light-weight and can be integrated easily to current pull-based systems with minimum modifications.

This study opens several interesting research questions that we would like to conduct. We plan to investigate the effect of the striping scheme on different chunk scheduling algorithms as well as the impact of varying partner assignment algorithms in our future work.

Acknowledgment. This work was supported by the German Academic Exchange Service (DAAD), Grant number A/09/97565.

References

1. Banerjee, S., Lee, S., Bhattacharjee, B., Srinivasan, A.: Resilient multicast using overlays. IEEE/ACM Trans. Netw. 14, 237–248 (2006)
2. Birrer, S., Lu, D., Bustamante, F.E., Qiao, Y., Dinda, P.A.: Fatnemo: Building a resilient multi-source multicast fat-tree. In: Chi, C.-H., van Steen, M., Wills, C. (eds.) WCW 2004. LNCS, vol. 3293, pp. 182–196. Springer, Heidelberg (2004)

3. Brinkmeier, M., Schafer, G., Strufe, T.: Optimally dos resistant p2p topologies for live multimedia streaming. IEEE Transactions on Parallel and Distributed Systems 20(6), 831–844 (2009)
4. Fischer, M., Grau, S., Nguyen, G., Schaefer, G.: Resilient and underlay-aware P2P live-streaming. Computer Networks 59, 122–136 (2014)
5. Hei, X., Liu, Y., Ross, K.: Iptv over p2p streaming networks: the mesh-pull approach. IEEE Communications Magazine 46(2), 86–92 (2008)
6. Hei, X., Liu, Y., Ross, K.: Inferring network-wide quality in p2p live streaming systems. IEEE JSAC 25(9), 1640–1654 (2007)
7. Kiraly, C., Abeni, L., Lo Cigno, R.: Effects of p2p streaming on video quality. In: IEEE ICC, pp. 1–5 (May 2010)
8. Li, B., Wang, Z., Liu, J., Zhu, W.: Two decades of internet video streaming: A retrospective view. ACM Trans. Multimedia Comput. Commun. Appl. 9(1s), 33:1–33:20 (2013)
9. Li, C., Chen, C., Chiu, D.: Buffer map message compression based on relevant window in p2p streaming media system. CoRR abs/1108.6293 (2011)
10. Liang, J., Nahrstedt, K.: Dagstream: locality aware and failure resilient peer-to-peer streaming. vol. 6071, p. 60710+. SPIE (2006)
11. Nguyen, G., Fischer, M., Strufe, T.: Ossim: A generic simulation framework for overlay streaming. In: Summer Computer Simulation Conference (2013)
12. Veloso, E., Almeida, V., Meira, W., Bestavros, A., Jin, S.: A hierarchical characterization of a live streaming media workload. In: Proceedings of the 2nd ACM SIGCOMM / IMW 2002, New York, NY, USA, pp. 117–130 (2002)
13. Wang, F., Liu, J., Xiong, Y.: Stable peers: Existence, importance, and application in peer-to-peer live video streaming. In: IEEE INFOCOM, pp. 1364–1372 (2008)
14. Wilkinson, B., Allen, M.: Parallel Programming: Techniques and Applications Using Networked Workstations and Parallel Computers. 2nd edn. Prentice-Hall, Upper Saddle River (2005)
15. Zegura, E.: Gt-itm: Georgia tech internetwork topology models (1996), http://www.cc.gatech.edu/fac/Ellen.Zegura/graphs.html
16. Zhang, X., Liu, J., Li, B., Yum, Y.S.: Coolstreaming/donet: A data-driven overlay network for peer-to-peer live media streaming. In: IEEE INFOCOM, vol. 3, pp. 2102–2111 (2005)
17. Zhou, Y., Chiu, D.M., Lui, J.C.S.: A simple model for chunk-scheduling strategies in p2p streaming. IEEE/ACM Trans. Netw. 19, 42–54 (2011)

On Stabilizing Departures in Overlay Networks

Dianne Foreback[1], Andreas Koutsopoulos[2], Mikhail Nesterenko[1],
Christian Scheideler[2], and Thim Strothmann[2]

[1] Kent State University
[2] University of Paderborn

Abstract. A fundamental problem for peer-to-peer systems is to maintain connectivity while nodes are leaving, i.e., the nodes requesting to leave the peer-to-peer system are excluded from the overlay network without affecting its connectivity. There are a number of studies for safe node exclusion if the overlay is in a well-defined state initially. Surprisingly, the problem is not formally studied yet for the case in which the overlay network is in an arbitrary initial state, i.e., when looking for a *self-stabilizing* solution for excluding leaving nodes. We study this problem in two variants: the *Finite Departure Problem ($\mathcal{FDP}$)* and the *Finite Sleep Problem ($\mathcal{FSP}$)*. In the $\mathcal{FDP}$ the leaving nodes have to irrevocably decide when it is safe to leave the network, whereas in the $\mathcal{FSP}$, this leaving decision does not have to be final: the nodes may resume computation if necessary. We show that there is no self-stabilizing distributed algorithm for the $\mathcal{FDP}$, even in a synchronous message passing model. To allow a solution, we introduce an oracle called $\mathcal{NIDEC}$ and show that it is sufficient even for the asynchronous message passing model by proposing an algorithm that can solve the $\mathcal{FDP}$ using $\mathcal{NIDEC}$. We also show that a solution to the $\mathcal{FSP}$ does not require an oracle.

1 Introduction

Peer-to-peer systems allow computers to interact and share resources without the need for a central server or centralized authority. This ability to self-organize makes peer-to-peer systems very popular. Since participation in such systems is usually voluntary, the peers may arrive and depart at any time. A peer may even leave the network without notice. Therefore, maintaining a connected overlay network is a challenging task. Many strategies help to alleviate this problem. They include using an overlay network with a high expansion or separating the peers into more reliable super-peers forming an overlay network on behalf of the other peers that just connect to one or more super-peers. While these strategies may work well in practice, rigorous research on when it is safe to leave the network is still in its infancy. The goal of this paper is to lay the foundation for a rigorous treatment of node departures in the context of self-stabilization. In fact, we are the first to provide answers to the question:

Is it possible to design a distributed algorithm that allows any collection of nodes to eventually leave a network from any initial state without losing connectivity?

Self-stabilization makes the above question non-trivial. A self-stabilizing algorithm recovers from an arbitrary initial state. Hence, a self-stabilizing node departure algorithm has to handle the states where the departing node is about to leave and may disconnect the network.

P. Felber and V. Garg (Eds.): SSS 2014, LNCS 8756, pp. 48–62, 2014.

1.1   System Model

We consider a distributed system consisting of a fixed set of processes with fixed identifiers, IDs for short, that are globally ordered. We refer to processes and their identifiers interchangeably. The system is controlled by an algorithm that specifies the variables and actions that are available in each process. In addition to the algorithm-based variables there is a process-based variable called *channel* whose values are sets of messages. The channel message capacity is unbounded, and messages will never get lost. We assume non-FIFO message delivery, fair-message receipt and point-to-point communications (multi-cast and broadcast primitives are not considered). We treat all messages sent to a process p as belonging to a single incoming channel C_p. Each process has a read-only boolean variable called *leaving*. If this variable is **true**, the process is *leaving*; the process is *staying* otherwise.

The format of an *action* is $\langle label \rangle : \langle guard \rangle \longrightarrow \langle command \rangle$. *label* is a name to differentiate actions. *guard* either detects the presence of a particular message type in the incoming channel, or it is a predicate over local variables. We call an action whose guard is simply **true** a *timeout* action. *command* is a sequence of statements that assigns new values to process variables or sends messages to other processes. Two other possible statements are **exit** and **sleep**. If a process executes **exit** it enters a designated *exit state*. Such a process is *gone*. If a process executes **sleep**, it enters the *sleep state*. Such a process is *asleep*. If a process is neither gone nor asleep, it is called *awake*.

The *system state* is an assignment of a value to every variable of each process and messages to each channel. An action in some process p is *enabled* in some system state if its guard evaluates to **true** in this state and p is awake, or its guard detects the presence of a particular message type in C_p and p is not gone. If in the latter case p is asleep, p becomes awake again, i.e., it leaves its sleep state. The action is *disabled* otherwise. Hence, while a gone process will never wake up again, an asleep process may wake up again when receiving an appropriate message.

A *computation* is an infinite fair sequence of states such that for each state s_i, the next sate s_{i+1} is obtained by executing an action that is enabled in s_i. This disallows the overlap of action execution. That is, action execution is *atomic*. We assume two kinds of fairness of computation: weak fairness of action execution and fair message receipt. *Weak fairness* of action execution means that if an action is enabled in all but finitely many states of the computation in which its process is awake, then this action is executed infinitely often. Hence, unless a process is gone or permanently asleep (i.e., it never wakes up again) at some point, its timeout action is executed infinitely often.

Fair message receipt means that if the computation contains a state where there is a message M in a channel C_p that enables at least one action in p, then there is also a later state in which either p is gone or M is not present in C_p, i.e., one of these actions is executed with M by p. Besides these fairness assumptions, we place no bounds on message propagation delay or relative process execution speeds, i.e. we consider fully asynchronous computations.

A *computation suffix* is a sequence of computation states past a particular state of this computation. In other words, the suffix of the computation is obtained by removing the initial state and finitely many subsequent states. Note that a computation suffix is also a computation.

We consider algorithms that do not manipulate the internals of process identifiers. Specifically, an algorithm is *copy-store-send* if the only operations that it executes on process IDs is copying them, storing them in local process memory and sending them in a message. That is, operations on IDs such as addition, radix computation, hashing, etc. are not used. In a copy-store-send algorithm, if a process does not store an ID in its local memory, the process may learn of this ID only by receiving it in a message. A copy-store-send algorithm cannot introduce new IDs to the system. It can only operate on the IDs that are already there.

1.2 Problem Statement

An algorithm is *self-stabilizing* if it satisfies the following two properties. *Convergence:* starting from an arbitrary system state, the algorithm is guaranteed to arrive at a legitimate state. *Closure:* starting from a legitimate state the algorithm remains in legitimate states thereafter. A self-stabilizing algorithm is thus able to recover from transient faults regardless of their nature. Moreover, a self-stabilizing algorithm does not have to be initialized as it eventually starts to behave correctly regardless of its initial state.

Before we define a legitimate state for the problems considered in this paper, we restrict the set of initial states to exclude trivially useless states. For this we first need some notation.

A (directed) *link* is a pair of identifiers (a, b) that is defined as follows: either a message carrying identifier b is in the incoming channel of process a, or process a stores identifier b in its local memory. We say that process a *points* to b or *has a link* to b. When we describe a link, we always state the pointing process first. The links form a directed *process (multi-)graph PG*. A *(weakly) connected component* in some directed graph G is a subgraph of G of maximum size so that for any two nodes u and v in that subgraph there is a (not necessarily) directed path from u to v. Two nodes that are not in the same weakly connected component are *disconnected*. A process p is *hibernating* if p is asleep and C_p is empty and all processes q that have a directed path to p in PG are also asleep and have an empty C_q.

Proposition 1. *For any copy-store-send algorithm and any system state of the algorithm in which process p is hibernating, p is permanently asleep.*

Proof. Let $PG(p)$ be the subgraph containing all processes q with a directed path to p. A process q in $PG(p)$ can only be woken up by a message, but such a message must arrive from a process q' outside of $PG(p)$. Hence, a link (q', q) in PG is required. Since such a link does not exist, the proposition follows.   □

Also initially gone processes are useless as they will never perform any computation. Hence, we assume that the initial state only consists of non-gone and non-hibernating processes. We also restrict the initial state to contain only messages that can trigger an action since the others will be ignored. Finally, we do not allow the presence of identifiers that do not belong to a process in the system. Their handling requires failure/presence detectors which is beyond the scope of this paper. From now on, an initial system state will always satisfy all of these constraints.

A system state is *legitimate* if (i) every staying process is awake, (ii) every leaving process is either hibernating or gone, and (iii) for each weakly connected component of the initial process graph, the staying processes in that component still form a weakly connected component. Now we are ready to formally state our two problems.

Finite Departure Problem ($\mathcal{FDP}$): eventually reach a legitimate state for the case that only the **exit** command is available.

Finite Sleep Problem ($\mathcal{FSP}$): eventually reach a legitimate state for the case that only the **sleep** command is available.

A self-stabilizing solution for these problems must be able to solve these from any initial state and to satisfy the closure property afterwards. Notice that (i) and (ii) can trivially be maintained in a legitimate state, so for the closure property one just needs to ensure that (iii) is also maintained.

In the following, a process is called *relevant* if it is neither gone nor hibernating. Otherwise we call it *irrelevant*. A process p can *safely* leave a system if the removal of p and its incident edges from PG does not disconnect any relevant processes. As we will see later, there is no distributed algorithm within our model that can decide when it is safe for a process p to leave the system. Hence, we need oracles.

1.3 Oracles

An *oracle* $\mathcal{O}$ is a predicate that depends on the system state and the process calling it. In the context of the $\mathcal{FDP}$, an oracle is supposed to advise a leaving process when it is safe to leave the network, so we restrict our attention to algorithms that *only* allow a leaving process to call **exit** if the oracle is **true** for it. Such an algorithm is also said to *rely* on the oracle. Moreover, we restrict our attention to oracles that *only* depend on the current process graph of the relevant processes and the calling process, i.e., the oracles are of the form $\mathcal{O}: \mathcal{PG} \times \mathcal{P} \to \{\textbf{true},\textbf{false}\}$ where $\mathcal{PG}$ is the set of process graphs and $\mathcal{P}$ is the set of processes. For example, we may define oracle $\mathcal{EXIT}$ to be **true** for some process u if u can safely leave the system. Certainly, this oracle needs global information and is therefore expensive to implement. So we are focusing on local oracles. To define these oracles we need to introduce additional notation.

A link (v, w) in PG with $v \neq w$ is *relevant* for some process u if $u = w$ and v is not gone, or it is implied by a message in C_u carrying the ID of w (i.e., $u = v$). Otherwise, the link is *irrelevant* for u. Note that the links implied by process IDs stored in u are also irrelevant (meaning that u does not have to learn about them since it already knows them).

An oracle $\mathcal{O}$ is *id-sensitive* for some process u if its output depends on links relevant for u. An oracle $\mathcal{O}$ is *strictly id-sensitive* if for every process u the oracle's output *only* depends on the links relevant for u. Hence, the oracle ignores irrelevant links. Note that an action that changes the system state without affecting relevant links also does not affect the output of a strictly id-sensitive oracle. Naturally, a strictly id-sensitive oracle is also (regularly) id-sensitive. An oracle is *id-insensitive* if it is not id-sensitive. That is, the output of an id-insensitive oracle does not depend on the links relevant for the process.

We define the following strictly id-sensitive oracles. Oracle $\mathcal{NID}$ (no identifiers) evaluates to **true** if the system does not contain an identifier of u in v or C_v for some relevant process $v \neq u$. Oracle $\mathcal{EC}$ (empty channel) evaluates to **true** for a particular process u if the incoming channel of u is empty. Oracle $\mathcal{NIDEC}$ is a conjunction of $\mathcal{NID}$ and $\mathcal{EC}$. That is, $\mathcal{NIDEC}$ evaluates to **true** if both $\mathcal{NID}$ and $\mathcal{EC}$ evaluate to **true**. Note that $\mathcal{NIDEC}$ is less powerful than $\mathcal{NID}$ and $\mathcal{EC}$ used jointly since the algorithm using $\mathcal{NIDEC}$ is not able to differentiate between the conditions separately reported by $\mathcal{NID}$ and $\mathcal{EC}$. Oracle $\mathcal{ONESID}$ evaluates to **true** for a process u if u shares relevant links with at most one relevant process.

Within a class of oracles $\mathcal{C}$, an oracle $\mathcal{O}$ is *necessary* for the $\mathcal{FDP}$ if for every algorithm $\mathcal{A}$ relying on an oracle $\mathcal{O'} \in \mathcal{C}$ with $\mathcal{O'}(s, u)$ =**true** while $\mathcal{O}(s, u)$ =**false** for some system state s and process u, $\mathcal{A}$ cannot be a self-stabilizing solution to the $\mathcal{FDP}$.

1.4   Our Contribution

First, we show that without an id-sensitive oracle there is no self-stabilizing solution for the $\mathcal{FDP}$ within our model. Afterwards we show that among all id-sensitive oracles $\mathcal{ONESID}$ is necessary to solve the $\mathcal{FDP}$. On the other hand, we prove that $\mathcal{NIDEC}$ is sufficient to solve the $\mathcal{FDP}$ by providing a self-stabilizing algorithm for the $\mathcal{FDP}$ relying on $\mathcal{NIDEC}$.

Problem $\mathcal{FSP}$, in contrast to the $\mathcal{FDP}$, does not require the processes to irrevocably exit the system. This will allow us to design a self-stabilizing algorithm for the $\mathcal{FSP}$ that does not need any oracle.

1.5   Related Work

The difficulty of the Finite Departure Problem resembles that of fault-tolerant agreement in distributed systems. Fault-tolerant agreement is studied in the context of the famous Consensus Problem. It is shown [17] that the problem is not solvable in an asynchronous system even if only a single process may crash, which implies that there is no self-stabilizing solution for the Consensus Problem. This impossibility is circumvented through the use of specialized oracles known as failure detectors [12].

Due to the popularity of peer-to-peer networks, the research literature on this subject is extensive [2,3,4,9,19,26,29,30,34]. While departure algorithms are proposed in these papers, none are self-stabilizing. In fact, a rigorous treatment of when it is safe to leave the system is not yet attempted. Cases in which the rate of churn is limited are already considered [1,20,25]. Kuhn et al [1,20,25] handle this limitation by organizing the nodes into cliques of $\Theta(\log n)$ size that they call super-nodes. Hayes et al. [20] handle limited churn with a topological repair strategy called Forgiving Graph. For the case that the nodes have a sufficient amount of time to react, Saia et al. [31] propose a network maintenance algorithm called DASH to repair the network resulting from an arbitrary number of deletions. Limited churn is studied in the context of adversarial nodes [5,6,32]. While there is no work on self-stabilizing node departures, several self-stabilizing peer-to-peer algorithms are proposed [10,11,13,14,21,22,27,24]. The studied topologies range from a simple line and ring [33,18], to skip lists and skip graphs [27,22], expanders [16], the Delaunay graph [23], hypertree [15], and Chord [7].

Also a universal algorithm for topological self-stabilization is known [8]. However, none of these provide any means to exclude nodes that want to leave the network.

2   Basic Properties of the $\mathcal{FDP}$

In this section we show that the $\mathcal{FDP}$ requires an id-sensitive oracle. Moreover, if only strictly id-sensitive oracles are considered, then $\mathcal{ONESID}$ is necessary. The below proposition is a restatement of the results obtained in [27,28]. Intuitively it says that once disconnected, the system may not be able to reconnect again.

Proposition 2. *[27,28] If a computation of a copy-store-send algorithm starts in a state where two processes u and v are disconnected in PG, u and v remain disconnected in PG in every state of this computation.*

Theorem 1. *Any self-stabilizing solution to the $\mathcal{FDP}$ has to rely on an id-sensitive oracle.*

Proof. Assume that algorithm $\mathcal{A}$ is a self-stabilizing solution to the $\mathcal{FDP}$ that relies on an id-insensitive oracle $\mathcal{O}$. We consider the following counter example. Consider a system of at least three processes. The computation of $\mathcal{A}$ starts in a state where all processes but one, process v, are weakly connected. Hence, by Proposition 2, v remains disconnected from the system for the rest of the computation. Among the connected processes, u is leaving. Since $\mathcal{A}$ is a solution to the $\mathcal{FDP}$, the computation will eventually reach a state s_1 in which u calls **exit** in some action A enabled in s_1. See Figure 1 for an illustration.

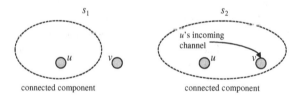

Fig. 1. Illustration for the proof of Theorem 1

We take s_1 and construct another state s_2 where there is a message carrying the ID of v in the incoming channel of process u. In s_2, all processes of the system are weakly connected. Observe that the process graphs PG_1 for state s_1 and PG_2 for state s_2 differ only by the new, relevant link (u, v). Since $\mathcal{O}$ is id-insensitive, both the state of u and the output of $\mathcal{O}$ for u are the same for s_1 and s_2. Hence, action A is also enabled in u, and it may execute in the same way in s_2 as in s_1, which implies that u may call **exit**. This disconnects v from the rest of the system. By Proposition 2, v remains disconnected from the system for the rest of the computation.

Hence, contrary to our initial assumption, $\mathcal{A}$ is not a self-stabilizing solution to the $\mathcal{FDP}$. A similar argument applies to the case in which process v or C_v holds an identifier of u.   □

Theorem 1 immediately implies the following corollary.

Corollary 1. *A self-stabilizing solution to the $\mathcal{FDP}$ is impossible without an oracle.*

Interestingly, the impossibility even holds in a synchronous communication model. Consider the model in which each round consists of two stages: in stage 1, every process receives all messages from the previous round, and in stage 2, every process executes any number of its enabled actions. Let us transform the state s_1 in the proof of Theorem 1 into a state s_2 in which v has a link to u. If this is the state of the initial round, u cannot receive a message from v in that round, since there was no prior round, so u still executes the **exit** statement. Hence, the system gets disconnected. We now address the strict id-sensitivity property of oracles.

Lemma 1. *If a self-stabilizing solution to the $\mathcal{FDP}$ relies on a strictly id-sensitive oracle, then this oracle evaluates to **true** only if a process has relevant links with at most one relevant process.*

Proof. Assume there exists an algorithm $\mathcal{A}$ that is a self-stabilizing solution to the $\mathcal{FDP}$ which uses a strictly id-sensitive oracle $\mathcal{O}$ such that there exists a state s_1 where the oracle evaluates to **true** for some leaving process u while it shares relevant links with at least two staying processes v and w. That is, either u has an identifier of v or w in its incoming channel or u's identifier is in the memory of v or w or their respective incoming channels. We construct state s_2 by removing all links from w except for the links to u. Since $\mathcal{O}$ is strictly id-sensitive, this does not change the output of $\mathcal{O}$. Notice that in s_2, process w is disconnected from the system except for the links to u.

Let us now consider a computation σ of $\mathcal{A}$ where u is leaving. Since $\mathcal{A}$ is a solution to the $\mathcal{FDP}$, u should eventually reach a state s_3 in σ in which it executes the **exit** statement in some enabled action A. Since A relies on $\mathcal{O}$, $\mathcal{O}$ must be true in this case.

We construct a system state s_4 where the state of u is the same as in s_3 while the state of the rest of the system is the same as in s_2. Since this does not change the links relevant for u compared to s_2, this does not change the output of $\mathcal{O}$ compared to s_2. On the other hand, the local state of u and the output of $\mathcal{O}$ for u is the same in s_4 as in s_3. Hence, action A must be enabled in s_4, and it may execute in the same way in s_4 as in s_3, which implies that u may call **exit**. This, however, disconnects process w from the rest of the staying processes. According to Proposition 2, w remains disconnected from the system for the rest of the computation. Thus, contrary to the initial assumption, $\mathcal{A}$ is not a self-stabilizing solution to the $\mathcal{FDP}$.   □

Lemma 1 leads to the following theorem.

Theorem 2. *Among all strictly id-sensitive oracles, the oracle $\mathcal{ONESID}$ is necessary to obtain a self-stabilizing solution to the $\mathcal{FDP}$.*

Since $\mathcal{NIDEC}$ is true only if $\mathcal{ONESID}$ is true, $\mathcal{NIDEC}$ is a potential candidate for solving the $\mathcal{FDP}$ problem, and the next section demonstrates that it is indeed sufficient.

3   Solution for the $\mathcal{FDP}$

In this section we present a self-stabilizing algorithm called $\mathcal{SDA}$ that solves the Finite Departure Problem with the help of $\mathcal{NIDEC}$. We focus on the case that PG consists of a single weakly connected component. However, the results transfer to PG being split up into multiple components. The algorithm is shown in Figure 2.

For ease of exposition, we write that identifier q is to the *right* of identifier p if $q > p$ and to the *left* of p if $q < p$. In algorithm $\mathcal{SDA}$, to maintain connectivity, each process p contains variables $left$ and $right$ that store process IDs that are less than resp. greater than p. If $left$ or $right$ does not contain an identifier, it contains $-\infty$ or $+\infty$ respectively. To ensure a safe process departure, $\mathcal{SDA}$ uses the $\mathcal{NIDEC}$ oracle.

Algorithm $\mathcal{SDA}$ uses two message types: *intro* and *reverse*. Message *intro* carries a single process ID and serves as a way to introduce processes to one another. Message *reverse* does not carry an ID. Instead, this message carries a boolean value denoted as **revright** or **revleft**. This message is a request for the receiving process to remove the respective left or right ID from its memory and send its own ID back.

We now describe the actions of the algorithm. Some of the actions contain message sending statements involving IDs stored in the $left$ and $right$ variables. If the variable contains $\pm\infty$, the sending action is skipped. To simplify the presentation of the algorithm, this is omitted in Figure 2.

The algorithm has three actions. The first action, called *timeout*, periodically introduces the process to its neighbors unless it is leaving. If the process is leaving, it sends messages to its neighbors requesting them to remove its ID from their memory. If additionally the $\mathcal{NIDEC}$ oracle signals that it is safe to leave, the process introduces its neighbors to each other to preserve system connectivity and then exits by executing the **exit** statement. The second action is *introduce*. It receives and handles *intro* messages received by a node. The operation of this action depends on the relation between the ID carried by the message and the IDs stored in $left$ and $right$. The process either forwards $intro(id)$ to its left or right neighbor to handle it; or, if id happens to be closer to p than $left$ or $right$, then p replaces the respective neighbor and instead introduces the old neighbor identifier to id. The third action, *reverse*, handles the neighbors' requests to leave, i.e. the *rev* messages received by a node. If p receives this message, it sets the respective variable to $+\infty$ or to $-\infty$ and, to preserve system connectivity, sends its own ID to this process. To break symmetry, if p itself is leaving, it ignores the request from its left neighbor.

3.1   Correctness Proof

For $\mathcal{SDA}$ to be a self-stabilizing solution to the $\mathcal{FDP}$ it remains to show two properties. *Safety*: $\mathcal{SDA}$ never disconnects any relevant processes. *Liveness*: All leaving processes eventually exit the system.

Lemma 2. *If a computation of $\mathcal{SDA}$ starts in a state where the graph PG of the non-gone processes is weakly connected, the graph PG of the non-gone processes remains weakly connected in every state of this computation.*

Proof. We demonstrate the correctness of the lemma by showing that none of the actions of $\mathcal{SDA}$ disconnects PG. Action *timeout* only adds links to PG if $\mathcal{NIDEC}$ is **false** and cannot disconnect it in this case. If $\mathcal{NIDEC}$ is **true**, PG does not contain links pointing to p and the only outgoing links are $(p, left)$ and $(p, right)$. If p is connected to the rest of PG by at most one link (i.e., $left$ or $right$ does not store an ID),

constant	p : process identifier
variables	*leaving* : *boolean*, read only, **true** when p wants to leave
	left : process ID less than p, $-\infty$ if undefined
	right : process ID greater than p, $+\infty$ if undefined
	$p.C$: channel of incoming messages of process p
messages	*intro(id)*, introduces process identifier
	rev(direction), requests recipient to reverse edge
	direction is **revleft** or **revright**

actions

timeout: **true** $\longrightarrow$
       if not *leaving* **then**
          send *intro(p)* **to** *left*,
          send *intro(p)* **to** *right*
       else // leaving
          send *rev*(**revleft**) **to** *right*
          send *rev*(**revright**) **to** *left*
    *   **if** $\mathcal{NIDEC}$ **then**
             if $left \neq -\infty$ **and** $right \neq +\infty$ **then**
                send *intro(left)* **to** *right*
                send *intro(right)* **to** *left*
   **   **exit**

introduce: *intro* $\in p.C \longrightarrow$
       receive *intro(id)*
       if $id < left$ **then**
          send *intro(id)* **to** *left*
       if $left < id < p$ **then**
          send *intro(left)* **to** *id*
          $left := id$
       if $p < id < right$ **then**
          send *intro(right)* **to** *id*
          $right := id$
       if $right < id$ **then**
          send *intro(id)* **to** *right*

reverse: *rev* $\in p.C \longrightarrow$
       receive *rev(direction)*
       if $direction =$ **revleft then**
          if not *leaving* **then**
             send *intro(p)* **to** *left*
             $left := -\infty$
       else // *direction* is **revright**
          send *intro(p)* **to** *right*
          $right := +\infty$

Fig. 2. Algorithm $\mathcal{SDA}$ for process p. $\mathcal{SSA}$ is obtained by omitting the line marked with * (i.e. the use of $\mathcal{NIDEC}$) and replacing the line indicated with ** (i.e. the **exit** command) by the **sleep** command

the departure does not disconnect PG. If both $left$ and $right$ store an ID, the leaving of p does not disconnect PG because p sends $intro(left)$ to $right$ and $intro(right)$ to $left$ and thereby preserves weak connectivity between the remaining processes.

Let us consider $introduce$. If the received id is the same as p or as $left$ or $right$, the message is ignored. However, this does not disconnect PG. Let us consider the case of $id < p$. The case of $id > p$ is similar. There are two sub-cases to address. In case $id < left$, p sends $intro(id)$ to $left$. That is, in PG, the link (p, id) is replaced with $(left, id)$. Since p stores the recipient identifier in $left$, i.e. PG has a link $(id, left)$, the graph connectivity is preserved. The other case is $left < id < p$. In this case, p replaces $left$ with id and forwards the old value to id. That is, the links (p, id) and $(p, left)$ are replaced by (p, id) and $(id, left)$. This replacement preserves PG connectivity.

The rev message received by a $reverse$ action may force p to set either $right$ or $left$ to infinity thus removing a link from PG. Let us consider the case of $right$ being set to $+\infty$, the other case is similar. This operation removes $(p, right)$ from PG. However, $reverse$ sends a message $intro(p)$ to $right$. That is, it replaces the link $(p, right)$ with $(right, p)$, so weak connectivity of PG is preserved.   □

The liveness part of the correctness proof is more involved. Due to the way IDs are handled by $\mathcal{SDA}$, the development of a link can be traced over the course of the computation. Recall that a link (p, q) is associated with an ID of q stored in p or a message in C_p. The actions of $\mathcal{SDA}$ may transform (p, q) into a different link (p', q'). Only the following cases can occur:

1. The $introduce$ action stores q in $left$ or $right$ or drops the q since it is equal to p, $left$ or $right$. In both cases, we stay with the link (p, q).
2. The $introduce$ action may delegate the ID of q to some process p': then (p, q) changes to (p', q). Note that whenever this happens, $p' \in [p, q]$.
3. The $reverse$ action reverses the link (p, q) to (q, p). Note that whenever this happens, p is staying or p is leaving and $p < q$.

The changes (i.e., cases 2 and 3) to a link (p, q) over time form a sequence of links $(p, q) = (p_0, q_0), (p_1, q_1), (p_2, q_2), \ldots$ that we call the $trace$ of (p, q). The cases listed above imply the following Monotonicity lemma.

Lemma 3. *(Monotonicity) For every (p', q') in the trace of (p, q), $p', q' \in [p, q]$.*

This and the fact that we have a finite number of processes may seem to imply that every trace is finite, but for now we cannot exclude the case that a link is reversed infinitely often between two processes. It will only be implied later when we know that eventually all leaving processes will exit the system.

Consider an arbitrary fixed computation of $\mathcal{SDA}$. A link that does not change any more is called *stable*. A *steady chain* of processes $x_k, \ldots, x_0$ is a sequence of leaving and not yet gone processes of increasing order with stable links (x_i, x_{i-1}). A steady chain is *maximal* if it cannot be extended to the left or right. See Figure 3 for an illustration. Note that at every state of the computation, every leaving process is part of at least one maximal steady chain (which might just be a chain consisting of itself). Also, the following holds:

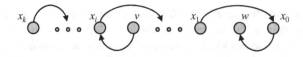

Fig. 3. Illustration of a steady chain

Lemma 4. *A maximal steady chain can only change in two ways: either (1) process x_k exits the system, or (2) the chain is extended to the left or right due to new stable edges.*

Since the number of processes is finite, this means that eventually a maximal steady chain is stable, i.e., it does not change any more for the rest of the computation. We call this a *stable chain*. Now, we can prove the following lemma.

Lemma 5. *In every computation of SDA, the only stable chain is the empty chain.*

Proof. Consider the contrary that we have a non-empty stable chain $x_k, \ldots, x_0$. Our goal will be to prove that eventually there is no incoming link from non-gone processes in PG to x_k. This implies that eventually x_k has no more messages to process, so $NIDEC$ will eventually be **true**. Therefore, x_k can exit the system, which contradicts our assumption that the chain is stable.

First, suppose there is an incoming link (p, x_k) with $p < x_k$. If there is a reversal in the trace of that link, then we end up with a link (x_k, p') with $p \leq p' < x_k$. If this causes x_k to delegate p' away, then due to the Monotonicity Lemma that link will never include x_k again. Otherwise, x_k stores p' in *left*, and since a leaving process never reverses its link to *left*, x_k either eventually delegates p' away, which will mean that the link never includes x_k again, or x_k holds on to that link, which means that (x_k, p') can never become an incoming link to x_k again. So suppose that there is no reversal in the trace of (p, x_k). Then its trace is finite, which means that eventually it becomes a stable link (p', x_k). We will argue via two cases that this cannot happen.

(1a) If p' is staying, then p' will eventually introduce itself to x_k. This will create a new edge (x_k, p') in PG. If this link is not delegated by x_k, x_k will eventually ask p' to reverse its link to x_k, which it will do, but this contradicts the assumption that (p', x_k) is stable. If x_k delegates (x_k, p'), then we keep track of that link until we get to a link (x, p') that gets reversed or is stable. In the former case, p' delegates x_k to x, and in the latter case, p' also either delegates x_k to x or reverses (p', x_k), depending on whether x is staying or leaving. Hence, in any case, (p', x_k) is not be stable, a contradiction.

(1b) If p' is leaving, then we distinguish between two cases. If x_k is not aware of p', then the chain can be extended to p' because (p', x_k) is stable, which contradicts our assumption to have a stable chain. If x_k is aware of p', then x_k will eventually ask p' to reverse its right edge, which will cause the link (p', x_k) to be reversed which again contradicts our assumption that (p', x_k) is stable.

Next, consider the case that there is an incoming link (p, x_k) with $p > x_k$. If there is a reversal in the trace of that link, we end up with a link (x_k, p') with $x_k < p' \leq p$. If this causes x_k to delegate p' away, then due to the Monotonicity Lemma the trace of that link will never include x_k again. Otherwise, it must hold that $x_k < p' \leq x_{k-1}$. If $p' = x_{k-1}$, the edge becomes stable, and otherwise, x_k delegates x_{k-1} to p', which contradicts the assumption that (x_k, x_{k-1}) is stable. So in any case this link will eventually not be an incoming link to x_k any more. Thus, suppose that there is no reversal in the trace of (p, x_k). Then its trace is finite, which means that eventually it becomes a stable link (p', x_k). We will again argue via two cases that this cannot happen.

(2a) If p' is staying, then p' eventually introduces itself of x_k. If $x_k < p' < x_{k-1}$, then x_k delegates x_{k-1} away, contradicting our assumption that (x_k, x_{k-1}) is stable. If $p' > x_{k-1}$, then similar arguments as for case (1a) above will show that (p', x_k) is not stable, also contradicting our assumption.

(2b) If p' is leaving, p' will eventually ask x_k to reverse its right edge, which it will do, contradicting our assumption that (x_k, x_{k-1}) is stable.

Moreover, x_k never creates an incoming link to itself since this occurs only if requested to reverse (x_k, x_{k-1}), but since (x_k, x_{k-1}) is stable, this does not happen. Hence, eventually x_k has no incoming link, which completes the proof. □

Lemmas 2 and 5 lead to the following theorem.

Theorem 3. *Algorithm $\mathcal{SDA}$ and the $\mathcal{NIDEC}$ oracle provide a self-stabilizing solution to the $\mathcal{FDP}$.*

4 Solution for the $\mathcal{FSP}$

We can overcome the use of oracles by changing to the Finite Sleep Problem. Algorithm $\mathcal{SSA}$, which solves this problem, is almost identical to $\mathcal{SDA}$ shown in Figure 2. The only differences are that no oracle is checked and that the **sleep** command is used instead of **exit**.

For the correctness proof of $\mathcal{SSA}$, we show that the safety and liveness properties hold. We first define and prove the conditions that must prevail for a process to remain permanently asleep.

Lemma 6. *In the $\mathcal{SSA}$ algorithm, a process p is permanently asleep if and only if p is hibernating.*

Proof. The backwards direction (if p is hibernating then p is permanently asleep) directly follows from Proposition 1. So it remains to prove the other direction.

Suppose that there is a process q that has a directed path along the processes $q_0 = q, q_1, \ldots, q_\ell = p$ to p and q is either not asleep, or C_q is non-empty. Without loss of generality, we may assume that for all other processes q_i with $i \geq 1$, C_q is empty. Hence, for all $i \geq 1$, q_{i+1} is initially stored in q_i. Since q is either awake and knows q_1, or C_q contains a message with q_1, q is guaranteed to eventually process the link (q, q_1) by either calling the *timeout* (which may contact q_1), *introduce* (which may contact or delegate q_1), or *reverse* action (which may contact q_1). If q_1 gets delegated, the receiving process is also guaranteed to process q_1. We continue the trace of (q, q_1) in this case until we reach a process q' where q_1 is not delegated any more. This must eventually happen since the number of processes is finite. Hence, q_1 is eventually contacted, which will wake up q_1. Since q_1 initially stores q_2, q_1 is therefore also guaranteed to eventually process the link (q_1, q_2). The same arguments as for q_1 then guarantee that also q_2 eventually processes the link (q_2, q_3). Hence, by induction, eventually p is woken up, which completes the proof. □

The lemma implies that given our initial state satisfies the conditions in Section 1.2, no process will initially be permanently asleep. Additionally, the following lemma holds, where we use $\mathcal{NIDEC}$ as a predicate and not an oracle.

Lemma 7. *For any process p that calls the* **sleep** *command in* timeout *it holds that p is hibernating afterwards if and only if $\mathcal{NIDEC}(p)$ is* **true**.

Proof. If $\mathcal{NIDEC}(p)$ is **true**, then no relevant process has a directed path to p, and there are no more messages in C_p, which means that p is hibernating.

On the other hand, if p is hibernating, then there is no directed path from a relevant node to p and no message in C_p, which means that $\mathcal{NIDEC}(p)$ is **true**.   □

Now we are ready to prove the following lemma.

Lemma 8. *If a computation of $\mathcal{SDA}$ starts in a state where the graph PG of the non-hibernating processes is weakly connected, the graph PG of the non-hibernating processes remains weakly connected in every state of this computation.*

Proof. We know from Lemma 2 that none of the actions of $\mathcal{SSA}$ disconnects the graph PG of the non-exited processes. Thus, as long as no process falls asleep after an action (which can only happen if a leaving process calls *timeout*), the lemma holds. Suppose now that a leaving process p calls *timeout*. Our first goal is to show that no other process can become hibernating in this case. Consider any process $q \neq p$ that is non-hibernating and that has a directed path from p. We distinguish between two cases.

(1) If the directed path from p to q leads through a process q' stored in a message in C_p, then p cannot become hibernating and therefore q cannot become hibernating as well.

(2) If the directed path from p to q leads though $left$ or $right$ of p, then q cannot become hibernating because p will contact $left$ and $right$ in *timeout*.

Hence, only p can potentially become hibernating. However, due to Lemma 7, this happens only if $\mathcal{NIDEC}(p)$ is **true**. Since we know from Lemma 2 that in this case p may even exit the system without causing a disconnection, we can also allow p to hibernate without risking disconnection from the non-hibernating processes.   □

Lemmas 6 and 8 imply safety. So it remains to prove liveness. Notice that due to Lemma 7, a process p calling **sleep** is permanently asleep if and only if $\mathcal{NIDEC}(p)$ is **true**. Hence, the liveness proof follows along the same lines as the liveness proof of $\mathcal{SDA}$, which implies the following theorem.

Theorem 4. $\mathcal{SSA}$ *provides a self-stabilizing solution to the $\mathcal{FSP}$.*

5   Conclusion

In this paper, we showed that among the strictly id-sensitive oracles, $\mathcal{ONESID}$ is necessary for a solution to the $\mathcal{FDP}$. We also showed that a more restrictive oracle, $\mathcal{NIDEC}$, is sufficient by presenting an algorithm that solves the $\mathcal{FDP}$ using $\mathcal{NIDEC}$. Note that there cannot be a more restrictive strictly id-sensitive oracle than $\mathcal{NIDEC}$

since $\mathcal{NIDEC}(p)$ is only true if there is no relevant link left for p. On the other hand, it would be interesting to find out whether $\mathcal{ONESID}$ is also sufficient for the $\mathcal{FDP}$ since it would allow nodes to leave earlier than $\mathcal{NIDEC}$.

Observe that the $\mathcal{SDA}$ algorithm, besides solving the $\mathcal{FDP}$, also organizes the staying processes in a sorted list. It would be interesting to consider building more complex and robust topologies such as the skip list or skip graph [13,27,24].

It would also be interesting to study the power of individual components of $\mathcal{NIDEC}$: $\mathcal{NID}$ and $\mathcal{EC}$. Specifically, we would like to determine the extent of the states from which the algorithm using only one of the components may recover.

References

1. Albrecht, K., Kuhn, F., Wattenhofer, R.: Dependable peer-to-peer systems withstanding dynamic adversarial churn. In: Kohlas, J., Meyer, B., Schiper, A. (eds.) Dependable Systems: Software, Computing, Networks. LNCS, vol. 4028, pp. 275–294. Springer, Heidelberg (2006)
2. Andersen, D., Balakrishnan, H., Kaashoek, F., Morris, R.: Resilient overlay networks. In: SOSP, pp. 131–145. ACM, New York (2001)
3. Aspnes, J., Shah, G.: Skip graphs. ACM Transactions on Algorithms 3(4), 37 (2007)
4. Awerbuch, B., Scheideler, C.: The hyperring: A low-congestion deterministic data structure for distributed environments. In: SODA, pp. 318–327. Society for Industrial and Applied Mathematics, Philadelphia (2004)
5. Awerbuch, B., Scheideler, C.: Towards scalable and robust overlay networks. In: IPTPS (2007)
6. Awerbuch, B., Scheideler, C.: Towards a scalable and robust dht. Theory Comput. Syst. 45(2), 234–260 (2009)
7. Benter, M., Divband, M., Kniesburges, S., Koutsopoulos, A., Graffi, K.: Ca-re-chord: A churn resistant self-stabilizing chord overlay network. In: NetSys, pp. 27–34 (2013)
8. Berns, A., Ghosh, S., Pemmaraju, S.V.: Building self-stabilizing overlay networks with the transitive closure framework. In: Défago, X., Petit, F., Villain, V. (eds.) SSS 2011. LNCS, vol. 6976, pp. 62–76. Springer, Heidelberg (2011)
9. Bhargava, A., Kothapalli, K., Riley, C., Scheideler, C., Thober, M.: Pagoda: A dynamic overlay network for routing, data management, and multicasting. In: SPAA, pp. 170–179. ACM, New York (2004)
10. Bianchi, S., Datta, A., Felber, P., Gradinariu, M.: Stabilizing peer-to-peer spatial filters. In: ICDCS, p. 27. IEEE Computer Society, Washington, DC (2007)
11. Caron, E., Desprez, F., Petit, F., Tedeschi, C.: Snap-stabilizing prefix tree for peer-to-peer systems. Parallel Processing Letters 20(1), 15–30 (2010)
12. Chandra, T.D., Toueg, S.: Unreliable failure detectors for reliable distributed systems. J. ACM 43(2), 225–267 (1996)
13. Clouser, T., Nesterenko, M., Scheideler, C.: Tiara: A self-stabilizing deterministic skip list and skip graph. Theor. Comput. Sci. 428, 18–35 (2012)
14. Dolev, D., Hoch, E.N., van Renesse, R.: Self-stabilizing and byzantine-tolerant overlay network. In: Tovar, E., Tsigas, P., Fouchal, H. (eds.) OPODIS 2007. LNCS, vol. 4878, pp. 343–357. Springer, Heidelberg (2007)
15. Dolev, S., Kat, R.I.: Hypertree for self-stabilizing peer-to-peer systems. In: NCA, pp. 25–32 (2004)
16. Dolev, S., Tzachar, N.: Spanders: Distributed spanning expanders. Sci. Comput. Program. 78(5), 544–555 (2013)

17. Fischer, M.J., Lynch, N.A., Paterson, M.S.: Impossibility of distributed consensus with one faulty process. J. ACM 32(2), 374–382 (1985)
18. Gall, D., Jacob, R., Richa, A., Scheideler, C., Schmid, S., Täubig, H.: Time complexity of distributed topological self-stabilization: The case of graph linearization. In: López-Ortiz, A. (ed.) LATIN 2010. LNCS, vol. 6034, pp. 294–305. Springer, Heidelberg (2010)
19. Harvey, N.J.A., Jones, M.B., Saroiu, S., Theimer, M., Wolman, A.: Skipnet: A scalable overlay network with practical locality properties. In: USENIX Symposium on Internet Technologies and Systems (2003)
20. Hayes, T.P., Saia, J., Trehan, A.: The forgiving graph: A distributed data structure for low stretch under adversarial attack. Distributed Computing 25(4), 261–278 (2012)
21. Herault, T., Lemarinier, P., Peres, O., Pilard, L., Beauquier, J.: Brief announcement: Self-stabilizing spanning tree algorithm for large scale systems. In: Datta, A.K., Gradinariu, M. (eds.) SSS 2006. LNCS, vol. 4280, pp. 574–575. Springer, Heidelberg (2006)
22. Jacob, R., Richa, A., Scheideler, C., Schmid, S., Täubig, H.: A distributed polylogarithmic time algorithm for self-stabilizing skip graphs. In: PODC, pp. 131–140 (2009)
23. Jacob, R., Ritscher, S., Scheideler, C., Schmid, S.: Towards higher-dimensional topological self-stabilization: A distributed algorithm for delaunay graphs. Theor. Comput. Sci. 457, 137–148 (2012)
24. Kniesburges, S., Koutsopoulos, A., Scheideler, C.: Re-chord: A self-stabilizing chord overlay network. In: SPAA, pp. 235–244 (2011)
25. Kuhn, F., Schmid, S., Wattenhofer, R.: Towards worst-case churn resistant peer-to-peer systems. Distributed Computing 22(4), 249–267 (2010)
26. Malkhi, D., Naor, M., Ratajczak, D.: Viceroy: A scalable and dynamic emulation of the butterfly. In: PODC, pp. 183–192. ACM, New York (2002)
27. Nor, R.M., Nesterenko, M., Scheideler, C.: Corona: A stabilizing deterministic message-passing skip list. In: Défago, X., Petit, F., Villain, V. (eds.) SSS 2011. LNCS, vol. 6976, pp. 356–370. Springer, Heidelberg (2011)
28. Nor, R.M., Nesterenko, M., Tixeuil, S.: Linearizing peer-to-peer systems with oracles. Technical Report TR-KSU-CS-2012-02, Dept. of Computer Science, Kent State University (July 2012)
29. Ratnasamy, S., Francis, P., Handley, M., Karp, R., Schenker, S.: A scalable content-addressable network. In: SIGCOMM, pp. 161–172. ACM, New York (2001)
30. Rowstron, A., Druschel, P.: Pastry: Scalable, decentralized object location, and routing for large-scale peer-to-peer systems. In: Guerraoui, R. (ed.) Middleware 2001. LNCS, vol. 2218, pp. 329–350. Springer, Heidelberg (2001)
31. Saia, J., Trehan, A.: Picking up the pieces: Self-healing in reconfigurable networks. In: IPDPS, pp. 1–12 (2008)
32. Scheideler, C.: How to spread adversarial nodes?: rotate. In: STOC, pp. 704–713 (2005)
33. Shaker, A., Reeves, D.S.: Self-stabilizing structured ring topology P2P systems. In: Peer-to-Peer Computing, pp. 39–46 (2005)
34. Stoica, I., Morris, R., Liben-Nowell, D., Karger, D.R., Kaashoek, M.F., Dabek, F., Balakrishnan, H.: Chord: A scalable peer-to-peer lookup protocol for Internet applications. IEEE/ACM Trans. Netw. 11(1), 17–32 (2003)

CloudSylla: Detecting Suspicious System Calls in the Cloud

Marc Kührer, Johannes Hoffmann, and Thorsten Holz

Horst Görtz Institute for IT-Security, Ruhr-University Bochum, Germany
{firstname.lastname}@ruhr-uni-bochum.de

Abstract. To protect computer systems against the tremendous number of daily malware threats, security software is typically installed on individual end hosts and the responsibility to keep this software updated is often assigned to (inexperienced) users. A critical drawback of this strategy, especially in enterprise networks, is that a single unprotected client system might lead to severe attacks such as industrial espionage. To overcome this problem, a potential approach is to move the responsibility to utilize the latest detection mechanisms to a centralized, continuously maintained network service to identify suspicious behavior on end hosts and perform adequate actions once a client invokes malicious activities. In this paper, we propose a security approach called *CloudSylla* (*Cloud-based SYscaLL Analysis*) in which we utilize a centralized network service to analyze the clients' activities directly at the API and system call level. This enables, among other advantages, a centralized management of signatures and a unified security policy. To evaluate the applicability of our approach, we implemented prototypes for desktop computers and mobile devices and found this approach to be applicable in practice as no substantial limitations of usability are caused on the client side.

1 Introduction

Malicious software needs to invoke API, respectively, system calls to cause substantial damage, thus monitoring these calls is a promising approach for detecting suspicious activities [1, 2]. Consequently, this technique is often adopted by security and malware protection services, which are typically deployed locally on end hosts. The drawback of this strategy is that each client is responsible for keeping its security software updated in short-time intervals to also detect latest zero-day attacks. When the software is not updated on a regular basis, the host might somehow get infected with malware. Especially in large-scale networks, this is a severe problem since an infected client machine might be used as an entrance point for more substantial attacks such as industrial espionage.

A reasonable approach is to move the identification of malicious activities to a centralized and more powerful network service. In the past, several approaches were proposed [3–5], in which the actual analysis process is performed in the Cloud. The clients are then no longer required to keep their detection mechanisms updated continuously, reducing the amount of required computing power

P. Felber and V. Garg (Eds.): SSS 2014, LNCS 8756, pp. 63–77, 2014.

on end hosts significantly—particularly important for mobile devices with limited power capabilities. Nevertheless, all these approaches operate on a rather coarse-grained level, e.g., CloudAV [3] only analyzes whether executables are detected by antivirus engines which might fail for obfuscated malware. To perform a more fine-granular inspection of the clients' behavior in the Cloud, we introduce an analysis mechanism that operates directly on API and system calls invoked on the end hosts. Outsourcing the inspection of these operations to a Cloud implies several benefits, yet might also induce serious drawbacks. To evaluate the applicability of our security mechanism, we implemented prototypes for desktop computers using Windows and mobile devices using Android and find our approach to efficiently detect malicious activities on the end hosts by analyzing invoked API and system calls at a centralized network service.

In summary, this paper makes the following contributions:
- We propose an approach to move the detection of malicious behavior from individual end hosts to a centralized network service. To perform a fine-granular inspection of end host activities, we analyze the corresponding API and system calls in the Cloud to determine if these activities are malicious.
- We implemented prototypes for desktop computers and mobile devices to monitor and forward invoked API and system calls to the Cloud service.
- In empirical evaluations, we demonstrate the feasibility of our approach. The typical runtime overhead of our implementation is negligible for already known applications due to efficient caching mechanisms. New and therefore unknown applications can still be analyzed in a satisfying amount of time.

2   General Approach

A fine-granular approach to improve the clients' security, particularly applicable in enterprise networks with good connectivity and low latency, is to outsource local malware detection to a less vulnerable and more powerful Cloud service that identifies malicious activities by inspecting API and system calls—both referred to as *syscall* in the following although we focus on API calls in our Windows prototype. This Cloud-based strategy reduces the administrative overhead significantly, since end hosts are no longer required to maintain local detection mechanisms and keep signatures updated in short-time intervals. Updating detection mechanisms can be accomplished more easily as changes need to be performed on the Cloud side only, which enables a unified security policy. This centralized analysis also enables a correlation of the behavior of all hosts that send data to the Cloud service, enabling detection mechanisms like BotMiner [6].

    To detect malicious activities, we require each end host to forward specific events at the API and system call level to the Cloud and await approval or denial to perform these actions locally. More specific, once a syscall is invoked by a client process, the corresponding syscall arguments (e.g., filenames and URLs) are individually looked up in locally stored caching instances, containing information for trusted, malicious, and analyzed but unsuspicious values. If not cached, the syscall including the arguments is forwarded to the Cloud. The Cloud first applies signatures matching, i.e., probes if the syscall is part of a signature, a sequence of consecutively invoked syscalls. Afterwards, the individual arguments are checked against blacklists and looked up at external sources. If no argument is found to indicate malicious behavior, the syscall is executed on the end host. If malicious behavior is identified, the end host terminates the malicious application or, more restrictive, is automatically blocked from accessing critical infrastructure such as the local network, depending on a specifiable local security policy.

Selecting a reasonable set of syscalls to monitor is a critical but necessary task to reduce the overall number of analysis requests forwarded to the Cloud. Monitoring irrelevant syscalls wastes network bandwidth and execution time of the clients, however, tracking an insufficient set of syscalls might miss important activities to detect malicious behavior. Modern operating systems provide a large number of syscalls, and in some cases, multiple syscalls perform almost the same operation (e.g., creating a process). We thus need to find basic syscalls (e.g., `ShellExecuteExW` which is called by `ShellExecuteA/W/ExA` on Windows) to significantly reduce the number of monitored syscalls. We also have to consider the frequency at which specific syscalls are triggered. To give a concrete example, let us assume we monitor the syscall `NtCreateFile`. When executing Office applications we might not experience a large number of new files, however, executing a web browser presumably increases the quantity of invocations considerably because of web content being cached. Furthermore, we have to select the syscalls based on the information they provide. Monitoring syscalls that solely pass handles or similar memory addresses might not be that effective since most of these addresses differ on each end host. Yet, intercepting syscalls operating on executable memory might lead to malicious activities on a client system. To comply with these restrictions, our approach mainly focuses on API and system calls that can be compared to blacklists, signatures, and reports gathered from automated malware analysis systems such as Anubis [7]. More precisely, we monitor syscalls providing information such as mutex-, file-, and service names, file hashes of executables, and IP addresses, domain names, URLs, and network messages to trace most of the outgoing communication to other end hosts such as botnet Command & Control (C&C) servers or SMTP servers for spam delivery.

3   Implementation

In this section, we introduce the caching mechanism utilized in our approach and describe the Cloud-to-client communication protocol. We then focus on the prototype of the Cloud service and the individual end host implementations.

3.1   Caching

When limiting the set of syscalls to those providing the information mentioned above, we would still have to handle a vast number of invocations by the client processes. To achieve a sufficient performance, our approach thus has to adopt an efficient caching strategy. As a result, the Cloud and the end host prototypes implement fast and cost-efficient Bloomfilter [8] caches to store and query already processed syscall arguments. Each prototype allocates three caching instances for every type of argument (e.g., filename and URL). Two instances store *trusted* ($\mathcal{T}$) and *malicious* ($\mathcal{M}$) entries, which are gathered from external sources. The third cache covers entries which are neither *trusted* nor *malicious* but were analyzed by the Cloud before. We name the last category *unsuspicious* ($\mathcal{U}$).

3.2 Communication

The communication between the Cloud and the clients is performed by interchanging a custom protocol that keeps the required network usage at a low level.

Notation: A syscall is denoted by its name and one or multiple arguments, defined as $\mathcal{S} := \{$ *name*, $\mathcal{A}^+$ $\}$. A syscall argument is represented by $\mathcal{A} := \{$ *type*, *data*, $\mathcal{L}$ $\}$. The parameter *type* denotes the argument type (e.g., filename or URL), and *data* contains the actual value of the argument. We define the label $\mathcal{L} := \mathcal{M} \mid \mathcal{T} \mid \mathcal{U} \mid \mathcal{TA} \mid \mathcal{ACP} \mid \mathcal{CR}$, whereas we distinguish between the categories *malicious, trusted, unsuspicious, temporarily approved, approved but caching prohibited,* and *caching revoked.*

Protocol: As shown in Figure 1, the protocol mainly utilizes five distinct message types. The message `client hello` is sent by each running and newly executed client process and includes its command line and the file hash of the corresponding executable. To complete the two-way hand-shake, the Cloud service looks up the command line and file hash in its caches and transmits the `server hello` message including the analysis result $\mathcal{L}$. When the process is associated to an already known malicious executable, $\mathcal{L}$ is defined as *malicious* and security measures are applied, defined by the specified security

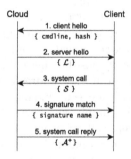

Fig. 1. Protocol

policies. If the file hash is not cached at the Cloud, the hash value is requested at external data sources and analysis modules. Depending on the security policies, the execution of the syscall is either denied or delayed to prioritize the safety of the end host or temporarily approved by setting the label to $\mathcal{TA}$ to avoid a delay on the client. Once we receive the analysis results from the external modules, we transmit an updated `server hello` message including the final label to the client. Update messages, however, might not be received by a device, e.g., during offline phases, hence the host could unknowingly perform malicious activities. We thus implemented fail-over solutions in the individual end host prototypes.

The remaining three messages are exchanged when end hosts forward invoked syscalls to the Cloud service as discussed in the following.

3.3 Cloud Implementation

The prototype of our Cloud service is implemented as a light-weight, extensible Python script and leverages an external database containing data from malware analysis systems and blacklists. We also utilize the third-party services VirusTotal [9] and Google Safebrowsing [10] to obtain details about syscall arguments.

Figure 2 illustrates the processing stages of the Cloud service once it receives a `system call` message from a client process (1). First, the syscall $\mathcal{S}$ is compared to locally stored signatures, characterizing malicious behavior and security policies. As signatures may consist of multiple consecutively executed syscalls, we verify if the currently processed syscall is part of a signature and whether

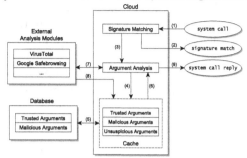

Fig. 2. Cloud implementation

additional syscalls are required to match the complete signature. When a complete signature is triggered, we forward the `signature match` message including the name of the triggered signature to the client, invoke security measures, and skip further analyses (2). If no signature is triggered but the syscall was part of a signature, the labels of all arguments in $\mathcal{S}$ are set to *approved but caching prohibited* ($\mathcal{ACP}$)—unless they are flagged as *malicious* in the succeeding analysis steps. When prohibiting caching of these arguments, we require the end hosts to always forward the corresponding syscalls to the Cloud for repeated analysis. In step (3), the syscall arguments are extracted from $\mathcal{S}$ and then individually checked against the caches (4). When an argument is not cached, the database is queried (5). If the query was successful, the result is added to the appropriate cache and written to the label $\mathcal{L}$ of the argument $\mathcal{A}$ (6). If the argument is neither cached nor stored in the database, we forward the argument (i.e., file hash, URL, domain, or IP address) to external analysis modules (7) and continue processing the next arguments. Once an analysis result from an external module is returned to the Cloud, it is added to the corresponding cache (8). When all arguments of $\mathcal{S}$ are analyzed locally and external modules still process arguments, we either decline or delay the execution of the syscall to ensure the end hosts' security or temporarily approve the syscall (9), similar to the `server hello` message.

On signature updates, we distribute *caching revoked* messages for all syscall arguments in the new signatures. This ensures that these arguments are removed from the client caches and always forwarded to the Cloud for signature matching.

3.4   Windows Implementation

Our prototype for desktop computers running Windows is split into two components, a background service and a syscall hooking library. The service is a light-weight application running in the background of each client system and utilizes the madCodeHook framework [11] to inject the library into each running and every new process. The hooking library is based on a heavily modified version of the `cuckoomon` library utilized by the Cuckoo Sandbox [12] and allocates a dedicated *hook function* for each monitored syscall. Once a syscall is invoked by a client process, the execution flow is redirected to the respective hook function, which first performs a look up of the syscall arguments in the locally stored caches. If not cached at the client, a `system call` message is sent to the Cloud. Depending on the results obtained from the caches or the Cloud, the execution of the native syscall function is then performed or prohibited.

As stated in Section 2, we have to closely select the monitored syscalls to achieve sufficient performance, thus we limit our monitoring to 29 syscalls and explain in the following the process how these system calls were chosen. To discover malware copying or renaming files to hide its presence, we monitor `NtCreateFile` and `NtFileOpen`. Hooking these syscalls, however, might induce a huge number of invocations, thus we limit the monitoring to two situations. We monitor `NtCreateFile` to obtain the filenames of newly created files. Note that we cannot perform any other investigations as no content is written yet. We also monitor both syscalls when the file contains a *Portable Executable* (PE) header, indicating a Windows executable. As the file paths provided by these syscalls might include client data such as the user name, we have to pre-process these paths and normalize user data with predefined values before forwarding the arguments to the Cloud to enable a comparison across multiple clients. We further hook syscalls responsible for DNS requests and opening URLs and monitor the socket functions `connect`, `send`, and `sendto` as these syscalls allow us to closely monitor target IPs and messages sent over the network. To only inspect the header data of a transmission, we limit the size of monitored messages to a minimum of 64 bytes and a maximum of 25% of the message length and only investigate the very first message sent over each socket. To protect the data privacy, we operate on hashed values only, thus split the network messages at specific delimiters, perform cryptographic hash operations on each argument individually, and look up every hash value in a cache covering malicious message fragments (e.g., keywords used by malware). As malware often creates distinct mutex names when probing for an already infected client system and installs itself as a service using a specific name, we also monitor syscalls related to these events. To detect and prevent the execution of malware at the earliest possible time, we trace `ShellExecuteExW` and `CreateProcessInternalW`.

To also track malicious activities in offline phases, we implement multiple failover solutions. First, we rely on adjustable security policies such as terminating the application or prohibiting specific types of syscalls (e.g., network operations) once uncached syscalls are invoked. Further, the hooking library maintains a local storage in which invoked syscalls are logged, while we approve or decline the syscalls depending on the security policies. Once the connection to the Cloud is restored, the recorded syscall information is replayed. The end host further logs invoked syscalls once a syscall is temporarily approved until an updated analysis result is received. To prevent manipulations by malware, we make use of *secure log files* [13] in which each entry is part of a cryptographic hash chain to validate all previous entries. We acknowledge that this solution does not protect the device against getting infected with malware, yet, the Cloud will block an infected device once the syscalls resembling the malicious behavior are replayed.

3.5   Android Implementation

To also evaluate our approach on mobile devices, we developed a prototype for Android, a middleware running a modified Linux kernel. We split our prototype into two components, a kernel module and a Java application. The kernel module is the sensitive part of our implementation since even minor issues can destabilize the entire OS. We thus implemented the syscall hooking in the kernel and moved less essential components such as caching and the Cloud communication into the app. Similar to Windows, we implemented hook functions to intercept syscall invocations. Again, these syscalls were systematically chosen to have only limited impact while maintaining a good visibility into the behavior of the system. To monitor file operations, we trace seven file syscalls (e.g., `sys_creat` and `sys_rename`). We again monitor the network operations `sys_connect`, `sys_send`, and `sys_sendto` and shorten the inspected messages. Equally to the Windows prototype, we also track the execution of new processes, defined by `sys_execve`. In order to filter syscalls of presumably benign default Android processes, we implemented a whitelist containing paths of common processes, files, and IP addresses used for inter-process communication. After whitelisting carefully-chosen services and filenames such as *SensorService* and */dev/urandom*, we were able to reduce the noise of syscall invocations considerably.

When a process invokes a monitored syscall, the name and path of the process and carefully-selected syscall arguments are checked against the whitelist. If whitelisted, the syscall is approved and the process execution is resumed immediately, otherwise the syscall is forwarded to the app, which checks if the syscall arguments are stored in the local caching instances. If not cached, we forward the syscall to the Cloud. Depending on the results obtained from the caches or the Cloud, the execution of the native syscall function is performed or prohibited.

Particularly for mobile devices, we cannot rely on a stable network connectivity and have to provide fail-over solutions during offline phases (e.g., loss of signal). Similarly to the Windows prototype, the app maintains a local storage in which invoked syscalls are logged using secure log files, while we approve or decline the syscalls depending on the security policies. Again, this information is replayed once the connection to the Cloud service is restored.

3.6   Signature Generation

There already exists a large body of work on signature generation based on syscalls [1, 14, 15], thus we do not focus on that part and stick to a straightforward way to generate the signatures for the evaluation of our approach. Note that arbitrary signature generation algorithms can be used. To generate signatures based on invoked syscalls, we execute samples of various malware families in a virtualized analysis environment and record the invoked syscalls. We then search for sequences of syscalls that can be found in a certain amount of the samples using a *longest common substring* (*LCS*) algorithm. If a LCS of syscalls is found, it is known to be characteristic for the specific malware family. We then apply the *Levenshtein* distance function to measure the similarity of these

LCS sequences and their arguments. Matching on syscall arguments, however, can be problematic as specific types of values are defined by a certain amount of randomness, e.g., file-, or mutex names. To compensate randomness, we first compute the LCS using the syscall names only (e.g., `NtCreateFile`), ignoring any arguments. Afterwards, we combine the syscall names with the set of arguments that have been observed. To perform signature matching, we again apply the distance function to detect similarities between signatures and invoked syscalls. We verified our signatures against benign sample sets as discussed in the next section to avoid side effects caused by common system operations.

4   Evaluation

We now discuss the results of the performed experiments to verify the applicability and reliability of our approach. The evaluation of our Windows prototype is conducted on a desktop computer using an Intel i7-2600 CPU with 3 GB of memory and Windows XP (SP 3)—later versions of Windows, however, can also be deployed. We chose Windows XP to leverage the analysis reports of various automated malware analysis systems such as Anubis, which are mostly still running Windows XP. The mobile prototype is evaluated on a *Samsung Galaxy Nexus* device using Android 4.1.2 and kernel version 3.0.31, utilizing WiFi to connect to the Cloud service. The prototype further supports the official Android emulator using Android 4.2 and kernel 2.6.29 to perform automated analyses of Android malware samples. During our evaluation, the network latency between the desktop computer and the Cloud, directly connected via LAN, resulted in an average of 0.52 ms, respectively, 11.7 ms between mobile device and the Cloud.

4.1   Caching

We first evaluate the influence of caching on the performance of the individual end host implementations. While conducting this experiment, we disabled external modules and signature matching to only measure the impact of our caching implementation and the Cloud-to-client communication. On the desktop computer,

Table 1. Performance impact of caching

Test	Native sec.	Disabled sec.	%	Cloud sec.	%	Full sec.	%
Windows:							
1000 Files	2.74	3.57	130	3.04	111	2.78	101
2000 Mutexes	0.03	1.17	3,900	0.82	2,733	0.03	100
100 Processes	0.52	0.69	133	0.65	125	0.64	123
1000 Sockets	0.31	0.79	255	0.68	219	0.31	100
Android:							
200 Files	0.20	1.89	945	1.76	880	0.37	185
100 Processes	2.55	5.71	224	5.62	220	2.59	102
200 Sockets	1.06	2.33	220	1.98	187	1.20	113

we perform the following experiment consisting of four different tests: i) we create empty files using unique filenames, ii) create a substantial number of unique mutexes, iii) repeatedly execute a dummy application that terminates right after invocation, and iv) allocate multiple sockets and establish connections to an external host in the local network without transmitting data. We repeat each test ten times and calculate the average on the measured execution times. To determine the impact of caching, we run this experiment four times: i) without injecting our hooking library (native Windows system), ii) injected library but disabled caches, iii) enabled caching at the Cloud, iv) enabled caching at the Cloud and the client side. We perform almost the same experiment on the Galaxy Nexus, except that we skip Test 2 as Android does not support mutexes. Before starting a test, we flush the caches to make sure each test run has the same preconditions.

As outlined in Table 1, each individual test lasts considerably longer when caching is disabled. Enabling the Cloud caches reduces the number of requests sent to the database as we can rely on already fetched results. Activating the caches on the client has the largest influence on the execution time since the client does not interrupt the execution to wait for analysis results from the Cloud. In fact, full caching improves the performance to a level where the execution times almost approximate to the results when no syscalls are monitored.

4.2   Windows

Caching has a huge impact on the performance of our Cloud-based approach, thus we attempt to cache as many syscall arguments as possible by creating a ground truth of trusted arguments, which can be used as initial values for the caching instances. To obtain a ground truth set, we set up a fresh installation of Windows, installed commonly used software such as browsers, file archivers, and Office software and executed each application for a few minutes.

Table 2. Cached (C) and uncached (U) syscalls invoked by Windows software

Software	C	U	Total
Adobe Reader	27	3	30
Google Chrome	98	10	108
Internet Explorer	62	5	67
Mozilla Firefox	13	0	13
Ms Media Player	15	1	16
Ms Paint	9	1	10
Notepad	8	0	8
Regedit	8	0	8
Services.msc	197	0	197
Skype	43	2	45
Taskmanager	2	0	2
WinZip	26	1	27
Total	508	23	531

Software: To determine the number of syscalls that still have to be forwarded to the Cloud when full caching is enabled, we enumerate the cached and uncached syscalls of common software, as depicted in Table 2. The software was already installed when generating the ground truth, thus each program was executed at least once. We find 508 syscalls cached at the client and 23 syscalls not stored in the caches. Without caching, we would have to forward 531 syscalls to the Cloud, thus caching reduces the communication between Cloud and clients significantly. Executing unknown software certainly requires a higher number of requests to the Cloud on the first execution, however, on second execution, most of these syscalls presumably are also cached.

Signatures: To evaluate the feasibility of a Cloud-based signature matching, we leverage the set S_{Mal} covering 1,508 clustered malware samples [16]. This set includes 13 malware families. To obtain signatures, we apply the algorithm introduced in Section 3.6 on all samples of each family using a Levenshtein-ratio of 90%. The signature length (i.e., the number of consecutive syscalls required by a signature) varies between one and nine syscalls.

To verify the correctness and detection capabilities of the signatures, we analyzed 234,829 samples randomly taken from the malware analysis service Anubis since August 2012 and obtained 18,493,498 syscalls to perform signature matching upon. When comparing our signatures against these syscalls, we find 3,323 signature matches. To verify that all matches hit a malicious executable, we request analysis results of various malware detection services from VirusTotal. As stated in Table 3, we find 3,406 Anubis samples to belong to one of the malware families in S_{Mal}, while the remaining samples are associated to other families not covered by our signature generation set. 2,140 matches (62.8%) are detected as the exact malware variant as found in S_{Mal} and are therefore considered correctly identified by our signatures. For 1,027 samples (30.2%), the signatures do not hit the exact variant of the family as stated in S_{Mal}, yet the VirusTotal results imply that we detected a different variant from the same family. This shows that our approach has the capability to tolerate differences malware authors presumably integrate to evade detection by antivirus software. For 156 signature matches (4.6%), VirusTotal results include different family names than stated by our signatures. When manually checking the samples, we discovered multiple *Sality* samples to be erroneously flagged by the antivirus vendors. Overall, our signatures correctly identified 97.6% of the malware samples as malicious. The false negative rate (i.e., the samples that are not detected by our signatures) is at 2.4%, which is mostly caused by the family *Spygames*. The signature is a single **send** call that transmits a partially randomized string. To detect this family we would have to set the *Levenshtein* ratio to a value below 50%, however, that would lead to thousands of false positives for the other signatures. Other malware families in the set S_{Mal} (e.g., *Adultbrowser*) are not included in the Anubis sample set at all, thus we cannot evaluate our signatures for these families.

Samples submitted to a malware analysis system commonly are of malicious character. Yet, according to VirusTotal the Anubis data set also contains 14,729 unsuspicious samples of which none is falsely classified to be malicious by our signatures. To further verify that our signatures are not triggered by benign software, e.g., ordinary Windows software, we perform three additional experiments: i) we prepare a system with five web browsers (i.e., Mozilla Firefox, Internet Explorer, Google Chrome, Opera, and Apple Safari), disable Flash, Java, and JavaScript and visit the Alexa Top 5,000 websites [17] twice with each browser, ii) repeat the experiment in i), whereas Flash, Java, and JavaScript are enabled, and iii) set up a fresh Windows host and manually install and execute several types of updates, commonly used software, and games. In total, 1,058 different applications are executed. While performing these experiments, we compared the invoked syscalls against our malware signatures. Overall, 81,256,875 syscalls with 624,125,933 individual arguments are invoked. As aimed for, we do not experience a single hit of a signature,

Table 3. Signature matching results (EF = Exact Family, FV = Family Variant, FM = Family Mismatch, FN = False Negative)

Family	#Samples	(in %)			
		EF	FV	FM	FN
Allaple	1,951	99.3	0.6	0.0	0.1
Bancos	33	9.1	36.4	54.5	0.0
Casino	27	0.0	100.0	0.0	0.0
Flystudio	38	0.0	10.5	89.5	0.0
Magiccasino	1	100.0	0.0	0.0	0.0
Poison	54	50.0	20.4	14.8	14.8
Porndialer	3	0.0	0.0	0.0	100.0
Sality	1,239	13.9	77.6	7.7	0.8
Spygames	60	0.0	0.0	0.0	100.0
Total	3,406	62.8	30.2	4.6	2.4

thus assume these signatures to be reliable to protect against known malware without classifying benign software to be malicious.

The third experiment simultaneously serves as a survey to evaluate the user experience, i.e., whether noticeable delays or problems are encountered. We repeat this test three times and find none of the 1,058 applications causing any problems such as crashes or error messages. For the majority of applications, we do not encounter any noticeable delays, however, while installing specific software (e.g., Microsoft Visual Studio 2012), which copies thousands of files onto the hard disk drive, we observe minor delays during the installation phase of the first run. These delays emerge as most of the accessed filenames are neither included in the initial ground truth nor cached at the Cloud service. When performing the second and third run, the filenames are still not included in the initial ground truth of the client (which is wiped after each run), but stored in the Cloud caches, resulting in almost no noticeable delays during these runs.

4.3   Android

We again build a ground truth data set containing syscall arguments of pre-installed and therefore likely benign software. Similarly to Windows, we execute these apps and classify each invoked syscall argument as trusted.

Table 4. Cached (C) and uncached (U) syscalls invoked by pre-installed apps

Application	C	U	Total
Browser	25	2	27
Calculator	25	1	26
Calendar	19	1	20
Contacts	20	1	21
Deskclock	20	1	21
Gallery	26	2	28
MMS	25	0	25
Settings	21	1	22
Videoeditor	23	1	24
Total	204	10	214

Apps: We execute nine pre-installed apps to determine how many syscalls are not covered by the ground truth and have to be analyzed by the Cloud. As shown in Table 4, we experience a small amount of uncached syscalls as most of the data is already stored in the caches.

Android is heavily built around the feature to install third-party apps, thus we also investigate how many syscalls are uncached when executing external apps for the first, respectively, second time as their syscall arguments might not be covered by the ground truth. As depicted in Table 5, we select ten commonly used apps and record the number of syscall invocations. We execute each app once to remove potential welcome screens and specify credentials of test accounts for specific apps (e.g., *Facebook* and *Twitter*). We then reset the caches to the initial ground truth values to ensure that none of the values got cached when preparing these apps. When executing the apps for the first time, 516 syscalls are already covered by the ground truth, yet we still have to analyze 221 unknown syscalls at the Cloud. When executing the apps a second time, the caching strategy requires merely 25 syscall analyses at all, most of them caused by *Instagram*. We thus argue that caching improves the performance of our approach significantly, on desktop computers and mobile devices for known and unknown software.

Signatures: To evaluate the Cloud-based signature matching on Android, we select two distinct malware families, namely the spy app *Gone in 60 seconds* (*Gi60s*) and the banking trojan *Carberp*. We execute one sample of each family and manually extract a signature based on the invoked syscalls. The signature of *Gi60s* depends on two consecutive `sys_sendto` syscalls that forward user data to external servers. The signature of *Carberp* is based on five syscalls invoked at the initialization phase of the app. To validate the signature matching we execute four different samples of *Gi60s* and two samples of *Carberp* on the mobile device and find our signatures to correctly classify all samples as malicious.

5 Discussion

The main argument to move the detection of malicious activities from end hosts to a Cloud service is that we assume the end hosts to be significantly less secure compared to the Cloud since a centralized system is maintained by experienced personal. Especially the currentness of detection algorithms and signatures is presumably better on a Cloud-based service than on individual end hosts, mostly maintained by regular users. Since operators have to maintain a single service only, updates of the detection mechanisms can be conducted in an easy way to quickly react to incidents or to enforce security policies. Further, the centralized strategy permits the operators to closely monitor and quarantine recently infected clients. If operators would have to be responsible for updating the security software on every client individually, they probably would be overwhelmed by the number of clients, especially when also considering mobile devices that are becoming more popular.

Table 5. Cached (C) and uncached (U) syscalls invoked by commonly used apps

Application	1st run			2nd run		
	C	U	Total	C	U	Total
Adobe Reader	11	3	14	14	0	14
Angry Birds	36	19	55	50	0	50
Google Chrome	46	71	117	108	3	111
Facebook	191	12	203	101	0	101
Mozilla Firefox	53	38	91	83	0	83
Instagram	31	18	49	33	18	51
Shazam	35	14	49	47	2	49
Twitter	47	7	54	38	0	38
VLC Player	4	4	8	27	1	28
Winamp	62	35	97	93	1	94
Total	516	221	737	594	25	619

The Cloud service is connected to existing firewall and intrusion detection systems to immediately apply security measures such as blocking a client from accessing particular infrastructure in the case of an incident. Further, when a client connects to the network, it is limited to communicate with the Cloud service at first. If the client does not instantiate a connection to the Cloud or stops communicating with the Cloud (e.g., after approving a syscall temporarily), the device is flagged as potentially dangerous and its network connectivity is revoked. A client not communicating with the Cloud can have multiple reasons: either the host is not participating in the Cloud-based security strategy yet (e.g., a new mobile device) or the device got infected during an offline phase and malware deactivated the security mechanisms. Nevertheless, as long as unprotected and infected clients are blocked from the network, no other clients can be harmed.

Applying a Cloud-based security approach, however, might also raise severe drawbacks. Forwarding syscalls to the Cloud and delaying the execution of end hosts' processes causes an overhead due to the high number of invoked syscalls on every client. Without selecting a partial set of syscalls to monitor and applying efficient caching, this would be a serious issue for the clients' performance and users' experience. Our approach thus makes exhaustively use of mechanisms to limit the number of requests to the Cloud. The evaluation results indicate that the overhead is reasonable in practice as almost no noticeable delays are induced.

A further limitation of a Cloud-based approach is the requirement of a continuous network connectivity, which cannot be guaranteed for specific types of end hosts like mobile devices. Still, we consider our approach to be feasible in well-established networks in which most of the clients such as desktop computers are permanently connected. Mobile devices could fall back to UMTS/GSM in areas without WiFi connectivity, however, GSM networks are significantly slower than WiFi connections. When evaluating the impact of caching in Section 4.1, creating 200 files or executing 100 processes both required 8 seconds using GSM and full caching. Yet, the number of uncached syscalls highly depends on the app, as shown in Table 5. Many apps invoke only a limited number of uncached syscalls that can also be transferred in a reasonable time using GSM networks.

A general limitation of a network service is the central point of failure. This problem can be avoided by providing fail over solutions to ensure the availability of the centralized system. Further, we can split the Cloud service into one master node and multiple slaves to distribute the load and to make the service resilient to faults of single servers. An additional benefit is that clients connect to the nearest node to reduce the network latency and the delay on the clients' side.

A centralized protection service is a promising target for adversaries, e.g., by infiltrating or taking down the service. The Cloud service thus has to be protected by reasonable security measures and monitored closely to identify and prevent attacks. It also has to be taken care of end hosts attempting to trick the Cloud, e.g., by malware taking over the clients' security application and emulating the communication to the Cloud. A solution includes the usage of a kernel-based client application. Encrypted and signed communication channels between Cloud and clients are mandatory to protect the integrity and confidentiality of the inter-communication. Secure channels also eliminate the risks of eavesdropping, replay, man-in-the-middle, and other serious attacks. We further have to address the issue of processing plain syscall arguments at a network service as proprietary data is relayed to a centralized system not under the control of the individual user. Yet, this drawback can be bypassed, e.g., by operating on hashed arguments only. Information sent to the Cloud thus cannot be converted back to plain text, hence we gain a privacy preserving approach, assuring the users' confidentiality. The functionality of detection mechanisms is not affected by hashed arguments, yet techniques such as blacklist comparison need to be altered to operate on hash values. When switching to hash functions, we have to ensure the hashes to be resilient against attacks, e.g., by applying *Hash-based Message Authentication Codes* [18] using individually shared keys between the Cloud and the end hosts.

6 Related Work

Analyzing system calls to detect malicious behavior has a long history on desktop computers. Some approaches [1, 19] develop benign behavior profiles based on multiple consecutively invoked system calls to identify anomalous behavior. Mutz *et al.* [20] analyze the relationship between system call arguments and the invocation context to detect malicious actions. Stinson and Mitchell [2] perform botnet detection based on system calls in combination with tainting untrusted memory values. Srivastava and Giffin [21] propose an approach that combines the analysis of network traffic with a hypervisor-based identification of malicious behavior at the user-, and kernel-level. Burguerae *et al.* [22] show that system call analysis is also feasible on mobile devices.

The idea of detecting malicious software at a centralized service is already explored in many approaches [3–5]. Oberheide *et al.* [3] present CloudAV, which utilizes a light-weight application running on end hosts to suspend the execution of an unknown binary, forward the binary to the Cloud, and perform or decline its execution based on the analysis result of the Cloud. Furthermore, Oberheide *et al.* [5] discuss an approach to move CloudAV from desktop computers to mobile devices. A more sophisticated approach is presented by Martignoni *et al.* [23] in which users may delegate the execution of potentially malicious applications to a Cloud service. As a result, the unknown process is executed in the Cloud, however, by interchanging specific system calls, the application acts like it is executed locally on the client.

7 Conclusion

We introduced a Cloud-based security approach to move the detection of malicious activities from individual end hosts to a centralized network service. To determine if activities on client systems are malicious, every end host forwards selected API and system calls to a Cloud service and awaits approval or denial to execute these operations locally. To evaluate the applicability of our approach, we implemented prototypes for desktop computers and mobile devices and found this protection strategy to be feasible in practice as almost no delays are caused on the client which would interfere with the usability of the end hosts.

Acknowledgment. This work was supported by the German Federal Ministry of Education and Research (Grants 16BY1110/MoBE and 16BY1020/MobWorm).

References

1. Forrest, S., Hofmeyr, S., Somayaji, A.: The Evolution of System-Call Monitoring. In: Proceedings of the 2008 Annual Computer Security Applications Conference, ACSAC 2008, pp. 418–430. IEEE Computer Society, Washington, DC (2008)
2. Stinson, E., Mitchell, J.C.: Characterizing Bots' Remote Control Behavior. In: Hämmerli, B.M., Sommer, R. (eds.) DIMVA 2007. LNCS, vol. 4579, pp. 89–108. Springer, Heidelberg (2007)
3. Oberheide, J., Cooke, E., Jahanian, F.: CloudAV: N-Version Antivirus in the Network Cloud. In: Proceedings of the 17th Conference on Security Symposium, SS 2008, pp. 91–106. USENIX Association, Berkeley (2008)

4. Harrison, K., Bordbar, B., Ali, S.T.T., Dalton, C.I., Norman, A.: A Framework for Detecting Malware in Cloud by Identifying Symptoms. In: Proceedings of the 2012 IEEE 16th International Enterprise Distributed Object Computing Conference, EDOC 2012, pp. 164–172. IEEE Computer Society, Washington, DC (2012)
5. Oberheide, J., Veeraraghavan, K., Cooke, E., Flinn, J., Jahanian, F.: Virtualized In-Cloud Security Services for Mobile Devices. In: Proceedings of the First Workshop on Virtualization in Mobile Computing, MobiVirt 2008, pp. 31–35. ACM, New York (2008)
6. Gu, G., Perdisci, R., Zhang, J., Lee, W.: BotMiner: Clustering Analysis of Network Traffic for Protocol- and Structure-Independent Botnet Detection. In: Proceedings of the 17th Conference on Security Symposium, SS 2008, pp. 139–154. USENIX Association, Berkeley (2008)
7. Bayer, U., Krügel, C., Kirda, E.: TTAnalyze: A Tool for Analyzing Malware. In: Proceedings of the 15th European Institute for Computer Antivirus Research (EICAR 2006) Annual Conference (April 2006)
8. Knuth, D.E.: The Art of Computer Programming, 2nd edn. Sorting and Searching, vol. 3. Addison Wesley Longman Publishing Co., Inc., Redwood City (1998)
9. Virustotal: VirusTotal Private API v2.0 (2014)
10. Google: Safe Browsing API v2.0 (2014)
11. Rauen, M.: madcodehook Framework (2014), http://madshi.net/
12. Guarnieri, C.: Cuckoo Sandbox (2014), http://www.cuckoosandbox.org/
13. Schneier, B., Kelsey, J.: Secure Audit Logs to Support Computer Forensics. ACM Trans. Inf. Syst. Secur. 2(2), 159–176 (1999)
14. Wang, L., Li, Z., Chen, Y., Fu, Z., Li, X.: Thwarting Zero-Day Polymorphic Worms With Network-Level Length-Based Signature Generation. IEEE/ACM Trans. Netw. 18(1), 53–66 (2010)
15. Wurzinger, P., Bilge, L., Holz, T., Goebel, J., Kruegel, C., Kirda, E.: Automatically Generating Models for Botnet Detection. In: Backes, M., Ning, P. (eds.) ESORICS 2009. LNCS, vol. 5789, pp. 232–249. Springer, Heidelberg (2009)
16. Rieck, K., Trinius, P., Willems, C., Holz, T.: Automatic Analysis of Malware Behavior using Machine Learning. J. Comput. Secur. 19(4), 639–668 (2011)
17. Alexa Internet, Inc.: Top 1,000,000 Websites (2014)
18. Bellare, M., Canetti, R., Krawczyk, H.: Keying Hash Functions for Message Authentication. In: Koblitz, N. (ed.) CRYPTO 1996. LNCS, vol. 1109, pp. 1–15. Springer, Heidelberg (1996)
19. Hofmeyr, S.A., Forrest, S., Somayaji, A.: Intrusion Detection using Sequences of System Calls. J. Comput. Secur. 6(3), 151–180 (1998)
20. Mutz, D., Robertson, W., Vigna, G., Kemmerer, R.A.: Exploiting Execution Context for the Detection of Anomalous System Calls. In: Kruegel, C., Lippmann, R., Clark, A. (eds.) RAID 2007. LNCS, vol. 4637, pp. 1–20. Springer, Heidelberg (2007)
21. Srivastava, A., Giffin, J.: Automatic Discovery of Parasitic Malware. In: Jha, S., Sommer, R., Kreibich, C. (eds.) RAID 2010. LNCS, vol. 6307, pp. 97–117. Springer, Heidelberg (2010)
22. Burguera, I., Zurutuza, U., Nadjm-Tehrani, S.: Crowdroid: Behavior-Based Malware Detection System for Android. In: Proceedings of the 1st ACM Workshop on Security and Privacy in Smartphones and Mobile Devices, SPSM 2011, pp. 15–26. ACM, New York (2011)
23. Martignoni, L., Paleari, R., Bruschi, D.: A Framework for Behavior-Based Malware Analysis in the Cloud. In: Prakash, A., Sen Gupta, I. (eds.) ICISS 2009. LNCS, vol. 5905, pp. 178–192. Springer, Heidelberg (2009)

Postman: An Elastic Highly Resilient Publish/Subscribe Framework for Self Sustained Service Independent P2P Networks*

Gil Einziger and Roy Friedman

Computer Science Department
Technion
Haifa 32000, Israel
{gilga,roy}@cs.technion.ac.il

Abstract. *Self sustained service independent P2P networks* aim to serve as a cheap alternative to traditional cloud providers. In such networks, users who add resources to the network are given strong (typically monetary) incentives to keep their devices connected for long periods of time. Further, in such networks, there is a decoupling between the machines that form the P2P network and the devices used to consume services from the network. In particular, users may access services offered by the network through their mobile devices. In fact, a user may obtain services even if he did not donate any resources, but is willing to pay for the services he consumes either through a service fee or by viewing ads, similarly to cloud services.

This work introduces Postman, a publish/subscribe architecture tailored for self sustained service independent P2P networks. Postman is designed to provide its users with a self-organizing, scalable, efficient and churn resilient publish/subscribe service. Postman achieves this using a novel client/mailbox architecture where a publish/subscribe system delivers content to a highly diverse set of mailboxes. Mailboxes are hosted on elastically selected set of peers and each mailbox accumulates multiple topics from many clients. Clients then fulfill their subscriptions by polling the relevant mailboxes, while the mailboxes act as subscribers of the actual publish/subscribe mechanism. Our experimental results show that the client/mailbox architecture significantly reduces the number of subscriptions the publish/subscribe mechanism handles. In addition, the publish/subscribe mechanism handles a much more uniform subscription pattern than the real subscription pattern, obtains very high delivery rates and is highly robust to failures and churn.

1 Introduction

Publish/subscribe is a popular programming paradigm for distributed computing as it offers decoupling of information producers from consumers [3,8,13]. Commercial applications in various domains such as social applications (e.g., micro blogging and status), finance (e.g., stock quotes), command and control (both military and civilian) utilize this paradigm. In particular, in publish/subscribe, information producers, called

---

* This work is partially supported by ISF grant 1247/09 and the Technion HPI center.

P. Felber and V. Garg (Eds.): SSS 2014, LNCS 8756, pp. 78–92, 2014.
© Springer International Publishing Switzerland 2014

publishers, publish events to the system, without knowing who exactly will receive it. Yet, the information is often characterized with one or more tags (sometimes also called *topics*). Information consumers, called *subscribers*, register subscriptions that describe the types of information they are interested in. It is then the job of the system, or middleware, to match published events to corresponding subscribers, and deliver each event to all of its subscribers. Publish/subscribe systems differ in the expressiveness power that they offer to their clients, as well as in their architecture, scalability and efficiency. Specifically, some systems only enable subscribers to register to a single topic and are referred to as *topic based publish/subscribe*. At the other extreme, subscriptions can refer to multiple topics and even be expressed as range queries on these topics, resulting in what is known as *content based publish/subscribe*. As an example, one may wish to register to all events that refer to weather forecasts for Hawaii that are issued on Mondays or Tuesdays with wind force above 10 Knots.

Publish/subscribe systems can be implemented centrally or in a distributed manner. Centralized systems have the advantage of retaining a global image of the system at all times, enabling intelligent optimizations during the matching process. However, providing scalable publish/subscribe in a centralized manner is costly.

Distributed, and in particular P2P-based, publish/subscribe systems have been introduced in the past to facilitate scalability at a greatly reduced cost compared to the centralized ones. However, in the vast majority of these systems, it is assumed that a user always consumes his content at the same peer. In particular, most P2P systems do not distinguish between the user and his/her hardware. Also, some of these systems assume that the entire P2P network is dedicated for the publish/subscribe application, and therefore manipulate the network's overlay to fit the publish/subscribe goals.

In contrast, we target a new generation of P2P systems in which individuals are given strong incentives to keep their donated machines and resources available to the P2P network for long periods of time. For example, owners of donated machines can be paid for the services they provide with money generated by the system, collected from the end users of the system either through subscription and usage fees or through advertisements.

This way, such P2P networks can serve as cheap alternatives to traditional cloud providers since it saves much of the expenses of buying and maintaining the cloud infrastructure. Further, this model decouples between the devices used to access the service and the machines used to run the service, which makes it adequate for the realm of mobile clients.

Virtual coins such as Bitcoin are a degenerated example that validate the promise of this model. People donate machines to the Bitcoin network in order to help mine Bitcoins and process Bitcoin transactions in exchange for being rewarded with Bitcoins. Another example is SpaceMonkey.com, which rents special storage devices that its customers place at their homes and connect to the Internet. Each such customer gets a cloud-like sharing and backup service with a very large capacity cheaper than the cost of similar true cloud based services. The data itself is replicated among the devices rented by other users.[1]

---

[1] Let us also mention AoTerra GmbH and the European ParaDIME project, in which a cloud is built from racks placed at people's houses in exchange for these racks serving as heating devices for these homes as a side effect of acting as cloud servers.

In these two example, the clients benefit from the service regardless of the devices they use to access the network, and there is a strong incentive to keep the machine available to the network as much as possible. Yet, in the full fledged version of the self sustained service independent P2P networks, the same P2P network can host multiple services rather than being dedicated to one of them. In this work, we investigate how to implement publish/subscribe systems over self sustained service independent P2P networks.

Specifically, we introduce *Postman*, a self-organizing elastic publish/subscribe service based on a flexible distributed architecture. Unlike most P2P systems however, and in accordance with the self-sustained P2P networks model, postman decouples the machines that operate the service from the users of the service. To that end, Postman envelops a traditional publish/subscribe mechanism with a layer of indirectness. The subscribers of the publish/subscribe mechanism are called *mailboxes* and each of them serves as a proxy (or rendezvous point) for many clients. Thus, instead of disseminating every event to a potentially large number of devices, in Postman an event is only propagated to a small set of relevant mailboxes. Interested clients fetch the events that match their interests by periodically polling only the corresponding mailboxes.

Below, we describe Postman, including its internals and its implementation and explore its performance characteristics. The performance study was carried by emulation, in which the actual implementation was run with both artificial and Twitter based traces, as well as large scale simulations using the same traces. The results show that Postman obtains very high delivery ratios. Moreover, the mailbox architecture reduces the scale of the publish/subscribe problem (w.r.t. traditional P2P approaches), making the delivery process highly efficient. Finally, since each mailbox aggregates multiple subscriptions, the subscription pattern exposed to the publish/subscribe infrastructure is much more uniform and stable than the subscription pattern exposed by any individual subscriber. This simplifies the dissemination mechanism and reduces the rate of changes that this mechanism needs to deal with.

An important aspect of Postman that becomes evident in our performance evaluation is its significant robustness to failures and churn. In particular, low rates of failures and churn make no noticeable impact on the delivery rates and latencies of Postman. Further, Postman is able to self recover from massive failure and churn events within several minutes of operation, as explained below. The rest of this paper is organized as follows: In Section 2, we present our basic assumptions and goals. We introduce Postman in Section 3. The experimental performance results are shown in Section 4. We discuss related work in Section 5 and conclude with a discussion in Section 6.

2   Assumptions and Goals

We assume a distributed network composed of *donated machines* that act as *peers* in the system. The P2P system serves as a substance for the implementation of multiple distributed services and applications. *Users* access the network from (potentially mobile) *client* devices, which are (potentially different) from the set of donated machines. Hence, peers are typically relatively strong computers connected to the Internet through a fixed broadband connection, whereas clients are often battery operated resource limited devices with intermitted connectivity and lower effective bandwidth.

Donated machines may fail by crashing or disconnecting from the network. Such disconnections may be temporary or permanent. In addition, new donated machines may be added to the network. The rate at which donated machines (new or old) connect and disconnect (or fail) is called the *churn rate* of the system. It is an a-priori unknown parameter that can change from one deployment to another as well as during the lifetime of the network.

The goal of this work is to implement an efficient, scalable, churn and failure resilient publish/subscribe service for this network. The service should be elastic is the number of donated machines it employs, reflecting the temporal load on the publish/subscribe service as well as the network conditions. Further, we rely on the existence of an underlying logical overlay [3,13,16]. Yet, as the service is only one of potentially many services running over the P2P network, its implementation should not alter the existing P2P infrastructure, as the latter could hurt the performance of other services utilizing it.

Given that the churn rate is unknown and can change over time, our solution should self-adapt to it. In particular, during *stable* periods, in which the churn rate is very low, we expect the publish/subscribe service to be communication efficient. In other times, we are willing to accept higher communication overheads in return for failure resiliency. This adaptivity should take place autonomously.

Finally, we assume the existence of an incentive based mechanism that motivates users to donate resources to the system, whose implementation is out of scope for this paper. An example to such a mechanism can be found in [9] that explain how to implement a P2P advertisement mechanism. Given the above mentioned incentive mechanism, our load sharing goal is simply to refrain from overloading nodes beyond what they are willing to tolerate rather than obtaining load balancing.

3   Postman

As mentioned above, in Postman we divide the notion of a subscriber into a *client* and a *mailbox*. Mailboxes are donated machines that are used as subscription proxies for clients, as depicted in Figure 1. Hence, Postman defines a unique way in which clients discover mailboxes and interact with them in order to register their subscriptions and obtain their corresponding events. As elaborated below, this mechanism is also the one that provides Postman with its elasticity property. In addition, Postman has a protocol for disseminating events among the relevant mailboxes in a way that is efficient when the system is static, yet is robust to failures and churn when they occur. To that end, the rest of this section is divided in two parts: Section 3.1 explains the interaction between clients and mailboxes while Section 3.2 presents the event dissemination protocol between mailboxes.

3.1   Client/Mailbox Interaction

Here, we focus on the clinet/mailbox interaction. This includes how to locate an existing mailbox and subscribing to it, prompting the creation of a new mailbox (when needed), as well as how subscribed clients obtain their corresponding events from the mailboxes.

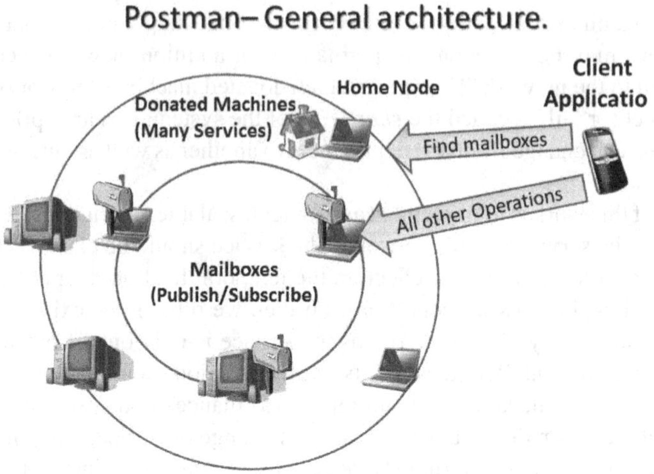

Postman– General architecture.

Fig. 1. General Postman architecture - clients use the home node to discover mailboxes, and then contact these mailboxes directly

Client Application and Home Node. As indicated above, a publish/subscribe client application is a light weight application, used to grant access to the network. The application is responsible for identifying the user and remembering the list of mailboxes the user is subscribed to. Machines running client applications are often not part of the network and cannot perform network related activities on their own. Instead, these applications contact one of the donated machines, e.g., through a REST API. We call the machine a client is connected to the *home node* for that client. This node can either come from some centralized bootstrap service publishing random node IP addresses, or be a machine that is owned by the client.

The client application discovers mailboxes through the home node. This is done using the *probabilistic lookup service (PLS)* described below. After mailboxes are discovered, the application accesses them directly. The applications maintain a data structure containing their subscriptions, the mailboxes that provide them and other topics these mailboxes provide. As we discuss in more details below, the client application polls these mailboxes in order to obtain events matching its subscriptions.

Probabilistic Lookup Service (PLS). In order to discover mailboxes, Postman uses a hints/random lookup technique. That is, each mailbox distributes a hint message of the form <Predicate, Owner> to all its overlay neighbors at a specific radius. The Predicate is a Bloom filter containing all the topics the Owner is subscribed to, while Owner contains the contact details of the mailbox that distributed the hint.

In order to discover mailboxes, we use a random walk message of the following form: <Origin, TTL, Topics, Visited, Hits, Message>. These random walk lookups are routed in the system until the TTL runs out, at which point they return back to the sender using the Origin field. Each node that participates in routing the lookup adds its ID to the Visited list. This way, lookup messages avoid revisiting nodes multiple times. Each node that receives a lookup message checks whether all the `Topics` included in the message are satisfied by the `Predicate` field of any of its stored hints. When a match is found, the lookup message is routed directly to the hint's `Owner`.

Since Bloom filters may have false positives, mailboxes have to check if they indeed provide the topics of the message (according to the `Topics` field). Mailboxes will add their contact details to the Hits field either if the mailbox is already subscribed to the lookup topics, or if the `Hits` field is empty and the mailbox is still available for handling additional topics (as described later). In case the mailbox is subscribed to the topic, it also records all other mailboxes included in the `Hits` field of the lookup as additional mailboxes subscribed to these topics for future dissemination.

Ultimately, at the end of the TTL, the lookup message is routed back to its original sender (according to its `Origin` field). We say that a random lookup was *successful* if it returned to the original sender with a non-empty list of mailboxes in the `Hits` field.

Finally, to overcome failures and churn, when a node discovers that a hint `Owner` is no longer online, it can simply remove the corresponding hint.

Client Application Subscribing Mechanism. For a client application, being subscribed to a topic means knowing at least a single mailbox that provides the topic. Thus, when the user orders the client application to subscribe to a new topic, the client application first checks if it is aware of a matching mailbox. If so, all the client application needs to do in order to subscribe is to ask this mailbox about the requested topic. Else, if the client application is not aware of a matching mailbox, it issues a small number of random lookups as described above and waits. These lookups are sent through the home node, and the result will be returned directly to the client. If any of the lookups succeeds, the client adds the mailboxes listed in the lookup `Hits` field to its data structure. The client is now subscribed to the topic and can contact these mailboxes to fetch publications. In addition, clients also ask mailboxes about all the topics they provide, for future use.

Polling and Temporary Subscribing. Mobile users are typically not connected continuously to the network and many may even connect for brief periods at a time. Hence, we combine two complementing mechanisms in order to ensure delivery of all relevant events to the client application. Specifically, mailboxes hold all publications they receive for a certain period, typically 24 hours (this corresponds to typical social network behavior, in which publications typically have a relatively short period of relevance). When a client logs into the network, it polls the mailboxes it is aware of for all matching publications it has not received since it was last updated.

In order to continue getting publications, the client can poll the mailboxes periodically. However, that would entail both a noticeable delay and excessive traffic when the rate of relevant events is low. Thus, instead, the client temporarily subscribes to the mailbox by sending a `<Predicate, Owner>` like hint to the mailbox. The mailbox maintains a list of all the clients that subscribed with a TTL of several minutes. When a publication arrives, the mailbox will distribute it to all subscribers based on their `Predicate` and `Owner` fields. Due to the temporary nature of this subscription, the client does not have to notify the mailbox if it leaves the network. Hence, clients that remain connected must renew their subscriptions before they expire. In order to avoid clock synchronization issues, each such subscription renewal also doubles as a polling request.

3.2 The Publish/Subscribe Mechanism

So far, we discussed the delivery mechanism between clients and mailboxes. Next, we describe how publications are disseminated between mailboxes. To that end, we use 3 complementing mechanisms that enable mailboxes to both learn about each other and disseminate publications among themselves. First, each mailbox that obtains a new publication disseminates it through a spanning tree of the mailboxes it is aware of that are also interested in the publication. Second, mailboxes send periodic PLS messages, disseminated as random walks, in order to both disseminate publications to interested mailboxes they are unaware of and learn on the fly about such mailboxes. Finally, in order to reduce the number of required PLS messages, and following the observation that clients in any case interact with multiple mailboxes, we transform clients interactions into an out-of-band gossip mechanism that helps disseminate publications to mailboxes and enable mailboxes to learn about each other. The rest of this section is devoted to explaining these mechanisms and their orchestration.

Specifically, when a user wishes to publish a new event, we assume the user is already subscribed to this event's topics. This means the user already knows a mailbox m for the topic. The user will send a publication message of the form <Topic, Content> to mailbox m. As a result, mailbox m will publish the message in two different ways. First, it uses the spanning tree distribution algorithm described in Section 3.2 to deterministically distribute the publication to all other mailboxes it is aware of in an efficient manner. Second, it sends a small number of PLS random walk messages in which the publication is stored in the Message field. However, in order to avoid reaching mailboxes that already appear in the spanning tree, the Visited and Hits fields of the PLS message is initiated with the list of the mailboxes known to this node.

Clearly, when a node receives a publication over the spanning tree, it continues its dissemination as well as forwards the publication to subscribed clients (if any) and storing it for possible future polling by clients. Yet, in the case of the first delivery of a PLS message for a given publication, the receiving node adds itself to the Hits list and forwards two copies of the PLS message to random unvisited nodes. Additionally, it extracts previously unknown mailboxes for this topic from the Hits list of the received PLS message.

Notice that when a mailbox subscribes to a topic, the PLS messages that it generates and the ones passed by it automatically notify this fact to other mailboxes. Hence, there is no need for a special mailbox subscribing mechanism.

Spanning Tree Distribution Algorithm. As all mailboxes that need to participate in the spanning tree are known to the mailbox that initiates the dissemination, any known deterministic construction of a spanning tree can be used. E.g., to generate a tree of degree k, the IDs of these mailboxes can be sorted into an array that is split into k equal

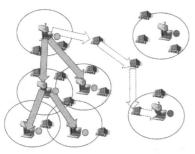 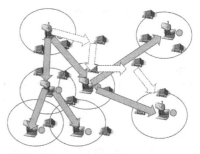

(a) Each publication is published to known mailboxes (green) on a spanning tree. In addition, a PLS message is routed attempting to discover unknown mailboxes (red). It is enough for a single PLS message from the green group to discover a single mailbox in the red group.

(b) In this case, both groups merge and subsequent publications reach the new group through the spanning tree.

Fig. 2. An example of the publish/subscribe mechanism

Algorithm 1. Handle Publish Algorithm

1: **function** HANDLEPUBLISH($LookupMessage\ lookup$)
2:     **if** $isNew(lookup.Messageh)$ **then**
3:         SpanningTreeDistribution(lookup.Message)
4:         ProbobalisticDistribution(lookup.Message)
5:         AddNewPublication(lookup.Message)
6:     **end if**
7:     **return**
8: **end function**

---

ranges. The message is then disseminated to the first node in each range. If the length of each range is more than k, this process repeats recursively until all nodes get their message.

Client/Mailbox Gossip Mechanism. As mentioned above, we utilize client polling messages as an out-of-band gossip mechanism to disseminate both publications and information about mailboxes. Recall that clients poll a different set of mailboxes every time they log-in. Each time the client contacts a mailbox, it shares with the mailbox some of the publications it has previously received. Mailboxes that missed publications can recover them this way. The client also notifies each such mailbox about other mailboxes it is aware of that handle the requested topic(s).

Typically, clients do not connect all the mailboxes every poll round. However, when the client encounters an unresponsive mailbox or a missed publication. The client perform an additional poll round, this time contacting all known mailboxes. This behaviour helps the client ensure that all relevant publications are delivered, it also improves the consistency of mailboxes.

Failure and Churn Recovery. In Postman, when all mailboxes are lost, a client simply resubscribes. In order to speed the mailbox heal rate, we allow clients to perform a second polling round in case resubscribing took place due to churn. The second polling round ensures that new mailboxes discovered or created by the resubscribing are also polled. This second polling significantly reduces the time it takes Postman to recover from failures and churn, since otherwise the client has to wait for the next polling round in order to satisfy all its subscriptions (typically, several minutes).

4   Experimental Results

In our experimental evaluation, we measure the delivery rate and message cost of our protocol. We also evaluate the merits of the Postman mailboxes approach, by comparing the mailboxes topic distributions and the amount of topics clients need to poll in order to satisfy their subscriptions, as well as study the ability of Postman to handle failures and churn, and in particular to recover from massive churn events.

Our measurements where performed over our Java based implementation of Postman [1] in two complementing settings: (1) a full implementation in which Postman was run above the [6] implementation of the Kademlia DHT [14] over a real LAN network, and (2) a simulated network setup in which Postman was run above a network simulation layer. Let us stress that both settings have exercised the actual Postman code! The simulated network setup enabled us to reach network sizes of tens of thousands of nodes. In contrast, due to resource constrains, using the full implementation we were only able to experiment with up to 1,500 nodes, but it served to validate the results of the simulated network settings.

We have used two sets of workloads: a synthetic workload in order to study the performance characteristics of our system as well as a real life Twitter trace containing the behavior of over 30k users produced by [20]. In the synthetic workload, we have generated subscriptions and events whose topics were chosen from the uniform distribution and the heavy-tailed Zipf-like distribution (with $\alpha = 0.9$). In the case of Twitter, the events and subscriptions were extracted from the trace as described below. As been reported in [12,17], Twitter subscription patterns contain two different kinds of user types, celebrities with thousands of followers and social users with a small number of followers. Last, we also implemented Quasar [19], and tested it as an example of a probabilistic publish/subscribe algorithm[2] (see Appendix).

4.1   Delivery Rate and Communication Load

In the following experiment, we give mailboxes 10 minutes to stabilize, and then publish a burst of publications. In the burst, each client publishes one event for each topic it

---

[2] We note that Quasar was developed with a social network graph in mind rather than a structured overlay

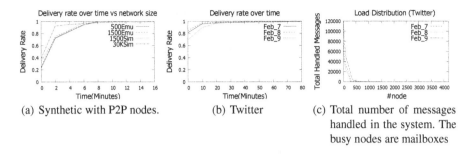

(a) Synthetic with P2P nodes.

(b) Twitter

(c) Total number of messages handled in the system. The busy nodes are mailboxes

Fig. 3. Delivery ratio as a function of preparation time

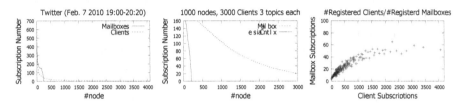

Fig. 4. Comparing the registration pattern of Postman to the client registration pattern in the system

is subscribed to. This is performed with 500 and 1,500 P2P nodes in the full implementation of the system as well as with 1,500 and 30,000 nodes in the case of the network simulator environment. In both settings, each node has 3 clients and each client is subscribed to 3 topics. Further, the mailbox polling frequency, which controls the delivery latency, is set to once every 10 minutes.

In addition, we have run Postman over a selected time period of the Twitter trace and measured delivery rate over time. Delivering events in this workload is tricky since we measure delivery rate until the sampling ends. Events that where not delivered during the sample are considered not delivered.

As can be seen from Figure 3, Postman achieves almost 100 percent delivery rate after 10-20 minutes. Also, the results of the full implementation and the network simulator environments are the same when ran with the same number of nodes.

The high delivery rate is coupled with a reasonable communication load. As can be seen in Figure 3(c), even the most congested mailboxes only handle several messages per second. Further, mailboxes can offload traffic from themselves by simply not answering some of the poll requests. In that case, the poll requests will either be delegated to another mailbox, or a new mailbox will be created.

4.2 Postman Subscription Pattern

We have studied both the client subscription patterns and the mailboxes subscription patterns. This was done by having all clients register to all their topics and examining the obtained pattern. As for the Twitter subscriptions, we have sampled the Twitter trace

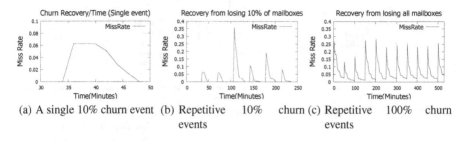

Fig. 5. Effect of suddenly mailbox churn on delivery rate

for one hour intervals and eliminated all users that where not active during this hour. The obtained registration pattern is the active set of topics during that hour.

As shown in Figure 4, in Postman, all subscriptions concentrate into a relatively small number of mailboxes. Consequently, the dissemination task of publications becomes much more manageable than if each event would have to be routed directly to its end clients. Further, as there is only a small number of mailboxes, there is also a high overlap between the dissemination trees, enabling sharing of resources and overheads between trees. Additionally, in the self sustained P2P network model, mailbox machines, being donated machines whose users are given strong incentives to keep them connected for long durations, are likely to have a much lower churn rate than client machines, enabling a more stable and efficient dissemination infrastructure.

Figure 4(c) exhibits another important angle of the subscription pattern. Here, the X-axis is the popularity of a given topic in terms of the number of clients interested in that topic. The Y-axis is the average number of mailboxes registered to the corresponding topic. As can be seen, there are much fewer mailboxes registered to each topic than clients, and this trend intensifies as the popularity of the topic increases reaching up to a two orders of magnitude reduction. In other words, the dissemination trees among mailboxes are fairly small, which was one of the main goals of our work.

4.3   Effects of Churn

In order to test our system's ability to sustain churn, we first added a small churn rate of around 1 percent of the mailboxes every 10 minutes to our Twitter runs. However, we have not seen any noticeable effect on the delivery rate. Hence, we then decided to experiment with much more dramatic churn rates.

In this test, we first let the system stabilize for 30 minutes and then every 35 minutes picked 10 percent of our mailboxes at random and crushed them as well as replaced 10 percent of our clients. We then have each client publish a single message on each of its topics. We measure the message delivery rate every two minutes.

As can be observed in Figure 5, removing 10 percent of the mailboxes only resulted in a slight increase in the miss rate, which returned to near zero within 20 minutes. The reason for this is that some of the clients maintain more than one mailbox per topic. In such a case, if a mailbox that disappeared is selected, after the timeout a new mailbox will be contacted, resulting in a slight delay of delivery but no loss. As for clients that know only a single mailbox, it will take these clients a few minutes to notice the unavailability of the mailbox, since clients only actively contact mailboxes every polling round (10 minutes in our configuration). After such a client discovers the churn, it will re-subscribe to the system. Further, if following such re-subscribing a new mailbox is created, then this mailbox needs some time to announce itself before it can recover all lost publications.

In order to further explore the capability of the architecture to repair itself, we decided to repeat the same experiment only this time we crushed 100 percent of our mailboxes every 50 minutes. The results of this experiment can be seen in Figure 5(c), indicating that Postman can even self recover from such a disastrous event. The churn resilience of our architecture comes from the inaccuracy of the PLS queries. Sometimes, when a client subscribes, it creates a new mailbox or causes a non full mailbox to subscribe to that topic even though a matching mailbox already exists in the system. In that case, we have more than one mailbox supplying each topic. These mailboxes will eventually find each other and each of them will tell its clients about the other one. Therefore, after the system stabilizes, all the clients are aware of the two mailboxes for that topic. In addition, we notice an increase in the number of mailboxes after a churn event, increasing the redundancy of the system.

Let us also note that during massive churn events, clients' resubscribing and the creation of new mailboxes generate a large number of PLS messages. The latter expedite the creation of an updated spanning tree including all new mailboxes.

5 Related Work

Numerous publish/subscribe systems have been implemented and published [3,8,13], therefore it is not practical to mention all of them. Instead, we discuss some of the systems that are closer to our work either in concepts or in their goals.

Quasar [19] is a probabilistic publish/subscribe protocol that uses attenuated Bloom filters [11], random walks and negative information in order to create a signature-less publish/subscribe mechanism. Quasar was tested on MySpace data and used the social graph as an overlay graph and yielded around 95 percent delivery rate. In contrast, our system utilizes the existing P2P overlay since in our model the overlay might be shared my multiple applications. Since both our scheme and Quasar use Bloom filters and random walks, in the experimental performance section we compare Postman to Quasar. Yet, our approach utilizes these concepts only for discovery and gossip, whereas Quasar employs them for data dissemination.

In [4], the cost of publish/subscribe on a structured overlay is reduced by reorganizing the overlay network in order to encourage nodes with similar topics subscriptions to form direct connection to each other. Such an approach is not applicable in our model (as described in Section 2), as we assume that the P2P overlay is shared by multiple services and therefore cannot be modified for the needs of a specific service.

SpiderCast constructs a distribution overlay with topic connectivity and low average node degree [5]. Such an overlay enjoys the benefit that the number of uninterested participants in the distribution process remains small and the size of the overlay is also kept small. SpiderCast is also capable of handling churn. The main difference between Postman and SpiderCast is the actual problem solved by each of them. SpiderCast can only deliver information to online users. Users cannot retrieve publications that were distributed when they where offline. Moreover, in SpiderCast there is no separation between a user and a machine. E.g., if the machine of the user is online, publications will be delivered to this machine even if the user is not there and vice versa.

Magnet focuses on reducing the distribution cost of publications using a special DHT named Oscar [10]. In Magnet subscriptions are transformed into a key, which places each node in the DHT such that its neighbors have similar interests. The join/leave operations in Magnet are relatively expensive and therefore Magnet is not suitable for our problem. In addition, Magnet builds and maintains a separate DHT just for the sake of the publish/subscribe service. In contrast, we envision publish/subscribe as being only one of many services offered by a larger system and therefore we rely on an unmodified "standard" DHT.

Corona [15] introduces the concept of cooperative polling. In Corona, a server coordinates the polling of existing RSS feeds over many peers. The coordination allows all peers to enjoy significantly quicker RSS updates and reduces the load on the RSS server. Corona's polling is somewhat similar to our client/mailbox interaction. Yet, Corona does not deal with disseminating the information to the mailboxes. It would be interesting in the future to combine our dissemination strategy with Corona's collaborative polling mechanism.

In Cuckoo [20], a hybrid central server and peer-to-peer infrastructure is suggested in order to reduce the load on a server using a peer to peer network. Using both a central server and a peer-to-peer methods, they manage to greatly reduce the requirements from the central server. This is different than our approach, which is pure P2P based.

In Pub2Sub [18], a virtual publish/subscribe network is deployed over an unstructured network. Their work shows an interesting alternative to gossiping as a delivery mechanism and results in reduced bandwidth and storage. In addition, their mechanism supports the usages of multiple publish/subscribe algorithms on the same network. Yet, in Pub2Sub subscribers are assumed to be available and connected all the time. Thus, information is disseminated immediately to all subscribers, whereas we hold events at mailboxes for future consumption by client devices.

Publish/subscribe is also widely utilized in data centers and cloud networks. In particular, these networks utilize publish/subscribe for resource monitoring [2], binding data centers together and synchronizing them with each other [7], maintaining a data storage with updates [21] and many more.

6   Conclusions

In this paper, we have presented Postman, a novel publish/subscribe mechanism for self sustained service independent P2P networks. Postman decouples between clients and donated P2P machines by utilizing mailboxes as aggregation services for subscriptions and publications. This architecture brings several advantages: As the number of mailboxes is much smaller than the number of nodes in the system, the scale of the publish/subscribe problem is greatly reduced. Further, as mailboxes are dedicated machines rather than client devices, their churn rate is likely to be lower than the one noticed in end-user devices. Another benefit is that since each mailbox aggregates multiple topics, the subscription patterns of mailboxes are much more uniform than the subscription patterns of individual clients, enabling sharing large parts of the dissemination trees and their overheads.

Postman is designed to be on one hand highly failure and churn resilient and on the other hand to have minimal message overheads. In order to do so, the distribution and consistency mechanisms adjust themselves to the actual behaviour of the network. In particular, for static networks dissemination of messages is done mainly on a spanning tree, as the random walks do not discover new mailboxes and are therefore never duplicated. Further, in such networks clients rarely miss publications, or discover unresponsive mailboxes and therefore only query a subset of their known mailboxes every poll round. However, when the network is dynamic, random walks often discover new mailboxes and their number increases. Further, clients often discover unresponsive mailboxes and therefore contact all their mailboxes every round in order to ensure both timely delivery and mailbox consistency.

We have also presented a performance study conducted on our real implementation using both synthetic workloads as well as Twitter based traces. The results of our study confirm the viability of Postman. They have also shown that low churn rates have no noticeable impact on Postman, and it can even recover quickly from massive failures and churn events.[3] Postman is currently implemented in Java over Kademlia [6] and is available in open source [1].

References

1. Postman implementation, `https://code.google.com/p/postman-pubsub/`
2. An, K., Pradhan, S., Caglar, F., Gokhale, A.: A publish/subscribe middleware for dependable and real-time resource monitoring in the cloud. In: Proc. of the Workshop on Secure and Dependable Middleware for Cloud Monitoring and Management, SDMCMM 2012, pp. 3:1–3:6. ACM, New York (2012)
3. Androutsellis-Theotokis, S., Spinellis, D.: A Survey of P2P Content Distribution Technologies. ACM Computing Survey 36, 335–371 (2004)
4. Baldoni, R., Beraldi, R., Querzoni, L., Virgillito, A., Italia, R.: Efficient publish/subscribe through a self-organizing broker overlay and its application to siena. The Computer Journal (2007)
5. Chockler, G., Melamed, R., Tock, Y., Vitenberg, R.: Spidercast: A scalable interest-aware overlay for topic-based pub/sub communication. In: Proc. of the 2007 Inaugural Int. Conf. on Distributed Event-Based Systems, DEBS 2007, New York, USA, pp. 14–25 (2007)
6. Einziger, G., Friedman, R., Kibbar, E.: Kaleidoscope: Adding colors to kademlia. In: 2013 IEEE Thirteenth Int. Conf. on Peer-to-Peer Computing (P2P), pp. 1–10 (September 2013)
7. Esposito, C., Ficco, M., Palmieri, F., Castiglione, A.: Interconnecting federated clouds by using publish-subscribe service. Cluster Computing, 1–17 (2013)
8. Eugster, P., Felber, P., Guerraoui, R., Kermarrec, A.-M.: The Many Faces of Publish/Subscribe. ACM Computing Surveys 35(2), 114–131 (2003)
9. Friedman, R., Libov, A.: An advertising mechanism for p2p networks. In: 2013 IEEE Thirteenth Int. Conf. on Peer-to-Peer Computing (P2P), pp. 1–10 (September 2013)

---

[3] "Neither snow nor rain nor heat nor gloom of night stays these couriers from the swift completion of their appointed rounds."

10. Girdzijauskas, S., Chockler, G., Vigfusson, Y., Tock, Y., Melamed, R.: Magnet: Practical subscription clustering for internet-scale publish/subscribe. In: Proc. of the Fourth ACM Int. Conf. on Distributed Event-Based Systems, DEBS 2010, New York, USA, pp. 172–183 (2010)

11. Kubiatowicz, J., Bindel, D., Chen, Y., Czerwinski, S.E., Eaton, P.R., Geels, D., Gummadi, R., Rhea, S.C., Weatherspoon, H., Weimer, W., Wells, C., Zhao, B.Y.: Oceanstore: An architecture for global-scale persistent storage. In: Proc. of the 9th Int. Conf. on Architectural Support for Programming Languages and Operating Systems (ASPLOS), pp. 190–201 (2000)

12. Kwak, H., Lee, C., Park, H., Moon, S.: What is twitter, a social network or a news media? In: Proc. of the 19th Int. Conf. on World Wide Web, WWW 2010, pp. 591–600. ACM, New York (2010)

13. Lua, E.K., Crowcroft, J., Pias, M., Sharma, R., Lim, S.: A Survey and Comparison of P2P Overlay Network Schemes. IEEE Comm. Surveys Tutorials 7(2), 72–93 (2005)

14. Maymounkov, P., Mazières, D.: Kademlia: A P2P Information System Based on the XOR Metric, 3rd edn., vol. 3279 (2005)

15. Ramasubramanian, V., Peterson, R., Sirer, E.G.: Corona: A high performance publish-subscribe system for the world wide web. In: Proc. of the 3rd Conf. on Networked Systems Design & Implementation, NSDI 2006, vol. 3, p. 2. USENIX Association, Berkeley (2006)

16. Rodrigues, R., Druschel, P.: P2p systems. Communications of the ACM 53(10), 72–82 (2010)

17. Sandler, D.R., Wallach, D.S.: Birds of a fethr: open, decentralized micropublishing. In: Proc. of the 8th Int. Conf. on P2P systems, IPTPS 2009, p. 1. USENIX Association, Berkeley (2009)

18. Tran, D.A., Pham, C.: Pub-2-sub: A content-based publish/subscribe framework for co-operative p2p networks. In: Fratta, L., Schulzrinne, H., Takahashi, Y., Spaniol, O. (eds.) NETWORKING 2009. LNCS, vol. 5550, pp. 770–781. Springer, Heidelberg (2009)

19. Wong, B., Guha, S.: Quasar: A probabilistic publish-subscribe system for social networks. In: Proc. of the 7th Int. Conf. on P2P Systems, IPTPS 2008, p. 2. USENIX Association, Berkeley (2008)

20. Xu, T., Chen, Y., Fu, X., Hui, P.: Twittering by cuckoo: decentralized and socio-aware online microblogging services. ACM SIGCOMM Computer Communication Review 41 (August 2010)

21. Zhu, Y., Wang, J., Wang, C.: Ripple: A publish/subscribe service for multidata item updates propagation in the cloud. Journal of Network and Computer Applications 34(4), 1054–1067 (2011)

A Self-stabilizing Algorithm for Edge Monitoring Problem

Brahim Neggazi[1], Mohammed Haddad[1], Volker Turau[2],
and Hamamache Kheddouci[1]

[1] University of Lyon, LIRIS UMR5205 CNRS, Claude Bernard Lyon 1 University
43 Bd du 11 Novembre 1918, F-69622, Villeurbanne, France
[2] Hamburg University of Technology, Institute of Telematics,
Schwarzenbergstraße 95, 21073, Hamburg, Germany

Abstract. Self-monitoring is a simple and effective mechanism for the security of wireless sensor networks (WSNs), especially to cope against compromised nodes. A node v can monitor an edge e if both end-nodes of e are neighbors of v; i.e., e together with v forms a triangle in the graph. Moreover, some edges need more than one monitor. Finding a set of monitoring nodes satisfying all monitoring constraints is called the *edge-monitoring problem*. The minimum edge-monitoring problem is long known to be NP-complete. In this paper, we present a novel silent self-stabilizing algorithm for computing a minimal edge-monitoring set. Correctness and termination are proven for the unfair distributed daemon.

Keywords: Edge-monitoring, Self-stabilization, Self-monitoring, Security, Sensor networks.

1 Introduction

A sensor network is a wireless ad-hoc network with a large number of nodes that are micro-sensors to collect and transmit environmental data autonomously. Often, the deployment of these sensor nodes is done in a random manner. Sensor networks find many applications such as military surveillance (detection intrusion, weapons locations, etc.), forest fire control, industrial process control, machine health monitoring, and so on.

The power limitation in wireless sensor networks (WSN) and hostile environments in which they can be deployed are factors that make this type of networks very vulnerable. Furthermore, the security of these networks is very important, especially for sensitive and critical applications.

One of the most difficult threats in the security of WSN is compromised nodes. Several attacks may use the compromised nodes to divert the proper functioning of the networks. Considering the real challenges to design security mechanisms against these attacks, many approaches have been proposed based on self-protection [16,17] and local monitoring (*a.k.a* watchdog) technique [1,8,10,11,14,12,13]. In sensor and ad-hoc networks, the concept of local monitoring was introduced by Marti et al. in [13].

P. Felber and V. Garg (Eds.): SSS 2014, LNCS 8756, pp. 93–105, 2014.

The basic idea of local monitoring is assigning monitoring roles to some of the nodes in the network. Usually, these monitors are placed somewhere in the intersection of the communication ranges of the sending (S) and the receiving nodes (R). Figure 1 illustrates the case where nodes $M1$ and $M2$ monitor the communication from S to R, by analyzing the traffic that R receives from S and forwards out to other nodes. In [13] these monitoring nodes are called watch-dogs. They monitor nodes by listening promiscuously to the transmissions of both nodes. When node S forwards a packet to R, the watchdog of this link ver-ifies that node R also forwards the packet. If R does not forward the packet, then it is misbehaving. Similar to this, monitoring nodes are able to detect any mali-cious actions such as delaying, dropping, modifying, or even fabricated packets [5,18]. The goal of monitoring considered in this paper is provide protection from transient faults (mainly memory corruption) and not from malicious behavior (*i.e.* Byzantine nodes). We assume that identifiers are not corrupted, *e.g.* they are stored in ROM as opposed to RAM. Our algorithm only determines the set of nodes that can monitor the edges, the actual monitoring task is a different subject and not part of our work. In this sense we assume that nodes execute their protocol as stated. Corruption of code, as a consequence of a fault or by a deliberate action, is clearly beyond the scope of this paper.

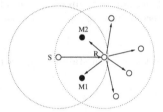

Fig. 1. Local monitoring

In dense networks with randomly deployed sensors nodes the selection of a minimal monitoring set of nodes is a challenging task, especially for large scale WSNs using only 1-hop knowledge. Consider for example the deployment in Figure 2. The black nodes can monitor all communication links depicted in bold. In [5,6], *Dong et al.* proved that finding a minimum set of monitoring nodes is NP-complete. The authors also propose two distributed polynomial algorithms with provable approximation ratio. However, the algorithms assume a synchronous model and distance-two knowledge. Moreover, their solution does not tolerate transient faults. Furthermore, distance-two knowledge is not a realistic solution in WSN. In this work, we assume the most general model that is asynchronous communication with distance-one knowledge.

One original approach proposed for dealing with fault-tolerance was proposed by Dijkstra [3], is called *self-stabilization*. A system is self-stabilizing if it can start from any possible configuration and converge to a correct behavior in finite time by itself without using any external intervention. Convergence is also guaranteed

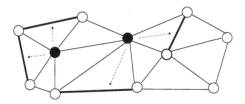

Fig. 2. Edge monitoring of a graph. The black nodes can monitors of the bold communication links.

when the system is affected by transient faults. This makes self-stabilization an elegant approach for non-masking fault-tolerance [4].

Hauck proposed the first self-stabilizing algorithm for the edge monitoring problem [9]. His algorithm uses the expression model [15] and converges in $O(n^2)$ moves under the central daemon. Using the transformer proposed by Turau in [15], the transformed algorithm converges in $O(mn^2)$ moves under the unfair distributed daemon.

In this paper, we improve the previous work by proposing a new algorithm that operates under the distributed daemon without using any transformer as it the case of Hauck's work. Moreover, our algorithm converges in $O(\Delta^2 m)$ moves where Δ is the maximum node degree in graph. Thus, in particular for networks with low maximal node degree our algorithm converges much faster.

The rest of this paper is organized as follows: the next section defines the used model and formally introduces the edges monitoring problem. In Section 3, we present our new self-stabilizing algorithm for finding a minimal edge-monitoring set. The proof of correctness is contained in Section 4 and the termination proof in Section 5. Finally, Section 6 concludes the paper.

2   Model and Definitions

In this section, we give formal definitions for the concepts used in this work.

2.1   Edge Monitoring Problem

We consider sensor networks in which all communications are bidirectional. We model the sensors network by a graph $G = (V, E)$ where sensors are represented by nodes, defined by the set V and their communications by edges, defined by the set E. Let $n = |V|$ and $m = |E|$. We assume each node to have a unique identifier (id) within a distance two from it [2]. We denote by $d(v)$ and $N(v)$ the degree and the open neighborhood of node v, respectively. Let Δ be the maximal degree of a node.

Definition 1. *A node $v \in V$ can* monitor *an edge* $e = \langle u, w \rangle \in E$, *if* $\langle v, u \rangle$, $\langle v, w \rangle \in E$, *i.e. the three nodes* v, u, w *form a triangle in* G.

Definition 2. *The edges* $\langle u, w \rangle \in E$ *where* $v, u,$ *an* w *form a triangle in* G *are called the* monitored edges *of* v.

In some applications some edges must be monitored by more than one node and others need no monitor at all. These situations are modeled by weighted graphs. The weight $\omega(e) \geq 0$ of an edge e denotes the number of nodes required to monitor e. The subset $E_M = \{e \in E : \omega(e) > 0\}$ represents the set of edges to be monitored. In the following we assume that nodes adjacent to an edge e are aware of $\omega(e)$.

Definition 3. *Let* $G = (V, E)$ *be an edge-weighted graph. The minimal edge monitoring problem consists of determining a minimal subset* V_M *of* V *such that for each edge* $e \in E$ *there are at least* $\omega(e)$ *nodes in* V_M *that can monitor* e.

Note that whether there exists a solution for the minimal edge monitoring problem depends of G and ω. In the following we assume that for a given weighted graph a solution exists. In other words, for each $e = \langle v, u \rangle \in E_M$ we have $|N(v) \cap N(u)| \geqslant \omega(e)$. Note that we can always define a solvable instance be setting $\omega'(e) = \min\{\omega(e), |N(v) \cap N(u)|\}$.

2.2 Self-stabilization

A system is self-stabilizing if it can start from any possible configuration and converges to a desired configuration in finite time by itself without using any external intervention. Convergence is also guaranteed when the system is affected by transient faults. This makes self-stabilization an elegant approach for non-masking fault-tolerance [4]. The concept of self-stabilization was first introduced by Dijkstra [3]. Every node has a set of local variables whose contents specify the *local state* of the node. The union of the local states of all nodes defines the system's *global state*. Each node has only a partial view of the system. Based on its local state and that of its neighbors, a node can decide to make *a move*. Therefore, self-stabilizing algorithms are given as a set of rules of the form [**If** $p(v)$ **then** M], where $p(v)$ is a predicate defined over v's local view and M is a move. Predicate $p(v)$ is true when the node's state v is locally illegitimate. In this case, v is called an *enabled*.

Self-stabilizing algorithms can be designed according to different *daemons* (a.k.a. schedulers). Two types of daemons are often assumed in the literature on self-stabilizing algorithms: *central* and *distributed* daemon. At each step, the central daemon selects exactly one enabled node to make a move. Whereas the distributed daemon selects in each step a non-empty subset of all enabled nodes to make their moves simultaneously. A taxonomy of existing daemons is proposed in [7].

Daemons are also associated with the notion of fairness. A daemon can be fair, or unfair. A daemon is fair if every node that is continuously enabled will eventually be selected. The unfair daemon on the other hand may delay the move of a node as long as there are other enabled nodes. Self-stabilizing algorithms are designed for a specific daemon and cannot trivially operate under a more general daemon. Obviously, an algorithm designed for an unfair distributed daemon will work with all other daemons. This paper assumes the most general daemon, the unfair distributed daemon. As a communication model the shared variable model is used.

3 Algorithm *SEMS*

This section presents the self-stabilizing algorithm *SEMS* for computing a minimal edge-monitoring set for a general graph G with edge weight function ω as introduced above. In this algorithm, each node v maintains a variable *state* with range $\{In, Wait, Out\}$. This variable indicates whether v belongs to the monitoring set or not. A node is called a *monitor* if its variable *state* has value IN. Thus, the edge-monitoring set D of G is defined by $D = \{v \in V : v.state = In\}$. The state $Wait$ is an intermediate state from state In to Out required for symmetry breaking. It is used to inform neighbors that this node is not required to be a monitor and can change its state to Out.

3.1 Informal Description of Algorithm *SEMS*

The monitors of an edge are administered by the end node with the smaller identifier. Neighbors of v that are either monitors or potential monitors of an edge adjacent to v are called *target monitors*. Thus, a node v maintains a set of target monitors for each of its adjacent edges which it is responsible for. For an edge $\langle v, u \rangle$, this includes all current monitors, i.e., all common neighbors of v and u with state In or $Wait$. If the number of these nodes is not sufficient (i.e., less than $\omega(v, u)$) then this set is supplemented by the smallest common neighbors of v and u with state Out until this set has $\omega(v, u)$ elements. If on the other hand the number of these nodes exceeds $\omega(v, u)$ then the set of target monitors is empty. Thus, the edge does not need this node as a monitor. The union of target monitors of all adjacent edges of a responsible node is called "*target monitoring set*" of the node.

Note that there is one small drawback with this notion: A node does not know the set of neighbors for each of its neighbors. This information is necessary to compute the target monitoring set of a node. A node can avoid this pitfall by exposing the set of neighbors in a variable and neighbors can use this variable for their computations. Since this variable can be corrupted by a transient fault, the target monitoring set may be faulty for some time.

The algorithm works as follows. Nodes keep a target monitoring set as well as the exposed set of neighbors always up-to-date. A node with state In that is not a target monitor for any of its neighbors will change its state. In order to avoid an oscillating behavior such a node does not immediately change its state to Out. It first transits into state $Wait$. In order to transit into state Out, all neighbors must give permission to do such transition. A node only gives this permission to the neighbor with state $Wait$ that has the smallest identifier among these nodes. This is realized by a public variable containing the identifier of the neighbor that can be removed from its monitoring set. So, only after all neighbors give this permission, a node may transit from state $Wait$ to state Out. If a node with state $Wait$ becomes a member of the target monitoring set of a neighbor then it transits back to state In. There is also a rule for changing the state from Out to In. The precondition for this rule is that the node is a target monitor of a neighbor and none of its neighbors is currently giving this node the above discussed permission.

3.2   Formal Description of Algorithm *SEMS*

Algorithm *SEMS* uses the following variables for each node v:

- S :: contains the open neighborhood of v.
- TM :: the set of target monitors. It is a set of neighbors that are either monitors or potential monitors of an edge adjacent to v. TM will contain a sufficient number of nodes to satisfy the monitor demands of all adjacent edges. Note that $|TM| \leq \Delta$.
- PO :: used to give permissions to change state to Out. It either contains the smallest identifier of all neighbors in state $Wait$ not contained in TM or $null$.

If $v.PO = u$ (resp. $u \in v.TM$) then we say v points at u to leave (resp. to enter) the monitoring set.

For a set X of node identifiers and a positive integer p denote by X^p the set of the p smallest identifiers contained in X. If $|X| \leq p$ then $X^p = X$. Thus

$$X^p = \begin{cases} X & \text{if } |X| \leq p \\ \text{the } p \text{ smallest elements of } X & \text{otherwise.} \end{cases}$$

In Algorithm *SEMS* a node v uses the three functions $Mon(v, u)$, $Candidate(v, u)$, and $TM_e(v, u)$, defined for all neighboring nodes $v, u \in V$. Function $Mon(v, u)$ returns the set of nodes that are supposingly monitoring edge $\langle v, u \rangle$. These are neighbors of v and most likely also of u that have state In or $Wait$. Formally,

$$Mon(v, u) = \{z \in N(v) \cap u.S \mid z.state = In \vee z.state = Wait\}$$

Function $Candidate(v, u)$ returns the set of nodes that are supposingly new candidates to monitor edge $\langle v, u \rangle$. These are neighbors of v and most likely also of u that have state Out. Formally,

$$Candidate(v, u) = \{z \in N(v) \cap u.S \mid z.state = Out\}$$

Function $TM_e(v, u)$ uses the first two functions to compute a target set of monitors for edge $\langle v, u \rangle$. It is used to keep $v.TM$ up-to-date. Formally,

if $(|Mon(v, u)| \leqslant \omega(v, u) \wedge v < u)$ **then**
  $TM_e(v, u) = Mon(v, u) \cup Candidate(v, u)^{\omega(v,u) - |Mon(v,u)|}$;

else
$$TM_e(v, u) = \emptyset;$$

Note that $TM_e(v, u) = \emptyset$ for an edge $\langle v, u \rangle$ if $v > u$.

Algorithm *SEMS* is specified by six rules that are divided into two categories. Rules **R1** and **R2** belong to the first category. They are used to update the values of the variables TM and PO.

Algorithm *SEMS*: Maintaining TM, PO and S

Nodes: v is the current node

$S \neq N(v) \quad \longrightarrow \quad S := N(v);$ **[R1]**

$TM \neq \bigcup_{u \in N(v)} TM_e(v, u) \vee PO \neq min\{u \in N(v) \mid u.state = Wait \wedge u \notin TM\}$

$\longrightarrow \quad TM := \bigcup_{u \in N(v)} TM_e(v, u);$

$\qquad PO := min\{u \in N(v) \mid u.state = Wait \wedge u \notin TM\} \; ;$ **[R2]**

The remaining four rules of the second category maintain variable *state*.

Algorithm *SEMS*: Maintaining *state*

Nodes: v is the current node

$state = Out \wedge \exists u \in N(v) : v \in u.TM \wedge \forall w \in N(v) : v \neq w.PO$

$\qquad\qquad\qquad\qquad\qquad\qquad\qquad \longrightarrow state := In;$ **[R3]**

$state = In \wedge \forall u \in N(v) : v \notin u.TM \qquad \longrightarrow state := Wait;$ **[R4]**

$state = Wait \wedge \exists u \in N(v) : v \in u.TM \qquad \longrightarrow state := In;$ **[R5]**

$state = Wait \wedge \forall u \in N(v) : v = u.PO \qquad \longrightarrow state := Out;$ **[R6]**

If more than one rule is enabled, we assume that the rule with the smallest number is executed.

3.3 Example

Figure 3 shows an execution of Algorithm *SEMS* under the synchronous daemon for a graph with six nodes. Two of the edges require each one monitor. In the initial configuration, all nodes are in state *Out* and the values of variable S are consistent with the neighborhood relation. Furthermore, we assume $v.TM = \emptyset$ and $v.PO = null$ for each node v.

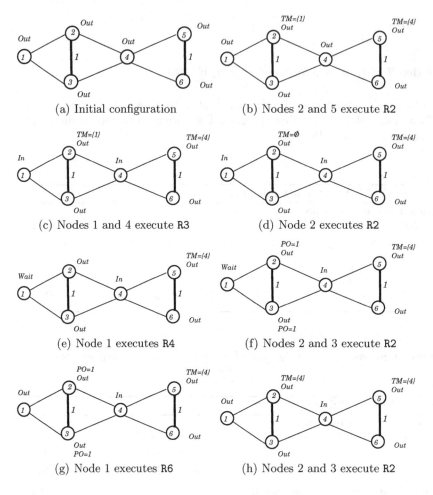

Fig. 3. Example of an execution of Algorithm *SEMS*

4   Proof of Correctness

First, we prove that in a configuration where no node is enabled, the set D forms a minimal edge monitoring set with respect to ω.

Lemma 1. *In a configuration with no enabled node, the following properties hold for each $v \in V$.*

(a) $v.S = N(v)$,
(b) if $v.state = Wait$ then $v \notin u.TM$ for all $u \in N(v)$,
(c) if $v.state = Out$ then $v \neq u.PO$ for all $u \in N(v)$,
(d) $v.state \in \{In, Out\}$.

Proof. Properties (a) and (b) are satisfied because rules R1 and R5 are disabled. Note that $v.PO = \{u \in N(v) : u.state = Wait \wedge u \notin v.TM\}$ since rule R2 is disabled for each node $v \in V$. Thus, $u.PO = null$ or $u.PO.state = Wait$. Hence, $v \neq u.PO$ since $v.state = Out$. This proves property (c).

Assume Property (d) is false. Among all nodes violating this property choose a node v with a minimal identifier. Then $v.state = Wait$. By minimality of v, if $v \notin u.TM$ for a node $u \in N(v)$ then $v = u.PO$. Since rule R6 is disabled there exists a node $u \in N(v)$ such that $v \neq u.PO$. Hence, $v \in u.TM$ and rule R5 is enabled. Contradiction.   □

Lemma 2. *In a configuration with no enabled node any edge has sufficiently many monitors, i.e.,* $|Mon(v, u)| \geqslant \omega(v, u)$ *for each* $\langle v, u \rangle \in E$.

Proof. The proof is by contradiction. Assume that there exists an edge $\langle v, u \rangle$ such that $|Mon(v, u)| < \omega(v, u)$. Without loss of generality, let $v < u$. By definition, $Mon(v, u) = \{z \in N(v) \cap u.S \mid z.state \in \{In, Wait\}\}$. Using properties (d) and (a) of Lemma 1, we have

$$Mon(v, u) = \{z \in N(v) \cap N(u) \mid z.state = In\}.$$

Since $|Mon(v, u)| < \omega(v, u)$ the set have $Candidate(v, u)^{\omega(v,u)-|Mon(v,u)|}$ is not empty (otherwise no solution would exist). Moreover, since rule R2 is disabled for v the following holds:

$$\emptyset \neq Candidate(v, u)^{\omega(v,u)-|Mon(v,u)|} \subseteq TM_e(v, u) \subseteq v.TM$$

This shows that there exists a node $z \in v.TM$ with $z.state = Out$. Also $z \neq w.PO$ for all $w \in N(z)$ by property (c) of Lemma 1. This yields that rule R3 is enabled for node z. Contradiction.   □

Lemma 3. *In a configuration with no enabled node, the set* $D = \{v \in V \mid state(v) = In\}$ *forms a minimal edge-monitoring set with respect to* ω.

Proof. According to Lemma 2, D is an edge-monitoring set. Thus, it is sufficient to prove that D is minimal. Assume there exists a node $v \in D$ such that $D' = D - \{v\}$ is an edge monitoring set of G with respect to ω (see Figure 4 for an example). So $v.state = In$. Then for any pair $u_1, u_2 \in N(v)$ with $u_1 < u_2$ edge $\langle u_1, u_2 \rangle$ has more than $\omega(u_1, u_2)$ monitors, i.e., $|Mon(u_1, u_2)| > \omega(u_1, u_2)$. Thus, $TM_e(u_1, u_2) = TM_e(u_2, u_1) = \emptyset$. Now, $v \notin u_1.TM$ and $v \notin u_2.TM$ since rule R2 is disabled for u_1 and u_2. Let $u_1 \in N(v)$ such that $N(u_1) \cap N(v) = \emptyset$. Then $v \notin u_1.TM$ by definition of $u_1.TM$ (note rules R1 and R2 are not enabled). Hence, $v \notin u.TM$ for any $u \in N(v)$. This implies that rule R4 is enabled for v. Contradiction.   □

5   Proof of Termination

It remains to prove that Algorithm *SEMS* stabilizes in finite time for any starting configuration under the distributed daemon. This will be accomplished by proving that every node makes only a finite number of moves, independently of its

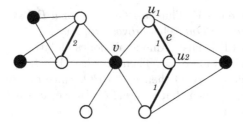

Fig. 4. Non-minimal edge-monitoring set. Monitoring nodes are depicted in bold and the edge labels denote ω. Node v is not needed as a monitor.

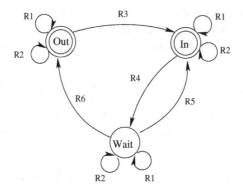

Fig. 5. State Transition Diagram of Algorithm *SEMS*

neighbor's concurrent moves or daemon's fairness assumptions. Figure 5 shows all transitions of a node with respect to variable *state* that can occur during an execution of Algorithm *SEMS*.

Let c be a configuration of the system. Let

$$D_c = \{v \in V \mid v.state \in \{In, Wait\}\}.$$

Observe that nodes do not enter or leave the set TM if they change their state from *Wait* to *In* or conversely.

The following lemma follows from the convention that rules with a higher priority have precedence.

Lemma 4. *Each node executes rule R1 at most once. If a node does execute R1 then in its first move.*

This lemma implies that if a node v executes rules R2 to R6 then $v.S = N(v)$.

A node v can change its state from *In* via *Wait* to *Out* because neighboring nodes signal to v that all their edges are sufficiently monitored. This information can be false because some neighbor u of v wrongly assumed that its neighbor u_1 could monitor edge $\langle u, u_2 \rangle$. The reason for such a wrong assumption is that $u_2 \in u_1.S$ but $u_2 \notin N(u_1)$. Once u_1 executes rule R1 node u will realize this and u can now consider v as a target monitor and include it into $u.TM$. This could then prompt v to change its state to In again. Now the situation is different, all neighbors of v have executed a rule in the mean time. Because of priority of rules then $u.S = N(u)$ holds for all $u \in N(v)$. If node v changes its state again to Out with rule R6 then it is because all neighbors indicated with their variable PO that their edges have a sufficient number of monitors without v. Since this number never will fall again under the value given by ω, node v will never move to state In again. This behavior is formally proved in the following two lemmas.

Lemma 5. *Each node executes R6 at most twice, i.e., it changes from state Wait to state Out at most twice.*

Proof. Let c be a configuration in which a node $v \in V$ has state $Wait$ and executes rule R6. For v to execute rule R6 again it must first change its state back to $Wait$. This can only be achieved by first changing to state In with rule R3 and then to state $Wait$ with rule R4. Note that $v = u.PO$ for all $u \in N(v)$ when v executed rule R6. For v to be enabled for rule R3 it is required that $v \neq u.PO$ for all $u \in N(v)$. Thus, all neighbors of v must have executed rule R2 before v can execute rule R3 again. A node executing rule R2 cannot be enabled for rule R1. Thus, each neighbor u of v satisfies $u.S = N(u)$ when u executes rule R2. Hence, those neighbors of v that are responsible for edges that v can monitor have all finally determined that v is not required as a monitor, i.e., v will never enter $u.TM$ for a neighbor u. Hence v will never change its state to In again. $\qquad\square$

Lemma 6. *Each node executes R3 at most three times, i.e., it changes from state Out to state In at most three times.*

Proof. A node executing rule R3 four times would execute rule R6 at least three times. This contradicts Lemma 5. $\qquad\square$

Lemma 7. *Each node executes R4 at most $6\Delta d(v)$ times, i.e., it changes from state In to state Wait at most $6\Delta d(v)$ times.*

Proof. A node v with state In executes rule R4 if v is not a target monitor of any of its neighbors, i.e., $v \notin u.TM$ for all $u \in N(v)$. In order to reenter state In at least one of v's neighbors must declare v as a target monitor, i.e., there must be a node $u \in N(v)$ with $v \in u.TM$. Note that for u to change its set of target monitors, a neighbor of u must change its state from Out to In or from $Wait$ to Out or execute rule R1. According to Lemmas 4 to 6, each neighbor of u can do this at most 6 times. Hence, node u can update $u.TM$ at most $6d(u)$ times. This implies that node v changes its state to $Wait$ at most $6\Delta d(v)$. $\qquad\square$

Lemma 8. *Each node executes R5 at most $6\Delta d(v) + 1$ times, i.e., it changes from state Wait to state In at most $6\Delta d(v) + 1$ times.*

Proof. Immediate consequence of Lemma 7. $\qquad\square$

Lemma 9. *Any node v can execute R2 at most $(6\Delta^2 + 9)d(v)$ times.*

Proof. Consider a node v. The execution of rule R2 depends on the values of $v.TM$ and $v.PO$. By definition, the value of $v.TM$ itself depends on $TM_e(v, u)$ for each neighbor u of v. $Mon(v, u)$ depends on the neighbors w of v which are in state *Wait* or *In*. Note that node w can change its value from state *Out* to *Wait* at most three times (Lemma 6) and from state *Wait* to *Out* at most twice (Lemma 5). Thus, each neighbor w of v changes $Mon(v, u)$ at most five times and once if $w.S$ is incorrect. So, for each of v's neighbor u, $TM_e(v, u)$ can change at most 6 times. Hence, we deduce that $v.TM$ can change at most $6d(v)$ times for each neighbor of v.

Next we consider variable $v.PO$. By definition, PO depends on the neighbors that have state *Wait*. Using Lemmas 5 and 8, each neighbor u of v changes its state from *Wait* to state *In* or *Out* at most $6\Delta d(u) + 3$ times. Thus, for each neighbor of v, the value of $v.PO$ can change at most $d(v)(6\Delta^2 + 3)$ times.

In summary, v can execute rule R2 at most $d(v)(6\Delta^2 + 9)$ times.   □

Lemma 10. *Algorithm* SEMS *terminates in* $O(\Delta^2 m)$ *moves under the unfair distributed daemon.*

Proof. Lemmas 4 to 9 stated upper bounds on the number of executions for each rule on each node. In the worst case these moves all occur sequentially. This gives the following upper bound for the total number of moves:

$$n + \sum_{v \in V}(6\Delta^2 + 9)d(v) + 3n + \sum_{v \in V} 6\Delta d(v) + \sum_{v \in V}(6\Delta d(v) + 1) + 2n \in O(\Delta^2 m)$$

□

Lemmas 3 and 10 yield our main result.

Theorem 1. *Algorithm* SEMS *is self-stabilizing algorithm for finding a minimal edge monitoring set for a given set of monitoring requirements of a general graph. It uses* $O(\Delta log\ n)$ *memory space per node and stabilizes in* $O(\Delta^2 m)$ *moves under the unfair distributed daemon.*

6   Conclusion

In this paper, we presented a novel self-stabilizing algorithm to find minimal edge-monitoring sets in general graphs. Such sets provide a valuable tool to implement a simple and effective mechanism for building secure wireless sensor networks. The algorithm has a lower move complexity as existing self-stabilizing algorithm. As future work, we aim to either improve the analysis of the presented algorithm, to come up with a more efficient algorithm or to prove that $\Omega(\Delta^2 m)$ moves is a lower bound of the problem for distributed daemon.

Acknowledgments. This work is partially supported by P2GE Rhone-Alpes Region project. Research of the third author was funded by the Deutsche Forschungsgemeinschaft (DFG), contract number TU 221/6-1.

References

1. Benahmed, K., Merabti, M., Haffaf, H.: Distributed monitoring for misbehaviour detection in wireless sensor networks. Security & Com. Netw. 6(4), 388–400 (2013)
2. Blair, J.R.S., Manne, F.: An efficient self-stabilizing distance-2 coloring algorithm. Theoretical Computer Science 444, 28–39 (2012)
3. Dijkstra, E.W.: Self-stabilizing systems in spite of distributed control. Commun. ACM 17(11), 643–644 (1974)
4. Dolev, S.: Self-stabilization. MIT Press (2000)
5. Dong, D., Liao, X., Liu, Y., Shen, C., Wang, X.: Edge self-monitoring for wireless sensor networks. IEEE Trans. on Parallel & Distr. Systems 22(3), 514–527 (2011)
6. Dong, D., Liu, Y., Liao, X.: Self-monitoring for sensor networks. In: Proc. 9th ACM Int. Symp. on Mobile Ad Hoc Networking and Computing, MobiHoc 2008, New York, USA, pp. 431–440 (2008)
7. Dubois, S., Tixeuil, S.: A taxonomy of daemons in self-stabilization. CoRR, abs/1110.0334 (2011)
8. Ganeriwal, S., Balzano, L.K., Srivastava, M.B.: Reputation-based framework for high integrity sensor networks. ACM Trans. Sen. Netw. 4(3), 15:1–15:37 (2008)
9. Hauck, B.: Time-and Space-Efficient Self-Stabilizing Algorithms. dissertation, Hamburg University of Technology (2012)
10. Khalil, I., Bagchi, S., Nina-Rotaru, C.: DICAS: Detection, Diagnosis and Isolation of Control Attacks in Sensor Networks. In: First Int. Conf. on Security and Privacy for Emerging Areas in Communications Networks, pp. 89–100 (2005)
11. Khalil, I., Bagchi, S., Shroff, N.: Liteworp: A lightweight countermeasure for the wormhole attack. In: Multihop Wireless Network, the International Conference on Dependable Systems and Networks (DSN), pp. 612–621 (2005)
12. Lian, S., Zhao, J., Zhao, X.: Near-optimal diagnosis system deployment in wireless sensor networks. Int. Journal of Distributed Sensor Networks (2013)
13. Marti, S., Giuli, T.J., Lai, K., Baker, M.: Mitigating routing misbehavior in mobile ad hoc networks. In: Proceedings of the 6th Annual International Conference on Mobile Computing and Networking, pp. 255–265 (2000)
14. Suk-Bok, L., Yoon-Hwa, C.: A resilient packet-forwarding scheme against maliciously packet-dropping nodes in sensor networks. In: Proc. 4th ACM Workshop on Security of Ad Hoc and Sensor Networks, New York, USA, pp. 59–70 (2006)
15. Turau, V.: Efficient transformation of distance-2 self-stabilizing algorithms. Journal of Parallel and Distributed Computing 72(4), 603–612 (2012)
16. Wang, D., Zhang, Q., Liu, J.: The self-protection problem in wireless sensor networks. ACM Transaction Sensor Networks 3(4) (October 2007)
17. Wang, Y., Li, M., Zhang, Q.: Efficient algorithms for p-self-protection problem in static wireless sensor networks. IEEE Transactions on Parallel and Distributed Systems 19(10), 1426–1438 (2008)
18. Wei, G., Zhu, Z., Mao, Y., Xiong, N.: A distributed node self-monitoring mechanism in wireless sensor networks. In: 2nd Int. Conf. on Information Science and Engineering, pp. 1684–1687 (December 2010)

Self-stabilizing Leader Election in Polynomial Steps*

Karine Altisen[1], Alain Cournier[2], Stéphane Devismes[1],
Anaïs Durand[1], and Franck Petit[3]

[1] VERIMAG UMR 5104, Université Grenoble Alpes, France
[2] MIS Lab., Université Picardie Jules Verne, France
[3] LIP6 UMR 7606, INRIA, UPMC Sorbonne Universités, France

Abstract. In this paper, we propose a silent self-stabilizing leader election algorithm for bidirectional connected identified networks of arbitrary topology. This algorithm is written in the locally shared memory model. It assumes the distributed unfair daemon, the most general scheduling hypothesis of the model. Our algorithm requires no global knowledge on the network (such as an upper bound on the diameter or the number of processes, for example). We show that its stabilization time is in $\Theta(n^3)$ steps in the worst case, where n is the number of processes. Its memory requirement is asymptotically optimal, *i.e.*, $\Theta(\log n)$ bits per processes. Its round complexity is of the same order of magnitude — *i.e.*, $\Theta(n)$ rounds — as the best existing algorithm [10] designed with similar settings. To the best of our knowledge, this is the first self-stabilizing leader election algorithm for arbitrary identified networks that is proven to achieve a stabilization time polynomial in steps. By contrast, we show that the previous best existing algorithm designed with similar settings [10] stabilizes in a non polynomial number of steps in the worst case.

1 Introduction

In distributed computing, the *leader election* problem consists in distinguishing one process, so-called the leader, among the others. We consider here identified networks. So, as it is usually done, we augment the problem by requiring all processes to eventually know the identifier of the leader. The leader election is fundamental as it is a basic component to solve many other important problems, *e.g.*, consensus, spanning tree constructions, implementing broadcasting and convergecasting methods, *etc*. *Self-stabilization* [11] is a versatile technique to withstand *any* transient fault in a distributed system: a self-stabilizing algorithm is able to recover, *i.e.*, reach a legitimate configuration, in finite time, regardless the *arbitrary* initial configuration of the system, and therefore also after the occurrence of transient faults. Thus, self-stabilization makes no hypotheses on the nature or extent of transient faults that could hit the system, and recovers from the effects of those faults in a unified manner. Such versatility comes at a price. After transient faults, there is a finite period of time, called the *stabilization phase*, before the system returns to a legitimate configuration. The *stabilization time* is

---

* This work has been partially supported by the LabEx PERSYVAL-Lab (ANR-11-LABX-0025-01) funded by the French program Investissement d'avenir and the AGIR project DI-AMS.

then the maximum time to reach a legitimate configuration starting from an arbitrary one. Notice that efficiency of self-stabilizing algorithms is mainly evaluated according to their stabilization time and memory requirement.

We consider (deterministic) asynchronous silent self-stabilizing leader election problem in bidirectional, connected, and identified networks of arbitrary topology. We investigate solutions to this problem which are written in the locally shared memory model introduced by Dijkstra [11]. In this model, the distributed unfair daemon is known as the weakest scheduling assumption. Under such an assumption, proving that a given algorithm is self-stabilizing implies that the stabilization time must be finite in terms of atomic steps. However, despite some solutions assuming all these settings (in particular the unfairness assumption) are available in the literature [8,9,10], none of them is proven to achieve a polynomial upper bound in steps on its stabilization time. Actually, the time complexities of all these solutions are analyzed in terms of rounds only.

Related Work. In [12], Dolev *et al* showed that silent self-stabilizing leader election requires $\Omega(\log n)$ bits per process, where n is the number of processes. Notice that *non-silent* self-stabilizing leader election can be achieved using less memory, *e.g.*, the non-silent self-stabilizing leader election algorithm for unoriented ring-shaped networks given in [5] requires $O(\log \log n)$ space per process.

Self-stabilizing leader election algorithms for arbitrary connected identified networks have been proposed in the message-passing model [1,4,6]. First, the algorithm of Afek and Bremler [1] stabilizes in $O(n)$ rounds using $\Theta(\log n)$ bits per process. But, it assumes that the link-capacity is bounded by a value B, known by all processes. Two solutions that stabilize in $O(\mathcal{D})$ rounds, where $\mathcal{D}$ is the diameter of the network, have been proposed in [4,6]. However, both solutions assume that processes know some upper bound D on the diameter $\mathcal{D}$; and have a memory requirement in $\Theta(\log D \log n)$ bits.

Several solutions are also given in the shared memory model [3,13,8,9,10,14]. The algorithm proposed by Dolev and Herman [13] is not silent, works under a *fair* daemon, and assume that all processes know a bound N on the number of processes. This solution stabilizes in $O(\mathcal{D})$ rounds using $\Theta(N \log N)$ bits per process. The algorithm of Arora and Gouda [3] works under a *weakly fair* daemon and assume the knowledge of some bound N on the number of processes. This solution stabilizes in $O(N)$ rounds using $\Theta(\log N)$ bits per process.

Datta *et al* [8] propose the first self-stabilizing leader election algorithm (for arbitrary connected identified networks) proven under the distributed unfair daemon. This algorithm stabilizes in $O(n)$ rounds. However, the space complexity of this algorithm is unbounded. (More precisely, the algorithm requires each process to maintain an unbounded integer in its local memory.)

Solutions in [9,10,14] have a memory requirement which is asymptotically optimal (*i.e.* in $\Theta(\log n)$). The algorithm proposed by Kravchik and Kutten [14] assumes a synchronous daemon and the stabilization time of this latter is in $O(\mathcal{D})$ rounds. The two solutions proposed by Datta *et al* in [9,10] assume a distributed unfair daemon and have a stabilization time in $O(n)$ rounds. However, despite these two algorithms stabilize within a finite number of steps (indeed, they are proven assuming an unfair daemon), no step complexity analysis is proposed. Finally, note that the algorithm proposed in [9] assumes that each process has a bit of memory which cannot be arbitrarily corrupted.

Contribution. We propose a silent self-stabilizing leader election algorithm for arbitrary connected and identified networks. Our solution is written in the locally shared memory model assuming a distributed unfair daemon, the weakest scheduling assumption. Our algorithm assumes no knowledge of any global parameter (*e.g.*, an upper bound on $\mathcal{D}$ or n) of network. Like previous solutions of the literature [9,10], it is asymptotically optimal in space (*i.e.*, it can be implemented using $\Theta(\log n)$ bits per process), and it stabilizes in $\Theta(n)$ rounds in the worst case. Yet, contrary to those solutions, we show that our algorithm has a stabilization time in $\Theta(n^3)$ steps in the worst case.

For fair comparison, we have also studied the step complexity of the algorithm given in [10], noted here $\mathcal{DLV}$. This latter is the closest to ours in terms of performance. We show that its stabilization time is not polynomial, *i.e.*, there is no constant α such that the stabilization time of $\mathcal{DLV}$ is in $O(n^\alpha)$ steps. More precisely, we show that fixing α to any constant greater than or equal to 4, for every $\beta \geq 2$, there exists a network of $n = 2^{\alpha-1} \times \beta$ processes in which there exists a possible execution that stabilizes in $\Omega(n^\alpha)$ steps. Due to the lack of space, this latter result is not presented here. Refer to the technical report online [2] for more details.

Roadmap. The next section is dedicated to computational model and basic definitions. In Section 3, we propose our self-stabilizing leader election algorithm. In Section 4, we outline the proof of correctness and the complexity analysis. A detailed proof of correctness and a complete complexity analysis are available in the technical report online [2]. Finally, we conclude in Section 5.

2   Computational Model

Distributed Systems. We consider *distributed systems* made of n *processes*. Each process can communicate with a subset of other processes, called its *neighbors*. We denote by $\mathcal{N}_p$ the set of neighbors of process p. Communications are assumed to be bidirectional, *i.e.* $q \in \mathcal{N}_p$ if and only if $p \in \mathcal{N}_q$. Hence, the topology of the system can be represented as a simple undirected connected graph $G = (V, E)$, where V is the set of processes and E is a set of edges representing (direct) communication relations. We assume that each process has a unique ID, a natural integer. IDs are stored using a constant number of bits, b. As commonly done in the literature, we assume that $b = \Theta(\log n)$. Moreover, by an abuse of notation, we identify a process with its ID, whenever convenient. We will also denote by ℓ the process of minimum ID. (So, the minimum ID will be also denoted by ℓ.)

Locally Shared Memory Model. We consider the *locally shared memory model* in which the processes communicate using a finite number of locally shared registers, called *variables*. Each process can read its own variables and those of its neighbors, but can only write to its own variables. The *state* of a process is the vector of values of all its variables. A configuration γ of the system is the vector of states of all processes. We denote by $\mathcal{C}$ the set of all possible configurations.

A distributed *algorithm* consists of one *program* per process. The program of a process p is a finite set of *actions* of the following form: $\langle label \rangle :: \langle guard \rangle \to \langle statement \rangle$. The *labels* are used to identify actions. The *guard* of an action in the program of process p is a Boolean expression involving the variables of p and its neighbors. If the guard of some action evaluates to true, then the action is said to be *enabled* at p. By extension, if at least one action is enabled at p, p is said to be enabled. We denote by $Enabled(\gamma)$ the set of processes enabled in configuration γ. The *statement* of an action is a sequence of assignments on the variables of p. An action can be executed only if it is enabled. In this case, the execution of the action consists in executing its statement.

The asynchronism of the system is materialized by an adversary, called the *daemon*. In a configuration γ, if $Enabled(\gamma) \neq \emptyset$, then the daemon selects a non empty subset S of $Enabled(\gamma)$ to perform an *(atomic) step*: $\forall p \in S$, p atomically executes one of its actions enabled in γ, leading the system to a new configuration γ'. We denote by $\mapsto$ the relation between configurations such that $\gamma \mapsto \gamma'$ if and only if γ' can be reached from γ in one (atomic) step. An *execution* is then a *maximal* sequence of configurations $\gamma_0, \gamma_1, \ldots$ such that $\gamma_{i-1} \mapsto \gamma_i, \forall i > 0$. The term "maximal" means that the execution is either infinite, or ends at a *terminal* configuration γ in which $Enabled(\gamma)$ is empty.

In this paper, the daemon is supposed to be *distributed* and *unfair*. "Distributed" means that while the configuration is not terminal, the daemon should select at least one enabled process, maybe more. "Unfair" means that there is no fairness constraint, *i.e.*, the daemon might never permit an enabled process to execute, unless it is the only enabled process.

Rounds. To measure the time complexity of an algorithm, we also use the notion of *round*. This latter allows to highlight the execution time according to the speed of the slowest process. If a process p is enabled in a configuration γ_i but not enabled in the next configuration γ_{i+1} and does not execute any action between γ_i and γ_{i+1}, we said that p is *neutralized* during the step $\gamma_i \mapsto \gamma_{i+1}$. The first round of an execution e, noted e', is the minimal prefix of e in which every process that is enabled in the initial configuration either executes an action or becomes neutralized. Let e'' be the suffix of e starting from the last configuration of e'. The second round of e is the first round of e'', and so forth.

Self-Stabilization. Let $\mathcal{A}$ be a distributed algorithm. Let $\mathcal{E}$ be the set of all possible executions of $\mathcal{A}$. A *specification SP* is a predicate over $\mathcal{E}$.

$\mathcal{A}$ is *self-stabilizing* for SP if and only if there exists a non-empty subset of configurations $\mathcal{L} \subseteq \mathcal{C}$, called *legitimate* configurations, such that:

– *Closure:* $\forall e \in \mathcal{E}$, for each step $\gamma_i \mapsto \gamma_{i+1} \in e$, $\gamma_i \in \mathcal{L} \Rightarrow \gamma_{i+1} \in \mathcal{L}$.
– *Convergence:* $\forall e \in \mathcal{E}, \exists \gamma \in e$ such that $\gamma \in \mathcal{L}$.
– *Correction:* $\forall e \in \mathcal{E}$ such that e starts in a legitimate configuration $\gamma \in \mathcal{L}$, e satisfies SP.

Every configuration that is not legitimate is called *illegitimate*. The *stabilization time* is the maximum time (in steps or rounds) to reach a legitimate configuration starting from any configuration.

Self-Stabilizing Leader Election. We define SP_{LE} the specification of the leader election problem. Let $Leader : V \mapsto \mathbb{N}$ be a function defined on the state of any process $p \in V$ in the current configuration that returns the ID of the leader appointed by p. An execution $e \in \mathcal{E}$ satisfies SP_{LE} if and only if:

1. For all configuration $\gamma \in e$, $\forall p, q \in V$, $Leader(p) = Leader(q)$ and $Leader(p)$ is the ID of some process in V.
2. For all step $\gamma_i \mapsto \gamma_{i+1} \in e$, $\forall p \in V$, $Leader(p)$ has the same value in γ_i and γ_{i+1}.

An algorithm $\mathcal{A}$ is *silent* if and only if every execution is finite [12]. Let γ be a terminal configuration. The set of all possible executions starting from γ is the singleton $\{\gamma\}$. So, if $\mathcal{A}$ is self-stabilizing and silent, γ must be legitimate. Thus, to prove that a leader election algorithm is both self-stabilizing and silent, it is necessary and sufficient to show that: (1) in every terminal configuration γ, $\forall p, q \in V$, $Leader(p) = Leader(q)$ and $Leader(p)$ is the ID of some process; (2) every execution is finite.

3   Algorithm $\mathcal{LE}$

In this section, we present a silent and self-stabilizing leader election algorithm, called $\mathcal{LE}$. Its formal code is given in Algorithm 1. Starting from an arbitrary configuration, $\mathcal{LE}$ converges to a terminal configuration, where the process of minimum ID, ℓ, is elected. More precisely, in the terminal configuration, every process p knows the identifier of ℓ thanks to its local variable $p.idR$. This means that, in particular, we instantiate the function $Leader$ of the specification as follows: $Leader(p) = p.idR$, $\forall p \in V$. Moreover, a spanning tree rooted at ℓ is defined using two variables per process: *par* and *level*. First, $\ell.par = \ell$ and $\ell.level = 0$. Then, for every process $p \neq \ell$, $p.par$ points to the parent of p in the tree and $p.level$ is the level of p in the tree.

We now present a simple algorithm for the leader election in Subsection 3.1. We show why this algorithm is not self-stabilizing in Subsection 3.2. We explain in Subsection 3.3 how to modify this algorithm to make it self-stabilizing.

3.1   Non Self-stabilizing Leader Election

We first consider a simplified version of $\mathcal{LE}$. Starting from a predefined initial configuration, it elects ℓ in all idR variables and builds a spanning tree rooted at ℓ. Initially, every process p declares itself as leader: $p.idR = p$, $p.par = p$, and $p.level = 0$. So, p satisfies the two following predicates: $SelfRoot(p) \equiv (p.par = p)$ and $SelfRootOk'(p) \equiv (p.level = 0) \wedge (p.idR = p)$. Note that, in the sequel, we say that p is a *self root* when $SelfRoot(p)$ holds. From such an initial configuration, our non self-stabilizing algorithm consists in the following single action:

$$J\text{-}Action' :: \exists q \in \mathcal{N}_p, (q.idR < p.idR) \rightarrow p.par \leftarrow \min_{\preceq}\{q \in \mathcal{N}_p\};$$
$$p.idR \leftarrow p.par.idR;$$
$$p.level \leftarrow p.par.level + 1;$$

where $\forall x, y \in V, x \preceq y \Leftrightarrow (x.idR \leq y.idR) \wedge [(x.idR = y.idR) \Rightarrow (x < y)]$

Informally, when p discovers that $p.idR$ is not equal to the minimum identifier, it updates its variables accordingly. Let q be the neighbor of p having idR minimum. Then, p selects q as new parent ($p.par \leftarrow q$ and $p.level \leftarrow p.par.level + 1$) and sets

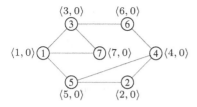

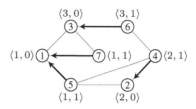

(a) Initial configuration. $SelfRoot(p) \wedge$ $SelfRootOk'(p)$ holds for every process p.

(b) 4, 5, 6, and 7 have executed $J\text{-}Action'$. Note that $J\text{-}Action'$ was not enabled at 2 because it is a local minimum.

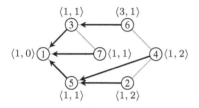

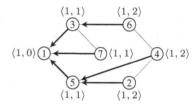

(c) 2, 3, and 4 have executed $J\text{-}Action'$. 3 joins the tree rooted at 1, but the new value of $3.idR$ is not yet propagated to its child 6.

(d) 6 has executed $J\text{-}Action'$. The configuration is now terminal, $\ell = 1$ is elected, and a tree rooted at ℓ is available.

Fig. 1. An example showing an execution of the non self-stabilizing algorithm. Process identifiers are given inside the nodes. $\langle x, y \rangle$ means $idR = x$ and $level = y$. Arrows represent par pointers. The absence of arrow means that the process is a self root.

$p.idR$ to the value of $q.idR$. If there are several neighbors having idR minimum, the identifiers of those neighbors are used to break ties.

Hence, the identifier of ℓ is propagated, from neighbors to neighbors, into the idR variables and the system reaches a terminal configuration in $O(\mathcal{D})$ rounds. Figure 1 shows an example of such an execution.

Notice first that for every process p, $p.idR$ is always less than or equal to its own identifier. Indeed, $p.idR$ is initialized to p and decreases each time p executes $J\text{-}Action'$. Hence, $p.idR = p$ while p is a self root and after p executes $J\text{-}Action'$ for the first time, $p.idR$ is smaller than its ID forever.

Second, even in this simplified context, for each two neighbors p and q such that q is the parent of p, it may happen that $p.idR$ is greater than $q.idR$ — an example is shown in Figure 1c, where $p = 6$ and $q = 3$. This is due to the fact that p joins the tree of q but meanwhile q joins another tree and this change is not yet propagated to p. Similarly, when $p.idR \neq q.idR$, $p.level$ may be different from $q.level + 1$.

According to those remarks, we can deduce that when $p.par = q$ with $q \neq p$, we have the following relation between p and q:

$$GoodIdR(p, q) \equiv (p.idR \geq q.idR) \wedge (p.idR < p)$$
$$GoodLevel(p, q) \equiv (p.idR = q.idR) \Rightarrow (p.level = q.level + 1)$$

3.2 Fake IDs

The algorithm presented in Subsection 3.1 is clearly not self-stabilizing. Indeed, in a self-stabilization context, the execution may start in any arbitrary configuration. In par-

$\langle 1,1 \rangle$ $\langle 3,0 \rangle$ $\langle 4,0 \rangle$ $\langle 1,1 \rangle$ $\langle 1,1 \rangle$ $\langle 1,2 \rangle$ $\langle 1,2 \rangle$ $\langle 1,1 \rangle$

②——③——④——⑤   ②◄——③——④——►⑤

(a) Illegitimate initial configuration, where 2   (b) 3 and 4 executed $J\text{-}Action'$. The configu-
and 5 have fake idR.   ration is now terminal.

Fig. 2. Example of execution that does not converge to a legitimate configuration

ticular, idR variables can be initialized to arbitrary natural integer values, even values
that are actually not IDs of (existing) processes. We call such values *fake IDs*.

The existence of fake IDs may lead the system to an illegitimate terminal configuration. Refer to the example of execution given in Figure 2: starting from the configuration
in 2a, if processes 3 and 4 move, the system reaches the terminal configuration given in
2b, where there are two trees and the idR variables elect the fake ID 1. In this example,
2 and 5 can detect the problem. Indeed, predicate $SelfRootOk'$ is violated by both 2
and 5. One may believe that it is sufficient to reset the local state of processes which detect inconsistency (here processes 2 and 5) to $p.idR \leftarrow p$, $p.par \leftarrow p$ and $p.level \leftarrow 0$.
After these resets, there are still some errors, as shown on Figure 3. Again, 3 and 4 can
detect the problem. Indeed, predicate $GoodIdR(p, p.par) \wedge GoodLevel(p, p.par)$ is
violated by both 3 and 4. In this example, after 3 and 4 have reset, all inconsistencies
have been removed. So let define the following action:

$R\text{-}Action' :: \big(SelfRoot(p) \wedge \neg SelfRootOk'(p)\big) \vee \big(\neg SelfRoot(p) \rightarrow p.par \leftarrow p;$
$\wedge \neg(GoodIdR(p, p.par) \wedge GoodLevel(p, p.par))\big) \qquad\qquad p.idR \leftarrow p;$
$\qquad\qquad\qquad\qquad\qquad\qquad\qquad\qquad\qquad\qquad\qquad\qquad\qquad p.level \leftarrow 0;$

$\langle 2,0 \rangle$ $\langle 1,2 \rangle$ $\langle 1,2 \rangle$ $\langle 5,0 \rangle$

②◄——③——④——►⑤

Fig. 3. One step after Figure 2b, 2 and 5 have reset

Unfortunately, this additional action does not ensure the convergence in all cases
— refer to the example in Figure 4. Indeed, if a process resets, it becomes a self root
but this does not erase the fake ID in the rest of its subtree. Then, another process can
join the tree and adopt the fake ID which will be further propagated, and so on. In the
example, a process resets while another joins its tree at lower level, and this leads to
endless erroneous behavior, since we do not want to assume any maximal value for
level (such an assumption would otherwise imply the knowledge of some upper bound
on n). Therefore, the whole tree must be reset, instead of its root only. To that goal, we
first freeze the "abnormal" tree in order to forbid any process to join it, then the tree is
reset top-down. The cleaning mechanism is detailed in the next subsection.

3.3 Cleaning Abnormal Trees

To introduce the trees, we define what is a "good relation" between a parent and its
children. Namely, the predicate $KinshipOk'(p, q)$ models that a process p is a *real
child* of its parent $q = p.par$. This predicate holds if and only if $GoodLevel(p, q)$ and
$GoodIdR(p, q)$ are true. This relation defines a spanning forest: a *tree* is a maximal set
of processes connected by *par* pointers and satisfying $KinshipOk'$ relation. A process p is a root of such a tree whenever $SelfRoot(p)$ holds or $KinshipOk'(p, p.par)$

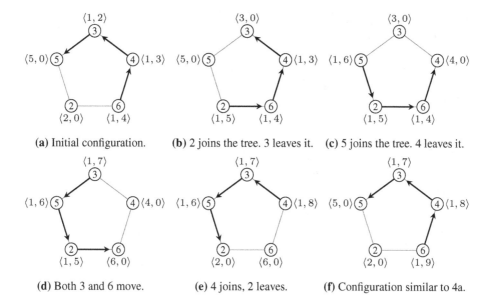

(a) Initial configuration.   **(b)** 2 joins the tree. 3 leaves it.   **(c)** 5 joins the tree. 4 leaves it.

(d) Both 3 and 6 move.   **(e)** 4 joins, 2 leaves.   **(f)** Configuration similar to 4a.

Fig. 4. The first process of the chain of bold arrows violates the predicate $SelfRootOk'$ and resets by executing $R\text{-}Action'$, while another process joins its tree. This cycle of resets and joins might never terminate.

is false. When $SelfRoot(p) \wedge SelfRootOk'(p)$ is true, p is a *normal root* just as in the non self-stabilizing case. In other cases, there is an error and p is called an *abnormal root*: $AbRoot'(p) \equiv \big(SelfRoot(p) \wedge \neg SelfRootOk'(p)\big) \vee \big(\neg SelfRoot(p) \wedge \neg KinshipOk'(p, p.par)\big)$. A tree is said to be *abnormal* (resp. *normal*) when its root is abnormal (resp. normal).

We now detail the different predicates and actions of Algorithm 1.

Variable status. Abnormal trees need to be frozen before to be cleaned in order to prevent them from growing endlessly (see 3.2). This mechanism is achieved using an additional variable, *status*, that is used as follows. If a process is clean (*i.e.*, not involved into any freezing operation), then its *status* is C. Otherwise, it has status EB or EF and no neighbor can select it as its parent. These two latter states are actually used to perform a "Propagation of Information with Feedback" [7] into the abnormal trees. Status EB means "Error Broadcast" and EF means "Error Feedback". From an abnormal root, the status EB is broadcast down in the tree. Then, once the EB wave reaches a leaf, the leaf initiates a convergecast EF-wave. Once the EF-wave reaches the abnormal root, the tree is said to be *dead*, meaning that there is no process of status C in the tree and no other process can join it. So, the tree can be safely reset from the abnormal root toward the leaves. Notice that the new variable *status* may also get arbitrary initialization. Thus, we enforce previously introduced predicates as follows. A self root must have status C, otherwise it is an abnormal root:

$$SelfRootOk(p) \equiv SelfRootOk'(p) \wedge (p.status = C)$$

Algorithm 1. Algorithm $\mathcal{LE}$ for every process p

Variables: $p.idR \in \mathbb{N}; p.par \in \mathcal{N}_p \cup \{p\}; p.level \in \mathbb{N}; p.status \in \{C, EB, EF\}$;

Macros:

$Children_p \equiv \{q \in \mathcal{N}_p \mid q.par = p\}$

$RealChildren_p \equiv \{q \in Children_p \mid KinshipOk(q, p)\}$

$p \preceq q \equiv (p.idR \le q.idR) \wedge [(p.idR = q.idR) \Rightarrow (p \le q)]$

$Min_p \equiv \min_{\preceq} \{q \in \mathcal{N}_p \mid q.status = C\}$

Predicates:

$SelfRoot(p) \equiv p.par = p$

$SelfRootOk(p) \equiv (p.level = 0) \wedge (p.idR = p) \wedge (p.status = C)$

$GoodIdR(s, f) \equiv (s.idR \ge f.idR) \wedge (s.idR < s)$

$GoodLevel(s, f) \equiv (s.idR = f.idR) \Rightarrow (s.level = f.level + 1)$

$GoodStatus(s, f) \equiv [(s.status = EB) \Rightarrow (f.status = EB)]$
$\qquad\qquad \vee [(s.status = EF) \Rightarrow (f.status \ne C)]$
$\qquad\qquad \vee [(s.status = C) \Rightarrow (f.status \ne EF)]$

$KinshipOk(s, f) \equiv GoodIdR(s, f) \wedge GoodLevel(s, f) \wedge GoodStatus(s, f)$

$AbRoot(p) \equiv [SelfRoot(p) \wedge \neg SelfRootOk(p)]$
$\qquad\qquad \vee [\neg SelfRoot(p) \wedge \neg KinshipOk(p, p.par)]$

$Allowed(p) \equiv \forall q \in Children_p, (\neg KinshipOk(q, p) \Rightarrow q.status \ne C)$

Guards:

$EBroadcast(p) \equiv (p.status = C) \wedge [AbRoot(p) \vee (p.par.status = EB)]$

$EFeedback(p) \equiv (p.status = EB) \wedge (\forall q \in RealChildren_p, q.status = EF)$

$Reset(p) \equiv (p.status = EF) \wedge AbRoot(p) \wedge Allowed(p)$

$Join(p) \equiv (p.status = C) \wedge [\exists q \in \mathcal{N}_p, (q.idR < p.idR) \wedge (q.status = C)]$
$\qquad\qquad \wedge Allowed(p)$

Actions:

$EB\text{-}action :: EBroadcast(p) \qquad\qquad \rightarrow p.status \leftarrow EB;$

$EF\text{-}action :: EFeedback(p) \qquad\qquad \rightarrow p.status \leftarrow EF;$

$R\text{-}action \quad :: Reset(p) \qquad\qquad \rightarrow p.status \leftarrow C; p.par \leftarrow p;$
$\qquad\qquad\qquad\qquad\qquad\qquad\qquad p.idR \leftarrow p; p.level \leftarrow 0;$

$J\text{-}action \quad :: Join(p) \wedge \neg EBroadcast(p) \rightarrow p.par \leftarrow Min_p; p.idR \leftarrow p.par.idR;$
$\qquad\qquad\qquad\qquad\qquad\qquad\qquad p.level \leftarrow p.par.level + 1;$

To be a real child of q, p should have a status coherent with the one of q. This is expressed with the predicate $GoodStatus(p, q)$ which is used to enforce the $KinshipOk(p, q)$ relation:

$$GoodStatus(p, q) \equiv [(p.status = EB) \Rightarrow (q.status = EB)]$$
$$\vee [(p.status = EF) \Rightarrow (q.status \ne C)]$$
$$\vee [(p.status = C) \Rightarrow (q.status \ne EF)]$$
$$KinshipOk(p, q) \equiv KinshipOk'(p, q) \wedge GoodStatus(p, q)$$

Precisely, when p has status C, its parent must have status C or EB (if the EB-wave is not propagated yet to p). If p has status EB, then the status of its parent must be EB because p gets status EB from its parent q and q will change its status to EF only after p gets status EF. Finally, if p has status EF, its parent can have status EB (if the EF-wave is not propagated yet to its parent) or EF.

Normal Execution. Remark that, after all abnormal trees have been removed, all processes have status C and the algorithm works as in the initial version. Notice that the guard of *J-action* has been enforced so that only processes with status C and which are not abnormal root can execute it, and when executing *J-action*, a process can only choose a neighbor of status C as parent. Moreover, remark that the cleaning of all abnormal trees does not ensure that all fake IDs have been removed. Rather, it guarantees the removal of all fake IDs smaller than ℓ. This implies that (at least) ℓ is a self root at the end of the cleaning and all other processes will elect ℓ within the next $\mathcal{D}$ rounds.

Cleaning Abnormal Trees. Figure 5 shows how an abnormal tree is cleaned. In the first phase (see Figure 5a), the root broadcasts status EB down to its (abnormal) tree: all the processes in this tree execute *EB-action*, switch to status *EB* and are consequently informed that they are in an abnormal tree. The second phase starts when the *EB*-wave reaches a leaf. Then, a convergecast wave of status *EF* is initiated thanks to action *EF-action* (see Figure 5b). The system is asynchronous, hence all the processes along some branch can have status *EF* before the broadcast of the *EB*-wave is done into another branch. In this case, the parent of these two branches waits that all its children in the tree (processes in the set *RealChildren*) get status *EF* before executing *EF-action* (Figure 5c). When the root gets status *EF*, all processes have status *EF*: the tree is dead. Then (third phase), the root can reset (safely) to become a self root by executing *R-action* (Figure 5e). Its former real children (of status *EF*) become themselves abnormal roots of dead trees (Figure 5f) and reset.

Finally, we used the predicate $Allowed(p)$ to temporarily lock the parent of p in two particular situations — illustrated in Figure 6 — where p is enabled to switch its status from C to EB. These locks impact neither the correctness nor the complexity of $\mathcal{LE}$. Rather, they allow us to simplify the proofs by ensuring that, once enabled, *EB-action* remains continuously enabled until executed.

4   Correctness and Complexity Analysis

First, remark that idR and $level$ can be stored in $\Theta(\log n)$ bits. So, the memory requirement of $\mathcal{LE}$ is $\Theta(\log n)$ bits per process.

Let us first distinguish between *clean* and *dirty* configurations. Given any configuration γ, γ is *clean* if and only if in γ, $\forall p \in V, \neg EBroadcast(p) \wedge p.status = C$. In other words, a configuration is clean if and only if it contains no abnormal trees. In particular, such a clean configuration does not contain fake IDs smaller than ℓ. Any configuration that is not clean is said to be *dirty*.

4.1   Correctness and Stabilization Time in Steps

Convergence from a Clean Configuration. Let us first consider any *clean* configuration, γ. As γ is clean, γ may contain some fake IDs, but all of them (if any) are greater than ℓ. This implies, in particular, that ℓ is a self root and $\ell.idR = \ell$ forever from γ. Moreover, in γ there are at most n different values disseminated into the idR variables. Every process $p \neq \ell$ can only decrease its own value of idR by executing *J-action* (all other actions are disabled forever at p because they deal with abnormal trees). Hence, overall after at most $\frac{(n-1) \times (n-2)}{2}$ executions of *J-action*, the configuration is terminal and ℓ is elected.

Convergence from an Arbitrary Configuration. The remainder of the proof consists in showing that, from any arbitrary configuration, a clean configuration is reached in $O(n^3)$ steps. So, let consider a dirty configuration γ. Then, γ contains some abnormal trees. In the following, we say that a process p is called *alive* if and only if $p.status = C$. Otherwise, it is said to be *dead*. By extension, a tree T is called an *alive tree* if and only if $\exists p \in T$ such that p is alive. Otherwise, it is called a *dead tree*.

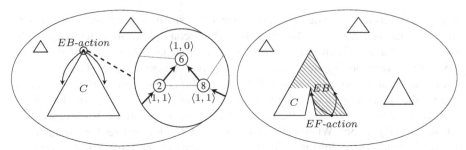

(a) When an abnormal root detects an error, it executes *EB-action*. The *EB*-wave is broadcast to the leaves. Here, 6 is an abnormal root because it is a self root and its *idR* is different from its ID ($1 \neq 6$).

(b) When the *EB*-wave reaches a leaf, it executes *EF-action*. The *EF*-wave is propagated up to the root.

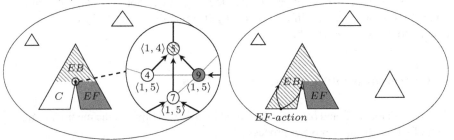

(c) It may happen that the *EF*-wave reaches a node, here process 5, even though the *EB*-wave is still broadcasting into some of its proper subtrees: 5 must wait that the status of 4 and 7 become *EF* before executing *EF-action*.

(d) *EB*-wave has been propagated in the other branch. An *EF*-wave is initiated by the leaves.

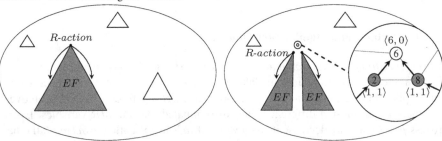

(e) *EF*-wave reaches the root. The root can safely reset (*R-action*) because its tree is dead. The cleaning wave is propagated down to the leaves.

(f) Its children become themselves abnormal roots of dead trees and can execute *R-action*: 2 and 8 can clean because their status is *EF* and their parent has status *C*.

Fig. 5. Schematic example of the cleaning mechanism. Trees are filled according to the status of their processes: white for C, dashed for EB, gray for EF.

We first show that no abnormal alive tree can be created from γ. So, as there are at most n abnormal alive trees in the initial configuration, and each of them may contain

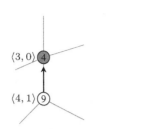

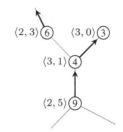

(a) 4 and 9 are abnormal roots. If 4 executes *R-action* before 9 executes *EB-action*, the kinship relation between 4 and 9 becomes correct and 9 is no more an abnormal root. Then, *EB-action* is no more enabled at 9.

(b) 9 is an abnormal root and Min_4 is 6. If 4 executes *J-action* before 9 executes *EB-action*, the kinship relation between 4 and 9 becomes correct and 9 is no more an abnormal root. Then, *EB-action* is no more enabled at 9.

Fig. 6. Example of situations where the parent of a process is locked

up to n processes, at most n^2 *EB-action*, *EF-action*, and *R-action* respectively are sufficient to freeze and remove all them. Notice that this way we clean abnormal trees is the main difference between our algorithm $\mathcal{LE}$ and the algorithm proposed in [10], $\mathcal{DLV}$. Indeed, we have shown that, contrary to $\mathcal{LE}$, the correction mechanism implemented in $\mathcal{DLV}$ can involve a non-polynomial number of correction actions (see [2]).

Nevertheless, processes can execute *J-action* during the removal of abnormal trees. In particular, a process p can leave an abnormal alive tree T by executing *J-action* to join another (normal or abnormal) tree. However, in this case the value of $p.idR$ necessarily decreases. Later p can join T again, but this may happen only if p executes actions *EB-action*, *EF-action*, and *R-action* at least once in the meantime. This means that p participates to the removal of some abnormal tree. Thus, each time p joins T again, the number of abnormal trees decreases, *i.e.*, p can join and leave T at most $n - 1$ times.

Thus, each process (n) can join each abnormal tree (at most n) at most $n - 1$ times using *J-action* which gives an overall number of *J-action*s in $O(n^3)$.

To sum up, starting from any configuration, a terminal configuration where ℓ is elected is reached in $O(n^3)$ steps. (We prove a tighter bound in [2].)

4.2 Stabilization Time in Rounds

Let us consider a clean configuration γ. Again, γ may contain some fake IDs, but all of them (if any) are greater than ℓ. This implies, in particular, that ℓ is a self root and $\ell.idR = \ell$ forever from γ. ℓ being the minimum value in idR variables, ℓ is propagated, from neighbors to neighbors, into the idR variables and the system reaches a terminal configuration in $O(\mathcal{D})$ rounds.

Consider now a dirty configuration γ. From γ, all abnormal trees are frozen and removed in parallel using three waves: (1) the broadcast of the value EB from the abnormal roots to the leaves, (2) a convergecast of the value EF from the leaves to the abnormal roots, and (3) finally, the cleaning is performed top-down. As the maximum height of a tree is n, each of these waves is done in at most n rounds. Overall, abnormal trees are removed in at most $3n$ rounds.

Hence, the stabilization time is at most $3n + \mathcal{D}$ rounds.

5 Conclusion

We proposed a silent self-stabilizing leader election algorithm, called $\mathcal{LE}$, for bidirectional connected identified networks of arbitrary topology. Starting from any arbitrary configuration, $\mathcal{LE}$ converges to a terminal configuration, where all processes know the ID of the leader, this latter being the process of minimum ID. Moreover, as in most of the solutions from the literature, a distributed spanning tree rooted at the leader is defined in the terminal configuration.

$\mathcal{LE}$ is written in the locally shared memory model. It assumes the distributed unfair daemon, the most general scheduling hypothesis of the model. Moreover, it requires no global knowledge on the network (such as an upper bound on the diameter or the number of processes, for example). $\mathcal{LE}$ is asymptotically optimal in space, as it requires $\Theta(\log n)$ bits per process, where n is the size of the network. We analyzed its stabilization time both in rounds and steps. We showed that $\mathcal{LE}$ stabilizes in at most $3n + \mathcal{D}$ rounds, where $\mathcal{D}$ is the diameter of the network. We have also proven in the technical report [2] that for every $n \geq 4$, for every $\mathcal{D}, 2 \leq \mathcal{D} \leq n - 2$, there is a network of n processes in which a possible execution exactly lasts this complexity.

Finally, we proved that $\mathcal{LE}$ achieves a stabilization time polynomial in steps. More precisely, we have shown in the technical report [2] that its stabilization time is at most $\frac{n^3}{2} + 2n^2 + \frac{n}{2} + 1$ steps. Still in [2], we have shown that for every $n \geq 4$, there exists a network of n processes (and of diameter 2) in which a possible execution exactly lasts $\frac{n^3}{6} + \frac{5}{2}n^2 - \frac{11}{3}n + 2$ steps, establishing then that the worst case is in $\Theta(n^3)$.

Perspectives of this work deal with complexity issues. In [10], Datta *et al* showed that it is easy to implement a silent self-stabilizing leader election which works assuming an unfair daemon, uses $\Theta(\log n)$ bits per process, and stabilizes in $O(D)$ rounds (where D is an upper bound on $\mathcal{D}$). Nevertheless, processes are assumed to *know* D. It is worth investigating whether it is possible to design an algorithm which works assuming an unfair daemon, uses $\Theta(\log n)$ bits per process, and stabilizes in $O(\mathcal{D})$ rounds without using any global knowledge. We believe this problem remains difficult, even adding some fairness assumption.

References

1. Afek, Y., Bremler-Barr, A.: Self-Stabilizing Unidirectional Network Algorithms by Power Supply. Chicago J. Theor. Comput. Sci. 1998 (1998)
2. Altisen, K., Cournier, A., Devismes, S., Durand, A., Petit, F.: Self-Stabilizing Leader Election in Polynomial Steps. Tech. rep., CNRS (2014),
   http://hal.archives-ouvertes.fr/hal-00980798
3. Arora, A., Gouda, M.G.: Distributed Reset. IEEE Trans. Computers 43(9), 1026–1038 (1994)
4. Awerbuch, B., Kutten, S., Mansour, Y., Patt-Shamir, B., Varghese, G.: Time Optimal Self-stabilizing Synchronization. In: STOC, pp. 652–661 (1993)
5. Blin, L., Tixeuil, S.: Brief Announcement: Deterministic Self-stabilizing Leader Election with O(log log n)-bits. In: PODC, pp. 125–127 (2013)

6. Burman, J., Kutten, S.: Time Optimal Asynchronous Self-stabilizing Spanning Tree. In: Pelc, A. (ed.) DISC 2007. LNCS, vol. 4731, pp. 92–107. Springer, Heidelberg (2007)
7. Chang, E.J.H.: Echo Algorithms: Depth Parallel Operations on General Graphs. IEEE Trans. Software Eng. 8(4), 391–401 (1982)
8. Datta, A.K., Larmore, L.L., Piniganti, H.: Self-stabilizing Leader Election in Dynamic Networks. In: Dolev, S., Cobb, J., Fischer, M., Yung, M. (eds.) SSS 2010. LNCS, vol. 6366, pp. 35–49. Springer, Heidelberg (2010)
9. Datta, A.K., Larmore, L.L., Vemula, P.: An O(n)-time Self-stabilizing Leader Election Algorithm. J. Parallel Distrib. Comput. 71(11), 1532–1544 (2011)
10. Datta, A.K., Larmore, L.L., Vemula, P.: Self-stabilizing Leader Election in Optimal Space under an Arbitrary Scheduler. Theor. Comput. Sci. 412(40), 5541–5561 (2011)
11. Dijkstra, E.W.: Self-stabilizing Systems in Spite of Distributed Control. Commun. ACM 17(11), 643–644 (1974)
12. Dolev, S., Gouda, M.G., Schneider, M.: Memory Requirements for Silent Stabilization. Acta Inf. 36(6), 447–462 (1999)
13. Dolev, S., Herman, T.: Superstabilizing Protocols for Dynamic Distributed Systems. Chicago J. Theor. Comput. Sci. (1997)
14. Kravchik, A., Kutten, S.: Time Optimal Synchronous Self Stabilizing Spanning Tree. In: Afek, Y. (ed.) DISC 2013. LNCS, vol. 8205, pp. 91–105. Springer, Heidelberg (2013)

Disconnected Components Detection and Rooted Shortest-Path Tree Maintenance in Networks[*]

Glacet Christian[1], Hanusse Nicolas[2], Ilcinkas David[2], and Johnen Colette[1]

[1] Univ. Bordeaux, LaBRI, UMR 5800, F-33400 Talence, France
[2] CNRS, LaBRI, UMR 5800, F-33400 Talence, France

Abstract. Many articles deal with the problem of maintaining a rooted shortest-path tree. However, after some edge deletions, some nodes can be disconnected from the connected component V_r of some distinguished node r. In this case, an additional objective is to ensure the detection of the disconnection by the nodes that no longer belong to V_r. Without any assumption on the asynchronous model (*unfair* daemon), with no knowledge of the network and within an anonymous network, we present a silent self-stabilizing algorithm solving this more demanding task and running in less than $2n + D$ rounds for a network of n nodes and hop-diameter D.

1 Introduction

Routing algorithms using the computation of distance/path vectors, like RIP (*Routing information protocol*) or BGP (*Border Gateway Protocol*), are based on the construction of shortest-path trees. For any destination r, a shortest-path tree rooted at r is implicitly built by the routing scheme. Because of the dynamicity of the network, it may happen that the network is disconnected. Routing to node r is only guaranteed from the nodes that belong to the same component as r, namely V_r. For the other nodes, one should remove, in the routing tables, information to reach r in order to prevent routing messages that will anyway never reach r, and thus to save some bandwidth. A legitimate configuration is characterized by the fact that every node that belongs to V_r knows a route to r and every other node detects that r is not in its own component. The difficulty of converging toward a legitimate configuration is called, in this context, the count-to-infinity problem [LGW04]: for nodes that do not belong to V_r, some control messages keep on being exchanged infinitely in order to find a path to r. At the same time, the updates of routing tables for nodes belonging to V_r should be done as fast as possible.

In practice, the most standard technics consist in exchanging distance/path vectors periodically and in using some timers in order to guess if a node is still within V_r. However, the convergence is not guaranteed without any assumption

[*] Partially supported by the ANR project DISPLEXITY (ANR-11-BS02-014). This study has been carried out in the frame of "the Investments for the future" Programme IdEx Bordeaux – CPU (ANR-10-IDEX-03-02).

P. Felber and V. Garg (Eds.): SSS 2014, LNCS 8756, pp. 120–134, 2014.

(i) on the asynchrony of the network and/or (ii) on some known upper bound on the diameter or the size of the network. The convergence toward a legitimate configuration can be often provided by self-stabilizing algorithms. However, solutions that can be found in the literature are dedicated to the maintenance of a BFS tree or shortest paths, but only for connected networks. Using them, we still face the count-to-infinity problem in the disconnected components.

In the routing context, it is not always required to store information for every node. In compact routing schemes [AGM+08, GGHI13], only some shortest-path trees completely spanning the connected components are built and need to be maintained. Given a set of roots $r_1, r_2, \ldots, r_k$, we aim at providing silent self-stabilizing algorithms that both maintain a shortest-path tree toward each r_i, for nodes of V_{r_i}, and detect the nodes that no longer belong to V_{r_i}. In the following, we present two algorithms for a single root for an *unfair daemon* but our solutions hold for any k. The identifiers of nodes do not need to be unique. Only r_i's identifiers should be different in order to distinguish the different roots. Thus, for $k = 1$, our self-stabilizing algorithms work in anonymous networks in the semi-uniform model.

1.1   Related Works

Self-stabilizing single-destination shortest-path constructions. The single-destination shortest-path problem is to find shortest paths from all vertices in the graph to a single destination vertex r. Edges can have weights and the length of a path corresponds to its sum of weights. The oldest distributed algorithms are inspired by the Bellman-Ford algorithm. In the articles dedicated to self-stabilizing algorithms, the difficulty is to find an algorithm running in the worst sequence of processes execution in an asynchronous setting. Models of processes execution are called *daemons*. In [CS94, HL02], self-stabilizing algorithms for the single-destination shortest-path problem are presented; both protocols require a central daemon, that is only one process can be executed at each instant. In [Hua05b], Tetz Huang proves that the algorithms in [CS94, HL02] also work under the unfair daemon, which is the most general daemon. However, no upper bounds on the time (rounds or number of execution steps) are given. The same author presents an algorithm under the read/write separate atomicity model (Dolev Model) in [Hua05a].

In [AGH90, CG02, JT03], self-stabilizing algorithms for the single-destination shortest-path problem are presented; these algorithms ensure the loop-free property: after any edge cost changes, even during the re-building phase, there is always a path from any node to the destination. To sum up, none of these articles provide tight bounds on the complexity of the convergence time in the most general asynchronous model, the unfair daemon, and the presented algorithms are not silent in the disconnected components.

Self-stabilizing breadth-first tree constructions. Whenever edges do not have any weight, shortest-path trees correspond to breadth-first trees. To our knowledge, this restriction does not help to get all the desirable guarantees. Chen et al.

present the first self-stabilizing BFS tree construction in [CYH91] under the central daemon. Huang et al. present the first self-stabilizing BFS tree construction in [HC92] under the unfair distributed daemon. In [CYH91, HC92], the exact network size has to be known by all nodes. Dolev, Israeli and Moran in [DIM93] present the first self-stabilizing BFS spanning-tree construction algorithm under read/write atomicity.

Blin et al. in [BPBRT10] present an universal transformer of self-stabilizing tree construction with any metric on semi-uniform networks to a loop-free super stabilizing algorithm under the fair daemon. All these cited works assume that the network is a connected graph.

Self-stabilizing routing algorithm. In [BDV07], Bein et al. present a self-stabilizing algorithm building local routing tables under the fair daemon (the tables ensure the routing from any node v to its t closest nodes) in $O(D)$ rounds in the connected component, in but $O(t)$ rounds within the disconnected component. Choosing the parameter t correctly helps to tackle the count-to-infinity problem. However, it means that in order to use their solution an upper bound on the network size has to be known.

Leader election algorithms. Surprisingly, one way to get closer to our goal is to focus on the problem of leader election, as in [DLV11, ACD$^+$14], under the very general daemon, the unfair one, without any knowledge about the network topology. In [DLV11] (resp. in [ACD$^+$14]), for each component, a BFS tree rooted at the selected leader is built within $4n + 11D + 4$ rounds (resp. $3n + D$ rounds). Note that D stands for the diameter of the unweighted network.

Since, in each component, the selected leader is the node with smallest identifier, one could change a little bit these uniform algorithms into semi-uniform algorithms, by forcing the node r to have the smallest identifier in adding a single bit to every identifiers. However, this trick can work only for $k = 1$ and it is not clear what would be the convergence time for a weighted network.

1.2   Model

A distributed system S is an undirected graph $G = (V, E)$ where vertex set V is the set of nodes and edge set E is the set of communication links. A link $\{u, v\}$ belongs to E if and only if u and v can directly communicate (links are bidirectional); so, u and v are neighbors. We note by $\Gamma(v)$ the set of v's neighbors: $\Gamma(v) = \{u \in V \mid \{u, v\} \in E\}$. Edges have positive weight. In the following, D stands for the hop-diameter of the underlying graph, that is the maximum over all pairs $\{u, v\}$ of the minimum number of edges in a shortest path from u to v.

Each node v maintains a set of shared variables such that v can read its own variables and those of its neighbors, but it can modify only its variables. The *state* of a node is defined by the values of its local variables. The union of states of all nodes determines the *configuration* of the system. The *program* of each node is a set of *rules*. Each rule has two parts, the guard and the action. The *guard* of a v's rule is a Boolean expression involving the state of the node v, and those of its neighbors. The *action* of a v's rule updates v's state. So, every rule will be graphically described by two braces. The first brace contains the predicates such that their conjunction is the rule guard; and the second brace contains the rule action (i.e. one or several local variable updates).

A rule can be executed only if it is *enabled*, i.e., its guard evaluates to true. A node is *enabled* if at least one of its rules is enabled. A configuration is said to be *terminal* if and only if no node is enabled. In a semi-uniform algorithm, all nodes except one, denoted r, perform the same distributed algorithm. V_r denotes the connected component of distinguished node r. In anonymous networks, nodes do not have distinct identifiers. However, we assume that a node can distinguish its neighbors since out-links of every node can be locally numbered.

During a *computation step under the daemon S*, $c_i \rightarrow^S c_{i+1}$, one or several enabled nodes in configuration c_i are selected by the daemon S. Theses nodes will simultaneously and atomically read their neighbors states and then perform their actions so that the system reaches the configuration c_{i+1} from c_i. An *execution e under daemon S* is a sequence of configurations $e = c_0, c_1, \cdots$, where c_{i+1} is reached from c_i by one computation step under S: $\forall i \geqslant 0, c_i \rightarrow^S c_{i+1}$. The centralized daemon selects at each computation step only one node. The fair daemon may select several nodes at each step, but it produces only fair executions (an always enabled node is eventually activated). There is no requirement on the unfair daemon; so unfair executions are produced by the unfair daemon.

We say that an execution e is *maximal* if it is infinite, or if it reaches a terminal configuration. We note by $\mathcal{C}$ the set of all possible configurations, and by $\mathcal{E}^S$ the set of all maximal executions under the daemon S. The set of maximal executions under the daemon S starting from a particular configuration $c \in \mathcal{C}$ is denoted $\mathcal{E}_c^S$.

Definition 1 (Silent Self-stabilization to $\mathcal{L}$). *Let $\mathcal{L}$ be a subset of $\mathcal{C}$, called set of legitimate configurations. A distributed system is silent and self-stabilizing under the daemon S to $\mathcal{L}$ if and only if the following conditions hold:*

- *all executions under S are finite;*
- *all terminal configurations belong to $\mathcal{L}$.*

Stabilization Time. We use the *round* notion to measure the time complexity. The first round of an execution $e = c_1, c_2, \cdots$ is the minimal prefix $e_1 = c_1, \cdots, c_j$, such that every node having an enabled rule in c_1 either executes a rule or is neutralized during a computation step of e_1. A node v is *neutralized* during a computation step $c_i \rightarrow c_{i+1}$, if v is enabled in c_i but not anymore in configuration c_{i+1}.

Let e' be the suffix of e such that $e = e_1 e'$. The second round of e is the first round of e', and so on.

The stabilization time is the number of rounds of an execution reaching a legitimate configuration from any initial one.

Definition 2 (Round of a component). *The end of the $i+1$-st round in the (connected) component $H \subseteq G$ in a computation e is defined recursively as the configuration of the execution e where every node $v \in H(V)$ that was enabled at the end of the i-th round of e in H have been either activated or neutralized once.*

We can notice that the i-th round in a component $H \subseteq G$ can end earlier than the i-th round (when the component is not explicitly given then the round is global).

Definition 3 (Node convergence). *A node v is said to have converged to its final state s under the daemon S at the configuration c_1 if along all executions under S from c_1, the node v keeps its state s.*

1.3 Our Contributions

We present two self-stabilizing silent algorithms on anonymous semi-uniform weighted networks working under the unfair daemon. Both algorithms build a shortest-path tree rooted at r in V_r, and isolate the nodes in the other connected components.

We first present a simple distributed algorithm, namely Algorithm DcD, which is quite natural. We show that the convergence time may unfortunately be as high as $\Omega(n^2)$ rounds in some n-node graphs of large diameter.

Changing a little bit this algorithm, we end up with a second algorithm FDcD. This latter algorithm converges to a legitimate configuration within less than $2n + D$ rounds in any n-node weighted graph of hop-diameter D.

2 Our Algorithms

This section is devoted to the presentation of our two algorithms, DcD (Disconnection Detection) and FDcD (Fast Disconnection Detection). These algorithms are using the same key idea and are thus very similar (although their performances are different).

The value of variable st indicates the status of the node: I for isolated (the node has no parent and no children); E for erroneous and C for correct.

A non-isolated node u ($st_u \neq I$) has two other meaningful variables: the variable d_u containing the shortest weighted distance to r, and the variable $parent_u$ containing a pointer to the first out-link on the shortest path to r. Thus, only non-isolated nodes can belong to a branch (i.e. have children and/or a parent).

The single rule for node r is the same for both algorithms (Figure 1).

Definition 4 (Children of node u). $children_u =$
$$\{v \in \Gamma(u) \mid (st_u \neq I) \wedge (st_v \neq I) \wedge (parent_v = u) \wedge (d_v \geq d_u + \omega\{u, v\})\}$$

Definition 5 (Correct state). *A node u is said to be in a correct state if:*

$$R_r \begin{cases} \begin{cases} P_{\text{root}}(u) \equiv (st_r \neq C) \vee (parent_r \neq r) \vee (d_r \neq 0) \end{cases} \\ \begin{cases} st_r \leftarrow C \\ parent_r \leftarrow r \\ d_r \leftarrow 0 \end{cases} \end{cases}$$

Fig. 1. Algorithm DcD or FDcD on node r

- *its status variable is C,*
- *its distance variable is set to $d(u,r)$ the weighted distance from u to r and*
- *the weighted distance $d(parent_u, r)$ of $parent_u$ to r is $d_u - \omega\{u, parent_u\}$.*

Definition 6 (Legitimate state). *A node u is said to be in a legitimate state if:*

- *it belongs to V_r and is in a correct state;*
- *or it does not belong to V_r and it has status I.*

Definition 7 (Legitimate configuration). *A legitimate configuration is a configuration where every node is in a legitimate state.*

2.1 A First and Simple Algorithm : Algorithm DcD

Algorithm DcD is given in figure 2. It is roughly based on the following idea. Whenever a node detects a local anomaly, it somehow detaches from its parent, warns its whole sub-tree, and then reconnects to another tree.

A given node u detects an anomaly in the relationship with its parent in four cases:

- the parent node is not in its neighborhood;
- it is not the best out-link for the destination r;
- the value of d_u is not coherent with the value of d_{parent_u};
- it, or its parent, has not status C.

When a node u detects an anomaly in the relationship with its parent, it takes the status E (rule R_C). Notice that the error status is propagated in sub-trees. When a leaf has the error status, then it can quit its tree: either it becomes isolated (rule R_I) or it joins a "correct" branch (rule R_C). So any erroneous sub-trees are eventually deleted.

Only nodes with status C may gain new children; and only nodes without children may change the value of their variable d or *parent* (rule R_C) to join a new branch. These two properties ensure that the execution of the rule R_C by a node u does not create anomaly (because a node u doing R_C during a computation step has no children and it cannot gain children during this step).

We can show that algorithm DcD converges to a legitimate configuration. However, for graphs with large diameter ($D = \Theta(n)$) it may converge in $\Omega(n^2)$ rounds. This lower bound is based on a graph $\mathcal{G}_n$ defined right after and presented in Figure 3. It uses several copies of the undermentioned graph H_i.

$$R_C \begin{cases} \begin{cases} P_{\text{update}}(u) \equiv (st_u \neq C) \wedge (children_u = \emptyset) \wedge (\exists v \in \Gamma(u) \mid st_v = C) \end{cases} \\ \\ \begin{cases} st_u \leftarrow C \\ parent_u \leftarrow \text{argmin}_{(v \in \Gamma(u)) \wedge (st_v = C)}(d_v + \omega\{u,v\}) \\ d_u \leftarrow d_{parent_u} + \omega\{u, parent_u\} \end{cases} \end{cases}$$

$$R_E \begin{cases} \begin{cases} P_{\text{fullError}}(u) \equiv \big[(parent_u \notin \Gamma(u)) \vee (st_{parent_u} \neq C) \\ \qquad\qquad \vee (d_{parent_u} + \omega\{u, parent_u\} \neq d_u) \\ \qquad\qquad \vee (\exists v \in \Gamma(u) \mid (st_v = C) \wedge (d_v + \omega\{u,v\} < d_u))\big] \\ \qquad\qquad \wedge (st_u = C) \end{cases} \\ \\ \begin{cases} st_u \leftarrow E \end{cases} \end{cases}$$

$$R_I \begin{cases} \begin{cases} P_{\text{isolate}}(u) \equiv (st_u = E) \wedge (children_u = \emptyset) \wedge (\forall v \in \Gamma(u) \mid st_v \neq C) \end{cases} \\ \\ \begin{cases} st_u \leftarrow I \end{cases} \end{cases}$$

Fig. 2. Algorithm DcD on node u

Definition 8 (Graph H). *The graph called H is a 5-node graph composed by a path (a, b, c, e) where node e and a are connected together via an intermediate node f.*

Definition 9 (Graph $\mathcal{G}_n$). *The graph $\mathcal{G}_n$ is composed of n copies of graph H: $H_0, H_1, \ldots, H_{n-1}$. To build $\mathcal{G}_n$ simply connect every H_i to H_{i+1} by merging nodes e_i and a_{i+1} (the index indicates the copy).*

This graph $\mathcal{G}_n$ has $4n + 1$ nodes and diameter $2n$.

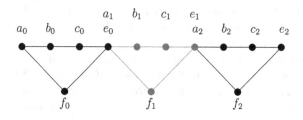

Fig. 3. $\mathcal{G}_3$ with the node names

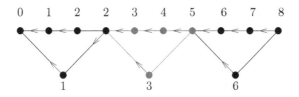

Fig. 4. Configuration X_1 of $\mathcal{G}_3$

Lemma 1. *For the graph $\mathcal{G}_n$ of $O(n)$ nodes, algorithm DcD may converge to a legitimate configuration within $\Omega(n^2)$ rounds.*

Proof. Let consider a graph $\mathcal{G}$ and set node a_0 to be the root of $\mathcal{G}_n$. In this proof we will mainly consider two possible configurations for any graph H_i:

- An *illegitimate configuration*, called ic, where nodes b_i, c_i, e_i, f_i have their parents variables respectively set to a_i, b_i, c_i, a_i, which leads node e_i to have its distance set to $d_{a_i} + 3$.
- And also the *legitimate configuration*, where nodes b_i, c_i, e_i, f_i have their parents variables respectively set to a_i, b_i, f_i, a_i and $d_{a_i} = 2i$. This leads node e_i to have its distance set to $2i + 2$.

First, we can notice that an illegitimate configuration can turn to a legitimate configuration for graph H_i only if node a_i already stores a distance of $2i$, which implies that every H_k such that $k < i$ is in legitimate state.

Let us define the configuration X_i for $0 \leq i \leq n$ as follow. The root node a_0 is in correct state, every H_k for $k < i$ is in the legitimate configuration and every H_j for $j \geq i$ is in the illegitimate configuration. The configuration X_1 is shown on figure 4 for $n = 3$. X_n is the legitimate configuration of $\mathcal{G}_n$.

We will study one execution from X_0 in which configurations X_i such that $i \in (1, 2, \ldots, n)$ are successively reached. This execution has n steps, during the ith step, configuration X_i is reached from configuration X_{i-1}.

Let us compute the number of rounds required to execute the $(i + 1)^{\text{th}}$ step. The node e_i has to switch its parent from c_i to f_i, resulting in changing its distance from $2i + 3$ to $2i + 2$. The difficulty is that to change its parent, node e_i must have the status I. The node e_i will get the status I only after the status E is propagated into e_i sub-tree which takes 3 rounds. After what, the status I is propagated from e_{n-1} to e_i which takes $3(n - i - 1)$ more rounds. Now, we need to bring every H_j such that $j > i$ into the illegitimate configuration. That can be done by activating successively, for every H_j such that $j > i$, every node except node f_j, after what the remaining nodes $(f_j \mid j > i)$ can be activated in an arbitrary order. Therefore, the $(i + 1)^{\text{th}}$ step takes at least $3(n - i - 1) + 3$ rounds.

In this execution, the total number of rounds needed to converge to the legitimate configuration on $\mathcal{G}_n$ is thus greater than $\sum_{i=1}^{n} 3(n - i)$. Which gives the lower bound of $\Omega(n^2)$. $\qquad\square$

2.2 A More Efficient Solution

With algorithm FDcD, presented in Figure 5, a node u joins a correct branch sooner than with algorithm DcD. Nevertheless, no anomaly is created when a node modifies the value of its variable d or *parent*.

When an anomaly is detected by a node u in the relationship with its parent, if there is an alternative parent to connect to, then u changes parent (rule R_C). Otherwise, u takes status E (rule R_E). Algorithm FDcD's rules are quite similar to DcD's, the only differences lie in R_C and R_E guards. A node p is an alternative parent for node u if it has status C and if :

- p is a better out-link than $parent_u$ (i.e. the cost of the path from u to r going through p is smaller than the cost of the path going through $parent_u$);
- or d_u matches d_p (i.e. $d_p + \omega\{p,u\} = d_u$).

Any configuration during the execution of algorithm FDcD induces a BFS tree rooted at node r that spans a subset of V_r, a forest rooted at different *illegal roots* and some isolated nodes.

$$
R_C \begin{cases}
\begin{cases}
P_{\text{create}}(u) \equiv (st_u \neq C) \wedge (children_u = \emptyset) \wedge (\exists v \in \Gamma(u) \mid st_v = C) \\
P_{\text{update}}(u) \equiv (\exists v \in \Gamma(u) \mid (st_v = C) \wedge (d_v + \omega\{u,v\} < d_u)) \\
P_{\text{correct}}(u) \equiv [\,(parent_u \notin \Gamma(u)) \vee (d_u \neq d_{parent_u} + \omega\{u, parent_u\}) \\
\qquad\qquad \vee (st_{parent_u} \neq C) \vee (st_u \neq C)\,] \\
\qquad\qquad \wedge [\exists v \in \Gamma(u) \mid (st_v = C) \wedge (d_v + \omega\{u,v\} = d_u)\,]
\end{cases} \\[2em]
\begin{cases}
st_u \leftarrow C \\
parent_u \leftarrow \text{argmin}_{(v \in \Gamma(u)) \wedge (st_v = C)}(d_v + \omega\{u,v\}) \\
d_u \leftarrow d_{parent_u} + \omega\{u, parent_u\}
\end{cases}
\end{cases}
$$

$$
R_E \begin{cases}
\begin{cases}
P_{\text{error}}(u) \equiv (st_u = C) \wedge (\forall v \in \Gamma(u) \mid (d_u < d_v + \omega\{(v,u)\}) \vee (st_v \neq C))
\end{cases} \\[1em]
\begin{cases}
st_u \leftarrow E
\end{cases}
\end{cases}
$$

$$
R_I \begin{cases}
\begin{cases}
P_{\text{isolate}}(u) \equiv (st_u = E) \wedge (children_u = \emptyset) \wedge (\forall v \in \Gamma(u) \mid st_v \neq C)
\end{cases} \\[1em]
\begin{cases}
st_u \leftarrow I
\end{cases}
\end{cases}
$$

Fig. 5. Algorithm FDcD on node u

3 Correctness and Convergence Time of Algorithm FDcD

All the proofs in this section hold for both algorithms, except Lemma 6 and thus Theorem 1, that hold only for Algorithm FDcD. We start this section by proving that the set of terminal configurations coincides with the set of legitimate configurations. This will be done thanks to the following two lemmas, the first one dealing with the connected components that do not contain node r, if some exist, and the second one dealing with the connected component V_r containing root node r.

Lemma 2. *For any connected component H not containing node r, any terminal configuration in H is a legitimate configuration.*

Proof. The proof is done by contradiction. So consider that for some connected component H not containing node r, there exists a terminal configuration in which at least one node has not status I.

Further assume that there exists some node that has status C. Consider the node $u \in H$ with status C having the smallest distance value d_u. By construction, u can apply rule R_E, which is in contradiction with the configuration being terminal. Therefore any node that does not have status I must have status E.

Consider now the node $u \in H$ that has status E having the largest distance value d_u. By construction and from the previous point, this node has no child and no neighbor have status C. Therefore node u can apply rule R_I, and we obtain again a contradiction, which concludes the proof of the lemma. $\square$

Lemma 3. *Any terminal configuration within the connected component V_r is legitimate.*

Proof. The proof is done by contradiction. Let consider it exists some non-legitimate terminal configuration of the connected component V_r.

Further, assume that there exists some node that has status E. Consider the node u of V_r with status E having the largest distance value d_u. Note that no node v that has status C can be a child of u, otherwise v could apply rule R_E or rule R_C. Therefore, node u has no child and thus can apply rule R_I or rule R_C, a contradiction.

Nodes have thus either status C or I. Assume now that there exists some node that has status I. Consider some node u with status I having at least one neighbor with status C. Such a neighbor node must exist because we are considering a connected component without any node with status E, but with at least one node that has status C, namely node r. Obviously, node u can apply rule R_C, a contradiction. So every node in V_r must have status C.

Now consider the node u in V_r having the smallest distance value d_u among the nodes in V_r that are not in a correct state. Then, either it exists some node v with status C in $\Gamma(u)$ such that $d_u \geq d_v + \omega\{u, v\}$, or not. If such a node v exists then node u can apply rule R_C. If it does not, then, by definition, it can apply rule R_E. In both those cases there is a contradiction, which concludes the proof. $\square$

After noticing that any legitimate configuration is a terminal one, we conclude with the following corollary.

Corollary 1. *The set of terminal configurations coincide with the set of legitimate configurations.*

We now prove that algorithm FDcD always terminates within $2n+D-2$ rounds under a fair daemon, where D is the hop-diameter of the connected component containing r. Before proceeding with the proof, let us introduce some useful concepts.

Definition 10 (Branch). *A branch is a maximal sequence of nodes $v_1, \cdots, v_k$, for some integer $k \geq 1$, such that none of the nodes have status I and, for every $i \leq k$, we have $v_i \in children_{v_{i+1}}$. The node v_i is said to be at depth $k - i$. If $v_k = r$ but the state of r is not terminal, or simply if $v_k \neq r$, the branch is said to be illegal, otherwise, the branch is said to be legal.*

The first lemma essentially claims that all nodes that are in illegal branches progressively switch to status E within n rounds, in order of increasing depth.

Lemma 4. *Fix any integer $i \geq 1$, and any connected component H. Starting from the beginning of round i in H, there does not exist any node of H both in state C and at depth less than $i - 1$ in an illegal branch.*

Proof. We prove this lemma by induction on i. The base case $i = 1$ is obvious so assume that the lemma holds for some integer $i \geq 1$. Consider any node u of H both with status C and depth $i - 1$ in an illegal branch. If $u = r$, then r executes R_r. Otherwise, by induction hypothesis, the parent of u is not in state C. Therefore u is enabled at the beginning of round i. During round i, it will either execute rule R_E and thus switch to state E, or it will execute rule R_C.

Note that, from the beginning of round i, no node can ever choose a parent which is at depth smaller than $i - 1$ in an illegal branch because those nodes will never be in state C, by induction hypothesis. Therefore, no node can become in state C at depth smaller than i. This is also true for node u if it applies rule R_C in round i. This concludes the proof of the lemma. $\square$

Root node r does not belong to an illegal branch after the first round. Therefore, after the first round, the number of nodes of an illegal branch cannot be more than $n - 1$. We thus obtain the following corollary.

Corollary 2. *For any connected component H, once round $n - 1$ in H has terminated, no node in an illegal branch in H has status C.*

The next lemma essentially claims that, within at most $n - 1$ subsequent rounds, the maximal length of an illegal branch progressively decreases until no illegal branches remain.

Lemma 5. *Fix any integer $i \geq 0$, any of the two algorithms, and any connected component H. Starting from the beginning of round $n + i$ in H, there does not exist any node of H at depth larger or equal to $n - i - 1$ in an illegal branch.*

Proof. We prove the lemma by induction on i. The base case $i = 0$ is obvious so assume that the lemma holds for some integer $i \geq 0$. By induction hypothesis, at the beginning of round $n + i$, no node is at depth larger or equal to $n - i - 1$.

Therefore, the nodes at depth $n - i - 2$ in an illegal branch have no children and are thus enabled at the beginning of round $n + i$. These nodes will thus all be executed within round $n + i$ (they cannot be neutralized as no children can connect to them). We conclude the proof by noticing that, from Corollary 2, once round $n - 1$ has terminated, every node in an illegal tree is in state E, and thus any node in an illegal branch that gets executed from this time will not be anymore in any illegal branch.   □

Corollary 3. *For any connected component H, once round $2n - 2$ in H has terminated, there are no illegal branches in H.*

Note that in a connected component that does not contain the root r, there are no legal branches. Since the only way for a node to be in no branch is to have status I, we obtain the following result.

Corollary 4. *For any connected component H not containing r, after $2n - 2$ rounds in H, every node v of H has status I.*

After $2n - 2$ rounds, the connected components not containing r are in a legitimate state. In the connected component V_r containing r, Algorithm FDcD may need additional rounds so that the correct distances to r are correctly propagated.

In the following lemma, we use the notion of hop-distance to r defined below.

Definition 11 (Hop-distance to the root node r). *A node v is said to be at k hops from r if k is the minimum number of edges of a shortest path from v to r.*

Lemma 6. *Consider any integer $i \geq 0$. For any execution of Algorithm FDcD, starting from the beginning of round $2n - 2 + i$, every node in component V_r at most i hops from r is in a correct state.*

Proof. Let us prove the lemma by induction on i. Firstly, we need to remark that after one single round, node r has necessary converged to the correct state. So the base case $i = 0$ holds, as we can assume n to be at least 2. Secondly, at round $2n-2$, from Corollary 3, every node either belongs to a legal branch or have status I, thus any node $v \in V_r$ always stores a distance d such that $d \geq d(v, r)$, its actual weighted distance to r. By induction hypothesis, every node at at most i hops from r has converged to a correct state before round $2n + i - 1$. Therefore, at the beginning of round $2n + i - 1$, every node v at $i + 1$ hops from r which is not in a correct state has rule R_C enabled. Thus, at the end of round $2n + i - 1$, every node at at most $i + 1$ hops from r is in a correct state (such nodes cannot be neutralized during this round). Also, these nodes will never change their state since there are no nodes other than their parent that can make them get closer to r than their current parent.   □

Note that algorithm DcD eventually reach an identical configuration where every node is either isolated or belongs to the tree rooted at r. But from this particular configuration algorithm DcD takes more time to converge to a legitimate state. We know from Lemma 1 that the convergence to a legitimate state can take at least $\Omega(n^2)$ additional rounds for some settings of graphs and configurations.

Putting together all the results of this section, we obtain, for algorithm FDcD, the following theorem.

Theorem 1. *Under a fair daemon, Algorithm* FDcD *always converges to a legitimate state within $2n + D - 2$ rounds, where D is the hop-diameter of the connected component V_r containing node r.*

4   Convergence under an Unfair Daemon

In this section, we will prove that algorithm FDcD always converges to a legitimate state, even under an unfair daemon. The proof, by contradiction, will go as follows. After noticing that a node activated infinitely often must execute rule R_C infinitely many times, we will prove that nodes activated infinitely often must have globally increasing distance values. This means that these nodes will eventually behave as if the nodes activated a finite number of times do not exist. This will lead to a contradiction, as we proved before that a connected component has to become silent after a finite number of rounds. Note that all the lemmas in this section also hold for Algorithm DcD.

Lemma 7. *If at some time a node has been executed k times, then it must have executed rule R_C at least $\left\lfloor \frac{k-2}{3} \right\rfloor$ many times.*

Proof. When a node with status E is enabled, it can either execute rule R_C or rule R_I. Moreover, a node with status I can only execute rule R_C. Thus between two consecutive executions of rule R_C by a node, only two other rule executions can happen.   □

Let us now introduce a useful notation for the next lemmas.

Definition 12. *A node u is said to execute a rule with (distance) value dist if the distance value d_u is equal to dist immediately after this rule execution.*

Lemma 8. *rule R_C cannot be executed infinitely often with the same distance value.*

Proof. For the purpose of contradiction, consider any (infinite) execution e of algorithm FDcD in which rule R_C is applied infinitely often with the same distance value. Let $d_{\min}$ be the minimum such infinitely often used value. Let v be some node applying infinitely often rule R_C with distance value $d_{\min}$. Now consider some suffix e' of e in which no node with a distance value smaller than $d_{\min}$ will ever apply any rule. Note that such a suffix e' must exist, by definition of $d_{\min}$.

Let consider the maximal suffix e'' of e' starting when node v has a parent u such that $d_u = d_{\min} - \omega\{u, v\}$. By definition of e', node u will remain in state C and be the better possible parent within e'', therefore node v will not apply any rule in e'', contradicting the assumption that node v applies infinitely often rule R_C.   □

We are now ready to conclude about the convergence under an unfair daemon.

Lemma 9. *Every execution is finite.*

Proof. For the purpose of contradiction, let us assume that there exists an infinite execution e. Let F, resp. $\overline{F}$, be the set of nodes executed finitely, resp. infinitely, many times in this execution, and let F' be the set of nodes in F that are neighbors of at least one node in $\overline{F}$. Note that the set F is necessarily non-empty as it contains at least node r.

Let execution e_1 be a suffix of e in which every node $v \in F$ is never executed. In e_1, only the nodes from $\overline{F}$ will be executed. Let $d_{\max}$ be the maximum distance stored in d_v for any node $v \in F$ within e_1. From Lemma 8, if a node executes an infinite number of steps during an execution of algorithm FDcD, then it will necessary change its distance an infinite number of times. Moreover, distances stored at a given node cannot be negative. Thus, there exists a suffix e_2 of e_1 such that for any node $\overline{v}$ in $\overline{F}$, $d_{\overline{v}} > d_{\max} + \omega_v$, where ω_v is the maximum weight of an edge incident to $\overline{v}$.

Within e_2, a node $v' \in F'$ cannot have status C, otherwise any node $\overline{v}$ that belongs to $\Gamma(v') \cap \overline{F}$ would apply R_C with distance value at most $d_{\max} + \omega\{\overline{v}, v'\}$ which would be in contradiction with the definition of e_2. Moreover, we have $d_{\overline{v}} > d_{v'}$, and thus v' does not belong to $children_{\overline{v}}$.

Looking at the algorithm, one can observe that, if a rule can be applied for a node $v \in \overline{F}$ during e_2, then it can still be applied after removing the nodes in F' from the graph. In other words, the nodes in $\overline{F}$ can have the same execution in the graph obtained after removing the nodes in F. Now consider any connected component H of $\overline{F}$. Since all nodes in H are activated infinitely many times, it means that there are an infinite number of rounds in H, without the nodes reaching a terminal configuration in H. This is in contradiction with Corollary 4, and this concludes the proof of this lemma.   □

Summarizing the results proved so far, we obtain the following main theorem.

Theorem 2. *Under an unfair daemon, Algorithm FDcD always converges to a legitimate state within a finite number of steps and in at most $2n + D - 2$ rounds, where D is the hop-diameter of the connected component V_r containing node r.*

References

[ACD+14]   Altisen, K., Cournier, A., Devismes, S., Durand, A., Petit, F.: Self-stabilizing leader election in polynomial steps. Technical Report hal-00980798, VERIMAG, MIS, LIP6, INRIA Rocquencourt (April 2014), http://hal.archives-ouvertes.fr/hal-00980798

[AGH90]   Arora, A., Gouda, M.G., Herman, T.: Composite routing protocols. In: The 2nd IEEE Symposium on Parallel and Distributed Processing (SPDP 1990), pp. 70–78 (1990)

[AGM+08]   Abraham, I., Gavoille, C., Malkhi, D., Nisan, N., Thorup, M.: Compact name-independent routing with minimum stretch. ACM Transactions on Algorithms 4(3), 37 (2008)

[BDV07]   Bein, D., Datta, A.K., Villain, V.: Self-stabilizing local routing in ad hoc networks. The Computer Journal 50(2), 197–203 (2007)

[BPBRT10] Blin, L., Potop-Butucaru, M.G., Rovedakis, S., Tixeuil, S.: Loop-free super-stabilizing spanning tree construction. In: Dolev, S., Cobb, J., Fischer, M., Yung, M. (eds.) SSS 2010. LNCS, vol. 6366, pp. 50–64. Springer, Heidelberg (2010)

[CG02]   Cobb, J.A., Gouda, M.G.: Stabilization of general loop-free routing. Journal of Parallel and Distributed Computing 62(5), 922–944 (2002)

[CS94]   Chandrasekar, S., Srimani, P.K.: A self-stabilizing distributed algorithm for all-pairs shortest path problem. Parallel Algorithms and Applications 4(1-2), 125–137 (1994)

[CYH91]   Chen, N.S., Yu, H.P., Huang, S.T.: A self-stabilizing algorithm for constructing spanning trees. Information Processing Letters 39, 147–151 (1991)

[DIM93]   Dolev, S., Israeli, A., Moran, S.: Self-stabilization of dynamic systems assuming only Read/Write atomicity. Distributed Computing 7(1), 3–16 (1993)

[DLV11]   Datta, A.K., Larmore, L.L., Vemula, P.: Self-stabilizing leader election in optimal space under an arbitrary scheduler. Theoretical Computer Science 412(40), 5541–5561 (2011)

[GGHI13]   Gavoille, C., Glacet, C., Hanusse, N., Ilcinkas, D.: On the communication complexity of distributed name-independent routing schemes. In: Afek, Y. (ed.) DISC 2013. LNCS, vol. 8205, pp. 418–432. Springer, Heidelberg (2013)

[HC92]   Huang, S.-T., Chen, N.-S.: A self-stabilizing algorithm for constructing breadth-first trees. Information Processing Letters 41(2), 109–117 (1992)

[HL02]   Huang, T.C., Lin, J.-C.: A self-stabilizing algorithm for the shortest path problem in a distributed system. Computers & Mathematics with Applications 43(1), 103–109 (2002)

[Hua05a]   Huang, T.C.: A self-stabilizing algorithm for the shortest path problem assuming read/write atomicity. Journal of Computer System Sciences 71(1), 70–85 (2005)

[Hua05b]   Huang, T.C.: A self-stabilizing algorithm for the shortest path problem assuming the distributed demon. Computers & Mathematics with Applications 50(5-6), 671–681 (2005)

[JT03]   Johnen, C., Tixeuil, S.: Route preserving stabilization. In: Huang, S.-T., Herman, T. (eds.) SSS 2003. LNCS, vol. 2704, pp. 184–198. Springer, Heidelberg (2003)

[LGW04]   Leon-Garcia, A., Widjaja, I.: Communication Networks, 2nd edn. McGraw-Hill, Inc., New York (2004)

Self-synchronized Cooperative Beamforming in Ad-Hoc Networks

Thomas Janson and Christian Schindelhauer

University of Freiburg,
Germany
{janson,schindel}@informatik.uni-freiburg.de

Abstract. We investigate the unicast problem for ad-hoc networks in the plane using MIMO techniques. In particular, we use the multi-node beamforming gain and present a self-synchronizing algorithm for the necessary carrier phase synchronization. First, we consider n nodes in a grid where the transmission power per node is restricted to reach the neighboring node. We extend the idea of multi-hop routing and relay the message by multiple nodes attaining joint beamforming gain with higher reception range. In each round, the message is repeated by relay nodes at dedicated positions after a fixed waiting period. Such simple algorithms can send a message from any node to any other node in time $\mathcal{O}(\log \log n - \log \lambda)$ and with asymptotical energy $\mathcal{O}(\sqrt{n})$, the same energy an optimal multi-hop routing strategy needs using short hops between source and target. Here, λ denotes the wavelength of the carrier. For $\lambda \in \Theta(1)$ we prove a tight lower time bound of $\Omega(\log \log n)$.

Then, we consider n randomly distributed nodes in a square of area n and we show for a transmission range of $\Theta(\sqrt{\log n})$ and for a wavelength of $\lambda = \Omega(\log^{-1/2} n)$ that the unicast problem can be solved in $\mathcal{O}(\log \log n)$ rounds as well. The corresponding transmission energy increases to $\mathcal{O}(\sqrt{n} \log n)$. Finally, we present simulation results visualizing the nature of our algorithms.

Keywords: Ad-hoc networks, unicast, MIMO, beamforming, signal-to-noise ratio, synchronization.

1 Introduction

Mobile devices reduce their wireless transmission power to prolong battery lifetime. An energy preserving extension of the transmission range is cooperative beamforming. Here, nodes cooperate by sending the same message and produce together a stronger signal than a single node. Without further adaption the different positions of the senders result in a delay skew such that the signals may not be correlated at some receiver positions. When the sending times are coordinated we achieve the so-called beamforming, where the radiant sender beams result in a strongly correlated signal towards a certain direction. In [4], we study fundamental features of phase-synchronized ad-hoc network nodes and show an exponential speedup for the broadcast operation of nodes placed on a line. Here, we are concerned in extending these observations to the two-dimensional plane.

P. Felber and V. Garg (Eds.): SSS 2014, LNCS 8756, pp. 135–149, 2014.

Unicast is defined as transfer of a message from a source node to a target node. For wireless communication the straight-forward solution is a direct transmission by increasing the signal strength at the sender such that the target node can receive the signal. While the message delay is optimal, the necessary transmission power is the drawback, since it quadratically increases with respect to the distance between sender and receiver.

In a power constraint scenario direct communication is not always available. Then, routes with multiple hops must be used. Messages are passed from the source via relay nodes towards the target. Regarding the sum of transmission energy, strategies with many short hops are better than single hop strategies. On the other hand, the delay increases with the number of hops. Here, we consider networks with n nodes in the plane placed on a $\sqrt{n} \times \sqrt{n}$ quadratic grid with unit distance between neighbored nodes. The delay or routing time for multi-hop routing with distances 1 each is $\mathcal{O}(\sqrt{n})$. The energy consumption compared to direct communication decreases by a factor of $\mathcal{O}(1/\sqrt{n})$.

Multi-hop routing implements time multiplexing, i.e. using several time slots, and spatial multiplexing by blocking a smaller area for communication compared to direct communication. However, the simultaneously sending nodes can do much better when one uses cooperative beamforming. One might expect that doubling the power of two senders increases the transmission range by a factor of $\sqrt{2}$. However, the superposition principle for electric fields implies that the signal strengths add up and this strength is proportional to the square root of the transmission energy. Therefore, the reception range of two close phase-synchronized senders increases by a factor of two [4].

This is the beamforming aspect of MIMO (multiple input/multiple output) technology in the line of sight case. Besides beamforming, MIMO allows to establish parallel channels with n senders (input) and m receivers (output), resulting up to $\min\{n, m\}$ parallel transmission channels. For this it is necessary that signals are reflected from obstacles in the environment, if the sender and receiver antennas are distant. However, MIMO signal processing is complex and MIMO does not work in the line-of-sight scenario with distant sender and receiver antenna arrays unlike beamforming.

In this paper we consider the line-of-sight model and beamforming. It is achieved by adjusting the sender time points such that the received signal consists of synchronized signals which add up because of the superposition principle. A message can be received if this signal strength is larger than a given value, i.e. the signal-to-noise ratio threshold.

Our main method is to assign rectangular areas for suitable relay nodes. These nodes cooperate for the beamforming of the unicast message. For this, nodes store the received message and resend it at time points depending on the reception times. We restrict the corresponding transmission power such that each node can only reach its neighborhood without beamforming. The overall goal is to minimize the transmission time of a single unicast message.

Due to page limitations some proofs are presented in a technical report [5].

2   Related Work

Gupta and Kumar [2] analyze the throughput capacity of wireless networks. The throughput capacity of a network node specifies the average data rate to a communication partner multiplied by the communication distance. For the case of nodes positioned independently at random in the plane and random communication pairings, they show that the capacity is $\Theta(\frac{1}{\sqrt{n \log n}})$ in the best case. Here, multiple hop routes using next neighbors turn out to be the best choice. It turns out that the communication bottleneck is a cut through the middle of the network, on which each node has to uphold $\mathcal{O}(\sqrt{n})$ connections throttling the throughput by a factor of $\mathcal{O}(\frac{1}{\sqrt{n}})$. It is necessary to increase the sending power by $\mathcal{O}(\log n)$ to guarantee network connectivity with high probability. By this, the throughput is further reduced by a factor of $\mathcal{O}(\frac{1}{\sqrt{\log n}})$. In such a model, our beamforming approach reaches only a throughput capacity comparable to direct point-to-point communication. Yet, for a scenario with only one point-to-point communication, where the transmission power is limited to $\Theta(\frac{\log n}{n})$ (the best case of [2]), the multi-hop scheme has a throughput of $\Theta(\frac{\sqrt{\log n}}{\sqrt{n}})$, while our unicast has a throughput of $\Theta(\frac{1}{\log \log n})$.

In [4] we present broadcasting algorithms for nodes on a line in the line-of-sight case. We prove that broadcasting can be done in $\mathcal{O}(\log n)$ rounds for n nodes regularly placed on a line, where each node alone can only reach its next neighbor. This is obtained by the beamforming gain and on-the-fly synchronization using only the reception time of the message. This scheme produces only constant factor increase of the energy consumption compared to direct neighbor communication, which needs $\mathcal{O}(n)$ rounds. Here, we consider the two dimensional setting for the same model and reuse the one-dimensional variant as a startup sub-routine.

In [7,8] communication schemes are presented that achieve order-optimal throughput by using MIMO techniques. Here, nodes in designated areas cooperate in order to increase the communication capacity resulting in higher bandwidth or increased transmission radius. In [7] the beamforming gain is exploited at designated areas of relay nodes between sender and receiver. In [8] diversity gain of highly parallel MIMO channels is used. An important step in many MIMO protocols is encoding and decoding the transmitted signal, which needs additional communication at the sender and receiver side. In practice, this is achieved by wiring the sender/receiver antennas into one device. For ad-hoc networks this step has to be emulated via wireless communication. The authors use a hierarchical approach, where the communication for the encoding at the sender nodes is organized by a recursive algorithm (and vice versa for the decoding at the receiver nodes). If this step can be done without a substantiate increase of the original message size (which may be doubted), then this achieves a capacity and time gain. The transmission time is $\mathcal{O}(\log n)$, which corresponds to the number of hierarchical steps and the capacity is up to linear depending on the path loss model. However, a minimum message length is required depending on the capacity and the authors assume a channel matrix with large eigenvalues, in contrast to the free-space model underlying this work. Here, we solve unicasting in time $\mathcal{O}(\log \log n)$ and the algorithms presented here are much simpler, since they do not use any MIMO encoding/decoding.

The authors of [6] use a similar approach by using beamforming of rectangular areas. Their algorithm spreads the information to a telescope-like region with increasing adjacent rectangles. Then, a mirrored construction is appended in order to reach the target node. They conclude that the beamforming gain is maximized up to a constant factor at each receiver as long as the area size of beamforming nodes is much smaller than $\sqrt{n}$ for n nodes in the network. The authors cannot give a closed form for the dimensions of the rectangles and refer to a Matlab program computing optimal sizes. An important difference to our approach is that they allow additional transmission power $a > 1$ for a short period $1/a$. Interestingly, their choice is $a = \Theta(1/n^{2/3})$ which results in throughput $T = \mathcal{O}(n^{2/3})$. We show that the choice of adjacent rectangles might be problematic, since our simulation results indicate that some receivers in the adjacent rectangle might not be reached. In this paper, we emphasize the large influence of the carrier wavelength and present a closed-form solution for the placement and dimensions of rectangular beam-forming areas. Furthermore, we present a solution which does not need the full channel state information.

3   Physical Model

The signal quality and the related transmission bandwidth of a communication channel between sender and receiver is difficult to model because of many effects arising in practice, e.g. multi-path propagation, diffraction, changing environment, node movement, etc. We neglect these effects and use the free-space model, where the signal strength as a function of the position of nodes in the network. Following [9], the signal output y at the receiver depends on the signal inputs at senders $x_1, \ldots, x_m$ as

$$y = \sum_{i=1}^{m} h_i \cdot x_i . \tag{1}$$

This establishes the physical input-output-model of a MISO channel (Multiple Input Single Output). Inputs and outputs are seen from the communication channel and not from the senders or receivers. We assume that all nodes emit the same input signal $x = x_i$ with the same transmission power but with a time shift in order to correlate the phases resulting in a beamforming gain at the target with output y. We denote by j the imaginary number ($j^2 = -1$). The baseband channel gain h_i for the i-th sender node is

$$h_i = \frac{1}{\|\mathbf{u_i}, \mathbf{v}\|} \cdot e^{-\frac{j2\pi}{\lambda} \cdot \|\mathbf{u_i}, \mathbf{v}\|}. \tag{2}$$

The attenuation factor $\|\mathbf{u_i}, \mathbf{v}\|^{-1}$ describes the path loss depending on the distance $\|\mathbf{u_i}, \mathbf{v}\|$ between the nodes at positions u_i and v. Since the power is proportional to the square of the signal strength this corresponds to the standard energy path loss model for line-of-sight and the far-field assumption with $\|\mathbf{u_i}, \mathbf{v}\| > 2\lambda$ where the energy decreases proportional to $\|\mathbf{u_i}, \mathbf{v}\|^{-2}$. The wavelength $\lambda = c/f$ of the carrier frequency f plays an important role for the beamforming. We denote by c the speed of light. In [3] we show that the sender geometry and the wavelength determine the width of the main beam, as well as the size of side beams. The distance between sender and receiver also results in a phase shift described by a rotation of the signal in complex space.

This signal value describes the electric field produced by the sender, and by the superposition principle the resulting field is the sum of the signals in Equation (1).

Interfering radio signals and errors occurring during the modulation and demodulation are modeled as being uncorrelated to the line-of-sight signal as additive white Gaussian noise w, which is Gaussian distributed $w \sim \mathcal{N}\left(0, \sigma^2\right)$ with variance σ^2. So, the received signal is described by $y + w$.

A signal can be received if the signal to noise ratio is larger than a threshold τ, i.e. SNR $= \frac{P}{N} \geq \tau$, where N is the energy of the noise.

We restrict the transmission power for each node in the grid such that only the vertical and horizontal neighbors in distance can be reached, if only a single sender is active. The received signal power is modeled by $P = |y|^2$.

So, we choose $\tau = 1$ and $|x_i| \leq 1$ to describe the situation in the grid. We also consider the random placement model, where we randomly position n nodes into a grid of area n. In [1] it is shown that the minimum transmission distance for achieving connectivity in this model is $\Omega(\sqrt{\log n})$. Therefore, we increase the maximum size $|x_i| \leq k(\log n)^{1/2}$ of the signal and let $\tau = 1$ for some constant k.

According to the Shannon-Hartley theorem, it is possible to achieve an information rate of $B \cdot \log\left(1 + \text{SNR}\right)$. So, a higher signal-to-noise ratio can increase the information rate. This effect is not used in this work, since at the relevant receiver antennas the received signal power is close to the SNR threshold.

4   Loglog n Unicast

The basic idea of our unicast algorithm is a multi-hop algorithm with relays between sender and receiver shown in Figure 1(a), but with the special property that each relay consists of multiple nodes which cooperate to perform joint sender beamforming, see Figure 1(b). With beamforming gain, the hop distance increases double exponentially such that this unicast algorithm needs $\mathcal{O}\left(\log \log n\right)$ hops from the source to the target.

We use beamforming for sending (MISO) which requires, when performed with several senders in parallel, the distribution of the message to all senders and phase synchronization between all senders. As Figure 1(b) indicates, we will show that we can broadcast a message from a sender to a receiver area with rectangular shape such that all nodes in the receiver area have the same message for cooperated sender beamforming in the next round. For synchronizing the sender phases, we present two algorithms. Algorithm 1 corrects the phase at the relay nodes using the position of the nodes, whereas Algorithm 2 is self-synchronizing. Algorithm 1 outperforms Algorithm 2 regarding the transmission time by a constant factor.

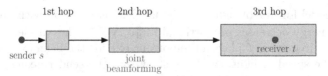

(a) Multi-hop between rectangles of beamforming senders.

(b) Beamforming from sender to receiver rectangle

Fig. 1. Scheme of the $\mathcal{O}(\log \log n)$-Unicast algorithm

We first describe the $\mathcal{O}(\log \log n)$-unicast algorithm in a network with $\sqrt{n} \times \sqrt{n}$ nodes placed in a grid. For unit grid distance we assume $\lambda \leq \frac{1}{2}$ to meet the far-field assumption. We start to describe the algorithm for a message transmission along the x-axis in the middle of the grid and generalize it for other coordinates, later on. The source node is at $s = (0,0)$ and the target node at $t = (\sqrt{n}, 0)$. The algorithm consists of two phases, an initial phase (Fig. 1(a) 1st hop) where we broadcast the message from the source to the first rectangle of relay nodes, and a second phase where we perform multi-hop with distributed beamforming (Fig. 1(a), 2nd, 3rd hop). The required rectangular area to be informed in phase 1 follows from the requirements of phase two, and thus we present phase 2 first.

We first describe how to set up phases for distributed beamforming when the senders are placed on a line along the x-axis (see Fig. 2) and extend that for rectangles in the plane, later on. Assume we have senders placed at $(i,0)$ with

Fig. 2. Synchronization in the one-dimensional case

$1 \leq i \leq n$ performing beamforming to a receiver r at $(r_x, 0)$ with $r_x > n$. To attain full beamforming gain, the senders start the transmission with a delay of $(n - i)/c$ for propagation speed c such that all transmissions arrive exactly at the same time and consequently in the same phase. We synchronize all senders with the initial signal containing the message. It is received at a node placed at $(i, 0)$ at time $t = i/c$ and if each node resends the message immediately, it sends the message with delay $-i/c$, which is the desired beamforming setup to receiver r. Hence, broadcasting along a line achieves self-synchronization for distributed beamforming.

For beamforming senders in a rectangle, we use the same synchronization setup, and each node u at coordinates (u_x, u_y) sends at time $t = u_x/c - t_0$ which only depends on the x-coordinate and offset time t_0 has to be chosen such that the sender with smallest u_x sends at time $t = 0$ without delay. If it holds $\|u, r\| = r_x - u_x$, which is the case for nodes along the x-axis, the synchronization is perfect. But for a rectangular area of nodes with width w_i and height h_i, the reception delay depends also on the y-coordinate. The delay function $\psi(i, r)$ computes for a receiver at coordinates $\mathbf{r} = (r_x, r_y)$ the delay to attain synchronization, which is phase angle $\arg[e^{-j2\pi r_x/\lambda}]$.

$$\psi(i, \mathbf{r}) = \frac{1}{f} + \frac{1}{2\pi f} \arg \left[\sum_{s \in (w_{i-1} \times h_{i-1})} \frac{e^{-j2\pi(\|\mathbf{s}, \mathbf{r}\| - r_x)/\lambda}}{\|\mathbf{s}, \mathbf{r}\|} \right] \quad (3)$$

When applying delay $\psi(i, r)$ at each receiver r, all nodes are synchronized for beamforming such that each node r sends with a delay of $-r_x/c$. By a proper choice of the dimensions of the rectangles (w_i, h_i), we can assure that the phase shift is less than $\pi/2$ and thus $\psi(i, \mathbf{r}) > 0$ (compare Lemma 1).

This leads to Algorithm 1 where the delay $\psi(i, r)$ is used in line 3 in order to synchronize the receivers in the i-th round for the $w_i \times h_i$-receiver area. The if-condition in Line 2 assures that only receivers in the correct receiver area process the message.

Algorithm 1. Unicast I

1: **procedure** RECEIVE(receiver r, message m, time t)
2:     **if** ISINRECTANGLE(round (t), r) **then**   ▷ only process in active rectangle
3:         WAIT(ψ (round (t), r))   ▷ phase correction
4:         SEND(m)   ▷ coordinated beamforming sending
5: **function** ISINRECTANGLE(round i, position p)   ▷ true for active receivers
6:     **return** $w_0 + w_i + 2\sum_{k=1}^{i-1} w_k \leq p_x \leq w_0 + 2\sum_{k=1}^{i} w_k$ & $0 \leq p_y \leq h_i$

The following Lemmas 1-3 specify the dimensions and distances between rectangles of relay nodes where the multi-hop procedure of Algorithm 1 with distributed sender beamforming is possible.

Lemma 1. *If a single sender s sends a signal to a $w \times h$ rectangular area in a distance of at least w (see Figure 3), then the phase shift with respect to the phase $2\pi r_x/\lambda$ is at any receiver node r inside the area at most α if $h^2 \leq \frac{\alpha}{\pi}\lambda w$.*

Proof: Let x denote the signal of the sender s and y the signal at r. Then,

$$y = \frac{x}{\|\mathbf{s}, \mathbf{r}\|} \cdot e^{-\frac{j2\pi}{\lambda} \cdot \|\mathbf{s}, \mathbf{r}\|} .$$

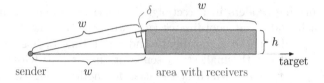

Fig. 3. Broadcast of an single sender (red) to receivers in the green area

Thus, the phase shift is described by $-\arg(\frac{y}{x}) = \frac{2\pi}{\lambda} \|\mathbf{s}, \mathbf{r}\|$. The difference of phase shifts is therefore

$$\delta = \frac{2\pi}{\lambda} \|\mathbf{s}, \mathbf{r}\| - \frac{2\pi x}{\lambda} = \frac{2\pi}{\lambda} \left(\sqrt{r_x^2 + r_y^2} - r_x \right) = \frac{2\pi}{\lambda} r_x \left(\sqrt{1 + \left(\frac{r_y}{r_x} \right)^2} - 1 \right) .$$

This phase difference is maximized for $r_y = h$ and $r_x = w$ and by applying the relation $\sqrt{1 + x^2} - 1 \leq \frac{x^2}{2}$ for all $x \geq 0$ (see [5]) we get

$$\delta \leq \frac{\pi}{\lambda} \frac{r_y^2}{r_x} = \frac{\pi}{\lambda} \frac{h^2}{w} .$$

From $h^2 \leq \frac{\alpha}{\pi} \lambda w$ it follows that $\delta \leq \alpha$.   □
Note that the difference between the signal and the offset is so small, e.g. for $\alpha \leq \pi/4$, that it is less than one wavelength. So, if we repeat the message transmission after a fixed time offset in the next round, then the message modulated upon the carrier wave is in sync with all the other sender nodes provided by using the same time offset.

Lemma 2. *A $w_i \times h_i$-rectangular area of beamforming senders S can reach any node in a $w_{i+1} \times h_{i+1}$ rectangle at distance w_{i+1} if*

$$h_{i+1} \geq h_i , \tag{4}$$

$$w_{i+1} \geq w_i , \tag{5}$$

$$w_{i+1} \leq \frac{1}{3\sqrt{2}} w_i h_i , \tag{6}$$

$$h_{i+1} \leq w_{i+1} , \quad and \tag{7}$$

$$h_{i+1}^2 \leq \frac{1}{4} \lambda w_{i+1} . \tag{8}$$

Proof: Remember that all sending nodes of a vertical column in the grid have the same phase. The received signal y at node r is

$$y = \sum_{s \in S} x_s \frac{e^{-\frac{j 2\pi}{\lambda} \cdot \|\mathbf{s}, \mathbf{r}\|}}{\|\mathbf{s}, \mathbf{r}\|} = \sum_{s \in S} e^{j \frac{2\pi u_x}{\lambda}} \frac{e^{-\frac{j 2\pi}{\lambda} \cdot \|\mathbf{s}, \mathbf{r}\|}}{\|\mathbf{s}, \mathbf{r}\|} = \sum_{s \in S} \frac{e^{-\frac{j 2\pi}{\lambda} \cdot \|\mathbf{s}, \mathbf{r}\| + j \frac{2\pi u_x}{\lambda}}}{\|\mathbf{s}, \mathbf{r}\|} .$$

And from Lemma 1 we get ($\alpha = \pi/4$) for

$$\beta_{s,r} := \frac{2\pi u_x}{\lambda} - \frac{2\pi}{\lambda} \cdot \|s, r\|$$

from $w_i \leq w_{i+1}$ and inequality (8)

$$0 \leq \beta_{s,r} \leq \frac{\pi}{4} . \tag{9}$$

We want to prove that $|y|^2 = \text{SNR} \geq \tau = 1$. For this it suffices to prove that for the real part of y, i.e. that $\Re(y) \geq 1$, since $|y|^2 = \Im(y)^2 + \Re(y)^2$.

Using, $\|s, r\| \leq w_i + 2w_{i+1} \leq 3w_{i+1} \overset{\text{by(6)}}{\leq} \frac{1}{\sqrt{2}} w_i h_i = \frac{1}{\sqrt{2}} |S|$ we get

$$\Re(y) = \sum_{s \in S} \frac{\Re(e^{-j\beta_{s,r}})}{\|s, r\|} = \sum_{s \in S} \frac{\cos \beta_{s,r}}{\|s, r\|} \geq \sum_{s \in S} \frac{1}{w_i + 2w_{i+1}} \cos \frac{\pi}{4} \geq \frac{w_i h_i}{3 w_{i+1}} \frac{1}{\sqrt{2}} \geq 1.$$

$\square$

Figure 4 illustrates the relation between the sender and the receiver area. The delay δ illustrates the largest possible value $\beta_{s,r}$ in the range of Eq. (9). If the

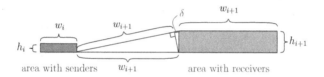

area with senders w_{i+1} area with receivers

Fig. 4. Area growth during broadcast step

sender and the receiver are at the margin of the grid, we cannot expand the height of the relay node areas symmetrically along the line of sight between sender and receiver. To apply the algorithm also at the margin of the network, we only expand the height of the rectangle in one direction, i.e. towards the center of the network. This has been already addressed in Equation (8).

This leads to the double exponential growth of the rectangles given in closed form in the following lemma.

Lemma 3. *The equations*

$$w_i = \left(\frac{72}{\lambda}\right) \left(\frac{\lambda}{72} w_0\right)^{(3/2)^i} , \tag{10}$$

$$h_i = \sqrt{18} \left(18^{-\frac{1}{2}} h_0\right)^{(3/2)^i} , \tag{11}$$

for $i \in \{1, 2, \ldots\}$ satisfy inequalities (4-8) for $h_0 \geq 18^{\frac{1}{2}}$, $w_0 \geq \frac{72}{\lambda}$ and $h_0^2 = \frac{1}{4} \lambda w_0$.

The proof can be found in [5].

So far, we assume that after the receipt of a message the relay node calculates the received phase from the senders' positions and readjusts the phase such that all vertical nodes are in phase. This step is not necessary, if the dimensions of the rectangles are chosen according to Lemma 4. Then, the received signal can be sent without phase correction from each relay node. The algorithm then reduces to two steps: If a message has been received, relay nodes check from the message header whether they are in the correct rectangles. Then, each relay node repeats the messages after the same time offset.

Algorithm 2. Unicast II

1: **procedure** RECEIVE(receiver r, message m, time t)
2:     **if** ISINRECTANGLE(round (t), r) **then**   ▷ only process in active rectangle
3:         SEND(m)   ▷ coordinated beamforming sending

Lemma 4. *If the phase errors are not corrected in this routing, then the correct signal can be received if we use the following inequality instead of (8).*

$$h_i^2 \leq \frac{3}{2\pi^2} \frac{1}{(i+1)^2} \lambda w_i \ . \tag{12}$$

The main idea is that the phase shifts in each round form a convergent series $\alpha_i = \frac{3\pi}{2} \cdot \frac{1}{\pi^2 i^2}$, such that the sum of all phases $\sum_{i=1}^r \alpha_i \leq \frac{\pi}{4}$ can be bound.

The dimensions of these rectangles can be chosen as follows.

Lemma 5. *The following recursions satisfy equations (4-7,12) for $h_0^2 = \frac{3}{2\pi^2} \lambda w_0$ for $w_0 \geq \frac{96\pi^2 e \cdot c_4}{\lambda}$, and $h_0 \geq 4\sqrt{18}$.*

$$w_{i+1} = \frac{1}{\sqrt{12\pi}} \cdot \frac{\sqrt{\lambda}}{i+1} \cdot w_i^{3/2} \tag{13}$$

$$h_{i+1} = 18^{-\frac{1}{4}} \frac{1+i}{2+i} \cdot h_i^{3/2} \ . \tag{14}$$

The recursions are satisfied by the following equations.

$$w_i \leq \left(\frac{\sqrt{\lambda}}{\sqrt{12\pi}}\right)^{2(3/2)^i - 2} \cdot c_2^{-(3/2)^i} \cdot w_0^{(3/2)^i} \ \text{ with } c_2 \geq 12.011 \tag{15}$$

$$w_i \geq \left(\frac{\sqrt{\lambda}}{\sqrt{12\pi}}\right)^{2(3/2)^i - 2} \cdot c_3^{-(3/2)^i} \cdot w_0^{(3/2)^i} \ \text{ with } c_3 \leq 1.58 \tag{16}$$

$$h_i = 18^{\frac{-(3/2)^i + 1}{2}} \cdot \left(\frac{i+1}{i+2}\right)^{\frac{1}{2}(i-1) \cdot i} \cdot h_0^{(3/2)^i} \tag{17}$$

Remember that we reach the constant length w_0 in a logarithmic number of rounds and therefore $\log_{3/2}(w_0 \cdot \lambda) = 25$ for a moderate expansion. The lengthy proofs of Lemma 4 and 5 are omitted here and can be found in [5].

It remains to show how to inform the first rectangle.

Lemma 6. *A start phase of $\mathcal{O}(-\log\lambda)$ rounds allows to inform an initial area of nodes with $w_0 > \frac{72}{\lambda}$, $h_0 \geq \sqrt{18}$, $h_0^2 \leq \frac{1}{4}\lambda w_0$, and $h_0 \leq w_0$.*

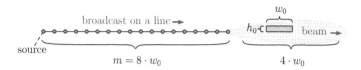

Fig. 5. Initial phase with a broadcast on the line to $m = 8w_0$ nodes followed by a last hop of cooperative beamforming to the first rectangle with dimensions $w_0 \times h_0$

Proof: To inform the first rectangle with dimensions $w_0 \times h_0$, we first inform $8w_0$ subsequent nodes placed on a line which together can inform and synchronize all nodes in the first rectangle with cooperative beamforming (compare Fig. 5). To initially inform a line of $m = 8w_0$ senders, we use the exponential broadcast algorithm of [4], which informs m nodes placed on a line in $\mathcal{O}(\log m)$ rounds. Note that the exponential broadcast algorithm has informed at least $(3/2)^i$ nodes after round i. We choose $m = 8w_0$ which results in a runtime $k \cdot \log\left(\frac{8 \cdot 72}{\lambda}\right) = \mathcal{O}(-\log\lambda)$ rounds for some constant k. Then, $8w_0$ nodes are in phase to inform not only the next $4w_0$ nodes on the line but also all other nodes in the beam including a rectangle with dimensions $w_0 \times h_0$. However, there will be a phase shift for the nodes of the rectangle, which are not on the line. By Lemma 1 this offset attenuates the signal by a factor of at most $\frac{1}{\sqrt{2}}$. Therefore, all nodes of this initial rectangle receive the message. We can compute the delay error for each node with an invariant of Equation (3) where the sender area is reduced to a line. $\qquad\square$

The above lemmas lead to our main result of $\mathcal{O}(\log\log n)$ unicast.

Theorem 1. *Given n nodes in a grid equipped with a transceiver with wavelength $\lambda \leq \frac{1}{2}$, placed within unit distance and possessing a transmission power only to reach each neighbor, any node can send a message to any other node in $\mathcal{O}(\log\log n - \log\lambda)$ rounds.*

Proof: The basic idea is, first to route on the x-axis until the correct y-coordinate has been reached and then to relaunch the algorithm orthogonally on the y-axis. Then, the claim follows by the above lemmas. $\qquad\square$

The energy is given by the sum of sending nodes, i.e. $\sum_{i=1}^{r} w_i h_i$ for r rounds, since each node sends with constant energy. Now, $w_i h_i = \mathcal{O}(w_{i+1})$, where $w_{r+1} = \mathcal{O}(d)$ and w_i grows double exponentially. So, for the sum of transmission energy the last term asymptotically bounds the sum.

Corollary 1. *The overall transmission energy consumed by the $\mathcal{O}(\log\log n)$ unicast algorithm for sending a message over distance d is $\mathcal{O}(d)$.*

Now, we apply this observation to randomly placed nodes in the grid. First, we establish a bound on the minimum number of nodes in some area.

Lemma 7. *Given n nodes randomly distributed in a square of area n with transmission range $k\sqrt{\log n}$ for some constant k. In every geometric object inside a square of an area of at least $k^2 \log n$ lie at least $\log n$ nodes with high probability, i.e. $1 - n^{-\ell}$ for some constant ℓ.*

If the transmission distance is asymptotically smaller, the network is disconnected with probability 1 in the limit [1].

Theorem 2. *Given n nodes randomly distributed in a square of area n with transmission range $k\sqrt{\log n}$ for some constant $k > 0$. Then, for wavelength $\lambda \geq \frac{3k}{\sqrt{\log n}}$ a node can send a message to any other node in time $\mathcal{O}(\log \log n)$ with high probability, i.e. $1 - n^{-\mathcal{O}(1)}$. The overall transmission energy for sending a message over distance d is $\mathcal{O}(d \log n)$.*

The proofs of Lemma 7 and Theorem 2 are presented in [5].

The transmission time of each hop in a multi-hop algorithm consists of the transmission delay between sender and receiver, the transmission of the message, and processing the message at the receiver. The following theorem shows that the double exponential growth of the transmission distance in the $\mathcal{O}(\log \log n)$ unicast algorithm is such large that the transmission delay dominates the propagation speed up to a constant factor (The proof is presented in [5]).

Theorem 3. *For $\lambda \in \Omega(1)$ and a quadratic grid with n nodes with unit node distance and unit transmission distance, it is possible to send a message from any node to any other node with a speed of $c(1 - o(1/n))$, where c is the speed of light.*

5   Lower Bound for Time

We now investigate the principal lower bound of rounds for disseminating a message in a two-dimension grid when each node has constant power P and an omnidirectional antenna in the line-of-side path-loss model. The following theorem shows the time optimality of our $\mathcal{O}(\log \log n)$ unicast algorithm.

Theorem 4. *In a grid with n nodes with constant transmission power, every unicast message takes at least $\Omega(\log \log n)$ rounds to reach its destination.*

Proof: Let u be the start node and let $C_d := \{v \in V : |u, v| \leq d\}$ denote all nodes within Euclidean distance at most d from u.

Now in round i, let d_i be the distance of the farthest node in this round carrying the (or some parts of the) message. Now consider a node v in distance $d' \gg d_i$.

The received energy is bounded by

$$P_v = |E_v^2| \leq \left| \sum_{u \in C_{d_i}} \frac{s_u}{\|u - v\|} \right|^2 \leq \left(\sum_{u \in C_{d_i}} \frac{\sqrt{P}}{d' - d_i} \right)^2 \leq P \frac{|C_{d_i}|^2}{(d' - d_i)^2} .$$

In order to receive the signal, this power must be larger than a constant $\tau > 0$. We want to investigate the case when we cannot receive a signal, i.e. $P_v \leq \tau$. Then, $d' \geq d_i + |C_{d_i}|\sqrt{\frac{\tau}{P}}$ which implies with $|C_d| \leq 2\pi d^2$ that

$$d' \geq d_i + 2\pi d_i^2 \sqrt{\tau/P} .$$

From this it follows that $d_{i+1} \leq k \cdot d_i^2$ for a constant $k > 0$ and thus

$$d_{i+1} \leq k^{2^i - 1}(d_1)^{2^i} .$$

Therefore, it takes at least some $k' \log \log d$ rounds (for a constant $k' > 0$) to inform a node in distance d.   □

(a) SNR with color range [orange,white) over threshold τ and [purple, cyan) under τ

(b) Phase error with angle range $[0, \pi)$ and colors [black, blue)

Fig. 6. Simulation of beamforming senders which are placed in a rectangle and produce a beam to the right. An animation with varying wavelength λ is available at www.youtube.com/watch?v=3TJ2Gz8uhbc

6   Simulation

We have simulated cooperative sender beamforming for nodes placed in a rectangle in the plane. The dimensions of the rectangles correspond to Unicast I (compare Fig. 1(b)). Figure 6 shows the signal strength respectively phase shift of a 1705×186 grid network with grid distance 1 (one pixel=1 node) and the wavelength is $\lambda = 0.1$. We see sender beamforming from a rectangle with 341×6=2046 nodes to a receiver area with 482×7=3374 nodes (the areas are white bordered).

The first picture 6(a) shows the signal strength where the blue color range depicts amplitudes under the SNR threshold $\tau = 1$ and the orange-white color range represents signal strengths over τ. We can spot a sharp beam around the receiver rectangle with a signal over the SNR threshold. The second figure 6(b) shows the phase shift for synchronized beamforming. The black corridor from sender to receiver rectangle makes clear, that all nodes receiving the message within this corridor will be synchronized for beamforming to the right. The blue lines around the corridor mark a phase shift of π and the subsequent next black rays around have a phase error of 2π, i.e. one period $1/f_c$ of carrier frequency

f_c. Notably, the spatial variation of the phases of the super-posed signal is much smaller than the wavelength (=0.1 pixels).

Figure 7(a) shows the beamforming gain for different wavelengths λ. The $n = 2048$ cooperating senders are selected according to Unicast I and highlighted with an orange rectangle on the left and the signal is over the SNR threshold in the blue colored area. We did not intend to show the special case where the wavelength is an integer multiple of the grid distance and thus added a small ϵ to the wavelength. The reception distance of the beam is nearly equal to n showing full beamforming gain in the middle of the beam. The height of the beam increases with the wavelength λ.

In a second experiment, we manipulate for a constant wavelength $\lambda = 0.5$ the ratio of the rectangle with factor k, i.e. $w := A/k$ and $h := A \cdot k$. When we increase the height, we can spot two effects. First, the beam is sharper and we cannot reach a rectangle with larger height in the multicast. In the examples $k \geq 4$ the height even shrinks. Second, the perception range decreases and we can only multicast to a short distance.

7 Conclusions

We present a unicast algorithm for ad-hoc networks on a grid with n nodes, which needs only $\mathcal{O}(\log \log n)$ rounds for wavelength $\lambda \in \Omega(1)$. This algorithm combines beamforming with multi-hop routing. Beamforming increases the hop distances to a double exponentially growth, i.e. $\mathcal{O}\left(w_0^{\left(b^i\right)}\right)$ for round i. This growing beamforming gain is realized by a set of increasing rectangular areas containing relay nodes. Similar results can be shown for randomly placed nodes in a square, if the transmission range is increased by a factor of $\Omega(\sqrt{\log n})$. The overall transmission velocity of such unicast algorithms converges towards the speed of light and for the grid we show the optimality of the routing time $\mathcal{O}(\log \log n)$. Such a unicast algorithm does not asymptotically use more energy than the basic multi-hop algorithm.

Unlike in the one-dimensional case, the wavelength plays a large role in the construction and performance of the algorithm. Short wavelengths compared to the node distance increase the run-time, since it takes longer until the double exponential growth phase begins. For random placement it is not clear how beamforming can be utilized for wavelengths shorter than $\mathcal{O}(1/\log n)$, while for larger wavelengths our algorithm provides a solution. In the grid, the unicast algorithm has only logarithmic run-time if the wavelength is $\mathcal{O}(1/n^c)$.

Since we only use beam-formed sending with Multiple Input Single Output (MISO), the main component of the algorithm is to obey a fixed time delay between receiving the message and residing it. Besides this, only a check is needed, whether the relay node is in one of the rectangles necessary for transport. This can be computed from the message header and the position information of the relay node. An exact position information is therefore not necessary. This is an extreme simplification compared to the way beamforming is usually achieved.

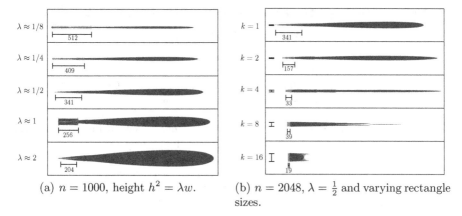

(a) $n = 1000$, height $h^2 = \lambda w$.

(b) $n = 2048$, $\lambda = \frac{1}{2}$ and varying rectangle sizes.

Fig. 7. Simulation of n beamforming senders placed in a rectangle (orange colored at the left) which produce a beam to the right

References

1. Gupta, P., Kumar, P.R.: Critical power for asymptotic connectivity in wireless networks. In: Stochastic Analysis, Control, Optimization and Applications, pp. 547–566. Springer (1998)
2. Gupta, P., Kumar, P.R.: The Capacity of Wireless Networks. IEEE Transactions on Information Theory 46, 388–404 (2000)
3. Janson, T., Schindelhauer, C.: Analyzing Randomly Placed Multiple Antennas for MIMO Wireless Communication. In: Fifth International Workshop on Selected Topics in Mobile and Wireless Computing (IEEE STWiMob), Barcelona (2012)
4. Janson, T., Schindelhauer, C.: Broadcasting in Logarithmic Time for Ad Hoc Network Nodes on a Line using MIMO. In: Proceedings of the 25th ACM Symposium on Parallelism in Algorithms and Architectures, SPAA 2013. ACM (July 2013)
5. Janson, T., Schindelhauer, C.: Ad-Hoc Network Unicast in O(log log n) using Beamforming, http://arxiv.org/abs/1405.0417 (May 2014)
6. Merzakreeva, A., Özgür, A., Lévêque, O.: Telescopic beamforming for large wireless networks. In: IEEE Int. Symposium on Information Theory, Istanbul (2013)
7. Niesen, U., Gupta, P., Shah, D.: On Capacity Scaling in Arbitrary Wireless Networks. IEEE Transactions on Information Theory 55(9), 3959–3982 (2009)
8. Özgür, A., Leveque, O., Tse, D.: Hierarchical Cooperation Achieves Optimal Capacity Scaling in Ad Hoc Networks. IEEE Transactions on Information Theory 53(10), 3549–3572 (2007)
9. Tse, D., Viswanath, P.: Fundamentals of wireless communication. Cambridge University Press, New York (2005)

Robots with Lights: Overcoming Obstructed Visibility Without Colliding

Giuseppe Antonio Di Luna[1], Paola Flocchini[2], Sruti Gan Chaudhuri[3],
Nicola Santoro[4], and Giovanni Viglietta[2]

[1] Dipartimento di Ingegneria Informatica, Automatica e Gestionale Antonio Ruberti, Università
degli Studi di Roma "La Sapienza", Rome, Italy
diluna@dis.uniroma1.it
[2] School of Electrical Engineering and Computer Science,
University of Ottawa, Ottawa ON, Canada
flocchin@site.uottawa.ca, viglietta@gmail.com
[3] Department of Information Technology, Jadavpur University, Kolkata, India
srutiganc@it.jusl.ac.in
[4] School of Computer Science, Carleton University, Ottawa ON, Canada
santoro@scs.carleton.ca

Abstract. *Robots with lights* is a model of autonomous mobile computational
entties operating in the plane in Look-Compute-Move cycles: each agent has an
externally visible light which can assume colors from a fixed set; the lights are
persistent (i.e., the color is not erased at the end of a cycle), but otherwise the
agents are oblivious. The investigation of computability in this model is under
way, and several results have been recently established. In these investigations,
however, an agent is assumed to be capable to see through another agent.

In this paper we start the study of computing when visibility is obstructable,
and investigate the most basic problem for this setting, *Complete Visibility*: The
agents must reach within finite time a configuration where they can all see each
other and terminate. We do not make any assumption on a-priori knowledge of the
number of agents, on rigidity of movements nor on chirality. The local coordinate
system of an agent may change at each activation. Also, by definition of lights,
an agent can communicate and remember only a constant number of bits in each
cycle. In spite of these weak conditions, we prove that COMPLETE VISIBILITY
is always solvable, even in the *asynchronous* setting, without collisions and using
a small constant number of colors. The proof is constructive. We also show how
to extend our protocol for COMPLETE VISIBILITY so that, with the same number
of colors, the agents solve the (non-uniform) CIRCLE FORMATION problem with
obstructed visibility.

1 Introduction

1.1 Framework

In the traditional model of distributed computing by mobile entities in the plane, called
robots or *agents*, each entity is modelled as a point; it is provided with a local coordinate system (not necessarily consistent with that of the other agents); it has sensorial
capabilities, called *vision*, enabling it to determine the position (within its own coordinate

P. Felber and V. Garg (Eds.): SSS 2014, LNCS 8756, pp. 150–164, 2014.

system) of the other agents. The agents are anonymous, they are indistinguishable, and they execute the same code.

Agents operate in *Look-Compute-Move* cycles: when becoming active, an agent uses its sensing capabilities to get a snapshot of its surroundings (Look), then this snapshot is used to compute a destination point (Compute), and finally it moves towards this destination (Move); after that, the agent becomes inactive. In the majority of investigations, the agents are assumed to be oblivious: at the beginning of each cycle, an agent has no recollection of its past observations and computations [11]. Depending on the assumptions on the activation schedule and the duration of the cycles, three main settings are identified. In the *fully-synchronous* setting, all agents are activated simultaneously, and each cycle is instantaneous. The *semi-synchronous* setting is like the fully synchronous one except that the set of agents to be activated is chosen by an adversary, subject only to a fairness restriction: each agent will be activated infinitely often. In the *asynchronous* setting, there is no common notion of time, and no assumption is made on timing of activation, other than fairness, nor on the duration of each computation and movement, other than it is finite.

Vision and mobility provide the agents with *stigmergy*, enabling the agents to communicate and coordinate their actions by moving and sensing their relative positions. The agents are otherwise assumed to be *silent*, without any means of explicit direct communication [11]. This restriction enables deployment in extremely harsh environments where communication is not possible, i.e an underwater deployment or a military scenario where wireless communication are impossible or can be jammed. Nevertheless, in many other situations it is possible to assume the availability of some sort of direct communication. The theoretical interest is obviously for weak communication capabilities.

A model employing a weak explicit communication mechanism is that of *robots with lights*: in this model, each agent is provided with a local externally visible *light*, which can assume colors from a fixed set; the agents explicitly communicate with each other using these lights [5, 6, 10, 12, 14, 16]. In this model, the lights are persistent (i.e., the color is not erased at the end of a cycle), but otherwise the agents are oblivious.

The classical model of silent entities and the more recent model of entities with visible lights share a common assumption, that *visibility is unobstructed*. That is, three or more collinear agents are assumed to be mutually visible. It can be easily argued against such an assumption, and for the importance of investigating computability when visibility is obstructed by presence of the agents: given three collinear agents, the one in the middle blocks the visibility between the other two and they cannot see each other.

Nothing is known on computing with *obstructed visibility* except for the study of uniformly spreading agents operating in a one dimensional space (i.e., on a line) [3], and the investigations on the so-called *fat agents* model, where agents are not points but unit discs (e.g., [1, 2, 4]). Notice that the fat agents model and our model do share the common assumption of visibility obstruction, but they are computationally orthogonal otherwise, and a solution in one model cannot generally be transformed into a solution in the other. A noticeable difference, for example, is regarding collisions: for fat agents collisions are allowed and can be used as an explicit computational tool, while for punctiform agents collisions create unbreakable symmetries and, unless this is the required outcome of the problem, their avoidance is required by all solution protocols.

In this paper we start to fill this void, and focus on agents with visible lights in presence of obstructed visibility.

The problem we investigate is perhaps the most basic in a situation of obstructed visibility, and it is the one of the agents reaching a configuration of complete unobstructeded visibility. More precisely, this problem, that we shall call COMPLETE VISIBILITY, requires the agents, starting from an arbitrary initial configuration where they are in distinct points but might be unable to see everybody and might not know the total number of agents[1], to reach within finite time a configuration in which every agent is in a distinct location from which it can see all other agents, and no longer move.

Among the configurations that achieve complete visibility, a special class is that where all agents are on the perimeter of a circle (not necessarily equally spaced). The problem of forming any such a configuration is called CIRCLE FORMATION and it has been extensively studied both in the classical model of silent agents and in the ones with visible lights (e.g., [7–9, 13, 15]). Unfortunately, none of these investigations consider obstructed visibility, and their algorithms do not work in the setting considered here.

1.2 Our Contributions

In this paper we study solving COMPLETE VISIBILITY by robots with lights. That is, we consider autonomous and anonymous agents, each endowed with a visible light that can assume a constant number of persistent colors, that are otherwise oblivious, and whose visibility is obstructed by other agents in the line of sight; and we investigate under what conditions they can solve COMPLETE VISIBILITY and at what cost (i.e., how many colors).

We do not make any assumptions on a-priori knowledge on the number of agents, nor on agreement on coordinate systems, unit of distance and chirality; actually, the local coordinate system of an agent may change at each activation. Neither we make any assumption on rigidity of movements; that is, a move may be stopped by an adversary before the agent reaches its destination; the only constraint is that, if interrupted before reaching its destination, the agent moves at least a minimum distance $\delta > 0$ (otherwise, no destination can ever be reached). Also, by definition of lights, an agent can communicate and remember only a constant number of bits in each cycle.

In spite of these weak conditions, we prove that COMPLETE VISIBILITY is always solvable, even in the *asynchronous* setting, without collisions and using a small constant number of colors. The proof is constructive. We first design a protocol that achieves complete visibility with six colors under a semi-synchronous scheduler. We then show how to transform it into an asynchronous algorithm with only four additional colors. We also show how to extend the protocol so that, under the same weak conditions and without increasing the number of colors, the agents can position themselves on the perimeter of a circle. In other words, we also show how to solve the (non-uniform) CIRCLE FORMATION problem with obstructed visibility.

Due to lack of space, some of the proofs are sketched and some omitted.

---

[1] The actual number of agents may be unknown for several reasons; e.g., if the deployment of agents has been done by an airplane, a subset of agents may be lost or destroyed during the landing process.

2   Model and Definitions

Consider a set of mobile anonymous agents $\mathcal{A} : \{a_1, a_2, .., a_n\}$. Each agent a_i has a persistent state variable s_i, which may assume any value in a finite set of *colors* C. We denote by $x_i(t) \in \mathbb{R}^2$ the position occupied by agent a_i at time t expressed in some global coordinate system (used only for description purposes, and unknown to the agents); when no ambiguity arises, we omit the indication of time. A *configuration* $\mathcal{C}$ is a set of n tuples in $C \times \mathbb{R}^2$ each defining the position and color of an agent; let $\mathcal{C}_t$ denote the configuration at time t.

Each agent a_i has its own system of coordinates centered in itself, which does not necessarily agree with those of the other agents, i.e. there is no common unit of measure and no common notion of clockwise orientation. Agents a_i and a_j are visible to each other at time t if and only if the segment $\overline{x_i(t)x_j(t)}$ does not contain any other agents. Let $\mathcal{C}_t[a_i]$ denote the set of the positions and colors of the agents visible to a_i at time t. We shall call such a set *local view*. A configuration $\mathcal{C}$ is said to be *obstruction-free* if $\forall a_i \in \mathcal{A}$ we have $|\mathcal{C}[a_i]| = n$; that is, if all agents can see each other. Two agents a_i and a_j are said to *collide* at time t if $x_i(t) = x_j(t)$.

At any time, agents can be active or inactive. When activated, an agent a_i performs a sequence of operations called *Look-Compute-Move*: it activates the sensors to obtain a snapshot (called *local view*) of the positions of the visible agents expressed in its own coordinate system (*Look*); it then executes an algorithm (the same for all agents) based on its local view, which returns a destination point $x \in \mathbb{R}^2$ and a color $c \in C$ (*Compute*); it then sets its own state variable to c and moves towards x (*Move*), these operations are considered atomic. The movement may be stopped by an adversary before the agent reaches its destination; the only constraint on the adversary is that, if interrupted before reaching its destination, a robot moves at least a minimum distance $\delta > 0$ (otherwise, no destination can ever be reached).

We consider two schedulers for the activation of the agents: *Semi-Synchronous* (*SSYNC*) and *Asynchronous* (*ASYNC*). In *SSYNC*, the time is discrete; at each time instant t (called a *round*) a subset of the agents is activated and performs its operational cycle instantaneously. The choice of the activation is done by an adversary, which however activates each agent infinitely often. In *ASYNC*, there is no common notion of time; each agent is activated independently, and each Compute and Move operation can take an unpredictable (but bounded) amount of time, unknown to the agent.

At the beginning (time $t = 0$), the agents start in an arbitrary configuration $\mathcal{C}_0$ occupying different positions, and they are *black* (the state variable of each one is set to a special symbol $\flat$). The goal is for the agents to reach, in finite time, an obstruction-free configuration without ever colliding. We call this problem COMPLETE VISIBILITY. An algorithm is said to solve the problem if it always achieves complete visibility regardless of the choices of the adversary, and from any initial configuration.

Let $\mathcal{H}_t$ be the convex hull defined by $\mathcal{C}_t$, let $\partial\mathcal{H}_t = \mathcal{V}_t \cup \mathcal{B}_t$ denote the agents on the border of $\mathcal{H}_t$, where $\mathcal{V}_t : \{v_1, \ldots, v_k\} \subseteq \mathcal{A}$ is the set of agents (*corner-agents*) located at the corners of $\mathcal{H}_t$ and $\mathcal{B}_t : \{b_1, \ldots, b_l\}$ is the set of those located on the edges of $\mathcal{H}_t$ (*edge-agents*); let $\mathcal{I}_t$ be the set of agents that are interior of $\mathcal{H}_t$ (*interior-agents*). Let $n_t = |\mathcal{V}_t|$ be the number of corners in $\mathcal{H}_0$. Given an agent $a_i \in A$, we denote by $\mathcal{H}_t[a_i]$ the convex hull of its local view $\mathcal{C}_t[a_i]$. Let $\mathcal{C}_t^c$ indicate the set of agents in $\mathcal{C}_t$ with color c at time t, similarly we define $\mathcal{H}_t^c[a_i]$ as the convex hull, of $\mathcal{C}_t^c[a_i]$. Analogously defined are the extensions of $\mathcal{V}_t, \mathcal{B}_t, \mathcal{I}_t$. Given a configuration $\mathcal{C}$, we indicate by $SEC(\mathcal{C})$ the smallest enclosing circle containing $\mathcal{C}$ (when no ambiguity arises we just use the term SEC). Given two points $x, y \in R^2$ with xy we indicate the line that contains them, and we use the operator $\cap$ to indicate the intersection of lines and segments. Let $d(x, y)$ indicate the Euclidean distance between two points (or a segment and a point); moreover, given $x, y, z \in R^2$ we use $\angle xyz$ to indicate the angle with vertex y and sides xy, yz. In the following, with an abuse of notation, when no ambiguity arises, we use a_i to denote both the agent and its position.

3   Complete Visibility in SSYNC

In this Section we provide an Algorithm that reaches Complete Visibility in the semi-synchronous setting. The algorithm is described assuming $|\mathcal{V}_0| \geq 3$; we will then show how the agents can easily move to reach this condition starting from a configuration with $|\mathcal{V}_0| = 2$.

Our algorithm works in two phases: (1) *Interior Depletion* (ID) and (2) *Edge Depletion* (ED). The purpose of the Interior Depletion phase is to reach a configuration $\mathcal{C}_{ID}$ in which there are no interior-agents. In this phase, the interior-agents move towards an edge they perceive as belonging to the border of the convex hull, and they position themselves between two corner-agents. At the end of this phase, all agents are on $\partial \mathcal{H}_0$. The goal of the Edge Depletion phase is to have all agents in $\mathcal{B}_{ID}$ to move so to reach complete visibility.

3.1   Phase 1: Interior Depletion Phase

Initially all agents are *black*. The objective of this phase is to have all agents on $\partial \mathcal{H}_0$, with the corner-agents colored *red* and the edge-agents colored *brown*.

Notice that corner (resp. edge) agents are able to recognize their condition in spite of possible obstructions. In fact, if a *black* agent a_i is activated at some round r, and it sees that $\mathcal{C}_r[a_i]$ contains a region of plane that is free of agents and wider than 180°, then a_i knows it is a corner and sets its variable s_i to *red*. A similar rule is applied to edge-agents; in this case, an edge-agent a_i sets its variable s_i to *brown* if $\mathcal{C}_r[a_i]$ contains a region of plane free of agents and wide exactly 180° (see Coloring Case of Figure 1).

In the ID phase, corner-agents color themselves *red*, and no longer move, while edge-agents color themselves *brown*. Each interior-agent a moves to position itself on one of its nearest visible edges of $\partial \mathcal{H}_0$; note that an edge of $\partial \mathcal{H}_0$ can be recognized in a's local view once it is occupied only by *brown* and *red* agents. To prevent collisions, the interior-agent moves towards the chosen edge e perpendicularly if and only if it is one with minimum distance to e and its destination on e is empty; otherwise it does not move. An edge-agent on the destination of an interior one, slightly moves to make room for the interior-agent. The INTERIOR DEPLETION algorithm is detailed in Figure 1.

It is easy to see that at the end of this phase, all the agents will be positioned on a convex hull.

Algorithm INTERIOR DEPLETION (for the generic agent a_i activated at round r)

- Coloring Case: if $(s_i = black)$ then:
  - If $(a_i$ is a corner-agent in $\mathcal{H}_r[a_i])$ then a_i sets $s_i = red$
  - If $(a_i$ is an edge-agent in $\mathcal{H}_r[a_i])$ then a_i sets $s_i = brown$
- Interior Case: if $(a_i$ is interior in $\mathcal{H}_r[a_i]$ and $s_i = black)$ then:
  - a_i uses its local view $\mathcal{C}_r[a_i]$ to determine the edges of $\partial\mathcal{H}_r[a_i]$.
  - If $(\exists e \in \partial\mathcal{H}_r[a_i]$ such that $\forall a_j \in \mathcal{I}_r[a_i], d(a_j, e) \leq d(a_i, e))$ then
    - $*$ a_i computes a point x of e such that $\overline{a_i x} \perp e$; if x is empty, then a_i moves toward x
- Obstructing Edge Case: if $(s_i = brown$) then:
  - Let e be the edge to which a_i belongs; if $(\exists a_j \in \mathcal{I}_r[a_i] \wedge s_j = black \wedge \overline{a_j a_i} \perp e)$, then a_i moves toward the nearest point $x \in e$ such that $\forall a_k \in \mathcal{I}_r[a_i], \overline{a_k x} \not\perp e$.

Fig. 1. Algorithm for the Interior Depletion Phase

Lemma 1. *For any initial configuration C_0 there exists a round $r \in \mathbb{N}^+$ such that in C_r we have that $\mathcal{I}_r = \emptyset$; furthermore, this occurs without collisions.*

Theorem 1. *There is a round $r \in \mathbb{N}^+$ such that the agents occupy different positions on $\mathcal{H}_r$. Moreover, the corner-agents are* red, *and the edge-agents are* brown.

3.2 Phase 2: Edge Depletion -ED

The purpose of the ED phase is to move the edge-agents out of the current convex hull to reach a final configuration whose convex hull includes $\mathcal{H}_0$ and all agents are on the corners, thus achieving complete visibility.

The algorithm makes an edge-agent move from its edge $e = \overline{v_0 v_1}$ to a point out of the current convex hull, but within a *safe zone*. Safe zones are calculated so to guarantee that *red* agents never cease to be located on corners of the current convex hull, in spite of the movement of the edge-agents. More precisely, the safe zone $S(e)$ of e consists of the portion of plane outside the current convex hull, such that $\forall x \in S(e)$ we have $\angle x v_0 v_1 < \frac{180° - \angle v_{-1} v_0 v_1}{4}$ and $\angle v_0 v_1 x < \frac{180° - \angle v_0 v_1 v_2}{4}$ (see Figure 2a).

Note that, due to the mutual obstructions that lead to different local views, edge-agents cannot always compute $S(e)$ exactly (see Figure 2b). In fact, only when there is a single edge-agent between the two *red* corner-agents on e, the computation of $S(e)$ is exact; in any case, we can show that the safe area $S'(e)$ computed by an agent is $S'(e) \subseteq S(e)$ and thus still safe.

The migration of edge-agents and their transformation into corner-agents occurs in steps: in fact, if the edge e contains more than one edge-agent, our algorithm makes them move in turns, starting from the two agents b_1 and b_0 that are immediate neighbors of the corners v_1 and v_0, respectively. Only once they are out of the convex hull and they are corner of a new edge e', other agents on e will follow, always moving perpendicularly to e'. Careful changes of colors are required to coordinate this process.

In fact, once the first pair is in position, the two agents will become *blue* to signal the other *brown* agents on e that it is their turn to move out; they will set their color to *red* only when there is no interior-agent in the space delimited by e' and e. Once *red*, their color will never change until completion.

Due to the different estimations of S, to semi-synchronicity, and to the unpredictable distance traversed by an agent (possibly stopped before destination), a variety of situations could disrupt this ideal behaviour. In particular, it could happen that only one of the two agents, say b_1, moves while the other stays still, or that b_1 moves further from e than b_0. In both cases this leads to a configuration in which b_0 becomes an interior or edge-agent. This problem is however adjusted by b_1 that, when noticing the situation, moves towards v_1 until b_0 becomes a corner in $\mathcal{H}[b_1]$. A further complication is that b_1 might wrongly perceive b_0 as a corner and thus decide not to move; this occurs if $v_0 b_0$ happens to be collinear with b_1 obstructing visibility; such a case is however detected by b_0 itself, which uses a different color (*orange*) to signal that b_1 has to move further towards v_1 to transform b_0 into a corner (see Figure 2d).

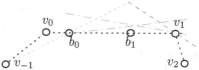

(**a**) Safe Area of edge $\overline{v_0 v_1}$: an agent moving inside the safe area cannot create collinearity with agents on the neighboring edges

(**b**) Approximation of the safe area computed by agent b_1 using as reference the two lines $v_1 v_2$ and $v_{-1} b_0$. This approximation is entirely contained in the real safe area

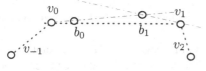

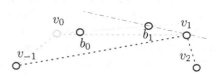

(**c**) Creation of a new edge, due to non-rigid movements or to different approximations of the safe area, agent b_1 could move making agent b_0 interior, this condition is adjusted by letting b_1 move towards v_1

(**d**) b_1 could move in such a way to become collinear to $v_0 b_0$, b_0 signals this condition by changing its color

Fig. 2. Edge Depletion Phase

The detailed algorithm for the ED phase is reported in Figure 3.

3.3 The case of $|\mathcal{V}_0| = 2$

The strategy of the previous Section works for $|\mathcal{V}_0| > 2$. It is however simple to have the agent move to reach such a condition from $|\mathcal{V}_0| = 2$, as described below.

When $|\mathcal{V}_0| = 2$ the agents are necessarily disposed forming a line and $|\mathcal{A}| \geq 2$. First notice that an agent a can detect that the configuration is a line, and whether it is an

Algorithm EDGE DEPLETION

For agent a_i activated at round r; to be executed if and only if $\nexists(black, a_j) \in C_r[a_i]$.

- Execute COMPUTE ORDER and appropriate case from the list below.

- BROWN EDGE CASE: a_i belongs to an edge e of $C_r[a_i]$ and $s_i = brown$.
  If a_i is the only agent on e then
  - a_i computes the angles $\alpha = 180° - \angle v_{-1}v_0a_i$, $\beta = 180° - \angle a_iv_1v_2$, and $\gamma = min(\frac{\alpha}{4}, \frac{\beta}{4})$; it then computes a point x such that $\angle xv_1a_i < \gamma$ and $\angle xv_0a_i < \gamma$.
  - a_i sets $s_i = yellow$.
  - a_i moves perpendicularly to e with destination x.

  If a_i is not the only non-*red* agent on e and one of its neighbors on e is *red* (by routine COMPUTEORDER, this agent is v_1) then: let b be its other neighbor;
  - a_i computes the two angles $\alpha = 180° - \angle a_iv_1v_2$, $\beta = 180° - \angle v_{-1}ba_i$, and $\gamma = min(\frac{\alpha}{4}, \frac{\beta}{4})$; it then computes a point x such that $\angle xv_1a_i < \gamma \wedge \angle xba_i < \gamma$.
  - a_i sets $s_i = yellow$.
  - a_i moves perpendicularly to e with destination x.

- YELLOW CASE: $s_i = yellow$.
  - if there is another *yellow* or *blue* agent a_j with $e^{a_i} = e^{a_j}$ then
    * if $a_iv_1 \cap a_jv_0 \notin (\overline{a_iv_1} \cup \overline{a_jv_0})$ then a_i sets $s_i = blue$
    * if $a_iv_1 \cap a_jv_0 \in \overline{a_iv_1}$ then a_i moves towards v_1 along $\overline{a_iv_1}$ of $\frac{d(a_i,v_1)}{2}$
    * if $a_j \in a_iv_1$ then a_i sets $s_i = orange$
  - else if $\nexists(s_j, a_j) \in C_r[a_i]$ with $a_j \neq a_i$ and $e^{a_i} = e^{a_j}$ and $\nexists(s_j, a_j) \in C_r[a_i] \cap e^{a_i}$ then
    * a_i set $s_i = red$

- ORANGE CASE: $s_i = orange$.
  - if there is another blue agent a_j with $e^{a_i} = e^{a_j}$ then
    * if $a_j \notin a_iv_1$ then a_i sets $s_i = blue$

- BLUE CASE: $s_i = blue$ and $a_i \in e$ with e edge of $C_r[a_i]$.
  - if there is another orange agent a_j with $e^{a_i} = e^{a_j}$ then
    * a_i moves along $\overline{a_iv_1}$ in direction of v_1 towards the point at distance $\frac{d(a_i,v_1)}{2}$
  - else if $\nexists(brown, a_j) \in C_r[a_i]$ such that a_j could move to e then
    * a_i sets $s_i = red$

- BROWN INTERIOR CASE: a_i is such that $s_i = brown$ and $a_i \in \mathcal{I}_r[a_i]$.
  - if there exists and edge $e' = \overline{a_xa_y}$ with $s_x = s_y = blue$ and a_i could move perpendicularly towards e' without crossing any segment delimited by two *red* agents, then a_i moves towards e'.
  - if $a_i \in e = \overline{a_0a_1}$ with $e \in \partial\mathcal{H}_r^{\{red,brown\}}[a_i]$ and $\exists x \in \mathbb{R}^2$ such that $a_0a_i \perp \overline{xa_i}$ and $\nexists a_j \in \angle a_0a_ix$ or $\nexists a_j \in \angle a_1a_ix$ then a_i executes the second subcase of the BROWN EDGE CASE.

- CORNER CASE: a_i is a corner of $C_r[a_i]$ and $s_i = red$.
  - a_i can check local termination and the global termination
    * a_i locally terminates when $s_i = red$
    * a_i detects the global termination of ED phase when $\nexists(s_j, a_j) \in C_r[a_i]$ with $s_j \neq red$

Fig. 3. Edge Depletion Phase algorithm

Procedure COMPUTE ORDER

- if a_i belongs to an edge e of $\mathcal{H}_r[a_i]$ and $s_i = brown$, it orders the *red* agents in its local view in a circular order, starting from the closest, $(v_1, v_2, \ldots, v_0)$.
- if $s_i \in \{orange, blue, yellow\}$, then a_i determines which of its current neighbors was v_1 in its previous computation and the edge $e^{a_i} = \overline{v_1 v_0}$ to which it belonged:
  - a_i computes the nearest edge $e = \{u, v\} \in \mathcal{H}_r^{red}[a_i]$
  - a_i computes the point $x \in \mathbb{R}^2$ such that is $uv \perp a_i x$
  - a_i sets $v_1 = u, v_0 = v$ if $\nexists a_j \in \angle uxa_i$ otherwise it sets $v_1 = v, v_0 = u$.
  - a_i sets $e^{a_i} = \overline{v_1 v_0}$

Color	Meaning	Transition to:
Black	initial color of all agents	{Red, Brown}
Brown	agents on edges or having to move to a new edge of $\mathcal{H}$	Yellow
Yellow	agents moving out of $\mathcal{H}$ to form a new edge	{Blue, Orange, Red}
Orange	agents needing to be transformed into corners	Blue
Blue	corner-agent now forming a new edge e, waiting for other agents to move to e	Red
Red	a stable corner-agent	–

Fig. 4. Colors used in the COMPLETE VISIBILITY algorithm

extremity (i.e., it sees only one other agents a'), or an internal agent (i.e., it is between two collinear agents). If a is an extreme, it does not move; if it is an internal agent, a it moves perpendicular to the segment $\overline{a'a}$. This means that, as soon as at least one of the internal agents is activated, it will move (or they will move) creating a configuration with $|\mathcal{V}| > 2$. At that point, the algorithm previously described is applied.

3.4 Correctness of the ED Phase

With the following lemma we show that the global absence of interior-agents with respect to the initial convex hull, can be locally detected by each agent.

Lemma 2. *Given an agent $a_i \in \mathcal{A}$ with $s_i \in \{red, brown\}$ and a round $r \in \mathbb{N}^+$, if $\nexists(black, a_j) \in \mathcal{C}_r[a_i]$ then $\mathcal{C}_r$ does not contain interior-agents with respect to $\mathcal{H}_0$.*

Proof. By contradiction, assume that $\nexists(black, a_j) \in \mathcal{C}_r[a_i]$ but there exists at least an interior-agent a with respect to $\mathcal{H}_0$. By the rules of the ID phase, agent a cannot change its color from *black* to another because it can detect it is neither a corner nor a border. Thus, a is not in $\mathcal{C}_r[a_i]$ because $\mathcal{C}_r[a_i]$, by assumption, does not contain *black* agents. Thus, it must exist an agent a_k that has color different from *black* and $a_k \in \overline{a_i a}$. But since a is interior then also a_k is interior, and so $s_k = black$. $\square_{Lemma\ 2}$

We now show that the safe area $S'(e)$ computed by an edge-agent on e is such that $S'(e) \subseteq S(e)$ and thus its movement is still safe (it does not transform a *red* corner into an interior or edge-agent).

Lemma 3. *Given a configuration C_r and an edge $e = \overline{v_0v_1}$ of $\mathcal{H}_r$, if an agent $a_j \in e$ moves from e, it moves inside the safe zone $S(e)$*

Proof. The case when there is a single edge-agent $b \in e$ is trivial because b can compute exactly $S(e)$. Consider now the case when there are two or more edge-agents on e; among those, let b_0 and b_1 be the two that are neighbors of v_0, v_1. Those agents move only when executing the Brown Edge Case or Brown Interior Case. Let us consider the movement of the first that is activated, say b_1. Agent b_1 has two neighbors on e: a *brown* neighbor b and the *red* corner v_1. Agent b_1 orders the corners in its view from v_1 to v_{last}, according to its local notion of clockwise, where v_{last} is the last corner before b, i.e. v_{-1} in Figure 2b. Following the rules of the algorithm, b_1 computes: $\alpha = 180° - \angle v_{last}bb_1$, $\beta = 180° - \angle b_1v_1v_2$, and $\gamma = min(\frac{\alpha}{4}, \frac{\beta}{4})$. Angle $\angle v_{last}bb_1$ is an upper bound on $\angle v_{last}v_0b_1$, otherwise we could get a contradiction since $v_{last}b$ and $v_{last}v_0$ will intersect in two points: one is v_{last} and the other one is after the intersection of $v_{last}v_0$ and v_0v_1, that is impossible. Thus, α is a lower bound on the angle that a single agent would compute on e, which implies that b_1 will move inside $S(e)$. The same holds for b_0. Notice that, given two points x and y inside the safe zone, any point $z \in \overline{xy}$ is still inside the safe zone, thus any agent that moves on the lines connecting two agents inside $S(e)$ will still be in $S(e)$, completing the proof. $\square$*Lemma 3*

The next lemma shows that the moves of our algorithm cannot transform any *red* corner-agents into an interior-agent.

Lemma 4. *Consider a corner-agent v_1 of $\mathcal{H}_{r'}$ with $s_1 = red$, we have that $\forall r \in \mathbb{N}^+$ with $r > r'$, v_1 is also a red corner-agent of $\mathcal{H}_r$.*

Proof. It is easy to see that during the ID phase we have that $\mathcal{H}_r = \mathcal{H}_0$ since the interior-agents will never trespass the edges of $\mathcal{H}_0$, so the hypothesis holds. We have to show that the same holds during the ED phase. We have that v_1 never moves after it sets $s_1 = red$ so if v_1 is a corner it cannot become interior as a consequence of its own move. Consider the two edges adjacent to v_1: $e_1 = \overline{v_0v_1}$ and $e_2 = \overline{v_1v_2}$. Assume, by contradiction, that there exists a round r in which the moves of a set X of agents on these two edges is such that v_1 is a corner-agent in $\mathcal{H}_{r-1}$ but not in $\mathcal{H}_r$. From Lemma 3 we have that agents in X move to points inside the safe zones $S(e_1)$ and $S(e_2)$ of e_1, e_2. Let us consider two points $x \in S(e_1)$ and $y \in S(e_2)$, such that agents on them will make v_1 interior. If v_1 is interior in $\mathcal{H}_r$, we have that $\angle xv_1y > 180°$. It is easy to see that $\angle v_0v_1x < \gamma$ (see Brown Edge Case and Brown Interior Case of Figure 3) and that $\gamma \leq \frac{180° - \angle v_0v_1v_2}{4}$, since $\gamma = min(\frac{\alpha}{4}, \frac{\beta}{4})$, and that at least one of the two among β, α is a lower bound on $180° - \angle v_0v_1v_2$. The same holds for y, so we have $\angle v_2v_1y \leq \frac{180° - \angle v_0v_1v_2}{4}$. Thus, we have $\angle v_0v_1x + \angle v_2v_1y + \angle v_0v_1v_2 < 180°$ and then $\angle xv_1y < 180°$, which is a contradiction. So, v_1 cannot be interior in $\mathcal{H}_r$. The same arguments hold if at round $r - 1$ we consider a set of agents X on two edges e', e'' that are not adjacent to v_1; this is easy to see since, given $x \in S(e')$ and $y \in S(e'')$ we have $\angle xv_1y \leq \angle v_0v_1v_2 < 180°$, which is another contradiction to the hypothesis of v_1 being interior in $\mathcal{H}_r$. $\square$*Lemma 4*

In the next sequence of lemmas, we show that, given an edge e in a configuration C of the ED phase, all edge-agents in e will eventually became *red* corners.

Lemma 5. *Given a configuration C_r and an edge e of $\mathcal{H}_r$ with a single brown agent b on e, eventually b will be a* red *corner.*

Proof. Since *red* corners never move and no interior-agents can be moving on e, while inactive, agent b maintains its single position inside e. When activated at some round r', agent b executes the Brown Edge Case with a single agent. Thus b switches color to *yellow* and it moves perpendicularly to e of at least $min(d(v_h, x), \delta)$. At round $r' + 1$, b is a corner-agent of $\mathcal{H}_{r'+1}$; in the next activation, after executing the Yellow Case code, b becomes *red*. $\square_{Lemma\ 5}$

Lemma 6. *Given a configuration C_r and an edge e of $\mathcal{H}_r$ with exactly two brown agents b_0, b_1 on e, eventually they will set their state variable to yellow and they will move outside e.*

Proof. Let b_1 be the first to be activated at some round $r' \geq r$. At that time, b_1 switches its color to *yellow* and it moves perpendicularly to e (see Brown Edge Case). Agent b_0 will do the same, no matter if it is activated in round r' or in some successive rounds (see Brown Edge Case and Brown Interior Case). $\square_{Lemma\ 6}$

Lemma 7. *Given a configuration C, any agent b_1 with $s_1 = yellow$ eventually becomes corner and will sets its state variable to red.*

Proof. If b_1 is *yellow* then a_1 has moved from an edge $e = \overline{v_0 v_1}$. If b_1 was not the only agent on e that could move, then there is (or there will be) another *yellow* agent b_0 moving from e. By construction, b_1 waits until it sees the other *yellow* agent b_0 (see Yellow Case). If both b_1 and b_0 realize to be corners of the current convex hull, then they eventually set their color to *blue* and then to *red*, thus the lemma is proved. However, due to the non-rigidity or the different local views of b_1 and b_0, the pathological case of Figure 2c may arise where one of the two, say b_0, becomes an interior-agent. This case is adjusted by the Yellow Case rule: each time a_1 is activated, it will move towards v_1 until a round r'' is reached when b_0 is not interior anymore in $C_{r''}[b_1]$. Note that, since b_1 moves always half of the distance $d(b_1, v_1)$, and the number of rounds until the next activation of b_0 is finite, we have that b_1 will never touch v_1. Two possible sub-cases may happen at round r'': (i) $b_1 v_1 \cap b_0 v_0 \notin (\overline{b_0 v_0} \cup \overline{b_1 v_1})$: in this case, in the subsequent activations, b_1 and b_0 will set their colors to *blue*; (ii) $b_1 \in b_0 v_0$: this might not be detected by the local view of b_1, but it is detected by b_0 that sets its color to *orange*; in the next activations b_1 will move so to transform b_0 into a corner and, after this move, an activation of b_0 will set $s_0 = blue$. So, in both sub-cases we eventually reach a configuration in which b_1 and b_0 are *blue* corner-agents. In the subsequent activations, they will set their color to *red*, proving the lemma. $\square_{Lemma\ 7}$

Lemma 8. *Given a configuration C, let $e = \overline{v_0 v_1}$ be an edge with $q > 2$ edge-agents on it. Eventually all these agents will become corners and set their color to* red.

Proof. The two edge-agents $b_0, b_1 \in e$ that are neighbors of *red* corners, execute the same code described in the previous lemma. So, they wil reach a configuration $C_{r'}$ in which b_0 and b_1 are *blue* corner-agents. In this case, they wait until all the agents on

e move on the segment $\overline{b_0 b_1}$; then, they set their color to *red* (see the rule 3 of Blue Case). It is straightforward to see that each remaining agent on e will move now towards this new edge without colliding, since all movements to the same edge are on parallels trajectories. It follows that, in finite time, a new edge e' is formed with $q - 2$ agents. Iterating the reasoning we will end up in a case where the number of edge-agents on the same edge is at most 2, hence, by Lemmas 5-7, the lemma follows. $\square_{Lemma\ 8}$

Theorem 2. *The* COMPLETE VISIBILITY *problem is solvable in SSYNC by a team of oblivious, obstructable agents, using five colors without creating any collision.*

Proof. From Theorem 1 we have that from any configuration $\mathcal{C}_0$ we reach a configuration $\mathcal{C}_{ID}$ where $\mathcal{I}_{ID} = \emptyset$. This is locally detected by agents (see Lemma 2), that start executing the ED phase. By Lemma 4 we have that the number of *red* corners is not decreasing during the execution of the algorithm. From Lemmas 5-8 we have that eventually each edge-agent a of $\mathcal{H}_{ID}$ will became a *red* corner. So we will reach a configuration $\mathcal{C}_{final}$ in which all agents are corner of $\mathcal{H}_{final}$, thus, they cannot obstruct each other. Moreover, It is easy to see that each agent is able to detect not only local termination, when it sets its color to *red*, but also global termination of ED phase, and thus of the algorithm, when each agent in its local view is *red*. $\square_{Theorem\ 2}$

4   Complete Visibility in ASYNC

In this section we consider the asynchronous model (ASYNC), where there is no common notion of time or rounds, there are no assumptions on time, on activation, on synchronization; moreover, each Compute and Move operation and inactivity may take an unpredictable (but finite) amount of time, unknown to the agent. As a consequence, agents can be seen while moving, and their computations and movements may be based on obsolete information.

Asynchronous Interior Depletion phase. The INTERIOR DEPLETION algorithm of Sec. 3.1 works also in ASYNC without modifications. We only need to show that the asynchronous behaviour of the agents, and in particular the asynchronous assignment of colors, cannot induce a collision among interior-agents. Since agents always move perpendicularly to the closest edge, it is easy to see that this does not happen and thus Lemmas 1 and Theorem 1 hold also in the asynchronous case.

Asynchronous Edge Depletion phase. The Edge Depletion phase has to be modified for ASYNC. To see why the EDGE DEPLETION algorithm would not work, consider, for example, the Yellow Case in Algorithm 3: it is possible that a moving *yellow* agent is seen by another *yellow* agent, this could lead to scenarios in which an agent assumes color *red* while it is on the edge of the convex hull and not on a corner.

The source of inconsistencies is the fact that agents can be seen while in transit. To prevent this problem we use new colors (*yellow_moving* and *blue_moving*) to signal that the agents are in transit; those agents will take color *yellow* (resp. *blue*) once as the movement is completed. Using these intermediate colors, we can simulate the ED phase of the previous Section (for $|\mathcal{V}_0| > 2$).

More precisely, in the *Edge Depletion* algorithm of Figure 3, instead of becoming *yellow*, a *brown* agent becomes *yellow_moving*, turning *yellow* at the next activation. Similarly, instead of becoming *blue*, a *yellow* agent becomes *blue_moving*, turning *blue* only when seeing that the "companion" agent is *blue_moving* or *blue*.

It is not difficult to see that, with these additional colors, since agents will always move inside the safe zones of $\mathcal{H}$, the validity of Lemmas 4, 7-8 holds also in ASYNC.

The case of $|\mathcal{V}_0| = 2$. When the agents initially form a line, the algorithm described for SSYNC where the agents first move to a configuration $|\mathcal{V}_0| > 2$, and then apply the general Algorithm, would not work. Consider, for example, the following scenario: both extreme agents compute and their destination is in opposite direction, but only one of them actually moves. At this point, the agents on the line set their color to *red* or *brown*, but they will became interior-agents as soon as the slower extreme agent moves from the line towards its destination, thus changing the convex hull.

The idea is to use a completely different algorithm in ASYNC when the initial configuration is a line (refer to Figure 5b). Two additional special colors (*line-extreme* and *line-moving*) are used. The color *line-extreme* is taken by the two agents a_1 and a_2 located at the extreme points of the line, x_1 and x_n, when activated; this color is used to acknowledge the line condition, and to define the smallest enclosing circle SEC with diameter $\overline{x_1, x_n}$. Notice that, due to obstructed visibility, the diameter, and thus SEC, is unknown to the agents. The two extreme agents will never move.

The general strategy is to have the other agents move to points on SEC. First notice that an agent a can detect that the configuration is a line, either by geometric conditions (i.e., it sees only one or two collinear agents), or by the special color of some visible agents (*line-extreme* or *line-moving*). If an uncolred agent a located in x sees a *line-extreme* agent (say a_1), then a changes its color to *line-moving* and it moves perpendicularly to xx_1 toward the perimeter of the circle whose diameter is identified by a_1 and the closest agent $b \neq a_1$ on the line xx_1 (note that there must be at least one, possibly the other extreme). A *line moving* agent follows similar rules; if it can detect SEC (e.g., it sees two *line-extreme*) it continues its perpendicular move towards it. Otherwise, it does not move. It can be shown that, at any time, there is at least one agent that, if activated, can move. A non extreme agent switches its color to *red* when it sees only agents on the SEC; an extreme agents switches its color to *red* when it sees only *red* or *line-extreme* agents.

It is not difficult to see that this set of rules will allow the agents to reach SEC in finite time becoming *red*, and thus to solve the COMPLETE VISIBILITY problem.

Theorem 3. *The* COMPLETE VISIBILITY *problem is solvable in ASYNC by a team of oblivious, obstructable agents, using eight colors without creating any collision.*

5   Circle Formation in ASYNC

When executing the previous algorithm, the agents reach a configuration $\mathcal{C}_{final}$ in which all agents are corners of $\mathcal{H}_{final}$. Starting from this particular configuration it is possible to arrange the agents in such a way to reach a configuration $\mathcal{C}_{circ}$ in which each agent is positioned on the $SEC(\mathcal{C}_{final})$. Note that the solution of the COMPLETE

VISIBILITY problem when $|\mathcal{V}_0| = 2$ already form a circle, hence we focus on the case $|\mathcal{V}_0| > 2$.

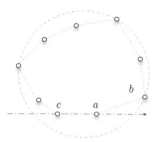
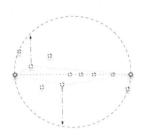

(a) CIRCLE FORMATION: Agent a is neighbor of an agent b on SEC, so it moves on line ca in direction of SEC. During this movement, the corner-agents of the convex hull are not modified, and visibility with the other agents is preserved.

(b) ASYNCH FORMATION FOR $|\mathcal{V}_0| = 2$: the two extreme agents signal the line configuration with color *line-extreme*, the other agents move perpendicularly to them until they reach the SEC whose diameter is defined by the extreme agents.

Fig. 5. Edge Depletion Phase

Notice that, when all agents are on ∂H_{final} they can compute the same $SEC(\mathcal{C}_{final})$ since all the local views are consistent. Moreover, there exists a set of agents $\mathcal{X} \subseteq \mathcal{A}$ that are already on SEC, and $|\mathcal{X}| \geq 2$. The idea of the algorithm is to move all agents on SEC in such a way that in each point of their trajectories they can see a subset of nodes $\mathcal{Y}$ such that $SEC(\mathcal{Y}) = SEC(\mathcal{X}) = SEC(\mathcal{C}_{final})$. More precisely, the moving rule allows agents to move towards SEC if they are "neighbors" (i.e., neighboring corner) of some agent on SEC in $\mathcal{C}_{final}$ (see Figure 5a). Let a be neighbor of some b already on SEC, and let c be its other neighbor: a will move toward SEC on line ca guaranteeing that the corner-agents of the convex hull stay corner-agents, and do not loose visibility with any other agent. Note that, unless in final position, there is always at least one agent that can move. The algorithm terminates when all the agents are on SEC.

It is not difficult to see that:

Theorem 4. *Starting from a configuration $\mathcal{C}_{final}$ in which all the agents are corners, there is an algorithm in ASYNC that makes the agents reach a configuration $\mathcal{C}_{circ}$ in which each agent occupies a different position on $SEC(\mathcal{C}_{final})$ without colliding.*

Acknowledgements. This work has been supported in part by the National Science and Engineering Research Council of Canada, under Discovery Grants, and by Professor Flocchini's University Research Chair.

References

1. Agathangelou, C., Georgiou, C., Mavronicolas, M.: A distributed algorithm for gathering many fat mobile robots in the plane. In: Proceedings of the 32nd ACM Symposium on Principles of Distributed Computing (PODC), pp. 250–259 (2013)

2. Bolla, K., Kovacs, T., Fazekas, G.: Gathering of fat robots with limited visibility and without global navigation. In: Int. Symp. on Swarm and Evolutionary Comp., pp. 30–38 (2012)
3. Cohen, R., Peleg, D.: Local spreading algorithms for autonomous robot systems. Theoretical Computer Science 399, 71–82 (2008)
4. Czyzowicz, J., Gasieniec, L., Pelc, A.: Gathering few fat mobile robots in the plane. Theoretical Computer Science 410(6-7), 481–499 (2009)
5. Das, S., Flocchini, P., Prencipe, G., Santoro, N., Yamashita, M.: The power of lights: Synchronizing asynchronous robots using visible bits. In: Proceedings of the 32nd International Conference on Distributed Computing Systems (ICDCS), pp. 506–515 (2012)
6. Das, S., Flocchini, P., Prencipe, G., Santoro, N.: Synchronized dancing of oblivious chameleons. In: Ferro, A., Luccio, F., Widmayer, P. (eds.) FUN 2014. LNCS, vol. 8496, pp. 113–124. Springer, Heidelberg (2014)
7. Datta, S., Dutta, A., Gan Chaudhuri, S., Mukhopadhyaya, K.: Circle formation by asynchronous fat robots. In: Hota, C., Srimani, P.K. (eds.) ICDCIT 2013. LNCS, vol. 7753, pp. 195–207. Springer, Heidelberg (2013)
8. Défago, X., Souissi, S.: Non-uniform circle formation algorithm for oblivious mobile robots with convergence toward uniformity. Theor. Comp. Sci. 396(1,3), 97–112 (2008)
9. Dieudonné, Labbani-Igbida, O., Petit, F.: Labbani-Igbida. Circle formation of weak mobile robots. ACM Transactions on Autonomous and Adaptive Systems 3(4), 1–16 (2008)
10. Efrima, A., Peleg, D.: Distributed models and algorithms for mobile robot systems. In: van Leeuwen, J., Italiano, G.F., van der Hoek, W., Meinel, C., Sack, H., Plášil, F. (eds.) SOFSEM 2007. SOFSEM, vol. 4362, pp. 70–87. Springer, Heidelberg (2007)
11. Flocchini, P., Prencipe, G., Santoro, N.: Distributed Computing by Oblivious Mobile Robots. Morgan & Claypool (2012)
12. Flocchini, P., Santoro, N., Viglietta, G., Yamashita, M.: Rendezvous of two robots with constant memory. In: Moscibroda, T., Rescigno, A.A. (eds.) SIROCCO 2013. LNCS, vol. 8179, pp. 189–200. Springer, Heidelberg (2013)
13. Katreniak, B.: Biangular circle formation by asynchronous mobile robots. In: Pelc, A., Raynal, M. (eds.) SIROCCO 2005. LNCS, vol. 3499, pp. 185–199. Springer, Heidelberg (2005)
14. Peleg, D.: Distributed coordination algorithms for mobile robot swarms: New directions and challenges. In: Pal, A., Kshemkalyani, A.D., Kumar, R., Gupta, A. (eds.) IWDC 2005. LNCS, vol. 3741, pp. 1–12. Springer, Heidelberg (2005)
15. Sugihara, K., Suzuki, I.: Distributed motion coordination of multiple mobile robots. In: Proceedings of 5th IEEE Int. Symposium on Intelligent Control, pp. 138–143 (1990)
16. Viglietta, G.: Rendezvous of two robots with visible bits. In: Flocchini, P., Gao, J., Kranakis, E., auf der Heide, F.M. (eds.) ALGOSENSORS 2013. LNCS, vol. 8243, pp. 291–306. Springer, Heidelberg (2014)

SMT-Based Synthesis of Distributed Self-stabilizing Systems

Fathiyeh Faghih[1] and Borzoo Bonakdarpour[2]

[1] School of Computer Science, University of Waterloo, Canada
ffaghihe@uwaterloo.ca
[2] Department of Computing and Software, McMaster University, Canada
borzoo@mcmaster.ca

Abstract. A *self-stabilizing* system is one that guarantees reaching a set of *legitimate states* from any arbitrary initial state. Designing distributed self-stabilizing protocols is often a complex task and developing their proof of correctness is known to be significantly more tedious. In this paper, we propose an SMT-based method that automatically synthesizes a self-stabilizing protocol, given the network topology of distributed processes and description of the set of legitimate states. We also report successful automated synthesis of Dijkstra's token ring and distributed maximal matching.

1 Introduction

Self-stabilization is a versatile technique for forward fault recovery. A self-stabilizing system has two key features:

- *Strong convergence.* When a fault occurs in the system and, consequently, reaches some arbitrary state, the system is guaranteed to recover proper behavior within a finite number of execution steps.
- *Closure.* Once the system reaches such good behavior, typically specified in terms of a set of *legitimate states*, it remains in this set thereafter in the absence of new faults.

Self-stabilization has a wide range of application domains, including networking [8] and robotics [17]. The concept of self-stabilization was first introduced by Dijkstra in the seminal paper [5], where he proposed three solutions for designing self-stabilizing token circulation in ring topologies. Twelve years later, in a follow up article [6], he published the correctness proof, where he states that demonstrating the proof of correctness of self-stabilization was more complex than he originally anticipated. Indeed, designing correct self-stabilizing algorithms is a tedious and challenging task, prone to errors. Also, complications in designing self-stabilizing algorithms arise, when there is no commonly accessible data store for all processes, and the system state is based on the valuations of variables distributed among all processes [5]. Thus, it is highly desirable to have

P. Felber and V. Garg (Eds.): SSS 2014, LNCS 8756, pp. 165–179, 2014.

access to techniques that can automatically generate self-stabilizing protocols that are correct by construction.

With this motivation, in this paper, we focus on the problem of automated *synthesis* of self-stabilizing protocols. Program synthesis (often called the holy grail of computer science) is an algorithmic technique that takes as input a logical specification and automatically generates as output a program that satisfies the specification. Automated synthesis is generally a highly complex and challenging problem due to the high time and space complexity of its decision procedures. For this reason, synthesis is often used for developing intricate but small-sized components of systems. Synthesizing self-stabilizing distributed protocols involves an additional level of complexity, due to constraints caused by read-write restriction of processes in the shared-memory model.

Based on the input specification and the type of output program, there are various synthesis techniques. Our technique in this paper to synthesize self-stabilizing protocols takes as input the following specification:

1. A *topology* that specifies (1) a finite set V of variables allowed to be used in the protocol and their respective finite domains, (2) the number of processes, and (3) read-set and write-set of each process; i.e., subsets of V that each process is allowed to read and write.
2. A set of *legitimate states* in terms of a Boolean expression over V.

Synthesis of a self-stabilizing protocol is a highly complex problem, since synthesizing strong convergence is shown to be NP-complete in the size of the state space, which itself is exponential in the size of variables of the protocol [14]. Our synthesis approach in this paper, is SMT[1]-based. That is, given the five above input constraints, we encode them as a set of SMT constrains. If the SMT instance is satisfiable, then a witness solution to its satisfiability is a distributed protocol that meets the input specification. If the instance is not satisfiable, then we are guaranteed that there is no protocol that satisfies the input specification. To the best of our knowledge, unlike the work in [3, 9], our approach, is the first sound and complete technique that synthesizes self-stabilizing algorithms. That is, our approach guarantees synthesizing a protocol that is correct by construction, if theoretically, there exists one.

Our technique for transforming the input specification into an SMT instance consists in developing the following two sets of constraints:

- *State and transition constraints* capture requirements from the input specification that are concerned with each state and transition of the output protocol. For instance, read-write restrictions constrain transitions of each process; i.e., in all transitions, a process should only read and write variables that it is allowed to. Encoding these constraints in an SMT instance is relatively straightforward.

---

[1] *Satisfiability Modulo Theories* (SMT) are decision problems for formulas in first-order logic with equality combined with additional background theories such as arrays, bitvectors, etc.

- *Temporal constraints* in our work are only concerned with ensuring closure and strong convergence. Our approach to encode weak/strong convergence in an SMT instance is inspired by *bounded synthesis* [11]. In bounded synthesis, temporal logic properties are first transformed into a universal co-Büchi automaton. This automaton is subsequently used to synthesize the next-state function or relation, which in turn identifies the set of transitions of each process.

Solving the satisfiability problem for the conjunction of all above state/transition and temporal properties results in synthesizing a stabilizing protocol. In order to demonstrate the effectiveness of our approach, we conduct a diverse set of case studies for automatically synthesizing well-known protocols from the literature of self-stabilization. These case studies include Dijkstra's token ring [5] (for the three-state machine) and maximal matching [16]. Given different input settings (i.e., in terms of the network topology), we report and analyze the total time needed for synthesizing these protocols using the constraint solver Alloy [13].

Organization The rest of the paper is organized as follows. In Section 2, we present the preliminary concepts on the shared-memory model and self-stabilization. Then, Section 3 formally states the synthesis problem in the context of self-stabilizing systems. In Section 4, we describe our SMT-based technique, while Section 5 is dedicated to our case studies. Related work is discussed in Section 6. Finally, we make concluding remarks and discuss future work in Section 7.

2   Preliminaries

2.1   Distributed Programs

Throughout the paper, let V be a finite set of discrete *variables*, where each variable $v \in V$ has a finite domain D_v. A *state* is a valuation of all variables; i.e., a mapping from each variable $v \in V$ to a value in its domain D_v. We call the set of all possible states the *state space*. A *transition* in the state space is an ordered pair (s_0, s_1), where s_0 and s_1 are two states. A *state predicate* is a set of states and a *transition predicate* is a set of transitions. We denote the value of a variable v in state s by $v(s)$.

Definition 1. *A* process *π over a set V of variables is a tuple $\langle R_\pi, W_\pi, T_\pi \rangle$, where*

- $R_\pi \subseteq V$ *is the* read-set *of π; i.e., variables that π can read,*
- $W_\pi \subseteq R_\pi$ *is the* write-set *of π; i.e., variables that π can write, and*
- T_π *is the transition predicate of process π, such that $(s_0, s_1) \in T_\pi$ implies that for each variable $v \in V$, if $v(s_0) \neq v(s_1)$, then $v \in W_\pi$.* ☐

Notice that Definition 1 requires that a process can only change the value of a variable in its write-set (third condition), but not blindly (second condition). We say that a process $\pi = \langle R_\pi, W_\pi, T_\pi \rangle$ is *enabled* in state s_0 if there exists a state s_1, such that $(s_0, s_1) \in T_\pi$.

Definition 2. *A distributed program is a tuple* $\mathcal{D} = \langle \Pi_\mathcal{D}, T_\mathcal{D} \rangle$, *where*

- $\Pi_\mathcal{D}$ *is a set of processes over a common set V of variables, such that:*
  - *for any two distinct processes* $\pi_1, \pi_2 \in \Pi_\mathcal{D}$, *we have* $W_{\pi_1} \cap W_{\pi_2} = \emptyset$
  - *for each process* $\pi \in \Pi_\mathcal{D}$ *and each transition* $(s_0, s_1) \in T_\pi$, *the following read restriction holds:*

$$\forall s'_0, s'_1 : (\forall v \in R_\pi : (v(s_0) = v(s'_0) \land v(s_1) = v(s'_1))) \land$$
$$(\forall v \notin R_\pi : v(s'_0) = v(s'_1))) \implies (s'_0, s'_1) \in T_\pi \qquad (1)$$

- $T_\mathcal{D}$ *is a transition predicate that is the union of transition predicates of all processes. I.e.,*

$$T_\mathcal{D} = \bigcup_{\pi \in \Pi_\mathcal{D}} T_\pi$$

□

Intuitively, the read restriction in Definition 2 imposes the constraint that for each process π, each transition in T_π depends only on reading the variables that π can read (i.e. R_π). Thus, each transition in $T_\mathcal{D}$ is in fact an equivalence class in $T_\mathcal{D}$, which we call a *group* of transitions. The key consequence of read restrictions is that during synthesis, if a transition is included (respectively, excluded) in $T_\mathcal{D}$, then its corresponding group must also be included (respectively, excluded) in $T_\mathcal{D}$. Also, notice that $T_\mathcal{D}$ is defined in such a way $\mathcal{D}$ resembles an asynchronous distributed program, where process transitions execute in an *interleaving* fashion.

Example We use the problem of distributed self-stabilizing *maximal matching* as a running example to describe the concepts throughout the paper. In an undirected graph a maximal matching is a maximal set of edges, in which no two edges share a common vertex. Consider the graph in Fig. 1 and suppose each vertex is a process in a distributed program. In particular, let $V = \{match_0, match_1, match_2\}$ be the set of variables and $\mathcal{D} = \langle \Pi_\mathcal{D}, T_\mathcal{D} \rangle$ be a distributed program, where $\Pi_\mathcal{D} = \{\pi_0, \pi_1, \pi_2\}$. We also have $D_{match_0} = \{1, \bot\}$, $D_{match_1} = \{0, 2, \bot\}$, and $D_{match_2} = \{1, \bot\}$. In other words, each process can be matched to one of its adjacent processes, or to no process (i.e., the value $\bot$). Each process π_i can read and write variable $match_i$ and read the variables of its adjacent processes. For instance, $\pi_0 = \langle R_{\pi_0}, W_{\pi_0}, T_{\pi_0} \rangle$, with $R_{\pi_0} = \{match_0, match_1\}$ and $W_{\pi_0} = \{match_0\}$. Notice that following Definition 2 and read/write restrictions of π_0, (arbitrary) transitions

$$t_1 = ([match_0 = match_2 = \bot, match_1 = 0], [match_0 = 1, match_1 = 0, match_2 = \bot])$$
$$t_2 = ([match_0 = \bot, match_1 = 0, match_2 = 1], [match_0 = match_2 = 1, match_1 = 0])$$

have the same effect as far as π_0 is concerned (since π_0 cannot read $match_2$). This implies that if t_1 is included in the set of transitions of a distributed program, then so should t_2. Otherwise, execution of t_1 by π_0 will depend on the value of $match_2$, which, of course, π_0 cannot read. Notice that the target state in t_2, where $match_0 = 1$, $match_1 = 0$, and $match_2 = 1$, is not a good matching state. However, such states in a distributed program may be reachable due to occurrence of faults or wrong initialization.

Fig. 1. Example of a maximal matching problem

Definition 3. *A computation of* $\mathcal{D} = \langle \Pi_{\mathcal{D}}, T_{\mathcal{D}} \rangle$ *is an infinite sequence of states* $\bar{s} = s_0 s_1 \cdots$, *such that: (1) for all* $i \geq 0$, *we have* $(s_i, s_{i+1}) \in T_{\mathcal{D}}$, *and (2) if a computation reaches a state* s_i, *from where there is no state* $\mathfrak{s} \neq s_i$, *such that* $(s_i, \mathfrak{s}) \in T_{\mathcal{D}}$, *then the computation stutters at* s_i *indefinitely. Such a computation is called a* terminating computation. □

As an example, in maximal matching, computations may terminate when a matching between processes is established.

We now define the notion of *topology*. Intuitively, a topology specifies only the architectural structure of a distributed program (without its set of transitions). The reason for defining topology is that one of the inputs to our synthesis solution is a topology based on which a distributed program is synthesized as output.

Definition 4. *A topology is a tuple* $\mathcal{T} = \langle V_{\mathcal{T}}, |\Pi_{\mathcal{T}}|, R_{\mathcal{T}}, W_{\mathcal{T}} \rangle$, *where*

- $V_{\mathcal{T}}$ *is a finite set of finite-domain discrete variables,*
- $|\Pi_{\mathcal{T}}| \in \mathbb{N}_{\geq 1}$ *is the number of processes,*
- $R_{\mathcal{T}}$ *is a mapping* $\{0 \ldots |\Pi_{\mathcal{T}}| - 1\} \mapsto 2^V$ *from a process index to its read-set,*
- $W_{\mathcal{T}}$ *is a mapping* $\{0 \ldots |\Pi_{\mathcal{T}}| - 1\} \mapsto 2^V$ *that maps a process index to its write-set, such that* $W_{\mathcal{T}}(i) \subseteq R_{\mathcal{T}}(i)$, *for all* i $(0 \leq i \leq |\Pi_{\mathcal{T}}| - 1)$. □

Example The topology of our matching problem is a tuple $\langle V, |\Pi_{\mathcal{T}}|, R_{\mathcal{T}}, W_{\mathcal{T}} \rangle$, where

- $V = \{match_0, match_1, match_2\}$, with domains $D_{match_0} = \{1, \bot\}$, $D_{match_1} = \{0, 2, \bot\}$, and $D_{match_2} = \{1, \bot\}$,
- $|\Pi_{\mathcal{T}}| = 3$,
- $R_{\mathcal{T}}(0) = \{match_0, match_1\}$, $R_{\mathcal{T}}(1) = \{match_0, match_1, match_2\}$, $R_{\mathcal{T}}(2) = \{match_1, match_2\}$, and
- $W_{\mathcal{T}}(0) = \{match_0\}$, $W_{\mathcal{T}}(1) = \{match_1\}$, and $W_{\mathcal{T}}(2) = \{match_2\}$.

Definition 5. *A* distributed program $\mathcal{D} = \langle \Pi_{\mathcal{D}}, T_{\mathcal{D}} \rangle$ has topology $\mathcal{T} = \langle V_{\mathcal{T}}, |\Pi_{\mathcal{T}}|, R_{\mathcal{T}}, W_{\mathcal{T}} \rangle$, iff

- *each process* $\pi \in \Pi_{\mathcal{D}}$ *is defined over* $V_{\mathcal{T}}$
- $|\Pi_{\mathcal{D}}| = |\Pi_{\mathcal{T}}|$
- *there is a mapping* $g : \{0 \ldots |\Pi_{\mathcal{T}}| - 1\} \mapsto \Pi_{\mathcal{D}}$ *such that*

$$\forall i \in \{0 \ldots |\Pi_{\mathcal{T}}| - 1\} : (R_{\mathcal{T}}(i) = R_{g(i)}) \wedge (W_{\mathcal{T}}(i) = W_{g(i)})$$ □

2.2   Self-Stabilization

Pioneered by Dijkstra [5], a *self-stabilizing system* is one that always recovers a good behavior (typically, expressed in terms of a set of *legitimate states*), even if it starts execution from any arbitrary initial state. Such an arbitrary state may be reached due to wrong initialization or occurrence of transient faults.

Definition 6. *A distributed program* $\mathcal{D} = \langle \Pi_{\mathcal{D}}, T_{\mathcal{D}} \rangle$ *is self-stabilizing for a set LS of legitimate states   iff   the following two conditions hold:*

- (Strong) convergence: *In any computation* $\overline{s} = s_0 s_1 \cdots$ *of* $\mathcal{D}$, *where* s_0 *is an arbitrary state of* $\mathcal{D}$, *there exists* $i \geq 0$, *such that* $s_i \in LS$. *That is, the* linear temporal logic *(LTL) [10] property:*

$$SC = \Diamond LS \tag{2}$$

- Closure: *For all transitions* $(s_0, s_1) \in T_{\mathcal{D}}$, *if* $s_0 \in LS$, *then* $s_1 \in LS$ *as well. That is, the LTL property:*

$$CL = LS \Rightarrow \bigcirc LS \tag{3}$$

□

Notice that the strong convergence property ensures that starting from any state, any computation will converge to a legitimate state of $\mathcal{D}$ within a finite number of steps. The closure property ensures that starting from any legitimate state, execution of the program remains within the set of legitimate states. Also, since all states in a self-stabilizing distributed program are considered as initial states, LTL formula 3 is evaluated over all possible states. This is why the formula is not of form $\Box(LS \Rightarrow \bigcirc LS)$.

Example In our maximal matching problem, the set of legitimate states is:

$$LS = \{ \ [match_0 = 1, match_1 = 0, match_2 = \bot],$$
$$[match_0 = \bot, match_1 = 2, match_2 = 1] \}$$

Notation We denote the fact that a distributed program $\mathcal{D}$ satisfies a temporal logic property φ by $\mathcal{D} \models \varphi$. For example, $\mathcal{D} \models SC$ means that distributed program $\mathcal{D}$ satisfies convergence.

3   Problem Statement

Our goal is to synthesize self-stabilizing distributed programs by starting from the description of its set of legitimate states and the architectural structure of processes. Formally, the goal is to devise a synthesis algorithm that takes the following as input:

- a topology $\mathcal{T} = \langle V, |\Pi_{\mathcal{T}}|, R_{\mathcal{T}}, W_{\mathcal{T}} \rangle$,
- a set LS of legitimate states,
- the LTL specification of self-stabilization,

and generates a distributed program as output that respects the above input specification.

4 SMT-Based Synthesis Solution

In this section, we propose a technique that transforms the synthesis problem stated in Section 3 into an SMT solving problem. An SMT instance consists of two parts: (1) a set of *entity* declarations (in terms of sets, relations, and functions), and (2) first-order modulo-theory *constraints* on the entities. An SMT-solver takes as input an SMT instance and determines whether or not the instance is satisfiable; i.e., whether there exists concrete SMT entities (also called an *SMT model*) that satisfy the constraints. We transform the input to our synthesis problem into an SMT instance. If the SMT instance is satisfiable, then the witness generated by the SMT solver is the answer to our synthesis problem. We describe the SMT entities obtained in our transformation in Subsection 4.1. SMT constraints appear in Subsection 4.2.

4.1 SMT Entities

Recall that the inputs to our problem are a topology $\mathcal{T} = \langle V, |\Pi_{\mathcal{T}}|, R_{\mathcal{T}}, W_{\mathcal{T}} \rangle$, and a set LS of legitimate states. Let $D = \langle \Pi_{\mathcal{D}}, T_{\mathcal{D}} \rangle$ denote the distributed program to be synthesized that has topology $\mathcal{T}$ and legitimate states LS. In our SMT instance, we include:

- A set D_v for each $v \in V$, which contains the elements in the domain of v.
- A set called S, whose cardinality is $\left| \prod_{v \in V} D_v \right|$ (i.e., the Cartesian product of all variable domains). This set represents the state space of the synthesized distributed program. Notice that in a self-stabilizing program, any arbitrary state can be an initial state and, hence, we need to include the entire state space in the SMT instance.
- An uninterpreted function v_val for each variable v, $v\_val : S \mapsto D_v$ that maps each state in the state-space to a valuation of that variable.
- A relation $T_{\mathcal{D}}$ that represents the transition relation of the synthesized distributed program (i.e., $T_{\mathcal{D}} \subseteq S \times S$). Obviously, the main challenge in synthesizing $\mathcal{D}$ is identifying $T_{\mathcal{D}}$, since variables (and, hence, states) and read/write-sets of $\Pi_{\mathcal{D}}$ are given by topology $\mathcal{T}$.
- A Boolean function $LS : S \mapsto \{0, 1\}$. $LS(s)$ is true iff s is a legitimate state.
- An uninterpreted function ψ, from each state to a natural number ($\psi : S \mapsto \mathbb{N}$). We will discuss this function in detail in Subsection 4.2.

Example In our maximal matching problem, the SMT entities are as follows:

- $D_{match_0} = \{\perp, 1\}$, $D_{match_1} = \{\perp, 0, 2\}$, $D_{match_2} = \{\perp, 1\}$
- set S, where $|S| = 12$
- $match_0\_val : S \mapsto D_{match_0}$, $match_1\_val : S \mapsto D_{match_1}$, $match_2\_val : S \mapsto D_{match_2}$
- $T_{\mathcal{D}} \subseteq S \times S$
- $\psi : S \mapsto \mathbb{N}$

4.2   SMT Constraints

In this section, we present the SMT constraints formulated based on our synthesis problem.

State Distinction. As mentioned, we specify the size of the state space in the model. The first constraint in our SMT instance stipulates that any two distinct states differ in the value of some variable:

$$\forall s_0, s_1 \in S \; : (s_0 \neq s_1) \implies (\exists v \in V \; : \; v\_val(s_0) \neq v\_val(s_1)) \qquad (4)$$

Example In our maximal matching problem, the state distinction constraint is:

$$\forall s_0, s_1 \in S \; : \; (s_0 \neq s_1) \implies (match_0\_val(s_0) \neq match_0\_val(s_1)) \; \vee$$
$$(match_1\_val(s_0) \neq match_1\_val(s_1)) \; \vee$$
$$(match_2\_val(s_0) \neq match_2\_val(s_1))$$

Closure (*CL*). The formulation of the *CL* constraint in our SMT instance is as follows:

$$\forall s, s' \in S \; : \; (LS(s) \wedge (s, s') \in T_{\mathcal{D}}) \implies LS(s') \qquad (5)$$

Strong Convergence (*SC*). Our formulation of the SMT constraints for *SC* is an adaptation of the concept of *bounded synthesis* [11]. Inspired by bounded model checking techniques [4], the goal of bounded synthesis is to synthesize an implementation that realizes a set of linear-time temporal logic (LTL) properties, where the size of the implementation is bounded (in terms of the number of states). One difficulty with bounded model checking and synthesis is to make an estimate on the size of reachable states of the program under inspection. We argue that this difficulty is not an issue in the context of synthesizing self-stabilizing systems, since it is assumed that any arbitrary state is either reachable or can be an initial state. Hence, the bound will be equal to the size of the state space; i.e., the size is a priori known by the input topology. The bounded synthesis technique for synthesizing a state-transition system from a set of LTL properties consists in two steps [11]:

– **Step 1: Translation to universal co-Büchi automaton.**   First, we transform each LTL property φ into a universal co-Büchi automaton B_φ. Roughly speaking, a universal co-Büchi automaton is a tuple $B_\varphi = \langle Q, Q_0, \Delta, G \rangle$, where Q is a set of states, $Q_0 \subseteq Q$ is the set of initial states, $\Delta \subseteq Q \times Q$ is a set of transitions, and G maps each transition in Δ to propositional conditions. Each state could be accepting (depicted by a circle), or rejecting (depicted by a double-circle). For instance, Fig. 2 shows the universal co-Büchi automaton for the strong convergence property $SC = \Diamond LS$.

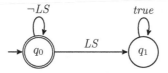

$Q = \{q_0, q_1\}$, $Q_0 = \{q_0\}$, $\Delta = \{(q_0, q_0), (q_0, q_1), (q_1, q_1)\}$, $G(q_0, q_0) = \{\neg LS\}$, $G(q_0, q_1) = \{LS\}$, $G(q_1, q_1) = \{true\}$

Fig. 2. Universal co-Büchi automaton for strong convergence $\varphi = \Diamond LS$

Let $ST = \langle S, S_0, T_{\mathcal{D}} \rangle$ be a state-transition system, where S is a set of states, $S_0 \subseteq S$ is the set of initial states, and $T_{\mathcal{D}} \subseteq S \times S$ is a set of transitions. We say that B_φ accepts ST iff on every infinite path of ST running on B_φ, there are only finitely many visits to the set of rejecting states in B_φ [15]. For instance, if a state-transition system is self-stabilizing for the set LS of legitimate states, all its infinite paths visit a state in $\neg LS$ only finitely many times. Hence, the automaton in Fig. 2 accepts such a system.

- **Step 2: SMT encoding.** In this step, the conditions for the co-Büchi automaton to satisfy a state-transition system are formulated as a set of SMT constraints. To this end, we utilize the technique proposed in [11] for developing an *annotation function* $\lambda : Q \times S \mapsto \mathbb{N} \cup \{\bot\}$, such that the following three conditions hold:

$$\forall q_0 \in Q_0 : \forall s_0 \in S_0 : \lambda(q_0, s_0) \in \mathbb{N} \tag{6}$$

If (1) $\lambda(q, s) \neq \bot$ for some $q \in Q$ and $s \in S$, (2) there exists $q' \in Q$ such that q' is an accepting state and $(q, q') \in \Delta$ with the condition $g \in G$, and (3) g is satisfied in the state s, then

$$\forall s' \in S : (s, s') \in T_{\mathcal{D}} \implies (\lambda(q', s') \neq \bot \land \lambda(q', s') \geq \lambda(q, s)) \tag{7}$$

and if q' is a rejecting state in the co-Büchi automaton, then

$$\forall s' \in S : (s, s') \in T_{\mathcal{D}} \implies (\lambda(q', s') \neq \bot \land \lambda(q', s') > \lambda(q, s)) \tag{8}$$

It is shown in [11] that the acceptance of a finite-state state-transition system by a universal co-Büchi automaton is equivalent to the existence of an annotation function λ. The natural number assigned to (q, s) by λ can represent the maximum number of rejecting states that occur on some path to (q, s) when running the state-transition system on the universal co-Büchi automaton.

To ensure that the synthesized distributed program $\mathcal{D} = \langle \Pi_{\mathcal{D}}, T_{\mathcal{D}} \rangle$ satisfies strong convergence, we use the bounded synthesis technique explained above. In the first step, we construct the universal co-Büchi automaton for the LTL property $\Diamond LS$ (see Fig. 2). The annotation constraints for the transitions in $T_{\mathcal{D}}$

with the set of states S for the automaton in Fig. 2 are as follows:

$$\forall s \in S \; : \; \lambda(q_0, s) \neq \bot \tag{9}$$

$$\forall s, s' \in S \; : \; (\lambda(q_0, s) \neq \bot \wedge LS(s) \wedge (s, s') \in T_{\mathcal{D}}) \implies$$
$$(\lambda(q_1, s') \neq \bot \wedge \lambda(q_1, s') \geq \lambda(q_0, s)) \tag{10}$$

$$\forall s, s' \in S \; : \; (\lambda(q_1, s) \neq \bot \wedge true \wedge (s, s') \in T_{\mathcal{D}}) \implies$$
$$(\lambda(q_1, s') \neq \bot \wedge \lambda(q_1, s') \geq \lambda(q_1, s)) \tag{11}$$

$$\forall s, s' \in S \; : \; (\lambda(q_0, s) \neq \bot \wedge \neg LS(s) \wedge (s, s') \in T_{\mathcal{D}}) \implies$$
$$(\lambda(q_0, s') \neq \bot \wedge \lambda(q_0, s') > \lambda(q_0, s)) \tag{12}$$

Notice that Constraint 9 is obtained from Constraint 6 (since in a self-stabilizing system, every state can be an initial state). Similarly, Constraints 10 and 11 are instances of Constraint 7 for transitions (q_0, q_1) and (q_1, q_1), respectively. Also, Constraint 12 is an instance of Constraint 8 for transition (q_0, q_0) (see Fig 2). We now claim that Constraints 10 and 11 can be eliminated.

Lemma 1. *There always exists a non-trivial annotation function λ, which evaluates Constraints 10 and 11 as true.*

Proof. We show that we can always find an annotation function that satisfies Constraints 10 and 11 without violating the other constraints. To this end, assume that there is an annotation that satisfies all properties except for the Constraint 10. Hence, we have:

$$\exists s, s' \in S \; : \; LS(s) \wedge (s, s') \in T_{\mathcal{D}} \wedge (\lambda(q_1, s') = \bot \vee \lambda(q_1, s') < \lambda(q_0, s))$$

We can simply assign $\lambda(q_0, s)$ to $\lambda(q_1, s')$, without violating Constraints 9 and 12. This assignment can be done in a fixpoint iteration, until no more violation exists. We can develop a similar proof for Constraint 11. Intuitively, for each state s, we assign to $\lambda(q_1, s)$, the maximum number assigned to $\lambda(q_1, s')$, for every state s' in any path reaching s. □

Following Lemma 1, since Constraints 10 and 11 can be removed from the SMT instance, all constraints involving λ will have q_0 as their first argument. This observation results in replacing λ by a simpler annotation function ψ as follows:

- Function ψ takes only one argument, since the state of the co-Büchi automaton is always q_0.
- Due to Constraint 9, the value $\bot$ is irrelevant in the range of the annotation functions. Hence, we define our annotation function as:

$$\psi \; : \; S \mapsto \mathbb{N} \tag{13}$$

As a result, one can simplify Constraints 9-12 as follows:

$$\forall s, s' \in S \; : \; \neg LS(s) \wedge (s, s') \in T_{\mathcal{D}} \implies \psi(s') > \psi(s) \tag{14}$$

The intuition behind Constraints 13 and 14 can be understood easily. If we can assign a natural number to each state, such that along each outgoing transition from a state in $\neg LS$, the number is strictly increasing, then the path from each state in $\neg LS$ should finally reach LS or get stuck in a state, since the size of state space is finite. Also, there can not be any loops whose states are all in $\neg LS$, as imposed by the annotation function.

Finally, the following constraint ensures that there is no deadlock state in $\neg LS$:

$$\forall s \in S \; : \; \neg LS(s) \implies \exists s' \in S \; : \; (s, s') \in T_{\mathcal{D}} \tag{15}$$

Constraints for an Asynchronous System. To synthesize an asynchronous distributed program, instead of a transition relation $T_{\mathcal{D}}$, we introduce a transition relation T_i for each process index $i \in \{0, \ldots, |\Pi_{\mathcal{T}}| - 1\}$ $(T_{\mathcal{D}} = T_0 \cup \cdots \cup T_{|\Pi_{\mathcal{T}}|-1})$, and add the following constraint for each transition relation:

$$\forall (s_0, s_1) \in T_i \; : \; \forall v \notin W_{\mathcal{T}}(i) \; : \; v\_val(s_0) = v\_val(s_1) \tag{16}$$

Constraint 16 ensures that in each relation T_i, only process π_i can execute. By introducing $|\Pi_{\mathcal{T}}|$ transition relations, we consider all possible interleaving of processes execution.

Example To synthesize an asynchronous version of our maximal matching example, we define three relations T_0, T_1, and T_2 and add a constraint for each to the SMT instance. For example, the constraint for T_0 is:

$$\forall (s_0, s_1) \in T_0 \; : \; (match_1\_val(s_0) = match_1\_val(s_1)) \land$$
$$(match_2\_val(s_0) = match_2\_val(s_1))$$

Read Restrictions. To ensure that $\mathcal{D}$ meets the read restrictions given by $\mathcal{T}$, we add the following constraint for each process index $i \in \{0, \ldots, |\Pi_{\mathcal{T}}| - 1\}$:

$$\forall (s_0, s_1) \in T_i : \; \forall s_0', s_1' \in S : \; (\forall v \in R_\pi : (v(s_0) = v(s_0') \; \land \; v(s_1) = v(s_1'))) \land$$
$$(\forall v \notin R_\pi : v(s_0') = v(s_1'))) \implies (s_0', s_1') \in T_i \tag{17}$$

which is similar to Condition 1 in Definition 2.

5   Case Studies and Experimental Results

We used the Alloy [13] model finder tool for our experiments. Alloy solver performs the relational reasoning over quantifiers, which means that we did not have to unroll quantifiers over their domains. All experiments in this section are run on a machine with Intel Core i5 2.6 GHz processor with 8GB of RAM. We note that since our synthesis method is deterministic, we do not replicate experiments for statistical confidence. We also conducted experiments using Z3 [2] and Yices [1] SMT solvers as well. In the majority of cases studies Alloy was the fastest solver.

5.1   Maximal Matching

Our first case study is our running example, distributed self-stabilizing *maximal matching* [12, 16, 18]. Table 1 presents our results for different sizes of line and star topologies. As expected, by increasing the number of processes, synthesis time also increases. Another observation is that synthesizing a solution for the star topology is in general faster than the line topology. This is because a protocol that intends to solve maximal matching for the star topology deals with a significantly smaller problem space.

Table 1. Results for synthesizing maximal matching

Topology	# of Processes	Time (sec)
line	3	0.19
star	4	2.95
line	4	3.5
star	5	53.75
line	5	65.88

5.2   Dijkstra's Token Ring with Three-State Machines

In the *token ring* problem, a set of processes are placed on a ring network. Each process has a so-called privilege (token), which is a Boolean function of its neighbors' and its own states. When this function is true, the process has the privilege.

Dijkstra [5] proposed three solutions for the token ring problem. In the *three-state token ring*, each process π_i maintains a variable x_i with domain $\{0, 1, 2\}$. The read-set of a process is its own and its neighbors' variables, and its write-set contains its own variable. As an example, for process π_1, $R_{\mathcal{T}}(1) = \{x_0, x_1, x_2\}$ and $W_{\mathcal{T}}(1) = \{x_1\}$. Token possession is formulated using the conditions on a machine and its neighbors [5]. Briefly, in a state s, process π_0 (called the *bottom* process) has the token, when $x_0(s) + 1 \mod 3 = x_1(s)$, process $\pi_{(|\Pi_{\mathcal{T}}|-1)}$ (called the *top* process) has the token, when $(x_0(s) = x_{(|\Pi_{\mathcal{T}}|-2)}(s)) \wedge (x_{(|\Pi_{\mathcal{T}}|-2)}(s) + 1 \mod 3 \neq x_{(|\Pi_{\mathcal{T}}|-1)}(s))$, and any other process π_i owns the token, when either $x_i(s) + 1 \mod 3$ equals to the variable of its left or right process. The set of legitimate states are those in which exactly one process has the token. For example, for a ring of size three, the set of legitimate states is formulated by the following expression:

$$((x_0(s) + 1 \mod 3 = x_1(s)) \wedge (x_1(s) + 1 \mod 3 \neq x_2(s))) \vee$$
$$((x_1(s) = x_0(s)) \wedge (x_1(s) + 1 \mod 3 \neq x_2(s))) \vee$$
$$((x_0(s) + 1 \mod 3 \neq x_1(s)) \wedge (x_1(s) + 1 \mod 3 = x_0(s))) \vee$$
$$(x_1(s) + 1 \mod 3 = x_2(s)))$$

Table 2. Results for synthesizing three-state token ring

# of Processes	Time (sec)
3	1.26
4	63.02

Table 2 presents the result for synthesizing solutions for the three-state version. We note that the synthesized stabilizing programs using our technique are identical to Dijkstra's solution in [5].

6 Related Work

In [14], the authors show that adding strong convergence is NP-complete in the size of the state space, which itself is exponential in the size of variables of the protocol. Ebnenasir and Farahat [9] also proposed an automated method to synthesize self-stabilizing algorithms. Our work is different in that the method in [9] is not complete for strong self-stabilization. This means that if it cannot find a solution, it does not necessarily imply that there does not exist one. However, in our method, if the SMT-solver declares "unsatisfiability", it means that no self-stabilizing algorithm that satisfies the given input constraints exists.

In bounded synthesis [11], given is a set of LTL properties, which are translated to a universal co-Büchi automaton, and then a set of SMT constraints are derived from the automaton. Our work is inspired by this idea for finding the SMT constraints for strong convergence. For other constraints, we used a different approach from bounded synthesis. The other difference of our work with bounded synthesis is that the main idea in bounded synthesis is to put a bound on the number of states in the resulting state-transition systems, and then increase the bound if a solution is not found. In our work, since the purpose is to synthesize a self-stabilizing system, the bound is the number of all possible states, derived from the given topology.

The other line of work related to the synthesis of self-stabilizing algorithms is the area of synthesizing fault-tolerant systems. The proposed algorithm in [3] synthesizes a fault-tolerant distributed algorithm from its fault-intolerant version. The distinction of our work with this study is (1) we emphasize on self-stabilizing systems, where any system state could be reachable due to the occurrence of any possible fault, (2) the input to our problem is just a system topology, and not a fault-intolerant system, and (3), the proposed algorithm in [3] is not complete. In [7], a synthesis algorithm is proposed to determine whether a fault-tolerant implementation exists for a fully connected topology and a temporal specification, and, in case the answer is positive, automatically derives such an implementation. Our work is different in (1) considering any kind of distributed topology, and (2) focusing on self-stabilizing systems.

7 Conclusion

In this paper, we proposed an automated technique for synthesis of finite-size self-stabilizing algorithms using SMT-solvers. The first benefit of our technique is that it is sound and complete; i.e., it generates distributed programs that are correct by construction and, hence, no proof of correctness is required, and if it fails to find a solution, we are guaranteed that there does not exist one. The latter is due to the fact that all quantifiers range over finite domains and, hence, finite memory is needed for process implementations. This assumption basically ensures decidability of the problem under investigation. Secondly, our method is fully automated and can save huge effort from designers, specially when there is no solution for the problem. Third, the underlying technique is based on SMT-solving, which is a fast evolving area, and hence, by introducing more efficient SMT-solvers, we expect better results from our proposed method.

For future work, we plan to work on synthesis of probabilistic self-stabilizing systems. Another challenging research direction is to devise synthesis methods where the number of distributed processes is parameterized as well as cases where the size of state space of processes is infinite. We would also like to investigate techniques such as counter-example guided inductive synthesis (CEGIS) that may be an interesting solution to the problem of scaling the synthesis process for larger number of processes.

Acknowledgements. This research was supported in part by Canada NSERC Discovery Grant 418396-2012 and NSERC Strategic Grant 430575-2012.

References

1. Yices: An SMT Solver, http://yices.csl.sri.com
2. Z3: An efficient theorem prover,
   http://research.microsoft.com/en-us/um/redmond/projects/z3/
3. Bonakdarpour, B., Kulkarni, S.S., Abujarad, F.: Symbolic synthesis of masking fault-tolerant programs. Springer Journal on Distributed Computing 25(1), 83–108 (2012)
4. Clarke, E.M., Biere, A., Raimi, R., Zhu, Y.: Bounded model checking using satis-fiability solving. Formal Methods in System Design 19(1), 7–34 (2001)
5. Dijkstra, E.W.: Self-stabilizing systems in spite of distributed control. Communications of the ACM 17(11), 643–644 (1974)
6. Dijkstra, E.W.: A belated proof of self-stabilization. Distributed Computing 1(1), 5–6 (1986)
7. Dimitrova, R., Finkbeiner, B.: Synthesis of fault-tolerant distributed systems. In: Liu, Z., Ravn, A.P. (eds.) ATVA 2009. LNCS, vol. 5799, pp. 321–336. Springer, Heidelberg (2009)
8. Dolev, S., Schiller, E.: Self-stabilizing group communication in directed networks. Acta Informatica 40(9), 609–636 (2004)
9. Ebnenasir, A., Farahat, A.: A lightweight method for automated design of con-vergence. In: Proceedings of the 25th IEEE International Parallel and Distributed Processing Symposium (IPDPS), pp. 219–230 (2011)

10. Emerson, E.A.: Handbook of Theoretical Computer Science. Temporal and Modal Logics, vol. B, ch. 16. Elsevier Science Publishers B. V., Amsterdam (1990)
11. Finkbeiner, B., Schewe, S.: Bounded synthesis. International Journal on Software Tools for Technology Transfer (STTT) 15(5-6), 519–539 (2013)
12. Hsu, S.-C., Huang, S.-T.: A self-stabilizing algorithm for maximal matching. Information Processing Letters 43(2), 77–81 (1992)
13. Jackson, D.: Software Abstractions: Logic, Language, and Analysis. MIT Press Cambridge (2012)
14. Klinkhamer, A., Ebnenasir, A.: On the complexity of adding convergence. In: Arbab, F., Sirjani, M. (eds.) FSEN 2013. LNCS, vol. 8161, pp. 17–33. Springer, Heidelberg (2013)
15. Kupferman, O., Vardi, M.Y.: Safraless decision procedures. In: Proceedings of 46th Annual IEEE Symposium on Foundations of Computer Science (FOCS), pp. 531–542 (2005)
16. Manne, F., Mjelde, M., Pilard, L., Tixeuil, S.: A new self-stabilizing maximal matching algorithm. Theoretical Computer Science 410(14), 1336–1345 (2009)
17. Ooshita, F., Tixeuil, S.: On the self-stabilization of mobile oblivious robots in uniform rings. In: Richa, A.W., Scheideler, C. (eds.) SSS 2012. LNCS, vol. 7596, pp. 49–63. Springer, Heidelberg (2012)
18. Tel, G.: Maximal matching stabilizes in quadratic time. Information Processing Letters 49(6), 271–272 (1994)

Stateless Stabilization Bootstrap[*]

(Extended Abstract)

Shlomi Dolev[1], Ramzi Martin Kahil[1], and Reuven Yagel[1,2]

[1] Department of Computer Science, Ben-Gurion University of the Negev, Beer-Sheva
84105, Israel
{dolev,kahilm,yagel}@cs.bgu.ac.il
[2] Software Engineering Department, Azrieli - College of Engineering, Jerusalem
9103501, Israel

Abstract. Stateless protocols, servers, services and programs are inherently *self-stabilizing* when repeatedly invoked, as any invocation starts from scratch. We suggest to augment a given stateful program with a stateless prefix that (upon invocation of the stateful program, and possibly periodically) verifies the consistency of the state of the stateful program prior to the execution of the stateful program.

We demonstrate the new *stateless stabilization bootstrap* paradigm by implementing stabilizing double linked list of the Linux kernel. In particular we focus on the KVM linked list data structure consistency.

1 Introduction

Writing code that matches the required specification is the goal of every programmer, but also a very challenging task. There are several reasons for the difficulty, such as, the human machine interface when specifying the requirement and the limited possible (rather than exhaustive) testing of the composed program. Therefore many methods, frameworks, and even languages have been developed trying to cope with mistakes that programmers make. Object oriented programming [14], Design by Contract [13] and Test-Driven-Development [1] are a few examples. Despite the fact that all these approaches reduced the amount of errors, and the required testing, systems accumulate faults during long enough runs, since they are not tested over all input lengths [3,12,10].

Related Work. *Stateless programs* are getting attention in the last few years, in several different scopes, including MapReduce framework, monads in functional programming, recovery oriented programming and reentrant code.

MapReduce design pattern [6] separates the *Map* part from the *Reduce* part, where each part is purely functional, and therefore a restartable process. From

---

[*] Partially supported by Orange Labs under external research contract number 0050012310-C04021, the Rita Altura Trust Chair in Computer Sciences, Lynne and William Frankel Center for Computer Sciences, and Israel Science Foundation (grant number 428/11).

P. Felber and V. Garg (Eds.): SSS 2014, LNCS 8756, pp. 180–194, 2014.

a stateful-stateless point of view MapReduce can be viewed as a design pattern which minimizes the state that is shared among the parts of the system, managing the state dependencies to allow independent computations in parallel.

Monads are used to pack inherently stateful tasks such as writing to a file, into a functional program [15]. This is achieved by encapsulating the state. It may therefore fit well into a multi-core architecture by allowing the migration of state from one core to another. Modeling state as a functional concept also allows a program to be abstracted as a mathematical entities, which is object useful for proving correctness [11,17].

Reentrant code [16] is code that can be re-executed while being executed, each execution starts in a different context, and still meets the semantics of a single execution, as if the other executions do not exist [15]. Reentrant code reconstructs a new state whenever executed, state that is independent of other past and concurrent execution instances.

Another path of research is *recovery oriented programming*, see [3] and the references therein, where procedures are augmented with code that ensures the recovery of the system upon violations of the desired properties.

Our Contribution. Writing software that respects the desired specifications, safety and liveness requirements, with no deadlocks and no livelocks is challenging. We suggest a design pattern in which a programmer adds a prefix segment of code to existing code. The prefix of the code, upon every invocation, checks and corrects the state of the existing code, ensuring convergence to the desired behavior. The added prefix can be executed as a periodical consistency check operation and/or as a triggered state consistency enforcement code segment executed just before the execution of an original code segment in scope. Our *stateless bootstrap stabilization* approach is a design pattern that can be implemented by adding code manually or automatically. An advantage of our design pattern is that no changes have to be made to the existing code. Thus making it applicable to working systems with minimal overhead, and no new bugs will be introduced into the system while adding typically simple stateless prefixes for consistency checks and enforcement.

Recovery code can be inserted by a compiler as suggested in [3]. While this is quite a general approach, we suggest a new scheme in which augmented code will be added as a prefix to existing code, where the added code is stateless. Our approach does not require the specification to be formalized and given as input to a compiler which augments the main code with recovery actions as suggested in [3]. In fact any stateless code which performs a consistency check and has appropriate recovery actions will do. Another aspect of our work is that re-execution of the (stateless) prefix has to be guaranteed, possibly, by using a watchdog timer and interrupts. Our stateless prefix stabilization bootstrap scheme can be automated by the use of a compiler that produces stateless prefix code, according to given invariants and recovery actions for setting the state of the relevant original code to a safe state.

We would like to emphasize that software segments designed for preserving system security are often the first targets in attacks on the system, because after subverting the security measures (e.g., anti-virus or kernel data structures) a malicious program is almost free to sabotage the target machine. In addition in most systems, a onetime manipulation of the state of some data structure will grant an attacker privileged access until a re-installation of the subverted module is performed. Therefore we believe that the system should be designed to be self-stabilizing, since a self-stabilizing system, by definition, does not assume that the state is correct, constantly ensures that the system converges to a safe state. In context of kernel-data-structures, we examine a scenario of virtualization with KVM/Linux, if an attacker has somehow manipulated the VM-list (Virtual Machine-list), is such a way as to cause the host to traverse the list forever, a self-stabilizing system should correct the VM-list to avoid such infinite loops, and to reach a legal state. Beyond ensuring the convergence of the state of the hypervisor to a safe state (including the VM-list) the self-stabilizing hypervisor should also ensure that the state of every VM is safe, and possibly restart a VM if the VM is corrupted (not acting as it should or even acting maliciously).

In the next section we define the system settings and requirements. Section 3 demonstrates the stateless stabilization bootstrap technique over an example in Java, which is merely an introduction to the full implementation of the stabilizing VM Linked List example that is detailed in Section 4. Section 4 fully details and demonstrates our framework in converting the linked list of the Linux kernel to a stabilizing version. Section 5 discusses briefly some more examples that have been implemented using our design pattern. Concluding remarks appear in Section 6. Details of the exact implementation of the linked lists in the Linux kernel appear in the Appendix.

2   Preliminaries and System Settings

A *Random Access Machine (RAM)* is a pair (CPU_c, MEM_m), where CPU_c is a state machine with c states and MEM_m is a finite tape of size m bits, with bounded access times. The *CPU* executes *assembly commands* whenever an internal clock pulse takes place, we use the term *atomic step* for the transition of the *RAM* due to the execution of a single assembly command. An atomic step, changes the state of the *CPU* and the content of the *MEM* according to the specifications of the *RAM* producer. The *State* is a pair $C = (cpu, mem)$ where *cpu* is the current state of the *CPU* and *mem* is the current content of *MEM*. The definition of an *execution* follows quite naturally as a (possibly infinite) sequence of states $C_1, C_2, ...$ where each state C_{i+1} is reached from C_i by the execution of a single atomic step (one assembly instruction). A *Legal Execution*, *LE*, is a set of sequenced states where the *RAM* exhibits a desired behavior. The definition of desired behavior is task specific. The *RAM* continuously executes an *operating system* and *applications*. Given an execution there is a mapping of steps and states that are related to the operating system, and steps and states that are related to the applications. Thus, an execution can be a legal execution for the operating system but at the same time be an illegal execution for an application.

A *self-stabilizing* program is a program that can be started in an arbitrary state and exhibits the desired behavior in any infinite execution suffix that follows a bounded number of steps.

A code segment *Seg* is *stateless* if: (1) *Seg* has reentrant properties, namely, defining and initializing all state variables before using them, and (2) the execution of *Seg* is *not* a function of the state of the processor and the operating system prior to the beginning of the execution of *Seg*. Thus, for example, the state of *Seg* is not uploaded from the stack.

An *Augmented program*, P, will be the concatenation of P_1 and P_2 where P_2 is the original program that does a certain task, and P_1 is the stateless prefix. For simplicity, we will assume that P_1 is written in *GCL* (*Guarded Commands Language*) [4]. Formally, we assume that P_1 is a sequence of n guards and commands, denoted as $guard_1 \rightarrow command_1, guard_2 \rightarrow command_2, ..., guard_n \rightarrow command_n$. Every guard will check some aspect of the state C and at least one will return true if the state of P_2 is not safe, and the corresponding command will be a procedure that corrects the state.

For simplicity we also assume that P_2 first loads its state to continue execution. Namely, program counter, stack, registers, etc. This assumption is based on how P_2 is executed if a scheduler and interrupt mechanism are present. Note that, we do not restrict our stateless bootstrap stabilization scheme to be implemented by a scheduler and interrupt mechanism.

We set apart the running time of P_1 and P_2. Since P_1 considers the memory *mem* of P_2 as input, we denote the upper bound on the running time of P_1 on memory *mem* as $t_1(|mem|)$, and the upper bound on the running time of P_2, when started in a safe state, on input x as $t_2(|x|)$. Obviously the running time of P on input x will be $t_1(|mem|) + t_2(|x|)$.

Stateless Stabilizing Bootstrap Design Pattern. In this section we formally define the *stateless stabilizing bootstrap* design pattern. The stateless stabilizing bootstrap is based on realizing the following requirements for any procedure or code segment P.

- *stateless prefix requirement*: We define that the *stateless prefix requirement* of a program P holds if P has two consecutive portions, P_1 and P_2, where P_1 is stateless.
- *repeated execution requirement*: We define the *repeated execution requirement* to hold if there is a mechanism which ensures that in any infinite execution the program counter infinitely often points to the first (assembly) command in P and the execution of P starts thereafter and executes for a sufficiently long period. We define "sufficiently long" as the period required for fully executing P_1 and then P_2, (when P_2 is in a safe state). Thus P_2's execution must be finite, bounded and predefined, when P_2 execution starts in a safe state.
- *composition* : If P_1 is proven to check the state of P_2 and enforce a safe state for P_2, then the execution continues with P_2, and then we say that the *composition requirement of P_1 and P_2* is met.

One possible way to implement these requirements is by using a reset to enforce invariants on the state, and by using the interrupt mechanism to ensure repeated execution of code segments.

Lemma 1. *Every execution of an augmented program P, which starts at P_1 (at the first assembly instruction) will result in an execution of P_2 starting in a safe state.*

Proof. The procedure P_1 is stateless, meaning that the state of the CPU is a pre-defined state. P_1 is proven to have a bounded number of steps, therefore P_2 will be reached eventually. In case the memory MEM_m is in a safe state, all guards in P_1 will return false, and the content of the memory will remain unchanged. In case the memory MEM_m has an invalid state, because P_1 starts from the first instruction, we know that every guard will be executed. Furthermore we know that if mem does not encode a safe state for P_2, then there exists a guard g_i which will return $true$ and the command c_i will change mem into a safe state mem'. After all guards have executed, the next instruction will be the first instruction of P_2, and MEM_m will have a safe state by then, which is actually a base for a legal execution of P_2 starting in a safe state.   □

Lemma 2. *Every infinite execution of an augmented program P, which satisfies the stateless prefix requirement, repeated execution requirement and composition requirement, will have a legal infinite execution suffix.*

Proof. Consider a program P that is the concatenation of two programs P_1, P_2, where P_1 is a stateless program that checks if P_2 is in a legal state and corrects it if necessary. Consider the execution of P at some random state $s = (cpu, mem)$. If s is a legal state, then an invocation of P_1 does not affect the memory tape MEM_m, and therefore P_2 is in a safe state when the execution of P_2 starts. Furthermore, any state change according to the correct execution of an assembly instruction from the program P_2 will result in a safe state by the correctness of P_2. If s is an illegal state, then an illegal state can be preserved until the invocation of P_1 which is within a bounded number of steps. From Lemma 1 we know that the execution of P_1 will result in an execution of P_2 that starts in a safe state. The execution of P ensures the stabilization of the execution of the original program P_2. In case the state s belongs to the execution of P_1 when it is corrupted, then P_2 may exhibit faulty behavior for at most $t_2(|x|)$ steps, then (upon an interrupt) P_1 will start again from the first assembly instruction, and by Lemma 1 this will result in P_2 executing correctly.

The worst case scenario is that the state s gets corrupted after the first instruction of P_1. In this case the system may be in a faulty state for $t_1(|mem|) + t_2(|x|) - 1$ steps. Since the execution of P_1 starts infinitely often, following the next execution of P_1 the execution of P_2 is a legal execution.   □

3   Stabilization Bootstrap for VM Linked List

The Linux kernel has an implementation for a linked list (located at `/include/linux/types.h`) which has the same structure as the presented Java example (See Figure 1), and this implementation is widely used throughout the kernel. For example, the *vm_list* is a doubly linked list used for maintaining the resources allocated to virtual machines by the KVM module [18], which is used for bookkeeping. A missing entry in the linked list may cause the user to be able to unload the KVM module (`rmmod kvm`) while a virtual machine is running. To demonstrate our conceptual approach we start with an example written in Java, then we turn the example into the KVM doubly linked list. The code for the Java example can be found in [20]. Note that this demonstration uses both implementation variants, namely, prefixing a code segment to ensure that each access after a fault is safe, and also periodical interrupts that ensure repeated execution that deals with corruptions which occur during an execution of pervious invocation of the prefix which has not terminated due to the corruption.

Please note that the example was written while holding in mind the implementation of the C code in the kernel. For example we do not assume that the Java class contains a *head* field, but rather receives a pointer to the head as an argument. This is done to adhere as much as possible to the original C implementation which will follow in the next section. A small flaw in the Java implementation is the fact that the delete method does not update the *head* pointer if it is deleted, this is dealt with in a different way in the C implementation, which has no similar Java variant. Please see the Appendix for details.

Listing 1. Implementation of a linked list (P_2)

```
1   public void _insert (Node⟨E⟩ newElem,
2                        Node⟨E⟩ prev, Node⟨E⟩ next){
3       next.prev = newElem;
4       newElem.next = next;
5       newElem.prev = prev;
6       prev.next = newElem;
7   }
8
9   public void insert (E o){
10      Node⟨E⟩ n = new Node⟨E⟩(o);
11      if(head == null){
12          this.head = n;
13          this.head.next = this.head;
14          this.head.prev = this.head;
15      }else{
16          Node⟨E⟩ newElem = new Node⟨E⟩(o);
17          this._insert (newElem, head, head.next);
18      }
19  }
20
21  public void delete (Node⟨E⟩ n) {
22      Node⟨E⟩ next = n.next;
23      Node⟨E⟩ prev = n.prev;
24      next.prev = prev;
25      prev.next = next;
26  }
27
28  public Node⟨E⟩ forEach(Operator o) {
29      if(head == null) return null;
30      Node⟨E⟩ current = head;
31      do{
32          o.action (current);
33          current = current.next;
34      }while(current != head);
35      return null;
36  }
37
38  Interface Operator{
39      action (Node⟨E⟩ n);
40  }
```

Assume we have a *node* object that stores data, a next pointer and a previous pointer. We define a *LinkedList* interface in Figure 1 assuming a non-empty

list. The case of an empty list can be solved with a simple if statement, and is
left out for clarity.

The code in Figure 1 performs well when no transient faults (accidentally
or maliciously) occur. To overcome transient faults there is a need for repeated
consistency enforcement. For example, if the faults caused the linked list to
contain a loop which does not contain the *head* then the *forEach* method may
imply an infinite loop.

Listing 2. Derived class for consistency (P_1)

```
 1 private void enforceConsistencyOnList(){
 2     if(super.head == null) return;
 3     // Nothing to correct - state is empty.
 4     Node⟨E⟩ current = super.head;
 5     do{
 6         if(current.next.prev != current){
 7             // Problem detected!
 8             // Trimming the rest of the list.
 9             current.next = super.head;
10             super.head.prev = current;
11             return;
12         }
13         current = current.next;
14     }while(current != super.head);
15 }
16
17 public void insert(E o){
18     this.enforceConsistency();
19     super.insert(o);
20 }
21
22 public void delete(Node⟨E⟩ o){
23     this.enforceConsistency();
24     super.delete(o);
25 }
26
27 public Node⟨E⟩ forEach(Operator o) {
28     this.enforceConsistency();
29     super.forEach(o);
30 }
```

We present in Figure 2 the following stateless consistency enforcement, which
checks if the linked list is in a consistent state, and if not, corrects it by trimming
the faulty section of the list. For simplicity we implement this by inheriting from
the previous class, and proxying all method calls, where the proxy invokes the
following method first, and then calls the parent method which does the actual
work.

The code in Figure 2 is an implementation of a prefix P_1 that ensures a safe
state for the code in Figure 1 that is the augmented code P_2. Lines 1-19 of Figure
1 are the *insert* method which adds one object to the end of the list. Lines 21-
26 are the *delete* method which when given a reference to a node, deletes the
node from the list. Lines 28-36 are the *forEach* method which takes an Operator
object, and applies it to all objects in the list. The execution of P_1 will guarantee
that the list is in a valid state, and the methods in P_2 will not enter an infinite
loop, or jump to a null pointer. We would like to emphasize the stateless aspect
of *enforceConsistency*, the only thing we access is the head of the list, and all

other decisions are made with no prior knowledge from past invocations of the method.

The composition of these procedures and the existence of a (watchdog) mechanism that ensures reexecution of the code from its first line, results in a self-stabilizing execution with respect to the required semantics of the vm_list. We prove the convergence following the arguments in Lemma 1 and 2.

We define a doubly linked list to be in a *safe state* iff there are $vm_1, vm_2, \ldots, vm_i$ such that the head of the list points to vm_1 and for every $1 \leq j < i : vm_j.next = vm_{j+1}$, for every $1 < j \leq i : vm_j.prev = vm_{j-1}$, $vm_i.next = vm_1$ and $vm_1.prev = vm_i$. We say that a list that fulfills the mentioned properties is safe since these are the properties needed by the methods of Figure 1 to function properly, without executing infinite loops or accessing invalid memory. For the *insert* and *delete* methods this property is important since they will preserve the structure that is around the said node, and the *forEach* method traverses the list till it finds the head again, using only the next pointer.

We would like to note that singly cyclic linked lists may get corrupted and have a cycle which does not include the head (e.g. $link_1 \to link_2 \to link_3 \to link_2$), but for doubly linked lists, given a finite amount of memory, the requirement that for every link accessible from the head, it holds that $vm_i \to next \to prev = vm_i$, also implies that the list is in a safe state. Furthermore we would like to note, that unlike a singly linked list, no cycle which is in a safe state can include a smaller cycle within it, which is also a required and sufficient property of a safe state. The equivalence of the properties that define a safe state is proved in two directions, clearly the definition based on $vm_1, vm_2, \ldots, vm_i$ ensures the $vm_i \to next \to prev = vm_i$, the other direction relies on Lemma 3. From Lemma 3 we know that there cannot be a cycle C' inside another cycle C and that both are in a safe state, from that we can conclude that if we check the invariant at each step, while iterating over the list, we will not enter an infinite loop. Furthermore, if there exists a pointer that just points outside the list to some random address, denote the vm that has a broken pointer as vm_x, then there will be two cases. (1) $vm_x \to next$ is pointing to a random address, then obviously that random address will not hold a structure which has a member named $prev$ which points back to vm_x. (2) If $vm_x \to prev$ is pointing to a random address, then the condition for vm_{x-1} will not hold, because $vm_{x-1} \to next$ points correctly to vm_x, but as assumed, $vm_x \to prev \neq vm_{x-1}$. Either way the condition at line 6 in Figure 2 will not hold and lines 9-11 will be executed. We would like to note that also the extreme case of vm_i and vm_1 satisfy this condition, because $vm_i \to next = vm_1$ and $vm_1 \to prev = vm_i$.

Lemma 3. *For every cycle $C = (vm_1, vm_2, ..., vm_k)$ that is in a safe state, no other cycle C' can be included in C and also be in a safe state.*

Proof. We assume that the cycle $C = (vm_1, vm_2, ..., vm_k)$ is in a safe state, namely, let vm_j be a vm from $[1, k]$ then $vm_j \to next \to prev = vm_j$. For the sake of contradiction we assume that there is a cycle C' that includes C. Let's denote vm_h a vm from $C' \setminus C$ such that $vm_h \to next = vm_j \in C$, because

$vm_j \in C$ we know that $vm_h \to prev \in C$ meaning $vm_h \to prev \neq vm_j$. Therefore C is not in a safe state. □

Now we would like to prove that the *stateless prefix requirement, repeated execution requirement* and *composition of P_1 and P_2 requirement* are being satisfied, and then leverage the proof from Section 2 to conclude that our example is self-stabilizing.

Lemma 4. *The prefix enforceConsistency from Figure 2 satisfies the stateless prefix, repeated execution and composition of P_1 and P_2 requirements.*

Proof. The *stateless prefix requirement* states that P has two consecutive portions, P_1 and P_2, where P_1 is stateless. Indeed the *enforceConsistency* method in Figure 2 does not assume any knowledge from previous invocations. It only gets a pointer to the head of the list, and starts checking consistency from scratch.

The *repeated execution requirement* states that we need a mechanism to ensure that the program counter points to the beginning of P_1 infinitely often. In an infinite execution the linked list should be addressed, by invocation of link operations, infinitely often. Since we prefixed the method calls with the *enforce-Consistency* method and then do the actual work, we conclude that P_1 will be executed infinitely often as required. We also want to note that the occurence of a transient fault during the execution of P_1 (which may cause it to enter an infinite loop) will be handled through an interrupt mechanism which will force a re-executed of the function, from the first assembly instruction, as required.

The *composition of P_1 and P_2 requirement* states that P_1 has to enforce a safe state on P_2. We prove that the list will be in a safe state by induction on the number of the algorithm's iterations.

Assume, that for all $l < k$, if the algorithm has not terminated, then the list is in a safe state. Namely, $\forall l < k, vm_l \to next \to prev = vm_l$.

Induction step, considering the k-th iteration. From lines 13 and 14 we can infer that at the k-th iteration, the variable *current* will point to vm_k. If the condition at line 6 is not met for vm_k then the assumption holds, and at line 13 the algorithm will advance *current* to the $vm_k \to next$ and at the next iteration vm_{k+1} will be checked. Therefore $vm_k \to next \to prev = vm_k$ as required. On the other hand, if the condition at line 6 is met, then we will trim the rest of the list and set $head \to prev = vm_k$ at line 10 and also set $vm_k \to next = head$ at line 9. By combining the two pointers assignments from lines 9, 10 one gets $vm_k \to next \to prev = vm_k$ which is the definition of a safe state for the list. □

4   Linux (KVM) Implementation

In this section we will convert the example from Section 3 into the linked list from the Linux kernel. A patch file can be found in [21]. The patch file can be run after downloading a fresh copy of the KVM module, and putting it outside the downloaded directory, then one can run `patch -p0 -s < linked-list.patch` to patch the code. The actual code for the linked list in the kernel is discussed in the Appendix. For the sake of demonstration it is enough to hold in mind that the structure is similar to the one presented in Section 3. Note that the differences are implementation related issues due to the differences between the Java and C languages. After translating the existing parts to C we discuss the running time implications, and suggest a possible solution. We then demonstrate that not only the structure, but also the data within the list should be and can be forced into a safe state.

This example illustrates the same approach as before, when applied to the *vm_list* in KVM/Linux. Since the *vm_list* and *mm_struct* are used to allocate resources to the VM, it is critical to the correct execution of the KVM module. For example, a transient fault or an attacker may cause a cycle which does not include the head to appear in the list, in which case any invocation of the *list_for_each_entry* macro will cause an infinite loop. The

Listing 3. VM-list stabilizing prefix

```
1  void enforceConsistency(
2              const struct list_head *head){
3      struct kvm *current;
4      int counter = 0;
5      current = head;
6      do{
7          if(current->next->prev != current){
8              // We have a problem,
9              // trimming the rest of the list.
10             current->next = head;
11             head->prev = current;
12             return;
13         }
14         current = current->next;
15         counter++;
16         if(counter > MAX_VMS){
17             head >next = head;
18             head->prev = head;
19         }
20     }while(current != head);
21 }
```

macros for initializing and accessing linked lists in the kernel are left for the Appendix, since they utilize some non-trivial arithmetic tricks.

The presented prefix to the macros in Figure 3 fulfills the stateless stabilization bootstrap requirements, and therefore if the macros are prefixed with this code, it will never enter an infinite loop.

The proof is in fact the same as the proof presented in the previous section, since we have the same prefix as in Figure 2 for the same data structure.

Despite having proved that no infinite loops can exists, one may wish to have an upper bound on a specific list, because, in practice, iterating over a large enough space of data is similar to entering an infinite loop. As a result lines 14-19 (which are new compared to the example in Figure 3) enforce a limit on the amount of elements in the list as an additional requirement. This is particularly applicable to virtual machines because one may limit each machine to run no more than, say, 1000 virtual machines.

We would like to note here that not all functions and macros have to be augmented by the same consistency check. For example, a *null* pointer passed to the *insert* function may cause invalid memory access, which in case of the KVM module may cause a *kernel oops*. On the other hand, augmenting it with a consistency check from Figure 3 will increase the running time from $O(1)$ to $O(length\ of\ the\ list)$, which is quite poor performance. In this case we may augment the *insert* method with a more local consistency check (see Figure 5 lines 1-8) that also runs in $O(1)$ just like the *insert* function itself, thus, avoiding heavy running time penalties. For the *delete* functions, similarly, if one of the pointers is pointing to *null*, we may get a *kernel oops*. Therefore, one may augment the *delete* function with a consistency check which appears in Figure 5 at lines 19-31, and leave the rest of the list for when the data is actually needed.

To further demonstrate the capabilities of our design pattern, one may add additional state checks that include the data records in the list to the *enforceConsistency* method. This consistency will be invoked upon data access, e.g. by using the *list_for_each_entry* macro. For example if we want to test that the number of allocated virtual cpus for each VM does not exceed the predefined *max_vcpus* constant, then we may use the code in Figure 4. The maximum possible value for *max_vcpus* can be re-

Listing 4. VM-list stabilizing prefix including data integrity check

```
1  void enforceConsistency(
2                  struct list_head *head){
3    struct kvm *current;
4    current = head;
5    do{
6      if(current->next->prev != current){
7        // We have a problem,
8        // trimming the rest of the list.
9        current->next = head;
10       head->prev = current;
11       return;
12     }
13     current = current->next;
14   }while(current != head);
15   list_for_each_entry(
16                  current, head, vm_list){
17     if (max_vcpu ≤
18                  kvm->online_vcpus.counter){
19       // Do something.
20     }
21   }
22 }
```

trieved using the KVM_CAP_MAX_VCPUS of the KVM_CHECK_EXTENSION ioctl() at run-time, see [18] file api.txt section 4.7. Note that lines 1-14 of Figure 4 are identical to those of Figure 3, for which we already proved that once executed the execution of *list_for_each_entry* macro will terminate. The new code in lines 15-20, uses the *list_for_each_entry* macro to traverse the list and check for each entry that the counter of virtual cpus does not exceed the upper limit.

In this case we demonstrate that not only the safety of the structure of the data structure be enforced, but also the content of the corresponding data. The prefix maybe, as suggested in [3], a compiled code from a formal specification of the system, or just a gross-grained invariant. It is up to the system administrator to decide to what extent the checks and enforcement are relevant to the system, making the design pattern widely configurable. Nonetheless, while writing the consistency enforcement rules one should keep in mind the self-stabilizing property, and make the system work towards a safe state, while ensuring progress in the system.

We would like to point out that instead of just trimming the list, one may also correct it. The simplest way to implement this would leave the *enforceConsistency* mainly as it is, but replace the body of the if statement at lines 6-10 in Figure 4 with code that assumes the rest of the list is a binary tree (with possible loops), and run an DFS exploration, numbering the nodes with discovered timestamps. After that one would re-build a (safe) list using the timestamps to order the nodes. That way only nodes that have absolutely no pointer pointing to them will be lost.

5   Expanding the KVM Example

To further demonstrate the power of our design pattern we introduce additional consistency checks on the *kvm struct*. These new checks show how one can enforce the consistency on the *vcpu*. Since the vcpu should always point to the kernel space of the system, we suggest enforcing this by a simple check while binding the pointer of the *vcpu* to its corresponding thread. The check can be done using a simple logical *and* operation, where we nullify all significant bits, which are over the CON-

Listing 5. VM-list insert stabilizing prefix

```
 1 void enforceConsistencyForInsert(
 2                      struct list_head *new,
 3                      struct list_head *head){
 4    struct kvm *next, *prev;
 5    if(head == null){
 6        head == new;
 7        return;
 8    }
 9    if(head->next == null || head->prev == null){
10        head->next = head;
11        head->prev = head;
12    }
13    if(head->next->prev != null){
14        head->next = head;
15        head->prev = head;
16    }
17    add_list(new, head);
18 }
19 void enforceConsistencyForDelete(
20                      struct list_head *entry){
21    if(entry == null){
22        return;
23    }
24    if(entry->next == null){
25        INIT_LIST_HEAD(entry->next);
26    }
27    if(entry->prev == null){
28        INIT_LIST_HEAD(entry->prev);
29    }
30    list_del(entry);
31 }
```

FIG_KERNEL_STACK_ORDER and check if we got a zero. Namely, once we have a pointer to a vcpu, we can check $(vcpu \ \& \ \sim mask) == 0$ while $mask = (1 << CONFIG\_KERNEL\_STACK\_ORDER) - 1$. This can be done in the *kvm_sched_in* procedure in the *virt/kvm/kvm_main.c* file.

The exact same method may be applied to the shadow pagetables which convert the guest's physical address into a host physical address. The shadow pagetable can be found in the *mm* field of the same *kvm* struct. Each page table entry (*pte*) is stored in the kernel space and serves only the kernel for dereferencing purposes. Therefore the exact same check can be invoked on each *pte* while it is being addressed.

Another kind of consistency check that can be performed by the kernel before invoking the *vm_enter* or *vm_exit*, is to make sure that no fault has changed the address of the function pointer. This can be done using the `kallsyms` file which specifies for each exported symbol, where it resides in the kernel. Therefore a simple comparison of two pointers will enforce that the jump into the function will be to the correct address.

6   Concluding Remarks

We have presented the *stateless self-stabilizing bootstrap* design pattern, which augments an existing code segment with a prefix that forces a safe state on the existing code segment. We have also defined the requirements that the prefix should fulfill, namely *stateless prefix requirement, repeated execution requirement* and *composition of P_1 and P_2 requirement*, to achieve self-stabilization. Furthermore we provided proof that a prefix augmenting an existing code segment which fulfills the mentioned requirements, will be self-stabilizing. Later we showed an example of how to stabilize the *list_head* struct, which is widely used in the Linux kernel, specifically in the KVM module. As a quick takeaway, we have presented a design pattern which will help developers make their working code self-stabilizing. While we proved the general correctness of the design pattern, its remains the developers duty to define what is a *safe state* for a given program, and to prove that the prefix indeed enforces a safe state from any given state. A natural path for future work would be the stabilization of other data structure like B-trees, Hashtables, etc. Also adding high level stabilization prefixes to kernel modules to make them self-stabilizing could be a promising direction for future work.

Acknowledgment. We thank with pleasure, Marc Lacoste for his comments on the paper.

References

1. Beck, K.: Test-Driven Development by Example. Addison Wesley-Vaseem (2003)
2. Brooks, F.: No silver bullet. University of North Carolina at Chapel Hill (1987)
3. Burkman, O., Dolev, S.: Recovery oriented programming: runtime monitoring of safety and liveness. International Journal on Software Tools for Technology Transfer, STTT 13(4), 377–395 (2011)
4. Dijkstra, E.W.: Guarded commands, nondeterminacy and formal derivation of programs. Communications of the ACM 18, 453–457 (1975)
5. Dijkstra, E.W.: Self-stabilizing systems in spite of distributed control. Communications of the ACM 17, 643–644 (1974)
6. Dean, J., Ghemawat, S.: MapReduce: simplified data processing on large clusters. In: The 6th Conference on Symposium on Opearting Systems Design and Implementation (OSDI), vol. 6, pp. 107–113 (2004)
7. Dolev, S.: Self-Stabilization. MIT press, Cambridge (2000)
8. Dolev, S., Welch, J.L.: Self-stabilizing clock synchronization in the presence of Byzantine faults. Journal of the ACM 51, 780–799 (2004)
9. Dolev, S., Israeli, A., Moran, S.: Self-stabilization of dynamic systems assuming only read/write atomicity. Distributed Computing 7, 3–16 (1993)
10. May, T.C., Woods, M.H.: Alpha-particle-induced soft errors in dynamic memories. IEEE Transactions Electron Devices 26, 2–9 (1979)
11. Moggi, E.: Notions of computation and monads. In: IEEE Symposium on Logic in Computer Science, vol. 93, pp. 55–92 (1991)

12. Musuvathi, M., Qadeer, S., Ball, T., Basler, G., Nainar, P.A., Neamtiu, I.: Finding and reproducing Heisenbugs in concurrent programs. In: Proceedings of the 8th USENIX Conference on Operating Systems Design and Implementation, pp. 267–280 (2008)
13. Rist, R., Terwilliger, R.: Object-oriented programming in Eiffel. Prentice Hall (1995)
14. Rumbaugh, J., Blaha, M., Premerlani, W., Eddy, F., Lorensen, W.: Object-Oriented Modeling and Design. Prentice-Hall (1991)
15. Sharma, A., Welch, S.: Preserving the integrity of enterprise platforms via an Assured eXecution Environment (AxE). In: The 7th Symposium on Operating Systems Design and Implementation, OSDI (2006)
16. Sloss, A.N., Symes, D., Wright, C., Rayfield, J.: ARM System Developer's Guide, pp. 342–346. Morgan Kaufmann Publications (2004)
17. Wadler, P.: Monads for functional programming. Advanced Functional Programming 925, 24–52 (1995)
18. KVM official documentation. See Documentation/virtual/kvm/ in
`git://git.kernel.org/pub/scm/virt/kvm/kvm.git`
19. `http://kernelnewbies.org/FAQ/LinkedLists`
20. `https://gist.github.com/RamziMartinKahil/11169599`
21. `https://gist.github.com/RamziMartinKahil/11083508`

A   Kernel Linked List

Kernel developers have unified the most common data structures, like linked lists, to reduce the amount of redundant code in the kernel. The code for cyclic linked lists appears in `/include/linux/list.h` and is made to be generic. Namely, it is independent of the enclosing struct. We would like to note that this Appendix was greatly influenced by [19] although no exact quotes are included.

List definition is done via the LIST_HEAD_INIT macro, which creates a list of one element.

```
19 #define LIST_HEAD_INIT(name)  { &(name), &(name) }
```

So if we have a struct called **mystruct** which has a `.data` field, and wish to make a list of it, we would embed a list_head pointer in it.

```
struct mystruct {
    int data ;
    struct list_head mylist ;
}
```

Note, that the mylist is not of type mystruct. This is the key to making the list independent of the struct in which it is embedded.

To initialize two elements we would do the following to create two nodes which point to themselves in the **next** and **prev** pointer.

```
struct mystruct first = {
    .data = 10,
    .mylist = LIST_HEAD_INIT(first.mylist)
}
struct mystruct second = {
    .data = 20,
    .mylist = LIST_HEAD_INIT(first.second)
}
```

There are also a few macros and functions for manipulating the lists. For example to add an element into a list there is the __list_add macro, which simply breakes the list between *next* and *prev* and inserts the new element at that point. Note that *next* and *prev* are assumed to be adjacent, therefore it is recommended to use the list_add macro.

```
37 static  inline  void  __list_add(struct  list_head  *new,
38                                   struct  list_head  *prev,
39                                   struct  list_head  *next)
40 {
41           next->prev = new;
42           new->next = next;
43           new->prev = prev;
44           prev->next = new;
45 }
```

Continuing our example we can initialize a list anchor and add the two elements to it with

```
LIST_HEAD(mylinkedlist) ;
list_add ( &first.mylist , &mylinkedlist ) ;
list_add ( &second.mylist , &mylinkedlist ) ;
```

The following macro expands to a simple for loop.

```
369 #define list_for_each(pos, head) \
370          for (pos = (head)->next; pos != (head); pos = pos->next)
```

The list_entry macro uses the container_of macro which is in common use in the kernel. The container_of macro returns the containing struct of a pointer. In our KVM example, given the location of a *vm_list* pointer, it returns the address of the enclosing *kvm* struct.

```
350 #define list_entry(ptr, type, member) \
351          container_of(ptr, type, member)
```

The container_of (defined in **/include/linux/kernel.h**) is a common technique in the kernel, it casts the 0 pointer to the desired type to get the offset of a member inside a struct, and subtracts that offset from the pointers location. The result of that computation will be the address of the containing struct.

```
684 #define container_of(ptr, type, member) ({                          \
685          const typeof( ((type *)0)->member ) *__mptr = (ptr);       \
686          (type *)( (char *)__mptr - offsetof(type,member) );})
```

Continuing the example, we could print the data from the list with the following code, which uses the list_for_each macro to iterate over the list elements, and list_entry to access the enclosing struct.

```
struct list_head *position = NULL ;
struct mystruct *datastructureptr = NULL ;
list_for_each ( position , & mylinkedlist )
   {
       datastructureptr = list_entry(position , struct mystruct , mylist );
       printk ("data = %d\n" , datastructureptr->data );
   }
```

To make things even easier for programmers, the list_for_each_entry macro combines the container_of macro with the list_for_each macro.

```
418 #define list_for_each_entry(pos, head, member)    \
419      for (pos = list_entry((head)->next, typeof(*pos), member);  \
420          &pos->member != (head);   \
421          pos = list_entry(pos->member.next, typeof(*pos), member))
```

Self-healing Computation[*][**]

George Saad and Jared Saia

Department of Computer Science, University of New Mexico
{saad,saia}@cs.unm.edu

Abstract. In the problem of reliable multiparty computation (RC), there are n parties, each with an individual input, and the parties want to jointly compute a function f over n inputs. The problem is complicated by the fact that an omniscient adversary controls a hidden fraction of the parties.

We describe a self-healing algorithm for this problem. In particular, for a fixed function f, with n parties and m gates, we describe how to perform RC repeatedly as the inputs to f change. Our algorithm maintains the following properties, even when an adversary controls up to $t \leq (\frac{1}{4} - \epsilon)n$ parties, for any constant $\epsilon > 0$. First, our algorithm performs each reliable computation with the following amortized resource costs: $O(m + n \log n)$ messages, $O(m + n \log n)$ computational operations, and $O(\ell)$ latency, where ℓ is the depth of the circuit that computes f. Second, the expected total number of corruptions is $O(t(\log^* m)^2)$, after which the adversarially controlled parties are effectively quarantined so that they cause no more corruptions.

Keywords: Self-Healing Algorithms, Threshold Cryptography, Leader Election.

1 Introduction

How can we protect a network against adversarial attack? A traditional approach provides robustness through redundant components. If one component is attacked, the remaining components maintain functionality. Unfortunately, this approach incurs significant resource cost, even when the network is not under attack.

An alternative approach is self-healing, where a network detects the damage made by attacks, inspects the corruption situation and automatically recovers. Self-healing algorithms expend additional resources only when it is necessary to repair from attacks.

In this paper, we describe self-healing algorithms for the problem of *reliable multiparty computation (RC)*. In the RC problem, there are n parties, each with an individual input, and the parties want to jointly compute a function f over n inputs. A hidden $1/4$-fraction of the parties are controlled by an omniscient Byzantine adversary. A party that is controlled by the adversary is said to be *bad*, and the remaining parties are said to be *good*. Our goal is to ensure that all good parties learn the output of f. [1]

RC abstracts many problems that may occur in high-performance computing, sensor networks, and peer-to-peer networks. For example, we can use RC to enable perfor-

---

[*] This research is partially supported by NSF grants: CISE-1117985 and CNS-1017509.
[**] The full paper is located at: http://cs.unm.edu/~saad/Papers/compute.pdf
[1] Note that RC differs from secure multiparty computation (MPC) only in that there is no requirement to keep inputs private.

P. Felber and V. Garg (Eds.): SSS 2014, LNCS 8756, pp. 195–210, 2014.
© Springer International Publishing Switzerland 2014

mance profiling and system monitoring, compute order statistics, and enable public voting.

Our main result is an algorithm for RC that 1) is asymptotically optimal in terms of total messages and total computational operations; and 2) limits the expected total number of corruptions. Ideally, each bad party would cause $O(1)$ corruptions; in our algorithm, each bad party causes an expected $O((\log^* m)^2)$ corruptions.

1.1 Our Model

We assume a *static* Byzantine adversary that takes over $t \leq (\frac{1}{4} - \epsilon)n$ parties before the algorithm begins, for any constant $\epsilon > 0$. As mentioned previously, parties that are compromised by the adversary are called *bad*, and the remaining parties are *good*. The bad parties may arbitrarily deviate from the protocol, by sending no messages, excessive numbers of messages, incorrect messages, or any combination of these. The good parties follow the protocol. We assume that the adversary knows our protocol, but is unaware of the random bits of the good nodes. We make use of a public key cryptography scheme, and thus assume that the adversary is computationally bounded.

Also, we assume a partially synchronous communication model, where any message sent from one good node to another good node requires at most h time steps to be sent and received, and the value h is known to all nodes. We allow the adversary to be *rushing* in the sense that the bad nodes receive all messages from good nodes in a round before sending out their own messages.

We further assume that each party has a unique ID. We say that party p has a link to party q if p knows q's ID and can thus directly communicate with node q.

In the reliable multiparty computation problem, we assume that the function f can be implemented with an arithmetic circuit over m gates, where each gate has two inputs and at most two outputs.[2] For simplicity of presentation, we focus on computing a single function multiple times (with changing inputs). However, we can also compute multiple functions with our algorithm.

1.2 Our Result

We describe an algorithm, *COMPUTE*, to efficiently solve reliable multiparty computation. Our main result is summarized in the following theorem.

Theorem 1. *Assume we have n parties providing inputs to a function f that can be computed by an arithmetic circuit with depth ℓ and containing m gates. Then COMPUTE solves RC and has the following properties: 1) in an amortized sense[3], any execution of COMPUTE requires $O(m+n \log n)$ messages sent by all parties, $O(m+n \log n)$ computational operations performed by all parties, and $O(\ell)$ latency; and 2) the expected total number of times COMPUTE returns a corrupted output is $O(t(\log^* m)^2)$.*

Due to space constraints, all proofs are provided in the full paper.

---

[2] We note that any gate of any fixed in-degree and out-degree can be converted into a fixed number of gates with in-degree 2 and out-degree at most 2.

[3] In particular, if we call *COMPUTE* $\mathcal{L}$ times, then the expected total number of messages sent will be $O(\mathcal{L}(m+n \log n)+t(m \log^2 n))$. Since t is fixed, for large $\mathcal{L}$, the expected number of messages per *COMPUTE* is $O(m+n \log n)$. Similar for the cost of computational operations.

1.3   Technical Overview

Our algorithms make critical use of quorums and a quorum graph.

Quorums and the Quorum Graph: We define a quorum to be a set of $\Theta(\log n)$ parties, of which at most $1/4$-fraction are bad. Many results show how to create and maintain a network of quorums [1,2,3,4,5,6,7]. All of these results maintain what we will call a *quorum graph* in which each vertex represents a quorum. The properties of the quorum graph are: 1) each party is in $\Theta(\log n)$ quorums; 2) for any quorum Q, any party in Q can communicate directly to any other party in Q; and 3) for any quorums Q and Q' that are connected in the quorum graph, any party in Q can communicate directly with any party in Q' and vice versa. Moreover, we assume that for any two parties x and y in a quorum, x knows all quorums that y is in.

Computing with Quorums: We maintain a quorum graph with $m + n$ nodes: m nodes for the gates of the circuit and n nodes for the inputs of the parties. The input nodes are connected to the gates using these inputs, and the gate nodes are connected as in the circuit. Quorums are mapped to nodes in this quorum graph as described above. For simplicity of presentation, we let the computation be performed from the left to the right, where the input quorums are the leftmost quorums and the output quorum is the rightmost quorum in the quorum graph.

Naive Algorithm: A correct but inefficient way to solve RC is as follows. Each party sends its input to all parties of the appropriate input quorum. Then the computation is performed from left to right. All parties in each quorum compute the appropriate gate operation on their inputs, and send their outputs to all parties in the right neighboring quorums via all-to-all communication. At the next level, all parties in each quorum take the majority of the received messages in order to determine the correct input for their gate. At the end, the parties in the rightmost quorum will compute the correct output of the circuit. They then forward this output back from right to left through the quorum graph using the same all-to-all communication and majority filtering.

Unfortunately, this naive algorithm requires $O((m + n) \log^2 n)$ messages and $O(m \log n)$ computational operations. Our main goal is to remove the logarithmic factors.[4]

Our Approach: A more efficient approach is for each quorum to have a leader, and for this leader to receive inputs, perform gate computations, and send off the output. Unfortunately, a single bad leader can corrupt the entire computation.

To address this issue, we provide *CHECK* (Section 2.3). This algorithm determines if there has been a corruption, and if so, it calls *UPDATE* (Section 2.4), which identifies at least one pair of parties that are in *conflict*. Informally, we say that a pair of parties are in conflict if they each accuse the other of malicious behavior. In such a situation, we know that at least one party in the pair is bad. Our approach is to mark both parties

---

[4] We note that such asymptotic improvements can be significant for large networks. For example, if $n = 64,000$, then we would expect our algorithm to reduce message cost by a factor of $\log^2 n = 255$.

in each conflicting pair, and these marked parties are prohibited from participating in future computation but they still can provide the inputs of the circuit. [5]

The basic idea of *CHECK* is to redo the computation through subsets of parties; one subset for each gate. *CHECK* runs in multiple rounds. Initially, all subsets are empty; and in each round, a new party is selected uniformly at random from each quorum to be added to each subset. We call these parties the *checkers*. For convenience of presentation, we will refer to the leaders as the checkers for round 0. For each round $i \geq 1$, all i checkers at gate g: 1) receive inputs to g from the checkers at each input gate for g; 2) compute the gate output for g based on these inputs; and 3) send this output to the checkers at each output gate for g. If a good checker ever receives inconsistent inputs, it calls *UPDATE*. Unfortunately, waiting until a round where each gate has had at least one good checker would require $O(\log n)$ rounds.

To do better, we use the following approach. Let G be the quorum graph as defined above and let the checkers be selected as above. Call a subgraph of G bad in a given round if all checkers in the nodes of that subgraph are bad; note that such a subgraph consists of the new checkers that are added to the subsets in that round. When the adversary corrupts an output of a bad subgraph of G in one round, it has to keep corrupting this output by nesting levels of bad subgraphs of G in all subsequent rounds.

Recall that in each round, new checkers are selected uniformly at random. When *CHECK* selects a good checker at a quorum, it is as removing the node associated with this quorum from the quorum graph. Thus, we can view *CHECK* as repeatedly removing nodes from increasingly smaller subgraphs of G until no nodes remain, at which the corruption is detected. A key lemma (Lemma 2) shows that for any rooted directed acyclic graph (DAG), with m nodes and maximum indegree 2, when each node is deleted independently with probability at least $1/2 + \epsilon$, for any constant $\epsilon > 0$, the probability of having a connected DAG, rooted at one node, with surviving nodes of size $\Omega(\log m)$, is at most $1/2$. By this lemma, we show that *CHECK* requires only $O(\log^* m)$ rounds to detect a corruption with constant probability. [6]

CHECK requires $O((m + n \log n)(\log^* m)^2)$ messages. Then, we can call it with probability $1/(\log^* m)^2$ and obtain asymptotically optimal resource costs for the RC problem, while incurring an expected $O(t(\log^* m)^2)$ corruptions.

1.4 Related Work

Our results are inspired by recent work on self-healing algorithms. Early work of [8,9,10,11,12] discusses different restoration mechanisms to preserve network performance by adding capacity and rerouting traffic streams in the presence of node or link failures. This work presents mathematical models to determine global optimal restoration paths, and provides methods for capacity optimization of path-restorable networks.

More recent work [13,14,15,16,17,18] considers models where the following process repeats indefinitely: an adversary deletes some nodes in the network, and the algorithm

---

[5] A technical point is that we may need to unmark all parties in a quorum if too many parties in that quorum become marked. However, a potential function argument (Lemma 8) shows that after $O(t)$ markings, all bad parties will be marked.

[6] This probability can be made arbitrarily close to 1 by adjusting the hidden constant in the $O(\log^* m)$ rounds.

adds edges. The algorithm is constrained to never increase the degree of any node by more than a logarithmic factor from its original degree. In this model, researchers have presented algorithms that ensure the following properties: the network stays connected and the diameter does not increase by much [13,14,15]; the shortest path between any pair of nodes does not increase by much [16]; expansion properties of the network are approximately preserved [17]; and keeping network backbones densely connected [18].

This paper particularly builds on [19]. That paper describes self-healing algorithms that provide reliable communication, with a minimum of corruptions, even when a Byzantine adversary can take over a constant fraction of the nodes in a network. While our attack model is similar to [19], reliable *computation* is more challenging than reliable communication, and hence this paper requires a significantly different technical approach. Additionally, we improve the fraction of bad parties that can be tolerated from $1/8$ to $1/4$.

Reliable multiparty computation (RC) is closely related to the problem of secure multiparty computation (MPC) which has been studied extensively for several decades (see e.g. [20,21,22,23,24] or the recent book [25]). RC is simpler than MPC in that it does not require inputs of the parties to remain private. Our algorithm for RC is significantly more efficient than current algorithms for MPC, which require at least polylogarithmic blowup in communication and computational costs in order to tolerate a Byzantine adversary. We reduce these costs through our self-healing approach, which expends additional resources only when corruptions occur, and is able to "quarantine" bad parties after $O(t(\log^* m)^2)$ corruptions.

1.5 Organization of Paper

The rest of this paper is organized as follows. In Section 2, we describe our algorithms. The analysis of our algorithms is shown in Section 3. Finally, we conclude and describe problems for future work in Section 4.

2 Our Algorithms

In this section, we describe our algorithms: *COMPUTE, COMPUTE-CIRCUIT, CHECK* and *UPDATE*.

Our algorithms aim at detecting corruptions and marking the bad parties. Note that the parties that are marked are not allowed to participate in the computation; but they still can provide inputs to the circuit. Note further that all parties are initially unmarked.

Recall that there are n parties, each provides an input to an input quorum, Q_i, for $1 \leq i \leq n$; and then the computation is performed through m quorums, Q_j's, for $n + 1 \leq j \leq m + n$. The result is produced at an output quorum Q_{m+n}, and it is sent back to the senders through the m quorums.

Before discussing our main *COMPUTE* algorithm, we describe that when a party x broadcasts a message msg, signed by the private key of a quorum Q, to a set of parties S, it calls $BROADCAST(msg, Q, S)$.

2.1 BROADCAST

In *BROADCAST* (Algorithm 1), we use threshold cryptography to avoid the overhead of Byzantine Agreement. In a (η, η')-threshold cryptographic scheme, a private key is distributed among η parties in such a way that 1) any subset of more than η' parties can jointly reassemble the key; and 2) no subset of at most η' parties can recover the key. The private key can be distributed using a *Distributed Key Generation* (DKG) protocol [26].

In particular, we use $(|Q|, \frac{3|Q|}{4} - 1)$-DKG to generate for each quorum Q the following: 1) a (distributed) private key of Q, where a private key share is generated for each party in Q; 2) a public key of Q to verify each message signed by the (distributed) private key of Q; and 3) a public key share for each party in Q in order to verify any message signed by the private key share of this party.

Note that for each quorum, Q, the public key of Q and the public key share of each party in Q are known to all parties in Q and all parties in the neighboring quorums.

Recall that a party x calls $BROADCAST(msg, Q, S)$ in order to send a message msg to all parties in S after signing msg by the private key of quorum Q. Signing a message msg, by the private key of Q, is formally stated in *SIGN* (msg, Q) (Algorithm 2). Note that we let the message msg be signed by the private key of Q in order to fulfill the following: 1) at least $3/4$-fraction of the parties in quorum Q have received the same message msg; 2) they agree upon the content of msg; and 3) they give permission to x to broadcast this message.

Algorithm 1. BROADCAST(msg, Q, S)   ▷ A party x sends message msg to a set of parties S after signing it by the private key of quorum Q.

1: Party x calls *SIGN* (msg, Q).   ▷ signs msg by the private key of quorum Q.
2: Party x sends this signed-message to all parties in S.

Each call to *BROADCAST* has $O(\log n + |S|)$ messages and $O(\log n)$ computational operations with latency $O(1)$.

Algorithm 2. SIGN(msg, Q)   ▷ Signs message msg by the private key of quorum Q.

1: Party x sends message msg to all parties in Q.
2: Each party in Q signs msg by its private key share to obtain its message share.
3: Each party in Q sends its message share back to party x.
4: Party x interpolates at least $\frac{3|Q|}{4}$ message shares to obtain a signed-message of Q.

2.2 COMPUTE

Now we describe our main algorithm, *COMPUTE* (Algorithm 3), which calls *COMPUTE-CIRCUIT* (Algorithm 4). In *COMPUTE-CIRCUIT*, the n parties broadcast their inputs to the input quorums; note that we assume that all parties provide their inputs to the circuit in the same round. The input quorums forward these inputs to a circuit of m leaders in order to perform the computation and provide the result to the output quorum. Then this result is sent back to all senders (all parties) through the same circuit. Note that we define a leader of a quorum as a representative party of all parties in this quorum, and its leadership is known to all parties in this quorum and the neighboring quorums.

Algorithm 3. COMPUTE   ▷ performs a reliable computation and sends the result reliably to all parties.

1: COMPUTE-CIRCUIT   ▷ computes and sends back the result through a circuit of leaders.
2: TRIGGER-CHECK   ▷ The output quorum triggers *CHECK* with probability $1/(\log^* m)^2$.

In the presence of an adversary, *COMPUTE-CIRCUIT* is vulnerable to corruptions. Thus, *COMPUTE* calls *TRIGGER-CHECK* (Algorithm 5), in which the parties of the output quorum decide together, to trigger *CHECK* (Algorithm 7) with probability $1/(\log^* m)^2$, using secure multiparty computation (MPC) [22,23,24]. *CHECK* is triggered in order to detect with probability at least $1/2$ if a computation was corrupted in the last call to *COMPUTE-CIRCUIT*.

Unfortunately, while *CHECK* can determine if a corruption occurred, it does not locate where the corruption originally occurred. Thus, when *CHECK* detects a corruption, *UPDATE* (Algorithm 11) is called. In each call to *UPDATE*, two neighboring quorums in the circuit are identified such that at least one pair of parties in these quorums is in conflict and at least one party in this pair is bad. Then the parties that are in conflict are marked in all quorums they are in, and in their neighboring quorums. Moreover, for each pair of leaders that are in conflict, their quorums elect a new pair of unmarked leaders uniformly at random. Note that if $(1/2 - \gamma)$-fraction of parties in any quorum have been marked, for any constant $\gamma > 0$, e.g., $\gamma = 0.01$, they are set unmarked in all their quorums and in all their neighboring quorums.

Moreover, we use *BROADCAST* in *COMPUTE-CIRCUIT* and *CHECK* in order to handle any accusation issued in *UPDATE* against the parties that provide the inputs to the input quorums, or those that receive the result in the output quorum.

Our model does not directly consider concurrency. In a real system, concurrent executions of *COMPUTE* that overlap at a single quorum may allow the adversary to achieve multiple corruptions at the cost of a single marked bad party. However, this does not effect correctness, and, in practice, this issue can be avoided by serializing concurrent executions of *COMPUTE*. For simplicity of presentation, we leave the concurrency aspect out of this paper.

2.3 *CHECK*

In this section, we describe *CHECK* algorithm, which is stated formally as Algorithm 7. In this algorithm, we make use of subquorums, where a subquorum is a subset of unmarked parties in a quorum. Let U_k be the set of all unmarked parties in quorum Q_k, for $1 \leq k \leq m + n$.

CHECK runs for $O(\log^* m)$ rounds. For each round i, the parties of the output quorum Q_{m+n} elect an unmarked party **r** from Q_{m+n} to be in charge of the recomputation in round i, where this election process is stated formally in *ELECT* (Algorithm 6). Then, the elected party **r** calls *REQUEST* (Algorithm 8) to send a request through a DAG of subquorums, S_j^A's, to the n senders in order to recompute. The recomputation process is stated formally as *RECOMPUTE* (Algorithm 9), in which each sender that receives this request provides its input to redo the computation through a DAG of subquorums, S_j^B's, producing the result at the output quorum. When **r** receives this result, it calls *RESEND-*

Algorithm 4. COMPUTE-CIRCUIT   ▷ performs a computation through a circuit of leaders producing a result at the output quorum; then the result is sent back through same circuit to all senders.

1: **for** $i = 1, \ldots, n$ **do**   ▷ provides the inputs to the circuit.
2:    Party s_i calls *BROADCAST* (a_i, Q_i, Q_i). ▷ s_i broadcasts its input a_i to all parties in Q_i.
3:    All parties in Q_i send a_i to the leaders of the right neighboring quorums of Q_i.
4: **end for**
5: **for** $i = n + 1, \ldots, m + n - 1$ **do**   ▷ performs the computation.
6:    Let $Q_{i'}$ and $Q_{i''}$ be the right neighboring quorums of Q_i in the circuit.
7:    **if** leader $q_i \in Q_i$ receives all its inputs **then**
8:        q_i performs an operation on its inputs producing an output, b_i.
9:        q_i sends b_i to leader $q_{i'} \in Q_{i'}$ and to leader $q_{i''} \in Q_{i''}$.
10:    **end if**
11: **end for**
12: **if** leader $q_{m+n} \in Q_{m+n}$ receives all its inputs **then**
13:    q_{m+n} performs an operation on its inputs producing an output, b_{m+n}.
14:    q_{m+n} broadcasts b_{m+n} to all parties in Q_{m+n}.
15: **end if**
16: **for** $i = m + n, \ldots, n + 1$ **do**   ▷ sends back the result to the leftmost leaders.
17:    Let $Q_{i'}$ and $Q_{i''}$ be the left neighboring quorums of Q_i in the circuit, for $n+1 \leq i', i'' \leq m + n$. *
18:    Leader $q_i \in Q_i$ sends b_{m+n} to leader $q_{i'} \in Q_{i'}$ and to leader $q_{i''} \in Q_{i''}$.
19: **end for**
20: **for** $i = 1, \ldots, n$ **do** ▷ sends result to all parties after broadcasting it to the input quorums.
21:    The leaders of Q_i's right neighboring quorums call *BROADCAST* (b_{m+n}, Q_i, Q_i).
22:    All parties in Q_i send b_{m+n} to sender s_i.
23: **end for**

* Recall that there are no leaders in the input quorums.

Algorithm 5. TRIGGER-CHECK ▷ The parties of the output quorum Q_{m+n} trigger *CHECK* with probability $1/(\log^* m)^2$.

1: Each party in Q_{m+n} chooses an input: a real number uniformly distributed between 0 and 1.
2: The parties of Q_{m+n} perform MPC to find the output, *prob*, which is the sum of all their inputs modulo 1.   ▷ *prob* is the fractional part of the sum of their inputs.
3: **if** $prob \leq 1/(\log^* m)^2$ **then**
4:    CHECK
5: **end if**

Algorithm 6. ELECT(Q)   ▷ Parties in Q elect an unmarked party in Q using MPC.

1: Let each party in the set of unmarked parties, $U \subset Q$, is assigned a unique integer from 0 to $|U| - 1$.
2: Each party in Q chooses an input: an integer uniformly distributed between 0 and $|U| - 1$.
3: The parties of Q perform MPC to find the output: the sum of all their inputs modulo $|U|$.
4: The party in U associated with this output number is the elected party.

Algorithm 7. CHECK   ▷ Party **r** calls *CHECK* to check for corruptions.

Declaration: Let U_k be the set of all unmarked parties in quorum Q_k, for $1 \leq k \leq m+n$. Also let m' be the maximum number of parties in any quorum. Further, let subquorums, S_j^A, S_j^B and S_j^C, be initially empty, for all $n+1 \leq j \leq m+n$.

1: **for** $i \leftarrow 1, \ldots, 8(\log^* m + 2(\log c + 1))^*$ **do**
2:     ELECT(Q_{m+n})   ▷ elects an unmarked party $\mathbf{r} \in Q_{m+n}$.
3:     Party **r** constructs A^i, B^i and C^i to be three, m by m', arrays of random integers.**
4:     REQUEST(i, A^i, B^i)   ▷ **r** requests all senders to recompute.
5:     RECOMPUTE   ▷ recomputes, producing the result, b_{m+n}^i, at **r**.
6:     RESEND-RESULT(i, C^i, b_{m+n}^i)   ▷ **r** sends back b_{m+n}^i to all parties.
7: **end for**

* $c = \frac{2(1+2p)}{\log e (1-2p)^2}$; note that for any quorum Q_k, $p \leq 1/2 - \epsilon$, is the probability of selecting a bad party u.a.r. from U_k, for a constant $\epsilon > 0$.
** $A^i[k, k']$, $B^i[k, k']$ and $C^i[k, k']$ are uniformly random integers between 1 and k', for $1 \leq k \leq m$ and $1 \leq k' \leq m'$.

Note that: if a party has previously received k_p, then it verifies each subsequent message with it; also if a party receives inconsistent messages or fails to receive and verify an expected message, then it initiates a call to *UPDATE*.

RESULT (Algorithm 10) in order to send the result back to the senders through a DAG of subquorums S_j^C's, for $n+1 \leq j \leq m+n$.

Note that in *ELECT* (Q), the parties of quorum Q perform MPC [22,23,24] to elect an unmarked party uniformly at random from Q. We know that at least half of the unmarked parties in Q are good. Thus, the elected party is good with probability at least $1/2$. MPC requires a message cost and a number of computational operations that are polylogarithmic functions in n, and it runs in $O(1)$ time.

Note further that during *CHECK*, if any party receives inconsistent messages or fails to receive and verify any expected message in any round, it initiates a call to *UPDATE*.

2.4 UPDATE

When a computation is corrupted and *CHECK* detects this corruption, *UPDATE* is called. The *UPDATE* algorithm is described formally as Algorithm 11. When *UPDATE* starts, all parties in each quorum in the circuit are notified.

The main purpose of *UPDATE* is to 1) determine the location in which the corruption occurred; and 2) mark the parties that are in conflict.

To determine the location in which the corruption occurred, *UPDATE* calls *INVESTIGATE* (Algorithm 12) to investigate the corruption situation by letting each party involved in *COMPUTE-CIRCUIT* or *CHECK* broadcast all messages they have received or sent. Then, *UPDATE* calls *MARK-IN-CONFLICTS* (Algorithm 13) in order to mark the parties that are *in conflict*, where a pair of parties is in conflict if at least one of these parties broadcasted messages that conflict with the messages broadcasted by the other party in this pair. Note that each pair of parties that are in conflict has at least one bad party. Recall that if $(1/2 - \gamma)$-fraction of parties in any quorum are marked, for any

Algorithm 8. REQUEST(i, A^i, B^i)   ▷ **r** requests n senders through a DAG of subquoums, S_j^A's, for $n + 1 \leq j \leq m + n$, to redo the computation.

1: Party **r** calls $SIGN([i, A^i, B^i, \mathbf{r}], Q_{m+n})$.   ▷ signs $[i, A^i, B^i, \mathbf{r}]$ by Q_{m+n}'s private key.
2: Party **r** sets $REQ^i = ([i, A^i, B^i, \mathbf{r}]_{k_s}, k_p)$.   ▷ (k_p, k_s) : public/private key pair of Q_{m+n}.
3: Party **r** sends REQ^i to all parties of quorum Q_{m+n}.
4: All parties in Q_{m+n} calculate party, $q_{m+n}^i \in U_{m+n}$, of index A_{m+n}^i to be added to S_{m+n}^A.*
5: **for** $j \leftarrow m + n, \ldots, n + 1$ **do**   ▷ sends REQ^i through a DAG of subquorums.
6:    Let $Q_{j'}$ and $Q_{j''}$ be the left neighboring quorums of Q_j in the circuit, for $n + 1 \leq j', j'' \leq m + n$. **
7:    All i parties in S_j^A calculate parties, $q_{j'}^i$ and $q_{j''}^i$, of indices $A_{j'}^i$ and $A_{j''}^i$, to be added to $S_{j'}^A$ and $S_{j''}^A$ respectively.
8:    Party q_j^i calculate all parties in $S_{j'}^A$ and $S_{j''}^A$ using $A_{j'}^1, \ldots, A_{j'}^i$ and $A_{j''}^1, \ldots, A_{j''}^i$.
9:    **for** $k \leftarrow 1, \ldots, i$ **do**   ▷ k refers to the rounds prior to round i.
10:        Party q_j^k sends REQ^k to parties $q_{j'}^i$ and $q_{j''}^i$.
11:        Party q_j^i sends REQ^i to parties $q_{j'}^k$ and $q_{j''}^k$.
12:    **end for**
13: **end for**
14: **for** $k \leftarrow n, \ldots, 1$ **do**   ▷ The input quorums forward REQ^i to all senders.
15:    Let $Q_{k'}$ and $Q_{k''}$ be the right neighboring quorums of Q_k in the circuit.
16:    All i parties in $S_{k'}$ and all parties in $S_{k''}$ call $BROADCAST(REQ^i, Q_k, Q_k)$.
17:    All parties in Q_k send REQ^i to sender s_k.
18: **end for**

* $A_j^i = A^i[j - n, |U_j|]$ is the index of the party, q_j^i, which is selected u.a.r. from the parties in U_j in round i of *REQUEST*; note that all parties in U_j are sorted by their IDs, for $n+1 \leq j \leq m+n$.
** Recall that there are no subquorums for the input quorums.

constant $\gamma > 0$, e.g., $\gamma = 0.01$, they are set unmarked. Also, for each pair of leaders that get marked, their quorums elect another pair of unmarked leaders.

3 Analysis

In this section, we sketch the proof of Theorem 1. Due to space constraints, all proofs are provided in the full paper. Throughout this section, all logarithms are base 2.

Recall that in each round of *CHECK*, a new unmarked party is selected u.a.r. from each quorum in the circuit forming a new DAG of unmarked parties.

Definition 1. *A Deception DAG, D_i, is the maximal subgraph of the new DAG of unmarked parties that are selected u.a.r. in round i, with the following properties: 1) it has only bad parties; 2) it receives all its inputs, and each input is provided correct by at least one good party; 3) it is rooted at one party, which does not provide the correct output to at least one good party; and 4) all other outputs this DAG has are provided correct.*

If the adversary corrupts the output of the root party in a deception DAG in any round, then it has to keep corrupting this output by a deception DAG in each subsequent round; otherwise, the good parties that expect to receive this output in each round will call *UPDATE* due to receiving inconsistent output messages.

Algorithm 9. RECOMPUTE   ▷ n senders provide inputs to a DAG of subquorums, S_j^B's, for $n + 1 \leq j \leq m + n$, to recompute, producing a result, b_{m+n}^i, at **r**.

1: **for** each sender s_j that receives REQ^i, for $1 \leq j \leq n$ and $n + 1 \leq j', j'' \leq m + n$ **do**
2:      s_j sets REC^i to be a message consisting of its input a_j and REQ^i.
3:      s_j broadcasts REC^i to all parties in Q_j.
4:      Let $Q_{j'}$ and $Q_{j''}$ be the right neighboring quorums of Q_j in the circuit.
5:      All parties in Q_j calculate parties, $q_{j'}^i$ and $q_{j''}^i$, of indices $B_{j'}^i$ and $B_{j''}^i$, to be added to $S_{j'}^B$ and $S_{j''}^B$ respectively.*
6:      All parties in Q_j send REC^i to all parties in $S_{j'}^B$ and to all parties in $S_{j''}^B$.
7:      All parties in Q_j send $REC^1, \ldots, REC^{i-1}$ to $q_{j'}^i$ and $q_{j''}^i$.
8: **end for**
9: **for** $j \leftarrow n + 1, \ldots, m + n - 1$ **do**   ▷ recomputes
10:      Let $Q_{j'}$ and $Q_{j''}$ be the right neighboring quorums of Q_j in the circuit.
11:      All i parties in S_j^B calculate parties, $q_{j'}^i$ and $q_{j''}^i$, of indices $B_{j'}^i$ and $B_{j''}^i$, to be added to $S_{j'}^B$ and $S_{j''}^B$ respectively.
12:      Party q_j^i calculate all parties in $S_{j'}^B$ and $S_{j''}^B$ using $B_{j'}^1, \ldots, B_{j'}^i$ and $B_{j''}^1, \ldots, B_{j''}^i$.
13:      for all $1 \leq k \leq i$, q_j^k performs its operation on its inputs producing an output, b_j^k.
14:      **for** $k \leftarrow 1, \ldots, i$ **do**
15:          q_j^k sends b_j^k and REC^k to parties $q_{j'}^i$ and $q_{j''}^i$.
16:          q_j^i sends b_j^i and REC^i to parties $q_{j'}^k$ and $q_{j''}^k$.
17:      **end for**
18: **end for**
19: All i parties in S_{m+n} broadcast b_{m+n}^i and REC^i to all parties in Q_{m+n}.
20: All parties in Q_{m+n} send b_{m+n}^i and REC^i to party **r**.   ▷ **r** receives the result.

* $B_j^i = B^i[j - n, |U_j|]$ is the index of the party, q_j^i, which is selected u.a.r. from the parties in U_j in round i of *RECOMPUTE*; note that all parties in U_j are sorted by their IDs, for $n + 1 \leq j \leq m + n$.

We say that a deception DAG, D_i, in round i extends in round $i + 1$ if there exists a deception DAG, D_{i+1}, in round $i + 1$ such that 1) there is at least one subquorum that has a party in D_i and a party in D_{i+1}; and 2) there is at least one subquorum that has a party in D_{i+1} but has no party in D_i.

Also, we say that a deception DAG, D_i, in round i shrinks in round $i + 1$ if there exists a deception DAG, D_{i+1}, in round $i + 1$ such that 1) each subquorum that has a party in D_{i+1} has a party in D_i; and 2) there is at least one subquorum that has a party in D_i but has no party in D_{i+1}.

Further, we say that a deception DAG, D_i, shrinks logarithmically from round i to round $i + 1$ if $|D_{i+1}| = O(\log |D_i|)$.

Note that in any round i, if a deception DAG, D_i, shrinks to a deception DAG, D_{i+1}, of size zero in round $i + 1$, then the good party that did not receive the correct output from D_i in round i will receive the correct output in round $i + 1$. As a result, this good party will call *UPDATE* declaring that it has received inconsistent output messages.

In the following lemmas, we first show that any deception DAG in any round never extends in any subsequent round. Then we show that with probability at least $1/2$, any

---

Algorithm 10. RESEND-RESULT(i, C^i, b^i_{m+n})   ▷ Party r sends back the result, b^i_{m+n}, through a DAG of subquorums, S^C_j's, to n senders, for $n + 1 \le j \le m + n$.

1: Party r calls $SIGN([i, C^i, b^i_{m+n}, \mathbf{r}], Q_{m+n})$.   ▷ signs it by Q_{m+n}'s private key.
2: Party r sets $RES^i = ([i, C^i, b^i_{m+n}, \mathbf{r}]_{k_s}, k_p)$. ▷ (k_p, k_s) : public/private key pair of Q_{m+n}.
3: Party r sends RES^i to all parties of quorum Q_{m+n}.
4: All parties in Q_{m+n} calculate party, $q^i_{m+n} \in U_{m+n}$, of index C^i_{m+n} to be added to S^C_{m+n}.*
5: **for** $j \leftarrow m + n, \ldots, n + 1$ **do**   ▷ sends back the result through a DAG of subquorums.
6:     Let $Q_{j'}$ and $Q_{j''}$ be the left neighboring quorums of Q_j in the circuit, for $n + 1 \le j', j'' \le m + n$. **
7:     All i parties in S^C_j calculate parties, $q^i_{j'}$ and $q^i_{j''}$, of indices $C^i_{j'}$ and $C^i_{j''}$, to be added to $S^C_{j'}$ and $S^C_{j''}$ respectively.
8:     Party q^i_j calculate all parties in $S^C_{j'}$ and $S^C_{j''}$ using $C^1_{j'}, \ldots, C^i_{j'}$ and $C^1_{j''}, \ldots, C^i_{j''}$.
9:     **for** $k \leftarrow 1, \ldots, i$ **do**   ▷ k refers to the rounds prior to round i.
10:        Party q^k_j sends RES^k to parties $q^i_{j'}$ and $q^i_{j''}$.
11:        Party q^i_j sends RES^i to parties $q^k_{j'}$ and $q^k_{j''}$.
12:     **end for**
13: **end for**
14: **for** $k \leftarrow n, \ldots, 1$ **do**   ▷ The input quorums forward RES^i to all senders.
15:     Let $Q_{k'}$ and $Q_{k''}$ be the right neighboring quorums of Q_k in the circuit.
16:     All i parties in $S_{k'}$ and all parties in $S_{k''}$ call $BROADCAST(RES^i, Q_k, Q_k)$.
17:     All parties in Q_k send RES^i to sender s_k.
18: **end for**

---

* $C^i_j = C^i[j - n, |U_j|]$ is the index of the party, q^i_j, which is selected u.a.r. from the parties in U_j in round i of *RESEND-RESULT*; note that all parties in U_j are sorted by their IDs, for $n + 1 \le j \le m + n$.
** Recall that there are no subquorums for the input quorums.

Algorithm 11. UPDATE   ▷ Party $q' \in Q'$ calls *UPDATE* after it detects a corruption.

1: q' broadcasts to all parties in Q' the fact that it calls *UPDATE* along with the messages it has received in this call to *COMPUTE*.
2: The parties in Q' verify that q' received inconsistent messages before proceeding.
3: Q' notifies all quorums in the circuit via all-to-all communication that *UPDATE* is called.
4: INVESTIGATE   ▷ investigates all participants to determine corruption locations.
5: MARK-IN-CONFLICTS   ▷ marks the parties that are in conflict.

Algorithm 12. INVESTIGATE   ▷ investigates the parties that have participated.

1: **for** each party, q, involved in the last call to *COMPUTE-CIRCUIT* or *CHECK* **do**
2:     q compiles all messages they have received (and from whom) and they have sent (and to whom) in the last call to *COMPUTE-CIRCUIT* or *CHECK*.
3:     q broadcasts these messages to all parties in its quorum and neighboring quorums.
4: **end for**

Algorithm 13. MARK-IN-CONFLICTS   ▷ marks the parties that are in conflict.

1: **for** each pair of parties, (q_x, q_y), that is in conflict*, in quorums (Q_x, Q_y) **do**
2:     party q_y broadcasts a *conflict* message, $\{q_x, q_y\}$, to all parties in Q_y.
3:     each party in Q_y forwards $\{q_x, q_y\}$ to all parties in Q_x.
4:     all parties in Q_x (or Q_y) send $\{q_x, q_y\}$ to the other quorums that has q_x (or q_y).
5:     each quorum has q_x or q_y sends $\{q_x, q_y\}$ to its neighboring quorums.
6: **end for**
7: **for** each party q that receives conflict message $\{q_x, q_y\}$ **do**
8:     q marks q_x and q_y in its marking table.
9: **end for**
10: **if** $(1/2 - \gamma)$-fraction of parties in any quorum have been marked, for $\gamma = 0.01$ **then**
11:     each of these parties is set unmarked in all its quorums.
12:     each of these parties is set unmarked in all its neighboring quorums.
13: **end if**
14: **for** each pair of leaders, (q_x, q_y), that is in conflict, in quorums (Q_x, Q_y) **do**
15:     ELECT(Q_x) and ELECT(Q_y) to elect a pair of unmarked leaders, (q'_x, q'_y).
16:     Q_x and Q_y notify their neighboring quorums with (q'_x, q'_y).
17: **end for**

* A pair of parties, (q_x, q_y), is *in conflict* if: 1) q_x was scheduled to send an output to q_y at some point in the last call to *COMPUTE-CIRCUIT* or *CHECK*; and 2) q_y does not receive an expected message from q_x in *INVESTIGATE*, or q_y receives a message in *INVESTIGATE* that is different than the message that it has received from q_x in the last call to *COMPUTE-CIRCUIT* or *CHECK*.

deception DAG shrinks logarithmically from round to round. This will imply that the expected number of rounds to shrink any deception DAG to size zero is $O(\log^* m)$.

Lemma 1. *Any deception DAG in any round never extends in any direction.*

Now we show that any deception DAG shrinks logarithmically from round to round with probability at least $1/2$.

Definition 2. Rooted Directed Acyclic Graph (R-DAG) *is a DAG in which, for a vertex u called the root and any other node v, there is at least one directed path from v to u.*

Lemma 2. *Given any R-DAG, of size n, in which each node has indegree of at most d and survives independently with probability at most p such that $0 < p \le \frac{1}{d} - \epsilon$, for any constant $\epsilon > 0$, then the probability of having a subgraph, rooted at some node, with surviving nodes, of size $\Omega(\frac{\log n}{(1-pd)^2})$ is at most $1/2$.*

Corollary 1. *For any R-DAG, of size n, the probability of having a subgraph, rooted at one node, with surviving nodes, of size at least $n/2$ is at most $1/2$.*

Now, if a deception DAG shrinks logarithmically in a successful step, then how many successful steps to shrink this deception DAG to a deception DAG of size zero or even of a constant size?

Lemma 3. *Assume that any deception DAG of size n' shrinks to a deception DAG of size $c \log n'$ in a successful step, for any constant $c \ge 1$. Then, for a deception DAG of* *size $n > c(2c + \log c + 1)$, after $\log^* n - \log^* (\log c + 1)$ successful steps, it shrinks to a deception DAG of size at most $c(2c + \log c + 1)$.*

Let p be the probability of selecting an unmarked bad party uniformly at random in any quorum. Recall that the fraction of bad parties in any quorum is at most $1/4$, and the fraction of unmarked parties in any quorum is at least $1/2 + \gamma$, for any constant $\gamma > 0$. Thus, $p \leq \frac{1/2}{1+2\gamma}$. Now we show the expected number of rounds to shrink any deception DAG to size zero.

Lemma 4. *With probability at least $1/2$, any deception DAG of size m shrinks to size zero in $8(\log^* m + 2(\log c + 1))$ rounds, where $c = \frac{2(1+2p)}{\log e(1-2p)^2}$ and $p \leq \frac{1/2}{1+2\gamma}$, for any constant $\gamma > 0$.*

Lemma 5. *For the adversary to maximize the expected number of rounds, in which no corruption detected, is to corrupt the output of the root party in the maximum deception DAG of the first round.*

The next lemma shows that *CHECK* catches corruptions with probability $\geq 1/2$.

Lemma 6. *Assume some party selected uniformly at random in the last call to COMPUTE-CIRCUIT has corrupted a computation. Then when the algorithm CHECK is called, with probability at least $1/2$, some party will call UPDATE.*

Lemma 7. *If some party selected uniformly at random in the last call to COMPUTE-CIRCUIT or CHECK has corrupted a computation, then UPDATE will identify a pair of neighboring quorums such that at least one pair of parties in these quorums is in conflict and at least one party in such pair is bad.*

The next lemma bounds the number of calls to *UPDATE* before all bad parties are marked.

Lemma 8. *UPDATE is called $O(t)$ times before all bad parties are marked.*

4   Conclusion and Future Work

We have presented algorithms for reliable multiparty computations. These algorithms reduce message cost and number of computational operations to be asymptotically optimal. The price we pay for this improvement is the possibility of computation corruption. In particular, if there are $t \leq (\frac{1}{4} - \epsilon)n$ bad parties, for any constant $\epsilon > 0$, our algorithm allows $O(t(\log^* m)^2)$ computations to be corrupted in expectation.

Many problems remain. First, it seems unlikely that the smallest number of corruptions allowable by an attack-resistant algorithm with optimal message complexity is $O(t(\log^* m)^2)$. Can we improve this to $O(t)$ or else prove a non-trivial lower bound? Second, we allow the inputs of parties to reveal. Can we maintain the privacy of these inputs? Finally, we assume a partially synchronous communication model, which is crucial for our *CHECK* algorithm to detect computation corruptions over rounds. Can we extend this algorithm to fit for asynchronous computations?

References

1. Fiat, A., Saia, J.: Censorship resistant peer-to-peer networks. Theory of Computing 3(1), 1–23 (2007)
2. Hildrum, K., Kubiatowicz, J.: Asymptotically efficient approaches to fault-tolerance in peer-to-peer networks. In: Fich, F.E. (ed.) DISC 2003. LNCS, vol. 2848, pp. 321–336. Springer, Heidelberg (2003)
3. Naor, M., Wieder, U.: A simple fault tolerant distributed hash table. In: Kaashoek, M.F., Stoica, I. (eds.) IPTPS 2003. LNCS, vol. 2735, pp. 88–97. Springer, Heidelberg (2003)
4. Scheideler, C.: How to spread adversarial nodes? rotate! In: STOC 2005, pp. 704–713 (2005)
5. Fiat, A., Saia, J., Young, M.: Making chord robust to Byzantine attacks. In: Brodal, G.S., Leonardi, S. (eds.) ESA 2005. LNCS, vol. 3669, pp. 803–814. Springer, Heidelberg (2005)
6. Awerbuch, B., Scheideler, C.: Towards a scalable and robust DHT. Theory of Computing Systems 45(2), 234–260 (2009)
7. King, V., Lonargan, S., Saia, J., Trehan, A.: Load balanced scalable Byzantine agreement through quorum building, with full information. In: Aguilera, M.K., Yu, H., Vaidya, N.H., Srinivasan, V., Choudhury, R.R. (eds.) ICDCN 2011. LNCS, vol. 6522, pp. 203–214. Springer, Heidelberg (2011)
8. Frisanco, T.: Optimal spare capacity design for various protection switching methods in ATM networks. ICC 1997, vol. 1, pp. 293–298 (1997)
9. Iraschko, R.R., MacGregor, M.H., Grover, W.D.: Optimal capacity placement for path restoration in STM or ATM mesh-survivable networks. IEEE/ACM Transactions on Networking 6(3), 325–336 (1998)
10. Murakami, K., Kim, H.S.: Comparative study on restoration schemes of survivable ATM networks. INFOCOM 1997, vol. 1, pp. 345–352 (1997)
11. Van Caenegem, B., Wauters, N., Demeester, P.: Spare capacity assignment for different restoration strategies in mesh survivable networks, ICC 1997, vol. 1, pp. 288–292 (1997)
12. Xiong, Y., Mason, L.G.: Restoration strategies and spare capacity requirements in self-healing ATM networks. IEEE/ACM Transactions on Networking 7(1), 98–110 (1999)
13. Boman, I., Saia, J., Abdallah, C.T., Schamiloglu, E.: Brief announcement: Self-healing algorithms for reconfigurable networks. In: Datta, A.K., Gradinariu, M. (eds.) SSS 2006. LNCS, vol. 4280, pp. 563–565. Springer, Heidelberg (2006)
14. Saia, J., Trehan, A.: Picking up the pieces: Self-healing in reconfigurable networks. In: IPDPS 2008, pp. 1–12 (2008)
15. Hayes, T., Rustagi, N., Saia, J., Trehan, A.: The forgiving tree: A self-healing distributed data structure. In: PODC 2008, pp. 203–212 (2008)
16. Hayes, T.P., Saia, J., Trehan, A.: The forgiving graph: A distributed data structure for low stretch under adversarial attack. In: PODC 2009, pp. 121–130 (2009)
17. Pandurangan, G., Trehan, A.: Xheal: localized self-healing using expanders. In: PODC 2011, pp. 301–310 (2011)
18. Sarma, A.D., Trehan, A.: Edge-preserving self-healing: keeping network backbones densely connected. In: IEEE Conference on Computer Communications Workshops (INFOCOM WKSHPS), pp. 226–231 (2012)
19. Knockel, J., Saad, G., Saia, J.: Self-healing of Byzantine faults. In: Higashino, T., Katayama, Y., Masuzawa, T., Potop-Butucaru, M., Yamashita, M. (eds.) SSS 2013. LNCS, vol. 8255, pp. 98–112. Springer, Heidelberg (2013)
20. Yao, A.C.: Protocols for secure computations. In: SFCS 1982, pp. 160–164 (1982)
21. Beaver, D.: Efficient multiparty protocols using circuit randomization. In: Feigenbaum, J. (ed.) CRYPTO 1991. LNCS, vol. 576, pp. 420–432. Springer, Heidelberg (1992)
22. Ben-Or, M., Goldwasser, S., Wigderson, A.: Completeness theorems for non-cryptographic fault-tolerant distributed computation. In: STOC 1988, pp. 1–10 (1988)

23. Rabin, T., Ben-Or, M.: Verifiable secret sharing and multiparty protocols with honest majority. In: STOC 1989, pp. 73–85 (1989)
24. Asharov, G., Lindell, Y.: A full proof of the BGW protocol for perfectly-secure multiparty computation. Electronic Colloquium on Computational Complexity (ECCC) 18, 36 (2011)
25. Prabhakaran, M., Sahai, A.: Secure Multi-Party Computation, vol. 10. IOS Press (2013)
26. Kate, A., Goldberg, I.: Distributed key generation for the internet. In: ICDCS 2009, pp. 119–128 (2009)

Optimal Gathering on Infinite Grids[*]

Gabriele Di Stefano[1] and Alfredo Navarra[2]

[1] Dipartimento di Ingegneria e Scienze dell'Informazione e Matematica,
Università degli Studi dell'Aquila, Italy
gabriele.distefano@univaq.it
[2] Dipartimento di Matematica e Informatica,
Università degli Studi di Perugia, Italy
alfredo.navarra@unipg.it

Abstract. The gathering problem has been largely studied in the last years with respect to various basic graph topologies. The requirement is to move a team of robots initially placed at different vertices of the input graph towards a common vertex, and to let them remain at such a vertex. Robots move based on the so called *Look-Compute-Move* model. Each time a robot wakes-up, it perceives the current configuration in terms of occupied vertices (Look), it decides whether to move towards one of its neighbors (Compute), and in the positive case it makes the computed move instantaneously (Move). All the phases are performed asynchronously for each robot. So far, the goal has been mainly to detect the minimal assumptions that allow to accomplish the gathering task, without taking care of any cost measure of the provided solutions. In this paper, we are interested in devising optimal algorithms in terms of total number of moves the robots have to perform in order to finalize the gathering. In particular, we consider infinite grids as input graphs, and we fully characterize when optimal gathering is achievable by providing a distributed algorithm.

1   Introduction

Robot-based computing systems have been largely addressed to the *gathering* (or *rendezvous*) problem either concerning open spaces or discrete representations. A team of robots, initially placed at different locations, have to gather at the same place (not determined in advance) and remain there. Many variants of the problem have attracted the interest of the research community (see e.g., [4, 7–10] and references therein).

In this paper, we consider infinite grids as input graphs where robots are initially placed at different vertices. Robots are assumed to be oblivious (without

[*] Work partially supported by the following Research Grants: 2010N5K7EB "PRIN 2010" ARS TechnoMedia (Algoritmica per le Reti Sociali Tecno-mediate) and 2012C4E3KT "PRIN 2012" Amanda (Algorithmics for MAssive and Networked DAta), both from the Italian Ministry of University and Research.

P. Felber and V. Garg (Eds.): SSS 2014, LNCS 8756, pp. 211–225, 2014.

memory of the past), uniform (running the same deterministic algorithm), autonomous (without a common coordinate system, identities or chirality), asynchronous (without central coordination), without the capability to communicate. Neither vertices nor edges are labeled and no local memory is available on vertices. Robots operate according to the so-called *Look-Compute-Move* cycles [3, 5, 11, 12, 14]. In each cycle, a robot wakes-up and takes a snapshot of the current global configuration (Look), then, based on the perceived configuration, decides either to stay idle or to move to one of its adjacent vertices (Compute), and in the latter case it makes an instantaneous move to this neighbor (Move). As moves are instantaneous, robots are always detected on vertices during the Look phase and not on edges. Cycles are performed asynchronously for each robot. This means that the time between Look, Compute, and Move phases is finite but unbounded, and is decided by the adversary for each robot. Hence, robots may move based on significantly outdated perceptions. Robots are oblivious, i.e., they do not have any memory of past observations. Thus, the target vertex (which is either the current position of the robot or one of its neighbors) is decided by the robot during a Compute phase solely on the basis of the location of other robots perceived during the Look phase. Robots are anonymous and execute the same deterministic algorithm. They cannot leave any marks at visited vertices, nor send any messages to other robots.

The problem has been largely studied on ring topologies (see, e.g., [2, 3, 11]), where another assumption has been proven to be necessary in order to allow the accomplishment of the task. Robots are in fact equipped with the so called *multiplicity detection* capability in one of its possible forms. This is the ability of robots to acquire information during the Look phase about the number of robots lying on a same vertex. A robot is always able to detect whether a vertex is empty or occupied but if it is empowered with the *global-strong* multiplicity detection, it is able to perceive the exact number of robots that occupy each vertex. In the *global-weak* version, a robot perceives only whether a vertex is occupied by one robot or if a multiplicity occurs, i.e., a vertex is occupied by an undefined number of robots greater than one. The *local* versions instead of global refer to the corresponding ability of a robot in perceiving the information about multiplicities only concerning the vertex where it currently lies. The relevance of the ring topology is motivated by its completely symmetric structure. It means that algorithms for rings are more difficult to devise as they cannot exploit any topological structure, assuming that all vertices look the same. In fact, the devised algorithms are only based on robots' disposal and not on topology.

In [1], gathering on finite grids has been fully characterized. In particular, even if the global-strong multiplicity detection is assumed, a configuration remains ungatherable if it is periodic (i.e., the same view can be obtained by rotating the grid around its geometric center of an angle smaller than 360 degrees) on a grid with at least an even side, or it is symmetric with respect to an axis of symmetry passing through edges. For all the other cases, a gathering algorithm has been provided which does not require any multiplicity detection (the only exception is represented by 2×2 grids with three robots). In this case, the chosen topology plays a central role in the designed algorithms. The main criticism with respect to the results in [1] has been that finite grids admit the existence of special vertices like corners that make the problem solvable even without any multiplicity detection.

In this paper, we are interested in infinite grids, that is no special vertices there exist as there are no borders. This clearly makes the problem more difficult as it was for rings where vertices look all the same and topological structure cannot be exploited. Moreover, in most of the previous results, the aim has been concerning the feasibility of the problem, without taking care of any cost measure for the devised solutions. Here, we are interested in optimal gathering algorithms with respect to the number of moves that robots have to perform.

Recently, in [6], basic results for optimal gathering have been introduced. Namely, gathering has been studied on finite graphs with respect to both its feasibility and the possibility to realize it by means of the minimum number of asynchronous moves performed by robots. The paper introduces the concept of Weber-point [13] on weighted graphs. A Weber-point for a discrete set of sample points in the Euclidean space is the point minimizing the sum of distances to the sample points. On graphs with robots, a Weber-point is a vertex of the graph that minimizes the sum of the length of the shortest paths from it to each robot. An algorithm that gathers all robots on a Weber-point via shortest paths is optimum w.r.t. the total number of moves.

Our Results. In this paper, we fully characterize optimal gathering on infinite grids where the topology does not help in detecting a gathering vertex. Nonetheless, the interest in infinite grids also arise by the fact they represent a natural discretization of the plane. More specifically, we extend the theory about optimal gathering to infinite grids. We detect all the specific configurations where gathering cannot be performed. For all other configurations, we devise a distributed algorithm that assures the gathering on a Weber-point by letting move robots along the shortest paths towards such a vertex, i.e., our algorithm is optimal in terms of moves.

Outline. In the next section, we introduce the notation used in the paper and give some basic definitions. In Section 3, we first provide few impossibility results, and then an optimal gathering algorithm for all the other cases is provided. In Section 4, we sketch on the general idea behind the correctness of the proposed algorithm. Finally, in Section 5, we conclude the paper.

2   Definitions and Preliminaries

In this section we provide all the basic definitions and notation necessary for the understanding of the proposed results.

Given a graph G, a function $\ell : V \longrightarrow \mathbb{N}$, represents the number of robots on each vertex of G, and we call (G, ℓ) a *configuration* whenever $k = \sum_{v \in V} \ell(v)$ is bounded and greater than zero. A configuration is *initial* if each robot lies on a different vertex (i.e., $\ell(v) \leq 1 \ \forall v \in V$). A configuration is *final* if all robots are on a single vertex u (i.e., $\ell(u) > 0$ and $\ell(v) = 0, \ \forall v \in V \setminus \{u\}$). The distance

$d(u, v)$ between two vertices u, v in V is the number of edges of a shortest path connecting u to v.

Two graphs $G = (V_G, E_G)$ and $H = (V_H, E_H)$ are *isomorphic* if there is a bijection φ from V_G to V_H such that $\{u, v\} \in E_G$ iff $\{\varphi(u), \varphi(v)\} \in E_H$.

An *automorphism* on a graph G is an isomorphism from G to itself, that is a permutation of its vertices mapping edges to edges and non-edges to non-edges.

We extend the concept of isomorphism to configurations in a natural way: two configurations (G, ℓ) and (G', ℓ') are isomorphic if G and G' are isomorphic via a bijection φ and for each vertex v in G, $\ell(v) = \ell'(\varphi(v))$. An *automorphism* on a configuration (G, ℓ) is an isomorphism from (G, ℓ) to itself and the set of all automorphisms of (G, ℓ) forms a group that we call *automorphism group* of (G, ℓ), denoted by $\mathrm{Aut}((G, \ell))$.

Given an isomorphism $\varphi \in \mathrm{Aut}((G, \ell))$, the *cyclic subgroup* of order p generated by φ is given by $\{\varphi^0, \varphi^1 = \varphi, \varphi^2 = \varphi \circ \varphi, \dots, \varphi^{p-1}\}$ where φ^0 is the identity.

If H is a subgroup of $\mathrm{Aut}((G, \ell))$, the *orbit* of a vertex v of G is $Hv = \{\gamma(v) \mid \gamma \in H\}$.

(G, ℓ) is said *asymmetric* if $|\mathrm{Aut}((G, \ell))| = 1$, *symmetric* otherwise.

Definition 1. *Let $\mathcal{C} = ((V, E), \ell)$ be a configuration. An isomorphism $\varphi \in \mathrm{Aut}(\mathcal{C})$ is called* partitive *if the cyclic subgroup $H = \{\varphi^0, \varphi^1 = \varphi, \varphi^2 = \varphi \circ \varphi, \dots, \varphi^{p-1}\}$ generated by φ has order $p > 1$ and is such that $|Hu| = p$ for each $u \in V'$.*

Note that, in the above definition, the orbits Hu, for each $u \in V$ form a partition of V. The associated equivalence relation is defined by saying that x and y are equivalent if and only if there exists a $\gamma \in H$ with $\gamma(x) = y$. The orbits are then the equivalence classes under this relation; two elements x and y are equivalent if and only if their orbits are the same; i.e., $Hx = Hy$. Moreover, note that $\ell(u) = \ell(v)$ whenever u and v are equivalent.

Let an infinite path be the graph $P = (\mathbb{Z}, E)$ with $E = \{\{i, i+1\} : i \in \mathbb{Z}\}$. An infinite grid is defined as the Cartesian product $G = P \times P$. A vertex of the grid is then an ordered pair of integers called *coordinates*.

If we assume the infinite grid embedded in a Cartesian plane, it is not difficult to see that it admits three types of automorphisms and combinations of them: *translations*, that is a shifting of the vertices by applying the same displacement to each vertex; *rotations*, defined by a center and an angle of rotation; *reflections*, defined by a reflection axis which acts as a mirror. In an infinite grid, the center of a rotation can be a vertex, or the center of an edge, or the center of the area surrounded by four vertices, whereas the angle of rotation can be of 90 or 180 degrees. Reflections axis can be horizontal (vertical), passing through vertices or through the middle of edges, or diagonal (45 degrees), passing through vertices. Regarding translations, even if they are possible for infinite grids, they do not belong to any automorphism group of configurations as these are defined for a finite number of robots. Moreover the automorphism group of a configuration with a finite number of robots is finite.

Definition 2. *Given a configuration* (G, ℓ), *with* $G = (V, E)$, *the* centrality *of each* $v \in V$, *is* $c_{G,\ell}(v) = \sum_{u \in V} d(u, v) \cdot \ell(u)$.

A vertex $v \in V$ *is a* Weber-point *if it has the minimal centrality, that is,* $c_{G,\ell}(v) = \min\{c_{G,\ell}(u) \mid u \in V\}$.

Whenever clear by the context, we refer to the centrality of a vertex v simply by $c(v)$. By definition, a Weber-point (WP) is a vertex that has the overall minimal distance from all the robots in the configuration.

Definition 3. *Given a configuration* $\mathcal{C} = (G, \ell)$, $G_{WP}(\mathcal{C})$ *is the subgraph induced by its WPs.*

An algorithm that gathers all robots on a WP via shortest paths is optimum w.r.t. the total number of moves. More formally, a gathering algorithm must define the sequence of moves for each robot, leading to a final configuration. A move is the change of the position of a single robot from a vertex u to an adjacent vertex v. This equals to change the configuration from, say (G, ℓ) to (G, ℓ'), where $\ell'(w) = \ell'(w) \; \forall w \in V \setminus \{u, v\}$, $\ell'(u) = \ell(u) - 1$ and $\ell'(v) = \ell(v) + 1$.

Let $S_{\mathcal{C}}$ be the minimal (finite) sub-grid containing all the occupied vertices of G, and $(S_{\mathcal{C}}, \ell)$ be the corresponding configuration. It is worth mentioning that $S_{\mathcal{C}}$ may change while robots move. As a consequence, even though $S_{\mathcal{C}}$ is a finite grid, the approach of [1] cannot be applied.

During the Look phase, a robot perceives $(S_{\mathcal{C}}, \ell)$ and it is able to recognize its position on $S_{\mathcal{C}}$ if (G, ℓ) is asymmetric. Whereas, if (G, ℓ) admits an isomorphism φ different from the identity, a robot cannot distinguish its position at u from $\varphi(u)$. As a consequence, two robots (e.g., one on u and one on $\varphi(u)$) can decide to move simultaneously, as any algorithm is unable to distinguish between them. This fact greatly increases the difficulty to devise a gathering algorithm for symmetric configurations.

If an algorithm allows at least two robots to move concurrently, then there might be a so called *pending* move. This occurs when, due to the asynchrony, one of the robots allowed to move performs its entire Look-Compute-Move cycle while one of the others does not perform the Move phase, i.e. its move is pending. Clearly, all the other robots performing their cycles are not aware whether there is a pending move.

A robot is said to *move back* if its movement is towards a direction not allowed by the algorithm. This definition is required for analysis purposes only.

We say that an algorithm *assures* the gathering if it achieves the gathering regardless any possible sequence of the moves it allows, and possible simultaneous moves. We propose to measure the efficiency of a gathering algorithm by counting the number of moves that it requires to gather all robots from an arbitrary initial configuration to a single vertex. We say that an algorithm is *optimal* if it requires the minimum possible number of moves. We say that an algorithm is *exact* if it achieves the gathering with a number of moves equal to the centrality of a WP in the initial configuration. Of course, this is a lower bound for each algorithm. In general, there might be cases where optimal algorithms are not exact. As we are going to see, this does not occur in infinite grids.

Theorem 1. *[6] Given a configuration $((V, E), \ell)$ with WPs in $X \subseteq V$, a move of a robot towards a WP x gives rise to a configuration $((V, E), \ell')$ with WPs in $X' \subseteq V$ such that: $c_{\ell'}(v) = c_\ell(v) - 1$ for each $v \in X'$; $x \in X'$; $X' \subseteq X$.*

When the configuration admits a unique WP, the above theorem suggests an exact gathering algorithm that also exploits concurrency among robots. In fact, regardless other robots, each one can move towards the only WP via the shortest path, until finalizing the gathering.

Corollary 1. *[6] If a configuration admits only one WP, and robots can detect it, then exact gathering can be assured.*

In what follows, configurations with one single WP are called of type S.

3   Gathering Algorithm

In this section, we first provide some impossibility results for the gathering task on infinite grids. Then, an exact resolution algorithm for the gatherable cases is provided, hence determining a full characterization of the problem.

3.1   Impossibility Results

Clearly, all the cases shown to be ungatherable in [1] for finite grids are inherited here, as the absence of borders can only make the problem more difficult. Assuming the global-strong multiplicity detection, the following theorems hold.

Theorem 2. *[6] If a configuration admits a partitive automorphism, then it is ungatherable.*

In infinite grids, the above theorem implies that all initial configurations with an axis of symmetry not passing through vertices or admitting a rotational center not coinciding with a vertex, are ungatherable. In fact, all such configurations are partitive with orbits of size at least two, and only those admitting rotations of 90 degrees have orbits of size four.

In what follows we say that a symmetry is *allowed* if it is not partitive.

Theorem 3. *If a configuration contains only two robots (or equivalently, two multiplicities of the same size), then it is ungatherable.*

Proof. Assume there exists an algorithm assuring the gathering of two robots and that the adversary prevents simultaneous moves. In order to accomplish the gathering task, robots must reach a configuration where they lie on two adjacent vertices, eventually. In this case, the configuration admits a reflection where the axis passes through the edge between the two occupied vertices, but not on vertices. This configuration admits a partitive automorphism of order two, then by Theorem 2 it is ungatherable.

Similar arguments can be applied when the initial configuration contains two multiplicities of the same size. □

Theorem 4. *If a configuration $\mathcal{C} = (G, \ell)$ contains only four robots (or equivalently, four multiplicities of the same size) disposed on the corners of $S_\mathcal{C}$, then $\mathcal{C}$ is ungatherable.*

Proof. If $S_\mathcal{C}$ has a side with an even number of vertices, $\mathcal{C}$ admits a partitive automorphism of order two, then by Theorem 2 the configuration is ungatherable.

Assume then all the sides of $S_\mathcal{C}$ have an odd number of vertices. Since $\mathcal{C}$ admits two orthogonal axes of reflections that meet at the central vertex of $S_\mathcal{C}$, any move can be made by all robots since they all look the same. The adversary can make move only two robots for which the movement is performed towards the same direction. This brings to a new configuration $\mathcal{C}'$ where $S_{\mathcal{C}'}$ has a side with a even number of vertices.

Similar arguments can be applied when the initial configuration contains four multiplicities of the same size. □

From now on, all initial configurations proved to be ungatherable are denoted by the set $\mathcal{U}$. It is worth noting that, differently from the finite grid case, the next theorem shows that the multiplicity detection is necessary.

Theorem 5. *If robots are not empowered by any multiplicity detection capability, then the gathering problem is unsolvable on infinite grids.*

Proof. The proof is by induction on the number of robots k. For $k = 2$, it follows from Theorem 3. Assume the statement true for a generic $k - 1$, and consider a gathering algorithm for $k > 2$ robots. Since the aim is to let robots meet at some vertex, there must be a moment in which a multiplicity is created. Since the system is asynchronous, the adversary can always decide to allow only one robot at time to move towards an adjacent vertex occupied by another robot. After this move, the number of vertices occupied by the robots decreases to $k-1$. As robots are assumed to not detect the multiplicity, they behave like the case of just $k - 1$ robots, as the adversary from now on can make synchronous the two robots on the multiplicity. By the inductive hypothesis gathering is thus impossible. □

It is worth noting that in [1], gathering on finite grids was possible without any multiplicity detection due to the existence of special vertices like corners. Here, we are assuming robots empowered by global-strong multiplicity detection. As shown by Figure 1, relaxing such an assumption makes ungatherable some configurations. In Figure 1.a, it is shown a symmetric configuration which may lead to two different configurations. Only two moves in fact can be defined in order to gather all robots at one of the nine WPs available, towards shortest paths. Any exact algorithm can allow each robot to move towards either the farthest or the closest robot that shares one coordinate with it, any other move would lead robots away from WPs. If all robots move synchronously, in the first case (in the second case, resp.) configuration of Figures 1.b (Figures 1.c, resp.) is reached. By Theorem 4, configuration in Figures 1.b is ungatherable. From configuration in Figures 1.c, only the move towards the center (the unique WP left) can be

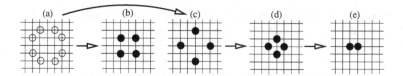

Fig. 1. Empty circles represent single robots; filled circles represent multiplicities. (a) Symmetric configuration with nine WPs in the center. (b) Symmetric configuration obtainable from (a) with nine WPs. (c) Symmetric configuration obtainable from (a) with one WP in the center. (d) Symmetric configuration obtainable from (c) with one WP recognizable only if robots are empowered by global-strong multiplicity detection. (e) Symmetric configuration obtainable from (d) with one WP recognizable only if robots are empowered by global-strong multiplicity detection.

allowed. If the adversary makes move all the robots for one step, configuration in Figures 1.d is obtained. From there, if all the robots but those belonging to only one multiplicity make another step, then configuration in Figures 1.e is reached. From there, without global-strong multiplicity detection, the two multiplicities are indistinguishable and by Theorem 3 the reached configuration in ungatherable.

3.2 Unidimensional Grids

We first consider infinite paths as grids with one row and infinite columns.

Lemma 1. *If the number of robots k is odd, then there exists only one WP. If k is even, then all vertices of the subpath delimited by the central robots (including the vertices where such robots lie) are WPs.*

Theorem 6. *Exact gathering on unidimensional grids is always achievable but for configurations with only two robots or admitting partitive automorphisms.*

Proof. The ungatherable cases simply follow from Theorem 2 and Theorem 3.

When the number of robots is odd, from Lemma 1 there exists only one WP.

When the number of robots is even, if the configuration is symmetric, then the subpath of WPs must be odd as otherwise the configuration is partitive. The idea is then to let move the robots delimiting the WPs towards the central vertex. If both move synchronously, the configuration remains symmetric but the interval of WPs is reduced until only the WP at the central vertex remains. If only one moves, it is possible to recognize the robot that has to move to re-establish the symmetry. In fact, considering the two intervals of free vertices neighboring the robots delimiting the WPs, the algorithm allows to move the robot delimiting the shortest interval.

When the number of robots is even, but the configuration is asymmetric, then either it is at one move from a possible symmetry which is allowed, or one of the two robots delimiting the WPs can be chosen to move towards the other one without creating a symmetry until only one WP remains.

Finally, when there is only one WP, from Corollary 1, all robots can move safely towards it. □

It is worth noting that the algorithm provided by the proof of Theorem 6 also works when the input configuration admits multiplicities.

3.3   Bidimensional Grids

In this section, we provide a general exact algorithm to solve the gathering problem for each configuration $C = (G, \ell)$ such that $C \notin \mathcal{U}$. From Corollary 1, if the configuration C admits only one WP (that is, $C \in S$), then exact gathering can be accomplished. Another characterization is provided by considering S_C, and in particular the projections of the robots to the two generating paths P_1 and P_2 of G. Given a robot on a generic vertex (i, j) of G, its projections on P_1 and P_2 are a robot on vertex i and a robot on vertex j, respectively. This gives rise to two configurations (P_1, ℓ_1) and (P_2, ℓ_2) such that $\ell_1(v) = \sum_j \ell((v, j))$ and $\ell_2(v) = \sum_i \ell((i, v))$. As the movements on a grid are either vertical or horizontal, solving the gathering with respect to the two dimensions separately, solves the general problem.

Theorem 7. *Given a configuration $C = (G, \ell)$ with $G = P_1 \times P_2$, if (P_1, ℓ_1) and (P_2, ℓ_2) are gatherable, then C is gatherable exactly.*

Proof. The exact gathering is obtained by simply considering (P_1, ℓ_1) and (P_2, ℓ_2) separately. Each time a robot wakes-up, it can move with respect to any of the two instances indiscriminately, as they are independent to each other. Theorem 6 guarantees exact gathering on both the instances even though they might contain multiplicities. □

The next theorem provides a useful characterization about the disposal of WPs in a configuration.

Theorem 8. *Given a configuration $C = (G, \ell)$ with $G = P_1 \times P_2$, $G_{\mathsf{WP}}(C)$ is a finite grid defined by the Cartesian product of the subpaths induced by the WPs belonging to (P_1, ℓ_1) and (P_2, ℓ_2).*

Proof. Let $v = (i, j) \in G$ be such that i is not a WP in P_1 or j is not a WP in P_2. Then, $c_{G,\ell}(v) = \sum_{u \in V} d(u, v) \cdot \ell(u) = c_{P_1,\ell_1}(i) + c_{P_2,\ell_2}(j) > \min_{x \in P_1} c_{P_1,\ell_1}(x) + \min_{y \in P_2} c_{P_2,\ell_2}(y)$. The last inequality holds as i or j is not a WP. Moreover, any vertex u in the grid defined by the Cartesian product of the subpaths induced by the WPs belonging to (P_1, ℓ_1) and (P_2, ℓ_2) has centrality $c_{G,\ell}(u) = \min_{x \in P_1} c_{P_1,\ell_1}(x) + \min_{y \in P_2} c_{P_2,\ell_2}(y)$ since the projections of u are WPs in (P_1, ℓ_1) and (P_2, ℓ_2), respectively. Hence, v is not a WP in G. □

By referring to Figure 2, it is worth noting that $G_{\mathsf{WP}}(C)$, for some configuration C, is in general a finite grid where robots can occupy only the corners. Moreover, all the vertices belonging to the strips from $G_{\mathsf{WP}}(C)$ to the borders of S_C cannot be occupied, but for the ones sharing coordinates with the border of $G_{\mathsf{WP}}(C)$. These robots will be said to *determine* $G_{\mathsf{WP}}(C)$. Note that, given a configuration C with k robots, evaluating the set of WPs has time complexity $O(|S_C| \times k)$.

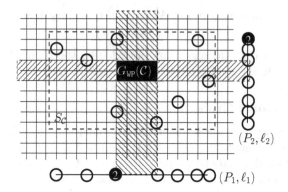

Fig. 2. A sample configuration $\mathcal{C}$ which induces $S_\mathcal{C}$, $G_{\text{WP}}(\mathcal{C})$, and its projections to the sides of $S_\mathcal{C}$

Corollary 2. *If the number of robots in a grid G is odd, then exact gathering can be accomplished.*

Proof. By Lemma 1, an odd number of robots implies a single WP for each instance on the two paths generating G. By Theorem 8, the Cartesian product of those two WPs constitutes the only WP of the configuration, hence by Corollary 1 exact gathering can be assured. □

3.4 Grids with an Even Number of Robots

In this section, we provide a general strategy that solves the exact gathering problem for all the configurations not in $\mathcal{U}$.

First of all, if $S_\mathcal{C}$ has both sides odd and the center is a WP then we can gather all the robots in the center. The idea at the basis of the strategy is to let move all the robots not determining the border of $S_\mathcal{C}$ towards the center that becomes the only WP of the current configuration. From there on, all the other robots can join the unique WP. This can be easily realized if the number of robots is "sufficiently" large, while for few robots specific strategies are required.

Lemma 2. *Let $\mathcal{C} = (G, \ell)$ be a configuration inducing $S_\mathcal{C}$ with both sides odd and the center being a WP, there exists an exact gathering algorithm, unless there are only four robots occupying the four corners of $S_\mathcal{C}$.*

Configuration admitting rotations but not in $\mathcal{U}$ are solved by the above lemma since their center is a vertex (i.e., $S_\mathcal{C}$ has both sides odd) and it is a WP.

Let us consider the case where $S_\mathcal{C}$ has at least one side even or its center is not a WP. Before proceeding with the characterization of the algorithm, we need to better specify the view of the robots during their Look phase when no multiplicities occur.

Let us consider the eight sequences of distances (number of empty vertices) between occupied vertices obtained by traversing S_C starting from its four corners and proceeding towards the two possible directions. Note that the two sequences associated to a corner occupied by a robot start with 0. We associate for each corner the lexicographically biggest sequence between the two readings from such corner. Note that, in square grids such two sequences are always different, but for the two corners through which passes a possible axis of symmetry. In rectangular grids, these two sequences can be equal, but we can distinguish one of them by assuming that if two sequences are equal, the one read in the direction of the largest side is bigger than the other.

We define the maximal sequence as the biggest one among the four sequences associated to the four corners. We refer to the corner(s) defining the biggest sequence as *preferred corner(s)*, and to the direction(s) that implies the biggest sequence as *preferred direction(s)*.

In Figure 2, the preferred corner of S_C is the bottom-leftmost one, the preferred direction is horizontal, and the maximal sequence is $(10, 11, 21, 34, 19, 12, 21, 7)$.

We are now ready to describe the gathering algorithm for each configuration $C \notin \mathcal{U}$ with more than one WP, where S_C has at least one side even or its center is not a WP.

In general, if a configuration is symmetric, the algorithm may allow to move two symmetric robots. If both move, the configuration remains symmetric. If only one moves, the algorithm always forces to move the one that can re-establish the symmetry. Moreover, it is possible to prove that from asymmetric configurations at one step from an allowed symmetry, it is always possible to detect one unique robot that has to move in order to (re)-establish the symmetry.

According to the number of corners of $G_{WP}(C)$ occupied by robots, different strategies are applied. See Figure 3 for a visualization of the configurations that will be considered.

Type F: No Corners Occupied. Among these configurations, $F1$ are the asymmetric ones, $F2$ the symmetric configurations with an horizontal/vertical axis, and $F3$ the symmetric configurations with a diagonal axis.

First we consider the cases when $G_{WP}(C)$ is not a path. If the configuration admits an axis of symmetry, then among the robots determining $G_{WP}(C)$, consider those closest to $G_{WP}(C)$ wrt the preferred direction. Ties are solved by considering those closest to the preferred corner. Such robot(s) moves towards $G_{WP}(C)$. In this case, either two symmetric robots move synchronously, or only one moves, and the other one (if any) is possibly pending. Eventually, this process leads to symmetric configurations with two corners of $G_{WP}(C)$ occupied and the axis reflecting them, or with one corner occupied by a multiplicity.

If the configuration is asymmetric at more than one step from an allowed symmetry, the closest robot to $G_{WP}(C)$ moves towards it. Ties are solved by considering the preferred direction and the preferred corner.

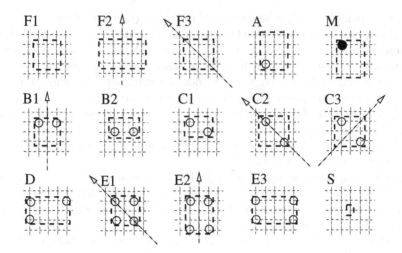

Fig. 3. Types of configurations according to the number of corners of $G_{WP}(\mathcal{C})$ occupied by robots/multiplicities. Dashed lines delimit $G_{WP}(\mathcal{C})$, empty circles represent single robots, and filled circles represent multiplicities.

When $G_{WP}(\mathcal{C})$ is constituted by just a path, the strategy is the same as above but limited to the robots determining the same direction of $G_{WP}(\mathcal{C})$ and not those determining its extremities.

Type A: One Corner Occupied by a Single Robot. If the configuration is asymmetric, first robots check whether an allowed symmetry can be (re-)established. This can be done by simulating the move back of the unique robot on the corner of $G_{WP}(\mathcal{C})$. If this occurs, then the possible pending robot is forced to perform its move. In any other case, the single robot on the corner moves in one of the two directions that reduce $G_{WP}(\mathcal{C})$, until obtaining only one WP.

Type M: One Corner Occupied by a Multiplicity. First, all robots sharing one coordinate with the multiplicity move in turn (i.e., without creating another multiplicity) until joining it, towards the shared coordinate. After that, if there are more than one WP, among the robots determining $G_{WP}(\mathcal{C})$, consider those closest to it. Such robots - at most four - move along the direction that reduces $G_{WP}(\mathcal{C})$, until they share one coordinate with the multiplicity.

Types B and C: Two Corners Occupied. Among these configurations we denote by B the set of configurations where the two corners occupied share one coordinate but for symmetric configurations with the axis passing through the two occupied corners. These last configurations and the remaining ones with two corners occupied are denoted by C. $B1 \subset B$ represents symmetric configurations,

---

Procedure: COMPUTE-PHASE
Input: $\mathcal{C} = ((V,E),\ell)$

1 Compute $S_{\mathcal{C}}$, $G_{\text{WP}}(\mathcal{C})$, and $k = \sum_{v \in V} \ell(v)$;
2 **if** $\mathcal{C} \notin \mathcal{U}$ **then**
3   **if** $\mathcal{C} \in S$ **then** any robot moves towards the unique WP;
4   **else**
5   **if** $S_{\mathcal{C}}$ *has both sizes odd* **then** Apply Lemma 2;
6   **else**
7   **case** $\mathcal{C} \in \mathcal{X}$, *with* $\mathcal{X} \in \{A,B,C,D,E,F,M\}$
8                  $\lfloor$ Apply the strategy designed for type $\mathcal{X}$;

Fig. 4. Procedure COMPUTE-PHASE

$B2 \subset B$ the asymmetric ones. $C1 \subset C$ represents asymmetric configurations, $C2 \subset C$ the symmetric ones with the axis passing through the occupied corners, and $C3 \subset C$ the remaining symmetric configurations.

From $B1$, the two robots on the axis move towards each other, still maintaining the symmetry. Note that, the two robots are separated by an odd path, as otherwise the configuration is ungatherable by Theorem 2.

From $B2$ and $C1$, the algorithm (re-)establish an allowed symmetry, if any. Otherwise, the robot closest to the preferred corner along the preferred direction moves towards the other robot avoiding ungatherable configurations.

From $C2$, the robot that moves is the one on the corner of $G_{\text{WP}}(\mathcal{C})$ closest to the corner of $S_{\mathcal{C}}$ associated with the biggest sequence among the two corners on the axis. The robot moves towards the other occupied corner of $G_{\text{WP}}(\mathcal{C})$.

From $C3$, the two robots on the corners of $G_{\text{WP}}(\mathcal{C})$ move towards the corner of $G_{\text{WP}}(\mathcal{C})$ on the axis, closest to the corner of $S_{\mathcal{C}}$ associated with the bigger sequence.

In all the cases, a configuration in S with a multiplicity occupying the only WP will be reached, eventually.

Type D: Three Corners Occupied. From D, the robot on the middle corner moves towards one of the two other occupied corners. This leads to a configuration with two corners occupied or with only one corner occupied by a multiplicity.

Type E: Four Corners Occupied. Among configurations E, we denote by $E1$ the symmetric ones with a diagonal axis, by $E2$ the remaining symmetric ones, and by $E3$ the asymmetric ones.

From $E1$, the robot on $G_{\text{WP}}(\mathcal{C})$ closest to the corner of $S_{\mathcal{C}}$ on the axis associated with the bigger sequence, moves reducing the WPs.

From $E2$, the two robots on $G_{\text{WP}}(\mathcal{C})$ closest to the preferred corners move towards each other. Note that, if both move synchronously, then a symmetric configuration with two corners occupied or with a multiplicity is obtained. If only one moves, then a configuration of type D is obtained. According to that case, the robot that will be allowed to move is the one with a possible pending move, hence it does not create ambiguities.

From $E3$, the robot on $G_{\mathrm{WP}}(\mathcal{C})$ closest to the preferred corner moves reducing the WPs.

4   Correctness

The general scheme of the algorithm is shown in Figure 4. Clearly, if $\mathcal{C} \in \mathcal{U}$ then robots do not move. When $\mathcal{C} \in S$, the correctness is guaranteed by Corollary 1. By Theorem 8, S includes all configurations with an odd number of robots.

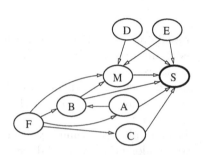

Fig. 5. Transitions among types of configurations allowed by the exact gathering algorithm

If $\mathcal{C}$ contains an even number of robots with $S_{\mathcal{C}}$ admitting both sides odd and its center being the non-unique WP, the correctness is guaranteed by Lemma 2.

When $S_{\mathcal{C}}$ has at least one even side or its center is not a WP, and there are more than one WP, we have defined different strategies according to the type of $\mathcal{C}$. The correctness proof is achieved by showing that all types of input configurations lead to S. From there, the correctness is then guaranteed by Corollary 1. All possible transitions among types of configurations are shown in Figure 5. The main difficulty faced concerns the design of an algorithm that avoids ambiguities. This means that each time a robot starts its Look-Compute-Move cycle, it must be sure whether it has to move or not, without leading to ungatherable configurations. This requires for instance to identify possible pending moves. Considering e.g., $\mathcal{C} \in B1$ with $G_{\mathrm{WP}}(\mathcal{C})$ composed of just two vertices, there are six possible moves back in order to detect whether $\mathcal{C}$ has been potentially obtained from a symmetric configuration, hence producing pending moves.

Our strategies guarantee the desired behavior and all moves are performed towards the final WP along shortest paths. Then, the next theorem holds.

Theorem 9 (Gathering). *Given an initial configuration $\mathcal{C} = (G, \ell)$ on an infinite grid G, exact gathering can be assured unless $\mathcal{C} \in \mathcal{U}$.*

5   Conclusion

We have studied the gathering problem under the Look-Compute-Move model with global-strong multiplicity detection on infinite grids. We have shown how the assumed model represents the minimal setting in order to assure exact gathering. This means that the number of moves required by the designed algorithm equals the minimal centrality among the vertices of the initial configuration.

We fully characterize exact gathering in terms of computed moves on infinite grids. This is one of the most important topologies for robot-based computing systems as it represents a natural discretization of the plane. Nonetheless, our algorithm also works for finite grids, hence improving the results on that respect to exact gathering. Other topologies might be worth investigating such as tori and hypercubes.

References

[1] D'Angelo, G., Di Stefano, G., Klasing, R., Navarra, A.: Gathering of robots on anonymous grids and trees without multiplicity detection. Theor. Comput. Sci. (to appear)

[2] D'Angelo, G., Di Stefano, G., Navarra, A.: Gathering on rings under the look-compute-move model. Distributed Computing 27(4), 255–285 (2014)

[3] D'Angelo, G., Di Stefano, G., Navarra, A.: Gathering asynchronous and oblivious robots on basic graph topologies under the look-compute-move model. In: Search Theory: A Game Theoretic Perspective, pp. 197–222. Springer (2013)

[4] Degener, B., Kempkes, B., Langner, T., Meyer, F.: A tight runtime bound for synchronous gathering of autonomous robots with limited visibility. In: Proc. of the 23rd ACM Symp. on Parallelism in Algorithms and Architectures (SPAA), pp. 139–148 (2011)

[5] Devismes, S., Lamani, A., Petit, F., Raymond, P., Tixeuil, S.: Optimal grid exploration by asynchronous oblivious robots. In: Richa, A.W., Scheideler, C. (eds.) SSS 2012. LNCS, vol. 7596, pp. 64–76. Springer, Heidelberg (2012)

[6] Di Stefano, G., Navarra, A.: Optimal gathering of oblivious robots in anonymous graphs. In: Moscibroda, T., Rescigno, A.A. (eds.) SIROCCO 2013. LNCS, vol. 8179, pp. 213–224. Springer, Heidelberg (2013)

[7] Dieudonné, Y., Pelc, A., Villain, V.: How to meet asynchronously at polynomial cost. In: Proc. of the 32nd ACM SIGACT-SIGOPS Symposium on Principles of Distributed Computing (PODC), pp. 92–99 (2013)

[8] Flocchini, P., Prencipe, G., Santoro, N.: Distributed Computing by Oblivious Mobile Robots. Synthesis Lectures on Distributed Computing Theory. Morgan & Claypool (2012)

[9] Flocchini, P., Prencipe, G., Santoro, N., Widmayer, P.: Gathering of asynchronous robots with limited visibility. Theor. Comput. Sci. 337, 147–168 (2005)

[10] Izumi, T., Izumi, T., Kamei, S., Ooshita, F.: Randomized gathering of mobile robots with local-multiplicity detection. In: Guerraoui, R., Petit, F. (eds.) SSS 2009. LNCS, vol. 5873, pp. 384–398. Springer, Heidelberg (2009)

[11] Klasing, R., Kosowski, A., Navarra, A.: Taking advantage of symmetries: Gathering of many asynchronous oblivious robots on a ring. Theor. Comput. Sci. 411, 3235–3246 (2010)

[12] Klasing, R., Markou, E., Pelc, A.: Gathering asynchronous oblivious mobile robots in a ring. Theor. Comput. Sci. 390, 27–39 (2008)

[13] Kupitz, Y., Martini, H.: Geometric aspects of the generalized Fermat-Torricelli problem. Intuitive Geometry, vol. 6. Bolyai Society Math Studies (1997)

[14] Suzuki, I., Yamashita, M.: Distributed anonymous mobile robots: Formation of geometric patterns. SIAM J. Comput. 28(4), 1347–1363 (1999)

Incremental Verification of Computing Policies

Ehab S. Elmallah[1], H.B. Acharya[2], and Mohamed G. Gouda[3]

[1] Department of Computing Science, University of Alberta
Edmonton, T6G 2E8, Canada
elmallah@ualberta.ca
[2] Indraprastha Institute of Information Technology
Delhi, India
acharya@cs.utexas.edu
[3] Department of Computing Science, University of Texas at Austin
Austin, Texas 78712, USA
gouda@cs.utexas.edu

Abstract. A computing policy is a sequence of rules, where each rule consists of a predicate and an action, which can be either "accept" or "reject". A policy P is said to accept (or reject, respectively) a request iff the action of the first rule in P, whose predicate matches the request, is "accept" (or "reject", respectively). An accept (or reject, respectively) property of a policy P is a set of requests that should be accepted (or rejected, respectively) by P. Policy P is said to satisfy an accept (or reject, respectively) property pp iff every request that is specified by property pp is accepted (or rejected, respectively) by policy P. In this paper, we outline efficient methods for verifying whether any given policy P satisfies any given property pp, provided that policy P results from changing only one rule in another policy that is known to satisfy property pp.

Keywords: Computing Policies, Access Control Policies, Routing Policies, Firewall Policies, Packet Classifiers, Logical Analysis, Incremental Verification, NP-hard.

1 Introduction

A computing policy is a filter that is placed at the entry point of some resource. Each request to access the resource needs to be first examined against the policy to determine whether to accept or to reject the request. The decision of a policy to accept or reject a request depends on two factors:

1. The values of some attributes that are specified in the request
2. The sequence of rules in the policy that are specified by the policy designer

Examples of computing polices are firewalls in the Internet, routing policies in the Internet, software-defined networks in the Internet, and access control policies [8].

P. Felber and V. Garg (Eds.): SSS 2014, LNCS 8756, pp. 226–236, 2014.

A rule in a policy consists of a predicate and an action, which is either accept or reject. To examine a request against a policy, the rules in the policy are considered one by one until the first rule, whose predicate satisfies the values of the attributes in the request, is identified. Then the action of the identified rule (whether accept or reject) is applied to the request.

Note that there are three sets of requests that are associated with each policy P: (1) the set of requests that are accepted by P, (2) the set of requests that are rejected by P, and (3) the set of requests that are neither accepted nor rejected by P. This third set is usually empty.

An accept (or reject, respectively) property of a policy P specifies a set of requests that should be accepted (or rejected, respectively) by P.

A policy P is said to satisfy an accept (or reject, respectively) property iff every request that is specified by the property is accepted (or rejected, respectively) by P.

The task of verifying whether a given policy satisfies a given property is not an easy one [5,6,9] especially when the policy has thousands of rules, as usually is the case.

In this paper, we outline efficient methods for verifying whether any given computing policy P satisfies any given property pp, provided that P results from adding or removing one rule from another policy that is known to satisfy property pp. We start our presentation by discussing a concrete example of a policy, four of its requests, and two of its properties.

Let u and v be two attributes whose integer values are taken from the interval $[1,9]$. A policy P over these two attributes can be defined as follows:

$$((u \in [1,4]) \wedge (v \in [8,9])) \rightarrow reject$$
$$((u \in [1,4]) \wedge (v \in [1,9])) \rightarrow accept$$
$$((u \in [5,8]) \wedge (v \in [4,4])) \rightarrow accept$$
$$((u \in [1,9]) \wedge (v \in [1,9])) \rightarrow reject$$

This policy P consists of four rules. The first rule states that each request (u,v), where the value of attribute u is an integer in the interval $[1,4]$ and where the value of attribute v is an integer in the interval $[8,9]$, is to be rejected. The second rule states that each request (u,v), that does not match the first rule and where the value of u is an integer in the interval $[1,4]$ and where the value of v is in the interval $[1,9]$, is to be accepted. And so on.

A request of policy P is a pair of values: a value of attribute u and a value of attribute v. Four request examples of policy P, named rq_1 through rq_4, are as follows:

$$rq_1 : (4,4)$$
$$rq_2 : (5,4)$$
$$rq_3 : (5,5)$$
$$rq_4 : (5,6)$$

Request rq_1 does not match the first rule of policy P, but it matches the second rule of P. Therefore P accepts request rq_1. Request rq_2 does not match the first and second rules of P, but it matches the third rule of P. Therefore, P accepts rq_2. Request rq_3 does not match the first, second, and third rules of policy P, but it matches the fourth rule of P. Therefore, P rejects rq_3. Similarly, request rq_4 does not match the first, second, and third rules of policy P, but it matches the fourth rule of P. Therefore, P rejects rq_3.

A property of policy P has the same syntax as a rule in P. Two property examples of policy P, named pp_1 and pp_2, are as follows:

$$pp_1 : ((u \in [4, 5]) \wedge (v \in [4, 4])) \rightarrow accept$$
$$pp_2 : ((u \in [5, 5]) \wedge (v \in [4, 6])) \rightarrow reject.$$

Policy P satisfies an accept (or reject, respectively) property pp iff P accepts (or rejects, respectively) every request that matches property pp. For example, there are two requests that match the accept property pp_1, namely requests $(4, 4)$ and $(5, 4)$, and because policy P accepts both these requests, we conclude that policy P satisfies the accept property $pp1$. Also, there are three requests that match the reject property pp_2, namely requests $(5, 4), (5, 5)$, and $(5, 6)$, and because policy P accepts at least one of these requests, namely request $(5, 4)$, we conclude that policy P does not satisfy the reject property pp_2.

2   Policy Preliminaries

In this section, we formally introduce the eight main concepts related to computing policies, or policies for short. These eight concepts are: Intervals, Attributes, Requests, Predicates, Actions, Rules, Properties, and Policies. We present these eight concepts one by one next.

2.1   Intervals

An interval is a finite and nonempty set of consecutive integers. An interval X can be denoted by a pair of integers $[y, z]$, where y is the smallest integer in X, and z is the largest integer in X. Note that an interval $[y, y]$ has only one integer y. Note also that any pair $[y, z]$, where $y > z$, is not an interval.

Two intervals $X = [y, z]$ and $X' = [y', z']$ are said to be overlapping iff one of the following two conditions holds: (1) $y \le y'$ and $y' \le z$, and (2) $y' \le y$ and $y \le z'$.

The intersection of two overlapping intervals $X = [y, z]$ and $X' = [y', z']$ is defined to be the interval $[\max(y, y'), \min(z, z')]$

2.2   Attributes

An attribute is a "variable" that has a "name" and has a "value". Throughout this paper, we assume that there are t attributes whose names are $a_1, a_2, \cdots, a_t$. The value of each attribute a_i is taken from an interval that is called the domain of attribute a_i and is denoted $D(a_i)$.

2.3 Requests

A request is a tuple $(v_1, \cdots, v_t)$ of t integers, where t is the number of attributes and each integer v_i is taken from the domain $D(a_i)$ of attribute a_i.

2.4 Predicates

A predicate is of the form $((a_1 \in X_1) \wedge \cdots \wedge (a_t \in X_t))$, where each a_i is an attribute, each X_i is an interval that is contained in the domain $D(a_i)$ of attribute a_i, and '$\wedge$' is the logical AND or conjunction operator.

The value of each conjunct $(a_i \in X_i)$ in a predicate is true iff the value of attribute a_i is an integer in interval X_i.

The value of a predicate is true iff the value of every conjunct $(a_i \in X_i)$ in the predicate is true.

A predicate $((a_1 \in X_1) \wedge \cdots \wedge (a_t \in X_t))$, where each interval X_i is the whole domain of the corresponding attribute a_i, is called the ALL predicate.

Let the pr and ps denote the following two predicates:

$$pr = ((a_1 \in X_1) \wedge \cdots \wedge (a_t \in X_t))$$
$$ps = ((a_1 \in Y_1) \wedge \cdots \wedge (a_t \in Y_t)).$$

We use next these two predicates to define two concepts: "two overlapping predicates" and "intersection of two predicates".

Predicates pr and ps are said to be overlapping iff every interval X_i in pr and every corresponding interval Y_i in ps are overlapping.

If predicates pr and ps are overlapping, then the intersection of predicates pr and ps is defined to be the predicate $((a_1 \in Z_1) \wedge \cdots \wedge (a_t \in Z_t))$ where every interval Z_i is the intersection of the two corresponding intervals X_i and Y_i.

A request $(v_1, \cdots, v_t)$ is said to match a predicate $((a_1 \in X_1) \wedge \cdots \wedge (a_t \in X_t))$ iff each integer v_i in the request is an element in the corresponding interval X_i in the predicate.

2.5 Actions

We assume that there are two distinct actions: "accept" and "reject". Henceforth, we write "accept" and "reject" with quotation marks to indicate the "accept" and "reject" actions, respectively. We also write accept and reject without quotation marks to indicate the English words accept and reject, respectively.

2.6 Rules

A rule (in a policy) is defined as a pair, one predicate and one action, written as follows:

$$< predicate > \rightarrow < action >$$

A rule whose action is "accept" is called an accept rule, and a rule whose action is "reject" is called a reject rule. An accept rule whose predicate is the

ALL predicate is called an *accept-ALL* rule, and a reject rule whose predicate is the ALL predicate is called the *reject-ALL* predicate.

A request is said to match a rule iff the request matches the predicate of the rule. (Note that each request matches every ALL rule.)

2.7   Properties

Like a rule, a property (of a policy) is defined as a pair, one predicate and one action, written as follows:

$< predicate > \rightarrow < action >$

A property whose action is "accept" is called an accept property, and a property whose action is "reject" is called a reject property.

A request rq is said to match a property pp iff rq matches the predicate of pp.

A rule r is said to overlap a property pp iff the predicate of r overlaps the predicate of pp.

If a rule r overlaps a property pp, then the intersection of r and pp is the rule whose predicate is the intersection of the two predicates of r and pp and whose action (accept or reject) is the same as the action of r.

2.8   Policies

A policy is a (possibly empty) sequence of rules. A policy P is said to accept (or reject, respectively) a request rq iff P has an accept (or reject, respectively) rule r such that request rq matches rule r and does not match any rule that precedes rule r in policy P.

A policy P is said to satisfy a property pp iff either pp is an accept property and P accepts every request that matches pp, or pp is a reject property and P rejects every request that matches pp.

3   Policy Verification Using the PSP Method

In this section, we briefly discuss a recent method [2] for verifying whether a policy P satisfies a property pp. For convenience, we refer to this method as the *Projection-Slicing-Probing* method, or the PSP method for short. Without any loss of generality, we focus our discussion of the PSP method on the case where pp is an accept property. (It is worth noting that the PSP method can also be used in detecting redundant rules in a policy [1, 7] and in determining whether any two given policies are equivalent.)

The PSP method for verifying whether a policy P satisfies an accept property pp consists of three steps: (More explanations about these steps are presented below.)

1. From policy P and the accept property pp, construct a new policy called the projection of policy P over property pp. This new policy is denoted P/pp

2. Divide the projection policy P/pp into a set of special policies $\{RS_1, \cdots, RS_k\}$ called the reject slices of the projection P/pp.
3. Check whether each reject slice RS_i rejects no request. If every reject slice RS_i is shown to reject no request, then policy P satisfies the accept property pp. Otherwise P does not satisfy pp.

Next we describe these three steps in more detail.

Algorithm 1: Projection
Input:
A policy P and an accept property pp

Output:
A new policy called the projection of policy P over property pp. This new policy is denoted P/pp

Step 1:
Add a reject-ALL rule at the end of policy P

Step 2:
Initially, P/pp is the empty policy

Step 3:
For every rule r in policy P do
  – If rule r overlaps property pp then add the intersection of rule r and property pp as a rule at the tail of policy P/pp
End Algorithm 1

The next theorem follows from Algorithm 1.

Theorem 1: A policy P satisfies an accept property pp iff the projection policy P/pp rejects no request.

Algorithm 2: Slicing
Input:
A projection policy P/pp of a policy P over an accept property pp

Output:
A set of policies $\{RS_1, \cdots, RS_k\}$, where each policy RS_i is called a reject slice of the projection policy P/pp and k is the number of reject rules in the projection policy P/pp

Step 1:
For each i in the range 1 to k do

- compute policy RS_i as the sequence of all accept rules that precede the i-th reject rule in policy P/pp followed by the i-th reject rule in policy P/pp

End Algorithm 2

The next theorem follows from Algorithm 2.

Theorem 2: The projection P/pp of a policy P over an accept property pp rejects no request iff every reject slice of the projection P/pp rejects no request.

Algorithm 3: Probing
Input:
A reject slice RS_i of the projection P/pp of policy P over an accept property pp

Output:
A determination of whether RS_i rejects no request

Step 1:
For each attribute x_j where j ranges from 1 to t do
  - Compute a set S_j of values of x_j as follows:
  - $S_j :=$ empty set
  - For each accept rule ar in RS_i do
      - If the predicate of ar has the conjunct $(x_j \in [u, v])$ then add element $(v + 1)$ to set S_j
    End for
  - If the predicate of the reject rule rr in RS_i has the conjunct $(x_j \in [u, v])$ then add element u to set S_j

Step 2:
Compute set S of all "probe requests" as the Cartesian product $(S_1 \times \cdots \times S_t)$

Step 3:
  - If no probe request in S is rejected by the reject slice RS_i then declare that slice RS_i rejects no request
  - Else declare that slice RS_i rejects at least one request

End Algorithm 3

The next theorem follows from Theorems 1 and 2 above.

Theorem 3: A policy P satisfies an accept property pp iff every reject slice of the projection P/pp rejects no request.

To verify whether a policy P satisfies an accept property pp, one needs to execute Algorithm 1 once, execute Algorithm 2 once, and execute Algorithm 3 on k reject slices, where $k \leq n$ and n is the number of rules in policy P. Because the time complexity of Algorithms 1 and of Algorithm 2 is $O(n*t)$, where t is the number of attributes, and because the time complexity of Algorithm 3 is $O(n^{t+1})$, the time complexity of verifying whether P satisfies pp is $O(n^{t+2})$.

This large time complexity is to be expected since it has been shown recently that the problem of verifying whether a policy satisfies a property is NP-hard [4]. (Beside resorting to the PSP method, it has been suggested [4] that the large time complexity of policy verification can be faced by using SAT solvers [10] or probabilistic verification techniques [3].)

4   Incremental Verification of Policies

Let P be a policy and let Q be a policy that results after modifying one rule in policy P, e.g. after adding one rule to policy P or after removing one rule from policy P. Also let pp be a property that is satisfied by policy P. There are two types of methods for verifying whether policy Q satisfies property pp: direct methods and incremental methods.

a. Direct Verification Methods:
To verify that policy Q satisfies property pp, a direct verification method takes into account only Q and pp. It completely ignores the two facts that (1) policy Q is obtained from policy P by modifying only one rule, and (2) policy P satisfies property pp.

b. Incremental Verification Methods:
To verify that policy Q satisfies property pp, an incremental verification method takes into account Q, pp, and the two facts that (1) policy Q is obtained from policy P by modifying only one rule, and (2) policy P satisfies property pp.

The main advantage of incremental methods over direct methods is that the time complexity of incremental methods tends to be smaller than that of direct methods.

An example of a direct verification method is the PSP method outlined in the previous section, and two examples of incremental verification methods are discussed in the next two sections.

5   Incremental Verification After Rule Addition

Let P be a policy and let Q be a policy that results after adding one reject rule rr **anywhere** in policy P. (Extending the discussion to the case where the added rule is an accept rule is straightforward.)

Also let pp be a property that is satisfied by policy P. Next, we describe an efficient method for verifying whether policy Q satisfies property pp.

First, observe that if pp is a reject property, then policy Q is guaranteed to satisfy pp. Henceforth, we assume that pp is an accept property.

Second, the PSP method can be used to verify whether policy Q satisfies the accept property pp by executing the following three steps:

(a) Compute the projection Q/pp
(b) Divide the projection Q/pp into a set **RS** of reject slices
(c) Check whether every reject slice in set **RS** rejects no request

Third, observe that set **RS** consists of all the reject slices of the projection P/pp plus a new reject slice denoted rs. The new reject slice rs consists of all the accept rules that precede the added reject rule rr in policy Q followed by rule rr.

Fourth, because policy P satisfies the accept property pp, then by Theorem 2 above every reject slice of the projection P/pp rejects no request. Therefore, the above three steps (a) to (c) for verifying whether policy Q satisfies the accept property pp can be reduced to the following three steps for incrementally verifying whether policy Q satisfies the accept property pp:

i. Construct the new reject slice rs to consist of all the accept rules that precede the added reject rule rr in policy Q followed by rule rr.
ii. Use Algorithm 3 above, to check whether the new reject slice rs rejects no request.
iii. Conclude that Q satisfies pp iff the new reject slice rs rejects no request

The time complexity for executing these three steps is dominated by the time complexity of executing Algorithm 3. Because the time complexity of executing Algorithm 3 is $O(n^{t+1})$, the time complexity for incrementally verifying whether policy Q satisfies the accept property pp is $O(n^{t+1})$, where n is the number of rules in policy Q and t is the number of attributes. This time complexity is better than $O(n^{t+2})$, which is the time complexity for directly verifying whether policy Q satisfies the accept property pp.

6   Incremental Verification After Rule Removal

Let P be a policy and let Q be a policy that results after removing one rule from policy P. Without any loss of generality, let the removed rule be an accept rule denoted ar. (Extending the discussion to the case where the removed rule is a reject rule is straightforward.)

Also let pp be a property that is satisfied by policy P. Next, we describe an efficient method for verifying whether policy Q satisfies property pp.

First, observe that if pp is a reject property, then policy Q is guaranteed to satisfy pp. Henceforth, we assume that pp is an accept property.

Second, the PSP method can be used to verify whether policy Q satisfies the accept property pp by executing the following three steps:

(a) Compute the projection Q/pp
(b) Divide the projection Q/pp into a set **RS** of reject slices
(c) Check whether every reject slice in set **RS** rejects no request

Third, observe that there is a one-to-one correspondence between the reject slices of the projection P/pp and those of the projection Q/pp. Each reject slice of projection Q/pp, whose corresponding slice of projection P/pp has the removed accept rule ar, is called an *affected* slice. Similarly, each reject slice of projection Q/pp, whose corresponding slice of projection P/pp does not have the removed accept rule ar, is called an *un-affected* slice.

Note that each affected slice of projection Q/pp is identical to its corresponding reject slice of projection P/pp with one exception, namely the removed accept rule ar does not occur in the affected slice even though it occurs in the corresponding reject slice. Note also that each un-affected slice of projection Q/pp is identical to its corresponding reject slice of projection P/pp. Finally note that the number of affected slices of projection Q/pp is at most $(m + 1)$, where m is the number of reject rules that follow the removed accept rule ar in policy P, and the $(m + 1)$st reject rule is added by Step 1 of Algorithm 1.

Fourth, because policy P satisfies the accept property pp, then by Theorem 2 above every reject slice of the projection P/pp rejects no request. Therefore, the above three steps (a) to (c) for verifying whether policy Q satisfies the accept property pp can be reduced to the following three steps for incrementally verifying whether policy Q satisfies the accept property pp:

   i. Construct all the affected slices of projection Q/pp. There are at most $(m + 1)$ of such slices, where m is the number of reject rules that follow the removed accept rule ar in policy P.
   ii. For each affected slice, use Algorithm 3 above, to check whether the affected slice rejects no request.
   iii. Conclude that Q satisfies pp iff every affected slice rejects no request.

The time complexity for executing these three steps is dominated by the time complexity of executing Algorithm 3 in Step ii. Because the time complexity of executing Algorithm 3 is $O(n^{t+1})$, the time complexity for incrementally verifying whether policy Q satisfies the accept property pp is $O(m * n^{t+1})$, where m is the number of reject rules that follow the removed accept rule ar in policy P, n is the number of rules in policy Q, and t is the number of attributes. This time complexity is better than $O(n^{t+2})$, which is the time complexity for directly verifying whether policy Q satisfies the accept property pp.

7   Concluding Remarks

The time complexity of the best known algorithm [2] for verifying whether a given policy P satisfies a given property pp is $O(n^{t+2})$ where n is the number of rules in policy P and t is the number of attributes. This time complexity is not likely to improve significantly in the future since the policy verification problem has been shown to be NP-hard [4].

In this paper, we show that the time complexity of verifying whether any policy P satisfies any property pp can be reduced to $O(n^{t+1})$ in the case where policy P is obtained by adding one rule to another policy that is known to satisfy property pp.

Also in this paper, we show that the time complexity of verifying whether any policy P satisfies any property pp can be reduced to $O(m * n^{t+1})$, where m is the number of rules that have the same action in policy P, in the case where policy P is obtained by removing one rule from another policy that is known to satisfy property pp.

It is straightforward to show that similar techniques to those discussed in this paper can be employed to reduce the time complexity of verifying whether any policy P satisfies any property pp in the following three cases: (1) policy P is obtained by flipping the action of one rule in another policy that is known to satisfy property pp, (2) policy P is obtained by weakening the predicate of one rule in another policy that is known to satisfy property pp, and (3) policy P is obtained by strengthening the predicate of one rule in another policy that is known to satisfy property pp.

References

1. Acharya, H.B., Gouda, M.G.: Firewall verification and redundancy checking are equivalent. In: Proceedings of the 30th IEEE International Conference on Computer Communication (INFOCOM). pp. 2123–2128 (2011)
2. Acharya, H.B., et al.: Projection and division: Linear space verification of firewalls. In: Proceedings of the 30th International Conference on Distributed Computing Systems (ICDCS), pp. 736–743 (2010)
3. Acharya, H.B., et al.: Linear-time verification of firewalls. In: Proceedings of the 17th IEEE International Conference on Network Protocols (ICNP), pp. 133–140 (2009)
4. Elmallah, E.S., Gouda, M.G.: Hardness of firewall analysis. In: Noubir, G., Raynal, M. (eds.) NETYS 2014. LNCS, vol. 8593, pp. 153–168. Springer, Heidelberg (2014)
5. Hoffman, D., Yoo, K.: Blowtorch: A framework for firewall test automation. In: Proceedings of the 20th IEEE/ACM International Conference on Automated Software Engineering, ASE 2005, pp. 96–103 (2005)
6. Kamara, S., Fahmy, S., Schultz, E., Kerschbaum, F., Frantzen, M.: Analysis of vulnerabilities in internet firewalls. Computers and Security 22(3), 214–232 (2003)
7. Liu, A.X., et al.: Complete redundancy removal for packet classifiers in TCAMs. IEEE Transactions on Parallel and Distributed Systems 21, 424–437 (2010)
8. Mayer, A., Wool, A., Ziskind, E.: Fang: A firewall analysis engine. In: IEEE Symposium on Security and Privacy, pp. 177–187 (2000)
9. Wool, A.: A quantitative study of firewall configuration errors. Computer 37(6), 62–67 (2004)
10. Zhang, S., Mahmoud, A., Malik, S., Narain, S.: Verification and synthesis of firewalls using SAT and QBF. In: 20th IEEE International Conference on Network Protocols (ICNP), pp. 1–6 (2012)

On the Synthesis of Mobile Robots Algorithms: The Case of Ring Gathering

Laure Millet[1,2], Maria Potop-Butucaru[1,2],
Nathalie Sznajder[1,2], and Sébastien Tixeuil[1,2,3]

[1] Sorbonne Universités, UPMC Univ Paris 06, UMR 7606, LIP6, F-75005, Paris, France
[2] CNRS, UMR 7606, LIP6, F-75005, Paris, France
[3] Institut Universitaire de France, France

Abstract. Recent advances in Distributed Computing highlight models and algorithms for autonomous swarms of mobile robots that self-organize and cooperate to solve global objectives. The overwhelming majority of works so far considers handmade algorithms and correctness proofs.

This paper is the first to propose a formal framework to automatically design distributed algorithms that are dedicated to autonomous mobile robots evolving in a discrete space. As a case study, we consider the problem of gathering all robots at a particular location, not known beforehand. Our contribution is threefold. First, we propose an encoding of the gathering problem as a reachability game. Then, we automatically generate an optimal distributed algorithm for three robots evolving on a fixed size uniform ring. Finally, we prove by induction that the generated algorithm is also correct for any ring size except when an impossibility result holds (that is, when the number of robots divides the ring size).

1 Introduction

The Distributed Computing community, motivated by the variety of tasks that can be performed by autonomous robots and their complexity, started recently to propose formal models for these systems and to design and prove protocols in these models. The seminal paper by Suzuki & Yamashita [24] proposes a robot model, two execution models, and several algorithms (with associated correctness proofs) for gathering and scattering a set of robots. In their model, robots are identical and anonymous (they execute the same deterministic algorithm and they cannot be distinguished using their appearance), robots are oblivious (they have no memory of their past actions) and they have neither a common sense of direction, nor a common handedness (chirality). Furthermore robots do not communicate in an explicit way. However they have the ability to sense the environment and see the position of the other robots, which lets them find their way in their environment. Also, robots execute three-phase cycles: *Look*, *Compute* and *Move*. During the *Look* phase robots take a snapshot of the other robots' positions. The collected information is used in the *Compute* phase in which robots decide to move or to stay idle. In the *Move* phase, robots may move to a new position computed in the previous phase. The two execution models are denoted (using recent taxonomy [13]) FSYNC, for fully synchronous, and SSYNC, for semi-synchronous. In the SSYNC

P. Felber and V. Garg (Eds.): SSS 2014, LNCS 8756, pp. 237–251, 2014.

model an arbitrary non-empty subset of robots execute the three phases synchronously and atomically. In the FSYNC model all robots execute the three phases synchronously.

A recent trend, motivated by practical applications such that exploration or surveillance, is the study of robots evolving in a discrete space with a *finite* number of locations. This discrete space is modeled by a graph, where nodes represent locations or sites, and edges represent the possibility for a robot to move from one site to the other. The discrete setting significantly increases the number of symmetric configurations when the underlying graph is also symmetric (*e.g.* a ring).

One of the benchmarking [13] problems for mobile robots evolving in a discrete space is that of *gathering*. Regardless of their initial positions, robots have to move in such a way that they are eventually located on the same location, not known beforehand, and remain there thereafter. The case of ring networks is especially intricate, since its regular structure introduces a number of possible symmetric situations, from which the limited abilities of robots make it difficult to escape. A particular disposal (or configuration) of robots in the ring is *symmetrical* if there exists an axis of symmetry, that maps single robots into single robots, multiplicities into multiplicities, and empty nodes into empty nodes. A symmetric configuration can be edge-edge, node-edge or node-node symmetrical if the axis goes through two edges, through one node and one edge, or through two nodes, respectively. A *periodic* configuration is a configuration that is invariant by non-trivial rotation.

On the negative side, it was shown [17] that gathering is impossible when the algorithm run by every robot is deterministic and there are only two robots, or if the initial configurations are periodic, or edge-edge symmetric, or if the ability for a robot to detect multiple robots on a single location (denoted as *multiplicity detection*) is not available. Running a probabilistic algorithm [20] permits to start from an arbitrary initial configuration (including periodic and edge-edge symmetric) but still requires multiplicity detection. In the deterministic setting, a number of ring gathering algorithms have been proposed in the literature [16,10,11,23,9] for the cases left open by impossibility results, focusing on the problem solvability for different initial configurations and different values for the size of the ring and the number of robots. When the robots are able to fully detect the number of robots in each location, a unified strategy was proposed [10]. When multiplicity detection is only available on the current position of each robot, more involved and specific approaches [14,15,16,9] are needed. Every aforementioned deterministic solution considers problem solvability with particular hypotheses, and does not consider performance issues (such as time needed to reach gathering, or the total number of moves before gathering is achieved). Also, only a handmade approach for both algorithm design and proof of correctness was considered in those works.

Most related to our concern are recent approaches to mechanizing the algorithm design or the correctness proof in the context of autonomous mobile robots [5,12,4,2]. Model-checking proved useful to find bugs in existing litterature [4] and formally assess published algorithms [12,4]. Proof assistants enabled the use of high order logic to certify impossibility results [2]. To our knowledge, the only previous attempt to automatically generate mobile robots algorithms (for the problem of perpetual exclusive exploration) is due to Bonnet *et al.* [5], but exhibits important limitations for studying the gathering problem. Indeed their approach is brute force (it generate every possible algorithm in a particular setting, regardless of the problem to solve) and specific to configurations where *(i)* a location can only host one robot (so, gathering cannot be expressed), and *(ii)* no symmetry appears.

Games and Protocols Synthesis. In the formal methods community, automatically synthesizing programs that would be correct by design is a problem that raised interest early [8,18,1,22]. Actually, this problem goes back to Church [7,6]. When the program to generate is intended to work in an open system, maintaining an on-going interaction with a (partially) unknown environment, it is known since [6] that seeing the problem as a *game* between the system and the environment is a successful approach. The system and its environment are considered as opposite players that play a game on some graph, the winning condition being the specification the system should fulfill however the environment behave. Then, the classical problem in game theory of determining winning strategies for the players is equivalent to find how the system should act in any situation, in order to always satisfy its specification. The case of mobile autonomous robots that we focus on in this paper falls in this category of problems: the robots may evolve (possibly indefinitely) on the ring, making decisions based on the global state of the system at each time instant. The vertices of graph on which the players will play would then be some representation of the different global positions of the robots on the ring. The presence of an opposite player (or environment) is motivated by the absence of chirality of the robots: when a robot is on an axis of symmetry, it is unable to distinguish its two sides one from another, hence to choose exactly *where* it moves ; this decision is supposed to be taken by the opposite player.

Our Contribution. In this paper, we introduce the use of formal methods for automatic synthesis of autonomous mobile robot algorithms, in the discrete space model. As a case study, we consider the problem of gathering all robots at a particular location, not known beforehand. Our contribution is threefold. First, we propose an encoding of the gathering problem as a reachability game, the players being the robot algorithm on the one side and the scheduling adversary (that is also capable for dynamically deciding robot chirality at every activation) on the other side. Our encoding is general enough to encompass classical FSYNC and SSYNC execution models for robots evolving on ring-shaped networks, including (and contrary to the existing ad hoc solution [5]) when several robots are located at the same node and when symmetric situations occurs. Then, in the FSYNC model, we automatically generate an *optimal* distributed algorithm for three robots evolving on a fixed size uniform ring. Our optimality criterion refers to the number of robot moves that are necessary to actually achieve gathering. Finally, we prove by induction that the mechanically generated algorithm is also correct for any ring size except when an impossibility result holds (that is, when the number of robots divides the ring size). Our method can be seen as a first step towards "correct by design" actual robot protocol implementations.

2 Background

In this section we present a formal model for a robot system evolving on a ring and definitions and notations for a reachability game.

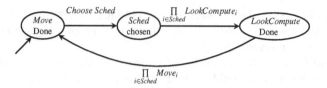

Fig. 1. The Semi-Synchronous Schedulers automaton

2.1   Robot Network Model

In the following we present the robots and system model using the formalism we proposed in [4]. We consider a set of robots evolving on a ring.

Robot Model. A robot behavior can be described by a finite automaton. Each robot executes a three-phase cycle composed of *Look, Compute, Move* phases. To start a cycle, a robot takes a snapshot of its environment, which is represented by a *Look* transition. Then it computes its future movement (*Compute* transition). Finally the robot moves according to its previous computation, this effective movement is represented by a *Move* transition, going back to its initial state. On a ring there are only three possibilities for the move: stay idle, move in the clockwise direction or in the counterclockwise direction. Note also that Look and Compute states can be merged in a single state - LookCompute.

Scheduler Model. The three existing asynchrony models fully synchronous (FSYNC), semi-synchronous (SSYNC) and asynchronous (ASYNC) in robot networks are called schedulers. The scheduler can be modeled by a finite automaton. The synchronization of these schedulers with robots automata is an automaton that represents the global behavior of robots in the chosen model.

   In the sequel we denote by $LookCompute_i$ (respectively $Move_i$), the *LookCompute* (resp. *Move*) phase of ith robot. And for a subset *Sched* of robots, we denote by $\prod_{i \in Sched} LookCompute_i$ (resp. $\prod_{i \in Sched} Move_i$) the synchronization of all $LookCompute_i$ (resp. $Move_i$) actions of all robots in *Sched*.

   In the SSYNC model, an arbitrary non-empty subset of robots is scheduled for execution at every phase, and operations are executed synchronously. In this case, the automaton consists of a cycle, where a set *"Sched"* is first chosen, then the *LookCompute* and *Move* phases are synchronized for this set. A generic automaton for SSYNC is described in Figure 1.

   The FSYNC model is a particular case of the SSYNC model, where all robots are scheduled for execution at every phase, and operate synchronously thereafter.

System model. A configuration of k robots on a ring of size n encodes the position of the robots in the ring. The system is modeled by the automaton obtained by the synchronized product of k robot automata and the possible configurations. The scheduler is used to define the synchronization function. The alphabet of actions is $A = \prod_i A_i$, with

$A_i = \{LookCompute_i, Move_i, idle\}$ for each robot i. From this definition, states are of the form $s = (s_1, \ldots, s_k, c)$ where s_i is the local state of robot i, and c the configuration. A transition of the system is labeled by a tuple $a = (a_1, \ldots, a_k)$, where $a_i \in A_i$ for all $1 \le i \le k$ and $(s_1, \ldots, s_k, c) \xrightarrow{a} (s_1', \ldots, s_k', c')$ iff for all i, $s_i \xrightarrow{a_i} s_i'$ and c' is obtained from c by updating the positions of all robots i such that $a_i = Move_i$. To represent the scheduling, we denote by $\prod_{i \in Sched} Act_i$ the action $(a_1, \ldots, a_k)$ such that $a_i = idle$ if $i \notin Sched$ and $a_i \in \{LookCompute_i, Move_i\}$ otherwise.

2.2   Reachability Games

In the following we revisit the reachability games. We present here classical notions on this subject. For more details, the interested reader can fruitfully consult the survey [19]. If A is a set of symbols, A^* is the set of finite sequences of elements of A (also called *words*), and A^ω the set of infinite such sequences, with ε the empty sequence. We note $A^+ = A^* \setminus \{\varepsilon\}$, and $A^\infty = A^* \cup A^\omega$. For a sequence $w \in A^\infty$, we denote its *length* by $|w|$. If $w \in A^*$, $|w|$ is equal to its number of elements. If $w \in A^\omega$, $|w| = \infty$. For all words $w = a_1 \cdots a_k \in A^*$, $w' = a_1' \cdots \in A^\infty$, we define the *concatenation* of w and w' by the word noted $w \cdot w' = a_1 \cdots a_k a_1' \cdots$. We sometimes omit the symbol and simply write ww'. If $L \subseteq A^*$ and $L' \subseteq A^\infty$, we define $L \cdot L' = \{w \cdot w' \mid w \in L, w' \in L'\}$.

A game is composed of an *arena* and *winning conditions*.

Arena. An arena is a graph $\mathcal{A} = (V, E)$ in which the set of vertices $V - V_p \uplus V_o$ is partitioned into V_p, the vertices of the protagonist, and V_o the vertices of the opponent. The set of edges $E \subseteq V \times V$ allows to define the set of successors of some given vertex v, noted $vE = \{v' \in V \mid (v, v') \in E\}$. In the following, we will only consider finite arenas.

Plays. To play on an arena, a token is positioned on an initial vertex. Then the token is moved by the players from one vertex to one of its successors. Each player can move the token only if it is on one of her own vertices. Formally, a play is a path in the graph, i.e., a finite or infinite sequence of vertices $\pi = v_0 v_1 \cdots \in V^\infty$, where for all $0 < i < |\pi|$, $v_i \in v_{i-1}E$. Moreover, a play is finite only if the token has been taken to a position without any successor (where it is impossible to continue the game): if π is finite with $|\pi| = n$, then $v_{n-1}E = \emptyset$.

Strategies. A strategy for the protagonist determines to which position she will bring the token whenever it is her turn to play. To do so, the player takes into account the history of the play, and the current vertex. Formally, a strategy for the protagonist is a (partial) function $\sigma : V^* \cdot V_p \to V$ such that, for all sequence (representing the current history) $w \in V^*$, all $v \in V_p$, $\sigma(w \cdot v) \in vE$ (i.e. the move is possible with respect to the arena). A strategy σ is *memoryless* if it does not depend on the history. Formally, it means that for all $w, w' \in V^*$, for all $v \in V_p$, $\sigma(w \cdot v) = \sigma(w' \cdot v)$. In that case, we may simply see the strategy as a function $\sigma : V_p \to V$.

Given a strategy σ for the protagonist, a play $\pi = v_0 v_1 \cdots \in V^\infty$ is said to be σ-*consistent* if for all $0 < i < |\pi|$, if $v_{i-1} \in V_p$, then $v_i = \sigma(v_0 \cdots v_{i-1})$. Given an initial vertex v_0, the *outcome* of a strategy σ is the set of plays starting in v_0 that are σ-consistent. Formally, given an arena $A = (V, E)$, an intial vertex v_0 and a strategy $\sigma : V^* V_p \to V$, we let $Outcome(A, v_0, \sigma) = \{v_0 \pi \in V^\infty \mid v_0 \pi \text{ is a play and is } \sigma\text{-consistent}\}$.

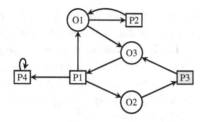

Fig. 2. A two-player game. In this figure protagonist vertices are represented by rectangles and antagonist vertices by circles. The winning condition is $Reach(\{P3\})$. Any path in the graph is a play. From P2 the protagonist has no winning strategy. From P1 a (memoryless) winning strategy is to go to O2. Winning positions are $\{P1, P3\}$.

Winning Conditions, Winning Plays, Winning Strategies. We define the *winning condition* for the protagonist as a subset of the plays $Win \subseteq V^{\infty}$. Then, a play π is *winning* for the protagonist if $\pi \in Win$. In this work, we focus on the simple case of reachability games: the winning condition is then expressed according to a subset of vertices $T \subseteq V$ by $Reach(T) = \{\pi = v_0 v_1 \cdots \in V^{\infty} \mid \exists 0 \leq i < |\pi| : v_i \in T\}$. This means that the protagonist wins a play whenever the token is brought on a vertex belonging to the set T. Once it has happened, the play is winning, regardless of the following actions of the players.

Given an arena $\mathcal{A} = (V, E)$, an initial vertex $v_0 \in V$ and a winning condition *Win*, a *winning strategy* σ for the protagonist is a strategy such that any σ-consistent play is winning. In other words, a strategy σ is winning if $Outcome(\mathcal{A}, v_0, \sigma) \subseteq Win$. The protagonist wins the game $(\mathcal{A}, v_0, Win)$ if she has a winning strategy for $(\mathcal{A}, v_0, Win)$. We say that σ is winning on a subset $U \subseteq V$ if it is winning starting from any vertex in U: if $Outcome(\mathcal{A}, v_0, \sigma) \subseteq Win$ for all $v_0 \in U$. A subset $U \subseteq V$ of the vertices is *winning* if there exists a strategy σ that is winning on U.

Solving a Reachability Game. Given an arena $\mathcal{A} = (V, E)$, a subset $T \subseteq V$, one wants to determine the set $U \subseteq V$ of winning positions for the protagonist, and a strategy $\sigma : V^* V_p \to V$ for the protagonist, that is winning on U for $Reach(T)$.

Figure 2 represents a reachability 2-player game. We recall now a well-known result on reachability games:

Theorem 1. *The set of winning positions for the protagonist in a reachability game can be computed in linear time in the size of the arena. Moreover, from any position, the protagonist has a winning strategy if and only if she has a memoryless winning strategy.*

3   Encoding the Gathering Problem into a Game

As we have claimed in the introduction, the gathering problem for synchronous robots is actually a game between the robots, that have an objective (winning condition) and evolve on a graph encoding the different configurations, and an opponent that can decide the actual movement of a disoriented robot, i.e. a robot whose observation of the ring is symmetrical, hence is unable to distinguish its two sides from one another. It may seem at first that the model actually needed is the one of *distributed games*, in which each robot represents a distinct player, all of them cooperating against a hostile environment. In distributed games, existence of a winning strategy for the team of players is undecidable [21]. However, the fact that the system is synchronous or semi-synchronous, and that the robots are able to sense their global environment, and thus to always know the global state of the system, allows us to stay in the framework of 2-player games, and to encode the set of robots as a single player. Of course, the strategy obtained will be centralized, but we will design the game in order to obtain only strategies that can be distributed amongst anonymous, memoryless robots without chirality. In the rest of the paper, we focus on the synchronous semantics for the system. With minor modifications, the game can be modified to handle the semi-synchronous semantics.

3.1 Encoding Robots Configurations: Symmetries and Equivalences

Consider a robot system consisting of k robots and n nodes ($k < n$). The configuration of such a system is represented by the tuple $(d_1, \cdots, d_k)$, such that $\Sigma_{i=1}^k d_i = n - k$, and $d_i \in \{-1, 0, \cdots, n-1\}$. Each value d_i represents the number of free nodes between the ith robot and the next robot in the clockwise direction. When the two robots occupy adjacent nodes, $d_i = 0$, and when these two robots occupy the same node, $d_i = -1$. Let $C = \{(d_1, \cdots, d_k) \mid \Sigma_{i=1}^k d_i = n - k \text{ and } d_i \in \{-1, 0, \cdots, n-1\}\}$ the set of all configurations (note that $|C| = C_{n+k-1}^n$). In a configuration, each robot can observe the entire ring, centered in its own position. Since the robots have no chirality, given a configuration $C = (d_1, \cdots, d_k)$, the *observation of robot i* is $obs_i(C) = \{(d_i, d_{i+1}, \cdots d_k, d_1, \cdots d_{i-1}), (d_{i-1}, \cdots, d_1, d_k, \cdots d_i)\}$. Let $Obs = \{obs_i(C) \mid C \in C, 1 \le i \le k\}$ be the set of all possible observations.

Several types of configurations can be distinguished (see Figure 3): *periodic*: if there are several axis of symmetry, *symmetric*: if there is only one axis of symmetry (edge-edge, node-edge, node-node), *rigid configurations*: all other configurations.

A configuration is called *tower configuration* if there are several robots on the same node. Robots constituting this tower are the ones such that at least one tuple of their observation begins with -1.

Since the robots take snapshots of the configuration, and their decisions are based on this information, the states of the arena must represent the different configurations of the ring. The robots are anonymous, hence, different rotations of a similar ring in fact represent the same configuration. We define the rotation relation $\circlearrowleft \subseteq C \times C$ as follows: for all configurations $C, C' \in C$, $C \circlearrowleft C'$ if and only if $C = (d_i, d_{i+1}, \cdots, d_{i+k-1})$ and $C' = (d_{i+1}, d_{i+2}, \cdots d_{i+k})$, where the addition symbol $+$ means sum modulo k. Since the robots have no chirality, one can easily observe that, for two configurations C and C', if $C = (d_1, \cdots, d_k)$ and $C' = (d_k, \cdots, d_1)$, then, for all robot i, $obs_i(C) = obs_i(C')$. We then define the mirror relation $\sim \subseteq C \times C$ by $C \sim C'$ if and only if $C = (d_1, \cdots, d_k)$ and $C' = (d_k, \cdots, d_1)$. From these two relations, we define an equivalence relation $\equiv \subseteq C \times C$ on the configurations, that identify all the configurations on which the robots should behave the same way: we let $\equiv \stackrel{\text{def}}{=} (\circlearrowleft \cup \sim)^*$.

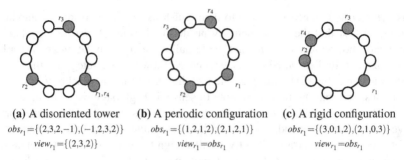

(a) A disoriented tower
$obs_{r_1} = \{(2,3,2,-1),(-1,2,3,2)\}$
$view_{r_1} = \{(2,3,2)\}$

(b) A periodic configuration
$obs_{r_1} = \{(1,2,1,2),(2,1,2,1)\}$
$view_{r_1} = obs_{r_1}$

(c) A rigid configuration
$obs_{r_1} = \{(3,0,1,2),(2,1,0,3)\}$
$view_{r_1} = obs_{r_1}$

Fig. 3. Robot observations and Views

The following lemma states that our equivalence relation is correct with respect to robots behavior.

Lemma 2. *For all $C \in \mathcal{C}$, $\bigcup_{1 \leq i \leq k} obs_i(C) = [C]_\equiv$.*

Then, an equivalence class of configurations can be seen as the set of observations for the robots in such a configuration.

We let $[C]_\equiv$ be the equivalence class of a configuration $C \in \mathcal{C}$, and we define an application $rep : \mathcal{C}/\equiv \to \mathcal{C}$, such that $rep([C]_\equiv) \in [C]_\equiv$ for all $C \in \mathcal{C}$, that associates to each equivalence class a unique representative in this class, say the smallest w.r.t lexicographic order on tuples. For the rest of the paper, when we use the sum symbol on indexes of elements of a configuration, it means sum modulo k.

3.2   Encoding the Moves of the Robots and Transitions between Configurations

To define precisely the transitions between the configurations, we need the following auxiliary notations. We let $\mathbb{M} = \{\curvearrowright, \curvearrowleft, \uparrow\}$ be the different possible moves for a robot, where, as one easily guesses, $\curvearrowright$ means that the robot moves in the clockwise direction, $\curvearrowleft$ means that it moves in the counter-clockwise direction, and $\uparrow$ means that the robot does not move. We will use the fact that, for robots on a tower, a deterministic algorithm will either make them all move, or none of them. However, if they are disoriented, they can move in different directions. When a robot i moves, it modifies the distances d_i and d_{i-1} (increasing one of these two distances by one, and decreasing by one the other). We can encode this by an algebraic notations, adding the configuration and one vector of movement for each robot: the effect on the configuration of the move $\curvearrowleft$ of robot i will be represented by the k-tuple $m^{i,\curvearrowleft}$, the effect of the move $\curvearrowright$ will be represented by $m^{i,\curvearrowright}$ and if the robot does not move, it will be represented by m^0. These tuples are defined as follows: for a robot $1 \leq i \leq k$, $m_i^{i,\curvearrowleft} = 1$ and $m_{i-1}^{i,\curvearrowleft} = -1$ and $m_j^{i,\curvearrowleft} = 0$ for all other $1 \leq j \leq k$. Similarly, $m_i^{i,\curvearrowright} = -1$ and $m_{i-1}^{i,\curvearrowright} = 1$ and $m_j^{i,\curvearrowright} = 0$ for all other $1 \leq j \leq k$. The last tuple is $m_j^0 = 0$ for all $1 \leq j \leq k$.

The idea is to add (in an element-by-element fashion) the current configuration to all the tuples representing the movements of the robots to obtain the next configuration. However, when the movements of two adjacent robots imply that they switch their positions in the ring, some absurd values (-2 or -3) may appear in the obtained configuration, if the sum is naively effected, so a careful treatment of these particular cases must be done. To obtain the correct configuration, one should recall that robots are anonymous, hence if two robots switch their positions, it has the same effect as if none of them has moved. Also, if in a tower, some robots want to move clockwise, and the others want to move counterclockwise, the exact robots that will move are of no importance: the only important thing is the number of robots that move. We will then reorganize the movements between the robots, in order to keep correct values in our configurations: in a tower, we will assume that the robots that will move in the counterclockwise direction will always be the bottom ones, and when a robot moves right and joins a tower, we will assume that it will be placed at the bottom of the tower, and when it moves left and joins a tower, it will be placed at the top of the tower. These conventions will ensure that when adding the configuration and the different movements, we will not obtain aberrant values.

Formally, given a configuration $C = (d_1, \ldots, d_k)$, we define $PosTower(C) = \{(i,j) \mid d_j \neq -1$ and $\forall i \leq \ell < j, d_\ell = -1\}$ that contains the positions of the towers, encoded by the position of the first and the last robot in it. We then define $Pos(C) = PosTower(C) \cup \{(i,i) \mid 1 \leq i \leq k, \forall 1 \leq \ell \leq k, (i,\ell), (\ell,i) \notin PosTower(C)\}$, that contains the positions of the towers, and the positions of the isolated robots. Given a tuple of movements $(m_i)_{1 \leq i \leq k}$, given $(i,j) \in Pos(C)$, $N_{(i,j)}^{\curvearrowright} = |\{m_\ell^{\curvearrowright} \mid i \leq \ell \leq j\}|$ and $N_{(i,j)}^{\curvearrowleft} = |\{m_\ell^{\curvearrowleft} \mid i \leq \ell \leq j\}|$. We first reorganize the movements of the robots in the towers: for all $(i,j) \in PosTower(C)$, we let $m_\ell' = m^{\ell,\curvearrowright}$ for all $i \leq \ell \leq (N_{(i,j)}^{\curvearrowleft} + i - 1)$ and $m_\ell' = m^{\ell,\curvearrowleft}$ for all $(N_{(i,j)}^{\curvearrowleft} + i) \leq \ell \leq j$. For all $(i,i) \in Pos(C) \setminus PosTower(C)$, $m_i' = m_i$. Now, we iteratively modify the tuple m'. Let $(i,j) \in Pos(C)$ be the element of $Pos(C)$ considered at the tth iteration and let m^t be the current tuple encoding the moves.

- If $d_j \neq 0$, $m^{t+1} = m^t$.
- Otherwise, let r such that $(j+1, r) \in Pos(C)$ (if $r = j+1$, the next robot is isolated, otherwise it is a tower).
  - If $N_{(i,j)}^{\curvearrowright} \geq N_{(j+1,r)}^{\curvearrowleft}$, then $m_\ell^{t+1} = m^{\ell,\curvearrowright}$ for all $j - N_{(i,j)}^{\curvearrowright} + N_{(j+1,r)}^{\curvearrowleft} + 1 \leq \ell \leq j$, $m_\ell^{t+1} = m^{\ell,0}$ for all $j - N_{(i,j)}^{\curvearrowright} \leq \ell \leq j - N_{(i,j)}^{\curvearrowright} + N_{(j+1,r)}^{\curvearrowleft}$ and for all $j+1 \leq \ell \leq j + N_{(j+1,r)}^{\curvearrowleft} - 1$, and $m_\ell^{t+1} = m_\ell^t$ for all other ℓ.
  - If $N_{(i,j)}^{\curvearrowright} < N_{(j+1,r)}^{\curvearrowleft}$, then the modification is symmetrical.

When all the elements of $Pos(C)$ have been visited, we obtain a tuple $(m_i^f)_{1 \leq i \leq k}$.

Proposition 3. *For all configurations* $C \in C$, *for all tuples* $(m_i)_{1 \leq i \leq k}$, $C + \sum_{i=1}^{k} m_i^f \in C$, *where* $(m_i^f)_{1 \leq i \leq k}$ *has been obtained as described above.*

Proof (sketch). Let $C = (d_1, \ldots, d_k)$. For all $1 \leq i \leq k$, if $d_i = 0$, then if the robot i wants to move in the clockwise direction, and the robot $i + 1$ wants to move in the counterclockwise direction, then by our construction, $m_i^f = m^{i,0}$ and $m_{i+1}^f = m^{i+1,0}$, and the resulting distance will stay 0. For all other decisions of the robots, the distance obtained will be positive. If $d_i = -1$, by the reorganization of the robots on a tower, it is impossible that robot i wants to move in the clockwise direction and that the robot $i + 1$

wants to move in the counterclockwise direction. Hence, the distance obtained is never less than -1. In all other cases, the obtained distance is necessarily positive.   □

Definition 4 (successor of a configuration). *Given a configuration $C \in C$ and a tuple of moves for the different robots $(m_i)_{i \in \{1,...,k\}} \in \mathbb{M}^k$, the successor configuration, noted*

$$C \oplus (m_i)_{i \in \{1,...,k\}} \text{ is obtained by } C + \sum_{i=1}^{k} m_i^f \in C, \text{ where } (m_i^f)_{1 \leq i \leq k} \text{ has been obtained as}$$

described above.

3.3 The Gathering Game

We build an arena for a reachability game, such that the protagonist has a winning strategy if and only if one can design an algorithm for the robots to gather on a single node, starting from any configuration. The possible decisions of movements taken by the robots will be noted by $\Delta = \{\curvearrowright, \curvearrowleft, \uparrow, ?\}$, which is the set $\mathbb{M}$ of possible movements, added by a special decision ?, taken by a disoriented robot that nevertheless wants to move. We will note $\overline{\curvearrowright} = \curvearrowleft$, $\overline{\curvearrowleft} = \curvearrowright$, $\overline{\uparrow} = \uparrow$ and $\overline{?} = ?$. We consider the arena $\mathcal{A}_{\text{gather}} = (V_p \uplus V_o, E)$, where the set of protagonist states is $V_p = (C/\equiv)$, the set of antagonist states is $V_o = C \times (\Delta^k)$, the size of the arena is thus linear in n and exponential in k.

The edge relation E will ensure a strict alternance between the two players: $E \subseteq (V_p \times V_o) \cup (V_o \times V_p)$ and will be detailed in the rest of the subsection.

From V_p to V_o From a protagonist position, representing an equivalence class of configurations, the play continues on an antagonist position memorizing the different movements decided by each robot. Such a move is possible if, in a given equivalence class of configurations, the robots with the same observation take the same decision. However, our definition of observation does not capture what happens when several robots are stacked to form a tower: consider two robots on a tower, in a configuration of the form $C = (-1, d_2, \cdots, d_k)$. Using our definition of observation, we obtain $obs_1(C) = \{(-1, d_2, \cdots, d_k), (d_k, \cdots, d_2, -1)\}$ and $obs_2(C) = \{(d_2, \cdots, d_k, -1), (-1, d_k, \cdots, d_2)\}$, hence $obs_1(C) \neq obs_2(C)$ whereas in reality they observe the same thing. Thus, we will use the notion of *view* for a robot, where, if a robot is part of a tower, the distance from other robots in the tower is removed from its observation. Formally, we define the *view* of the robot i as follows:

Definition 5 (view). *Let $C \in C$ and $1 \leq i \leq k$ be a robot. Let $(d_1, \ldots, d_k) \in obs_i(C)$ be the smallest observation of C, with respect to the lexicographic order. We define the view of robot i by $view_i(C) = \{(d_i, \ldots, d_j), (d_j, \ldots, d_i)\}$, where $i < j$ are respectively the smallest and greatest index such that $d_i \neq -1$ (respectively $d_j \neq -1$).*

We let $\mathcal{V} = \{view_i(C) \mid C \in C, 1 \leq i \leq k\}$ be the set of all possible views.

Note that if robot i does not belong to a tower then $view_i(C) = obs_i(C)$. Also, when $|view_i(C)| = 1$, the robot is disoriented (see Figure 3). For $o \in Obs$ an observation, we let $p(o) \in \mathcal{V}$ be the projection from an observation to obtain a view.

A *decision function* is a function that suggests a movement to a robot, according to its view.

Definition 6 (decision function). *A decision function is a function* $f : \mathcal{V} \to \Delta$ *such that, for all* $V \in \mathcal{V}$, *if* $|V| = 1$, *then* $f(V) \in \{\uparrow, ?\}$ *and if* $f(V) =?$ *then* $|V| = 1$.

Given a configuration $C = (d_1, \ldots, d_k) \in \mathcal{C}$, we translate a decision function f into a real movement of each robot. For all $1 \leq i \leq k$, let $f(C, i)$ be defined as follows. If $(d_i, \cdots, d_k, d_1, \cdots d_{i-1})$ is the smallest element of $view_i(C) = \{(d_i, \cdots, d_k, d_1, \cdots d_{i-1}), (d_{i-1}, \cdots, d_1, d_k, \cdots d_i)\}$ in the lexicographic order, then $f(C, i) = f(view_i(C))$. Otherwise, $f(C, i) = \overline{f(view_i(C))}$. This is so because, when applying the real movements on a real configuration, the game (that makes the robots move) must be coherent on a common direction.

We are able to determine now the edge relation from a protagonist state to an antagonist state: for all $v \in V_p, v' \in V_o$, $(v, v') \in E$ if and only if there exists a decision function f such that $v' = (C, (a_1, \ldots, a_k))$ defined as follows: $C = rep(v) = (d_1, \ldots, d_k)$ and, for all $1 \leq i \leq k$, $a_i = f(C, i)$.

From V_o to V_p The moves of the antagonist lead the game into the following configuration of the system resulting of the application of the decisions of all the robots. If one robot decides to move, but is disoriented, then the antagonist chooses the actual move ($\curvearrowright$ or $\curvearrowleft$) the robot will make. The next configuration reached by the robots is then determined by the actions chosen and by the decisions taken by the antagonist.

Definition 7. *For a state* $v' = (C, (a_1, \ldots, a_k))$, *we say that a tuple* $(m_i)_{i \in \{1, \ldots, k\}}$ *is* v'-*compatible if,*

- *for all* $1 \leq i \leq k$ *such that* $a_i \neq ?$, $m_i = a_i$,
- *for all* $1 \leq i \leq k$ *such that* $a_i = ?$, $m_i \neq \uparrow$.

A v'-compatible tuple is then a tuple in which the antagonist has chosen in which directions disoriented robots will move.

Then, we can formally define the edge relation from an antagonist state to a protagonist state: for all $v \in V_p$, $v' = (C, (a_1, \ldots, a_k)) \in V_o$, $(v', v) \in E$ if and only if there exists a v'-compatible tuple $(m_i)_{i \in \{1, \ldots, k\}}$ such that $v = [C \oplus (m_i)_{i \in \{1, \ldots, k\}}]_\equiv$.

To sum up, in $\mathcal{A}_{gather}{}^1$,

$$E = \{(v, v') \in V_p \times V_o \mid$$

there exists a decision function f such that $v' = (rep(v), (f(C, 1), \ldots, f(C, k)))\}$

$\cup \{(v', v) \in V_o \times V_p \mid v' = (C, (a_i, \ldots, a_k))$

and there exists a v'-compatible tuple $m_{(i)i \in \{1, \ldots, k\}}, v = [C \oplus (m_i)_{i \in \{1, \ldots, k\}}]_\equiv\}$.

We now state the result that validates the construction: solving the reachability game that we have just defined amounts to automatically synthesizing a deterministic algorithm achieving the gathering for this system. Let $W = [(-1, \cdots, -1, n-1)]_\equiv \in V_p$ be the equivalence class of all the configurations representing the case where all the robots are positioned on a single node.

Theorem 8. *The winning region for the game* $(\mathcal{A}_{gather}, W)$ *corresponds exactly to the set of configurations from which the robots can achieve the gathering.*

---

[1] To handle the semi synchronous semantics, the antagonist should also choose at each step the subset of robots that will be activated.

Proof (Sketch). An algorithm $\mathcal{F}$ can be turned into a decision function $f : \mathcal{V} \to \Delta$ as follows: let $\{view_1, view_2\} \in \mathcal{V}$, and assume that $view_1 < view_2$ with $<$ being the lexicographic order. Let $o \in p^{-1}(view_1)$ be an observation compatible with the view $view_1$ (we recall that p is the projection of an observation for a robot in a tower to its view that removes the elements equal to -1). Then $f(\{view_1, view_2\}) = \mathcal{F}(o)$. Since the algorithm $\mathcal{F}$ takes the same decision for all the robots in a tower, hence for all $o \in p^{-1}(view_1)$, this definition indeed translates the algorithm into a decision function. The strategy that chooses this decision function will visit the same configurations as the algorithm on the real ring. Reciprocally, a winning strategy from a configuration class gives a decision function. To turn the decision functions for each configuration class into a distributed algorithm, we remark, thanks to Lemma 2, that one observation for a robot belongs to exactly one equivalence class of configurations. To determine the movement a robot takes according to its observation of the ring, it suffices to translate the decision function associated to the corresponding equivalence class into a movement in the ring. Then one can show that any sequence of configurations obtained by the algorithm corresponds to a play in the game, visiting the same configurations.   □

4   Synthesis of 3-Robots Gathering Protocol

In the case of a system with three robots, there are 6 distinct types of configuration classes:

- The 3-robots tower configuration, which is the configuration to reach: $[(-1, -1, n - 1)]_\equiv$. From this class of configuration the edge leads to $(C, (a_1, a_1, a_1))$ with $a_1 \in \{\uparrow, ?\}$. However, this edge is not of interest for us since the gathering property is verified.
- The disoriented tower is a configuration where there is an axis of symmetry passing through the tower and the isolated robot. This configuration belongs to the class $[(-1, \frac{n-1}{2}, \frac{n-1}{2})]_\equiv$ and occurs only when n is odd. In this case, all robots are disoriented and thus the outgoing edges lead to all the states $\{(-1, \frac{n-1}{2}, \frac{n-1}{2}), (a_1, a_1, a_2)\}$ with $a_1, a_2 \in \{\uparrow, ?\}$.
- The tower configurations are the configurations of the classes $[(-1, d_2, d_3)]_\equiv$, with $rep([(-1, d_2, d_3)]_\equiv) = (-1, d_2, d_3)$ and $-1 < d_2 < d_3 \in \mathbb{N}$. The edges lead to all the states $\{(-1, d_2, d_3), (a_1, a_1, a_2\}$ with $a_1, a_2 \in \{\curvearrowright, \curvearrowleft, \uparrow\}$.
- The symmetrical configurations, which is in $[(d_1, d_1, d_2)]_\equiv$ with $-1 \neq d_1 \neq d_2$ and $-1 \neq d_2$. Recall that when k is odd and there is an axis of symmetry, the axis goes through an occupied node. If $d_1 < d_2$, the edges lead to $(C, (a_1, a_2, a_1)$ with $a_1 \in \{\curvearrowright, \curvearrowleft, \uparrow\}$ and $a_2 \in \{\uparrow, ?\}$, otherwise edges lead to $(C, (a_1, a_1, a_2)$ with $a_1 \in \{\curvearrowright, \curvearrowleft, \uparrow\}$ and $a_2 \in \{\uparrow, ?\}$.
- The rigid configurations are all other configurations. For a class $\mathbb{C}$ such that $rep(\mathbb{C}) = C$ does not fall into any of the above categories, the outgoing edges go to states $(C, (a_1, a_2, a_3))$ with $a_1, a_2, a_3 \in \{\curvearrowright, \curvearrowleft, \uparrow\}$.

We implemented the arena for three robots and different ring sizes, in the game-solver tool UPPAAL TIGA [3]. We verified the impossibility of the gathering from periodic configurations. Moreover we obtained that there is a winning strategy from all protagonist vertices except from the periodic configurations, and we identified in the edges relation that the edges that lead to $\{(C,(a,a,a))\}$ with $a \in \mathbb{M}$ are not part of any winning strategy.

The arena without the periodic class of configuration $\{[(d,d,d)]_{\equiv}\}$, and the edges that lead to $\{(C,(a,a,a))\}$ with $a \in \mathbb{M}$ from a protagonist vertex $[C]_{\equiv}$, is the graph such that all protagonist vertices are winning. In order to find the best winning strategies, weights are added on the edges. In order to minimize the number of robot moves, each edge is weighed by the number of robots that move. A strategy is a shortest path algorithm on this graph such that the protagonist vertices and opponent vertices are handled differently. The distance between a protagonist vertex and the configuration to reach is the minimum distance, and the distance between an opponent vertex and this configuration is the maximal distance between them.

We obtained all the optimal strategies, for each class of configurations $[(d_1,d_2,d_3)]_{\equiv}$, the edge relation is restricted. From these strategies we outline the following pattern of strategy.

- If all robots form a tower nobody moves. From $[(-1,-1,n-1)]_{\equiv}$ the edge relation leads to $((-1,-1,n-1),(\uparrow,\uparrow,\uparrow))$.
- If 2 robots form a tower the last robot takes the shortest path to the tower. From $[(-1,d_1,d_2)]_{\equiv}$ with $-1 < d_1 < d_2$, the edge relation leads to $((-1,d_1,d_2),(\uparrow,\uparrow,\frown$ $))$. And from $[(-1,\frac{n-1}{2},\frac{n-1}{2})]_{\equiv}$ the edge relation leads to $((-1,\frac{n-1}{2},\frac{n-1}{2}),(\uparrow,\uparrow,?))$.
- If the configuration is symmetrical, in $[(d_1,d_1,d_2)]_{\equiv}$ with $-1 < d_1 < d_2$, the proposed strategy depends on whether $rep([(d_1,d_1,d_2)]_{\equiv}) = (d_1,d_1,d_2)$ or (d_2,d_1,d_1).
  • If $rep([(d_1,d_1,d_2)]_{\equiv}) = (d_1,d_1,d_2)$ then the two symmetrical robots get closer to the last robot. The edge relation leads to $((d_1,d_1,d_2),(\frown,\uparrow,\frown))$.
  • If $rep([(d_1,d_1,d_2)]_{\equiv}) = (d_1,d_1,d_2)$ then the disoriented robot moves. The edge relation leads to $((d_2,d_1,d_1),(\uparrow,\uparrow,?))$.
- If the configuration is rigid (in $[(d_1,d_2,d_3)]_{\equiv}$ with $-1 < d_1 < d_2 < d_3$)the edge relation leads to three possibilities :
  • The robot with the minimum view gets closer to its nearest neighbor. In this case the edge relation leads to $((d_1,d_2,d_3),(\frown,\uparrow,\uparrow))$.
  • The robot with the maximum view gets closer to its nearest neighbor.In this case the edge relation leads to $((d_1,d_2,d_3),(\uparrow,\uparrow,\frown))$.
  • The robot with the minimum view and the robot with the maximum view get closer to their nearest neighbor. In this case the edge relation leads to $((d_1,d_2,d_3),(\frown,\uparrow,\frown))$. This strategy is the two above strategies made simultaneously.

Thus the edge relation for rigid configuration leads to: $\{((d_1,d_2,d_3),(a_1,\uparrow,a_2))\}$, with $a_1 \in \{\frown,\uparrow\}$, $a_2 \in \{\uparrow,\frown\}$ and $a_1 \neq a_2$.

From Theorem 8, one can translate the decision functions for each configuration into a distributed algorithm. Among the possible strategies we present below the strategy that moves the robot with the minimum view and the robot with the maximum view closer to their nearest neighbor in the rigid configurations. Thus we obtain the following distributed algorithm: if the view of the robot r is $view(r) = \{(y,-1,z),(z,-1,y)\}$ with $y < z$, r robot moves in order to increment z and decrement y. If $view(r) = \{(x,x,z), (z,x,x)\}$ with $x < z$ then r moves to increment z and decrement x,if $view(r) = \{(z,x,z), (z,x,z)\}$ with $x < z$ then r moves in any direction,if $view(r) = \{(x,y,z),(z,y,x)\}$ with

$x < y < z$ then r moves to increment z and decrement x, if $view(r) = \{(y,x,z),(z,x,y)\}$ with $x < y < z$ then r moves to increment z and decrement y, and when r has a different view than the above, it remains idle.

The above algorithm is correct by construction for various values of n ($3 \le n \le 15$, $n = 100$). The following theorem proves that it is also correct for any ring of size n. Due to space limitation the proof by induction of the theorem is omitted.

Theorem 9. *In a ring of any size $n > 3$ starting from any configuration (except periodic ones) the above 3-gathering algorithm eventually reaches a gathering configuration.*

5　Conclusions and Discussions

We proposed a formal method based on reachability games that permits to automatically generate distributed algorithms for mobile autonomous robots solving a global task. The task of gathering on a ring-shaped network was used as a case study. We hereby discuss current limitations and future works.

While our construction generates algorithms for a particular number of robots k and ring size n, the game encoding we propose enables to easily tackle the gathering problem for any given k and n, provided as inputs, since k and n are parameters of the arena described in Section 3. Also, we focused on the atomic FSYNC and SSYNC models. Breaking the atomicity of Look-Compute-Move cycles (that is, considering automatic algorithm production for the ASYNC model [13]) implies that robots cannot maintain a current global view of the system (their own view may be outdated), nor be aware of the view of other robots (that may be outdated as well). Then, our two-players game encoding is not feasible anymore. A natural approach would be to use distributed games, but they are generally undecidable as previously stated. So, a completely new approach is required for the automatic generation of non-atomic mobile robot algorithms.

The problem of synthesis for parameterized systems is a challenging path for future research. Also, the size of the game increases quickly with the number of robots; it is expected that to-be-discovered optimizations and/or heuristics will help bringing algorithm production more practical. Finally, we believe that part of our encoding (typically, configurations and transitions between configurations) can be reused for different problems on ring-shaped networks, such as exploration with stop or perpetual exploration and easily extended to other topologies.

References

1. Abadi, M., Lamport, L., Wolper, P.: Realizable and unrealizable specifications of reactive systems. In: Ronchi Della Rocca, S., Ausiello, G., Dezani-Ciancaglini, M. (eds.) ICALP 1989. LNCS, vol. 372, pp. 1–17. Springer, Heidelberg (1989)
2. Auger, C., Bouzid, Z., Courtieu, P., Tixeuil, S., Urbain, X.: Certified impossibility results for byzantine-tolerant mobile robots. In: Higashino, T., Katayama, Y., Masuzawa, T., Potop-Butucaru, M., Yamashita, M. (eds.) SSS 2013. LNCS, vol. 8255, pp. 178–190. Springer, Heidelberg (2013)
3. Behrmann, G., Cougnard, A., David, A., Fleury, E., Larsen, K.G., Lime, D.: UPPAAL-Tiga: Time for playing games! In: Damm, W., Hermanns, H. (eds.) CAV 2007. LNCS, vol. 4590, pp. 121–125. Springer, Heidelberg (2007)
4. Bérard, B., Millet, L., Potop-Butucaru, M., Tixeuil, S., Thierry-Mieg, Y.: Vérification formelle et robots mobiles. In: Proc. of Algotel 2013 (2013)

5. Bonnet, F., Défago, X., Petit, F., Potop-Butucaru, M.G., Tixeuil, S.: Brief announcement: Discovering and assessing fine-grained metrics in robot networks protocols. In: Richa, A.W., Scheideler, C. (eds.) SSS 2012. LNCS, vol. 7596, pp. 282–284. Springer, Heidelberg (2012)
6. Büchi, J.R., Landweber, L.H.: Solving sequential conditions by finite-state strategies. Trans. Amer. Math. Soc. 138, 295–311 (1969)
7. Church, A.: Logic, arithmetics, and automata. In: Proc. of Int. Congr. of Mathematicians, pp. 23–35 (1963)
8. Clarke, E.M., Emerson, E.A.: Design and synthesis of synchronization skeletons using branching time temporal logic. In: Kozen, D. (ed.) Logic of Programs 1981. LNCS, vol. 131, pp. 52–71. Springer, Heidelberg (1982)
9. D'Angelo, G., Navarra, A., Nisse, N.: Gathering and exclusive searching on rings under minimal assumptions. In: Chatterjee, M., Cao, J.-n., Kothapalli, K., Rajsbaum, S. (eds.) ICDCN 2014. LNCS, vol. 8314, pp. 149–164. Springer, Heidelberg (2014)
10. D'Angelo, G., Di Stefano, G., Navarra, A.: How to gather asynchronous oblivious robots on anonymous rings. In: Aguilera, M.K. (ed.) DISC 2012. LNCS, vol. 7611, pp. 326–340. Springer, Heidelberg (2012)
11. D'Angelo, G., Stefano, G.D., Navarra, A., Nisse, N., Suchan, K.: A unified approach for different tasks on rings in robot-based computing systems. In: IPDPS Workshops, pp. 667–676 (2013)
12. Devismes, S., Lamani, A., Petit, F., Raymond, P., Tixeuil, S.: Optimal grid exploration by asynchronous oblivious robots. In: Richa, A.W., Scheideler, C. (eds.) SSS 2012. LNCS, vol. 7596, pp. 64–76. Springer, Heidelberg (2012)
13. Flocchini, P., Prencipe, G., Santoro, N.: Distributed Computing by Oblivious Mobile Robots. Morgan & Claypool Publishers (2012)
14. Izumi, T., Izumi, T., Kamei, S., Ooshita, F.: Mobile robots gathering algorithm with local weak multiplicity in rings. In: Patt-Shamir, B., Ekim, T. (eds.) SIROCCO 2010. LNCS, vol. 6058, pp. 101–113. Springer, Heidelberg (2010)
15. Kamei, S., Lamani, A., Ooshita, F., Tixeuil, S.: Asynchronous mobile robot gathering from symmetric configurations without global multiplicity detection. In: Kosowski, A., Yamashita, M. (eds.) SIROCCO 2011. LNCS, vol. 6796, pp. 150–161. Springer, Heidelberg (2011)
16. Kamei, S., Lamani, A., Ooshita, F., Tixeuil, S.: Gathering an even number of robots in an odd ring without global multiplicity detection. In: Rovan, B., Sassone, V., Widmayer, P. (eds.) MFCS 2012. LNCS, vol. 7464, pp. 542–553. Springer, Heidelberg (2012)
17. Klasing, R., Markou, E., Pelc, A.: Gathering asynchronous oblivious mobile robots in a ring. Theor. Comput. Sci. 390(1), 27–39 (2008)
18. Manna, Z., Wolper, P.: Synthesis of communicating processes from temporal logic specifications. ACM Trans. Program. Lang. Syst. 6(1), 68–93 (1984)
19. Mazala, R.: Infinite games. In: Grädel, E., Thomas, W., Wilke, T. (eds.) Automata, Logics, and Infinite Games. LNCS, vol. 2500, pp. 23–38. Springer, Heidelberg (2002)
20. Ooshita, F., Tixeuil, S.: On the self-stabilization of mobile oblivious robots in uniform rings. In: Richa, A.W., Scheideler, C. (eds.) SSS 2012. LNCS, vol. 7596, pp. 49–63. Springer, Heidelberg (2012)
21. Peterson, G.L., Reif, J.H.: Multiple-person alternation. In: Proc. of FOCS 1979, pp. 348–363. IEEE Computer Society Press (1979)
22. Pnueli, A., Rosner, R.: On the synthesis of a reactive module. In: Proc. of POPL 1989, pp. 179–190. ACM (1989)
23. Di Stefano, G., Navarra, A.: Optimal gathering of oblivious robots in anonymous graphs. In: Moscibroda, T., Rescigno, A.A. (eds.) SIROCCO 2013. LNCS, vol. 8179, pp. 213–224. Springer, Heidelberg (2013)
24. Suzuki, I., Yamashita, M.: Distributed anonymous mobile robots: Formation of geometric patterns. SIAM Journal on Computing, 1347–1363 (1999)

Synthesizing Self-stabilization through Superposition and Backtracking

Alex Klinkhamer and Ali Ebnenasir *,**

Department of Computer Science
Michigan Technological University, Houghton MI 49931, USA
{apklinkh,aebnenas}@mtu.edu

Abstract. While the design of self-stabilization is known to be a hard problem, several sound (but incomplete) heuristics exist for algorithmic design of self-stabilization. This paper presents a sound and *complete* method for algorithmic design of self-stabilizing network protocols. The essence of the proposed approach is based on variable superposition and backtracking search. We have validated the proposed method by creating both a sequential and a parallel implementation in the context of a software tool, called Protocon. Moreover, we have used Protocon to automatically design self-stabilizing protocols for the problems that all existing heuristics fail to solve.

1 Introduction

Self-stabilization is an important property of today's distributed systems as it ensures *convergence* in the presence of transient faults (e.g., loss of coordination and bad initialization). That is, from *any* state/configuration, a Self-Stabilizing (SS) system recovers to a set of legitimate states (a.k.a. *invariant*) in a finite number of steps. Moreover, from its invariant, the executions of an SS system satisfy its specifications and remain in the invariant; i.e., *closure*. Design and verification of convergence are difficult tasks [10,16,23] in part due to the requirements of (i) recovery from *any* state; (ii) recovery under distribution constraints, where processes can read/write only the state of their neighboring processes (a.k.a. their *locality*), and (iii) the non-interference of convergence with closure. This paper presents a novel method for algorithmic design of self-stabilization by variable superposition [9] and a *complete* backtracking search.

Most existing methods for the design of self-stabilization are either manual [5, 7, 10, 16, 18, 29, 31] or heuristics [1, 2, 13, 14] that may fail to generate a solution for some systems. For example, Awerbuch *et al.* [7] present a method based on distributed snapshot and reset for locally correctable systems; systems in which the correction of the locality of each process results in global recovery to invariant. Gouda and Multari [18] divide the state space into a set of supersets of

---

* This work was sponsored by the NSF grant CCF-1116546.
** **Superior**, a high performance computing cluster at Michigan Technological University, was used in obtaining the experimental results presented in this paper.

P. Felber and V. Garg (Eds.): SSS 2014, LNCS 8756, pp. 252–267, 2014.

the invariant, called *convergence stairs*, where for each stair closure and convergence to a lower level stair are guaranteed. Stomp [29] provides a method based on ranking functions for design and verification of self-stabilization. Gouda [16] presents a theory for design and composition of self-stabilizing systems. Methods for algorithmic design of convergence [1,2,13,14] are mainly based on sound heuristics that search through the state space of a non-stabilizing system in order to synthesize recovery actions while ensuring non-interference with closure. However, the aforementioned methods may fail to find a solution while there exists one; i.e., they are sound but incomplete.

This paper proposes a sound and complete method for the synthesis of SS systems. The essence of the proposed approach includes (1) systematic introduction of computational redundancy by introducing new variables, called *superposed variables*, to an existing protocol's variables, called *underlying variables*, and (2) an intelligent and parallel backtracking method. The backtracking search is conducted in a parallel fashion amongst a fixed number of threads that simultaneously search for an SS solution. When a thread finds a combination of design choices that would result in the failure of the search (a.k.a. *conflicts*), it shares this information with the rest of the threads, thereby improving resource utilization during synthesis.

The contributions of this work are multi-fold. First, the proposed synthesis algorithm is complete; i.e., if there is an SS solution, our algorithm will find it. Second, we relax the constraints of the problem of designing self-stabilization by allowing new superposed behaviors inside the invariant. This is in contrast to previous work where researchers require that during algorithmic design of self-stabilization no new behaviors are included in the invariant. Third, we provide three different implementations of the proposed method as a software toolset, called Protocon (`http://cs.mtu.edu/~apklinkh/protocon/`), where we provide a sequential implementation and two parallel implementations; one multi-threaded and the other an MPI-based implementation. Fourth, we demonstrate the power of the proposed method by synthesizing four challenging network protocols that all existing heuristics fail to synthesize. These case studies include the 3-bit (8-state) token passing protocol (due to Gouda and Haddix [17]), coloring on Kautz graphs [21] which can represent a P2P network topology, ring orientation and leader election on a ring.

Organization. Section 2 introduces the basic concepts of protocols, transient faults, closure and convergence. Section 3 formally states the problem of designing self-stabilization. Section 4 presents the proposed synthesis method. Section 5 presents the case studies. Section 6 summarizes experimental results. Section 7 discusses related work. Finally, Section 8 makes concluding remarks and presents future/ongoing work.

2   Preliminaries

In this section, we present the formal definitions of protocols and self-stabilization. Protocols are defined in terms of their set of variables, their actions and their processes. The definitions in this section are adapted from [5,10,16,26].

For ease of presentation, we use a simplified version of Dijkstra's token ring protocol [10] as a running example.

Protocols. A *protocol* p comprises N processes $\{P_0, \cdots, P_{N-1}\}$ that communicate in a shared memory model under the constraints of an underlying network topology T_p. Each process P_i, where $i \in \mathbb{Z}_N$ and $\mathbb{Z}_N$ denotes values modulo N, has a set of local variables V_i that it can read and write, and a set of *actions* (a.k.a. *guarded commands* [11]). Thus, we have $V_p = \cup_{i=0}^{N-1} V_i$. The domain of variables in V_i is non-empty and finite. T_p specifies what P_i's neighboring processes are and which one of their variables P_i can read; i.e., P_i's *locality*. Each action of P_i has the form $grd \rightarrow stmt$, where grd is a Boolean expression specified over P_i's locality, and $stmt$ denotes an assignment statement that atomically updates the variables in V_i. A *local state* of P_i is a unique snapshot of its locality and a *global state* of the protocol p is a unique valuation of variables in V_p. The *state space* of p, denoted S_p, is the set of all global states of p, and $|S_p|$ denotes the size of S_p. A *state predicate* is any subset of S_p specified as a Boolean expression over V_p. We say a state predicate X *holds in a state* s (respectively, $s \in X$) *if and only if (iff)* X evaluates to true at s. A *transition* t is an ordered pair of global states, denoted (s_0, s_1), where s_0 is the source and s_1 is the target state of t. A *valid* transition of p must belong to some action of some process. The set of actions of P_i represent the set of all transitions of P_i, denoted δ_i. The set of transitions of the protocol p, denoted δ_p, is the union of the sets of transitions of its processes. A *deadlock state* is a state with no outgoing transitions. An action $grd \rightarrow stmt$ is *enabled* in a state s iff grd holds at s. A process P_i is *enabled* in s iff there exists an action of P_i that is enabled at s.

Example: Token Ring (TR). The Token Ring (TR) protocol (adapted from [10]) includes three processes $\{P_0, P_1, P_2\}$ each with an integer variable x_j, where $j \in \mathbb{Z}_3$, with a domain $\{0, 1, 2\}$. The process P_0 has the following action (addition and subtraction are in modulo 3):

$$A_0 : \quad (x_0 = x_2) \qquad \longrightarrow \qquad x_0 := x_2 + 1$$

When the values of x_0 and x_2 are equal, P_0 increments x_0 by one. We use the following parametric action to represent the actions of processes P_j for $1 \leq j \leq 2$:

$$A_j : \quad (x_j \neq x_{(j-1)}) \qquad \longrightarrow \qquad x_j := x_{(j-1)}$$

Each process P_j copies x_{j-1} only if $x_j \neq x_{j-1}$, where $j = 1, 2$. By definition, process P_j *has a token* iff $x_j \neq x_{j-1}$. Process P_0 *has a token* iff $x_0 = x_2$. We define a state predicate I_{TR} that captures the set of states in which only one token exists, where I_{TR} is

$$((x_0 = x_1) \wedge (x_1 = x_2)) \vee ((x_1 \neq x_0) \wedge (x_1 = x_2)) \vee ((x_0 = x_1) \wedge (x_1 \neq x_2))$$

Each process P_j is allowed to read variables x_{j-1} and x_j, but can write only x_j. Process P_0 is permitted to read x_2 and x_0 and can write only x_0.   ◁

Minimal Actions. Notice that the guard of an action $A : grd \rightarrow stmt$ of a process P_i can be specified in terms of a proper subset of V_i. In such cases, the action A is the union of a set of $k > 1$ minimal actions $grd_1 \rightarrow stmt_1, \cdots, grd_k \rightarrow stmt_k$, where $grd \equiv grd_1 \vee \cdots \vee grd_k$, and each grd_j ($1 \leq j \leq k$) is specified in terms of the values of all variables in V_i (where $i \in \mathbb{Z}_N$). More precisely, a *minimal* action of a process P_i includes a single valuation of all readable variables for P_i in its guard and a single valuation of all writable variables for P_i in its assignment statement. For example, consider an action $x_0 = 0 \to x_0 := x_2$ in the TR protocol. This action is the union of the minimal actions $x_0 = 0 \land x_2 = 0 \to x_0 := x_2$, $x_0 = 0 \land x_2 = 1 \to x_0 := x_2$, and $x_0 = 0 \land x_2 = 2 \to x_0 := x_2$. The proposed synthesis algorithm by superposition and backtracking in Section 4 explores the space of all minimal actions that can be included in a solution.

Computations. Intuitively, a computation of a protocol p is an *interleaving* of its actions. Formally, a *computation* of p is a sequence $\sigma = \langle s_0, s_1, \cdots \rangle$ of states that satisfies the following conditions: (1) for each transition (s_i, s_{i+1}) in σ, where $i \geq 0$, there exists an action $grd \to stmt$ in some process such that grd holds at s_i and the execution of $stmt$ at s_i yields s_{i+1}, and (2) σ is *maximal* in that either σ is infinite or if it is finite, then σ reaches a state s_f where no action is enabled. A *computation prefix* of a protocol p is a *finite* sequence $\sigma = \langle s_0, s_1, \cdots, s_m \rangle$ of states, where $m > 0$, such that each transition (s_i, s_{i+1}) in σ (where $i \in \mathbb{Z}_m$) belongs to some action $grd \to stmt$ in some process. The *projection* of a protocol p on a non-empty state predicate X, denoted $\delta_p|X$, consists of transitions of p that start in X and end in X.

Specifications. We follow [25] in defining a safety specification *sspec* as a set of bad transitions in $S_p \times S_p$ that should not be executed. A computation $\sigma = \langle s_0, s_1, \cdots \rangle$ satisfies *sspec* from s_0 iff no transition in σ is in *sspec*. A liveness specification *lspec* is a set of infinite sequences of states [4]. A computation $\sigma = \langle s_0, s_1, \cdots \rangle$ satisfies *lspec* from s_0 iff σ has a suffix in *lspec*. A computation σ of a protocol p satisfies the specifications *spec* of p from a state s_0 iff σ satisfies both safety and liveness of *spec* from s_0.

Closure and Invariant. A state predicate X is *closed in an action grd* $\to$ *stmt* *iff* executing *stmt* from any state $s \in (X \land grd)$ results in a state in X. We say a state predicate X is *closed in a protocol* p *iff* X is closed in every action of p. In other words, *closure* [16] requires that every computation of p starting in X remains in X. We say a state predicate I is an *invariant* of p *iff* I is closed in p and every computation of p that starts in some state in I satisfies its specifications. TR Example. Starting from a state in the predicate I_{TR}, the TR protocol generates an infinite sequence of states, where all reached states belong to I_{TR}.   ◁

Remark. In the problem of synthesizing self-stabilization (Problem 1), we start with a protocol that satisfies its liveness specifications from its invariant. Since during synthesis by superposition and backtracking we preserve liveness specifications in the invariant, we do not explicitly specify the nature of liveness specifications.

Convergence and Self-Stabilization. A protocol p *strongly converges* to I iff from any state in S_p, every computation of p reaches a state in I. A protocol p *weakly converges* to I iff from any state in S_p, there is a computation of p that reaches a state in I. We say a protocol p is strongly (respectively, weakly) self-stabilizing to I iff I is closed in p and p is strongly (respectively, weakly) converging to I. For ease of presentation, we drop the term "strongly" wherever we refer to strong stabilization.

3   Problem Statement

In this section, we state the problem of incorporating self-stabilization in non-stabilizing protocols using superposition. Let p be a non-stabilizing protocol and I be an invariant of p. When we fail to synthesize a self-stabilizing version of p, we *manually* expand the state space of p by including new variables. Such *superposed variables* provide computational redundancy in the hopes of giving the protocol sufficient information to detect and correct illegitimate states without forming livelocks. Let p' denote the self-stabilizing version of p that we would like to design and I' represent its invariant. $S_{p'}$ denotes the state space of p'; i.e., the expanded state space of p. Such an expansion can be captured by a function $\mathcal{H} : S_{p'} \to S_p$ that maps every state in $S_{p'}$ to a state in S_p. Moreover, we consider a one-to-many mapping $\mathcal{E} : S_p \to S_{p'}$ that maps each state $s \in S_p$ to a set of states $\{s' \mid s' \in S_{p'} \wedge \mathcal{H}(s') = s\}$. Observe that $\mathcal{H}$ and $\mathcal{E}$ can also be applied to transitions of p and p'. That is, the function $\mathcal{H}$ maps each transition (s'_0, s'_1), where $s'_0, s'_1 \in S_{p'}$, to a transition (s_0, s_1), where $s_0, s_1 \in S_p$. Moreover, $\mathcal{E}((s_0, s_1)) = \{(s'_0, s'_1) \mid s'_0 \in S_{p'} \wedge s'_1 \in S_{p'} \wedge \mathcal{H}((s'_0, s'_1)) = (s_0, s_1)\}$. Furthermore, each computation (respectively, computation prefix) of p' in the new state space $S_{p'}$ can be mapped to a computation (respectively, computation prefix) in the old state space S_p using $\mathcal{H}$. Our objective is to design a protocol p' that is self-stabilizing to I' when transient faults occur. That is, from any state in $S_{p'}$, protocol p' must converge to I'. In the absence of faults, p' must behave similar to p. Thus, each computation of p' that starts in I' must be mapped to a unique computation of p starting in I. This means that while we can have new computations in the invariant I', each new computation should be mapped to a computation of p in I (using $\mathcal{H}$). We state the problem as follows[1]: (The function $\mathsf{Pre}(\delta)$ takes a set of transitions δ and returns the source states of δ.)

Problem 1. **Synthesizing Self-Stabilization.**

- **Input:** A protocol p and its invariant I for specifications *spec*, the function $\mathcal{H}$ and the mapping $\mathcal{E}$ capturing the impact of superposed variables.
- **Output:** A protocol p' and its invariant I' in $S_{p'}$.
- **Constraints:**
  1. $I = \mathcal{H}(I')$
  2. $\forall s \in \mathsf{Pre}(\delta_p) \cap I : \mathcal{E}(s) \subseteq \mathsf{Pre}(\delta_{p'})$
  3. $\delta_p | I = \mathcal{H}(\{(s'_0, s'_1) \mid (s'_0, s'_1) \in (\delta_{p'} | I') \wedge \mathcal{H}(s'_0) \neq \mathcal{H}(s'_1)\})$
  4. $\forall s \in \mathsf{Pre}(\delta_p) \cap I : \delta_{p'} | \mathcal{E}(s)$ is cycle-free
  5. p' strongly converges to I'

The first constraint requires that no states are added/removed to/from I; i.e., $I = \mathcal{H}(I')$. The second constraint requires that any non-deadlocked state in I should remain non-deadlocked. The third constraint requires that any transition in $\delta_p | I$ should correspond to some transitions in $\delta_{p'} | I'$, and each transition included in $\delta_{p'} | I'$ must be mapped to a transition (s_0, s_1) in $\delta_p | I$ while ensuring

---

[1] This problem statement is an adaptation of the problem of adding fault tolerance in [26].

$s_0 \neq s_1$. Implicitly, this constraint requires that no transition in $\delta_{p'}|I'$ violates safety of *spec*. The fourth constraint stipulates that, for any non-deadlock state $s \in I$, the transitions included in the set of superposed states of s must not form a cycle; otherwise, liveness of *spec* may not be satisfied from I'. Notice that (i) the combination of Constraints 3 and 4 allows the inclusion of transitions $(s_0', s_1') \in \delta_{p'}|I'$ where $\mathcal{H}(s_0') = \mathcal{H}(s_1')$ under the constraint that such transitions do not form a cycle, and (ii) the combination of Constraints 1 to 4 ensure that p' would satisfy *spec* from I'. Finally, p' must converge to I'.

Example 1. Token ring using one bit per process

Consider the non-stabilizing token ring protocol p with N processes, where each process P_i owns a binary variable t_i and can read t_{i-1}. P_0 is said to have a token when $t_{N-1} = t_0$ and each other process P_i is said to have a token when $t_{i-1} \neq t_i$. P_0 and the other processes P_i (where $i > 0$) have the following actions:

$$P_0 : t_{N-1} = t_0 \longrightarrow t_0 := 1 - t_0;$$
$$P_i : t_{i-1} \neq t_i \longrightarrow t_i := t_{i-1};$$

Let I denote the legitimate states, where exactly one process has a token, written $I \equiv \exists! \; i \in \mathbb{Z}_N : ((i = 0 \wedge t_{i-1} = t_i) \vee (i \neq 0 \wedge t_{i-1} \neq t_i))$, where the quantifier $\exists!$ means there exists a unique value of i. The above protocol is a special case of the Token Ring protocol presented in Section 2 except that $N > 3$ and t_i is a binary variable. Dijkstra [10] has shown that such a protocol is non-stabilizing. In Section 5, we discuss how we automatically generate a constant state space token ring, where the size of the local state space of each process is constant, but N grows.

Deterministic, Self-Disabling Processes. The following theorem shows that the assumptions of deterministic and self-disabling processes do not impact the completeness of any algorithm that solves Problem 1. In general, convergence is achieved by collaborative actions of all processes. That is, each process partially contributes to the correction of the global state of a protocol. As such, starting at a state $s_0 \in \neg I$, a single process may not be able to recover the entire system single-handedly. Thus, even if a process executes consecutive actions starting at s_0, it will reach a local deadlock from where other processes can continue their execution towards converging to I. The execution of consecutive actions of a process can be replaced by a single write action of the same process. As such, we assume that once a process executes an action it will be disabled until the actions of other processes enable it again. That is, processes are *self-disabling*.

Theorem 1. *Let p be a non-stabilizing protocol with invariant I. There is an SS version of p to I iff there is an SS version of p to I with deterministic and self-disabling processes. (See proof in [24])*

4   Synthesis Using Backtracking

We present an efficient and complete backtracking search algorithm to solve Problem 1. Backtracking search is a well-studied technique [28] which is easy to implement and can give very good results. Throughout this section, we use actions and minimal actions interchangeably (unless otherwise stated).

4.1   Overview of the Search Algorithm

Like any other backtracking search, our algorithm incrementally builds upon a guess, or a partial solution, until it either finds a complete solution or finds that the guess is inconsistent. We decompose the *partial solution* into two pieces: (1) an *under-approximation* formed by making well-defined decisions about the form of a solution, and (2) an *over-approximation* which is the set of remaining possible solutions (given the current under-approximation). In a standard constraint satisfaction problem, a backtracking search builds upon a partial assignment to problem variables. The partial assignment is inconsistent in two cases: (i) the constraints upon assigned variables are broken (i.e., the under-approximation causes a conflict), or (ii) the constraints cannot be satisfied by the remaining variable assignments (i.e., the over-approximation cannot contain a solution). Each time a choice is made to build upon the under-approximation, the current partial solution is saved at decision level j and a copy which incorporates the new choice is placed at level $j + 1$. If the guess at level $j + 1$ is inconsistent, we move back to level j and discard the choice which brought us to level $j + 1$. If the guess at level 0 is found to be inconsistent, then enough guesses have been tested to determine that no solution exists. In the context of our work, we apply a backtracking search in the space of all valid minimal actions that can be included in a solution. Specifically, we use a set of actions, called `delegates`, that plays the role of the under-approximation, and another set of actions, called `candidates`, that contains the remaining actions to potentially include in `delegates`. Thus, the set (`delegates` ∪ `candidates`) constitutes the over-approximation.

Figure 1 represents an abstract flowchart of the proposed backtracking algorithm. We start with the non-stabilizing protocol p, its invariant I (which is closed in p), the topology, and the mappings to ($\mathcal{E}$) and from ($\mathcal{H}$) its expanded state space. Note that the inclusion of superposed variables is done manually and the designer is responsible to use his/her experience in determining the superposed variables and their domain sizes. Our approach has been to start with the fewest variables and smallest domains. If no solution is found, we gradually grow variable domains or add new variables. The algorithm in Figure 1 starts by computing all *valid* candidate actions (in the expanded state space) that adhere to the read/write permissions of all processes. The initial value of `delegates` is often the empty set unless there are specific actions that must be in the solution (e.g., to ensure the reachability of particular states). The algorithm in Figure 1 then calls ReviseActions to remove self-loops from `candidates` (since they violate convergence), and checks for inconsistencies in the partial solution. The designer may give additional safety specifications that forbid certain actions.

In general, ReviseActions (see the bottom dashed box in Figure 1) is invoked whenever we strengthen the partial solution by adding to the under-approximation or removing from the over-approximation. It may further remove from the over-approximation by enforcing the determinism and self-disablement constraints (see Theorem 1). Then ReviseActions computes the largest possible invariant I' which could be used by the current partial solution. That is, it finds the weakest predicate I' for which the constraints of Problem 1 can be satisfied using some set of transitions $\delta_{p'}$ permissible by the partial solution. The

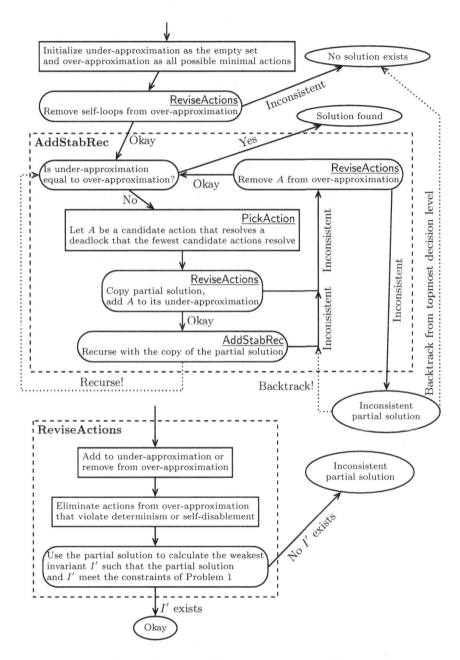

Fig. 1. Overview of the backtracking algorithm.

partial solution requires $\delta_{p'}$ to include all transitions corresponding to actions in delegates. Additionally, $\delta_{p'}$ can include any subset of transitions corresponding to actions in candidates. For example, Constraint 5 of Problem 1 stipulates that the transitions of delegates are cycle-free outside of I' and that the transitions of delegates $\cup$ candidates provide weak convergence to I'. If such an I' does not exist, then the partial solution is inconsistent.

If our initialized delegates and candidates give a consistent partial solution, then we invoke the AddStabRec routine. The objective of AddStabRec (see the top dashed box in Figure 1) is to go through all actions in candidates and check their eligibility for inclusion in the self-stabilizing solution. In particular, AddStabRec has a loop that iterates through all actions of candidates until it becomes empty or an inconsistency is found. In each iteration, AddStabRec picks a candidate action to resolve some remaining deadlock at the next decision level. In general, the candidate action can be randomly selected. However, to limit the possible choices, we use an intelligent method for picking candidate actions described in Section 4.2. After picking a new action A, we invoke ReviseActions to add action A to a copy of the current partial solution by including A in the copy of delegates and removing it from the copy of candidates. If the copied partial solution is consistent, then AddStabRec makes a recursive call to itself, using the copied partial solution for the next decision level. If the copied partial solution is found to be inconsistent (either by a call to ReviseActions or by the exhaustive search in the call to AddStabRec), then we remove action A from candidates using ReviseActions. If after removal of A the partial solution is consistent, then we continue in the loop. Otherwise, we backtrack since no stabilizing protocol exists with the current under-approximation.

Theorem 2 (Soundness and Completeness). *The algorithm in Figure 1 is sound and complete. (See proof in [24])*

4.2   Picking Actions via the Minimum Remaining Values Method

The worst-case complexity of a depth-first backtracking search is determined by the branching factor b and depth d of its decision tree, evaluating to $O(b^d)$. We can tackle this complexity by reducing the branching factor. To do this, we use a minimum remaining values (MRV) method in PickAction. MRV is classically applied to constraint satisfaction problems [28] by assigning a value to a variable which has the minimal remaining candidate values. In our setting, we pick an action which resolves a deadlock with the minimal number of remaining actions which can resolve it.

Algorithm 1 shows the details of PickAction that keeps an array deadlock_sets, where each element deadlock_sets[i] contains all the deadlocks that are resolved by exactly i candidate actions. We initially start with array size |deadlock_sets| = 1 and with deadlock_sets[0] containing all unresolved deadlocks. We then loop through all candidate actions, shifting deadlocks to the next highest element in the array (bubbling up) for each candidate action which resolves them. After building the array, we find the lowest index i for which the deadlock set deadlock_sets[i] is nonempty, and then return an action which can resolve some deadlock in that set. Line 21 can only be reached if either the remaining deadlocks cannot be resolved (but ReviseActions catches this earlier) or all deadlocks are resolved.

Algorithm 1. Pick an action using the minimum remaining values method.

PickAction(p: protocol, $\mathcal{E}$: mapping $S_p \rightarrow S_{p'}$, delegates, candidates: set of minimal actions, I': state predicate)

Output: Next candidate action to pick.

1. **let** deadlock_sets be a single-element array, where deadlock_sets[0] holds a set of deadlocks in $\neg I' \cup \mathcal{E}(\mathsf{Pre}(\delta_p))$ which actions in delegates do not resolve.
2. **for all** action $\in$ candidates **do**
3.   **let** $i := |\text{deadlock\_sets}|$
4.   **while** $i > 0$ **do**
5. $i := i - 1$
6.   **let** resolved := deadlock_sets[i] $\cap$ Pre(action)
7.   **if** resolved $\neq \emptyset$ **then**
8.   **if** $i = |\text{deadlock\_sets}| - 1$ **then**
9.   **let** deadlock_sets[$i + 1$] := $\emptyset$ {Grow array by one element}
10.   **end if**
11.   deadlock_sets[i] := deadlock_sets[i] \ resolved
12.   deadlock_sets[$i + 1$] := deadlock_sets[$i + 1$] $\cup$ resolved
13.   **end if**
14.   **end while**
15. **end for**
16. **for** $i = 1, \ldots, |\text{deadlock\_sets}| - 1$ **do**
17.   **if** deadlock_sets[i] $\neq \emptyset$ **then**
18.   **return**   An action from candidates which resolves a deadlock in deadlock_sets[i].
19.   **end if**
20. **end for**
21. return An action from candidates. {This line may never execute!}

4.3 Optimizing the Decision Tree

This section presents the techniques that we use to improve the efficiency of our backtracking algorithm.

Conflicts. Every time a new candidate action is included in delegates, ReviseActions checks for inconsistencies, which involves cycle detection and reachability analysis. These procedures become very costly as the complexity of the transition system grows. To mitigate this problem, whenever an inconsistency is found, we record a minimal set of decisions (subset of delegates) that causes it. We reference these *conflict sets* to remove candidate actions which would cause an inconsistency.

Randomization and Restarts. When using the standard control flow of a depth-first search, a bad choice near the top of the decision tree can lead to infeasible runtime. This is the case since the bad decision exists in the partial solution until the search backtracks up the tree sufficiently to change the decision. To limit the search time in these branches, we employ a method outlined by Gomes et al. [15] which combines randomization with restarts. In short, we limit the amount of backtracking to a certain height (we use 3). If the search backtracks past the height limit, it forgets the current decision tree and restarts from the root. To avoid trying the same unfruitful decisions after a restart, PickAction randomly selects a candidate action permissible by the MRV method.

Parallel Search. In order to increase the chance of finding a solution, we instantiate several parallel executions of the algorithm in Figure 1; i.e., *search diversification*. The parallel tasks avoid overlapping computations due to the randomization used in PickAction. Further, the parallel tasks share conflicts with each other to prevent the re-exploration of branches that contain no solutions. In our MPI implementation, conflict dissemination occurs between tasks using a virtual network topology formed by a generalized Kautz graph [21] of degree 4. This topology has a diameter logarithmic in the number of nodes and is fault-tolerant in that multiple paths between two nodes ensure message delivery. That is, even if some nodes are performing costly cycle detection and do not check for incoming messages, they will not slow the dissemination of new conflicts.

5   Case Studies

In this section, we investigate the feasibility of designing a constant space token ring protocol using the proposed algorithm. Section 5.1 presents a 4-state token ring, Section 5.2 discusses how we automatically design the 8-state token ring presented in [17], and Section 5.3 introduces a 6-state token ring synthesized by Protocon. We also provide an overview of other case studies [24] we have conducted (which have been omitted due to space constraints).

5.1   4-State Token Ring

To generate a stabilizing version of the 2-state token ring of Example 1, we add a superposed binary variable x_i to each process P_i. Each process P_i can also read its predecessor's superposed variable x_{i-1}. One such protocol is stabilizing for rings of size $N = 2, \ldots, 7$ but contains a livelock when $N = 8$. It is defined as follows for process P_0 and other processes P_i where $i > 0$:

$$
\begin{aligned}
&P_0 : t_{N-1} = 0 \wedge && t_0 = 0 && \longrightarrow t_0 := 1; \\
&P_0 : t_{N-1} = 1 \wedge x_{N-1} = 0 \wedge t_0 = 1 && && \longrightarrow t_0 := 0; \ x_0 := 1 - x_0; \\
&P_0 : t_{N-1} = 1 \wedge x_{N-1} = 1 \wedge t_0 = 1 \wedge x_0 = 1 && \longrightarrow t_0 := 0; \\
&P_i : \ t_{i-1} = 0 \wedge && t_i = 1 && \longrightarrow t_i := 0; \ x_i := 1 - x_i; \\
&P_i : \ t_{i-1} = 1 \wedge \ x_{i-1} = 1 \wedge t_i = 0 && && \longrightarrow t_i := 1; \\
&P_i : \ t_{i-1} = 1 \wedge \ x_{i-1} = 0 \wedge (t_i = 0 \vee x_i = 1) && \longrightarrow t_i := 1; \ x_i := 0;
\end{aligned}
$$

5.2   8-State Token Ring

We further expand the state space by giving each process a third binary variable $ready_i$ which no other process can read. This way, each process can read $2^5 = 32$

unique valuations and can assign variables in $2^3 = 8$ unique ways, giving it $2^8 = 256$ possible minimal actions. Process P_0 remains distinguished and may act differently from other processes. With the superposed variable $ready_i$, the backtracking synthesis algorithm begins with $2(2^8) = 512$ candidate actions, and it generates several solutions similar to the 3-bit token ring of Gouda and Haddix [17]. To our knowledge, no previous method has been able to synthesize such protocols automatically.

5.3   6-State Token Ring

In order to investigate the existence of a constant space token ring with fewer than 8 states, we expand the domain of x_i to $\{0, 1, 2\}$ and remove $ready_i$. This way, each process has variables t_i and x_i, comprising 6 states. Thus, each process can read $6^2 = 36$ valuations of its 4 readable variables and can assign its 2 writable variables in 6 unique ways, giving it $6^3 = 216$ possible actions. Process P_0 remains distinguished and may act differently from other processes. The algorithm starts with $2(6^3) = 432$ candidate actions and generates a 6-state self-stabilizing protocol.

5.4   Other Case Studies

Due to space constraints, we have omitted the actions of the 6-state token ring and other case studies including coloring on Kautz graphs, ring orientation and leader election on a ring. (Please see [24] for details.)

6   Experimental Results

We synthesized Huang's leader election [20] on a ring size 6, which gives an agreement protocol as 6 is not prime. This ring size is chosen for its difficulty, since a ring of size 5 is usually solved within 8 restarts. For this ring of size 6, we performed 25 trials of the parallel search using different numbers of MPI processes to measure the effect of parallelism on runtime. Averaging the times taken by 8, 16, 32, and 64 MPI processes, we get 2468.36, 1120.76, 659.96, and 371.96 seconds respectively, giving a reasonable speedup. Using the specifications in Section 5, we found that no single protocol is a stabilizing 4-state token ring for sizes $2, \ldots, 8$ or more, but we did synthesize 6-state and 8-state versions which we believe to be generalizable (verified up to size 25). Some of these converge to having one enabled process like Dijkstra's stabilizing toking ring [10]. We are currently working on mechanical verification of their correctness for arbitrary numbers of processes. Finally, we synthesized an odd-sized ring orientation protocol using the topology of Hoepman [19]. It was verified as self-stabilizing up to rings of size 11.

7 Related Work and Discussion

This section discusses related work on manual and automated design of fault tolerance in general and self-stabilization in particular. Manual methods are mainly based on the approach of *design and verify*, where one designs a fault-tolerant system and then verifies the correctness of (1) functional requirements in the absence of faults, and (2) fault tolerance requirements in the presence of faults. For example, Liu and Joseph [27] provide a method for augmenting fault-intolerant systems with a set of new actions that implement fault tolerance functionalities. Katz and Perry [22] present a general (but expensive) method for global snapshot and reset towards adding convergence to non-stabilizing systems. Varghese [30] and Afek *et al.* [3] provide a method based on local checking for global recovery of locally correctable protocols. Varghese [31] also proposes a counter flushing method for detection and correction of global predicates.

Methods for automated design of fault tolerance can be classified into specification-based and model repair techniques. In specification-based methods [6] the inter-process synchronization mechanisms of programs are derived from formal specifications often specified in some variant of temporal logic. By contrast, in model repair one incorporates fault tolerance functionalities in an existing system while ensuring that the resulting program would still satisfy its specifications in the absence of faults. For example, Kulkarni and Arora [26] study the addition of three different levels of fault tolerance, namely failsafe, nonmasking and masking fault tolerance. A *failsafe* protocol meets its safety specifications under all circumstances (i.e., in the absence and in the presence of faults), whereas a *nonmasking* protocol ensures recovery to invariant from the set of states that are reachable in the presence of faults (but not necessarily equal to the entire state space). A *masking* fault-tolerant program is both failsafe and nonmasking. Ebnenasir [12] has investigated the automated addition of recovery to distributed protocols for types of faults other than transient faults. Nonetheless, their method has the option to remove deadlock states by making them unreachable. A similar choice is utilized in Bonakdarpour and Kulkarni's work [8] on adding progress properties to distributed protocols. This is not an option in the addition of self-stabilization; recovery should be provided from any state in protocol state space.

Since it is unlikely that an efficient method exists for algorithmic design of self-stabilization [23], most existing techniques [1, 2, 13, 14, 32] are based on sound heuristics. For instance, Abujarad and Kulkarni [1, 2] present a heuristic for adding convergence to locally-correctable systems. Zhu and Kulkarni [32] give a genetic programming approach for the design of fault tolerance, using a fitness function to quantify how close a randomly-generated protocol is to being fault-tolerant. Farahat and Ebnenasir [14] provide a lightweight method for designing self-stabilization even for non-locally correctable protocols. They also devise [13] a swarm method for exploiting the computational power of computer clusters towards automated design of self-stabilization. While the swarm synthesis method inspires the proposed work in this paper, it has two limitations: it is incomplete and forbids any change in the invariant.

8   Conclusions and Future Work

This paper presents a method for algorithmic design of self-stabilization based on variable superposition and backtracking. Unlike existing algorithmic methods [1, 2, 13, 14] the proposed approach is sound and complete; i.e., if there is an SS solution, our algorithm will find it. We have devised sequential and parallel implementations of the proposed method in a software tool, called Protocon. Variable superposition allows us to systematically introduce computational redundancy where existing heuristics fail to generate a solution. Afterwards, we use the backtracking search to intelligently look for a self-stabilizing solution. The novelty of our backtracking method lies in finding and sharing design conflicts amongst parallel threads to improve the efficiency of search. We have used Protocon to automatically generate self-stabilizing protocols that none of the existing heuristics can generate (to the best of our knowledge). For example, we have automatically designed an 8-state self-stabilizing token ring protocol for the same topology as the protocol manually designed by Gouda and Haddix [17]. We have even improved this protocol further by designing a 6-state version thereof available at `http://cs.mtu.edu/~apklinkh/protocon/`. Besides token rings, we have synthesized other protocols such as coloring on Kautz graphs, ring orientation and leader election on a ring [24].

We are currently investigating several extensions of this work. First, we would like to synthesize protocols such as Dijkstra's 4-state token chain and 3-state token ring [10], where the invariant and legitimate behavior cannot be expressed using the protocol's variables without essentially writing the self-stabilizing version. Second, we are using theorem proving techniques to figure out why a synthesized protocol may not be generalizable. Then, we plan to incorporate the feedback received from theorem provers in our backtracking method. A third extension is to leverage the techniques used in SAT solvers and apply them in our backtracking search.

References

1. Abujarad, F., Kulkarni, S.S.: Multicore constraint-based automated stabilization. In: Guerraoui, R., Petit, F. (eds.) SSS 2009. LNCS, vol. 5873, pp. 47–61. Springer, Heidelberg (2009)
2. Abujarad, F., Kulkarni, S.S.: Automated constraint-based addition of nonmasking and stabilizing fault-tolerance. Theoretical Computer Science 412(33), 4228–4246 (2011)
3. Afek, Y., Kutten, S., Yung, M.: The local detection paradigm and its application to self-stabilization. Theoretical Computer Science 186(1-2), 199–229 (1997)
4. Alpern, B., Schneider, F.B.: Defining liveness. Information Processing Letters 21, 181–185 (1985)
5. Arora, A., Gouda, M.G.: Closure and convergence: A foundation of fault-tolerant computing. IEEE Transactions on Software Engineering 19(11), 1015–1027 (1993)
6. Attie, P.C.: anish Arora, and E. A. Emerson. Synthesis of fault-tolerant concurrent programs. ACM Transactions on Programming Languages and Systems (TOPLAS) 26(1), 125–185 (2004)

7. Awerbuch, B., Patt-Shamir, B., Varghese, G.: Self-stabilization by local checking and correction. In: Proceedings of the 31st Annual IEEE Symposium on Foundations of Computer Science, pp. 268–277 (1991)
8. Bonakdarpour, B., Kulkarni, S.S.: Revising distributed UNITY programs is NP-complete. In: Baker, T.P., Bui, A., Tixeuil, S. (eds.) OPODIS 2008. LNCS, vol. 5401, pp. 408–427. Springer, Heidelberg (2008)
9. Chandy, K.M., Misra, J.: Parallel Program Design: A Foundation. Addison-Wesley (1988)
10. Dijkstra, E.W.: Self-stabilizing systems in spite of distributed control. Communications of the ACM 17(11), 643–644 (1974)
11. Dijkstra, E.W.: A Discipline of Programming. Prentice-Hall (1990)
12. Ebnenasir, A.: Automatic Synthesis of Fault-Tolerance. PhD thesis, Michigan State University (May 2005)
13. Ebnenasir, A., Farahat, A.: Swarm synthesis of convergence for symmetric protocols. In: Proceedings of the Ninth European Dependable Computing Conference, pp. 13–24 (2012)
14. Farahat, A., Ebnenasir, A.: A lightweight method for automated design of convergence in network protocols. ACM Transactions on Autonomous and Adaptive Systems (TAAS) 7(4), 38:1–38:36 (2012)
15. Gomes, C.P., Selman, B., Kautz, H.A.: Boosting combinatorial search through randomization. In: Mostow, J., Rich, C. (eds.) AAAI/IAAI, pp. 431–437. AAAI Press / The MIT Press (1998)
16. Gouda, M.G.: The theory of weak stabilization. In: Datta, A.K., Herman, T. (eds.) WSS 2001. LNCS, vol. 2194, pp. 114–123. Springer, Heidelberg (2001)
17. Gouda, M.G., Haddix, F.F.: The stabilizing token ring in three bits. Journal of Parallel and Distributed Computing 35(1), 43–48 (1996)
18. Gouda, M.G., Multari, N.J.: Stabilizing communication protocols. IEEE Transactions on Computers 40(4), 448–458 (1991)
19. Hoepman, J.-H.: Uniform deterministic self-stabilizing ring-orientation on odd-length rings. In: Tel, G., Vitányi, P. (eds.) WDAG 1994. LNCS, vol. 857, pp. 265–279. Springer, Heidelberg (1994)
20. Huang, S.-T.: Leader election in uniform rings. ACM Transactions on Programming Languages and Systems (TOPLAS) 15, 563–573 (1993)
21. Imase, M., Itoh, M.: A design for directed graphs with minimum diameter. IEEE Trans. Computers 32(8), 782–784 (1983)
22. Katz, S., Perry, K.: Self-stabilizing extensions for message passing systems. Distributed Computing 7, 17–26 (1993)
23. Klinkhamer, A.P., Ebnenasir, A.: On the hardness of adding nonmasking fault tolerance. IEEE Transactions on Dependable and Secure Computing (in press, 2014)
24. Klinkhamer, A.P., Ebnenasir, A.: Synthesizing self-stabilization through superposition and backtracking. Technical Report CS-TR-14-01, Michigan Technological University (May 2014), http://www.mtu.edu/cs/research/papers/pdfs/CS-TR-14-01.pdf
25. Kulkarni, S.S.: Component-based design of fault-tolerance. PhD thesis, Ohio State University (1999)
26. Kulkarni, S.S., Arora, A.: Automating the addition of fault-tolerance. In: Joseph, M. (ed.) FTRTFT 2000. LNCS, vol. 1926, pp. 82–93. Springer, Heidelberg (2000)
27. Liu, Z., Joseph, M.: Transformation of programs for fault-tolerance. Formal Aspects of Computing 4(5), 442–469 (1992)

28. Russell, S., Norvig, P.: Artificial Intelligence: A Modern Approach, 3rd edn. Prentice Hall Press, Upper Saddle River (2009)
29. Stomp, F.: Structured design of self-stabilizing programs. In: Proceedings of the 2nd Israel Symposium on Theory and Computing Systems, pp. 167–176 (1993)
30. Varghese, G.: Self-stabilization by local checking and correction. PhD thesis, MIT (October 1992)
31. Varghese, G.: Self-stabilization by counter flushing. In: The 13th Annual ACM Symposium on Principles of Distributed Computing, pp. 244–253 (1994)
32. Zhu, L., Kulkarni, S.: Synthesizing round based fault-tolerant programs using genetic programming. In: Higashino, T., Katayama, Y., Masuzawa, T., Potop-Butucaru, M., Yamashita, M. (eds.) SSS 2013. LNCS, vol. 8255, pp. 370–372. Springer, Heidelberg (2013)

Configuration Hopping: A Secure Communication Protocol without Explicit Key Exchange

Yue Qiao[1], Kannan Srinivasan[1], and Anish Arora[1,2]

[1] Department of Computer Science and Engineering,
The Ohio State Univeristy, Columbus, OH 43210, USA
[2] The Samraksh Company, Dublin, OH 43017, USA

Abstract. By changing one or more physical layer parameters (such as spreading code, symbol duration, symbol constellation, center frequency, modulation method, transmission power, etc.) in an agreed upon manner between two communication parties, we are able to realize communication that is hard to detect, identify, and decode. We present a formal link layer protocol for secure communication based on this idea that, along with the use of channel reciprocity, notably eschews the use of cryptographic keys. We prove the security properties of the protocol in the Canetti-Krawczyk framework and study the feasibility of changing several physical layer parameters at the link packet level in Software Defined Radios.

1 Introduction

Secret communication had been explored extensively before the theory of modern cryptography emerged. The basis of secret communication (including cryptography) is to encode plain messages into a form that is unbreakable by the adversary [10]. Traditional cryptographic techniques focus on converting a plaintext into a ciphertext that is decodable only by authorized parties. These cryptographic conversions are typically performed at a logical level even though conversions at the physical level are also possible. We hypothesize that the main reason for favoring the higher (logical) layers in the past is that manipulating signals at the physical layer has not been as easy as encoding data bits. The recent developments in Software-Defined Radios (SDRs), however, make physical layer conversion much more convenient.

In fact, physical layer encryption is not new: hiding transmissions using spread spectrum was done during World War II. However, physical layer encryption is not as popular as cryptographic techniques that work with bits at the higher layers. SDRs have opened up the physical layer and have fueled physical layer systems research. Although nowadays SDRs are more expensive than existing network devices, there is a growing tendency of employing SDRs because of the emergence of low-cost SDRs and the promising prospect. This is why we believe that it is timely to revisit physical layer encryption.

P. Felber and V. Garg (Eds.): SSS 2014, LNCS 8756, pp. 268–282, 2014.

Since SDRs provide many opportunities for physical (PHY) layer encryption beyond the traditionally used spread spectrum, we propose a generic hop-by-hop secure communication protocol that adapts various PHY parameters on a per link packet basis. We refer to this sort of PHY layer adaptation as Configuration Hopping. Many PHY parameters can be adapted. For instance, modulation constellation can be remapped in an agreed upon manner between two communicating ends in order to confuse the attackers. Pseudorandom number (PN) sequences used in direct sequence spreading spectrum (DSSS) can also be adapted in a similar way. We discuss other feasible PHY layer encodings in Section 5.

Combining all the possible encodings at the link packet level (or possibly even at the sub-packet level), we can achieve secure communication at a relatively low cost compared to traditional cryptography. By adapting PHY parameters, i.e., changing configurations during wireless communication, radios can send and receive packets in a protected way without involving much computation and communication overhead. In addition to cost considerations, PHY layer protection is also graceful for the following reasons: First of all, it requires attackers to spend more energy and effort to detect the communication as signals could be sent in different frequencies, and/or spread by different PN codes. Secondly, even if an attacker succeeds in detection, decoding still remains to be solved. Without knowing the exact configuration in which signals are sent, an attacker must decode by brute-force search. Last but not least, localization and identification also become hard for the adversary. A transmitter-receiver pair will not be traced by its communication mode as it keeps changing during communication.

To realize the idea of configuration hopping in a link layer protocol for secure communication, we propose two core modules. One adapts configuration parameters for each link layer packet (we note that this adaptation is feasible at a finer granularity as well, such as per symbol or per block, but we will not dwell on this refinement in the paper). The other provides a mechanism of securely exchanging the mutually agreed upon configurations online between the two communicating parties. We design a protocol called Configuration Hopping that exploits channel reciprocity to exchange the configuration implicitly. In Sections 4 and 5, we prove the security properties and study the implementation feasibility of Configuration Hopping in SDRs.

2   Background

Goal. Our main goal is to propose a protocol which allows protected hop-to-hop communication by adapting configurations at a fine granularity in a key-free manner. To achieve a key-free exchange of adaptation values, we leverage channel reciprocity. As the channel between two nodes is stable only for a short time, to get matching estimates of the channel, the times at which the two nodes measure the channel need to be as close as possible to each other. To realize this, we adopt full-duplex techniques such as in-band full-duplex [9] and dialog codes [4] in our protocol. In addition to enabling matching channel estimates, full-duplex techniques also provide extra jamming-like protection against eavesdroppers.

Channel Reciprocity. In wireless communications, multi-path fading leads to the fact that the signal observed by a wireless receiver is the superposition of multiple copies of the transmitted signal that have propagated over different paths. In other words, the output signal carries the information of the propagation paths. More importantly, if there is a propagation path from Alice to Bob, then there must be an identical reverse path from Bob to Alice. Therefore, the paths of electromagnetic wave propagation are identical in both directions between the two communicating ends (henceforth called Alice and Bob). This phenomenon is commonly known as channel reciprocity. In addition, as channels decorrelate rapidly over space, wireless channel can act as a common random source between two communicating parties and eavesdroppers which are half a wavelength away from them will see uncorrelated channels [15]. So in a scattering environment, it is infeasible for the eavesdroppers to derive the channel between legitimate users even with collusion. A significant body of prior research [5,11–13] has considered the extraction of secrets by exploiting channel reciprocity.

Full-duplex Radios. Note that if Alice and Bob wish to exploit channel reciprocity to obtain matching measurements of the channel, they need to receive signals from each other over a period of time in which the channel does not change significantly. The time for which the wireless channel remains coherent is called *coherence time*. The coherence time T_c is related to the maximum Doppler frequency f_d. In Clarke's model, the 50% coherence time is defined by $T_c \approx \frac{0.423}{f_d}$ [15]. In other words, Alice and Bob need to observe the channel between them within the coherence time, which can be short in a mobile environment. Full-duplex techniques [4,9] allow radios to transmit and receive at the same time. Thus, two communicating radios can measure the channel between them at (almost) the same time by performing simultaneous transmissions in both directions. We, therefore, use two full-duplex radios in our communicating parties. The two radios, Alice and Bob, exchange information in the same time slot. Then, based on the messages they receive and the channel information they derive from the signals, Alice and Bob could communicate with each other in a protected and key-free way using our protocol.

3   System Model

Assumptions on the Knowledge and Capability of Legal Users. Given two wireless nodes that are within each other's transmission region, they share a common configuration for the initial stage of communication. They are both able to hop among different PHY layer configurations. The capability of such configuration hopping is defined by the SDRs used. Generally speaking, most SDRs are able to adapt PHY parameters like frequency, modulation method, symbols duration, PN sequences, and rotations of constellation maps (cf. Section 5.3). These parameters individually have a number of options whose count ranges from tens to hundreds. The combinatorial number of parameter options thus yield a relatively large configuration hopping space. A more detailed discussion of parameter change is given in Section 5.

Attacker Model. Cryptographic protocols often formalize the adversary at the network, session, or application layer. A powerful, standard cryptographic adversary model is the Canetti Krawczyk(CK)-framework [7]. In the CK-framework, a concurrent man-in-the-middle (CMIM) adversary $\mathcal{A}$ controls all the communication links. It can listen to all the transmissions, change transmitted messages and inject its own traffic. It is also in charge of message passing and scheduling of all protocol events. Besides these basic attacker capabilities, the adversary is able to obtain secret information too. It has access to secret information via three types of attacks:

1. Session-state leakage: the adversary gets the internal state of an incomplete session;
2. Session-key query: the adversary queries the value of the session key generated by a completed session;
3. Corruption query: all of the information stored in the memory of the corrupted parties is leaked to the adversary.

For our purposes, we will refine the CK-model to apply to the link layer, as follows. We instantiate the CK-adversary actions on messages to corresponding actions on link layer packets. And we instantiate the CK-adversary actions on sessions to periods of time where the Configuration Hopping protocol uses the same secret key (generated from the physical layer). We can thus analyze the security of session keys in our protocol in the presence of the CK-adversary.

The security of our protocol relies on the secretly agreed upon configurations, which are conceptually analogous to "session keys". To break the system, attackers need to compromise these session keys. We will show in Section 4 that the complexity of discovering the configuration for the attackers is no less than that of compromising the session key, as long as the size of the configuration space is the same as the session key space.

Jamming is also a primary threat for a wireless protocol. Our adversary model thus allows flexible narrow band jamming. Intuitively speaking, the Configuration Hopping protocol tolerates even adaption in narrow band jamming since the configuration used by the two communicating ends hop across a wide band in an unpredictable, random manner. That said, more powerful wide band jamming is a challenging problem, which all wireless communication suffers from, but is beyond the scope of our paper.

SK-security Within the CK-framework. In the CK-framework, the input of a session in a key-exchange (KE) protocol is of the form $(P_i, P_j, s, role)$, where P_i or P_j is the identity of a party, s is the identity of a session, and $role$ is either *initiator* or *responder*. A session of input $(P_i, P_j, s, initiator)$ and a session of input $(P_j, P_i, s, responder)$ are collectively called a *matching*. In our proposed protocol, the two nodes, Alice and Bob, transmit and listen in an in-band full-duplex channel, so it may seem that there is no *initiator* or *responder*. However, these roles are chosen in a higher layer before the communication stream commences. Therefore, ignoring the role, we define two sessions are matching as long as the two parties are matching and the session ids are identical.

Definition 1. *A session is called* complete *when a key establishment event is recorded.*

Definition 2. *A session is called* locally exposed *if it or its matching session is subject to one or more of the three attacks.*

Definition 3. *The session-key security (SK-security) within the CK-framework is captured as follows: a key-exchange (KE) protocol is secure as long as for any unexposed complete session adaptively selected by* $\mathcal{A}$*, referred as the test session, it holds with overwhelming probability that:*

1. *The test session and its matching session output the same session-key.*
2. *The adversary* $\mathcal{A}$ *cannot distinguish the session-key output by the test session from a random value.*

4   Protocol

In this section, we first propose an abstract protocol which achieves secure communication by letting Alice and Bob iterate through configurations in an agreed upon manner. We then analyze its security properties and give the security proof under the CK-framework. Our protocol provides a link layer solution that protects communication from active adversaries in a manner that can be integrated with many existing link layer standards, such as 802.11. The coordination and synchronization issues associated with our link layer protocol exchange would be handled per these link layer standards.

4.1   Protocol Schema

Alice and Bob communicate with each other in the full-duplex mode, which allows them to exchange messages msg_{A_i} and msg_{B_i} in parallel. We define the parallel exchange of a message pair as spanning one round of communication. In each round, Alice and Bob are assumed to get the same channel information upon reception. Leveraging this, they can share the configuration of the next round implicitly based on the channel information. While in the first round, the configuration needs to be predetermined since configurations cannot be derived without any information exchanged. Alice and Bob also exchange two parameters r_{A_i} and r_{B_i} in each round. The configuration of the ith round is derived not only from the channel information $ch_{A_{i-1}}/ch_{B_{i-1}}$ of the previous round, but also from the parameters $r_{A_{i-1}}$ and $r_{B_{i-1}}$ chosen and sent by Alice and Bob respectively in the previous round. We will explain the role of $r_{A_{i-1}}$ and $r_{B_{i-1}}$ in Section 4.2. Figures 1 and 2 depict the protocol schema, where authentication functions f and g take $r_{A_{i-1}}$, $r_{B_{i-1}}$, $ch_{A_{i-1}}$, and $ch_{B_{i-1}}$ as keys to encode msg_{A_i}, msg_{B_i}, r_{A_i}, or r_{B_i}. The authentication functions f and g provide extra protection

Table 1. Notations

A,B	Communicating parties
i	Index of the communication round
msg_{A_i}, msg_{B_i}	Message sent by Alice and Bob respectively
r_{A_i}, r_{B_i}	Random number generated by Alice and Bob respectively
ch_{A_i}, ch_{B_i}	Secret derived from the channel by Alice and Bob respectively
$conf_{A_i}$, $conf_{B_i}$	Configurations used by Alice and Bob respectively
$conf(\cdot)$	Deterministic function which maps the input $(r_{A_i}, r_{B_i}, ch_{A_i})$ or $(r_{A_i}, r_{B_i}, ch_{B_i})$ to one of the pre-defined configurations
$f(\cdot)$, $g(\cdot)$	Authentication functions

from certain attackers (e.g., impersonation). It is worth noting that this schema allows for several realizations. In the analysis of the security of Configuration Hopping, we will simply treat f and g as commonly used MAC functions. For an active eavesdropper (Eve) who tries to hijack during the ith round by guessing the configuration and then impersonating Alice or Bob, Eve needs to successfully guess $r_{A_{i-1}}$ or $r_{B_{i-1}}$, too. In our protocol, $r_{A_{i-1}}$ and $r_{B_{i-1}}$ play a role of authenticators which provide a proof that the one that Alice/Bob is talking to at the moment is the one Alice/Bob talked to in the previous round. A formal description of the protocol schema is presented below; Table 1 lists the notations used in the protocol schema.

- **1st round:**
  Alice $\rightarrow$ Bob : $f(msg_{A_1}, r_{B_0})$, $g(r_{A_1}, r_{B_0})$ with configuration $= conf(r_{A_0}, r_{B_0})$
  Bob $\rightarrow$ Alice : $f(msg_{B_1}, r_{A_0})$, $g(r_{B_1}, r_{A_0})$ with configuration $= conf(r_{A_0}, r_{B_0})$
- **ith round ($i \geq 2$):**
  Alice $\rightarrow$ Bob : $f(msg_{A_i}, r_{B_{i-1}}, ch_{A_{i-1}})$, $g(r_{A_i}, r_{B_{i-1}})$

  $$with\ configuration = conf(ch_{A_{i-1}}, r_{A_{i-1}}, r_{B_{i-1}})$$

  Bob $\rightarrow$ Alice : $f(msg_{B_i}, r_{A_{i-1}}, ch_{B_{i-1}})$, $g(r_{B_i}, r_{A_{i-1}})$

  $$with\ configuration = conf(ch_{B_{i-1}}, r_{A_{i-1}}, r_{B_{i-1}})$$

4.2   Security Properties

We can see that $conf_{A_i}$ might not be equal to $conf_{B_i}$ in every single round since there is a possibility that Alice and Bob's observations of the channel are slightly different. Disagreement in the configuration in the next round may also happen if r_{A_i} or r_{B_i} is not correctly received. When disagreement occurs, both parties will likely not hear from each other. Fortunately, this lack of communication is symmetric, i.e., when Alice does not hear from Bob then Bob also does not hear from Alice. In other words, they detect the error simultaneously. We address this protocol issue with a simple recovery mechanism that lets them retransmit the

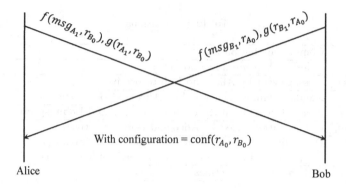

Fig. 1. 1st Round

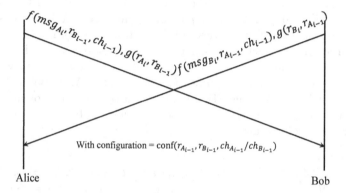

Fig. 2. ith Round

messages using the latest successful configuration. The procedure is shown in Figure 3. We define a complete round, or a complete matching session as one in which two parties could hear from each other and record the new configuration establishment. Note that whether or not the messages are correctly received does not matter. Higher layer retransmission mechanisms would resolve the issue.

In this section, we first show that $conf_{A_i}/conf_{B_i}$ plays the role of a session key. Then, we prove that the protocol meets the SK-security requirement in the CK-framework. It is worth noting that the initial phase of authentication is assumed, but the more detailed treatment of which is out of scope of our paper. This is because, although PHY layer authentication approaches have been defined, this is still an active area of research in terms of robustly tolerating a rich class of attacks. And one can also resort to complementary approaches (i.e. crypto-based) as well. Note that authentication can be used to seed the initial randoms. Alternatively, the initial random numbers may even be distributed publicly without affecting the security of our system since the security of the first round is guaranteed by the authentication procedure and the security of the following rounds

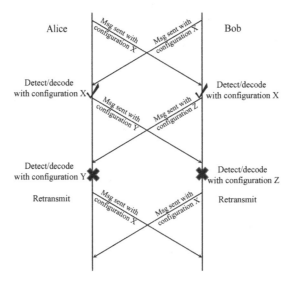

Fig. 3. Retransmission

is guaranteed by PHY layer assumptions and our protocol. And as our protocol allows two communicating parties to agree upon new configurations implicitly without exchanging any key materials, it follows that our protocol is key-free.

Claim. $conf_{A_i}$ and $conf_{B_i}$ represent session keys.

The rationale for this claim is as follows. In each session, the session key determines the way to encode messages in a logical layer. Similarly, $conf_{A_i}/conf_{B_i}$ determine the way to encode the signal corresponding to a link layer packet at the PHY layer. Without knowing the configuration (session key) used by the encoder, the adversary cannot decode the received signals unless it applies a brute-force search.

Claim. Let $|Conf|$ be the size of the configuration space and $|Sk|$ be the session key space. If $|Conf| = |Sk|$, then the hardness of applying brute-force search to decode signals encoded with an unknown configuration is at least equal to decoding bits encoded with an unknown session key.

The rationale for this claim is as follows. If $|Conf| = |Sk|$, then the number of possible ways to decode signals at PHY layer is the same as that to decode bits at logic layer. Assume the transmitted signal is X, the received signals is Y and the digit representation of Y is Z. The three variables form a Markov chain $X \to Y \to Z$. For each try in brute-force search at PHY layer, the decoder needs to deal with Y while a logic-layer brute-force decoder only needs to deal with Z, which is a sufficient statistic of X and less noisy than Y. Although we do not know the appropriate metric to compare the effort made at the PHY layer and the logic layer, it is clear that the former is no less than the latter.

Ignoring the retransmission part, let us write the protocol in the following form, where $E_{conf}(m)$ stands for a PHY layer encryption function which encrypts m with a configuration $conf$:

- **1st round:**
  Alice $\rightarrow$ Bob :
  $E_{conf_{A_1}}(f(msg_{A_1}, r_{B_0}), g(r_{A_1}, r_{B_0}))$, where $conf_{A_1}$ is predefined.
  Bob $\rightarrow$ Alice :
  $E_{conf_{B_1}}(f(msg_{B_1}, r_{A_0}), g(r_{B_1}, r_{A_0}))$, where $conf_{B_1}$ is predefined.
- **ith round $(i \geq 2)$:**
  Alice $\rightarrow$ Bob :
  $E_{conf_{A_i}}(f(msg_{A_i}, r_{B_{i-1}}, ch_{A_{i-1}}), g(r_{A_i}, r_{B_{i-1}}))$

  $$where\ conf_{A_i} = conf(ch_{A_{i-1}}, r_{A_{i-1}}, r_{B_{i-1}})$$

  Bob $\rightarrow$ Alice :
  $E_{conf_{B_i}}(f(msg_{B_i}, r_{A_{i-1}}, ch_{B_{i-1}}), g(r_{B_i}, r_{A_{i-1}}))$

  $$where\ conf_{B_i} = conf(ch_{B_{i-1}}, r_{A_{i-1}}, r_{B_{i-1}})$$

We can see that as long as $conf_{A_i}$ and $conf_{B_i}$ are kept from Eve, Eve could not do anything better than a random guess to detect and decode the signals. In other words, proving the security of the session key $conf_{A_i}/conf_{B_i}$ is sufficient to prove that the communication is protected. In the following part, we analyze the SK-security of the protocol in CK-framework.

SK-security Analysis in the CK-framework. Now we prove that our protocol is robust against attackers in CK model with the following assumption:

Assumption 1. *Eavesdroppers that are at least a half-wavelength away from legitimate users will see uncorrelated channels. As a result, eavesdroppers at this distance cannot successfully guess the secrets derived from the channel between two communicating parties with a non-negligible probability.*

According to the definition of SK-security in the CK-framework, we need to prove that Configuration Hopping satisfies the following two requirements in the presence of the CK-adversary:

Req. 1: If two parties, Alice and Bob, complete matching sessions, then their session keys are the same.
Req. 2: There is no feasible adversary that could succeed in distinguishing the session key of an unexposed session with a non-negligible probability.

Lemma 1. *When Alice and Bob complete the $(i-1)$th round of communication, for $i > 0$, they derive the same configuration for the ith round of communication, i.e., $conf_{A_i} = conf_{B_i}$.*

Proof. In the first round, configuration is predetermined. Therefore,

$$conf_{A_1} = conf_{B_1}.$$

If Alice and Bob complete the $(i-1)$th round, then it means that

$$conf_{A_{i-1}} = conf_{B_{i-1}}.$$

In the next round of exchanging messages, either Alice and Bob could hear from each other, or they could not. In the first case, $conf_{A_i} = conf_{B_i}$. In the second case, they both retransmit using the configuration $conf_{A_i}/conf_{B_i}$, which is equal to $conf_{A_{i-1}}/conf_{B_{i-1}}$. In both the cases, the ith complete round ends in

$$conf_{A_i} = conf_{B_i}.$$

By mathematical induction, we have proved Lemma 1

Lemma 2. *No feasible adversary in CK-model can distinguish the session key of an unexposed session with a non-negligible probability.*

Proof. Let us check what secret information adversaries can obtain by the three types of attacks allowed in CK model:

Consider Eve picks ith session between Alice and Bob as a test session, and assume that she can distinguish a random value from the session key of $(i+1)$th round generated by the test session with a non-negligible probability. With session-key query, she has access to any session keys generated by all the previous ones, including $(i-1)$th session, so the transmission of the ith session is public. It implies that she can obtain r_{A_i} and r_{B_i}. Since the $(i+1)$th session key $conf_{A_{i+1}}$ and $conf_{B_{i+1}}$ are respectively generated by one-way MAC function $conf(ch_{A_i}, r_{A_i}, r_{B_i})$ and $conf(ch_{B_i}, r_{A_i}, r_{B_i})$, Eve must be able to guess ch_{A_i} or ch_{B_i} successfully with a non-negligible probability. This contradicts Assumption 1, therefore the claim is wrong.

Session-state leakage does not help Eve to access secret information. But in half-duplex model, knowing the session state might help Eve to know the exact time point to hijack the communication. For instance, in ith round, if Eve replies to Alice before Bob, with $r_{A_{i-1}}$, $ch_{B_{i-1}}$, and the right configuration obtained by session-key query, then she can impersonate Bob. As Alice and Bob work in full-duplex model, however, Eve cannot inject his own traffic without being exposed.

Corruption query does not help Eve either, since our protocol is pair-wise. No corrupted party would reveal secret information between Alice and Bob to Eve. $\frac{1}{|Conf|}$, where $|Conf|$ is the cardinality of the space of configurations.

Theorem 1. *Configuration Hopping achieves SK-security in the CK-framework.*

Proof. The proof follows directly from Lemma 1, Lemma 2 and the requirements of SK-security in the CK-framework.

Forward Secrecy. In cryptography, forward secrecy requires that a session key derived from a set of long-term keys will not be compromised if one of the long-term keys is compromised in the future. To be more specific, it could be obtained by using new key materials for each session. In our protocol, the key material ch changes when the channel between Alice and Bob changes. So, a compromised key would affect Configuration Hopping only in a bounded time. We call this type of forward secrecy as Bounded-Time Forward Secrecy (BTFS). Fortunately the coherence time in which a channel remains stable is rather short in practical environments. As a result, a leaked key would only affect the system for the rather short time (on the scale of tens or hundreds of milliseconds [15]). Therefore, we have the following claim:

Claim. Configuration Hopping achieves Bounded-Time Forward Secrecy in the presence of the active adversary.

Protection Provided by PHY Layer. PHY layer encryption provides three levels of protection in Configuration Hopping. First, in-band full-duplex prevents the adversary from overhearing the communication. Similar Wyner-style techniques like Dialog Codes [4] have previously evidenced feasibility of protecting decodability for certain classes of adversary. Note that if an eavesdropper is very close to the transmitter, then the protection provided by full-duplex radios vanishes. But that still does not compromise the security of our protocol. Second, PHY layer encryption mechanisms such as changing PN sequences make signal detection hard for eavesdroppers. Third, localization is also made hard since power level and other location-dependent measurements are not predictable. We discuss details regarding choices of PHY layer parameters in Section 5.

4.3 Overhead Comparison

The cost of hop-to-hop secure communication in our protocol consists of two parts: the cost of distributing shared keys, and the cost of encryption in PHY layer. Let us first look at the first part. Since the keys are extracted from the channel information contained in the received signals, no extra messages are needed to share keys beyond normal data transmissions. In contrast, to share keys in traditional cryptography without violating perfect forward secrecy, communicating parties have to exchange new key materials. Therefore, at least two additional messages have to be exchanged for key sharing (cf. Diffie-Hellman key exchange [8]). And about the encryption part, as the configuration hopping idea encrypts signals by hopping among different PHY parameters, little computation is involved. Therefore the computational overhead of our protocol is trivial compared to traditional cryptography.

5   Implementation Feasibility

In this section, we first discuss the architecture of our proposed system, and then discuss the feasibility of adapting different PHY parameters in SDRs. Finally, we propose a configuration hopping scenario which is easy to implement.

5.1 Architecture

Figure 4 shows the implementation architecture. The adaptation control module lies below MAC and higher layers. The module determines at what granularity (symbol, block or packet) the PHY parameters would be adapted. In the next, the PHY parameter control module chooses the PHY parameters according to the adaptation values, which should be agreed upon between the two communicating parties. Then, data are processed at the PHY layer according to the PHY parameters chosen by the control modules. The PHY parameters include standard ones like modulation, error correction coding method, carrier frequency, and TX power control, and others like symbol duration and spreading code.

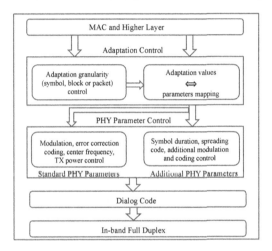

Fig. 4. Fine grain adaptive radio architecture

5.2 Feasibility of PHY Parameter Adaptations

Our previous work, Puzzle [14] shows that extracting secret from wireless channel is feasible. In a 20MHz band, two communicating parties can share a 5-bit secret per coherence interval using Puzzle with a mismatch rate below 5%. With the assumption that the failure of the protocol is caused mainly by the disagreement of the secret extracted from the wireless channel at two communicating ends, the probability of failure of the protocol is below 5%. Experiments also show that the secrets produced by Puzzle are robust against eavesdropping. Sub-packet adaptation of PHY layer parameters is possible according to our preliminary study of different software-defined radios (SDRs) [1, 3]. While adaptations of some PHY layer parameters are straightforward, this is not the case for others.

One type of adaptation is coding. For example, when encoding data, nodes can choose different kinds of modulations and simultaneously change the duration of each symbol. Even within one modulation method, remapping the constellation to different symbols is feasible and easy to implement. If two communicating ends adopt DSSS technique, they can also update the PN code for each symbol. All of these coding layer configuration hopping techniques provide obscurity against eavesdroppers, and in addition, PN sequence hopping makes detection harder for eavesdroppers, too.

Power level is also a choice for configuration adaptation. NI PXIe-1082 [1], an SDR from National Instruments, can easily change transmit gain between 1 and 231. From the perspective of communication, randomly changing power level may not appear at first blush to be reasonable, but from the perspective of security, varying power level can hide the existence and identities of transmitters from eavesdroppers. For instance, with fixed transmission power, it is easy for eavesdroppers to estimate the number of transmitters, and even to tell each captured packet belongs to which transmitter. And, clearly, localization is also harder for attackers.

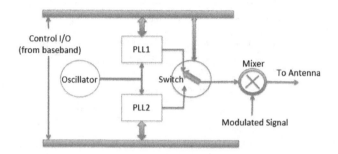

Fig. 5. Sub-Packet Adaptive Center Frequency Circuitry. PLLs can take time to stabilize frequency source output. Provisioning multiple PLLs allows a radio to keep the next frequency ready for the next symbol.

All of the above operations can be done in the digital domain, so they are easy to realize. But adaptations in the (analog) RF domain need more effort. Take frequency adaptation as an example. It is possible to change the frequency in baseband. But, for center frequency variations beyond a certain range, the change needs to be done in RF domain. To be more specific, phase locked loops (PLLs) would lose the lock for a large jump in frequency. So, we need to send control signals from the baseband to tune the PLL circuitry. As the PLLs take time to stabilize, which is typically in the order of several microseconds (comparable to a symbol duration), no data can be transmitted during the switch [6]. In other words, a long switching time will reduce data rate. Therefore, fast FHSS can only be implemented in narrow band with single PLL. We propose a design that has two PLLs to avoid extensive time delays for the PLLs to settle. Figure 5 shows our design. The first PLL is used for the current symbol. Meanwhile, the second PLL is tuned to the frequency to be used for the next symbol. At the end of the current symbol, a switch triggers the connection to the second PLL thus changing the frequency used for the next symbol. Here, the transition time between the PLLs is dictated by the switch. There are commercial switches [2] available that have a transition time in the order of nanoseconds. Note that if the PLL's tuning time is larger than the smallest symbol duration, then more than two PLLs can be tuned in advance and switched in a round-robin fashion. Since the center frequencies for different symbols within a packet are derived from the configuration, these values are available before sending a packet.

5.3   Example: Constellation Hopping

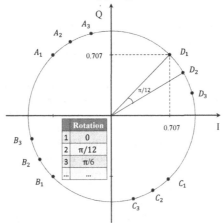

Fig. 6. Constellation is redefined by rotation

Constellation can be redefined by rotating the original constellation for modulation with different angles. In Figure 6, A_1, B_1, C_1 and D_1 represent the four ideal points in a QPSK constellation. By rotating the constellation with $\frac{\pi}{12}$, we get a synonymous constellation with four ideal points A_2, B_2, C_2 and D_2. Continuing this rotation, we can get 24 different constellations for QPSK and then modulation can be done according to the constellation chosen by the adaptation control module. A transmitter can hop among these synonymous constellations and the receiver who knows the rule of the hopping can decode the corresponding packets easily. But an eavesdropper with no information about the chosen constellation needs to collect a large amount of symbols to decide where the ideal points are, since it receives noisy versions of the ideal points. Even with the right ideal points, it still needs to go through all the four possible mappings between the ideal points and the digital data bits.

6   Conclusion

In this paper, we proposed a secure communication protocol that takes advantage of PHY layer operability provided by extant SDRs. We proved the security properties of our link layer protocol and also discussed the protection provided by configuration hopping at the PHY layer. We find that changing configurations with in-band full-duplex prevents eavesdroppers from decoding messages. And moreover, the adaptation that accommodates extant DSSS techniques can provide transmission with low signal to noise ratio (SNR) and therefore make transmission detection correspondingly harder. Frequency hopping also increases the degree of difficulty of detectability against eavesdroppers. In addition, changing transmission gain helps hide the geolocation of a transmission source for those cases where transmissions are detected.

References

1. NI PXIe-1082 user manual, http://www.ni.com/pdf/manuals/372752b.pdf
2. RF-switches, http://www.analog.com/en/switchesmultiplexers/rf-switches
3. USRP N210, https://www.ettus.com/product/details/UN210-KIT
4. Arora, A., Sang, L.: Dialog codes for secure wireless communications. In: Proceedings of the 2009 International Conference on Information Processing in Sensor Networks, IPSN 2009, pp. 13–24. IEEE Computer Society (2009)
5. Azimi-Sadjadi, B., Kiayias, A., Mercado, A., Yener, B.: Robust key generation from signal envelopes in wireless networks. In: Proceedings of the 14th ACM Conference on Computer and Communications Security, CCS 2007 (2007)
6. Best, R.E.: Phase-Locked Loops. Professional Engineering. Mcgraw-hill (2003)
7. Canetti, R., Krawczyk, H.: Analysis of key-exchange protocols and their use for building secure channels. In: Pfitzmann, B. (ed.) EUROCRYPT 2001. LNCS, vol. 2045, pp. 453–474. Springer, Heidelberg (2001)
8. Diffie, W., Hellman, M.E.: New directions in cryptography. IEEE Transactions on Information Theory 22(6), 644–654 (1976)
9. Jain, M., Choi Il, J., Kim, T., Bharadia, D., Seth, S., Srinivasan, K., Levis, P., Katti, S., Sinha, P.: Practical, real-time, full duplex wireless. In: Proceedings of the 17th Annual International Conference on Mobile Computing and Networking, MobiCom 2011 (2011)
10. Katz, J., Lindell, Y.: Introduction to Modern Cryptography (Chapman & Hall/Crc Cryptography and Network Security Series). Chapman & Hall/CRC (2007)
11. Madiseh, M.G., McGuire, M.L., Neville, S.S., Cai, L., Horie, M.: Secret key generation and agreement in UWB communication channels. In: Proceedings of the Global Communications Conference, GLOBECOM 2008, pp. 1842–1846. IEEE (2008)
12. Mathur, S., Trappe, W., Mandayam, N., Ye, C., Reznik, A.: Radio-telepathy: extracting a secret key from an unauthenticated wireless channel. In: Proceedings of the 14th ACM International Conference on Mobile Computing and Networking, MobiCom 2008 (2008)
13. Patwari, N., Croft, J., Jana, S., Kasera, S.K.: High-rate uncorrelated bit extraction for shared secret key generation from channel measurements. IEEE Transactions on Mobile Computing 9(1), 17–30 (2010)
14. Qiao, Y., Srinivasan, K., Arora, A.: Shape matters, not the size: A new approach to extract secrets from channel. In: The Proccedings of the First ACM Workshop on Hot Topics in Wireless, HotWireless 2014 (2014)
15. Rappaport, T.: Wireless Communications: Principles and Practice, 2nd edn. Prentice Hall PTR (2001)

Dependable Decentralized Cooperation
with the Help of Reliability Estimation*

Seda Davtyan[1], Kishori M. Konwar[2], and Alexander A. Shvartsman[1]

[1] Department of Computer Science & Engineering, University of Connecticut,
Storrs CT 06269, USA
{seda,aas}@engr.uconn.edu
[2] University of British Columbia, Vancouver BC V6T 1Z3, Canada
kishori@mail.ubc.ca

Abstract. Internet supercomputing aims to solve large partitionable computational problems by using vast numbers of computers. Here we consider the abstract version of the problem, where n processors perform t independent tasks, with $n \leq t$, and each processor learns the results of all tasks. An adversary may cause a processor to return incorrect results, and to crash. Prior solutions limited the adversary by either (i) assuming the average probability of returning incorrect results to always be inferior to $\frac{1}{2}$, or (ii) letting each processor know such probabilities for all other processors. This paper presents a new randomized synchronous algorithm that deals with stronger adversaries while achieving efficiency comparable to the weaker solutions. The adversary is constrained in two ways. (1) The set of non-crashed processors must contain a *hardened* subset H of the initial set of processors P, for which the *average* probability of returning a bogus result is inferior to $\frac{1}{2}$. Notably, crashes may *increase* the average probability of processor misbehavior. (2) The adversary may crash a set of processors F, provided $|P - F|$ is bounded from below. We analyse the algorithm for three bounds on $|P - F|$: (a) when the bound is linear in n the algorithm takes $\Theta(\frac{t}{n} \log n)$ communication rounds, has work complexity $\Theta(t \log n)$, and message complexity $O(n \log^2 n)$; (b) when the bound is polynomial ($|P - F| = \Omega(n^a)$, for a constant $a \in (0, 1)$), the algorithm takes $O(\frac{t}{n^a} \log n \log \log n)$ rounds, with work $O(t \log n \log \log n)$, and message complexity $O(n \log^2 n \log \log n)$; ($c$) when the bound is polylog in n, it takes $O(t)$ rounds, has work $O(t \cdot n^a)$, and message complexity $O(n^{1+a})$, for $a \in (0, 1)$.

1 Introduction

Cooperative network supercomputing is becoming increasingly popular for harnessing the power of the global Internet computing platform. A typical Internet supercomputer, e.g., [1,2], consists of a master computer and a large number of computers called workers, performing computation on behalf of the master. Despite the simplicity and benefits of a single master approach, as the scale of such computing environments grows, it becomes unrealistic to assume the existence of the infallible master that is able to coordinate the activities of multitudes of

---

* This work is supported in part by the NSF award 1017232.

P. Felber and V. Garg (Eds.): SSS 2014, LNCS 8756, pp. 283–298, 2014.

workers. Large-scale distributed systems are inherently dynamic and are subject to perturbations, such as failures of computers and network links, thus it is also necessary to consider fully distributed peer-to-peer solutions.

One could address the single point of failure issue by providing redundant multiple masters, yet this would remain a centralized scheme that is not suitable for big data processing that involves a large amount of input and output data. For example, consider applications in molecular biology that require large reference databases of gene models or annotated protein sequences, and large sets of unknown protein sequences [11]. Dealing with such voluminous data requires a large scale platform providing the necessary computational power and storage. Therefore, a more scalable approach is to use a decentralized system, where the input is distributed and, once the processing is complete, the output is distributed across multiple nodes.

Interestingly, computers returning bogus results is a phenomenon of increasing concern. While this may occur unintentionally, e.g., as a result of over-clocked processors, workers may in fact wrongly claim to have performed assigned work so as to obtain incentives associated with the system, e.g., higher rank. To address this problem we introduced a decentralized approach [6,4]. Here, our synchronous algorithms perform all tasks correctly with high probability (*whp*), while dealing with misbehaving processors under a strong assumption that the average probability of returning incorrect results remains inferior to $\frac{1}{2}$. Thus the adversary is severely limited in its ability to crash processors that normally return correct results. We also considered a linearly-bounded model [7], where the average probability of returning bogus results can become greater than $\frac{1}{2}$. However, a strong assumption is made that each processor knows the probability of misbehavior for *all* processors. We addressed this assumption by developing an algorithm that computes an (ϵ, δ)-approximation of such probabilities [5].

Here we present a decentralized algorithm that deals with much stronger types of adversaries, where the adversary causes failure patterns that may *increase* the average probability of processors returning bogus results above $\frac{1}{2}$.

Contributions. We consider the problem of performing t tasks in a distributed system of n workers *without* centralized control. The tasks are independent, and any task can be performed by one or more workers in constant time. The point-to-point message-passing system is synchronous and reliable. The failure model allows crash-prone workers to return incorrect results. Initially, the average probability of worker misbehavior is inferior to $\frac{1}{2}$, however crashes can increase this probability. We present a randomized algorithm and analyze it for three adversaries of increasing strength. Here all surviving processors may return bogus results with unconstrained probabilities, except that in each execution there is a "hardened" subset of surviving processors that are likely to return correct results. In more detail our contributions are as follows.

1. We define the following failure model. Given the initial set of processors P, with $|P| = n$, and the initial average probability of worker misbehavior being inferior to $\frac{1}{2}$, we begin to constrain the adversary in one of three ways with respect to the set F of processors that may crash: *a*) The adversary is constrained by a linear fraction, where $|P - F| \geq cn$, with a constant $c \in (0, 1)$ (as in [6]);

b) the adversary is constrained by a fractional polynomial, where $|P - F| = \Omega(n^a)$, for a constant $a \in (0,1)$; and *c)* the adversary is constrained by a poly-log, where $|P - F| = \Omega(\log^c n)$, for a constant $c \geq 1$ (as in [4]). Additionally, the adversary may assign an arbitrary constant probability $p_i < 1$ to each processor $i \in P$ of returning an incorrect result, except that in each execution there exists some, unknown to the algorithm, *hardened subset H* of remaining survivors, where $H \subseteq P - F$, with $|H| \geq h|P - F|$ for some constant $h \in (0,1)$, such that processors in H return bogus results with the *average* probability inferior to $\frac{1}{2}$.

2. We provide a randomized algorithm that works in synchronous rounds and consists of two phases. In the *estimation* phase, the probabilities of each processor computing the result of a task incorrectly is estimated as in [5]. Our presentation concentrates on the *computation* phase. Here processors perform tasks and share their knowledge until the termination conditions are satisfied. Since for live processors the average probability of misbehavior can become *greater* than $1/2$, the challenge is to determine for each task the set of processors whose results will contribute to the calculation of the final result. Doing so efficiently and correctly is a major departure from prior work. We formulate a new method that chooses a correct subset of processors that satisfy the needed constraints.

3. We analyze the algorithm for each adversarial constraint and show that workers obtain the correct results of all tasks *whp* (with high probability). We show that the time complexity R (in terms of rounds), work complexity W, and message complexity M hold *whp* as follows. **a)** For the linearly constrained model: $R = \Theta(\frac{t}{n} \log n)$, $W = \Theta(t \log n)$, and $M = O(n \log^2 n)$. **b)** For the polynomially constrained model we have: $R = O(\frac{t}{n^a} \log n \log \log n)$, $W = O(t \log n \log \log n)$, and $M = O(n \log^2 n \log \log n)$. **c)** For the poly-log constrained model: $R = O(t)$, $W = O(t \cdot n^a)$, and $M = O(n^{1+a})$, where $a \in (0,1)$. **Prior work.** Earlier approaches explored ways of improving the quality of the results obtained from untrusted workers in the settings where a bandwidth-unlimited and infallible master is coordinating the workers. Fernandez et al. [9,8] and Konwar et al. [12] designed algorithms that help the master determine correct results *whp*, while minimizing work. The failure models assume that some fraction of processors exhibits faulty behavior. Recent work by Christoforou et al. [3] pursues a game-theoretic approach. Paquette and Pelc [13] study fault-prone systems where a decision has to be made on the basis of unreliable information and design a deterministic strategy for deciding correctly *whp*.

Our prior work [6,4] introduced the decentralized approach and provided synchronous algorithms for the problem under a strong assumption that the average probability of non-crashed processors returning incorrect results remains inferior to $\frac{1}{2}$. We addressed this assumption by developing a decentralized algorithm that estimates such probabilities [5] using an (ϵ, δ)-approximation, for $0 < \epsilon < 1$ and $\delta > 0$, that estimates the mean of a random variable.

A related problem, called Do-All [10], also deals with cooperative execution of tasks, but the processors need not learn the results of the computation.

Document Structure. Section 2 states models and definitions. Section 3 presents our algorithm; its analysis is in Section 4. We conclude in Section 5.

2   Model of Computation and Definitions

We deal with a system, where a collection of not-entirely-dependable processors cooperatively perform a large number of computation-intensive tasks.

System Model. There are n processors, each with a unique identifier (id) from set $P = [n]$. We refer to the processor with id i as processor i. The fully-connected message-passing system is synchronous and point-to-point reliable. However, we do not assume that broadcast is reliable, i.e., if a processor that sends a message to multiple destinations crashes, then the message may be delivered only to an arbitrary subset of destinations. Computation is structured in terms of *rounds*. The duration of each round is sufficient for a processor to (1) send messages, (2) receive messages, and (3) perform one task and some local computation, where the local computation time is assumed to be negligible compared to message latency and the time required to perform the task. Messages sent at the beginning of a round are received before the end of the same round.

Tasks. There are t tasks to be performed, each with a unique id from set $T = [t]$. We assume that tasks can be obtained from some repository. We refer to the task with id j as task j. The tasks are (1) similar, meaning that any task can be done in constant (possibly large) time by any processor, (2) independent, meaning that each task can be performed independently, and (3) idempotent, meaning that the tasks admit at-least-once semantics and can be performed concurrently. The problem is most interesting when there are at least as many tasks as there are processors, thus we consider $t \geq n$.

Models of Adversity. Processors misbehave in two ways: (1) processors may crash, and (2) processors may return incorrect results for tasks. (Clearly the failure model is weaker than the byzantine model.) Once crashed, a processor performs no further actions. We refer to non-crashed processors as *live*. The adversary is oblivious in that it decides prior to the computation what processors to crash and when. For an execution of an algorithm, we let F be the set of processors that crash. The maximum number of processors that can crash is established by three specific adversarial models.

Model $\mathcal{F}_{\ell f}$: The adversary is constrained by a *linear fraction* of the number of processors: $|P - F| \geq cn$, where $c \in (0, 1)$.

Model $\mathcal{F}_{fp}$: The adversary is constrained by a *fractional polynomial*: $|P - F| = \Omega(n^a)$, for a constant $a \in (0, 1)$.

Model $\mathcal{F}_{pl}$: The adversary is constrained by a *poly-logarithm*: $|P - F| = \Omega(\log^c n)$, for a constant $c \geq 1$.

For each processor $i \in P$, we define p_i to be the probability of processor i returning incorrect results, independently of other processors. Initially the average probability of processors in P returning incorrect results is inferior to $\frac{1}{2}$, i.e., $\frac{1}{|P|} \sum_{i \in P} p_i < \frac{1}{2} - \zeta$, for a certain small $\zeta > 0$, ensuring that this average probability does not become arbitrarily close to $\frac{1}{2}$ as n tends to infinity. We define a subset H of processors to be a *hardened set* if $H \subseteq P - F$, i.e., no processors in H crash, and $|H| \geq h|P - F|$ for some constant $h \in (0, 1)$, and $\frac{1}{|H|} \sum_{i \in H} p_i < \frac{1}{2} - \zeta$. Neither the existence of set H, not its cardinality are known to any processor.

We choose ζ to be some multiple of Δ, where Δ, the chosen precision, is at least the smallest floating point number supported across all nodes. (Any $\zeta > 0$ works for proving correctness, and assessing work, rounds, and message complexities. The choice of Δ affects only the local computation as will be made clear in the analysis.) For simplicity, in the remainder of the paper we assume $\zeta = \Delta$.

We note that while the average probability of returning incorrect results for processors in a hardened set is inferior to $\frac{1}{2}$, the overall average probability of all non-crashed processors returning result incorrectly can be *greater* than $\frac{1}{2}$.

Measures of Efficiency. We evaluate algorithms using three measures of efficiency: *communication rounds, work,* and *message complexity*. *Communication rounds* measure assesses the worst case number of rounds executed by an algorithm. *Work complexity* accounts for the total number of tasks (counting multiplicities) performed by the algorithm. We assess *message complexity* as the number of point-to-point messages sent during an execution. Lastly, we use the common definition of *an event $\mathcal{E}$ occurring with high probability (whp)* to mean that $\mathbf{Pr}[\mathcal{E}] = 1 - O(n^{-\alpha})$ for some constant $\alpha > 0$.

3   Algorithm Description

We now present algorithm DARE (for Decentralized Algorithm with Reliability Estimation). We first detail the algorithm for n processors and $t = n$ tasks, then we generalize it for t tasks, where $t \geq n$. Algorithm DARE is given in Figure 1.

The algorithm consists of two phases: *estimation* and *computation*. In the *estimation* phase, processors estimate the probabilities of computing the result of a task correctly for all processors. This phase begins by executing algorithm A_{est} of [5], then each processor i calculates the estimates of probabilities of computing results incorrectly and stores these probabilities in the array $E_i[\ ]$. If it is detected that processor j crashed, then this is recorded by setting $E_i[j]$ to -1.

The *computation* phase is the focus of our presentation. The main data structure at each processor is an array of size linear in n used to accumulate knowledge gathered by the processors. The phase is structured as a loop. Each processor starts as a *worker*, and in each iteration, it performs one randomly selected task and sends its knowledge to one randomly selected processor. When a worker obtains "enough" knowledge about the tasks, it computes the final results, and becomes enlightened. Such processors "profess" their knowledge to other processors by means of multicasts to exponentially increasing random sets of processors. The loop terminates when a certain number of messages is received from enlightened processors. We now detail the algorithm.

Local Knowledge and State Variables. Every processor i maintains the following information. Array of results $R_i[1..t]$, where element $R_i[j]$, for $j \in T$, is a set of results for $Task[j]$. Each $R_i[j]$ is a set of triples $\langle v, k, r \rangle$ representing the result v computed for $Task[j]$ by processor k in round r (this ensures that results computed by processor k in different rounds are included). Array $Results_i[1..t]$ stores the final results. Array $E_i[1..n]$ stores the estimates of probabilities p_j, rounded to the numerical precision Δ for each $j \in P$. If a crash of processor j is

Procedure for processor i;
   external n, t, k_m, k_t /* n processors and t tasks; k_m, k_t are constants */
   $Task[1..t]$ /* set of tasks */
   $E_i[1..n]$ **init** $\perp$ /* estimates of p_j for each $j \in P$ */
   $R_i[1..t]$ **init** $\emptyset^n$ /* set of collected results */
   $Results_i[1..t]$ **init** $\perp$ /* array of results */
   $prof\_ctr$ **init** 0 /* number of **profess** messages received */
   r **init** 0 /* round number */
   ℓ **init** 0 /* number of **profess** messages to send */
   worker init true /* initially each processor is a worker */

ESTIMATION PHASE

   Use procedure A_{est} [5] to compute $Estimate_i[1..n]$
   /* $Estimate_i[q]$ = **if** q crashes **then** -1 **else** (ϵ, δ)-approximation of $1 - p_q$ */
   for each $j \in P$ **do** /* Prob. of computing incorrectly */
      $E_i[j] \leftarrow$ **if** $Estimate_i[j] \neq -1$ **then** $1 - Estimate_i[j]$ **else** -1
      /* Here $E_i[j]$ is rounded to the numerical precision Δ */

COMPUTATION PHASE

   while $prof\_ctr < k_m \log n$ **do**
      Send:
1:      **if** worker **then**
2:         Let q be a randomly selected processor from P
3:         Send $\langle$share, $R_i[\ ]\rangle$ to processor q
4:      **else**
5:         Let D be a set of $2^\ell \log n$ randomly selected processors from P
6:         Send $\langle$profess, $R_i[\ ]\rangle$ to processors in D
7:         $\ell \leftarrow \ell + 1$
      Receive:
8:      Let M be the set of received messages
9:      $prof_ctr \leftarrow prof_ctr + |\{m : m \in M \wedge m.type = $ profess$\}|$ /* count msgs */
10:     **for all** $j \in T$ **do** /* update knowledge */
11:        $R_i[j] \leftarrow R_i[j] \cup (\bigcup_{m \in M} m.R[j])$
      Compute:
12:     $r \leftarrow r + 1$
13:     **if** worker **then**
14:        Randomly select $j \in T$ and compute the result v_j for $Task[j]$
15:        $R_i[j] \leftarrow R_i[j] \cup \{\langle v_j, i, r\rangle\}$
16:        **for all** $j \in T$ **do**
17:           Let $Q = \{s : \langle \_, s, \_\rangle \in R_i[j]\}$
18:           $S \leftarrow$ SELECT$(Q, R_i[j], E_i[\ ], 2\zeta)$
19:           Let $K_j = \{\langle v, s, q\rangle : \langle v, s, q\rangle \in R_i[j] \wedge s \in S\}$
20:        **if** $\min_{j \in T}\{|K_j|\} \geq k_t \log n$ **then** /* sufficient results for all tasks */
21:           **for all** $j \in T$ **do**
22:              $Results_i[j] \leftarrow u$ such that triples $\langle u, \_, \_\rangle$ form a plurality in K_j
23:           worker $\leftarrow$ false /* worker is enlightened */
  end.

Fig. 1. Algorithm DARE for $t = n$ at processor i for $i \in P$

detected, $E_i[j]$ is set to -1. The $prof\_ctr$ stores the number of messages received from enlightened processors. Variable r is the round (iteration) number that is used by *workers* to timestamp the computed results. Variable ℓ is the exponent that controls the number of messages multicast by enlightened processors.

Control Flow. The *computation* phase consists of the main while-loop, where each *iteration* consists of three stages, viz., *Send, Receive,* and *Compute.* Processors communicate by means of messages m that contain pairs $\langle type, R[\ ]\rangle$. Here $m.R[\ ]$ is the sender's array of results. When a processor is a worker, it sends messages with $m.type = $ share. When a processor becomes enlightened, it sends messages with $m.type = $ profess. The loop is controlled by counter *prof_ctr* that records the number of received profess messages. (In Section 4 we reason about the compile-time constant k_m, and establish that $k_m \log n$ profess messages are sufficient for our claims.) We next detail the stages.

Send **stage:** Any *worker* chooses a target processor q at random and sends it the array of results $R[\ ]$ in a share message. Any enlightened processor chooses a set $D \subseteq P$ of processors at random and sends them the array of results $R[\ ]$ in a profess message. The size of the set D is $2^\ell \log n$, where initially $\ell = 0$, and ℓ is incremented by 1 in every round.

Receive **Stage:** Processor i receives messages (if any) sent to it in the preceding *Send* stage. The processor increments its *prof_ctr* by the number of profess messages received. For each task j, the processor updates its $R_i[j]$ by including the results received in all messages.

Compute **Stage:** Any worker randomly selects task j, computes the result v_j, and adds the triple $\langle v_j, i, r\rangle$ for round r to $R_i[j]$. For each task the worker computes the set of results received from the processors chosen in procedure SELECT (discussed below). Once at least $k_t \log n$ results for each task are obtained, the worker stores the final results in $Results_i[\ ]$ by taking the plurality of results for each task, and becomes enlightened. (In Section 4 we reason about the compile-time constant k_t, and establish that $k_t \log n$ results are sufficient for our claims.) Enlightened processors rest in subsequent *Compute* stages.

Procedure SELECT in Figure 2 is called in line 18 of algorithm DARE. Recall that we *do not* require the average probability of returning bogus results to be inferior to $\frac{1}{2}$ (in contrast with [4,6]). Hence, the challenge for each worker is to find, for each task, a "good" subset S of processors, whose set of computed results can be used to determine the final result for the task. As will be shown in the analysis, the selected subset S is such that: 1) each $s \in S$ has computed a result for task j, and 2) S is the maximal subset of P such that *whp* $\frac{1}{|S|}\sum_{s \in S} p_s < \frac{1}{2} - \zeta$, where $\{p_s\}$ is the probability of processors s returning bogus results.

Procedure SELECT$(Q, Z, E[\ ], \eta)$
    S_1, S_2 **init** $\emptyset$ /* *subsets of selected processors* */
1:   $S_1 \leftarrow \{s \mid s \in Q \wedge E[s] \leq \frac{1}{2} - \eta\}$
2:   $Q' \leftarrow Q \setminus S_1$
3:   Let $\ell = |Q'|$ and $\langle s_1, ..., s_\ell\rangle$ be some ordering of $s_k \in Q'$
4:   Let $\mathbf{w} = \langle E[s_1] - \frac{1}{2} + \eta, \ldots, E[s_\ell] - \frac{1}{2} + \eta\rangle$ /* *the weight vector for $s_k \in Q'$* */
5:   Let $\mathbf{v} = \langle \lambda_1, \cdots, \lambda_\ell\rangle$, where $\lambda_k = |\{\tau \mid \tau = \langle \_, s_k, \_\rangle \in Z\}|$
        /* *λ_k is the number of results in Z calculated by processor $s_k \in Q'$* */
6:   $W \leftarrow \sum_{s \in S_1}(\frac{1}{2} - \eta - E[s])$
7:   $S_2 \leftarrow$ BINARYKNAPSACK$(\mathbf{v}, \mathbf{w}, W)$
8:   **return** $S_1 \cup S_2$

Fig. 2. SELECT returns $S = S_1 \cup S_2 \subseteq P$ s.t. $\frac{1}{|S|}\sum_{s \in S} p_s < \frac{1}{2} - \eta$.

Algorithm SELECT returns the set of processors that satisfies the constraint on the average probability, and also the set of results computed by the selected processors is the maximal. Note that simply taking the maximum subset of results is not enough since we want the average probability of the processors erring to be inferior to $\frac{1}{2}$. Therefore, for any task, we achieve our goal of computing the final result correctly *whp*, and at the same time with as few tasks as possible. Note that in order to provide the *whp* guarantee we need the average probability constraint, and for probability amplification process (by taking the majority) we need the number of results to be on the order of $\log n$. In order to to be able to decide on the final result for a task we search such a set of results using SELECT. We accomplish this with the help of a solution to the 0-1 Knapsack problem as we detail in the next section. Once a sufficient number of results is obtained, SELECT returns a set of processors that satisfy our model constraint.

Additional Implementation Detail. It is possible for processors to exit the *estimation* phase and enter the *computation* phase at different times. The durations of all rounds are identical, thus the actions of processors within rounds are synchronized. We assume that processors ignore "out of phase" messages, but we do not explicitly model this to avoid clutter. This is easily done by including a phase indicator in each message, so that "out of phase" messages are ignored.

Extension for $t \geq n$. We now modify the algorithm to handle any t tasks, where $t \geq n$. We segment the t tasks into chunks of $\lceil t/n \rceil$ tasks, and construct a new array of chunk-tasks with identifiers in $[n]$, and so each chunk-task can be performed in $\Theta(t/n)$ time by any processor. We now use algorithm DARE, where the only difference is that each *Compute* stage is extended by $\Theta(t/n)$ rounds to perform a chunk-task (no communication is carried out during these rounds).

4 Complexity Analysis

We analyze algorithm DARE in our three failure models. In each we first carry out the analysis for n tasks, then extend the results for $t \geq n$ tasks.

The *estimation* phase is based on algorithm A_{est} [5], where we showed that for the given $\delta > 0$ and $\epsilon > 0$ chosen by the user, algorithm A_{est} obtains estimates $\tilde{q}_i$ that obey the following bound: $\mathbf{Pr}[q_i(1 - \epsilon) \leq \tilde{q}_i \leq q_i(1 + \epsilon)] > 1 - \delta$, where $q_i = 1 - p_i$ is the probability of worker i returning correct result. The analysis of algorithm A_{est} is given in [5] (Theorems 2, 3, and 4). These results translate to the *estimation* phase of algorithm DARE as summarized in Theorem 1.

Theorem 1. *Algorithm A_{est} computes for every processor $i \in P - F$ an (ϵ, δ)-approximation of $q_i = 1 - p_i$, for given $\epsilon, \delta > 0$, within the following bounds:.*
• *Model $\mathcal{F}_{cf}$: Time $T(n) = O(\log n)$, work $W(n) = O(n \log n)$, and message complexity $M(n) = O(n \log^2 n)$;* • *Model $\mathcal{F}_{fp}$: $T(n) = O(n^{1-a} \log n \log \log n)$, $W(n) = O(n \log n \log \log n)$, and $M(n) = O(n \log^2 n \log \log n)$;* • *Model $\mathcal{F}_{pl}$: $T(n) = O(n)$, $W(n) = O(n^{1+a})$, $M(n) = O(n^{1+a})$.*

We proceed to analyze the *computation* phase. The heart of the analysis rests in the properties of procedure SELECT. The first lemma shows that, for any task,

SELECT returns a subset S of processors such that the average probability of processors in S erring is inferior to $\frac{1}{2}$, and that the set of results computed for the task by processors in such S is the largest among all subsets of P that satisfy the above constraint. In the sequel, for each $s \in P$, we let $\tilde{p}_s$ stand for the value of $E[s]$, the probability approximation computed in the *estimation* phase.

Lemma 1. *If processor i invokes* SELECT$(Q, Z = R_i[j], E[\ ] = E_i[\ ], \eta = 2\zeta)$, *then it returns set $S \subseteq Q$, such that, $\frac{1}{|S|} \sum_{s \in S} \tilde{p}_s \leq \frac{1}{2} - 2\zeta$, where $\tilde{p}_s$ is the value of $E[s]$. Additionally, the subset of results from Z, computed by the processors in S, is maximal among all subsets $X \subseteq Q$, such that $\frac{1}{|X|} \sum_{s \in X} \tilde{p}_s \leq \frac{1}{2} - 2\zeta$.*

Proof. SELECT defines λ_s in line 5 as the number of results from Z computed by a processor $s \in Q$ for task j. The procedure is invoked with $\eta = 2\zeta$. With these we have the following optimization problem.
$$\max_{S \subseteq Q} \sum_{s \in S} \lambda_s \text{ such that } \frac{1}{|S|} \sum_{i \in S} \tilde{p}_i \leq \frac{1}{2} - 2\zeta = \frac{1}{2} - \eta$$
Here $\sum_{s \in S} \lambda_s$ is the number of results in Z, computed by processors in S. This problem can be written as
$$\max_{S \subseteq Q} \sum_{s \in S} \lambda_s \text{ such that } \sum_{s \in S}(\tilde{p}_s - \frac{1}{2} + \eta) \leq 0 .$$
We partition set Q into sets $S^- = \{s : s \in S \text{ and } \tilde{p}_s - \frac{1}{2} + \eta \leq 0\}$ and $S^+ = \{s : s \in S \text{ and } \tilde{p}_s - \frac{1}{2} + \eta > 0\}$, where S^- and S^+ correspond to S_1 and S_2 in Figure 2, respectively. Any optimal solution S^* to this problem must include S^-, i.e., $S^- \subseteq S^*$. To see this, suppose there exists a processor $s' \in S^-$ such that $s' \notin S^*$. Since s' is in S^- we have, by definition, $\tilde{p}_{s'} - \frac{1}{2} + \eta \leq 0$. We can create a new solution $X = S^* \cup \{s'\}$. Note that $\lambda_{s'}$ is positive, since there is at least one result computed for task j by every $s \in Q$. Hence, we have $\sum_{s \in X} \lambda_s > \sum_{s \in S^*} \lambda_s$ and X also satisfies the constraint $\sum_{s \in X}(\tilde{p}_s - \frac{1}{2} + \eta) \leq 0$. Therefore, X contains more results from Z than the solution S^*, a contradiction. Hence $S^- \subseteq S^*$.

Line 1 of SELECT gives S^- as it is a part of any optimal solution as argued above. What remains is to select processors from S^+ such that the average probability constraint is satisfied and the number of results computed by the selected processors is the largest. Notice, that the sets of results, for task j, in Z computed by any two distinct processors are disjoint. We select the processors from S^+ as a solution to the next optimization problem
$$\sum_{s \in S^-} \lambda_s + \max_{S \subseteq S^+} \sum_{s \in S} \lambda_s \text{ such that } \sum_{s \in S \cup S^-}(\tilde{p}_s - \frac{1}{2} + \eta) \leq 0$$
that can be written as
$$\sum_{s \in S^-} \lambda_s + \max_{S \subseteq S^+} \sum_{s \in S} \lambda_s \text{ such that } \sum_{s \in S}(\tilde{p}_s - \frac{1}{2} + \eta) \leq \sum_{s \in S^-}(\frac{1}{2} - \eta - \tilde{p}_s).$$
By letting W stand for $\sum_{s \in S^-}(\frac{1}{2} - \eta - \tilde{p}_s)$ and noting that $W > 0$, we have
$$\sum_{s \in S^-} \lambda_s + \max_{S \subseteq S^+} \sum_{s \in S} \lambda_s \text{ such that } \sum_{s \in S}(\tilde{p}_s - \frac{1}{2} + \eta) \leq W.$$
Therefore, we would like to find the subset S of S^+, that solves the following optimization problem.
$$\max_{S \subseteq S^+} \sum_{s \in S} \lambda_s \text{ such that } \sum_{s \in S}(\tilde{p}_s - \frac{1}{2} + \eta) \leq W \tag{1}$$

This is an instance of 0-1 Knapsack problem, where, as defined in lines 4 to 6 of procedure SELECT, $\mathbf{v} = \{\lambda_s\}_{s \in S^+}$ are the values of the items, $\mathbf{w} = \{(\tilde{p}_s - \frac{1}{2} + \eta)\}_{s \in S^+}$ are the set of weights of the items, and W is the capacity of the knapsack. (Although the Knapsack optimization problem is NP-hard, we show in Lemma 2 that it takes polylogarithmic time to solve our instance.) In SELECT the solution to the Knapsack problem is computed in line 7, and the resulting solution, set S_2, is included in the returned set in line 8.   □

We next reason that *whp* procedure SELECT takes local polylogarithmic time to terminate for each task, thus each processor does not expend more than the polynomial local computation time alloted to it by our model.

Lemma 2. *Any invocation of* SELECT *with the results parameter* Z, *such that* $|Z| = O(\log n \cdot \log \log n)$, *returns in local polylogarithmic time for each task whp.*

We next show that the needed maximal set S returned by SELECT satisfies the constraint on the average probability, *whp*. Note that satisfying the average probability constraint by the estimated values $\tilde{p}_i$ does not automatically imply that the constraint is satisfied for the actual probabilities p_i, $i \in P$.

Lemma 1 shows that the estimates $\tilde{p}_s$ satisfy $\frac{1}{|S|}\sum_{s \in S}\tilde{p}_s \leq \frac{1}{2} - 2\zeta$. The following lemma shows that this implies that the actual probabilities p_s, satisfy the condition, $\frac{1}{|S|}\sum_{i \in S}p_s \leq \frac{1}{2} - \zeta$, *whp* (note the ζ vs. 2ζ difference).

Lemma 3. *The subset* S *returned by* SELECT *for any task* j, *satisfies* $\frac{1}{|S|}\sum_{s \in S}p_i \leq \frac{1}{2} - \zeta$, *whp*.

Proof. The *estimation* phase computes $\tilde{p}_s$, the probability of processor s returning bogus results, as $1 - \tilde{q}_s$, where $\tilde{q}_s$ is the estimate of the probability of s returning correct results as computed by A_{est} [5]. As follows from the analysis in [5], each estimation $\tilde{q}_s$ satisfies $\mathbf{Pr}[q_s(1 - \epsilon) \leq \tilde{q}_s \leq q_s(1 + \epsilon)] > 1 - \delta$, for any chosen constant $\epsilon > 0$, and some $\delta > 0$. Moreover, it is shown that by picking $\delta = \frac{1}{n^\alpha}$, for some $\alpha > 1$ we have $q_s(1 - \epsilon) \leq \tilde{q}_s \leq q_s(1 + \epsilon)$ *whp*, conversely, we have $p_s(1 - \epsilon) \leq \tilde{p}_s \leq p_s(1 + \epsilon)$ *whp*.

We know that for $s \in S$, we have $\mathbf{Pr}\left(p_s(1 - \epsilon) \leq \tilde{p}_s \leq p_s(1 + \epsilon)\right) > 1 - \frac{1}{n^\alpha}$, for $\alpha > 1$. Let us denote by $\mathcal{E}_s$ the event $\{\tilde{p}_s \geq p_s(1 - \epsilon)\}$ and let us denote by $\bar{\mathcal{E}}_s$ the complement of that event. It follows from above that, $\mathbf{Pr}[\bar{\mathcal{E}}_s] \leq \frac{1}{n^\alpha}$, for $\alpha > 1$. Now, by Boole's inequality we have $\mathbf{Pr}[\cup_s\bar{\mathcal{E}}_s] \leq \sum_s \mathbf{Pr}[\bar{\mathcal{E}}_s] \leq \frac{1}{n^\beta}$, where $\beta = \alpha - 1 > 0$, hence $\mathbf{Pr}[\cap_s\mathcal{E}_s] = \mathbf{Pr}[\overline{\cup_s\bar{\mathcal{E}}_s}] = 1 - \mathbf{Pr}[\cup_s\bar{\mathcal{E}}_s] \geq 1 - \frac{1}{n^\beta}$.

Given that $\cap_s\mathcal{E}_s = \bigcap_{s \in S}\{p_s(1 - \epsilon) \leq \tilde{p}_s\}$, it follows that $\sum_{s \in S}p_s(1 - \epsilon) \leq \sum_{s \in S}\tilde{p}_s \leq |S|(\frac{1}{2} - 2\zeta)$, where the second inequality comes from the properties of the set S as returned by SELECT and the result of Lemma 1. Therefore, we have $\frac{1}{|S|}\sum_{s \in S}p_s \leq \left(\frac{1}{2} - 2\zeta\right)(1 - \epsilon)^{-1} \leq \left(\frac{1}{2} - 2\zeta\right)(1 + O(\epsilon)) \leq \left(\frac{1}{2} - \zeta\right)$, for sufficiently small constant $\epsilon > 0$, *whp*, because $\mathbf{Pr}[\cap_s\mathcal{E}_s] \geq 1 - \frac{1}{n^\beta}$.   □

Remark: The choice of the precision Δ affects only the local time of procedure SELECT, but does not affect the correctness (*whp*) of the algorithm. This is because we call SELECT with 2ζ (*i.e.*, 2Δ) as the value of the fourth parameter, resulting in a more stringent constraint on probabilities than ζ. The choice of Δ is completely immaterial in the analysis of the rounds and message complexities.

Next we analyze the performance of the *computation* phase. The complete analysis of the performance is then obtained by adding the relevant complexities of the two phases. Note that it is possible for processors to enter the *computation* phase in different rounds. However, all processors enter the phase *whp* in $O(\log n)$ rounds after the first processor that computes the estimates (Lemma 4 in [5]). In our analysis we assume without loss of generality that all live processors start the *computation* phase together. In essence, this discounts any potential computational progress made by the processors that start the phase "early." We will show that our algorithm takes at least $\log n$ rounds, and thus any "wasted" work and communication done by "early" processors can be absorbed into the respective complexities of the *computation* phase. We next show that if $\Theta(n \log n)$ profess messages are sent in the *computation* phase by the enlightened processors, then every live processor terminates *whp*.

Lemma 4. *Let r be the first round by which the total number of* profess *messages is $\Theta(n \log n)$. Then by the end of this round every live processor halts whp.*

Lemmas 4 is proved along the lines of Lemmas 2 of [4]. (The constant k_m from the proof is used as a compile-time constant in algorithm DARE.)

Lemma 5. *Once a processor $v \in P - F$ becomes enlightened, every live processor halts in additional $O(\log n)$ rounds whp.*

Proof. Per Lemma 4 if $\Theta(n \log n)$ profess messages are sent then every processor halts *whp*. Given that processor v does not crash it takes v at most $\log n$ rounds to send $\Theta(n \log n)$ profess messages (line 5 in Figure 1), regardless of the actions of other processors. Hence, *whp* every live processor halts in $O(\log n)$ rounds. $\square$

We denote by L the number of iterations of the *computation* phase required for a processor from the hardened set H to become enlightened. Let us further denote by F_r the set of processors crashed before round r.

We will analyze the value of L for models $\mathcal{F}_{\ell f}$, $\mathcal{F}_{fp}$ and $\mathcal{F}_{pl}$. The compile-time constant k_t appearing in algorithm DARE is computed as $\max\{k_1, k_2, k_3\}$, where k_1, k_2 and k_3 are from the proofs of Lemmas 6, 8, and 12.

Here it is sufficient to be concerned with the tasks that are performed by the hardened processors before any of them becomes enlightened, and by the processors that computed more results than some hardened processors. The latter is interesting because it is possible that for a task j SELECT returns a subset of processors that performed task j, yet $H \not\subseteq S$. Lemmas 1 and 3 teach that for the task j subset S is the maximal subset that satisfied the problem constraint. Hence, if some processor $w \in H$ is not included in S, then there exists another processor $v \in P - H$ that obtained more results for task j, and moreover, the inclusion of v in S does not violate the constraint on average probability.

Analysis for Model $\mathcal{F}_{\ell f}$. Here $|F_r|$ is bounded as in model $\mathcal{F}$ of [6] with at most a linear fraction of processor crashes. We show that L needs to be $\Theta(\log n)$. Next two lemmas can be respectively proved along the lines of the proofs of Lemmas 5.1 and 5.2 in [6].

Lemma 6. *In the computation phase of algorithm DARE every task is performed $\Theta(\log n)$ times whp in $\Theta(\log n)$ rounds by the processors in H.*

Lemma 7. *In the computation phase of algorithm* DARE, *if every task becomes performed* $\Theta(\log n)$ *times by workers in* H, *then whp in additional* $\Theta(\log n)$ *rounds at least one worker in* H *becomes enlightened.*

Lemma 5 shows that once a processor in H becomes enlightened, then every live processor halts in $\Theta(\log n)$ rounds *whp*. It remains to show that the correct result for each task is obtained from the collectively computed results by processors in subset S returned by SELECT just before *Results* are computed.

Theorem 2. *Algorithm* DARE *performs all* n *tasks correctly, and the results are known at every live processor in* $\Theta(\log n)$ *rounds whp.*

The next theorem assesses work and message complexities.

Theorem 3. *Algorithm* DARE *in adversarial model* $\mathcal{F}_{\ell f}$ *takes* $\Theta(\log n)$ *rounds, with work complexity* $\Theta(n \log n)$ *and message complexity* $O(n \log^2 n)$.

Last, we assess the efficiency of algorithm DARE for t tasks, where $t \geq n$. As discussed earlier, we extend each round by $\Theta(t/n)$ rounds during which a chunk of t/n tasks are performed without any communication. Then the following result is simply obtained from Theorem 3 for $t = n$ by multiplying the number of rounds and work complexities by $\Theta(t/n)$; the message complexity is unchanged.

Theorem 4. *For* $t \geq n$ *algorithm* DARE *in model* $\mathcal{F}_{\ell f}$ *takes* $\Theta(\frac{t}{n} \log n)$ *rounds, with work complexity* $\Theta(t \log n)$ *and message complexity* $O(n \log^2 n)$.

Analysis for Model $\mathcal{F}_{fp}$. Here we have $|F| \leq n - n^a$. For the purpose of analysis we divide an execution of the algorithm into two epochs: epoch $\mathfrak{a}$ consists of all rounds r where $|F_r|$ is at most linear in n, so that the number of live processors is at least $c'n$ for some suitable constant c'; epoch $\mathfrak{b}$ consists of all rounds r, starting with the first round r' (it can be round 1) when the number of live processors drops below some $c'n$ and becomes $b'n^a$ for some suitable constant b'. For the small number of failures in epoch $\mathfrak{a}$, we anchor the analysis to model $\mathcal{F}_{\ell f}$. We analyze the cost of epoch $\mathfrak{b}$ below. The final message and work complexities will be at most the worst case complexity for model $\mathcal{F}_{\ell f}$ plus the additional costs incurred while $|P - F| = \Omega(n^a)$ per model $\mathcal{F}_{fp}$.

We show that *whp* it takes $L = \Theta(n^{1-a} \log n \log \log n)$ rounds for a "hardened" worker to become enlightened.

Lemma 8. *In* $O(n^{1-a} \log n)$ *rounds of the algorithm every task is performed* $\Theta(\log n)$ *times whp by processors in* H.

We now focus only on the hardened set H with $|H| \geq cn^a$. Our goal is to show that in $O(n^{1-a} \log n \log \log n)$ rounds of the computation phase of algorithm DARE at least one processor from H becomes enlightened.

We first show that in the computation phase any triple $\tau = \langle x, y, z \rangle$ generated by a processor in H is known to all processors in H in $O(n^{1-a} \log n \log \log n)$ iterations. We denote by $S(d) \subseteq H$ the set of processors that know a certain triple τ by round d, and let $s(d) = |S(d)|$. Next lemma shows that after $r_1 = O(n^{1-a} \log n \log \log n)$ rounds $s(r_1) = \Theta(\log^3 n)$.

Lemma 9. *After $r_1 = O(n^{1-a} \log n \log \log n)$ rounds of the computation phase whp $s(r_1) = \Theta(\log^3 n)$.*

Next we reason about the growth of $s(r_1)$ after round r_1.

Lemma 10. *Let r_2 be the first iteration after round r_1 in the computation phase, such that $r_2 - r_1 = \Theta(n^{1-a} \log n)$. Then $s(r_2) \geq \frac{3}{5}|H|$ whp.*

Next we calculate the number of rounds in the computation phase required for the remaining $\frac{2}{5}|H|$ processors in H to learn τ.

Lemma 11. *Once every task is performed $\Theta(\log n)$ times by processors in H then at least one worker from H becomes enlightened whp in $O(n^{1-a} \log n \log \log n)$ rounds of the computation phase of algorithm DARE.*

Lemmas 8, 9, 10, and 11 can be respectively proved by arguing along the lines of Lemmas 5, 6, 7 and 8 in [4].

Theorem 5. *Algorithm DARE performs n tasks correctly in the computation phase, making the results known to all live processors in $O(n^{1-a} \log n \log \log n)$ rounds whp.*

According to Lemma 11, after $O(n^{1-a} \log n \log \log n)$ rounds of the computation phase, at least one processor in H becomes enlightened. Then, per Lemma 5, after $\Theta(\log n)$ rounds every live processor becomes enlightened and then terminates, *whp*. Next we assess work and message complexities.

Theorem 6. *Algorithm DARE in model $\mathcal{F}_{fp}$ takes $O(n^{1-a} \log n \log \log n)$ rounds and its work complexity is $O(n \log n \log \log n)$, and message complexity $O(n \log^2 n \log \log n)$.*

Lastly, we evaluate algorithm DARE for t tasks such that $t \geq n$ using the techniques we discussed earlier.

Theorem 7. *For $t \geq n$ algorithm DARE in model $\mathcal{F}_{fp}$ takes $O(\frac{t}{n^a} \log n \log \log n)$ rounds, with work and message complexities $O(t \log n \log \log n)$ and $O(n \log^2 n \log \log n)$, respectively.*

Failure Model $\mathcal{F}_{pl}$. Here we have $|P - F| = \Omega(\log^c n)$. We let $|P - F|$ be at least $b \log^c n$, for specific constants b and c satisfying the model constraints. For the purpose of analysis we divide an execution of the algorithm into two epochs: epoch $\mathfrak{b}'$ consists of all rounds r where $|F_r|$ remains bounded as in model $\mathcal{F}_{fp}$ (for reference, this epoch combines epoch $\mathfrak{a}$ and epoch $\mathfrak{b}$ defined above); epoch $\mathfrak{c}$ consists of all rounds r starting with the first round r'' (it can be round 1) when the number of live processors drops below $b'n^a$, where b' and a are specified by the failure model $\mathcal{F}_{fp}$, but remains $\Omega(\log^c n)$ per model $\mathcal{F}_{pl}$. Observe that since we are concerned with model $\mathcal{F}_{pl}$, in the sequel we can chose any a, such that $0 < a < 1$. Also note that either epoch may be empty.

In epoch $\mathfrak{b}'$ the algorithm incurs costs exactly as in model $\mathcal{F}_{fp}$. If algorithm DARE terminates in round r'', the first round of the epoch, the costs remain the same as the costs analyzed for $\mathcal{F}_{fp}$ above.

If it does not terminate, it incurs additional costs associated with the processors in $P - F_{r''}$, where $b \log^c n \leq |P - F_{r''}| \leq b'n^a$. We analyze the costs for epoch $\mathfrak{c}$ next. The final message and work complexities are then at most the worst case complexity for epoch $\mathfrak{b}'$ plus the additional costs for epoch $\mathfrak{c}$.

The next lemma shows that within $O(n)$ rounds of the computation phase every task t is chosen for execution $\Theta(\log n)$ times by processors in H whp.

Lemma 12. *In $O(n)$ rounds of the computation phase every task is performed $\Theta(\log n)$ times whp by processors in H.*

Next we show that once each task is done a logarithmic number of times, then every processor in H will acquire a sufficient collection of triples in linear number of rounds to become enlightened.

Lemma 13. *Once every task is performed $\Theta(\log n)$ times in the computation phase, by processors in H then at least one worker in H becomes enlightened whp in $O(n)$ rounds.*

Lemmas 12 and 13 can be respectively proved by arguing along the lines of Lemmas 9 and 10 in [4].

Theorem 8. *Algorithm DARE performs n tasks correctly in the computation phase, making the results known to all live processors in $O(n)$ rounds whp.*

According to Lemma 13, after $O(n)$ rounds of the computation phase at least one processor in H becomes enlightened, and according to Lemma 5 after $O(\log n)$ additional rounds of the computation phase every live processor becomes enlightened and then terminates, *whp*. Next we assess time, work and message complexities (this is done similarly to Theorem 6).

Theorem 9. *Algorithm DARE, in model $\mathcal{F}_{pl}$, takes $O(n)$ rounds, with work complexity $O(n^{1+a})$ and message complexity $O(n^{1+a})$.*

Remark. It should be possible to derive tighter bounds than above because we only assume for epoch $\mathfrak{c}$ that the number of live processors is bounded by the generous range $b \log^c n \leq |P - F_r| \leq b'n^a$. E.g., if in epoch $\mathfrak{c}$ there are $\Theta(poly \log n)$ live processors, then work and message complexities become $O(n \, poly \log n)$.

Finally, we consider algorithm DARE for t tasks such that $t \geq n$ using the techniques we discussed earlier.

Theorem 10. *For $t \geq n$, in model $\mathcal{F}_{pl}$, algorithm DARE takes $O(t)$ rounds, with work $O(t \cdot n^a)$ and message complexity $O(n^{1+a})$.*

Remark. In our analysis we let ϵ and ζ be constants based on the chosen floating point precision Δ. However, one can pick ϵ and ζ to be $O(\frac{1}{\log n})$, requiring, for large n, an algorithmic implementation of arithmetic operations. This can be done in a straightforward manner in $O(\log^2 n)$ time per operation using polynomial representation of values. This cost can be lowered with an FFT-based multiplication algorithms. In this case the complexity bounds for the estimation phase would increase, e.g., for model $\mathcal{F}_{\ell f}$ the time will increase by a factor of $\log^2 n$. Also, the time required for solving Knapsack in procedure SELECT will increase, but remain polylogarithmic. The desired precision should guide the selection of ϵ and ζ, and this affects only the local computation at the nodes.

5   Conclusion

We presented and analyzed a synchronous decentralized algorithm for the network supercomputing problem. The algorithm copes with erring and crashing processors by estimating processor reliability. The algorithm tolerates crashes that may increase the average overall probability of processors returning wrong results. Of independent interest, we presented an optimization technique for extracting correct results from the collections of results of unknown quality.

References

1. Distributed.net, http://www.distributed.net/
2. Seti@home, http://setiathome.ssl.berkeley.edu/
3. Christoforou, E., Anta, A.F., Georgiou, C., Mosteiro, M.A., Sánchez, A(A.): Reputation-based mechanisms for evolutionary master-worker computing. In: Baldoni, R., Nisse, N., van Steen, M. (eds.) OPODIS 2013. LNCS, vol. 8304, pp. 98–113. Springer, Heidelberg (2013)
4. Davtyan, S., Konwar, K., Russell, A., Shvartsman, A.: Dealing with undependable workers in decentralized network supercomputing. Technical report, Preliminary results appear in Frey, D., Raynal, M., Sarkar, S., Shyamasundar, R.K., Sinha, P. (eds.) ICDCN 2013. LNCS, vol. 7730, pp. 27–41. Springer, Heidelberg (2013); Preprint submitted to Elsevier, arXiv:1407.0442[cs.DC]
5. Davtyan, S., Konwar, K.M., Shvartsman, A.A.: Estimating reliability of workers for cooperative distributed computing. Technical report, Extended abstract appeared in Proc. of ISPDC 2013 (2013) arXiv:1407.0696 [cs.DC]
6. Davtyan, S., Konwar, K.M., Shvartsman, A.A.: Robust network supercomputing without centralized control. In: Fernàndez Anta, A., Lipari, G., Roy, M. (eds.) OPODIS 2011. LNCS, vol. 7109, pp. 435–450. Springer, Heidelberg (2011)
7. Davtyan, S., Konwar, K.M., Shvartsman, A.A.: Decentralized network supercomputing in the presence of malicious and crash-prone workers. In: ACM PODC 2012, Madeira, Portugal, pp. 231–232 (2012)
8. Fernandez, A., Georgiou, C., Lopez, L., Santos, A.: Reliably executing tasks in the presence of malicious processors. Technical Report RoSaC-2005-9, Sistemas y Comunicaciones, Univ. Rey Juan Carlos (2005)
9. Fernandez, A., Georgiou, C., Lopez, L., Santos, A.: Reliably executing tasks in the presence of untrusted entities. In: SRDS, pp. 39–50 (2006)
10. Georgiou, C., Shvartsman, A.A.: Cooperative Task-Oriented Computing; Algorithms and Complexity. Morgan & Claypool Publishers (2011)

11. Hanson, N.W., Konwar, K.M., Wu, S.-J., Hallam, S.J.: Metapathways v2.0: A master-worker model for environmental pathway/genome database construction on grids and clouds. In: IEEE Conf. on Comput. Intelligence in Bioinf. and Comput. Biology, Hawaii (to appear, 2014)
12. Konwar, K.M., Rajasekaran, S., Shvartsman, M.M.A.A.: Robust network supercomputing with malicious processes. In: Dolev, S. (ed.) DISC 2006. LNCS, vol. 4167, pp. 474–488. Springer, Heidelberg (2006)
13. Paquette, M., Pelc, A.: Optimal decision strategies in byzantine environments. Parallel and Distrib. Computing 66(3), 419–427 (2006)

Snap-Stabilizing PIF on Non-oriented Trees and Message Passing Model

Florence Levé, Khaled Mohamed, and Vincent Villain

Laboratoire MIS, Université de Picardie, 33 Rue St Leu,
80039 Amiens Cedex 01, France
{florence.leve,khaled.mohamed,vincent.villain}@u-picardie.fr

Abstract. Starting from any configuration, a *snap-stabilizing protocol* guarantees that the system always behaves according to its specification while a *self-stabilizing protocol* only guarantees that the system will behave according to its specification in a finite time. So, a snap-stabilizing protocol is a time optimal self-stabilizing protocol (because it stabilizes in 0 rounds). That property is very suitable in the case of systems that are prone to transient faults. There exist a lot of approaches of the concept of self-stabilization, but to our knowledge, snap-stabilization is the only variant of self-stabilization which has been proved power equivalent to self-stabilization in the context of the state model (a locally shared memory model) and for non anonymous systems. So the problem of the existence of snap-stabilizing solutions in the message passing model is a very crucial question from a practical point of view. In this paper, we present the first snap-stabilizing propagation of information with feedback (PIF) protocol for non-oriented trees in the message passing model. Moreover using slow and fast timers, the round complexity of our algorithm is in $\theta(h \times k)$ and $\theta((h \times k) + k^2)$, respectively, where h is the height of the tree and k is the maximal capacity of the channels. We conjecture that our algorithm is optimal.

1 Introduction

The concept of Propagation of Information with Feedback (PIF) has been introduced by Chang [7] and Segall [20]. The PIF scheme can be described as follows: a node, called root or initiator, initiates a wave by broadcasting a message m into the network (broadcast phase). Each non root processor acknowledges to the root the receipt of m (feedback phase). The wave terminates when the root has received an acknowledgment from all other processors [13].

Self-stabilization has been introduced by Dijsktra in 1974 [18]. A distributed algorithm is self-stabilizing if, starting from any arbitrary global state, the system is able to recover itself in finite time. This property is crucial when considering systems after any faulty behavior (even any byzantine behavior). In that case, the resulting configurations (unexpected messages and memory states) can be arbitrary and self stabilizing algorithms eventually recover without any external action. So it is one of the most versatile techniques to handle transient faults arising in distributed systems. Recently, snap-stabilization has been introduced

P. Felber and V. Garg (Eds.): SSS 2014, LNCS 8756, pp. 299–313, 2014.

by Bui *et al.* [4]. A distributed algorithm is snap-stabilizing if starting from any arbitrary global state the system always satisfies the specification. In other words, a snap-stabilizing algorithm is a self-stabilizing algorithm that stabilizes in 0 rounds, i.e., it is optimal in terms of the stabilization time. For example, after some transient faults, when a user starts a self-stabilizing PIF algorithm he is not sure to receive the right feedback of all the processors at the first attempt, and it is generally the same for all the other attempts until the algorithm stabilizes. Moreover the number of attempts that fail can be not bounded depending on the algorithm. On the contrary, if the algorithm is snap-stabilizing, the first attempt is the *right one.*

There exist a lot of approaches of the concept of self-stabilization, some of them try to overcome some of its drawbacks like a high complexity [16], some of them try to make it stronger [17]. Snap-stabilization belongs to the second family and enhances the safety of the system since the stabilization time is nul. To our knowledge, snap-stabilization is the only variant of self-stabilization which has been proved power equivalent to self-stabilization in the context of the state model (a locally shared memory model) and for non anonymous systems, meaning that each problem that admits a self-stabilizing solution also admits a snap-stabilizing solution and reciprocally [10]. So the existence of snap-stabilizing solutions in the message passing model is a very crucial problem from a practical point of view.

Related work. Several snap-stabilizing PIF protocols have been proposed for oriented trees [4,19,6], for non-oriented trees [5,9,11,6], for full-connected networks [15], and for general networks [8,3,13]. In [10,12,14] snap-stabilizing PIF protocols are the key tools of the transformation of protocols into snap-stabilizing versions. But all the literature above is written in the state model.

To the best of our knowledge there only exist two snap-stabilizing protocols in the message passing model. A snap-stabilizing propagation of information with feedback (PIF) protocol for full-connected networks has been presented in [15]. Another one for oriented trees has been evoked in [19] but no protocol nor proof are provided.

Contributions. In this paper, we present the first snap-stabilizing PIF algorithm for non-oriented trees in the message-passing model. Following the impossibility result in [15] we consider that the capacity of the channels is bounded. Moreover in order to tolerate message losses after the occurence of transient faults our algorithm uses timers that regularly send duplicate messages. With slow timers, we show that the round complexity of a complete execution is in $\theta(h \times k)$ where h and k are the height of the tree and the maximal capacity of the channels, respectively. With fast timers, the round complexity only gets k^2 as an additionnal term and is in $\theta((h \times k) + k^2)$. We conjecture that our algorithm is optimal in terms of round complexity. That result is coherent with the round complexity in [5] and [6] since they achieve $\theta(h)$ in the state model.

Outline of the paper. The paper is organized as follows. In Section 2 we present the model assumed in this paper. We then present the snap-stabilizing PIF algorithm and its proof in Section 3 and discuss the complexity in Section 4. We then conclude in the last section.

2   Preliminaries

Notations. We consider a network as an undirected connected graph $G = (V, E)$ where V is a finite set of nodes (or *processors*) ($|V| = n$) and E is the set of *bidirectional asynchronous communication links.* A bidirectional communication link $\{p, q\}$ exists iff p and q are neighbors, in this case p and q can communicate together by sending messages through the link. This link can be viewed as two *channels* (p, q) and (q, p), one by direction. The capacity of the channels is bounded, otherwise no deterministic snap-stabilizing solution is available [15]. To simplify the presentation, we assume that the bound is the same for every channel and is denoted by k. Channels are not reliable so messages can be lost but they are *fair*, i.e., if a processor sends infinitely many messages through a channel, then the channel will deliver infinitely many of them. Messages can be lost when the channel has a faulty behavior or is full. When they are not lost, messages transmitted through a channel are received in a finite but not bounded time, moreover they arrive in the order they have been sent (FIFO). Every processor p can distinguish and number all its channels from 0 to $\delta - 1$, where δ is the number of neighbors of p. For sake of simplicity, we sometimes refer to a link $\{p, q\}$ (or a channel (p, q)) of a processor p by the label q instead of its local number. We consider networks which are *tree structured*, so $|E| = n - 1$. Our algorithm will not use any identity for the processors except the one called the *root* or r. Any other processor p is called an *internal* processor if it has at least two neighbors, and a *leaf* processor otherwise.

We will call the neighbor of a processor p ($p \neq r$) which is on the path from r to p the *topological parent* of p. We will call any of the other neighbors of p a *topological child*. In non-oriented trees, p does not know which of its neighbors is its topological parent.

Programs. In our model, protocols are *semi-uniform*, i.e., according to δ, each processor executes the same program except r. So, aside from r, we distinguish between the case of internal processors ($\delta > 1$) and leaf processors ($\delta = 1$). We consider the message-passing model of computation. The message receptions are sequentially taken into account by the processors and the set of actions associated to a message reception is atomically executed.

To compute the time complexity, we use the notion of *round*. Since in asynchronous systems, the local execution time is considered as null, the definition of a *round* captures the execution rate of the slowest messages in any computation.

Definition 1 (Round). *Given an execution e of a protocol P, the* first round *of e (let us call it e') is the minimal prefix of e containing the reception or the loss of every message sent or already in a channel from the initial configuration. Let e'' be the suffix of e such that $e = e'e''$. The* second round *of e is the first round of e'', and so on.*

We assume that during a round the timers of every processor involved in the execution are activated at least once.

PIF. PIF is a well-known problem, so we simply specify the problem as follows:

Specification 1 (PIF). *An algorithm is a PIF algorithm if it satisfies the two following conditions:*

[PIF1] *r initiates a PIF by broadcasting a message m,*
[PIF2] *after the initialization, PIF terminates at r and when that happens, all processors have acknowledged the receipt of m.*

Remark 1. In practice, to prove that a PIF protocol is snap-stabilizing we have to show that every execution of the algorithm satisfies these two conditions: (i) if r has a message m to broadcast, it will do it in a finite time, and (ii) starting from any configuration where r broadcasts m, the system satisfies Specification 1.

3   Snap-Stabilizing PIF Algorithm

3.1   Algorithm Description

We call our algorithm *PIF*, the formal description is given in Algorithms 1, 2, 3, and 4. The main idea follows that of [4,6] while cleaning the channels follows that of [15] based itself on a sequence of integers as in [2,1]. Roughly speaking, our algorithm is based on the sending of broadcast messages with timestamp (Messages *("B",X)*) in order to stabilize the channels. An internal processor must wait for a broadcast message with Timestamp $M - 2$ before it begins to propagate the broadcast. The value M is discussed below in paragraph *Any Initial Configuration*. In order to avoid wrong feedbacks, a processor which has received the feedback (Message *("F")*) of all its children must wait for an application (Message *("B",M − 1)*) from its parent before it sends it a feedback. We describe our algorithm more precisely in the two following paragraphs.

Safe Initial Configuration. Starting from a safe configuration, *i.e.*, no processor is involved in any execution of *PIF* (so Boolean *End* is *True*) and every channel is empty, r sends *("B",0)* to all its topological children, see Actions *Spontaneously* and *Timer[C]=0* in Algorithm 2 and Macro *InitBroadcast()* in Algorithm 1.
   At the reception of *("B",0)* from channel C, a neighbor p of r sets $parent_p$ to C, $S_p[C]$ to 0, and sends *("ACK",0)* to r by C, see Action *At the reception of ("B",X) from C* in Algorithms 4 or 3. At the reception of *("ACK",0)* from channel C, r sets $S_r[C]$ to 1 and sends *("B",1)* to C, see Action *At the reception of ("ACK",X) from C* in Algorithm 2. This exchange of messages goes on on every channel of r. When for some C, $S_r[C]$ reaches $M - 2$, r sends *("B",M-2)* to C. When receiving this message, the neighbor p at the end of C sends *("ACK",M-2)* to r, sets $S_p[C]$ to $M - 2$, and starts broadcasting *("B",0)* to all its topological children. At the reception of *("ACK",M-2)*, r sets $S_r[C]$ to

$M - 1$ and sends *("B",M-1)* to C. When p receives this message, it sets $S_p[C]$ to $M - 1$ meaning that r is now waiting for the feedback message *("F")* of p. The broadcast goes on along the paths from r to the leaves. When a leaf has received the sequence of *("B",0), ("B",1),..., ("B",M-1)* from its unique channel 0, it sends back *("F")*, see *At the reception of ("B",X) from C* in Algorithm 3. After they send their sequence of *("B",0), ("B",1),..., ("B",M-1)*, the internal processors wait for a *("F")* from their topological children. Once an internal processor p has received a *("F")* from all its children, $S_p[C]$ equals M for all its children, so that p satisfies the predicate *EndWaitFeedback* and it can sends *("F")* to its topological parent. We can remark that $S_p[parent_p]$ can be equal to $M - 2$ only because the system is asynchronous. In this case p waits for the reception of *("B",M-1)* from its parent before p sends *("F")*. Finally, the *("F")* messages go up to r and the execution terminates.

Any Initial Configuration. Starting from any configuration, the channels can contain some residual messages (messages already in the channels at the initial configuration). Since $M = (2k + 1) + 2$ where k is the channel capacity, the sequence of *("B",0), ("B",1),..., ("B",M-2)* ensures that when the sender receives the last acknowledgment *("ACK",M-2)* the receiver has received at least *("B",M-2)* and that *("ACK",M-2)* is really an acknowledgment to this message.

But cleaning the channels is not enough to ensure a good behavior of the algorithm, because residual messages may have bad consequences when proceeding by a processor. The role of messages *("Broadcast?"), ("B:No"),* and *("Withdraw")* is to limit the effects of a possible dysfunction. A broadcasting internal processor p regularly sends *("Broadcast?")* to its neighbor $parent_p$ to be sure that $parent_p$ is really broadcasting a message to p. If $parent_p$ is still broadcasting to p then $parent_p$ does not answer directly to the question since it will eventually send a broadcast message to p. Otherwise, $parent$ sends a *("B:No")* message to p. When a processor p, which is not involved in any *PIF* execution (*i.e.*, End_p is *True*), receives a *("B",M-2)* message from a neighbor q (*i.e.*, q is waiting for a feedback), it sends a *("Withdraw")* message to q, because the broadcast is not valid. These messages allow to remove abnormal broadcasts, *i.e.*, broadcasts the source of which is not r.

3.2   Proof of Snap-Stabilization

To simplify the proofs, we will reduce the tree to a chain where r is the processor at the top of the chain and the unique leaf is the processor at the bottom of the chain. The validity of our results on trees is simply ensured by the synchronization of the *("F")* sending, driven by the predicate *EndWaitFeedback*.

We now present several definitions before we prove our algorithm.

Definition 2 (Residual Message). *A message which is already in a channel in the initial configuration is called a* residual *message.*

Definition 3 (Working Message). *A message* m *received by p is a* working *message if p executes at least one state change at the reception of* m.

Algorithm 1. Environment

```
Constant  :
        M                                    // M=(2k+1)+2 where k is an integer bounding the channel capacity
        α: positive integer                                        // waiting time value of the timer
        δ: positive integer                              // number of neighbors of the processor
Messages :
        ("B",X) where X ∈ {0,..., M − 1}
        ("ACK",X) where X ∈ {0,..., M − 2}
        ("F")
        ("F_ACK")
        ("Broadcast?")
        ("Withdraw")
        ("B:No")
Variables :
        C, parent, i: channel number
        S[0...δ − 1]: array of values in {0,..., M}
        End: boolean
        Prev: in {0,..., M}
Predicates:
        Broadcast[C] ≡ (S[C] ≤ M − 2)                                                // r
        Broadcast[C] ≡ (S[parent] ∈ {M − 2, M − 1} and S[C] ≤ M − 2)      // internal proc.
        WaitFeedback[C] ≡ (S[C] = M − 1)                                         // r
        WaitFeedback[C] ≡ (S[parent] ∈ {M − 2, M − 1} and S[C] = M − 1)  // internal proc.
        EndWaitFeedback ≡ (∀i ∈ {0,..., δ − 1}, S[i] = M)                      // r
        EndWaitFeedback ≡ (∀i ∈ {0,..., δ − 1} \ {parent}, S[i] = M and S[parent] = M − 1)
// internal proc.
        EndWaitFeedback ≡ (S[0] = M − 1)                                         // leaves
        Error ≡ (S[parent] ∉ {M − 2, M − 1} and ∃C ∈ {0,..., δ − 1} \ {parent} : S[C] ≠ 0)// internal
proc.
Macros   :
        ExecEnd() : (∀i ∈ {0,..., δ − 1}(S[i] ← 0); End ← True)        // leaves and internal proc.
        InitBroadcast() : (∀i ∈ {0,..., δ − 1}(S[i] ← 0; Timer[i] ← 0))            // r
        InitBroadcast(C) : (∀i ∈ {0,..., δ − 1} \ {C}(S[i] ← 0; Timer[i] ← 0))     // internal proc.
```

Algorithm 2. r code

```
• Spontaneously
if End or EndWaitFeedback then
 |   end ← False ; InitBroadcast() ;
end

• At the reception of ("ACK",X) from C
if ¬(End) then
 |   if S[C]=X then
 |    |   S[C] ← S[C]+1;
 |    |   if Broadcast[C] or WaitFeedback[C] then
 |    |    |   Timer[C] ← 0;                                          // Send (''B'', S[C]) to C
 |    |   end
 |   end
end

• At the reception of ("F") from C
if ¬(Broadcast[C]) then
 |   Send("F_ACK") to C;
 |   if ¬(End) and WaitFeedback[C] then
 |    |   S[C] ← M;
 |    |   if EndWaitFeedback then
 |    |    |   ExecEnd();
 |    |   end
 |   end
end

• At the reception of ("Broadcast?") from C
if End or EndWaitFeedback then
 |   Send("B:No") to C;
end

• At the reception of ("Withdraw") from C
if ¬(Broadcast[C]) and ¬(End) then
 |   ExecEnd();
end

• Timer[C]=0
if ¬(End) then
 |   if Broadcast[C] or WaitFeedback[C] then
 |    |   Send("B",S[C]) to C;
 |   end
 |   Timer[C] ← α;
end
```

Algorithm 3. Leaves code

```
• At the reception of ("B",X) from C                                    // C=0
if End then
    if X=M-1 then
    |    Send("Withdraw") to 0 ;
    else
    |    if X < M-1 then
    |    |    End ← False ;
    |    end
    end
else
    Prev ←S[0] ;
    S[0] ← X ;
    if S[0] > M-1 or S[0] < Prev then
    |    ExecEnd() ;
    else
    |    if S[0] < M-1 then
    |    |    Send ("ACK", X) to 0 ;
    |    else// S[0]=M-1
    |    |    Send ("F") to 0 ;
    |    end
    end
end
• At the reception of ("F_ACK") from C                                  // C=0
if ¬(End) then
|    ExecEnd() ;
end
• At the reception of ("Broadcast?") from C                             // C=0
Send ("B:No") to 0 ;
```

Definition 4 (Real Broadcast). *Let p and q be two neighboring processors. A ("B",X) message received by p from channel (q,p) is a* real broadcast *if it has been sent by q.*

Definition 5 (Real Acknowledgment). *Let p and q be two neighboring processors. A ("ACK",X) message received by p from channel (q,p) is a* real acknowledgment *if it has been sent by q at the reception of a real broadcast ("B",X) sent by p.*

Definition 6 (Real Feedback). *Let p and q be two neighboring processors. A ("F") message received by p from channel (q,p) is a* real feedback *if it has been sent by q at the reception of a real broadcast ("B",M-1) sent by p.*

Definition 7 (Right Feedback). *Let p and q be two neighboring processors. A ("F") message received by p from channel (q,p) is a* right feedback *if it is a real feedback sent by q and q satisfies one of the two following conditions:*

1. *q is a leaf,*
2. *q is not a leaf. Let q' be the topological child of q. The last ("F") message q has accepted is a right feedback from q'.*

Roughly speaking a ("F") message is a right feedback if this message is a real feedback which has originally been generated by the leaf.

We define an *abnormal root* as an internal processor which is broadcasting while it must not. More formally:

Definition 8 (Abnormal Root). *Let p be an internal processor. Processor p is an abnormal root if all the following conditions are satisfied:*

Algorithm 4. Internal Processors code

```
• At the reception of ("B",X) from C
if End then
    if X=M-1 then
    |   Send("Withdraw") to C ;
    else
    |   if X < M-1 then
    |   |   End ← False ; parent ← C ;
    |   end
    end
end
if ¬(End) and C=parent then
    Prev ← S[C] ; S[C] ← X ;
    if S[C] > M − 1 or S[C] < Prev or (S[C] = M − 1 and Prev < M − 2) or Error then
    |   ExecEnd();
    else
    |   if S[C] < M − 1 then
    |   |   Send ("ACK",X) to C ;
    |   |   Timer[C] ← α ;                                    // Avoid to send (''Broadcast?'') to parent
    |   |   if S[C] = M − 2 and S[C] ≠ Prev then
    |   |   |   InitBroadcast(C) ;
    |   |   end
    |   else// S[C]=M-1
    |   |   if EndWaitFeedback then
    |   |   |   Send("F") to C ;
    |   |   end
    |   end
    end
end
• At the reception of ("ACK",X) from C ∈ {0,...,δ − 1} \ {parent}
if ¬(End) then
    if S[C]=X then
    |   S[C] ← S[C]+1 ;
    |   if Broadcast[C] or WaitFeedback[C] then
    |   |   Timer[C] ← 0 ;                                    // Send (''B'', S[C]) to C
    |   end
    end
end
• At the reception of ("F") from C ∈ {0,...,δ − 1} \ {parent}
if ¬(Broadcast[C]) then
    Send("F_ACK") to C ;
    if ¬(End) and WaitFeedback[C] then
    |   S[C] ← M ;
    |   if EndWaitFeedback then
    |   |   Send("F") to parent ;
    |   end
    end
end
• At the reception of ("F_ACK") or ("B:No") from parent
if ¬(End) then
|   ExecEnd();
end
• At the reception of ("Broadcast?") from C
if ¬(Broadcast[C]) and ¬(WaitFeedback[C]) then
|   Send("B:No") to C ;
end
if C=parent then
|   ExecEnd() ;
end
• At the reception of ("Withdraw") from C
if ¬(Broadcast[C]) and ¬(End) then
|   ExecEnd();
end
• Timer[C]=0
if ¬(End) then
    if Error then
    |   ExecEnd() ;
    else
    |   if Broadcast[C] or WaitFeedback[C] then
    |   |   if C ≠ parent then
    |   |   |   Send("B",S[C]) to C ;
    |   |   else
    |   |   |   Send("Broadcast?") to C ;
    |   |   end
    |   end
    end
    Timer[C] ← α;
end
```

1. $\neg End_p$,
2. $Broadcast_p \vee WaitFeedback_p$,
3. $Error_q \vee End_q \vee (\neg End_q \wedge (parent_q = p)) \vee (\neg End_q \wedge (parent_q \neq p) \wedge (S_q[p] = M))$ where $q = parent_p$.

Processor p is a top abnormal root *or a* bottom abnormal root *if q is the topological parent of p or a topological child of p, respectively.*

Definition 9 (Down and Up Broadcast). *Let p be either r or a top abnormal root (respectively a bottom abnormal root). If p is sending ("B",X) messages, this broadcast is called a* down broadcast *(respectively an* up broadcast*).*

Definition 10 (Up-Free Configuration). *A configuration is called an* up-free *configuration if it does not contain any* bottom abnormal root *nor any* up broadcast *message.*

We will often assume in the proofs that a processor which starts or has started a broadcast is never disrupted by its parent (that is trivially satisfied by r since it has no parent). We call such a processor a *stop-free processor.*

Definition 11 (Stop-Free Processor). *Let p be a processor, p is a* stop-free *processor if one of the two following conditions is satisfied:*

1. *p is* r,
2. *p is not* r *and all the following conditions are satisfied:*
   - *p never receives from its parent a message ("B",X) followed by ("B",Y) with $X > Y$,*
   - *p never receives from its parent any message ("F_ACK"), ("B:No"), ("Withdraw").*

In order not to overload the proofs, since after one round, every processor does not satisfy *Error* forever, we now assume that no processor will satisfy *Error* forever.

Lemma 1 (Abnormal Root Life). *Let p be an* abnormal root. *Processor p cannot remain an* abnormal root *forever.*

Proof. Assume, by the contradiction, that p remains an *abnormal root* forever. Let q be the neighbor of p such that $parent_p = q$. Then p sends *("Broadcast?")* infinitely often to q. By fairness of (p,q), q will receive *("Broadcast?")* infinitely often. Since p is an *abnormal root* forever, when q receives *("Broadcast?")* from (p,q), q follows one of these three cases:

- End_q is satisfied,
- q is not r and $(\neg End_q \wedge (parent_q = p))$ is satisfied,
- q is not r and $(\neg End_q \wedge (parent_q \neq p) \wedge (S_q[p] = M))$ is satisfied.

In all cases q sends *("B:No")* to p. So q sends *("B:No")* infinitely often to p and by link fairness, p receives *("B:No")* infinitely often. Since at the reception of *("B:No")* p executes $ExecEnd()$, p will stop being an *abnormal root* in a finite time. A contradiction.   □

The following lemma can be easily proved by induction on the distance to the leaves:

Lemma 2 (Bottom Abnormal Root Appearance). *Let p be an internal processor. Processor p cannot become a* bottom abnormal root *infinitely often.*

From Lemmas 1 and 2 we can easily deduce the following lemma:

Lemma 3 (No More Bottom Abnormal Root). *The number of* bottom abnormal roots *is nul in a finite time.*

Since *up broadcast* messages can be only generated by *bottom abnormal roots*, we can easily deduce the following corollary from Lemma 3.

Corollary 1 (No More Up Broadcast). *The system does not contain any message of an* up broadcast *in a finite time.*

We first show that starting from an *up-free* configuration our algorithm always satisfies Specification 1 (from Lemma 4 to Theorem 1). We then prove that the result still holds from any initial configuration so even if this configuration contains *bottom abnormal roots*.

Lemma 4 (Broadcast Progress). *Let p and q be two neighboring processors such that p sends* ("B",X) *($X \in \{0, \ldots, M-2\}$) to q from an* up-free *configuration. If p is stop-free it will eventually receive* ("ACK",X) *by channel (q,p).*

Proof.   Assume that p never receives any message *("ACK",X)* from q. So p sends infinitely many *("B",X)* to q. Since (p,q) is fair, q receives infinitely many *("B",X)*. The configuration is *up-free*, so $parent_q$ cannot be set to another neighbor than p. Depending of the initial state of q, q can execute $ExecEnd()$ at the reception of the first *("B",X)* from p. But at each new reception q sends *("ACK",X)* to p. So q sends infinitely many *("ACK",X)* and by fairness of (q,p) p will eventually receive infinitely many *("ACK",X)*. A contradiction.   □

The following lemma states that if a processor sends all its *("B",X)* messages to a neighbor, then it is ensured that its neighbor has received *("B",M - 2)*.

Lemma 5 (Snap Local Broadcast). *Let p and q be two neighboring processors such that p starts broadcasting to q (it sends* ("B",0) *to q) from an* up-free *configuration. If p is stop-free it will eventually send* ("B",M - 2) *to q and, for this message, it will receive a* real acknowledgment *from q.*

Proof.   From our algorithm, since p is stop-free, p increments $S_p[q]$ at the reception of *("ACK",X)* from q, then sends *("B",$S_p[q]$)* to q and goes on until it receives *("ACK",M-2)* from channel (q,p). Thus from Lemma 4, if the processor

p starts broadcasting to q, we know that p will eventually receive a message *("ACK",M-2)* by channel (q,p). Since $M - 2 = 2k + 1$ where k is the channel capacity, this message cannot be a residual channel message, it has necessarily been generated by q. □

The following lemma can be formally proved by induction on the distance to the farthest leaf.

Lemma 6 (Partial Snap Up-Free PIF). *Let p be a processor such that p is not a leaf and p starts a* down broadcast *(it sends* ("B",0) *to its topological child) from an* up-free *configuration. If p is stop-free it will eventually receive a unique working* ("F") *message and this message is a* right feedback.

Since by Definition 11 r is stop-free, r satisfies Lemma 6 and *[PIF2]* of Specification 1 holds. Moreover, if r is already involved in Algorithm *PIF* in the initial *up-free* configuration, it is easy to show with a reasoning similar to that of the proof of Lemma 6 that r will be able to initiate a complete *PIF* in a finite time, so the following result holds:

Lemma 7 (Up-Free PIF1). *Starting from an* up-free *configuration, Algorithm* PIF *satisfies* [PIF1] *of Specification 1.*

The following theorem is a corollary of Lemmas 6 and 7:

Theorem 1 (Snap Up-Free PIF). *Starting from an* up-free *configuration, Algorithm* PIF *is snap-stabilizing.*

We now generalize Lemma 6 and Theorem 1 to any initial configuration.

Lemma 8 (Partial Snap PIF). *Let p be a processor such that p is not a leaf and p starts a* down broadcast *from any initial configuration. If p is stop-free it will eventually receive a unique working* ("F") *message and this message is a* right feedback.

Proof. We know from Lemma 6 that if a non-leaf processor p starts a *down broadcast* from an *up-free* configuration, and if p is stop-free, it will eventually accept a unique *("F")* message and this message is a *right feedback*.

Now consider the case when there exist abnormal roots in the configuration. A top abnormal root does not cause any problem to the execution of the algorithm since messages *("B",X)* coming from its parent are working messages (when its state is different from X). Assume that q and q' are two neighboring processors, such that q starts a down broadcast towards q' and q' is a bottom abnormal root (w.l.o.g. we can suppose there is no bottom abnormal root on the topological path from the root to q'). No message can prevent q from broadcasting because:

- Since q' is not the parent of q, if q receives *("B",No)* from q', it does not take it into account.
- Since $S_q[q'] < M - 1$, if q receives *("Withdraw",)* from q', it does not take it into account.

 – Since q satisfies *Broadcast*, if q receives *("F")* from q', it does nothing.
 – Since the parent of q is stop-free, it does not send *("F_ACK")* to q until it receives F from q.

From Lemma 3, we know that the number of bottom abnormal roots is nul in a finite time. Thus the broadcast will go on towards the leaves and, from Lemma 6, p will eventually receive a unique working *("F")* message and this message is a *right feedback.*   □

Since r is stop-free, r satisfies Lemma 8 and *[PIF2]* of Specification 1 holds. Moreover, as previously, if r is already involved in Algorithm *PIF* in the initial configuration, it is easy to show that r will be able to initiate a complete *PIF* in a finite time, so the following result holds:

Lemma 9 (PIF1). *Starting from any configuration, Algorithm* PIF *satisfies* [PIF1] *of Specification 1.*

The following theorem is a corollary of Lemmas 8 and 9:

Theorem 2 (Snap PIF). *Algorithm* PIF *is snap-stabilizing.*

4   Complexity

Variable $S[0\ldots\delta-1]$ which is an array of values in $\{0,\ldots,M\}$ has the highest complexity: $\theta(\delta \times log(M))$ or $\theta(\delta \times log(k))$ since M is proportionnal to k. So the memory space needed on each processor is in $\theta(\delta \times log(k))$.

In order not to mix up the network's performances with the algorithm's performances, we assume in the rest of the paper that the only losses of messages are due to full channels, this case can appear when timers are faster than a round. However, as we will see, the round complexity is sensitive to the speed of the timers. So we will consider two cases, the first one is *slow timers* (with a period of the order of k rounds or a speed of the order of the speed of k rounds) and the second one is *fast timers* (with a period at most of the order of a round or a speed at least of the order of the round speed). We show that the round complexity of Algorithm *PIF* is in $\theta(h \times k)$ and $\theta((h \times k) + k^2)$ with slow and fast timers, respectively, Of course in order to get the best performance of a system the users have to adjust the speed of the timers to the expected average frequency of message losses.

Lemma 10 (Round Complexity of Message Delivering). *Let p and q be two neighboring processors. Let M be a message sent by p to q, then q will receive M in $\theta(k)$ rounds where k is the maximal capacity of the channels. More precisely, the number of rounds is less than or equal to $k+1$.*

Proof.   In the worst case Channel (p,q) is full and only one message is consumed from (p,q) by round. So M reaches q in $k+1$ rounds.   □

Corollary 2 (Round Complexity of Neighboring Broadcast). *Let p and q be two neighboring processors. Assume that p starts to send* ("B",0) *to q and any message* ("B",X) *($X \in \{0, \ldots, M-2\}$) from p is a working message for q, then p will receive the acknowledgement of its message* ("B",M-2) *in $\theta(k)$ rounds and $\theta(k^2)$ rounds with slow and fast timers, respectively, where k is the maximal capacity of the channels.*

Proof. In the worst case, when p starts to send *("B",0)*, the channel is full in both directions and contains neither *("B",0)* (in (p,q)) nor *("ACK",0)* (in (q,p)). Moreover each *("B",0)* is a working message for q. From Lemma 10, p will receive *("ACK",0)* in $2k+2$ rounds.

With slow timers when p receives the first *("ACK",0)*, (p,q) and (q,p) contain at most a constant number of *("B",0)* and *("ACK",0)*, respectively. So when p starts to send *("B",1)*, it will receive the first *("ACK",1)* in a constant number of rounds. By induction on X it is clear that p sends $\theta(1)$ times each of its $M-2$ messages *("B",X)* ($X \in \{1, \ldots, M-2\}$). Finally it will receive the acknowledgement of its message *("B",M-2)* after $\theta(k)$ rounds.

With fast timers when p receives the first *("ACK",0)*, (p,q) is full of *("B",0)* and (q,p) is full of *("ACK",0)*. So when p starts to send *("B",1)*, the situation is similar to that above and p will receive *("ACK",1)* in $\theta(k)$ rounds. By induction on X it is clear that p sends $\theta(k)$ times each of its $M-1$ messages *("B",X)* ($X \in \{0, \ldots, M-2\}$). Since $M = 2k+3$, it will receive the acknowledgement of its message *("B",M-2)* after $\theta(k^2)$ rounds. $\square$

The following lemma can be formally proved for *bottom abnormal roots* by induction on the distance to the farthest leaf and the result can be extended to *top abnormal roots*.

Lemma 11 (Round Complexity of the Disappearance of the Abnormal Roots). *Starting from any configuration, the system will never contain abnormal roots in $\theta(h \times k)$ rounds, where h and k are the height of the tree and the maximal capacity of the channels, respectively.*

Let us call *parasite messages* the messages which do not concern the broadcast coming from r. After the disappearance of the abnormal roots, the only parasite messages can be *("B",M-1)*, *("ACK",X)*, *("F")*, *("F_ACK")*, *("B:No")*, *("Broadcast?")*, or *("Withdraw")*. Among those messages only *("B",M-1)*, *("F")*, and *("Broadcast?")* can generate some response: *("Withdraw")*, *("F_ACK")*, and *("B:No")*, respectively. So from Lemma 10 in $\theta(k)$ rounds, the system contains no parasite messages until a new broadcast starts from r and the channels between two processors satisfying *End* are empty whichever timer you use.

Now it is easy to see that the round complexity can be reduced to the round complexity of the propagation of the broadcast, the extra term for fast timers is due to the initial broacast in a full channel.

Theorem 3 (Round Complexity of Algorithm *PIF*). *Starting from any configuration, the round complexity of Algorithm PIF is in $\theta(h \times k)$ and $\theta((h \times$*

$k) + k^2$) *rounds with slow and fast timers, respectively, where h is the height of the tree and k is the maximal capacity of the channels.*

We think that snap-stabilization of channels is unavoidable in order to get a snap-stabilizing algorithm in the message passing model, so we conjecture that Algorithm *PIF* is an optimal snap-stabilizing algorithm in terms of round complexity.

5   Conclusion

There exist a lot of approaches of the concept of self-stabilization, but to our knowledge, snap-stabilization is the only variant of self-stabilization which has been proved power equivalent to self-stabilization in the context of the state model (a locally shared memory model) and for non anonymous systems [10]. Moreover snap-stabilization enhances the safety of the system since the stabilization time is nul. So the problem of the existence of snap-stabilizing solutions in the message passing model is a very crucial question from a practical point of view. In this paper, we have presented the first snap-stabilizing propagation of information with feedback (PIF) protocol for non-oriented trees in the message passing model. Following the impossibility result in [15] we consider that the capacity of the channels is bounded. Using slow and fast timers, we show that the round complexity of our algorithm is in $\theta(h \times k)$ and $\theta((h \times k) + k^2)$, respectively, where h is the height of the tree and k is the maximal capacity of the channels. We conjecture that our algorithm is optimal in terms of round complexity. The next problem to solve is the design of a snap-stabilizing *PIF* algorithm for arbitrary networks and then to get the power equivalence with self-stabilization in the message passing model.

References

1. Afek, Y., Brown, G.M.: Self-stabilization over unreliable communication media. Distributed Computing 7(1), 27–34 (1993)
2. Awerbuch, B., Patt-Shamir, B., Varghese, G.: Self-stabilization by local checking and correction (extended abstract). In: 32nd Annual Symposium on Foundations of Computer Science (FOCS), pp. 268–277. IEEE Computer Society (1991)
3. Blin, L., Cournier, A., Villain, V.: An improved snap-stabilizing PIF algorithm. In: Huang, S.-T., Herman, T. (eds.) SSS 2003. LNCS, vol. 2704, pp. 199–214. Springer, Heidelberg (2003)
4. Bui, A., Datta, A.K., Petit, F., Villain, V.: State-optimal snap-stabilizing pif in tree networks. In: Workshop on Self-stabilizing Systems (WSS), pp. 78–85. IEEE Computer Society (1999)
5. Bui, A., Datta, A.K., Petit, F., Villain, V.: Snap-stabilizing pif algorithm in the tree networks without sense of direction. In: SIROCCO 1999, 6th International Colloquium on Structural Information & Communication Complexity, Lacanau-Ocean, France, July 1-3, pp. 32–46. Carleton Scientific (1999)
6. Bui, A., Datta, A.K., Petit, F., Villain, V.: Snap-stabilization and pif in tree networks. Distributed Computing 20(1), 3–19 (2007)

7. Chang, E.J.H.: Echo algorithms: Depth parallel operations on general graphs. IEEE Trans. Software Eng. 8(4), 391–401 (1982)
8. Cournier, A., Datta, A.K., Petit, F., Villain, V.: Snap-stabilizing pif algorithm in arbitrary networks. In: 22nd International Conference on Distributed Computing Systems (ICDCS), pp. 199–208 (2002)
9. Cournier, A., Datta, A.K., Petit, F., Villain, V.: Optimal snap-stabilizing pif in un-oriented trees. In: Proceedings of the 5th International Conference on Principles of Distributed Systems OPODIS 2001, Manzanillo, Mexico, December 10-12, pp. 71–90. Studia Informatica Universalis (2001)
10. Cournier, A., Datta, A.K., Petit, F., Villain, V.: Enabling snap-stabilization. In: 23rd International Conference on Distributed Computing Systems (ICDCS 2003), Providence, RI, USA, May 19-22, pp. 12–19. IEEE Computer Society (2003)
11. Cournier, A., Datta, A.K., Petit, F., Villain, V.: Optimal snap-stabilizing pif algorithms in un-oriented trees. J. High Speed Networks 14(2), 185–200 (2005)
12. Cournier, A., Devismes, S., Villain, V.: From self- to snap- stabilization. In: Datta, A.K., Gradinariu, M. (eds.) SSS 2006. LNCS, vol. 4280, pp. 199–213. Springer, Heidelberg (2006)
13. Cournier, A., Devismes, S., Villain, V.: Snap-stabilizing pif and useless computations. In: 12th International Conference on Parallel and Distributed Systems (ICPADS 2006), Minneapolis, Minnesota, USA, July 12-15, pp. 39–48. IEEE Computer Society (2006)
14. Cournier, A., Devismes, S., Villain, V.: Light enabling snap-stabilization of fundamental protocols. TAAS 4(1), 1–27 (2009)
15. Delaët, S., Devismes, S., Nesterenko, M., Tixeuil, S.: Snap-stabilization in message-passing systems. In: Garg, V., Wattenhofer, R., Kothapalli, K. (eds.) ICDCN 2009. LNCS, vol. 5408, pp. 281–286. Springer, Heidelberg (2008)
16. Devismes, S., Petit, F., Villain, V.: Autour de l'autostabilisation 1. techniques généralisant l'approche. Technique et Science Informatiques 30(7), 873–894 (2011)
17. Devismes, S., Petit, F., Villain, V.: Autour de l'autostabilisation 2. techniques spécialisant l'approche. Technique et Science Informatiques 30(7), 895–922 (2011)
18. Dijkstra, E.W.: Self-stabilizing systems in spite of distributed control. Commun. ACM 17(11), 643–644 (1974)
19. Dolev, S., Tzachar, N.: Empire of colonies: Self-stabilizing and self-organizing distributed algorithms. In: Shvartsman, M.M.A.A. (ed.) OPODIS 2006. LNCS, vol. 4305, pp. 230–243. Springer, Heidelberg (2006)
20. Segall, A.: Distributed network protocols. IEEE Transactions on Information Theory 29(1), 23–34 (1983)

Edge Coloring Despite
Transient and Permanent Faults

Alexandre Maurer[1] and Toshimitsu Masuzawa[2]

[1] UPMC Sorbonne Universités, France
[2] Osaka University, Japan
alexandre.maurer@lip6.fr,
masuzawa@ist.osaka-u.ac.jp

Abstract. We consider the problem of edge coloring in the presence of transient and permanent faults: we must achieve a stable edge coloring despite any initial state, and despite an unbounded number of Byzantine nodes. In this paper, we consider that no local variable is allowed: we only use the colors of the edges. We give a general algorithm to achieve edge coloring at distance 2 of Byzantine failures. Then, we give a Byzantine insensitive algorithm for edge coloring on a ring (we achieve a stable coloring on the correct subgraph).

This paper is a regular submission, and should be considered for the best student paper award (full-time student at the time of submission: Alexandre Maurer). If this submission is not selected for a regular presentation, it should also be considered for a brief announcement.

1 Introduction

We consider the problem of *edge coloring*: in a network, each communication channel (or *edge*) must be attributed a number (or *color*) such that two adjacent edges do not have the same color. This problem is more difficult than other similar problems, such as node coloring or dining philosophers. Indeed, it requires that two neighbor nodes agree on a same color for their common edge, without disrespecting the aforementioned condition. This problem has many applications, such as resource allocation in distributed systems – for instance, frequency or time slot allocation in wireless networks.

Related Works

In this paper, we consider that the network can be subject to unbounded transient faults: in the initial configuration, the nodes can have any state. The paradigm of *self-stabilization* [2,3] ensures that in a finite time, the network satisfies the specification of the problem, despite the arbitrary initial configuration. Self-stabilizing algorithms for the edge coloring problem have been proposed in [9,5,8,1].

P. Felber and V. Garg (Eds.): SSS 2014, LNCS 8756, pp. 314–327, 2014.

To be more general, we also consider that the network can be subject to unbounded permanent faults: some nodes can be malicious (*Byzantine*) and have an arbitrary behavior. Therefore, tolerating Byzantine faults implies to ensure that there exists no strategy, however unlikely it may be, enabling the Byzantine nodes to destabilize the network. Combining self-stabilization and Byzantine resilience provides the strongest possible guarantees in the field of fault tolerance. Self-stabilizing algorithms resilient to unbounded Byzantine failures have been proposed in [4,7,8].

To our knowledge, only two papers consider the problem of edge coloring in such an unfavourable setting. A first paper [7] studies edge coloring in oriented tree networks, but assumes that each node has a unique identifier. A second paper [6] relaxes this requirement, but uses local variables. Our objective here is to relax both requirements.

Our Contribution

In this paper, we consider the problem of self-stabilizing Byzantine resilient edge coloring in anonymous networks without local variables: we only use the colors of the edges.

We first give an algorithm for edge coloring at distance 2 of Byzantine nodes. We study its correctness under different schedulers, depending on the *fairness* and the *centrality* hypotheses.

Then, we consider the more difficult problem of Byzantine insensitive edge coloring: all correct edges should be correctly colored. We give a Byzantine insensitive algorithm for edge coloring on a ring topology.

Organization of the Paper

The paper is organized as follows:

- In Section 2, we present the setting of the problem.
- In Section 3, we study edge coloring at distance 2 of Byzantine nodes.
- In Section 4, we study Byzantine insensitive edge coloring.

2   Setting

In this section, we present the setting of the problem and give some general definitions.

2.1   Graph

Let $G = (V, E)$ be the undirected graph representing the network. V is the set of *nodes*, and $E \subseteq V \times V$ is the set of *edges*. Two nodes p and q are *neighbors* when $\{p, q\} \in E$. Let N_p be the set of neighbors of a node p. Let Δ be the maximal degree of the network (that is, the maximal number of neighbors per node).

2.2 Identification of Edges

As edge coloring is a local probem, we do not want to make the hypothesis that each node has a unique identifier. However, the nodes need a way to distinguish their neighbors. Therefore, we assume that each node attributes a number $i \in \{1, \ldots, \Delta\}$ to each one of its edges (port numbering model).

If p and q are 2 neighbor nodes, let $e_p(q)$ be the number attributed by p to the edge $\{p, q\}$. This is illustrated in Figure 1. We assume that p also knows $e_q(p)$ (and reciprocally). Let E_p and E_q be the edge numbers used by p and q.

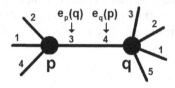

Fig. 1. Identification of edges

2.3 Correct and Byzantine Nodes

Some nodes are *correct*, and follow a given algorithm. The other are *Byzantine*, and behave arbitrarily. The correct nodes do not know which nodes are Byzantine. We do not put any limit to the number of Byzantine nodes.

2.4 Scheduling

We consider several schedulers in this paper. The hypotheses are on the *fairness* and the *centrality* of the scheduler.

Fairness. We say that the scheduler is...

- *Weakly fair* if each correct node is activated infinitely often.
- *Unfair* if, when a correct node is continuously enabled, then eventually, an enabled correct node is activated (but not necessarily this node).

The condition for a correct node to be *enabled* depends on the algorithm. This condition must be chosen carefully: otherwise, the unfair scheduler can activate a certain subset of nodes endlessly, and ignore the other correct nodes.

Centrality. We say that the scheduler is...

- *Locally central* when two neighbor nodes are never activated in the same time.
- *Periodically locally central* when two neighbor nodes can be activated in the same time, but each node is activated independently of its neighbors infinitely often.
- *Non locally central* otherwise.

2.5   Edge Coloring

Colors. Let $\{1, \ldots, C_p\}$ be the set of *colors* that a node p can manipulate. The usual assumption for the edge coloring problem is to assume that $\forall p \in V$, $C_p = 2\Delta - 1$. However, it requires the nodes to know Δ, which is a global network parameter.

To avoid making this assumption, we assume that $C_p = 2\Delta_p - 1$, where $\Delta_p = \max_{q \in N_p \cup \{p\}} |N_q| \leq \Delta$. Thus, p only requires knowledge about the degree of its direct neighbors. Note that all the following is also correct if we simply assume that $\forall p \in V$, $C_p = 2\Delta - 1$.

State. The *state* of a node p is a function $c_p : E_p \rightarrow \{1, \ldots, C_p\}$ that associates a color to each edge number. We make the usual assumption for self-stabilizing algorithms, that is: a correct node that is activated can read the state of its neighbors. Let $c(p, q) = c_p(e_p(q))$.

Definition 1 (Edge coloring). *Let us define the following two predicates:*

- *distinct(p): $\forall q \in N_p$, $\forall r \in N_p$, $q \neq r \Rightarrow c(p, q) \neq c(p, r)$*
- *colored(p, q): $c(p, q) = c(q, p)$*

We say that a graph $G = (V, E)$ is colored *when:*

1. *$\forall p \in V$, distinct(p)*
2. *$\forall \{p, q\} \in E$, colored(p, q)*

This is illustrated in Figure 2.

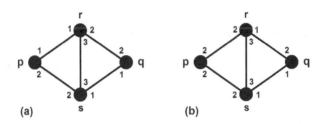

(a)   s   (b)   s

Fig. 2. Example of edge coloring. Graph (a) is colored. Graph (b) is not colored, as we do not have *distinct(p)* and *colored(r, q)*.

Definition 2 (Stable coloring). *Let $G = (V, E)$ be a colored graph. We say that this coloring is* stable *when the colors of the edges do not change, that is: $\forall \{p, q\} \in E$, the value of $c(p, q)$ always remains the same.*

2.6   Self-Stabilization

The property of *self-stabilization* ensures that, from any initial configuration, the system eventually comes back to a legitimate configuration.

Nesterenko and Arora [7] generalized this property to *strict stabilization*, in order to encompass the presence of permanent Byzantine failures. In this new setting, we ensure that the system eventually comes back to a legitimate configuration at a certain *distance* of Byzantine failures. Therefore, we introduce the notion of *R-confined* graph (for a non-negative integer R).

Definition 3 (R-confined graph). *For a given graph $G = (V, E)$ and a given set of Byzantine nodes $B \subseteq V$, the R-confined graph is the graph obtained from G after the removal of the Byzantine nodes and the correct nodes at distance R or less from the Byzantine nodes (with their adjacent edges).*

Definition 4 (Strict stabilization). *An algorithm is* strictly stabilizing *for the edge coloring problem with a containment radius R if for any graph G and for any initial configuration, we always eventually reach a configuration where:*

1. *We have a stable coloring on the R-confined graph G' extracted from G.*
2. *The state of the nodes of G' does not change.*

Strictly stabilizing edge coloring with a containment radius of 0 may be difficult or impossible, as the Byzantine nodes may force their correct neighbors to recolor their common edge endlessly. Thus, the following definition was introduced in [6].

Definition 5 (Byzantine insensitiveness). *An algorithm is* Byzantine insensitive *for the edge coloring problem if for any graph G and for any initial configuration, we always eventually reach a configuration where:*

1. *We have a stable coloring on the 0-confined graph extracted from G.*
2. *The state of the nodes without Byzantine neighbors does not change.*

3   Strictly Stabilizing Edge Coloring

In this section, we present a strictly stabilizing algorithm for edge coloring with a containment radius of 1 (see 3.1). That is, we reach a stable coloring on the graph formed by the correct nodes at distance 2 or more from Byzantine nodes.

We then study the correctness of this algorithm under different schedulers:

- Locally central weakly fair scheduler (see 3.2)
- Locally central unfair scheduler (see 3.3)
- Periodically locally central unfair scheduler (see 3.4)
- Non locally central unfair scheduler (see 3.5)

3.1   Algorithm

Let $choice(p, q)$ be the smallest integer $c \geq 1$ such that:

1. $\forall i \in E_p - \{e_p(q)\}, c_p(i) \neq c$
2. $\forall i \in E_q - \{e_q(p)\}, c_q(i) \neq c$

As C_p (resp. C_q) $\geq 2\max(|N_p|, |N_q|) - 1$, the color c can be manipulated by both p and q.

When a correct node p is activated, it executes the following 3 steps. Informally:

- Step 1 eliminates the edges that have the same color.
- Step 2 colors an edge as soon as it is possible.
- Step 3 prepares the non colored edges for the next activation.

Step 1. If $distinct(p)$ is false, then $\forall k \in E_p$, $c_p(k) := k$.

Step 2. If there exists $q \in N_p$ such that $\forall r \in N_p$, we have $c(p, r) \neq c(q, p)$, then $c(p, q) := c(q, p)$.

Step 3. For each neighbor q of p, taken in the order defined by the edge numbering: if $colored(p, q)$ is false, then $c(p, q) := choice(p, q)$.

3.2   Locally Central Weakly Fair Scheduler

We first assume a locally central weakly fair scheduler.

As the scheduler is weakly fair, we use *asynchronous rounds* to evaluate the time complexity of our algorithm. An asynchronous round is the minimum period necessary for each correct node to be activated at least once.

Let $G' = (V', E')$ be the 1-confined graph obtained from G (see Definition 3). Let us show that we reach a stable coloring on G' in at most $\Delta + 1$ asynchronous rounds.

Lemma 1. *After one asynchronous round, for each correct node p, $distinct(p)$ is always true.*

Proof. During the first asynchronous round, p is activated and executes step 1 of the algorithm. Thus, $distinct(p)$ becomes true. Then, note that no step of the algorithm can invalidate this predicate. Thus, $distinct(p)$ always remains true in the following of the execution.

Lemma 2. *Let p and q be two correct neighbors. After the first asynchronous round, if $colored(p, q)$ is true, then $colored(p, q)$ always remains true in the following of the execution.*

Proof. According to Lemma 1, after the first asynchronous round, the condition of step 1 of the algorithm is never satisfied anymore. Thus, only step 2 and 3 can be executed. Then, note that step 2 and 3 cannot invalidate $colored(p, q)$. Thus, the result.

Lemma 3. *Let $p \in V'$. After $\Delta+1$ asynchronous rounds, $\forall r \in N_p$, $colored(p, r)$ is and remains true.*

Proof. As $p \in V'$, all the neighbors of p are correct. Let q be a neighbor of p such that $colored(p, q)$ is false after the first asynchronous round. As q has been activated previously, according to step 3 of the algorithm, we have $c(q, p) = choice(q, p)$. Thus, when p is activated in the second asynchronous round, the condition of step 2 is satisfied, and there is a neighbor r of p (possibly q) such that $colored(r, q)$ becomes true. According to Lemma 2, $colored(r, q)$ remains true in the following of the execution.

The same reasoning works for the following asynchronous rounds. As there are at most Δ neighbors r of q, after $\Delta + 1$ asynchronous rounds, $\forall r \in N_q$, $colored(r, q)$ is and remains true.

Theorem 1. *We have a stable coloring on G' after $\Delta+1$ asynchronous rounds, and the algorithm is strictly stabilizing with a containment radius of 1.*

Proof. Let p in V'. After $\Delta + 1$ asynchronous rounds:

- According to Lemma 1, $distinct(p)$ is true.
- According to Lemma 3, $\forall r \in N_p$, $colored(p, r)$ is and remains true.

Thus, G' is colored. Besides, as $\forall r \in N_p$, $colored(p, r)$ is and remains true, according to the algorithm, p never changes of state anymore. Therefore, the coloring is stable, and the algorithm is strictly stabilizing with a containment radius of 1.

3.3   Locally Central Unfair Scheduler

Now, let us assume an unfair scheduler. We say that a correct node p is *enabled* when the activation p can change the state of p.

As we consider coloring at distance 2 from Byzantine nodes, we have no guarantees on the behavior of correct nodes at distance 1. In particular, it is possible that the Byzantine nodes perturb their correct neighbor such that the unfair scheduler can activate them endlessly and ignore other correct nodes. Therefore, we make the following restriction on the unfair scheduler: when a node of V' is continuously enabled, then eventually, an enabled node of V' is activated.

The asynchronous round complexity is not appropriate for the unfair scheduler. Instead, we us the number of activations of node. Let us show that we reach a stable coloring in at most $|V| + |E|$ activations of nodes of V'.

Lemma 4. *If G' is not colored, then a node of V' is eventually activated.*

Proof. Let us suppose that G' is not colored.

First, let us suppose that there exists a node $p \in V'$ such that $distinct(p)$ is false. Thus, if p is activated, p can execute step 1 of the algorithm and change its state. Then, $p \in V'$ is continuously enabled until it is activated. Thus, a node of V' is eventually activated.

Now, let us suppose that $\forall p \in V'$, $distinct(p)$ is true. As G' is not colored, it implies that there exists an edge $\{p, q\} \in E'$ such that $colored(p, q)$ is false. Thus, if p is activated:

– Either p can execute step 2 of the algorithm and change its state.
– Or p cannot execute step 2 of the algorithm. Then, if p executes step 3 of the algorithm, p necessarily changes its state.

The same reasoning stands for q. Thus, as long as p and q are not activated, p and q are continuously enabled. Thus, a node of V' (possibly p or q) is eventually activated.

Now, let us define the following two metrics:

– A, the set of correct nodes that are "not enabled" at least once.
– B, the set of edges $\{p, q\}$ such that p and q are correct and $distinct(p)$, $distinct(q)$ and $colored(p, q)$ are true.
– $M = |A| + |B|$

Lemma 5. *When a node $p \in V'$ is activated, M increases.*

Proof. If $p \notin A$ when activated, then p is added to A, and $|A|$ increases.

If $p \in A$ when activated:

– Either this is the first time p is activated.
– Or p has been activated before. As the scheduling is locally central, after the last activation of p, p is not enabled.

Thus, in all cases, p is not enabled, then enabled, then activated. As p becomes enabled, it implies that a set of nodes $X \subseteq N_p$ changes their states.

As $p \in V'$, the nodes of X are correct. Thus, as the nodes of X change of state, they are necessarily activated and execute step 3 of the algorithm. Therefore, when p is activated, p can execute step 2 of the algorithm, and there exists a neighbor $q \in X$ such that $colored(p, q)$ becomes true. Besides, as p and q are activated at least once, $distinct(p)$ and $distinct(q)$ are true. Thus, $|B|$ increases.

Therefore, as either $|A|$ and $|B|$ increase, M increases.

Lemma 6. $|A|$, $|B|$ *and M cannot decrease.*

Proof. $|A|$ cannot decrease by definition. Now, let us show that $|B|$ cannot decrease.

Let us suppose the opposite: $|B|$ decreases. For a correct node p, no step of the algorithm can invalidate $distinct(p)$. Thus, there exists an edge $\{p, q\}$ such that p and q are correct, $distinct(p)$ and $distinct(q)$ are true, and $colored(p,q)$ becomes false. Let $r \in \{p,q\}$ be a node activated when $colored(p,q)$ becomes false. The only step of the algorithm that can invalidate $colored(p,q)$ is step 1, so r necessarily executes step 1. However, as $distinct(r)$ is true, r cannot execute step 1 of the algorithm: contradiction.

Thus, $|B|$ cannot decrease. Thus, the result.

Theorem 2. *We reach a stable coloring on G' after $|V| + |E|$ activations of nodes of V', and the algorithm is strictly stabilizing with a containment radius of 1.*

Proof. M is bounded by $|V| + |E|$. According to Lemma 4 and Lemma 5, as long as G' is not colored, a node of V' is eventually activated, and M eventually increases. Besides, according to Lemma 6, M cannot decrease.

Therefore, after at most $|V|+|E|$ activations of nodes of V', M cannot increase anymore. According to Lemma 5, it implies that no node $p \in V'$ is activated anymore. According to Lemma 4, it implies that G' is colored.

Besides, as no node $p \in V'$ is activated anymore, the state of p does not change anymore. Therefore, the coloring is stable, and the algorithm is strictly stabilizing with a containment radius of 1.

3.4   Periodically Locally Central Unfair Scheduler

Now, let us assume that the scheduler is only periodically locally central (see 2.4). Let us show that we reach a stable coloring in at most $(\Delta + 1)n$ locally central activations of nodes of V'.

First, let us notice that the proof of Lemma 6 remains valid, as it does not use the locally central hypothesis.

Lemma 7. *When a node $p \in V'$ is activated independently of its neighbors, M increases.*

Proof. The proof of Lemma 5 remains true, as p is activated independently of q.

Theorem 3. *We have a stable coloring on G' after $|V'| + |E'|$ locally central activations of nodes of V', and the algorithm is strictly stabilizing with a containment radius of 1.*

Proof. The proof is the same as in Theorem 2, if we replace Lemma 5 by Lemma 7.

3.5   Non Locally Central Unfair Scheduler

At last, let us remove the locally central hypothesis: some nodes may never be activated independently of their neighbors.

It was shown in [6] that no deterministic algorithm can solve this problem. Therefore, we modify our algorithm to make it probabilistic. The new algorithm is as follows: when a correct node is activated, then with equal probability, it chooses to do nothing or to execute the previous algorithm.

Let us show that the expected number of activations of nodes of V' to have a stable coloring on G' is at most $4(|V'| + |E'|)$.

Lemma 8. *When a node $p \in V'$ is activated, then with a probability of at least $1/4$, M increases.*

Proof. The proof of Lemma 5 remains true provided that, when p is activated, p executes the algorithm and q does not executes the algorithm in the same time. When p is activated, p executes the algorithm with probability $1/2$. If q is activated in the same time, q does not execute the algorithm with probability $1/2$. Therefore, M increases with a probability of at least $1/4$.

Theorem 4. *The expected number of activations of nodes of V' to have a stable coloring on G' is at most $4(|V'| + |E'|)$.*

Proof. As stated in Theorem 2, M is bounded by $|V'| + |E'|$. According to Lemma 6 and Lemma 8, the expected number of activations of nodes of V' for M to increase is at most 4. Thus, the expected number of activations of nodes of V' for M to reach its maximal value is at most $4(|V'| + |E'|)$. Thus, the result, for the same argument as in Theorem 2.

4   Byzantine Insensitive Edge Coloring on a Ring

In this section, we propose a Byzantine insensitive edge coloring algorithm for ring topologies.

4.1   Preliminaries

In the previous section, we considered strict stabilization with a containment radius of 1, and proposed an algorithm working in the general case.

Now, we would like to have a Byzantine insensitive algorithm (see Definition 5). This is a more difficult problem, and the previous algorithm does not work in this new setting. Indeed, let p and q be two correct nodes with Byzantine neighbors. In this new setting, we must satisfy $colored(p, q)$. However, when p (for instance) wants to color the edge $\{p, q\}$, a Byzantine neighbor r of p can propose the same color as q, and p may choose to color $\{p, r\}$ instead of $\{p, q\}$. The same situation is possible for q. Thus, this malicious strategy can be repeated endlessly.

In this paper, we propose a first solution to this problem on a *ring* topology, in the case where no local variable is used.

Definition 6 (Ring topology). *A ring is a graph formed by a sequence of nodes $(u_1, \ldots, u_n)$ such that:*

- $\forall i \in \{1, \ldots, n-1\}$, u_i and u_{i+1} are neighbors.
- u_1 and u_n are neighbors.

As each node of a ring has exactly two neighbors, $\forall p \in V$, we have $C_p = 3$. A simple justification of this is that it is impossible to color a ring of 3 nodes with only 2 colors.

4.2   Algorithm

To solve this problem, we modify step 2 of the algorithm, and introduce a mechanism of priority. This mechanism is such that, for a given node p, a given edge cannot have the priority endlessly. A similar mechanism (based on a queue) is proposed in [6], but uses local variables. As local variable are not allowed in our setting, this priority is based on the previous colors used by p.

For instance, let us suppose that p and q are two correct neighbors, and that r is a Byzantine neighbor of p. In the worst case, the edge $\{p, r\}$ may have the priority, but eventually, the priority is given to another edge. Thus, as p has only two neighbors on a ring topology, the priority is necessarily given to the correct edge $\{p, q\}$.

More formally, here is how step 2 should be modified:

Step 2 (modified). If $distinct(p)$ is true, let q and r be the two neighbors of p, such that $c(p, q) > c(p, r)$. We then execute the two following actions:

1. If $c(p, r) \neq c(q, p)$, then $c(p, q) := c(q, p)$.
2. If $c(p, q) \neq c(r, p)$, then $c(p, r) := c(r, p)$.

4.3   Correctness Proof

We assume a locally central weakly fair scheduler (see 2.4). Let us show that we reach a stable coloring after 3 asynchronous rounds.

First, let us notice that the proofs of Lemma 1 and Lemma 2 are still valid despite the modification of step 2 of the algorithm.

Lemma 9. *Let p and q be two neighbor correct nodes. Let r be the other neighbor of p. If $c(p, q) > c(p, r)$ at the end of the ith asynchronous round $(i \geq 1)$, then $colored(p, q)$ is true at the end of the $(i + 1)^{th}$ asynchronous round.*

Proof. When p is activated in the $(i + 1)^{th}$ asynchronous round, as $c(p, q) > c(p, r)$, p first executes step 2.1 of the algorithm. Then, as q has been activated previously and has executed step 3 of the algorithm, $colored(p, q)$ becomes true. Thus, the result.

Lemma 10. *Let p and q be two neighbor correct nodes such that $colored(p, q)$ is false. Let r be the other neighbor of p, and let s be the other neighbor of q. Then, if $c(p, r) > c(p, q)$ and $c(q, s) > c(q, p)$, we are in one of the following situations:*

1. $c(p,r) = 2$, $c(p,q) = 1$, $c(q,p) = 2$ and $c(q,s) = 3$.
2. $c(p,r) = 3$, $c(p,q) = 2$, $c(q,p) = 1$ and $c(q,s) = 2$.
3. $c(p,r) = 3$, $c(p,q) = 1$, $c(q,p) = 2$ and $c(q,s) = 3$.
4. $c(p,r) = 3$, $c(p,q) = 2$, $c(q,p) = 1$ and $c(q,s) = 3$.

Proof. As $c(p,r) > c(p,q)$ and $c(q,s) > c(q,p)$, $c(p,q)$ and $c(q,p)$ cannot take the value 3. As $colored(p,q)$ is false, one of these values is 2 and the other is 1. Then, only the 4 aforementioned situations remain.

Lemma 11. *If we are in situation 1 or 2, then after at most 2 asynchronous rounds, $colored(p,q)$ is true.*

Proof. Let us suppose the opposite: $colored(p,q)$ is not true after 2 asynchronous rounds. As situations 1 and 2 are symmetric, we only consider situation 1.

Let us suppose that p is activated before q. When p is activated, as $c(p,r) > c(p,q)$, if the condition of step 2.2 is satisfied, then $colored(p,q)$ becomes true. Thus, the assumption that this condition cannot be satisfied implies that $c(p,r) = c(q,p) = 2$ after step 2.1. Therefore, after the execution of step 3, we still are in situation 1. Thus, in all cases, when q is activated in the first round, we still are in situation 1.

When q is activated in the first round, as $c(q,s) > c(q,p)$, if the condition of step 2.2 is satisfied, then $colored(p,q)$ becomes true. Thus, the assumption that this condition cannot be satisfied implies that $c(q,s) = c(p,q) = 1$ after step 2.1. Therefore, after the execution of step 3, we have $c(q,p) = 3$ and $c(q,s) = 1$. Thus, as $c(q,p) > c(q,s)$, according to Lemma 9, $colored(p,q)$ is true in the next asynchronous round: contradiction. Thus, the result.

Lemma 12. *If we are in situation 3 or 4, then after at most 2 asynchronous rounds, $colored(p,q)$ is true.*

Proof. Let us suppose the opposite: $colored(p,q)$ is not true after 2 asynchronous rounds. As situations 3 and 4 are symmetric, we only consider situation 3.

Let us suppose that p is activated before q. When p is activated, as $c(p,r) > c(p,q)$, if the condition of step 2.2 is satisfied, then $colored(p,q)$ becomes true. Thus, the assumption that this condition cannot be satisfied implies that $c(p,r) = c(q,p) = 2$ after step 2.1. Therefore, after the execution of step 3, we reach situation 1. Thus, the result, according to the proof of Lemma 11.

Now, let us suppose that q is activated before p. When q is activated, as $c(q,s) > c(q,p)$, if the condition of step 2.2 is satisfied, then $colored(p,q)$ becomes true. Thus, the assumption that this condition cannot be satisfied implies that $c(q,s) = c(p,q) = 1$ after step 2.1. Therefore, after the execution of step 3, $c(q,p) = 2$ and $c(q,s) = 1$. Thus, as $c(q,p) > c(q,s)$, according to Lemma 9, $colored(p,q)$ is true in the next asynchronous round: contradiction. Thus, the result.

Lemma 13. *Let p and q be two correct neighbors. After at most 3 asynchronous rounds, $colored(p,q)$ is true.*

Proof. Let us suppose the opposite: $colored(p, q)$ does not become true in 4 asynchronous rounds.

Let r be the other neighbor of p, and let s be the other neighbor of q. According to Lemma 1, after one asynchronous round, $distinct(p)$ and $distinct(q)$ are true, implying that $c(p, r) \neq c(p, q)$ and $c(q, s) \neq c(q, p)$. Thus, two possibilities:

- Either $c(p, q) > c(p, r)$ or $c(q, p) > c(q, s)$. Thus, we are in a situation such as described in Lemma 9. Then, according to Lemma 9, $colored(p, q)$ is true after 2 asynchronous rounds.
- Or $c(p, r) > c(p, q)$ and $c(q, s) > c(q, p)$. Thus, we are in one of the 4 situations described in Lemma 10. Then, according to Lemma 11 and Lemma 12, $colored(p, q)$ is true after 3 asynchronous rounds.

Theorem 5. *We reach a stable coloring after 3 asynchronous rounds, and the algorithm is Byzantine insensitive.*

Proof. Let p and q be two correct neighbors. According to Lemma 1, 2 and 13, after 3 asynchronous rounds, $distinct(p)$, $distinct(q)$ and $colored(p, q)$ are true and always remain true. Besides, for the same argument as in Theorem 1, this coloring is stable.

At last, let p be a node without Byzantine neighbors. As $\forall r \in N_p$, $colored(p, r)$ is and remain true, p is never activated anymore, and never changes of state anymore. Thus, the result.

5   Conclusion

In this paper, we considered the problem of Byzantine resilient edge coloring without local variables. We proposed a general algorithm with a containment radius of 1, and a specific Byzantine insensitive algorithm for ring topologies. We also showed that this problem could be probabilistically solved without the locally central hypothesis, in an expected linear time.

As we can see, a challenging open problem is the existence of a general Byzantine insensitive algorithm in this setting. If a general algorithm does not exist, an open question is the class of network topologies where this problem can be solved.

References

1. Jiang, J.-R., Tzeng, C.-H., Huang, S.-T.: A self-stabilizing (delta+4)-edge-coloring algorithm for planar graphs in anonymous uniform systems. Information Processing Letters 101(4), 168–173 (2007)
2. Dijkstra, E.W.: Self-stabilizing systems in spite of distributed control. Commun. ACM 17(11), 643–644 (1974)
3. Dolev, S.: Self-Stabilization. MIT Press (2000)
4. Dubois, S., Masuzawa, T., Tixeuil, S.: Bounding the impact of unbounded attacks in stabilization. IEEE Transactions on Parallel and Distributed Systems, TPDS (2011)

5. Huang, S.-T., Tzeng, C.-H.: Distributed edge coloration for bipartite networks. In: 8th International Symposium on Stabilization, Safety and Security of Distributed Systems, pp. 363–377 (2006)
6. Masuzawa, T., Tixeuil, S.: Stabilizing link-coloration of arbitrary networks with unbounded byzantine faults. International Journal of Principles and Applications of Information Science and Technology (PAIST) 1(1), 1–13 (2007)
7. Nesterenko, M., Arora, A.: Tolerance to unbounded byzantine faults. In: 21st Symposium on Reliable Distributed Systems (SRDS 2002), pp. 22–29. IEEE Computer Society (2002)
8. Sakurai, Y., Ooshita, F., Masuzawa, T.: A self-stabilizing link-coloring protocol resilient to byzantine faults in tree networks. In: Higashino, T. (ed.) OPODIS 2004. LNCS, vol. 3544, pp. 283–298. Springer, Heidelberg (2005)
9. Pirwani, I., Herman, T., Pemmaraju, S.: Oriented edge coloring and link scheduling in sensor networks. In: International Conference on Communication Software and Middleware, pp. 1–6 (2006)

Tight Bounds for Stabilizing Uniform Consensus in Mobile Networks

Hung Tran-The and Luís Rodrigues

INESC-ID, Instituto Superior Técnico, Universidade de Lisboa
tran.thehung@gsd.inesc-id.pt,
ler@ist.utl.pt

Abstract. This paper addresses the problem of solving stabilizing uniform consensus in mobile networks. In this problem, the input of nodes may change multiple times before they eventually stabilize. However, when the system stabilizes all correct nodes output a value and there are no two non-crashed nodes (whether faulty or not) that output different values. In contrast to stabilizing consensus, stabilizing uniform consensus is not solvable with Byzantine faults. So we consider here weaker kinds of faults, namely crash faults and omission faults. We show that for crash and send-omission faults, $n > 2t$ is a necessary and sufficient condition for solving stabilizing uniform consensus, where n is the total number of mobile nodes, out of which t may be faulty. Interestingly, when the input of nodes are fixed, stabilizing uniform consensus is solvable with crash faults for $n > t$ and with send-omission faults for $n > 2t$ (for $t > 1$). When considering general omission faults, we show that stabilizing uniform consensus is not solvable, even for fixed inputs and $t = 1$.

1   Introduction

In this paper we address the problem of coordinating mobile nodes equipped with sensors (for instance, autonomous robots). We consider that each node is equipped with a sensor that captures information from the external world. In this case, it is natural that during transition periods in the environment, the input from the sensors flickers before stabilizing. For instance, a light sensor may detect if the node is operating during the day (input 1) or the night (input 0). However, during sunset, and depending on the movement of the node among regions of light and shadow, the sensor may change its input multiple times before it stabilizes to 0.

Further, we assume that mobile nodes are not permanently within contact with every other node. However, their movement ensures that eventually, every node encounters every other node infinitely often. This should allow nodes to cooperate and take coordinated actions based on the values of the stabilized inputs. For instance, all correct nodes should be able to coordinate in order to perform some action after the night has settled.

This realistic problem can be captured by an abstraction that has been named *stabilizing consensus in mobile networks* [1]. In this paper we study a stronger

P. Felber and V. Garg (Eds.): SSS 2014, LNCS 8756, pp. 328–342, 2014.
© Springer International Publishing Switzerland 2014

version, that we name *stabilizing uniform*, inspired by the classical uniform variant of the problem [11]. Informally, in the uniform consensus, no two nodes (whether faulty or not) output different values. In the stabilizing setting, this means that a faulty (non-crashed) node may never decide but, in any case, should never stabilize its output to a value different from the stabilized output of correct nodes. In detail, this paper is concerned with identifying the conditions for which it is possible to solve stabilizing uniform consensus in mobile networks.

The consensus problem: The consensus problem occurs in many contexts and has therefore been extensively studied in the literature (e.g.,[2], [13],[16]). Relevant applications of consensus are the consolidation of replicated states and the synchronization of nodes. It is usually trivial to reach agreement in a reliable system composed of n nodes, for example by performing a leader election. However, if there are $t < n$ faulty nodes, the consensus problem becomes much harder. Nodes in the system are liable to fail by halting prematurely (crash faults), by omitting to send messages (send-omission faults), by omitting to send or receive messages (general omission faults), or by behaving arbitrarily (Byzantine faults). Fischer, Lynch, and Paterson [8] showed that, in a fully asynchronous environment, there is no solution to the consensus problem even with a single crash fault ($t = 1$). In a synchronous environment, where all nodes run at the same speed, consensus is solvable for $n > t$, even for omission faults. For Byzantine faults, consensus is only solvable if $n > 3t$ [12].

Uniform consensus: For many applications, the regular version of the agreement condition of consensus, namely "no two correct nodes decide differently", is inadequate as it does not restrict the decision values of faulty nodes. A strengthen version of consensus, namely the *uniform* consensus problem, is considered in [11]. It requires that no two nodes (whether faulty or not) decide differently. Clearly, uniform consensus is trivially not solvable with Byzantine faults, because faulty nodes have no constraints on their possible behaviors. In synchronous systems, for crash faults only, it is not difficult to solve both consensus and uniform consensus in the presence of any number of faulty nodes. Interestingly, Guerraoui [9] showed that in most partially synchronous systems, any algorithm that solves consensus also solves uniform consensus. For general omission faults, Neiger and Toueg [15] showed that uniform consensus can be solved if and only if $n > 2t$. When $n > 2t$, they also showed that any algorithm that solves uniform consensus in the crash fault model is converted by means of this translation into an algorithm that solves uniform consensus and tolerates omission faults.

Consensus in mobile networks: Fault-tolerance issues in mobile networks started to be addressed in more recent years. A survey of fault tolerance in mobile wireless networks is provided in [3]. For crash faults, [4,5] presented consensus protocols using failure detectors. Randomization is also used for consensus with omission faults and Byzantine faults in [14]. Beside using synchronization, failure detectors and randomization, stabilization is also a viable way of circumventing the impossibility result of Fischer, Lynch, and Paterson [8], specially in mobile environments. The problem of stabilizing consensus in mobile networks has been addressed for the first time in [1]. Stabilizing consensus requires non-faulty nodes to eventually agree on one of their inputs, but nodes do not necessarily know when agreement is reached. It is possible to solve the regular version of consensus with Byzantine nodes for $n > 3t$, as shown in [1]. More recently, [7] considered the stabilizing consensus problem in the synchronous model and a T-bounded adversary that knows the entire state of the system at the end of each communication round and may corrupt the state of up to T nodes in an arbitrary way before the next round starts.

Stabilizing uniform consensus: When considering stabilizing inputs, the "standard" definition of uniform consensus cannot be applied. In fact, at a given time all nodes may have the same input (say 0), which requires them to also output 0. Then a single node crashes and the inputs of all correct nodes flip to 1. In this case, correct nodes must output 1 and must necessarily diverge from the (past) output of the crashed node. However, for stabilizing inputs, it makes sense to consider a stabilizing version of uniformity, that excludes crashed nodes but still considers nodes subject to more benign faults. Informally, we say that an output is stabilizing uniform if eventually, no two (correct or not) non-crashed nodes do not stabilize their outputs to different values (a more precise definition is given in Section 2). Unfortunately, as we show in this paper, even this weaker variant of uniformity is difficult to achieve.

Contributions: We address the problem of stabilizing the outputs in face of stabilizing inputs. We do not address self-stabilizing, in the classical sense [6], as we do not address the problem recovering from arbitrary state-corruptions (instead, we model an abritrary state corruption as a Byzantine fault). As discussed before, uniform consensus is not solvable with Byzantine faults and, in its classical formulation, does not make sense in face of stabilizing inputs. So we consider here a variant, named *stabilizing uniform consensus* in the presence of crash faults and omission faults. We show that for crash and send omission faults, $n > 2t$ is a necessary and sufficient condition for solving stabilizing uniform consensus, where n is the total number of mobile nodes, out of which t may be faulty. Interestingly, when the input of the nodes are fixed, stabilizing uniform consensus is solvable with crash faults for $n > t$ and with send-omission faults for $n > 2t$ (for $t > 1$). However, when considering general omission faults, we show that stabilizing uniform consensus is not solvable, even for fixed inputs and $t = 1$. These results are summarized in Table 1 (entries that correspond to new results are depicted with shaded background). Our results show that in contrast to synchronization, stabilization is not sufficient to assure the agreement of nodes (faulty or not) in the presence of general omission faults. To the best of our knowledge, this is the first paper that investigates the stabilizing uniform consensus problem.

Roadmap: The remainder of the paper is structured as follows. Section 2 provides a precise definition of the system model and of the problem we are tackling.

Table 1. Necessary and sufficient conditions on the number of nodes for solving the uniform consensus in a system of n nodes and tolerating t faulty nodes

	Synchronous Network	Mobile Network	
	Fixed Inputs (Uniform)	Fixed Inputs (Uniform)	Stabilizing Inputs (Stabilizing Uniform)
Crash	$n > t$ [15]	$n > t$ [1]	$n > 2t$
Send-Omission	$n > t$ [15]	$n > 2t$ for $t > 1$ $n \geq 2$ for $t = 1$	$n > 2t$
General Omission	$n > 2t$ [15]	Impossible	Impossible

Then, Section 3 derives a number of new impossibility results for the problem of stabilizing uniform consensus in mobile networks. An algorithm that solves stabilizing uniform consensus with crash and send-omission faults is presented in Section 4. Finally, Section 5 concludes the paper.

2   Model and Definitions

We consider a set of mobile nodes *with distinct identifiers* that may establish pairwise interactions whenever their mobility pattern allows them to *encounter* each other. An *encounter* is a directed interaction among two nodes, where one node is denoted the *initiator* and the other is denoted the *recipient*. We say that a node i encounters node j, when i is the initiator and j the recipient. When an encounter occurs, the initiator sends a message to the recipient.

Network Fault Model We assume a wireless channel that is unable to store messages. Messages may get lost, but we assume that if node i sends a message to j infinitely often (as a result of multiple encounters), j receives the message infinitely often. If a fault occurs during an encounter, that prevents the message from being received by the recipient, the message is lost and a new message will need to be created and sent in the next encounter.

Node Fault Model We consider 3 different types of faults in this paper (if a node never becomes faulty we say that it is correct):

- *Crash Faults*: A node that suffers a crash fault operates correctly until a point where it *crashes*. After crashing, the node stops operating. A crashed node does not output any value, no longer encounters any other node, and is no longer encountered by any other node.
- *Send-Omission Faults*: A node that suffers from send-omission faults, when it encounters other nodes, it may fail to send information to the recipient, even if the recipient is correct. Nodes subject to send-omission faults, may fail to send messages infinitely often.

- *General Omission Faults*: A node that suffers from general omission faults may fail to send information to the recipient when it plays the role of the initiator and/or fail to receive the information that was sent by the initiator, when it plays the role of the recipient. It may do so infinitely often.

Note that, since the network is unreliable, nodes cannot distinguish an encounter with a correct node where the network drops a message from an encounter with a node subject to send-omission faults. We say that i encounters *successfully* j if the message sent by i is received by j (i.e., no faults occur during the encounter, either in the network or in the nodes).

Mobility and Fairness Condition The mobility model considers node movement and also captures the fact that to maintain bi-directional wireless communication for an extended period may be hard to enforce in a real setting. Thus, a node i may encounter node j at a given time, and its is possible that node j only encounters i at a later time. Also, after node i encounters node j there is no pre-defined time limit for node i to encounter any other node k (including j again). Thus, the system is asynchronous. In fact, the mobility of nodes is controlled by an adversary, but we assume the following fairness condition:

Local fairness: *Every node encounters every other node infinitely often.*

Note that while an individual encounter is directed, the fairness condition guarantees eventually bidirectional communication.

Stabilizing Uniform Consensus Each node has access to an input whose value may be read but may not be changed by the protocol. The values of the inputs may change multiple times but eventually stabilize. Unlike classical consensus, the output of nodes may be written many times but eventually, stabilize. More precisely: A configuration includes the local state of all nodes (the state of a node may change after each encounter where that node participates). A configuration C is said to be output-stable if in all possible executions starting from C, the output values of all nodes never change. If every correct node outputs v in an output-stable configuration C, we say the outputs stabilize to v in C.

Definition 1. *A protocol solves the stabilizing uniform consensus problem if the following 3 properties are satisfied:*

- **Stabilization:** *If the inputs of the nodes stabilize, the system eventually reaches an output-stable configuration.*
- **Validity:** *If all nodes have inputs stabilizing to the same value v, the outputs of all correct nodes eventually stabilize to v.*
- **Stabilizing Uniform Agreement:** *In any reachable output-stable configuration, no two (correct or not) non-crashed nodes have different outputs (note that crashed nodes have no output).*

3   Impossibility Results

In this section, we provide bounds for the impossibility of solving stabilizing uniform consensus in face of different types of faults.

3.1   Notation

We consider the configuration of the system at the end of each interaction. Such configuration is composed of the state of each node. We say that a configuration C is v-*valent* in some set of executions E, if in every execution of E starting from C the only stable output value of all nodes is v. A configuration C is v-*valent* if in all possible executions starting from C the only stable output value of all nodes is v. C is *bivalent* if there is an execution where C is v-valent and another execution where C is v'-valent such that $v' \neq v$.

Let n be the number of nodes, t of which may be subject to faults. Consider the case where $n = 2t$ and let $G = G_0 \cup G_1$ in which G_0 is the set of t nodes with initial input 0, and G_1 is the set of t nodes with initial input 1. For simplicity, in the impossibility results section we only consider binary protocols P solving the stabilizing uniform consensus in the presence of up to t faults. For a configuration C of G, we denote the sub-configuration of G_0 by C^0, sub-configuration of G_1 by C^1. Let I be the initial configuration of G. We denote by $E(I)$ the set of all possible executions of P starting from I and by $F(I)$ the set of fault-free executions of P starting from I.

For the crash failure model: we denote by $\alpha(C^0)$ (resp., $\alpha(C^1)$) the set of executions starting from configuration C, in which t nodes in G_1 (resp., G_0) are crashed. If C is v-valent in $\alpha(C^0)$ (resp., $\alpha(C^1)$), we say that C_0 (resp., C_1) is v-valent.

For the send omission failure model: we denote by $\beta(C^0)$ (resp., $\beta(C^1)$) set of all possible executions starting from configuration C, in which no message from group G_1 (resp., G_0) is delivered to the group G_0 (resp., G_1). This is possible because t nodes in G_1 may be subject to send omission faults. If C is v-valent in $\beta(C^0)$ (resp., $\beta(C^1)$), we say that C^0 (resp., C^1) is v-valent. Let $\beta(C) = \beta(C^0) \cup \beta(C^1)$. We say that C is bivalent in $\beta(C)$ if there exist v, v' such that (1) C^0 is v-valent, C^1 is v'-valent and (2) $v \neq v'$.

From these notations, we obtain the following simple lemmas:

Lemma 1. *If C is bivalent in $\beta(C)$ then C is bivalent.*

Lemma 2. *For the crash failure model, if a configuration C can be reached in a fault-free execution, then i) $\alpha(C^0) \in E(I)$ (resp., $\alpha(C^1) \in E(I)$), and ii) if the inputs stabilize starting from C then C^0 (resp., C^1) is either 0-valent, or 1-valent.*

Lemma 3. *For the send omission failure model, if a configuration C can be reached in a fault-free execution, then i) $\beta(C^0) \in E(I)$ (resp., $\beta(C^1) \in E(I)$) are possible in P, and ii) if the inputs stabilize starting from C then C^0 (resp., C^1) is either 0-valent, or 1-valent.*

3.2   Stabilizing Uniform Consensus with Crash Faults

Theorem 1. *There is no protocol that solves stabilizing uniform consensus with crash faults if the inputs are not fixed and $n \leq 2t$.*

Proof. It suffices to prove there is no protocol for stabilizing consensus when $n = 2t$. Assume by contradiction that there exists such a protocol P. Consider the system G as described in Section 3.1, where $G = G_0 \cup G_1$ and $|G_0| = |G_1| = t > 0$. By Lemma 4, there is some reachable configuration C such that configuration C^1 of G_1 is 0-valent. Recall that by definition, C^1 is 0-valent means that C is 0-valent in $\alpha(C^1)$. Consider a possible execution β of P starting from C such that all nodes in G_0 change their inputs to 1 and then crash. In this execution, all nodes have inputs stabilizing to 1, so by the validity property of consensus, the outputs of correct nodes eventually stabilize to 1 in β. But, nodes in G_1 cannot distinguish β from an execution in $\alpha(C^1)$ where nodes in G_0 keep input 0 and crash. So they eventually output 0 in β. Contradiction.   □

Lemma 4. *There is some configuration C reached in a fault-free execution such that C^1 is 0-valent.*

Proof. Given Lemma 2 every configuration C reached in a fault-free execution is either 0-valent or 1-valent. Assume by the sake of contradiction that C^1 is 1-valent. Consider executions in $F(I)$ where the inputs of G are fixed. The system must eventually reach some output stable configuration D in $F(I)$. Without loss of generality, assume the stable output value in D is $v = 0$. By hypothesis, we have D^1 is 1-valent. This means that there is an execution β in $\alpha(D^1)$ where the output of nodes in G_1 eventually stabilizes to 1 after some point T. On the other hand, consider a fault-free partial execution starting from D until point T such that it is similar to β but nodes in G_0 do not crash, instead, they do not encounter nodes in G_1 and nodes in G_1 do not encounter nodes in G_0. By definition of D, nodes in G_1 output 0 at T. But, nodes in G_1 cannot distinguish execution this execution from β, so they output 1 at T. Contradiction.   □

3.3   Stabilizing Uniform Consensus with Send-Omission Faults

For the case of send-omission faults, we start by considering first the case where $n \leq 2t, n \geq 4$ and $t \geq 2$ and later the particular case where $n = 3$ and $t = 2$. Here, we use the bivalent argument and the contradiction argument by constructing a fault-free execution that (1) satisfies the local fairness and the condition that if a node i sends a message to a node j infinitely often, j receives the message infinitely often, and that (2) violates the stabilization condition. We first consider the case where $n \leq 2t, n \geq 4$ and $t \geq 2$. We prove the following lemmas:

Lemma 5. *I^0 is 0-valent and I^1 is 1-valent.*

Proof. The lemma holds due to the validity condition of stabilizing uniform consensus. The proof is omitted due to space constraints.   □

We denote by $\theta(G_0)$ (resp., $\theta(G_1)$) the following execution (that we call a partitioned execution): first, all nodes in each group encounter successfully nodes also in that group only one time. Next, all nodes in group G_0 (resp., G_1) encounter all nodes in group G_1 (resp., G_0) only one time but all messages from G_0 (resp., G_1) to G_1 (resp., G_0) are not delivered. Finally we choose determinatively a couple nodes i, j where i in G_1 (resp., G_0) and j in G_0 (resp., G_1) and node i encounter successfully j. We denote by $\theta(C^0)$ (resp., $\theta(C^1)$) the set of executions starting from C, in which we repeat the partitioned execution $\theta(G_0)$ (resp., $\theta(G_1)$) infinitely often and choose valid couples i, j such that every node in G_1 (resp., G_0) encounters successfully other nodes in G_0 (resp., G_1) infinitely often. It is easy to see that the executions in $\theta(C^0)$ (resp., $\theta(C^1)$) satisfy the local fairness condition and $\theta(C^0) \subset \beta(C^0)$, $\theta(C^1) \subset \beta(C^1)$.

Lemma 6. *Consider a configuration C where C^0 is v-valent and C^1 is v'-valent ($v \neq v'$). Then there is a reachable configuration A in $\theta(C^0)$ such that: i) A^1 is v'-valent; ii) for every configuration B reached from A by one encounter where the initiator is in G_0, the recipient is in G_1, then B^1 is always v-valent.*

Proof. Since C^0_k is 0-valent, then in every execution in $\beta(C^0_k)$, the only stable output value of all nodes is 0. In particular, it is also true for a subset $\theta(C^0_k)$ of $\beta(C^0_k)$. By the argument similar to Lemma 4, for executions in $\theta(C^0_k)$, there is a configuration C reached from C_k, where C^1 is 0-valent. Since C^1_k is 1-valent and C^1 is 0-valent, there is reachable configurations E and F such that F reached from E by an encounter e and E^1 is still 1-valent, F^1 is 0-valent. Moreover, for encounter e, the initiator must be in G_0 and the recipient must be in G_1. Indeed, recall if E^1 is 1-valent then E is 1-valent in $\beta(E^1)$. It means that in every possible execution in which all messages from G_0 to G_1 are not delivered, then configurations reached from E is still 1-valent. Hence, in order that F^1 is 0-valent, the initiator of e must be in G_0 and the recipient of e must be in G_1.

By definition of $\theta(C^0)$, such an encounter e is deterministically chosen. Hence by the deterministic choice, the system may reach some configuration A such that (1) A^1 is still 1-valent and (2) every configuration B reached from A by one encounter where the initiator is in G_0, the recipient is in G_1 then B^1 is always 0-valent. □

Similarly, we also get:

Lemma 7. *Consider configuration C where C^0 is v-valent and C^1 is v'-valent ($v \neq v'$). Then there is a reachable configuration A in $\theta(C^1)$ such that: i) A^0 is v-valent; ii) for every configuration B reached from A by one encounter where the initiator is in G_1, the recipient is in G_0, then B^0 is always v'-valent.*

Lemma 8. *There is no protocol solving stabilizing uniform consensus with send-omission faults for $n \leq 2t$, $t \geq 2$ and $n \geq 4$.*

Proof. It suffices to prove there is no protocol for stabilizing consensus when $n = 2t$. Assume by contradiction that there exists a protocol P solving stabilizing

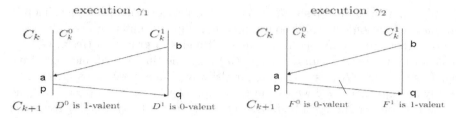

Fig. 1. An example of $n = 4, t = 2$. $G_0 = \{a, p\}$ and $G_1 = \{b, q\}$

consensus. The idea of the proof is to construct a fault-free execution in which there is an infinite sequence of bivalent configurations C_k. This contradicts the stabilization condition of stabilizing uniform consensus.

Let $C_0 = I$. Then C_0 is the bivalent configuration. Now, assume we constructed a bivalent configuration C_k ($k \geq 0$) by a fault-free execution. Assume without loss of generality that in C_k, C_k^0 is 0-valent, C_k^1 is 1-valent. We will show that there is an execution of P such that from C_k, we can reach another bivalent configuration C_{k+1}. If k is even we consider executions in $\beta(C_k^0)$, else we consider executions in $\beta(C_k^1)$ (the odd even check is to guarantee the local fairness condition).

Assume without loss of generality that k is even. We choose deterministically a couple nodes p, q where p in G_0 and q in G_1. Let $S_k = G_0 \setminus \{p\}$ and $P_k = G_1 \setminus \{q\}$. By Lemma 6, there is configuration A reached in some execution α in $\theta(C^0)$ such that (1) A^1 is 1-valent, and (2) for configuration B reached from A by encounter e between p and q, B^1 is 0-valent. Let θ be the partitioned execution in $\theta(C^0)$ that e belongs to. Consider a partial execution γ_1 starting from C_k such that it is similar to execution α except that all messages from nodes in P_k sent to nodes in S_k in the partial execution θ are delivered. Clearly, in this partial execution, all nodes still execute correctly and due to the fact that $|S_k|, |P_k| \geq 1$, there is at least one node in G_1 that encounters a node in G_0. Let D be the obtained configuration after p encounters q. Since nodes in G_1 cannot distinguish this execution from execution α, D^1 must be 0-valent. We consider the two cases: i) if D^0 is 1-valent then let $C_{k+1} = D$; ii) if D^0 is 0-valent then consider execution γ_2 that is similar to γ_1 except that message from p to q is not delivered. Let F be configuration obtained after p encounters q. Clearly, F^1 is 1-valent and $F^0 = D^0$ is 0-valent. Let $C_{k+1} = F$.

In both cases, C_{k+1} is obtained by a fault-free execution and it is bivalent (see Figure 1). Hence, by induction, we obtain a fault-free execution in which there is an infinite sequence of bivalent configurations C_i, where $i \geq 0$. It remains to show that such an execution satisfies the local fairness condition and the condition that if a node i sends a message to a node j infinitely often, j receives the message infinitely often. Indeed, if k is odd, as noticed above, nodes in each group encounter successfully each other and we can choose deterministically the sets S_k, P_k and assure that nodes from P_k always encounter successfully nodes in S_k. Similarly, if k is even, nodes in each group encounter successfully each other and we can choose deterministically the sets S_k, P_k and assure that nodes from S_k encounter successfully nodes in P_k.   □

Lemma 9. *There is no protocol that solves stabilizing uniform consensus with send-omission faults for $t = 2$ and $n = 3$ even with fixed inputs.*

Proof. (the proof is omitted due to space constraints).   □

Thus, for send-omission faults, we get the following impossibility:

Theorem 2. *Stabilizing uniform consensus is unsolvable with send-omission faults if $t \geq 2$ and $n \leq 2t$ even inputs are fixed.*

Proof. This result derives from Lemma 8 and Lemma 9.   □

3.4 Stabilizing Uniform Consensus with General Omission Faults

Theorem 3. *There is no protocol solving stabilizing uniform consensus in the presence of one node subject to general omission faults, even if inputs are fixed.*

Proof. Assume by contradiction that there exists a protocol P solving stabilizing consensus in the presence of one node subject to general omission fault and with inputs of nodes are fixed. By the bivalency argument, it is not difficult to prove that there are two initial configurations C and C' which differ only by the initial value of some node i and such that I is 0-valent and I' is 1-valent. Consider the set α of executions of P in which node i is subject to general omission faults end fails to send/receive all messages to/from other nodes. There must be some output stable configuration D reached after some point T in α. Without loss of generality, assume this stable output value is $v = 1$.

We choose deterministically a node j other than i. Then we get that j outputs 1 at T. Consider the set β of executions of P starting from point T, in which node j subjects to general omission faults and fails to send/receive all messages to/from other nodes. There must be some reachable output stable configuration D' after some point T' by some execution β_1 in β. Without loss of generality, assume this stable output value is v'. By stabilizing uniform consensus, node j outputs either v', or $\perp$. Now consider a partial execution from T to T' such that it is similar to execution β_1 but node j does not fail to send/receive all messages to/from other nodes, instead, all messages sent to/from j get lost. Node j cannot distinguish the partial execution from execution β_1 from T to T', so it outputs either v', or $\perp$ in this partial execution. On the other hand, node j cannot distinguish this partial execution from a possible execution in α where node i subjects to general omission faults, so it outputs 1 at T' in the partial execution. Thus, $v' = 1$.

Note that such a partial execution from T to T' can be simulated by an execution where nodes are not subject to faults given that, in a finite period, a node may fail to send/receive messages due to network omissions. Repeating fault-free partial executions similar to above one infinitely often such that all nodes can be chosen infinitely often, we obtain a fault-free execution that satisfies the local fairness condition and the condition that if a node i sends a message to a node j infinitely often, j receives the message infinitely often. Moreover, all nodes do not have the stable output 0. This contradicts the hypothesis that I is 0-valent, i.e., every possible fault-free execution starting from I, the only stable value of nodes is 0.   □

4   Solving Stabilizing Uniform Consensus with Crash and Send-Omission Faults

The stabilizing uniform consensus algorithm tolerating crash faults and considering fixed inputs is similar to the one in [1]. For send-omission faults and fixed inputs, if $t = 1$ and $n = 2$, the consensus algorithm is trivial. Thus, we only consider the algorithm with stabilizing inputs tolerating t crash or send-omission faults, assuming $n > 2t$, where $t \geq 1$ and n is the total number of nodes. When considering the case where inputs of nodes are fixed as in classical models, it is not difficult to obtain consensus by using the majority and a *flood set* strategy [10]. However, when inputs are not fixed, it is very difficult to use this strategy on inputs. We here use a counter array to keep track of the number of times the other nodes change their inputs. Since our solution relies on the value of these counters being correctly initialized, our algorithm is not self-stabilizing, in the classical sense [6], since it cannot recover from arbitrary state-corruptions.

Each node i maintains the following variables: my_input_i denotes the current reading of the input port. A matrix $inputs_i[][]$ is used to maintain an estimate of the input values known by every node (the line $inputs_i[i][]$ keeps the values known by i). An array $C\_INPUT_i[]$ to maintain consistent input values of all nodes. The counter array $c_i[]$ to keep track of the number of times each node changes its input. In particular, $c_i[i]$ is used to keep track of how many times the local input has changed. The details of the algorithm are presented in Figure 2. In each encounter, the initiator sends arrays $inputs_i[i][]$ and $c_i[]$ to the recipient. When node i is the recipient, it updates the array $c_i[]$, the matrix $inputs_i[][]$, and also $C\_INPUT_i[]$. The update of $c_i[]$ is based on the increasing order of the counter and the update of $C\_INPUT[]$ is based on the majority of values in $inputs_i[][]$. Eventually, correct nodes obtain an array $C\_INPUT_i[]$ containing consistent values for the inputs.

Lemma 10. *For any i, $c_i[i]$ eventually stabilizes.*

Proof. Since the input of node i can only change a finite number of times, variable $c_i[i]$ is bounded. Moreover, this variable cannot decrease. Thus, $c_i[i]$ eventually stabilizes.   □

Lemma 11. *For any i, j, $c_i[j]$ eventually stabilizes.*

```
Code for node i
Variables:
1   my_input_i, c_i[], inputs_i[][], C_INPUT_i[]

Initialization:
2   for all k, j: inputs_i[k][j] = 0, C_INPUT_i[k] = 0, c_i[k] = 0

State update:
3   when inputs_i[i, i] ≠ my_input_i
4       c_i[i] = c_i[i] + 1
5       inputs_i[i][i] = my_input_i
6   when node i encounters node j
7       i sends inputs_i[i][], c_i[] to j
8   when node i receives inputs_j[j][], c_j[] from j do
9       inputs_i[j][] = inputs_j[j][]
10      for all k ≠ i:
11          if c_j[k] > c_i[k] then
12              c_i[k] = c_j[k]
13              inputs_i[i][k] = inputs_j[j][k]

Output:
14  for all j
15      if ∃v : |k : inputs_i[k][j] = v| ≥ n − t then C_INPUT[j] = v else C_INPUT[j] = 0
16  if ∃v : |k : C_INPUT_i[k] = v| ≥ n − t then outputs v else outputs 0
```

Fig. 2. Stabilizing uniform consensus algorithm for $n > 2t$

Proof. If $j = i$ then by Lemma 10, $c_i[i]$ eventually stabilizes. Consider case where $j \neq i$. By Lemma 10, $c_j[j]$ eventually stabilizes to some value after some time t. Let c_j be this value. Clearly, at any time $c_j[j] \leq c_j$. Moreover, at any time for any k: $c_k[j] \leq c_j[j]$. Hence, at any time for any k: $c_k[j] \leq c_j[j]$. After time t, variable $c_i[j]$ cannot decrease, so $c_i[j]$ eventually stabilizes. □

Lemma 12. *For any i, j, $input_i[i][j]$ eventually stabilizes.*

Proof. Since the input of node i can only change a finite number of times, $inputs_i[i][i]$ must stabilize. Consider $j \neq i$: By Lemma 11, $c_i[j]$ eventually stabilizes. It follows that eventually node i stops updating variable $inputs_i[i][j]$. □

By Lemmas 11 and 12, we get that for any i, j: $c_i[j], input_i[i][j]$ eventually stabilizes. Let T be a time where for any i, j: $c_i[j], input_i[i][j]$ stabilizes.

Lemma 13. *Assume i to be a correct node and that $inputs_i[i][i]$ stabilizes to v_i. Then for any j: $input_j[j][i]$ eventually stabilizes to v_i.*

Proof. By Lemma 11 $c_j[i]$ eventually stabilizes. Thus, node j eventually stops updating variable $input_j[j][i]$. Since node i is correct and my_input_i stabilizes to v_i, node j eventually is encountered by i and sets $input_j[j][i] = v_i$. □

Lemma 14. *If j, k are correct nodes then for any i if $input_j[j][i]$ stabilizes to v_j and $input_k[k][i]$ stabilizes to v_k then $v_j = v_k$.*

Proof. If $i = k$ or $j = k$ then by Lemma 13, the lemma holds. Consider the case where $i \neq j, k$. Assume $c_j[i]$ stabilizes to c_j and $c_j[i]$ stabilizes to c_k. There are two cases to consider: *case 1)* $c_k \neq c_j$ then without loss of generality, assume $c_k > c_j$. Since j, k are correct, j encounters successfully i and i encounters successfully j infinitely often. After T, when k receives messages from j, it will set $c_k[i] = c_j[i]$ and $inputs_k[k][i] = input_j[j][i]$ at lines 12,13. Thus, $c_k = c_j$ and $v_k = v_j$. *case 2)* $c_k = c_j$. There is some time t_j where node i has $c_i[i] = c_j$ and $inputs_i[i][i] = v_j$ and an other time t_k where node i has $c_i[i] = c_k$ and $inputs_i[i][i] = v_k$. Since $c_i[i]$ only increase over time if node i changes its input, if $c_k = c_j$ then $v_k = v_j$. □

Lemma 15. *For any i, j, k: $inputs_i[j][k]$ stabilizes after time T.*

Proof. It is direct from Lemma 12 □

Lemma 16. *For any i, j: $C\_INPUT_i[j]$ stabilizes after T.*

Proof. By Lemma 15, for any i, j, k: $inputs_i[k][j]$ eventually stabilizes after T. Consider some time t_1 after T:

If there is some value v s.t $|k : input_i[k][j] = v| \geq n - t$ then it sets $C\_INPUT_i[j]$ to v. We prove that this value will not be changed any more. Indeed, assume node i will changes this value at some time $t' > t_1$. There are only two possibilities:

  – there is some value v' s.t $|k : input_i[k][j] = v'| \geq n - t$ at time t'. Thus, there must be at least some node u s.t that $inputs_i[u][j] = v$ at t and $inputs_i[u][j] = v'$ at t'. This is a contradiction because after T, $inputs_i[u][j]$ stabilizes.
  – $v \neq 0$ and $|k : inputs_i[k][j] = v| < n - t$ at time t'. Let $S = \{k : inputs_i[k][j] = v$ at time $t\}$. Thus there must a some node $u \in S$ s.t at time t', $inputs_i[u][j] \neq v$. This is a contradiction because after T, $inputs_i[u][j]$ stabilizes.

If there is not a value v s.t $|k : inputs_i[k][j] = v| \geq n - t$. Then node i sets $C\_INPUT_i[j] = 0$. So if node i changes this value then there must be some $t'' > t_1$ s.t there is some $v'' \neq 0$ and $|k : inputs_i[k][j] = v''| \geq n - t$. Since after T, for any i, j, k: $inputs_i[k][j]$ eventually stabilizes, if at time $t'' > T$ we have $inputs_i[k][j] = v''$ then at time $t_1 > T$ we also have $inputs_i[k][j] = v''$. Thus, at time t_1, we have $|k : input_i[k][j] = v''| \geq n - t$ and node i sets $C\_INPUT_i[j]$ to v'', contradicting that $v'' \neq 0$. Thus, $C\_INPUT_i[j]$ stabilizes to 0. □

Lemma 17. *Assume i be a correct node and my_input_i stabilizes to v_i. For any j, $C\_INPUT_j[i]$ eventually stabilizes to v_i.*

Proof. By Lemma 13, $inputs_k[k, i]$ eventually stabilizes to v_i for every correct node k. Consider any node j. If k is correct then after T, node j receives all messages from k and so node j will have that $inputs_j[k][i] = v_i$. Moreover, since there are at least $n - t$ correct nodes, eventually the condition at line 15 is satisfied and node j will have that $C\_INPUT_j[i] = v_i$. □

Lemma 18. *For any i, j, k, if $C\_INPUT_j[i]$ stabilizes to v_j and $C\_INPUT_k[i]$ eventually stabilizes to v_k then $v_j = v_k$.*

Proof. If $INPUT_j[i]$ stabilizes to v_j then after T we have that $|k : inputs_j[k][i] = v_j| \geq n - t$. Since $n - t \geq t + 1$, there must is at least some correct node u such that $inputs_j[u][i] = v_j$. It follows that $inputs_u[u][k] = v_j$. By Lemma 13, for every correct node p: $inputs_p[p][i]$ eventually stabilizes to v_j. Similarly for node k, we also have that for every correct node p: $inputs_p[p][i]$ eventually stabilizes to v_k. Since there is at least $n - t$ correct nodes, there must be some correct node q s.t $inputs_q[q][i]$ eventually stabilizes to v_j and $inputs_q[q][i]$ eventually also stabilizes to v_k. Thus, $v_j = v_k$. □

Theorem 4. *The stabilizing uniform consensus with send-omission faults is solvable if $n > 2t$.*

Proof. We will prove that three conditions of stabilizing uniform consensus are satisfied:

Stabilization condition: the proof is similar to Lemma 16. We omit the proof due to space constraints.

Validity condition: if all nodes have the inputs stabilizing to v then by Lemma 17, for any correct node i and any node k, we get that $C\_INPUT_k[i]$ eventually stabilizes to v after T. Since there are at least $n - t$ correct nodes, at any time t after T, node k eventually has that $|i : C\_INPUT_k[i] = v| \geq n$ t. Thus, it outputs v.

Agreement condition: Assume for the sake of contradiction that the outputs of two nodes i and j stabilize to different values, v_i and v_j. Thus, either $v_i \neq 0$ or $v_j \neq 0$. Without loss of generality suppose that $v_i \neq 0$. Thus, at some time after T, we have that $|k : C\_INPUT_i[k] = v_i| \geq n - t$. Let $S = \{k : C\_INPUT_i[k] = v_i\}$. By Lemma 18, for every $k \in S$: $C\_INPUT_j[k]$ also stabilizes to v_i. Thus, eventually node j will have that $|k : C\_INPUT_j[k] = v_i| \geq n - t$ and it eventually outputs v_i. Thus, $v_j = v_i$. □

5 Conclusions

This paper addressed a variant of stabilizing consensus in mobile networks that we have named stabilizing uniform consensus. Perhaps surprisingly, we show that the problem is impossible to solve if a single node suffers from general omission faults, even if the inputs are stable. Further, we identify the tight conditions for solving the problem for more benign faults, such as crash and send-omissions.

Acknowledgments. We are grateful to the anonymous reviewers for their help in improving the paper. This work was partially supported by Fundação para a Ciência e Tecnologia (FCT) via the project PEPITA (PTDC/EEI-SCR/2776/2012) and via the INESC-ID multi-annual funding through the PIDDAC Program fund grant, under project PEst-OE/EEI/LA0021/2013.

References

1. Angluin, D., Fischer, M.J., Jiang, H.: Stabilizing consensus in mobile networks. In: Gibbons, P.B., Abdelzaher, T., Aspnes, J., Rao, R. (eds.) DCOSS 2006. LNCS, vol. 4026, pp. 37–50. Springer, Heidelberg (2006)
2. Attiya, H., Welch, J.: Distributed Computing: Fundamentals, Simulations and Advanced Topics. John Wiley & Sons (2004)
3. Basile, C., Killijian, M.-O., Powell, D.: A survey of dependability issues in mobile wireless networks. Technical report (2003)
4. Bonnet, F., Ezhilchelvan, P., Vollset, E.: Quiescent consensus in mobile ad-hoc networks using eventually storage-free broadcasts. In: Proc. of the 21st ACM SAC, Dijon, France, pp. 670–674 (2006)
5. Chockler, G., Demirbas, M., Gilbert, S., Newport, C., Nolte, T.: Consensus and collision detectors in wireless ad hoc networks. In: Proc. of the 24th ACM PODC, Las Vegas, NV, USA, pp. 197–206 (2005)
6. Dijkstra, E.: Self-stabilizing systems in spite of distributed control. Commun. ACM 17(11), 643–644 (1974)
7. Doerr, B., Goldberg, L., Minder, L., Sauerwald, T., Scheideler, C.: Stabilizing consensus with the power of two choices. In: Proc. of the 23rd ACM SPAA, San Jose, California, USA, pp. 149–158 (2011)
8. Fischer, M., Lynch, N., Paterson, M.: Impossibility of distributed consensus with one faulty process. Journal of the ACM 32(2), 374–382 (1985)
9. Guerraoui, R.: Revisiting the relationship between non-blocking atomic commitment and consensus. In: Helary, J.-M., Raynal, M. (eds.) WDAG 1995. LNCS, vol. 972, pp. 87–100. Springer, Heidelberg (1995)
10. Guerraoui, R., Rodrigues, L.: Introduction to Reliable Distributed Programming. Springer-Verlag (2006)
11. Hadzilacos, V.: On the relationship between the atomic commitment and consensus problems. In: Simons, B., Spector, A. (eds.) Fault-Tolerant Distributed Computing. LNCS, vol. 448, pp. 201–208. Springer, Heidelberg (1990)
12. Lamport, L., Shostak, R., Pease, M.: The Byzantine generals problem. ACM Transactions on Programming Languages and Systems 4(3), 382–401 (1982)
13. Lynch, N.: Distributed Algorithms. Morgan Kaufmann Publishers Inc., San Francisco (1996)
14. Moniz, H., Neves, N., Correia, M.: Byzantine fault-tolerant consensus in wireless ad hoc networks. IEEE Transactions on Mobile Computing 99(PrePrints), 1 (2012)
15. Neiger, G., Toueg, S.: Automatically increasing the fault-tolerance of distributed algorithms. J. Algorithms 11(3), 374–419 (1990)
16. Pease, M., Shostak, R., Lamport, L.: Reaching agreement in the presence of faults. Journal of the ACM 27(2), 228–234 (1980)

Brief Announcement: Publish/Subscribe on Virtual Rings

Gerry Siegemund[1], Khaled Maâmra[2], and Volker Turau[1]

[1] Institute of Telematics, Hamburg University of Technology, Hamburg, Germany
{gerry.siegemund,turau}@tu-harburg.de
[2] PRiSM Reseach Group, University of Versailles St-Quentin, Versailles, France
khaled.maamra@prism.uvsq.fr

Abstract. This paper introduces a scalable, self-stabilizing, channel-based publish/subscribe system for wireless sensor networks. As base structure a virtual ring is maintained. We consider message and memory corruptions and also respect dynamic network changes, such as, node and link removals and additions.

Keywords: Self-stabilization, publish/subscribe, wireless sensor networks.

1 Introduction

Wireless sensor networks (WSN) are resource-constrained and operate based on multi-hop relay and ad hoc routing rather than on a robust infrastructure as the Internet. Many applications of WSNs require data generated at a given node to be efficiently forwarded to all nodes interested in that data. Publish/subscribe systems provide an effective solution for this task [1]. They allow a group of content publishers to notify content subscribers in an asynchronous style without knowing the identities of the interested nodes. There are two roles in such systems *publishers* and *subscribers*. Publishers publish messages without knowing the identities of the receivers - the subscribers. Subscribers register their interests in a category of information and asynchronously receive messages matching their subscriptions. Interests can be specified with respect to the message's content using some form of patterns or by referring to a categorization of messages carried out by the publishers. Such categories are called channels. In any case messages do not contain destination addresses. The system must provide an infrastructure to route a message from the publisher to all matching subscribers.

2 Overview

The publsih/subscribe system is build upon several foundations. Foremost, a virtual ring layer. This is a kind of overlay network where all nodes are arranged on a ring. Messages are routed on this ring. Scalability is achieved by using so called *shortcuts*, these help to avoid sections of the ring with no subscribers for a particular channel. The maintenance of the virtual ring layer is based on a spanning tree layer. Which is realized using a well-known self-stabilizing spanning

P. Felber and V. Garg (Eds.): SSS 2014, LNCS 8756, pp. 343–345, 2014.

tree algorithm. The lowest layer provides a stable and scalable neighborhood relation. This is achieved with the self-stabilizing neighborhood protocol Mahalle$^+$ [3] that achieves agility and stability at the same time. An important feature of Mahalle$^+$ is that it allows to specify an upper bound C_N for the number of neighbors of each node. The value C_N allows to trade the average route length of publications for memory space required for routing tables. Memory consumption grows quadratically with C_N while routing tables for a single channel grow linearly. We expect C_N to be in the range of 5 to 10. Thus, the size of a message and the required storage fit the capabilities of current hardware used in WSNs. Additionally, larger values of C_N increase the number of shortcuts.

To achieve self-stabilization we use next to classical techniques the concept of *leasing*, in particular for routing entries and subscriptions [2]. A routing entry must be renewed before the leasing period expires to protect it from being discarded. If a routing entry or a subscription is not renewed in time, it is removed from the corresponding table. Such removals trigger update operations for the virtual ring and the shortcuts.

3   Overall Approach

Routing of Publish/Subscribe Messages. The distributed system is modeled as an undirected graph $G = (V, E)$. Nodes in this graph are responsible for forwarding subscriptions to all nodes and for delivering publications to subscribers. In our model all nodes participate in the routing process. We aim to balance the amount of memory used for routing tables and the number of messages used for forwarding subscriptions and publications. This way, we can adopt to the varying resources found in WSNs.

Ideally, only nodes that are subscribers of a channel are involved in forwarding publications for that channel. Obviously, this is not achievable in general. We use an overlay network in the form of a ring. Since not every topology does contain a ring with each node appearing exactly once we propose to use a virtual ring. The main difference is that each node can appear more than once on the ring. The total size of the ring is $2(n - 1)$ with $n = |V|$, i.e., on average each node appears twice on the ring. Routing is performed counter clockwise on this ring. A message is discarded just before it is forwarded to the originating node again.

Since this simple approach does not provide scalability we use *shortcuts* on the virtual ring. A shortcut skips some nodes on the ring. For publications we must guarantee that a shortcut does not jump over a subscriber for the corresponding channel. To do so, each node maintains, for each of its positions and for each channel, the position of the neighbor that comes closest to the next subscriber for that channel on the virtual ring in a table F. On average, a node has to maintain two forwarding positions per node. With this information routing becomes as simple as a single look-up in this table. The main challenge is to keep F up-to-date with respect to (un)subscriptions and transient faults. To perform this in a distributed algorithm, each node must maintain two lists with positions: list P with the own positions and R with those of all neighbors.

Example. The routing of publications is explained by the example given in Fig. 1. Here, one publisher is indicated by P at Position 1 and 7. Furthermore, there are two subscribers indicated by S at Position 25 and 27, respectively. Note, that the actual node id is transparent to the publish/subscribe layer.

In Fig. 1 for all circled positions the routing table F (current position pos and the message forwarding position $fPos$) is depicted as well, for other positions it is omitted for readability. Publishing always begins at the smallest position of a node. In this case it is Posi-

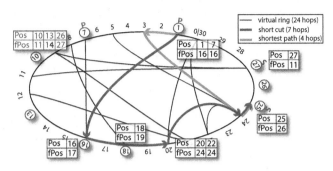

Fig. 1. Routing a publication to a single subscriber

tion 1. Thus, the publication is forwarded to Position 16. Since there exists no shortcut from 16, messages will be forwarded to 17, as depicted in the routing table next to Position 16. Routing proceeds in this style (i.e., without shortcuts) until the message reaches Position 20. Now the forwarding position is 24. In the next step Position 25 - one of the subscribers - is reached, the publication is delivered, and the message will be forwarded until it reaches Position 27. Here, the message is delivered once again and then discarded, because the forwarding position of Position 27 is Position 11, which lies beyond the origin, i.e., Position 1. The figure furthermore depicts the traveled path from P to the first S, its length is 7 hops, even though this is much shorter than using the virtual ring in the typical way (24 hops), it is not the shortest path (4 hops).

4 Outlook

We will investigate some super-stabilizing aspects of the given protocol. Currently we are evaluating an implementation of the middleware in a simulation and later in a real deployment. This will permit us to derive values for the lengths of the various leading periods used.

Acknowledgments. Funded by Deutsche Forschungsgemeinschaft (TU 221/6-1).

References

[1] Eugster, P.T., Felber, P.A., Guerraoui, R., Kermarrec, A.M.: The many faces of publish/subscribe. ACM Comput. Surv. 35(2), 114–131 (2003)

[2] Gray, C., Cheriton, D.: Leases: An efficient fault-tolerant mechanism for distributed file cache consistency. SIGOPS Oper. Syst. Rev. 23(5), 202–210 (1989)

[3] Siegemund, G., Turau, V., Weyer, C., Lohs, S., Nolte, J.: An agile and stable neighborhood protocol for wSNs. In: Higashino, T., Katayama, Y., Masuzawa, T., Potop-Butucaru, M., Yamashita, M. (eds.) SSS 2013. LNCS, vol. 8255, pp. 376–378. Springer, Heidelberg (2013)

Brief Announcement: Sweep Coverage with Mobile and Static Sensors

Barun Gorain and Partha Sarathi Mandal

Department of Mathematics
Indian Institute of Technology Guwahati, India
{b.gorain,psm}@iitg.ernet.in

Abstract. The objective of a sweep coverage problem is to find the minimum number of mobile sensors to ensure the periodic monitoring for a given set of points of interest. In this paper we have remarked on the flaw of approximation algorithms proposed in the paper [1] for sweep coverage with mobile sensors and proposed a 3-approximation algorithm to guarantee sweep coverage with mobile and static sensors.

Keywords: Sweep Coverage, TSP tour, Approximation Algorithm, WSNs.

1 Introduction

Sweep coverage concept is recently introduced in the literature where periodic patrol inspections are sufficient for a given set of points of interest (PoIs) by a set of mobile sensors [1]. A point is said to be $t-sweep\ covered$ if and only if at least one mobile sensor visits the point within every t time period, where t is called *sweep period* of the point. Objective of the sweep coverage problem is to find minimum number of mobile sensors to guarantee sweep coverage for the set of PoIs. Li et al. in [1] proved that finding minimum number of mobile sensors to sweep cover a set of PoIs is NP hard and proposed a $(2 + \epsilon)-$approximation and a $3-$approximation algorithm to find minimum number of mobile sensors. Each algorithm in [1] computes approximate TSP tour through all the PoIs and divides the tour into equal parts of length $\frac{vt}{2}$, where v is the uniform speed of the mobile sensors and t is the sweep period for all the PoIs. Then one mobile sensor is deployed in every partition and let the mobile sensors move back and forth to sweep cover all PoIs of the corresponding partitions. But there is a serious flaw of the approximation algorithms proposed in [1] as explained below. In general, if the distance between the PoIs is large compare to the length of the partitions then there may not exist any PoI on some of the parts. For example, assume there are only two PoIs on a plane, the distance between them is 100 meter and vt is 20 meter. Therefore, the length of the TSP tour is 200 meter and according to the algorithms mentioned in [1], the total number of mobile sensors needed is $200/\frac{vt}{2}$ = 200/10=20. But practically it is sufficient to place only two sensors to monitor two PoIs respectively and thus two sensors can guarantee sweep coverage. Hence

P. Felber and V. Garg (Eds.): SSS 2014, LNCS 8756, pp. 346–348, 2014.

the algorithms proposed by Li et al. in [1] does not provide a solution which achieve approximation factors $(2 + \epsilon)$ or 3.

In this paper we introduce a variation of sweep coverage named as GSweep coverage problem, where the PoIs are represented by vertices of a weighted graph. We propose a 3−approximation algorithm to guarantee sweep coverage of all vertices of the graph with mobile and static sensors.

2   GSweep Coverage

Let $G = (U, E)$ be a weighted graph, where weight of an edge (u_i, u_j) for $u_i, u_j \in U$ is denoted by $|(u_i, u_j)|$. Let n be the total number of vertices in G. For any subgraph H of G, we denote $|H|$ as the sum of the edge weights of H. The definition of GSweep coverage is given below.

Definition 1. *Let* $\mathcal{U} = \{u_1, u_2, \cdots, u_n\}$ *be the vertices of a weighted graph,* $S = \{s_1, s_2, \cdots, s_p\}$ *and* $M = \{m_1, m_2, \cdots, m_q\}$ *be the sets of static and mobile sensors respectively. The mobile sensors move with a uniform speed* v *along edges of the graph. A vertex* u_i *is said to be* $t-$*GSweep covered with (mobile and/or static) sensors iff either at least one mobile sensor* m_j *visits* u_i *in every* t *time period or one static sensor* s_j *is deployed at* u_i *which periodically monitors* u_i *in every* t *time period.*

The objective of GSweep coverage problem is to find minimum number of sensors, combination of static and mobile sensors, such that each vertex is $t-$GSweep covered. The problem is NP hard, follows from the hardness proof given in [1].

We propose Algorithm 1: GSWEEPCOVERAGE to find minimum number of sensors for GSweep coverage problem. First two steps of the algorithm executes n iterations for finding the best possible solution i.e., number of sensors. In kth iteration $(1 \leq k \leq n)$, the minimum spanning forest F_k with k connected components $C_1, C_2, \cdots, C_k$ is computed. After that k disjoint tours $T_1, T_2, \cdots, T_k$ are found by doubling all edges of each component. Partition each T_i into $\left\lceil \frac{|T_i|}{vt} \right\rceil$ parts of length vt. Total number of partitions for an iteration is equal to the number of sensors required for that iteration. Minimum over the number of sensors of all iterations is chosen as the solution of our Algorithm 1. Initial positions of mobile and static sensors are calculated in steps 5-13 of the algorithm with movement scheduling of the mobile sensors.

Lemma 1. *Let* opt *be the minimum number of sensors needed in the optimal solution. Let* opt' *be the minimum number of paths of length* $\leq vt$ *which span* U *on* G*. Then* $opt \geq opt'$*.*

Proof. Let us assume that $opt < opt'$. Consider the path of movements by the mobile and static sensors in the optimal solution during any time period $[t_0, t_0 + t]$, where the path for a static sensor is of length zero. Let $P_1, P_2, \cdots, P_{opt}$ be the movement paths of the sensors with $|P_i| \leq vt$. Since each vertex is visited by a sensor at least once in time period t therefore $\bigcup P_i$ spans all the vertices of U. Hence, $\{P_1, P_2, \cdots, P_{opt}\}$ is a collection of paths with $|P_i| \leq vt$ that spans U, which contradicts the fact that $opt < opt'$. Therefore $opt \geq opt'$. $\square$

Algorithm 1: GSWEEPCOVERAGE

1: **for** $k = 1$ *to* n **do**
2:    Find the minimum spanning forest F_k on G with $n - k$ edges. Let $C_1, C_2, \cdots, C_k$ be

   the connected components of F_k. $N_k = \sum_{i=1}^{k} \left\lceil \frac{2|C_i|}{vt} \right\rceil$.

3: **end for**
4: Let j be the index $\in [1, 2, \cdots, n]$ such that $N_j = \min\{N_1, N_2, \cdots, N_n\}$
5: Let $C_1, C_2, \cdots, C_j$ be the connected components of F_j.
6: **for** $i = 1$ to j **do**
7:    **if** C_i is a component having more than one vertices **then**
8:       Find a tour T_i on C_i by doubling each edges of C_i. Partition the tour into $\left\lceil \frac{|T_i|}{vt} \right\rceil$
      parts and deploy one mobile sensor at each of the partitioning points.
9:    **else**
10:       Deploy one static sensor at the vertex of C_i.
11:    **end if**
12: **end for**
13: All mobile sensors start moving at the same time along the respective tours in same
   direction.

Theorem 1. *The Algorithm 1 is a 3 factor approximation algorithm.*

Proof. Let opt be the minimum number of sensors required in the optimal solution and opt' be the minimum number of paths of length $\leq vt$ which span U on G. Then by Lemma 1, $opt' \leq opt$.

Algorithm 1 chooses the minimum over all N_k for $k = 1$ to n. Let us consider the iteration of the algorithm when $k = opt'$. Let Min_path be the total sum of the length of the edges in opt'. Then $Min\_path \leq k \times vt$. Again as there are k disjoint connected components in opt' and F_k is the minimum spanning forest with k connected components, we have $|F_k| \leq Min\_path$. After doubling edges in step 8, the total length of the movement paths of the sensors is $\leq 2|F_k|$. Since $\left\lceil \frac{|T_i|}{vt} \right\rceil \leq \frac{|T_i|}{vt} + 1$, the number of sensors needed in our solution is $N \leq \frac{2|F_k|}{vt} + k \leq \frac{2Min\_path}{vt} + k \leq 3k \leq 3opt$. Therefore the approximation factor of the Algorithm 1 is 3.   □

3   Conclusion

In this paper we overcome the limitation of a previous study [1] on sweep coverage. The key argument is that when the graph is sparse, it is better to provide sweep coverage with a combination of static and mobile sensors, instead of using only mobile sensors as was done in the the previous study. We have proposed a 3-approximation algorithm to solve this NP hard problem. Our solution overcomes the flaw of the previous solution and it is more efficient in terms of cost and energy utilization for sweep coverage.

Reference

1. Li, M., Cheng, W.-F., Liu, K., Liu, Y., Li, X.-Y., Liao, X.: Sweep coverage with mobile sensors. IEEE Trans. Mob. Comput. 10(11), 1534–1545 (2011)

Brief Announcement: Designing Dining-Philosophers to Optimize Experimental Performance*

Jordan Adamek[1], Mikhail Nesterenko[1], and Sébastien Tixeuil[2,**]

[1] Kent State University, Kent, OH 44242, USA
[2] UPMC Sorbonne Universités & IUF, Paris, France

We evaluate five of the most widely known self-stabilizing solutions to the Dining-Philosophers Problem. For the purposes of presentation we call them LRA [2], Fuzzy [3], Transformation [5], Alternator [4], and Refinement [6].

In a dining-philosophers algorithm, processes compete for critical section (CS) access. A solution to dining-philosophers ensures *safety*: only neighbor process at at time is allowed to enter the CS; and *liveness*: every requesting process is eventually allowed to enter the CS.

We determine that Transformation, Fuzzy and LRA are incorrect. All three violate the safety of the Dining-Philosophers Problem even if no faults are injected. Even though the algorithms are incorrect, we still consider them in case they are used for applications that do not require perfect safety compliance.

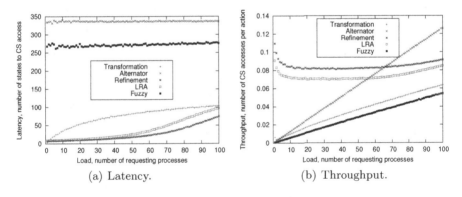

(a) Latency.　　　　　(b) Throughput.

Fig. 1. Functional characteristics under no faults

We evaluate the dining-philosophers algorithms in all three common execution semantics (also called schedulers or demons): *interleaving* (*centralized*), *powerset* (*distributed*), and (*maximally*) *synchronous*. In interleaving semantics, all process actions are executed sequentially. We present results for this semantics only. See [1] for complete results.

---

* Refer to [1] for details.
** This work was supported in part by LINCS.

P. Felber and V. Garg (Eds.): SSS 2014, LNCS 8756, pp. 349–351, 2014.
© Springer International Publishing Switzerland 2014

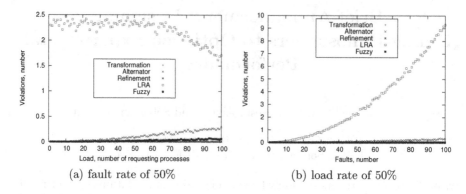

(a) fault rate of 50%   (b) load rate of 50%

Fig. 2. Safety violations

We evaluate algorithms using computations of 1,000 states. A single fault of varying extent is injected at a random state of the computation. For each particular data point, we run 1,000 simulated computations. For each computation we generate a new random graph topology.

For the simulated algorithms, we estimate two functional and one fault-tolerance metric. The functional metrics are: *latency* — the average number of states between request and corresponding CS access, and *throughput* — the average number of CS accesses per action. Fault-tolerance of self-stabilizing algorithms is usually measured in the number of states until the algorithm reaches correct state. The standard metric is, however, inapplicable as three of the algorithms we evaluate are incorrect. Hence, we measure the number of safety violations per computation instead. The results of our evaluation are shown in Figures 2 and 1.

Considering the functional properties of the two correct algorithms: Alternator and Refinement, neither has a clear advantage. The throughput of Refinement is better under low load while Alternator outperforms it under high load. Observing this dichotomy, we design Combined Algorithm that computes the system load and, depending on the load, switches between Alternator and Refinement.

Combined Algorithm is shown in Figure 3. The algorithm assumes there is a rooted tree. Processes report their load up the tree. The root process evaluates the accumulated load information and decides which basic algorithm, Alternator or Refinement, to execute. To eliminate thrashing, the switching is done when the load exceeds configurable thresholds *low* and *high*. This decision propagates down the tree. To ensure safety, a process executes the CS only when all of its neighbors are executing the same basic algorithm. Theorem 1 states the correctness of the combined algorithm. If load keeps changing fast enough, Combined Algorithm may preclude some process from entering the CS indefinitely. Hence, the theorem states that the algorithm satisfies the liveness and safety properties only when the load is high (every process is requesting) or low (a single process is requesting).

process P_i
constants
// identifier of father process, for root $f = i$
f,

// basic algorithm switch thresholds:
$low, high : 1 \le low < high \le n$

variables
$basic_i$, // executed algorithm, either **a** or **r**
$load_i$, // branch load

actions
$load_i \ne$ **sum**(load of children) + request $\longrightarrow$
$\quad load_i :=$ **sum**(load of children) + request

$f = i \wedge load_i \ge high \wedge basic \ne$ **a** $\longrightarrow$
$\quad basic_i :=$ **a**

$f = i \wedge load \le low \wedge basic \ne$ **r** $\longrightarrow$
$\quad basic_i :=$ **r**

$f \ne i \wedge basic_f \ne basic_i \longrightarrow$
$\quad basic_i := basic_f$

process P_i
parameter $j : (P_i, P_j) \in N$
variables private
// private copy of neighbor P_j
// basic algorithm mode
$bc_i.j$

// controls correct switch start, either **a** or **r**
$switch_i$

actions
// modified Refinement request initiating action
$basic_i =$ **r** $\wedge$ request initiating predicate $\longrightarrow$
$\quad switch_i :=$ **r**
$\quad$ request initiating command

// modified Refinement CS execution action
CS execution predicate $\longrightarrow$
$\quad$ **if** $switch_i =$ **r** $\wedge basic_i =$ **r** $\wedge$
$\quad\quad (\forall k : bc_i.k =$ **r**$)$ **then**
$\quad\quad\quad$ critical section
$\quad\quad$ CS execution command

// modified Refinement synchronization action
predicate $\longrightarrow$
$\quad$ command,
$\quad bc_i.j := basic.j$

// added action
$bc_i.j \ne basic.j \longrightarrow$
$\quad bc_i.j := basic.j$

Fig. 3. Combined Algorithm, refinement and switching parts

Theorem 1. Under high and low load, Combined Algorithm satisfies safety and liveness properties of the Dining-Philosophers Problem.

References

1. Adamek, J., Nesterenko, M., Tixeuil, S.: Comparing self-stabilizing dining philosophers through simulation. Technical Report TR-KSU-CS-2013-01, Kent State University (August 2013)
2. Cantarell, S., Datta, A.K., Petit, F.: Self-stabilizing atomicity refinement allowing neighborhood concurrency. In: Huang, S.-T., Herman, T. (eds.) SSS 2003. LNCS, vol. 2704, pp. 102–112. Springer, Heidelberg (2003)
3. Huang, S.-T.: The fuzzy philosophers. In: Rolim, J. (ed.) IPDPS 2000 Workshop. LNCS, vol. 1800, pp. 130–136. Springer, Heidelberg (2000)
4. Kulkarni, S.S., Bolen, C., Oleszkiewicz, J., Robinson, A.: Alternators in read/write atomicity. Information Processing Letters 93(5), 207–215 (2005)
5. Mizuno, M., Nesterenko, M.: A transformation of self-stabilizing serial model programs for asynchronous parallel computing environments. Information Processing Letters 66(6), 285–290 (1998)
6. Nesterenko, M., Arora, A.: Stabilization-preserving atomicity refinement. Journal of Parallel and Distributed Computing 62(5), 766–791 (2002)

Brief Announcement:
Introducing Recurrence in Self-Stabilization*

Oday Jubran and Oliver Theel

Carl von Ossietzky Universität Oldenburg, 26111 Oldenburg, Germany
{jubran,theel}@informatik.uni-oldenburg.de

Abstract. We introduce the notion of recurrence, which denotes how frequent a condition is satisfied in an execution of a system. We use this notion in self-stabilization to address the convergence of a system to a behavior that guarantees a minimum recurrence. We apply this notion to show how the design of distributed mutual exclusion algorithms can be altered, to achieve a high recurrence of granting unique privilege to processes, under various time and space requirements.

Keywords: Self-Stabilization, Recurrence, Performance, Mutual Exclusion.

1 Introduction

Self-stabilization ensures that a system's desired behavior is eventually obtained and never voluntarily violated regardless of the system's initial behavior. Self-stabilization requires that once the desired property is satisfied in a configuration, any following configuration has to satisfy the property. With this classical definition of self-stabilization, liveness properties, that do not necessarily need to be satisfied in each configuration, are not covered. Such properties may be the core of the system performance evaluation.

In this work, we introduce the notion of *recurrence* in self-stabilization, which describes (1) how frequent a global condition is satisfied in an execution, and (2) the convergence time to reach a configuration, from which a minimum recurrence is guaranteed. We apply this notion to show how the design of synchronous distributed mutual exclusion algorithms can be altered to achieve high recurrence of granting unique privilege, under various time and space requirements.

We consider the classical shared memory model: the *topology* is a connected graph, whose vertices are called *processes*, and each process has a unique id in $\{0, ..., n-1\}$. A *distributed algorithm* is a set of *sub-algorithms*, executed by the processes. A *configuration* γ is a vector of the local states of all processes. An *execution* is a sequence of configurations $\gamma_1, \gamma_2, ...$ such that for $i \geq 1$, γ_{i+1} is reachable from γ_i by executing guarded commands. An execution is *synchronous* iff in each step, all processes with enabled commands execute their actions.

---

* This work was partially supported by the German Research Foundation (DFG) as part of the Transregional Collaborative Research Center "Automatic Verification and Analysis of Complex Systems" (SFB/TR 14 AVACS, http://www.avacs.org/).

P. Felber and V. Garg (Eds.): SSS 2014, LNCS 8756, pp. 352–354, 2014.

2   Recurrence in Self-Stabilization

Recurrence addresses the ratio of configurations, that satisfy some condition (i.e. predicate) over configurations, in an execution. This ratio is a means to cover finite and infinite executions.

DEFINITION 1 (RECURRENCE). *Let con be a condition over configurations, and let $\Xi : \gamma_i, \gamma_{i+1}, ...$ be an execution. The recurrence of con in Ξ, denoted by $Rec_{con,\Xi}$, is the ratio of the configurations satisfying con in Ξ.*   ◇

By Definition 1, considering subsequent configurations satisfying *con*: if a condition is not satisfied infinitely often, or if the time between two subsequent satisfactions of the condition increases with no bounds, then recurrence approaches 0. If a condition holds in each configuration, then recurrence is 1.

Using recurrence, we define properties over executions as follows: the recurrence of some condition in an execution is equal to Δ, where $\Delta \in [0,1]$. Our concern is to measure the worst case convergence (i.e. stabilization) time to an execution suffix, that satisfies having Δ recurrence of some condition *con*. We denote such convergence time by Δ_{con}-*Convergence time*. Recall that in the classical self-stabilization, the desired condition to be satisfied has to hold in each configuration after the system stabilizes. This indicates that the recurrence of the condition is required to be 1.

DEFINITION 2 (Δ_{con}-CONVERGENCE TIME). *Let A be an algorithm, con be a condition, and $\Delta \in [0,1] \subset \mathbb{R}_0^+$.*

- *An execution $\Xi : \gamma_0, \gamma_1, ...$ is said to have a Δ_{con}-Convergence time of k steps iff k is the minimum number, such that $\Delta = Rec_{con,\Xi'}$ for the execution suffix $\Xi' : \gamma_k, \gamma_{k+1}, ...$ of Ξ.*
- *Algorithm A is said to have Δ_{con}-Convergence time of k steps iff k is the maximum Δ_{con}-Convergence time among all executions.*   ◇

Considering distributed algorithms that are defined by guarded commands, recurrence can be used to measure the frequency of running particular commands, by analyzing the recurrence of their guards. In the following, we apply recurrence to alter the design of distributed mutual exclusion algorithms.

3   Mutual Exclusion Algorithms

We use [1, Algorithm 3], which is designed for synchronous environments, to design three synchronous mutual exclusion algorithms. Mutual Exclusion, denoted by *ME*, comprises two properties: (1) Safety: at most one process is privileged in each configuration, and (2) Liveness: each process is privileged infinitely often. We also aim to satisfy that the recurrence of granting unique privilege is 1. We follow a similar approach to [2] to design our algorithms.

[1, Algorithm 3] results in an incrementing system with a finite domain. Each process p has a variable r_p, that is incremented modulo n, such that in a

Table 1. Time and Space Complexities of Algorithms 1-3

Algorithm	ME-Convergence Time	$1_{privileged}$-Convergence Time	Space
1	$diam(G)-1$	$2diam(G)$	$diam(G)+n$
2	$\lceil diam(G)/2\rceil -1$	$> 2diam(G)$	$2diam(G)+n$
3	$2diam(G)-1$	$2diam(G)$	$n+1$

legitimate behavior, (1) the value of r_p is equal to the value of r_q for each process q, and (2) the value of r_p is incremented in each step. We extend this system as follows: (1) In the legitimate behavior, the value of r_p has to be in $\{0, ..., n-1\}$. (2) A process is privileged if and only if the id of p is equal to r_p. This ensures that the algorithm is self-stabilizing wrt. ME. In addition, since these processes' ids are $\{0, ..., n-1\}$, in each step, exactly one process is privileged. In other words, the recurrence of granting a unique privilege is 1. We write "$1_{privileged}$" to denote this. Due to limited space, we only show the time and space complexity results of our three algorithms. The algorithms are presented in detail in [3].

Table 1 presents the time and space complexities of the three algorithms. Considering the safety property of ME (granting unique privilege), Algorithm 2 has the shortest convergence time. However, the convergence time to $1_{privileged}$ is the largest. On the other hand, Algorithm 3 has the largest ME-Convergence time, but the $1_{privileged}$-Convergence time is shorter than the one of Algorithm 2. In particular, besides space requirements, the overall convergence time to achieve both ME and $1_{privileged}$ in Algorithm 3 is less than the time required by Algorithm 2. In other words, Algorithm 3 guarantees to start granting unique privilege, safely, before Algorithm 2 does, and with less space requirements.

4   Optimality of $\lceil \frac{diam(G)}{2}\rceil -1$ ME-Convergence Time

As a particular interest, the convergence time wrt. ME, observed in Algorithm 2, slightly improves the state-of-the-art $\lceil diam(G)/2\rceil$, introduced in [2]. In addition, this result rectifies [2, Theorem 4] that $\lceil diam(G)/2\rceil$ is a lower bound; in the proof of [2, Theorem 4], the issue, that the privilege condition of a process p may also cover the states of the neighbors of p, is missing. Considering this point, while following the steps of the proof of [2, Theorem 4], we conclude that $\lceil diam(G)/2\rceil -1$ is optimal for synchronous executions. Details are found in [3].

References

[1] Boulinier, C., Petit, F., Villain, V.: Synchronous vs. Asynchronous Unison. Algorithmica 51(1) (2008)
[2] Dubois, S., Guerraoui, R.: Introducing Speculation in Self-Stabilization - An Application to Mutual Exclusion. CoRR, abs/1302.2217 (2013)
[3] Jubran, O., Theel, O.: Introducing Recurrence in Self-Stabilization. Technical Report No. 101 of SFB/TR 14 AVACS (July 2014), http://www.avacs.org/

Brief Announcement:
Tamper-Evident Stabilization

Reza Hajisheykhi[1], Ali Ebnenasir[2], and Sandeep S. Kulkarni[1]

[1] Michigan State University, Houghton, MI 49931, USA
[2] Michigan Technological University, East Lansing, MI 48824, USA

Abstract. We propose the notion of tamper-evident stabilization –that combines stabilization with the concept of tamper-evidence– for computing systems. On the first glance, these notions are contradictory; stabilization requires that eventually the system functionality is fully restored whereas tamper-evidence requires that the system functionality is permanently degraded in the event of tampering. Tamper-evident stabilization captures the intuition that the system will tolerate perturbation upto a limit. In the event that it is perturbed beyond that limit, it will exhibit permanent evidence of tampering, where it may provide reduced (possibly none) functionality.

1 Introduction

A tamper-resistant system ensures that an effort to tamper with the system makes the system less inoperable (e.g., by zeroing out sensitive data in a chip or voiding the warranty). The notion of tamper resistance is contradictory to the notion of stabilization in that the notion of stabilization requires that in spite of any possible tampering the system inherently acquires its usefulness eventually.

We envision that if the system is outside its normal legitimate states, it is in one of two modes: *recovery mode*, where it is trying to restore itself to a legitimate state, or *tamper-evident mode*, where it is trying to make itself inoperable. The recovery mode is similar to the typical stabilizing systems in that the recovery should be guaranteed after external perturbations stop. However, in the tamper-evident mode, it is essential that the system makes itself inoperable even if outside perturbations continue.

2 Tamper-Evident Stabilization Definition

Our program modeling utilizes standard approach for defining interleaving programs and stabilization [1, 3, 4] and active stabilization [2]. Thus, a program includes a finite set of variables with (finite or infinite) domain. A program also includes *guarded commands* [3] that update those program variables atomically. Since these internal variables are not needed in the definitions involved in this section, we describe a program in terms of its state space S_p, and its transitions $\delta_p \subseteq S_p \times S_p$, where S_p is obtained by assigning each variable in p a value from its domain.

P. Felber and V. Garg (Eds.): SSS 2014, LNCS 8756, pp. 355–358, 2014.

Definition 1 (Convergence). *Let p be a program with state space S_p and transitions δ_p. Let S and T be state predicates of p; i.e., any subset of S_p. We say that T converges to S in p iff*

- $S \subseteq T$,
- *S is closed in p, (S is closed in p iff $\forall s_0, s_1 \in S_p :: (s_0 \in S \wedge (s_0, s_1) \in \delta_p) \Rightarrow (s_1 \in S))$*
- *T is closed in p, and*
- *For any sequence σ ($=\langle s_0, s_1, s_2, ... \rangle$) if $s_0 \in T$ and σ is a computation of p then there exists l such that $s_l \in S$.*

Definition 2 (Stabilization). *Let p be a program with state space S_p and transitions δ_p. We say that program p is stabilizing for invariant S iff S_p converges to S in p.*

Definition 3 (Adversary). *We define an adversary for program $p = \langle S_p, \delta_p \rangle$ to be a subset of $S_p \times S_p$.*

Note that the above definition is general in that an adversary may include any set of possible transitions. However, realizing a tamper-evident stabilizing system would be feasible only when the power of the adversary is reasonable. In particular, the motivation of tamper-evident stabilization is that if a system is perturbed beyond an acceptable limit then it should become inoperable/less useful. Moreover, an adversary should not be able to prevent this. Of course, in order for this to be feasible, adversary must not have unrestricted power that allows it to perturb the system to any state.

Definition 4 ($\langle p, adv, k \rangle$-computation). *Let p be a program with state space S_p and transitions δ_p. Let adv be an adversary for program p. And, let k be an integer greater than 1. We say that a sequence $\langle s_0, s_1, s_2, ... \rangle$ is a $\langle p, adv, k \rangle$-computation iff*

- $\forall j \geq 0 :: s_j \in S_p$, *and*
- $\forall j \geq 0 :: (s_j, s_{j+1}) \in \delta_p \cup adv$, *and*
- $\forall j \geq 0 :: ((s_j, s_{j+1}) \notin \delta_p) \Rightarrow (\forall l \mid j < l < j + k :: (s_l, s_{l+1}) \in \delta_p)$

Observe that a $\langle p, adv, k \rangle$-computation guarantees that there are at least $k - 1$ program transitions/actions between any two adversary actions for $k > 1$. Moreover, the adversary is not required to execute in a $\langle p, adv, k \rangle$-computation.

Definition 5 (Convergence in the presence of adversary). *Let p be a program with state space S_p and transitions δ_p. Let S and T be state predicates of p. Let adv be an adversary for p and let k be an integer greater than 1. We say that T $\langle adv, k \rangle$-converges to S in p in the presence of adversary adv iff*

- $S \subseteq T$,
- *S is closed in $p \cup adv$,*
- *T is closed in $p \cup adv$, and*

- For any sequence σ $(=\langle s_0, s_1, s_2, ...\rangle$ $)$ if $s_0 \in T$ and σ is a $\langle p, adv, k\rangle$-computation then there exists l such that $s_l \in S$.

Definition 6 (Tamper-evident stabilization). *Let p be a program with state space S_p and transitions δ_p. Let adv be an adversary for program p. And, let k be an integer greater than 1. We say that program p is* k-tamper-evident stabilizing *with adversary adv for* invariants $\langle S1, S2 \rangle$ *iff there exists T*

- T converges to $S1$ in p
- $\neg T$ $\langle adv, k\rangle$-converges to $S2$ in p.

Notice that the definition of tamper-evident stabilization provides no guarantees about program behaviors if the adversary executes in T.

Relation between Stabilization, Tamper-Evident Stabilization and other variations of Stabilization. Due to reasons of space, we cannot provide detailed results about the relation between stabilization, tamper-evident stabilization and other variations such as weak stabilization, active stabilization, multitolerant stabilization, etc. The details of this comparison can be found in [5]. Also, in [5], we have identified an example of tamper-evident stabilizing programs. We have also identified how tamper-evident stabilizing programs can be composed with parallel or sequential composition and evaluated properties such as transitivity. While many of these properties are similar to that of stabilization, we find that composing tamper-evident stabilizing programs introduces certain new challenges that are absent in composing stabilizing programs.

3   Future Work

We are currently investigating the design and analysis of tamper-evident stabilizing System-on-Chip (SoC) systems in the context of the IEEE SystemC language. Our objective here is to design systems that facilitate reasoning about what they do and what they do not do in the event of tampering. Second, we will leverage our existing work on model repair and synthesis of stabilization in automated design of tamper-evident stabilization. Third, we plan to study the application of tamper-evident stabilization in game theory (and vice versa).

Acknowledgements. This work has been supported by National Science Foundation awards CNS-1329807 and CNS-1318678, and CCF-1116546.

References

1. Arora, A., Gouda, M.G.: Closure and convergence: A foundation of fault-tolerant computing. IEEE Transactions on Software Engineering 19(11), 1015–1027 (1993)
2. Bonakdarpour, B., Kulkarni, S.S.: Active stabilization. In: Défago, X., Petit, F., Villain, V. (eds.) SSS 2011. LNCS, vol. 6976, pp. 77–91. Springer, Heidelberg (2011)
3. Dijkstra, E.W.: A Discipline of Programming. Prentice-Hall (1990)

4. Dolev, S.: Self-Stabilization. MIT Press (2000)
5. Hajisheykhi, R., Ebnenasir, A., Kulkarni, S.: Tamper-evident stabilization. Technical Report MSU-CSE-14-4, Department of Computer Science, Michigan State University, East Lansing, Michigan (June 2014)

Brief Announcement: A Stabilizing Algorithm for Finding Two Node-Disjoint Paths

Hadid Rachid[1], Mehmet Hakan Karaata[2], and Vincent Villain[3]

[1] Department of Computer Engineering, Istanbul Aydin University, Beşyol Mah.
İnönü Cad. No:38 Küçükçekmece, Istanbul, Turkey
[2] Department of Computer Science P.O. Box 5969, Safat, Kuwait
[3] MIS, Université de Picardie Jules Verne, 33, Rue St Leu, Amiens Cedex 01, France

Abstract. We present the first adaptive stabilizing algorithm for finding *two node disjoint* paths in anonymous arbitrary networks. Given a graph $G = (V, E)$, two paths from source $s \in V$ to target $t \in V$ are said to be node disjoint if they do not share any nodes except for the endpoints. The proposed algorithm adapts to topology changes in the form of process/link crashes and additions, i.e., upon a topology change, it finds two disjoint paths from s to t. The algorithm has a wide range of applications in ensuring reliability and security of sensor, mobile and fixed communication networks.

Keywords: Two node disjoint paths, distributed systems, stabilization.

1 Introduction

The two node disjoint paths problem is one of the fundamental problems with several applications in diverse areas including VLSI layout, reliable network routing, secure message transmission, and network survivability. The first distributed algorithm for finding two node disjoint paths in arbitrary network is proposed in [2]. The first self-stabilizing distributed algorithm for finding all node disjoint paths in mesh networks is presented in [3]. In this paper, we present the first stabilizing distributed algorithm for finding two node disjoint paths between two distinct nodes s and t in anonymous arbitrary networks. This work was initially proposed in [4]. Since the proposed solution is self-stabilizing [1], it does not require initialization and withstands transient faults.

2 Basis of Algorithm

Let $G = (V, E)$ be a graph with two distinct vertices $s, t \in V$ such that G contains two node-disjoint paths between s and t. Let $\mathcal{P}$ be a path between s and t and ds_v the distance of vertex v on $\mathcal{P}$ from vertex s. A *link path* of path $\mathcal{P}$ in G is a path disjoint from $\mathcal{P}$ except for its endpoints that extends from a vertex o on $\mathcal{P}$ to a vertex w on $\mathcal{P}$ such that w is the farthest vertex reachable from o, i.e., distance from o to w is maximum. Let us now define $\mathcal{SP} = P_1, P_2, ..., P_k$

P. Felber and V. Garg (Eds.): SSS 2014, LNCS 8756, pp. 359–361, 2014.
© Springer International Publishing Switzerland 2014

to be a maximal sequence of link paths of path $\mathcal{P}$ in G each of which has its endpoints on $\mathcal{P}$ such that the following four conditions are satisfied by $\mathcal{SP}$.
(I) P_1 is the first link path with origin $o_1(=s)$ and terminus w_1. *(II)* Each link path P_{i-1} where $1 < i \leq k$ has a successor link path P_i that extends from its origin o_i to its terminus w_i such that $ds_{o_1} < ds_{o_2} < ds_{w_1}$ $(i = 2)$ and $ds_{w_{i-2}} \leq ds_{o_i} < ds_{w_{i-1}}, 2 < i \leq k$, holds. *(III)* For each i, $1 < i \leq k$, vertex o_i on $\mathcal{P}$ is selected to maximize ds_{w_i}. *(IV)* The terminus of the last link path P_k is target $w_k = t$. In order to illustrate the above concepts, Figure 1 depicts a graph with source s, target t, and its four link paths P_1, P_2, P_3, and P_4 on path $\mathcal{P}$ from s to t.

We now present the basis of the algorithm in the form of the following theorem.

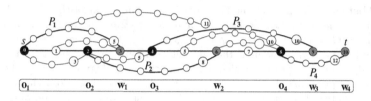

Fig. 1. A graph with origins and terminus of its link paths P_1, P_2, P_3, and P_4

Theorem 1. *A Graph $G = (V, E)$ contains two node disjoint paths $\mathcal{P}_1$ and $\mathcal{P}_2$ between two arbitrary but distinct vertices $s, t \in V$ iff there exists a maximal sequence of link paths $\mathcal{SP} = P_1, P_2, ..., P_k$ on $\mathcal{P}$ in G satisfying the above four conditions for being a sequence of link paths.*

Proof. For the "if" direction, we prove the contrapositive. We assume that the sequence of link paths $\mathcal{SP} = P_1, P_2, ..., P_k$ does not exist and we show that two disjoint paths do not exist. Observe that the sequence $\mathcal{SP} = P_1, P_2, ..., P_k$ does not exist if at least one of the link paths $P_i, \leq i \leq k$ do not exit. First, if the link path P_1 does not exist, then the successor of s on $\mathcal{P}$ is common for all the paths starting from s. Now, consider the case where link paths $P_1, P_2, ...P_i, 1 < i < k$, exist and the next link path P_{i+1} does not exist. Analogously to the above, the terminus of P_i is common for all the paths starting from s. Thus, in both cases, two disjoint paths between s and t cannot exist, hence the result. For the "only if" direction, we prove by construction. First, we need the following definitions. $\mathcal{P}[v, w]$ denotes the subpath of $\mathcal{P}$ with origin v and terminus w. On the other hand, $\mathcal{P}[v, w)$, $\mathcal{P}(v, w]$, and $\mathcal{P}(v, w)$ denote the same subpath excluding the terminus, the origin, and both the origin and the terminus of the subpath $\mathcal{P}[v, w]$, respectively. We assume that the sequence of link paths $\mathcal{SP} = P_1, P_2, ..., P_k$ exists, then two disjoint paths $\mathcal{P}_1$ and $\mathcal{P}_2$ exist and can be constructed as follows: (i) If k is even $(k = 2l)$, then $\mathcal{P}_1 = P_1, \mathcal{P}(w_1, o_3), P_3, \mathcal{P}(w_3, o_5), ..., P_{2i+1}, \mathcal{P}(w_{2i+1}, o_{2i+3}), ..., P_{2l-1}, \mathcal{P}(w_{2l-1}, w_{2l} = t]$ and $\mathcal{P}_2 = \mathcal{P}[o_1 = s, o_2), P_2, \mathcal{P}(w_2, o_4), P_4, .., \mathcal{P}(w_{2i}, o_{2i+2}), P_{2i+2}, ..., \mathcal{P}(w_{2l-2}, o_{2l}), P_{2l}$ (see Figure 1).

(ii) Otherwise, i.e., k is odd $(k = 2l+1)$, then $\mathcal{P}_1 = P_1, \mathcal{P}(w_1, o_3), P_3, \mathcal{P}(w_3, o_5)$, $P_5, ..., \mathcal{P}(w_{2i+1}, o_{2i+3}), P_{2i+3}, ..., \mathcal{P}(w_{2l-1}, o_{2l+1}), P_{2l+1}$ and $\mathcal{P}_2 = \mathcal{P}[o_1 = s, o_2), P_2$, $\mathcal{P}(w_2, o_4), P_4, \mathcal{P}(w_4, o_6), ..., P_{2i}, \mathcal{P}(w_{2i}, o_{2i+2}), ..., P_{2l}, \mathcal{P}(w_{2l}, w_{2l+1} = t]$.

3   Self-stabilizing Algorithm

The proposed algorithm constructs two node disjoint paths $\mathcal{P}_1$ and $\mathcal{P}_2$ between $s \in V$ and $t \in V$ in the following four phases. In the first phase a self stabilizing BFS tree construction gives a shortest path $\mathcal{P}$ between source s and target t. During the second phase, a maximal BFS forest stabilizing construction where each process on $\mathcal{P}$ but s are the root of a tree and a leaf of another tree allows the discover of all the link paths. Moreover each process p in the system knows its predecessor in the link path it belongs to, if any. In the third phase of the algorithm, based on the previous two phases, the terminuses $w_1, w_2, ..., w_k$ on $\mathcal{P}$ of the link paths $P_1, P_2, ..., P_k$, respectively, satisfying the above four conditions (see Section 2) are gradually *identified* and *marked* one after the other. In the fourth phase, the two node-disjoint paths $\mathcal{P}_1$ and $\mathcal{P}_2$ are constructed from target t towards source s as follows. The first process of each of the two disjoint paths $\mathcal{P}_1$ and $\mathcal{P}_2$ is determined to be t. Then, the second process of $\mathcal{P}_1$ is assumed to be the predecessor of t in the link path to which t belongs. However, the second process of $\mathcal{P}_2$ is determined to be the predecessor of t on $\mathcal{P}$. After determining the first two processes of $\mathcal{P}_1$ and $\mathcal{P}_2$, disjoint paths $\mathcal{P}_1$ and $\mathcal{P}_2$ are extended concurrently in the same manner as follows. Let p be the last process of the disjoint path, either $\mathcal{P}_1$ or $\mathcal{P}_2$, constructed thus far. Observe that process p can either be a process on $\mathcal{P}$ or on a link path P_i, $1 \leq i \leq k$. We first consider the case where p is on path $\mathcal{P}$. If p is a terminus of a link path P_i, then the next process is determined to be the predecessor of p in the link path to which process p belongs to. Otherwise, the next process is the predecessor of p on $\mathcal{P}$. We now consider the case where process p is on a link path P_i, $1 \leq i \leq k$. Then, the successor of process p on a link path P_i, hence on $\mathcal{P}_1$ or $\mathcal{P}_2$, is the predecessor of p in the link path to which process p belongs to. This approach is repeated and the construction of each disjoint path, either $\mathcal{P}_1$ or $\mathcal{P}_2$, terminates after the source process s is added to the path.

References

1. Dijkstra, E.W.: Self-stabilizing in spite of distributed control. Commun. Assoc. Comput. Mach. 17(11), 643–644 (1974)
2. Mohanty, H., Bhattacharjee, G.P.: A distributed algorithm for edge-disjoint path problem. In: Nori, K.V. (ed.) FSTTCS 1986. LNCS, vol. 241, pp. 344–361. Springer, Heidelberg (1986)
3. Hadid, R., Karaata, M.H.: An adaptive stabilizing algorithm for finding all disjoint paths in anonymous mesh networks. Computer Communications 32(5), 858–866 (2009)
4. Karaata, M.H., Hadid, R.: Brief Announcement: A Stabilizing Algorithm for Finding Two Disjoint Paths in Arbitrary Networks. In: Guerraoui, R., Petit, F. (eds.) SSS 2009. LNCS, vol. 5873, pp. 789–790. Springer, Heidelberg (2009)

Brief Announcement:
Region-Adherent Algorithms – Bounding the Impact of Faults in Space*

Jan Steffen Becker, Dilshod Rahmatov, and Oliver Theel

Carl von Ossietzky University of Oldenburg, D-26111 Oldenburg, Germany
www.svs.informatik.uni-oldenburg.de

1 Introduction

Self-stabilizing systems are famous realizations of non-masking fault-tolerant systems. Such a system is always live, but due to faults or improper initialization, it might not be safe. But because of its "inner design," a self-stabilizing system – as long as it is not in a state from whereon it exhibits safe behavior – autonomously works towards establishing or reestablishing this safe behavior. And importantly, it does so in an upper-bounded number of execution steps (in the absence of newly occuring faults), a property called *convergence* (see Figure 1). Thus, one can regard self-stabilizing systems as systems that limit the invalidation of their safety property *in time*. An alternative, though, of restricting the invalidation of the safety property in time is restricting it *in space*.

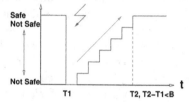

Fig. 1. Behavior of a Self-Stabilizing System over Time

2 Notion of Region Adherence

Clearly, a system that is live and safe should provide the system service the user is interested in. In this case, we assume that the system is delivering 100% of service quality. For example, the system correctly sorts all the values given to it in an increasing manner, if the system's service is "integer sorting, increasing." If faults occur, then this intended system behavior might be compromised. The rationale behind restricting a system's safety property invalidation *in space* is to upper-bound the reduction of service quality of the system *per fault* of the underlying fault model, which can – for obvious reasons – not be as strong as the standard fault model used for self-stabilizing

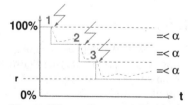

Fig. 2. Worst Case and Particular Behavior of a Region-Adherent System over Time

* The work is partially supported by the German Research Foundation in the scope of DFG GRK 1765/1 SCARE, DFG SFB/TR AVACS 14/3 and the European Commission's Erasmus Mundus TARGET II program.

P. Felber and V. Garg (Eds.): SSS 2014, LNCS 8756, pp. 362–365, 2014.

systems. A particular behavior of such a system over time is given in Figure 2. The solid blue line indicates the lower bound of service quality at a given time. At the beginning, the system exhibits 100% service quality – it is live and safe. After the first fault has occured (thunderbolt 1), the system is guaranteed to exhibit a service quality of *at least* $100\% - \alpha$. Assuming a maximal service quality reduction per fault of $\alpha = 25\%$, then the system is able to "survive" three faults (of the underlying fault model) and is still able to provide a system service above 0%, here, a "residual" quality of at least $r = 25\%$. The dashed blue line indicates a possible run of the system, represented by the actual service quality provided at a particular time. Note, that in the example run given, the system could survive more faults and still deliver a service quality of greater than 0%, but without any *a priori known* minimal service quality above 0%. Furthermore, notice that the actual service quality is always above the solid blue line. Figure 3 gives a topological interpretation of the behavior of a region-adherent system.

In the absence of any fault, the system is required to always stay in a region of the state
space where the system is guaranteed to provide a service quality of 100%, indicated by
the innermost region in the figure. When the
first fault happens, then – by the effect of
the fault – the system may be "thrown" into
the neighboring region of the state space (but
not any further). Here, a service quality of at
least $100\% - \alpha$ is guaranteed. An alternative
also allowed (and not shown by the sample

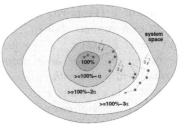

Fig. 3. Topological Interpretation of a Region-Adherent System

run of the system indicated by the blue dashed line) is that the system remains in the region, including included regions. Thus, after a second fault, the system is allowed to adopt system states belonging to any of the three innermost regions, thereby exhibiting a system quality of $100\% - 2 \cdot \alpha$ minimum. So, contrary to a self-stabilizing system, where no minimum service quality can be assumed (for some time) even after the first fault, a region-adherent system, per fault up to some maximal number of faults, at most enters a neighboring region of the state space with a guaranteed quality-of-service behavior. Thus, the system behavior is *restricted in space* since it is not allowed to transit into *any other outer region*. In this sense, the system adheres to regions of known system quality. In the following, we give a more formal and more general definition of region adherence.

3   Definition of Region Adherence

We perceive a (distributed) system P as a finite set of n processes $\{P_0, \ldots, P_{n-1}\}$. The state of a process is given by the valuation of a Cartesian product of its variables. A Cartesian product of the states of all n processes defines the configuration of the system. Let C be the set of all possible configurations of the system. $c_0 \in C_0 \subseteq C$ is an initial configuration of the set of initial configurations C_0. Every process executes a local algorithm in atomic steps according to the read/write atomicity paradigm. An atomic step leads to a state change transferring the distributed system from the current configuration c to some subsequent configuration c'. The set of all possible (fault-free) transitions of configurations according to the algorithm is A. It presents the algorithm of the system. We denote a configuration transition due to A from c to c' by $c \rightarrow_A c'$. It is also called *computation step*. The fault model F can be regarded as a specification of all possible configuration transitions from a configuration c to a configuration c' due to a fault of the model, denoted by $c \rightarrow_F c'$. It is also called *fault step*. A fault step, in our model, is also assumed to be an atomic step.

A nonempty sequence of configurations $\gamma = c_o c_1 \cdots c_n \in C^+$ with c_o being an initial configuration and configuration $c_i, i > 0$, leading to a configuration c_{i+1} by either A or F is called an *execution*. Every non-empty prefix of an execution is also an execution. Executions can be finite or infinite. A configuration is called *reachable* if there exists a finite execution ending in it.

Definition 1 (General Region Adherence of a System). *We assume a system with configurations C, initial configurations C_0 and algorithm A under fault model F. Let $g : C \mapsto [0,1]$ be a function stating the service quality of the system and let f be a natural number. $r : \{0, \ldots, f\} \mapsto [0,1)$ is a non-decreasing function with $r(0) = 0$ and $r(f) < 1$. Algorithm A is called f-region-adherent wrt. g, r, and F, if and only if for all reachable configurations $c \in C$, all initial configurations $c_0 \in C_0$ and all executions $\gamma = c_0 \cdots c$ ending in c with $\#_{F \backslash A}(\gamma) \leq f$, the following holds:*

$$g(c) \geq 1 - r\left(\#_{F \backslash A}(\gamma)\right), \tag{1}$$

where $\#_{F \backslash A}(\gamma)$ represents the number of fault steps of execution γ. A system executing an f-region-adherent algorithm is also called f-region-adherent.

A fault (step) having the same effect as computation step does not count as fault (step). This is indicated by the "$F \backslash A$" subscript of the $\#$ function. The value of g may also be interpreted as a percentage. The function r can be perceived as the service's *loss* or *reduction of quality* with $r(i)$, $0 \leq i \leq f$, upper-bounding the loss due to the i-th fault. Note that an f-region-adherent system is able to tolerate at least f faults and is still exhibiting a service quality higher than 0%. For example, a loss-of-quality function r with $r(i) = i \cdot \alpha$ for $i = 0, \ldots, f$ with $f = 3$ and $\alpha = 0.25 < 1/f$ describes the non-masking fault-tolerance behavior of the example system of Figures 2 and 3 as 3-region-adherent.

4   Further Work

Clearly, a region-adherent system exhibits desirable fault tolerance properties. When region adherence is realized in a system, it manifests gracefully degrading, quantified quality-of-service guarantees in case up to f faults happen. Thus, at any time – knowing the number of faults that have happened –, the system user can take an a priori known minimal service quality for granted: a very valuable information in various critical settings! Similar to self-stabilizing systems, the construction of region-adherent systems is not an easy task and requires careful algorithm design. In the future, we will report on example systems that we have developed as well as on a design and verification methodology of region-adherent systems along with a deeper analysis of accompanying system properties, fault models and a suitable "self-stabilization co-design."

Brief Announcement:
Entropy Adaptive On-Line Compression

Shlomi Dolev[1,*], Sergey Frenkel[2], and Marina Kopeetsky[3]

[1] Department of Computer Science , Ben-Gurion University of the Negev,
Beer-Sheva, 84105, Israel
dolev@cs.bgu.ac.il
[2] Institute of Informatics Problems, Russian Academy of Sciences, Moscow, Russia
fsergei51@gmail.com
[3] Department of Software Engineering, Shamoon College of Engineering, Beer-Sheva,
84100, Israel
marinako@sce.ac.il

Introduction. Self-organization is based on adaptivity. Adaptivity should start with the very basic fundamental communication tasks such as encoding the information to be transmitted or stored. One of the most challenging task of communicating entities in distributed systems and computer communication networks is the way information is compressed. The sole traditional requirement for the optimality of lossless data compression schemes is the stationary ergodic nature of the information source. Nevertheless, due to the wide deployment of multimedia networks, heterogeneous ad-hoc network, and the wide range of communication tasks, the efficient compression techniques of the dynamic (non-stationary) sources are of a special interest now-days. In particular, dynamic sources that are characterized by non-stationary probability distribution and non constant entropy, are the typical sources that transmit on-line multimedia (voice, video) traffic.

Lempel and Ziv introduced compression algorithm defining a rule for parsing strings of symbols from a finite alphabet into substrings, or words of bounded length, and a coding scheme which maps these substrings sequentially into uniquely decipherable codewords of fixed length over the same alphabet. It has been demonstrated that for a stationary ergodic source as the input size and the sliding window size both tend to infinity, the compression ratio approaches the constant source entropy.

We consider the non-asymptotic case, which is characterized by a restricted memory size at the encoder and the decoder sides. To the best of our knowledge, we provide the first Entropy Adaptive on-line Compression (EAC) scheme. EAC is practical and efficient on-line adaptive scheme that tracks the variable entropy rate of the source and provides optimal compression of fixed-size data blocks on-

* Partially supported by Deutsche Telekom, Rita Altura Trust Chair in Computer Sciences, Israeli Internet Association, Israeli Ministry of Science, Lynne and William Frankel Center and Israel Science Foundation (grant number 428/11). The second author has partially been supported by the Russian Foundation for Basic Research under grant RFBR 12-07-00109. The third author has partially been supported by the internal research program of the Shamoon College of Engineering.

P. Felber and V. Garg (Eds.): SSS 2014, LNCS 8756, pp. 366–368, 2014.
© Springer International Publishing Switzerland 2014

line without performing computationally and time expensive preprocessing. The simulation results demonstrate that the EAC scheme can perform in many cases better than $LZ77$ and achieves higher compression ratio on-line, comparing with the standard $LZ77$ compression scheme.

Description of the EAC scheme. $LZ77$ uses lookahead for finding the longest match in the previous window and the next information to encode. In real time transmission the lookahead is bonded by the maximal latency (say at most B bits). We suggest to optimize the window size each time new B bits are about to be sent, and therefore react to the changing entropy in an adaptive fashion. Apparently, the number of possible relevant window sizes is logarithmic in the maximal window size. The detailed description of the scheme is presented in Figure 1. Let the information source generate a random (may be non-stationary) finite length string. Let the initial sliding window size $N_0 = n_{w_0}$ be set according to (say, twice)the $LZ77$ (fixed) window definition. The first n_{w_0} bits of the initial window from the input are sent from the encoder E to the decoder D (by using an agreed upon efficient algorithm (e.g., $LZ77$)), (lines 2-8). Upon accumulating the next B bits, generated by the source, the encoder E searches for the optimal window size N for encoding these new accumulating B bits. The search starts using $LZ77$ with a dictionary of the recent window of N_0 bits, which we call the pyramid base, then repeatedly tries smaller windows (each time halving the size of the previous used window).

The initial window N_0 is used as a pyramid base for testing all possible smaller windows. The test stage for the current portion of size B bits is performed by trying all windows of sizes $N_0/2^i$ for every $0, \ldots, \log N_0$. The EAC algorithm starts using a dictionary of $N_0/2^i$ bits from the previously received and compressed B bits, and then shift the window which is also of size $N_0/2^i$ until the algorithm is done with the current portion of B bits (lines 8-10, 14-29). The total length of each encoded phrase is composed from comma free binary encoding of its length L_i (denoted by $e(L_i)$), and the length of the binary encoding of the corresponding index m_i. The total length of the compressed string determines the redundancy that has been removed from the original uncompressed B bits string. The window size $N = n_{w_i}$, that satisfies the shortest length of the compressed string (and corresponding maximal compression ratio), is determined as the current optimal size (lines 30-33). The current portion of B bits is compressed using the optimal N and sent to D (line 10). Information concerning the chosen size of the optimal window is sent as a prefix of the encoded B bits.

Experimental results and conclusions. The EAC scheme was tested with different real-life files of different types (docx, ppt, jpeg, xls), and some artificial ones generated as segments of homogeneous Markov Chains. In order to fairly compare the EAC and $LZ77$ algorithms, the fixed window size n_w, used by the $LZ77$ algorithm, is equal to the maximal window size (pyramid base), applied in our scheme.

The experimental results demonstrate that the EAC scheme can provide a higher compression ratio (compared with the $LZ77$ algorithm) for rather short

```
 1. EAC scheme for encoder E
 2. Loop over whole file for each portion of B bits
 3. int B
 4. /* number of look ahead buffered bits respecting the maximal allowed latency */
 5. int N₀ initial window size
 6. int N_prev window size optimal for compression of the previous portion of B bits
 7. /* Bootstrap stage – establishing the first dictionary */
 8. Compress the first N₀ bits by agreed upon efficient algorithm (e.g., LZ77) and send to
    decoder D
 9. Upon the arrival of the next B bits of the (streaming) file
10. TestCompress(B, N₀, Output)
11. Send Output to decoder D
12.
13.
14. Procedure TestCompress(LA, PB, Output)
15. /* Procedure TestCompress: search for the optimal window size N ≤ PB
16. for the portion of LA bits from input/*
17. Input:
18. int LA length in bits of InputString for compression
19. N₀ = PB initial window size (pyramid base)
20. Perform LZ77 compression of LA bits using the last N₀ bits of previous LA
21. as the dictionary
22. CompressedString = Output
23. /* CompressedString – LA bits, compressed in optimal window */
24. Compute A – length of CompressedString in bits
25. for int i = 1 .. log PB
26.     Perform LZ77 compression of LA bits using the last PB/2^i bits of previous LA
27.     as the dictionary and
28.     Compute length Lᵢ of string CompressedStringᵢ
29.     using window of size n_{wᵢ} = PB/2^i bits
30.     N = PB
31.     /* N optimal window size for LA bits */
32.     if Lᵢ < A
33.         Set A = Lᵢ, N = n_{wᵢ}, CompressedString = CompressedStringᵢ
34. if N = N_prev
35. Output = (N, CompressedString)
```

Fig. 1. Entropy Adaptive Compression Scheme

sequences since the asymptotic properties of the $LZ77$ are still not satisfied. In addition, there is also an improvement in the compression ratio for long files.

Acknowledgment. We thanks Asaf Cohen for useful remarks and discussions. We thanks Dmitry Zbarsky for implementing and testing our Entropy Adaptive Compression scheme.

Reference

1. Dolev, S., Frenkel, S., Kopeetsky, M.: Entropy Adaptive On-line Compression, Technical Report 14-04, Department of Computer Science, Ben Gurion University of the Negev, Beer Sheva, Israel (2014)

1. EAC scheme for encoder E
2. Loop over whole file for each portion of B bits
3. int B
4. /* number of look ahead buffered bits respecting the maximal allowed latency */
5. int N_0 initial window size
6. int N_{prev} window size optimal for compression of the previous portion of B bits
7. /* Bootstrap stage – establishing the first dictionary */
8. Compress the first N_0 bits by agreed upon efficient algorithm (e.g., $LZ77$) and send to decoder D
9. Upon the arrival of the next B bits of the (streaming) file
10. $TestCompress(B, N_0, Output)$
11. Send $Output$ to decoder D
12.
13.
14. Procedure $TestCompress(LA, PB, Output)$
15. /* Procedure $TestCompress$: search for the optimal window size $N \leq PB$
16. for the portion of LA bits from input/*
17. Input:
18. int LA length in bits of $InputString$ for compression
19. $N_0 = PB$ initial window size (pyramid base)
20. Perform $LZ77$ compression of LA bits using the last N_0 bits of previous LA
21. as the dictionary
22. $CompressedString = Output$
23. /* $CompressedString$ – LA bits, compressed in optimal window */
24. Compute A – length of $CompressedString$ in bits
25. for $int\ i = 1 .. \log PB$
26.   Perform $LZ77$ compression of LA bits using the last $PB/2^i$ bits of previous LA
27.   as the dictionary and
28.   Compute length L_i of string $CompressedString_i$
29.   using window of size $n_{w_i} = PB/2^i$ bits
30. $N = PB$
31.   /* N optimal window size for LA bits */
32.   if $L_i < A$
33.   Set $A = L_i$, $N = n_{w_i}$, $CompressedString = CompressedString_i$
34. if $N = N_{prev}$
35. $Output = (N, CompressedString)$

Fig. 1. Entropy Adaptive Compression Scheme

sequences since the asymptotic properties of the $LZ77$ are still not satisfied. In addition, there is also an improvement in the compression ratio for long files.

Acknowledgment. We thanks Asaf Cohen for useful remarks and discussions. We thanks Dmitry Zbarsky for implementing and testing our Entropy Adaptive Compression scheme.

Reference

1. Dolev, S., Frenkel, S., Kopeetsky, M.: Entropy Adaptive On-line Compression, Technical Report 14-04, Department of Computer Science, Ben Gurion University of the Negev, Beer Sheva, Israel (2014)

line without performing computationally and time expensive preprocessing. The simulation results demonstrate that the EAC scheme can perform in many cases better than $LZ77$ and achieves higher compression ratio on-line, comparing with the standard $LZ77$ compression scheme.

Description of the EAC scheme. $LZ77$ uses lookahead for finding the longest match in the previous window and the next information to encode. In real time transmission the lookahead is bonded by the maximal latency (say at most B bits). We suggest to optimize the window size each time new B bits are about to be sent, and therefore react to the changing entropy in an adaptive fashion. Apparently, the number of possible relevant window sizes is logarithmic in the maximal window size. The detailed description of the scheme is presented in Figure 1. Let the information source generate a random (may be non-stationary) finite length string. Let the initial sliding window size $N_0 = n_{w_0}$ be set according to (say, twice)the $LZ77$ (fixed) window definition. The first n_{w_0} bits of the initial window from the input are sent from the encoder E to the decoder D (by using an agreed upon efficient algorithm (e.g., $LZ77$)), (lines 2-8). Upon accumulating the next B bits, generated by the source, the encoder E searches for the optimal window size N for encoding these new accumulating B bits. The search starts using $LZ77$ with a dictionary of the recent window of N_0 bits, which we call the pyramid base, then repeatedly tries smaller windows (each time halving the size of the previous used window).

The initial window N_0 is used as a pyramid base for testing all possible smaller windows. The test stage for the current portion of size B bits is performed by trying all windows of sizes $N_0/2^i$ for every $0, \ldots, \log N_0$. The EAC algorithm starts using a dictionary of $N_0/2^i$ bits from the previously received and compressed B bits, and then shift the window which is also of size $N_0/2^i$ until the algorithm is done with the current portion of B bits (lines 8-10, 14-29). The total length of each encoded phrase is composed from comma free binary encoding of its length L_i (denoted by $e(L_i)$), and the length of the binary encoding of the corresponding index m_i. The total length of the compressed string determines the redundancy that has been removed from the original uncompressed B bits string. The window size $N = n_{w_i}$, that satisfies the shortest length of the compressed string (and corresponding maximal compression ratio), is determined as the current optimal size (lines 30-33). The current portion of B bits is compressed using the optimal N and sent to D (line 10). Information concerning the chosen size of the optimal window is sent as a prefix of the encoded B bits.

Experimental results and conclusions. The EAC scheme was tested with different real-life files of different types (docx, ppt, jpeg, xls), and some artificial ones generated as segments of homogeneous Markov Chains. In order to fairly compare the EAC and $LZ77$ algorithms, the fixed window size n_w, used by the $LZ77$ algorithm, is equal to the maximal window size (pyramid base), applied in our scheme.

The experimental results demonstrate that the EAC scheme can provide a higher compression ratio (compared with the $LZ77$ algorithm) for rather short

Author Index